W9-AXQ-873

THE WORD BIBLE HANDBOOK

THE WORD BIBLE HANDBOOK

Lawrence O. Richards

WORD BOOKS
PUBLISHER
WACO, TEXAS

Library of Congress Cataloging in Publication Data
Richards, Larry, 1931–
  The Word Bible handbook.
  Includes index.
  1. Bible—Introductions. I. Title.
BS475.2.R52   220.6′01   81–22007
ISBN 0–8499–0279–7   AACR2

Acknowledgments

The author expresses special appreciation to the publishers of the NEW INTERNATIONAL VERSION Bible. I have quoted extensively from this excellent version of the Scriptures, and recommend it highly for use as a study and devotional Bible.

I also wish to express appreciation to the staff of editors at Word Publications, coordinated for this project by Al Bryant, for their usual outstanding and supportive work on this Bible Handbook.

The photographs used in this book were supplied by Dr. Howard A. Hanke. The illustrations were done by my son, Paul.

Contents

CONTENTS

Illustrations

Maps

Charts

Theology in Brief

THE WORD
BIBLE
HANDBOOK

UNDERSTANDING YOUR BIBLE

What Kind of Book?

Some have described the Bible as a "collection of religious writings." It is a collection. There are 66 books. They were written by 40 different persons, over a span of some 1,500 years. The writers were fishermen and farmers, political leaders and kings. A few were highly educated philosophers. One writer was a medical doctor. Three different languages were used in its writing: Hebrew, Aramaic, and Greek. And yet the Bible is essentially one Book, and it tells a unified salvation story.

Most people recognize the Bible as something more than "religious writings." But not everyone. There are three dominant ideas about the Bible commonly held today.

1. It is a record of man's search for God. In this view, the Bible is simply history. It's a moving report by religious men of their struggles to understand themselves and the universe. Such a Bible may be of interest to us if we're religiously minded. But this kind of Bible holds no real answers for people today. The men who wrote it were struggling, just as we are, with what must always remain Mystery. To those who hold this view, the Bible can never be authoritative. It may be worth reading. But, in this view, the Bible is simply the thinking of fallible human beings, and its guesses about God are no better than our own.

2. It is a record of man's experience with God. In this view the Bible was written about real "experiences" with God. The writers then tried to describe their own or their nation's experiences, and offered explanations of what these experiences meant. In this view, while the experiences of the writers were real, the words and ideas reporting them are strictly human. This kind of Bible is not necessarily authoritative, or even reliable. Did God *really* part the Red Sea? Or was the description just one writer's attempt to express for his readers a sense of how powerful God is?

Those who see the Bible simply as a report of religious experiences believe it has great value for people today. Reading it, we too may meet God and have our own experiences with him. But the concepts and the ideas of the Bible writers are not necessarily accurate, even though the God hidden behind them is real.

3. It is God's revelation to man. This third view is dramatically different from the first two. This kind of Bible is wholly authorita-

tive: a means to bring us to salvation and guide us in the life of faith. In this kind of Bible we both meet God and come to know about him. In this kind of Bible, we are introduced to a personal relationship with God, and we hear his thoughts expressed in words that reliably portray hidden realities. What we could never discover by ourselves, or even imagine, God has communicated to us in the words of the Scripture (1 Cor. 2:9–13).

This is the kind of Bible that Scripture claims to be. We glance through the Old Testament* and find that claim on page after page. Over 2,600 times the writers claim to be writing or speaking not their words, but God's! "The Word of the Lord came to Jeremiah . . ."; "Thus saith the Lord . . ."; "Hear the word of the Lord. . . ." Certainly the writers of the Bible had no doubts about what they were recording. They were writing what they firmly believed to be the message of God to man.

This is how we need to understand the Bible. And, because the Bible is written revelation, God's communication in human language, we come to Scripture with excitement and with expectation. What does God have to say to us?

How Did God Speak?

God has a message for us. But how has he communicated it? The Bible tells us of many ways that God has disclosed himself— in dreams, by prophets and seers, in mighty acts, in the outworking of history, and ultimately in the person of his Son, Jesus. The creation itself is an unveiling, a disclosure by God of his power and wisdom (Ps. 19:1–6; Rom. 1:18–20). The word for God's disclosure of himself and of his message is "revelation."

The primary mode of self-disclosure, which draws on the other forms of revelation, is the written Word. The whole Scripture, we are told, was "God-breathed," and is "useful for teaching, rebuking, correcting and training in righteousness, so that the man of God may be thoroughly equipped for every good work" (2 Tim. 3:16,17). The word that speaks of God's work in giving the Scripture is "inspiration."

Inspiration does not suggest dictation. Some have thought that dictation was required, and imagined that somehow the human writer's personality was blanked out: that God moved hands and minds without human involvement. But each writer of the Bible

---

* From this point on, we will abbreviate Old Testament OT and New Testament NT.

has his own literary style. Each reflects the language patterns of his culture. Each uses language that reveals his education and background. No, inspiration simply affirms that God the Holy Spirit quietly worked within the personalities of the writers, so that what they wrote accurately communicates what he intended. Inspiration is not a statement about the psychological state of the writers. Inspiration is a statement about the writings. The doctrine of inspiration guarantees that the writings themselves, as they came from the authors' pens, reliably communicate the message God intended to share.

The recent past has seen dispute about the extent to which inspiration guarantees the reliability of the Scriptures. All who believe that God has spoken to us in his Word are confident that the Bible accurately communicates the message about God he intends us to have. But some are less sure that inspiration means the human writers of the Bible were preserved from other kinds of errors. For instance, they suggest that a writer might have been mistaken about a historical fact, or might have expressed an unscientific notion common to his culture, without in any way reflecting on the truth of the Bible's teachings.

Actually, the more archaeology reveals about the background of the Bible, the more the evidence mounts the Scriptures are historically accurate. Supposed errors have over and over again been shown to reflect misunderstandings, or a lack of information available to the critics. We should never let such criticism distract us from the most important truth about our Bible. When God acted to communicate his message to us, he chose to present and preserve it in written form. By the Holy Spirit's ministry of inspiration, he guaranteed that process of writing. In our Scripture we have a revelation we can trust.

For you and me, what is important when we read our Bible is not the debates of the scholars, but the wonderful realization that this Book is without question the authoritative, reliable, and relevant source of our faith. It is God's Book, about himself, and about us. In every matter touching our relationship with God we can be completely confident that what the Bible says we are to appropriate by faith.

Origin of Our Bible

Content. The Bible collects, and presents as a unit, 66 separate writings, completed over a great span of time. These books are the "canon" of Scripture. The word "canon" in Greek means "measuring rod." So to talk of a "canon of Scripture" indicates that there are certain writings uniquely recognized as the yardstick by which belief and practice are to be measured.

Well before the time of Jesus the books included in our OT were recognized by the Hebrew people as authoritative words from God. Statements in the Bible indicate the writers themselves claimed to present God's Word. Jesus certified the canonicity of most of the OT books by his reference to and use of them. And lists, from Jewish and Christian sources that range from the early second century B.C. to the fifth century A.D., attest the modern 39 OT books.

Other early Hebrew writings were considered spiritually profitable. But only the 39 in the Bible we use today were revered as God's authoritative Word. Those 39, with the abbreviations we'll use for them in this book, are:

Genesis	Gen.	Proverbs	Prov.
Exodus	Exod.	Ecclesiastes	Eccl.
Leviticus	Lev.	Song of Solomon	S. of Sol.
Numbers	Num.	Isaiah	Isa.
Deuteronomy	Deut.	Jeremiah	Jer.
Joshua	Josh.	Lamentations	Lam.
Judges	Judg.	Ezekiel	Ezek.
Ruth	Ruth	Daniel	Dan.
1 Samuel	1 Sam.	Hosea	Hos.
2 Samuel	2 Sam.	Joel	Joel
1 Kings	1 Kings	Amos	Amos
2 Kings	2 Kings	Obadiah	Obad.
1 Chronicles	1 Chron.	Jonah	Jonah
2 Chronicles	2 Chron.	Micah	Mic.
Ezra	Ezra	Nahum	Nah.
Nehemiah	Neh.	Habakkuk	Hab.
Esther	Esth.	Zephaniah	Zeph.
Job	Job	Haggai	Hag.
Psalms	Pss.	Zechariah	Zech.
		Malachi	Mal.

The canon of the NT is similarly attested by the early Christian community. An important factor in recognizing these books was their antiquity, and apostolic authorship. Later writings offered insights and instruction, even as devotional books and commentaries do today. But the believing community came to a consensus about those books which were inspired by God and thus authoritative. These books, and the abbreviations that represent them, are:

Matthew	Matt.	1 Timothy	1 Tim.
Mark	Mark	2 Timothy	2 Tim.
Luke	Luke	Titus	Titus
John	John	Philemon	Philem.
Acts	Acts	Hebrews	Heb.
Romans	Rom.	James	James
1 Corinthians	1 Cor.	1 Peter	1 Pet.
2 Corinthians	2 Cor.	2 Peter	2 Pet.
Galatians	Gal.	1 John	1 John
Ephesians	Eph.	2 John	2 John
Philippians	Phil.	3 John	3 John
Colossians	Col.	Jude	Jude
1 Thessalonians	1 Thes.	Revelation	Rev.
2 Thessalonians	2 Thes.		

Accuracy. One question the doctrine of Inspiration raises is important. Perhaps the original writings were the Word of God. But do the contents of these 66 canonical books today accurately represent the original text? To answer this we need to know something about how we got our present text, and something about the different translations available today.

In seminary bookstores today you can pick up a Hebrew text of the OT as well as Greek texts of the NT. When you hold one of these in your hands what you have is, amazingly, substantially what the authors first wrote!

In its earliest time the OT text was often threatened. Once the Scriptures were lost for decades, until a copy was rediscovered when reconstructing the Temple. Jeremiah's freshly written prophecies were ripped up and burned by an angry king, only to be rewritten by the prophet. A few hundred years before Christ, foreign conquerors searched out and tried to destroy all copies of the Scriptures. But God did preserve the text. For hundreds of years scribes copied and recopied manuscripts, laboriously counting the number of letters in each line, then on each page, and also in each book—checking to make sure that nothing had been changed. Minor changes did creep into various copies. But these were studied and a standard Hebrew text, called the Massoretic text, was developed about 100 years after Christ. For a long time the earliest copy of that text we possessed was penned about A.D.

1100. Then the Dead Sea scrolls were discovered in 1947. Among these scrolls dating from before Christ were copies of OT books in Hebrew which showed amazing agreement with the Massoretic text.

The NT was completed within the span of a hundred years. Afterward multiplied copies were made and circulated to churches around the world. Thousands of portions of NT manuscripts, copied by hand before the invention of printing, are still in existence.

There are minor variations in these Greek manuscripts, as there were in the Hebrew. But the science of textual criticism, which makes careful comparisons of the manuscripts to determine what readings best represent the original, has reached the point where not one word in a thousand is seriously questioned. And no basic teaching of Scripture is in doubt because of uncertainty about the correctness of the text!

We can be confident that the Greek and Hebrew texts in our hands today reliably reproduce the words and message of the original.

Our English Bibles

Today we can hold Hebrew and Greek texts that accurately reproduce the original. But most of us can't read them! We must rely on translations of these texts into English. This raises another vital question. When we read an English version, how confident can we be that it communicates what God has said? And, with so many English versions to choose from, which should we use for study?

This latter question becomes more important when we realize that no less than 43 different English versions of the Bible were published between 1950 and 1979.

The tradition of English translation stretches back to Bishop Aldheim of Sherborne, who died in A.D. 709. He translated the Psalms into Anglo-Saxon. John Wycliffe published the first complete English Bible in 1382, and organized a group of lay preachers to travel across England preaching God's Word in the common tongue. By 1611 the classic King James version, the work of 54 scholars, was completed. And today we have dozens of translations and paraphrases from which to choose.

Translation vs. *paraphrase*. It's important when you pick up a version of the Bible to know whether you have a translation or a paraphrase. Generally speaking, a translation attempts word for word, or meaning for meaning transfer of the original into English equivalents. A paraphrase is a free rendering of the original, with an effort to interpret. The paraphrase does not give you what the original *says,* but tells you what the translator thinks the original *means.*

Normally translations are the work of teams of scholars, who sometimes work together for decades on the best way to express the original in English. A good translation, like the RSV (Revised Standard Version) or NIV (New International Version) tries to help you see, when you read the English text, what the first Greek or Hebrew readers saw in their languages. Normally a paraphrase is the work of a single individual, and the effect is to have you see what the paraphraser sees in the text.

What should we use? Both translations and paraphrases have a place in our exploration of the Bible. Paraphrases can suggest fresh insights, or state old truths in lively new ways. But when you study the Bible to grasp what God actually has said, it is best to rely on a good translation. For personal or group Bible study, a good translation is a must.

What are the best versions of the Bible to use? Among the best, and the version quoted most frequently in this Handbook, is the recent NIV translation.

J. B. Phillips *The New Testament in Modern English* is a dynamic paraphrase. The very popular *Living Bible,* paraphrased by Ken Taylor, is heavily biased by the author's interpretations. It, like all other paraphrases, should be checked against a good translation.

With this warning about paraphrases, we can come to an encouraging conclusion. The original text of the OT and NT are well established today, and well translated by RSV and NIV scholars. As we read either of them, we can be confident that we have God's Word expressed in our very own tongue.

How Can I Understand It?

So far we've seen a number of exciting truths about our Bible. It is a Book of revelation. In it God discloses himself and his thoughts. Inspired by the Holy Spirit, the writings that make up our Scriptures are fully authoritative, a trustworthy means to bring us to salvation and guide us in the life of faith.

Only the books that make up our Bible have been recognized for millennia by the community of faith as God's Word to us. What's more, the science of textual criticism has been successful in reproducing the Hebrew and Greek texts substantially as they came from the pens of their authors!

But with this said, there are still questions. One of the most important is this: Can I understand what the Bible is saying?

God's unveiling. Earlier we saw that the Bible is written revelation. It is an unveiling by God of information that, apart from his communication, would have remained hidden. It follows that if God's intention is to unveil, the Bible cannot be obscure or impossible for us to understand!

You may wonder about that if you've ever opened Scripture to some list of apparently meaningless names, or to a poetic passage such as Job, or to a prophecy that speaks of nations and races that long ago passed into oblivion. But nevertheless it's true. While there are different literary forms in the Bible, and while there are passages that one needs background information to interpret, the Bible's message is really not a hidden one. The Bible is an open book. You need not go to a seminary, or be a scholar, to understand its teachings or to hear God speak to you personally.

Bible Handbook. One value of this Bible Handbook is that it provides most of the background data you'll need to understand a passage of Scripture. There's information about the culture and the times in which a book of Scripture was written. There's an overview of every unit of thought in the entire Scripture, to orient you as you read the inspired Word. With this Handbook, and by following a few simple rules for personal study, you'll find the Bible opens up to you in a truly exciting way.

Interpretation. What are the simple rules for interpretation to follow as you study the Bible?

1. *Don't look for hidden meanings.* Normally you will take the Bible words in their ordinary sense, as plain talk.

2. *Don't read verse by verse.* Read the Bible in paragraphs. The verse divisions in today's Bibles, and even the chapter divisions, were not in the original but were added by translators. So study with versions of the Bible that organize the verses into paragraphs, and read whole paragraphs.

This is really important. Most parts of the Bible are written in units of thought. Scripture is not lists of unrelated ideas. So to understand a particular verse you need to see how it fits into the larger unit of thought. If you can learn to concentrate on understanding these larger units, you'll be much less likely to miss the meaning.

3. *Don't jump to conclusions.* This means read the Bible intelligently, thinking about what a passage is actually saying. For instance, in Mark, Jesus tells a rich young man to sell what he has and then to follow him (10:21). Does that mean everyone

should sell all his possessions to become a follower of Jesus? Looking at the passage we note that Jesus did not say this to all his followers—just to one individual. That individual had asked what he should do to obtain eternal life. When he was commanded to sell all his possessions the young man refused, and revealed what Christ had intended to teach him—his money was more important to him than God. So the command to sell all was not a general command for all believers, but a specific instruction given an individual to show him his need for salvation.

Reading intelligently involves stopping to think about what we see in the Bible, and not jumping to conclusions that ignore important details.

4. *Don't read the Bible as a duty.* Read God's Word expectantly. Realize that it is God who has given us the Bible, and that he meets us in its pages. Expect God to touch your heart and your mind, and be open to what God's Spirit wants you to learn. If you read the Bible carefully, following the flow of thought expressed in its paragraphs, take its words in their plain sense, and ask God to speak to you through this unique revelation, you find that you *do* begin to understand the Bible. As you come to know the Bible better and better the excitement and the joy will mount. God will be speaking to *you!*

Experiencing God's Truth

The Bible is a Book you can understand. But it's also a Book you can experience. This too sets the Bible apart from all other literature.

We need to be very clear about this. God didn't share his Word with us simply to give us information. He didn't even reveal his thoughts so we could believe correctly. God gave us his Word to bring us into a transforming relationship with him.

We can read the Bible intelligently and carefully, and understand what it has to say. But what we read will not be of value to us unless it takes root in our hearts and lives. So the final thing we need to explore about the Bible before launching into the Scripture itself is this: How should I read it? How do I approach the Word of God so that it will shape and enrich my experience?

Read with faith. The Bible is a deeply personal document. As many have noted, it is a "letter from God," directed to each one of us. We can come to Scripture with the confidence that God is, that he loves us, and that in Jesus Christ he has called us into a personal, saving relationship with him.

Faith in Jesus as a living person who loves you and forgives you doesn't have to precede study of the Bible. Many have found that relationship with God while reading it. But the point is that the Bible is a Book of personal relationship with God. We can never really know what the Bible is talking about until we come to Jesus by faith and invite him into our lives as Savior and Lord.

When that personal relationship with God through Christ has been established, we have the Author of the Bible with us as we read, to help us understand and live the words he has given.

Read with an open life. How you or I feel subjectively or what we are currently experiencing need not affect our interpretation of the Scripture. But it will affect our application.

Interpretation has to do with the basic meaning of a passage or section of the Bible. Interpretation is something we can establish objectively, and so we can speak of "the faith" as something believers of all time affirm [see *Biblical Faith,* p. 562]. But application has to do with experiencing God's truth personally, and will have subjective elements.

We interpret the Bible to see what Scripture means.

We apply the Bible to learn what God is saying through the Scripture to us personally.

In application an open life is important. By "open" I mean that when we come to the Bible, you or I come with an awareness of our needs, of decisions we face, of tensions and problems that exist. As we read, we ask God to speak to us through his Word. We consciously seek to relate what we read to our daily life.

This Handbook will help you in application as well as in interpretation. Frequently the symbol of an open Bible appears, followed by questions that you can keep in mind as you study the passage discussed. These questions will help you become sensitive to areas of your life to which the passage may apply. The questions will show you how to look at the passage to discover what God may be saying to you.

So one key to application is coming to the Bible with an open life, willing to let God's Word touch and probe your joys and sorrows, your strengths and weaknesses.

Read with readiness to respond. The Bible is a relational Book. Through it God speaks to us individually and personally, as well as with his message to all mankind. God's Spirit seeks to apply his words to each of our personal lives.

When we read the Bible with open lives we'll hear him speaking to us. It's then that response is vital. Both the Old and New Testaments emphasize the importance of an obedient response to God.

"In keeping them," the psalmist says about God's words, "there is great reward" (Ps. 19:11). Jesus portrays the wise man as one who "hears my sayings and does them" (Luke 6:47, RSV). Thus we are all called by Scripture to pattern our lives on the moral and spiritual teachings of the Bible, and to be responsive to the voice of God when he speaks to us with personal applications.

Readiness to respond to what we see in the Scriptures and sense of God's leading has a great impact on our lives. It also has an impact on our personal relationship with God. Jesus told his disciples, "If anyone loves me, he will obey my teaching. My father will love him, and we will come to him and make our home with him" (John 14:23). Our obedient response to God's Word is not, then, something that flows from terror or some sense of obligation. Our response to God and his Word is marked by love.

God, who reveals himself to us in the Word, speaks out of a deep love for us, and a desire for our best. As we become more and more confident in that love, and learn to love him in return, the Scriptures become a rich source of wisdom and guidance. God's Word marks out a pathway, love motivates us to travel its leading, and our lives move on into an ever deepening relationship with the Lord.

Old Testament Overview

The OT contains 39 books. They are books of history, poetry, and prophetic utterance. The books were written by many different authors over the span of a thousand years. They tell a gradually unfolding story of God's relationship with human beings.

It is important to recognize the gradual and unfolding nature of the OT. The full picture of God and his purposes, which we have now, simply was not available to God's people in the past. Instead, new insights and information were given step by step, with revelations of ten hundreds of years apart. Often the promises and the prophecies could not really be understood by those to whom they were given until history filled in the shadows with solid reality.

In general the OT knows of two major historical ages. The first age is one of unspecified thousands of years, stretching from the Creation to the call of Abraham. This period was one in which God related directly to the whole human race, calling them to faith through the traditions passed on from the beginning. The first eleven chapters of the OT deal with this vast age.

The rest of the OT focuses on a single race and family. With

Abraham, God initiates a plan to bring redemption to all men through the line of one individual, to whom he makes a series of Covenant promises, or oaths. The rest of the OT tells the story of that family, and of how God works across the centuries to gradually reveal through them more and more of his character and of his purposes and plans.

Because of the historical nature of this revelation, we can best understand the OT by mastering ten critical periods of time, in which the progressive revelations came. If these time periods, their emphases, key persons and events, and the books related to them are mastered, then the sweep and scope of the OT will be understood.

The chart on the next two pages identifies these ten periods and their emphases. It lists key persons, and identifies key events. In addition, these OT books written in the period or dealing with it are listed. OT books are not found in the Bible in historical sequence. You can quickly locate any portion of the OT in its appropriate time period by using this chart.

Period, Dates	Description	OT Books	Persons/Events
I PRIMEVAL –2000	God deals with all mankind, showing his love and his judgment to fallen humanity.	Genesis 1–11	Adam, Eve The Fall The Flood
II PATRIAR-CHAL 2000–1500	God chooses Abraham's family, and gives him a Covenant which reveals his purposes.	Genesis 12–50 Job	Abraham, Isaac, Jacob Abrahamic Covenant
III EXODUS 1500–1400	God frees his people from Egyptian slavery. The Law is given, and the shape of Israel as a nation determined.	Exodus Leviticus Numbers Deuteronomy	Moses, Aaron Deliverance Miracles Passover Law, Priesthood, Sacrificial system
IV CONQUEST 1400–1390	The land promised Abraham is taken and occupied by his descendants.	Joshua	Joshua Conquest of Canaan (Palestine)
V JUDGES 1390–950	The people apostatize in the land, and experience cycles of defeat and restoration.	Judges Ruth	Gideon Jephthah Samson Ruth Eli Samuel

Period, Dates	Description	OT Books	Persons/Events
VI **UNITED** **KINGDOM** 950–931	Israel becomes a monarchy and grows to power and prosperity under David and Solomon.	1, 2 Samuel 1 Chronicles 2 Chron. 1–20 1 Kings 1–11 Proverbs, Psalms Song of Sol. Ecclesiastes	Samuel Saul David Solomon Jerusalem Temple Davidic Covenant
VII **DIVIDED** **KINGDOM** 931–722	On Solomon's death the nation divides into two kingdoms: Northern (Israel), and Southern (Judah). The north is conquered by Assyria.	1 Kings 12– 2 Kings 2 Chronicles 10–29 (N) Jonah, Amos, Obadiah, Hosea (S) Isaiah, Micah, Joel	Asa, Jehoshaphat, Joash False worship system of Jeroboam I Assyrians deport citizens of the Northern kingdom
VIII **SURVIVING** **KINGDOM** 722–586	Judah continues as a nation but only until its own exile at the hands of the Babylonian conqueror, Nebuchadnezzar.	2 Kings 18–25 2 Chronicles 30–36 Habakkuk, Nahum, Jeremiah, Zephaniah	Hezekiah, Josiah New Covenant Temple destroyed People deported
IX **CAPTIVITY** 605–536	The people of Judah are held captive in Babylon for 70 years	Ezekiel Daniel Lamentations	Jeremiah, Daniel, Ezekiel
X **THE** **RETURN** 537–400	A remnant returns to resettle the land and to rebuild Jerusalem.	Ezra, Nehemiah Haggai, Zechariah, Esther, Malachi	Ezra, Nehemiah, Esther The Temple rebuilt Jerusalem rebuilt

GENESIS
The Book of Origins

Genesis takes its name from the Bible's first Hebrew word, usually translated "in the beginning." The word may also be rendered "to begin with": an affirmation that to understand ourselves and our universe, we must begin with the fact of Creation. On the foundation of Creation the Bible builds its unique picture of life and death, sin and redemption, history, and the future triumph of good over evil in God's eternal kingdom.

Structure. Genesis is divided into two major sections. Chapters 1–11 present the personal nature of God's creation and his relationship with human beings. Chapters 12–50 present the purposive nature of God's creation, revealed through Covenant promises which God makes to Abraham. In spite of the way sin has distorted the beauty of the original creation described here, God intends to bring blessing to all mankind. Thus Genesis reveals God as a Person who is lovingly, intimately, and totally involved in the beginnings of our universe, and also in the outworking of history. We can outline Genesis around these two Creation themes: our universe is personal, and purposive, for it has its origin in a personal and loving God.

Outline

I. Revelation of Personal Origins
   1. of the physical universe: 1:1–2:3
   2. of humankind: 2:4–25
   3. of sin: 3:1–24
   4. of death: 4:1–26
   5. of judgment: 5:1–9:28
   6. of peoples and cultures: 10:1–11:32
II. Revelation of Purpose in Origins
   1. through Abraham 12–25
   2. through Isaac 25–28
   3. through Jacob 28–36
   4. through Joseph 37–50

Source. Jews and Christians from earliest times have regarded Moses as author of the first five books of the OT. Thus the earliest

possible date for Genesis' existence in its present written form is
c. 1450 B.C. Much in Genesis surely existed earlier as part of the
vital, living tradition of the Hebrew people, shared verbally across
the generations. Most significant is the fact that throughout history
believers have remained confident that Genesis, as all Scripture,
is God's own reliable and relevant revelation of reality.

Chapter 1. The Personal Origins of the Physical Universe

In the beginning, God. The first words of Genesis immediately
confront the dominant modern world view, which assumes that
life sprang from random motion in dead, impersonal matter. Mod-
erns explain origins in the chance interplay of mindless atoms:
the Bible presents an all-powerful Person, who calls the physical
universe into being.

Scripture's view of creation has always been radical. While the
OT does reflect the culture of its human writers, the Genesis version
of Creation is joltingly different from the myths of the ancient
world. The Bible alone introduces a single God, who towers above
nature, and whose personal action explains all beginnings.

Ancient Concepts of Origins

	Mesopotamian	Egyptian	Greek	Genesis
VIEW OF GOD(S)	Many competing gods/goddesses	Many related gods/goddesses	Many warring gods/goddesses	One God
NATURE GOD(S)	Good/evil petty, warring	Represents natural phenomena & abstract ideas	Adulterous, petty, limited	A good, all-powerful Being
RELATION MAN/GOD(S)	Man vastly inferior; from blood of murdered god Kingu	Little moral or personal relationship	Both subject to fate; gods capriciously intervene	Mankind is created and loved by God
SOURCE OF MATERIAL UNIVERSE	Corpse of slain deity, Tiamat	Five myths give different explanations	Universe pre-existed the gods	The One God is creator and designer

What does the fact that we live in a universe shaped by
God mean to us, and how do we respond to God as Creator?
You'll find beautiful insights in Psalms 104 and 148 and in Isaiah
40.

Heavens and earth: 1,2. God's creative act did involve bringing the universe into being from nothing. But in Genesis 1 the emphasis is on God's work of shaping the universe. Some have attempted to divide verses one and two and to insert geologic eras and prehistoric animals in the "gap." The structure of the Hebrew sentence does not support this interpretation. And the Genesis language rivets our attention on a single theme: our universe was structured to the design of a God who brings order and meaning to all existence. It is valid to raise questions about the relationship of Genesis to scientific theories (see *The Seven Days: the Bible and Science*). But we are not to be distracted from the primary goal of Bible study. We come to Scripture to discern God's message to us, and to meet him.

The NT enlarges our Creator's portrait. We're told he is the one who, as Jesus Christ, came to reveal God's love. We're taught that our universe is even today upheld and sustained by his power. You can see this in John 1:1–14; Colossians 1:15–20; Hebrews 1:1–4, 10–12.

God in Genesis 1. An overview of this chapter reveals much about God as a Person. (1) The text says several times that God "separated" [lit., "made a distinction between"] aspects of creation. He planned a complex world marked by great diversity, yet stable and dependable. (2) The chapter repeats God's evaluation of his workmanship: "it was good." (3) The chapter stresses God's active involvement in Creation. "God" appears 32 times here, in nearly every case as subject of some active verb. The God of Genesis 1 plans and establishes a complex yet stable order, makes moral and esthetic value judgments, and cares enough about the universe to shape it in person. This God is no absentee landlord, nor one who retreats to some "spiritual" realm to escape involvement with the material. Distinct from the universe, yes. Greater than the universe, yes. But the God of Genesis 1 cares, and is involved!

The Seven Days: the Bible and Science

The Genesis creation story raises questions about the relationship between the Bible and science. The world view presented in Genesis stands in direct conflict with the present "scientific" view of the universe. The Bible presents the universe and life as direct creations of a living, personal God, in opposition to the notion that life was spontaneously generated from non-living matter in a cold, impersonal universe.

Actually, the evolutionary view is not "scientific." It is merely the theory accepted by most modern scientists. As history shows, scientific theories constantly change! The change of scientific theories is one reason why we should not try to interpret the Bible to make it "fit" some contemporary view. This is particularly true when Bible scholars differ on just how to understand the details of a passage like our creation story. For instance, six different theories have been suggested as interpretations of this passage. (1) The gap theory proposes an original creation ruined by Satan, and a seven-day process setting it to rights. (2) The indefinite age theory suggests that "day" is figurative and represents geologic eras. (3) The day-age theory supposes a twenty-four hour period to introduce vegetation, for instance, and then millenia for development before the next day. (4) Creation *in situ* assumes seven literal days a few thousand years ago, with coal, fossils, etc. created in place to give the appearance of age. (5) The revelatory day theory suggests the seven were days in which God revealed his work to Moses. (6) The revelatory device theory says the human author simply used "days" to organize his material.

What about Bible/science conflicts? Neither the scientist nor the believer has enough data to speak confidently about the "how" of origins. But in the true conflict, between world views, we can affirm confidently that the Bible's teaching is trustworthy. God is! He is the Creator, and he is the source of our life.

Day one, two; 3–8. The foundation for life on earth is laid as light is created, the earth set spinning, and the waters divided. The passage uses phenomenological language: that is, it describes events from the viewpoint of an observer on earth. Thus the writer describes alternating night and day as separation of light and darkness, and describes water condensing to fill the seas and to fill the skies as clouds of water vapors being "under" and "above."

Day three, four; 9–9. The organization of the earth for habitation is described. Dry land rises, is seeded with vegetation, and the pattern of alternating seasons controlled by sun and moon is established.

Day five, six; 20–31. The population of the earth takes place. First comes creation of all sorts of living creatures. Then as a separate and culminating act, God stoops to shape human beings. God's words of evaluation show this is the culmination of creation. The other days' work is pronounced good: the work of making mankind is "very good." It is this description of the origin of humanity that we must begin with if we are to realize who we really are. (See *Human Nature: Man in the Image of God.*)

"Let us." The language of God's statement has been noted by many. "Let us make man" suggests to some simply the plural of majesty: the monarch's way of saying "we" rather than "I." Others see this language as early evidence of the Trinity, a doctrine which

emerges gradually through later revelation. The word "God" in Genesis 1, Elohim, is also a plural form.

Dominion. God's gift of dominion implies responsibility. God has given us authority over his creation; we are responsible to guard our environment. The Christian is to have an ecological concern. We are to exercise our dominion responsibly.

Day seven: 2:1–3. God's rest. Jewish commentators made much of the fact that no "morning and evening" statement mark this day as closed.

Hebrews 4:1–10 says we can share God's rest today. The thought is that Creation involved a complete plan for the ages. God cannot be surprised by an event. When we trust God, and respond with obedient confidence that he is in control, we experience his rest.

Chapter 2. The Personal Origins of Humankind

Genesis 1 gives an overview of the sequence of Creation events. Genesis 2 returns to the Creation of mankind, to provide more detail. The description given of Eden, the environment God designed for the first pair, is particularly revealing.

Location of Eden: 8–14. Eden was located to the east of the OT writer, at the origin of four rivers. Two, known today as the Tigris and Euphrates, originate in the general area of Armenia, in the Fertile Crescent where civilization's earliest records are found (see *Archaeology,* p. 36,37). The other two rivers cannot be identified, and possibly were affected by later topographical changes.

Human Nature: Man in the Image of God

Who are we? To some you and I are simply animals, descended from single-celled ancestors. To others we are merely fallen creatures, with sinfulness being man's defining characteristic. But to the psalmist we are the focus of God's concern, "crowned with glory and honor" (Ps. 8:5). The biblical view of mankind reflects a confidence that, with all our failings, we are special. We bear the "image and likeness" of God. This is the place we must begin to understand mankind.

This phrase, "image and likeness," is best understood as a statement about personhood. We share with God capacities that only persons possess: we think, we feel, we value, we choose. It is because we are, like God, persons, that we have the capacity for fellowship with God and for meaningful relationships with each other.

Many have been troubled by man's capacity for hatred, brutality, and crime. Certainly sin (see *Sin: OT,* p. 33) has twisted us. But sin has not robbed us of personhood, or of the potential for fellowship with God. It is in the Bible's revelation of our origin in God's gift of personhood that we grasp the Source of our capacity for love, self-sacrifice, appreciation for truth and beauty, creativity, worship, and moral sensibility. The good in mankind is adequately explained only by our origin at God's own hand.

The Bible, like our newspapers, testifies to the damage sin does in human experience. We carry God's likeness imperfectly. But the basic fact is that we human beings have the potential for restoration. God's image has not been eradicated (cf. Gen. 9; James 3:9). We are created in the image of God, and thus have infinite worth and value. Our respect for others, our acceptance of ourselves, and our sense of the worth of every individual, rest on this foundation.

For study: Psalm 8; Hebrews 2:5–18.

Eden's design: 4–20. The pre-Flood world described in Genesis is quite different from the world we know. Heavy cloud cover softens the light that reaches earth. The land is watered by evening mists rather than rains, the subterranean waters bubble in multiplied springs and streams. These unique conditions are sketched but not fully described.

What is most significant here is the way God designed the garden (LXX, "park of delight") for habitation. Each detail seems planned to encourage full development of human potential. There is beauty to nurture man's aesthetic capacities (9); there are natural resources to use (11); there are opportunities to exercise creativity (19, 20); meaningful work to do (15) and another person with whom to share all the good gifts of God. In the environment God planned, capacities which God himself exercised in creating, and which he shared with humankind, are given full scope for development.

The tree of knowing good and evil: 15–17. Some have seen placement of the tree of the knowledge of good and evil in Eden as some sort of trap. We need to understand it in the context of God's design of Eden. It too is an opportunity provided by God. Man's moral nature must be exercised if he is to fulfill his potential as a person. Placement of the tree is no trap, but provision of an opportunity for moral fulfillment.

There is, by the way, no indication of the length of time Adam and Eve lived in the Garden, and obeyed God's command, before their fall.

Creation of woman: 19–23. This description of the origin of the sexes is particularly significant (see *Male and Female,* p. 32). In the passage, note that (1) Adam was told to search for a companion in the animal world before Eve's creation. None were suitable. Only one who was as fully a person as Adam could possibly share a significant relationship with him. (2) The Genesis story stresses the identity shared by woman and man, not differences between them. Adam explicitly recognizes this identity in his statement, "this is now bone of my bones and flesh of my flesh" (23). This is the necessary starting point for all our understanding of man/woman relationships: we are, together, persons made in the image of God, each with a full share of every potential that God has given to the human race.

Marriage: 25. This brief statement shows the family to be the first institution to be established by God.

Reviewing this chapter on the origins of humankind, we see again the early Genesis stress on the personal. It is God, not mindless nature, who lovingly designs mankind for fellowship with himself. In the description of Eden we see God's deep concern that our potential as persons be fully realized, in the company of others for whom we can care deeply, and with whom we can share God's good gifts.

Chapter 3. The Personal Origins of Sin

Genesis now describes sin's entry. Man was given true moral responsibility. He used that freedom to choose, but chose the wrong path.

Satan: 1. Scripture identifies Satan as the one acting through the serpent (2 Cor. 11:3; Rev. 12:9). The principles of evil had entered the universe earlier, before Eden's creation (see *Satan,* p. 245). Now, as humanity is subverted from allegiance to God, sin introduces evil into human experience by the personal choice of the first pair.

Temptation: 1–6. Satan's strategy is always to drive a wedge of doubt into man's relationship with God. God's word is questioned (2), his motives and love subtly denied (5), and his warnings flatly contradicted. Eve set aside confidence in God's wisdom and love, as greed for sensory pleasure and position controlled (6). The pattern is often repeated (see Matt. 4:1–11; 1 John 1:15–17; James 1:13–15).

Male and Female

Hebrew culture was patriarchal (father-centered). In such a culture there was little emphasis on women, nor opportunity for careers outside the home. Thus it is striking to see in Genesis a strong affirmation of woman's worth as a person. (1) The common identity of men and women as persons made in God's image is unequivocally taught. (2) Women are given full share in humanity's dominion over God's creation. The partnership established by God was soon distorted by sin. But the ideal of full equality as persons is clearly taught.

Genesis 3:16 contains God's announcement of one impact of sin on human experience. The intended equality will be distorted; domination and subordination will mar relationships between the sexes.

Loss of the ideal is even reflected in certain OT laws which place women in a weaker legal position (cf. Num. 5:11–31; 30:1–15). Yet other laws affirm equality (cf. Exod. 20:12; Deut. 21:18–21). Undoubtedly women had more rights in Israel, and were granted more respect, than among other ancient peoples.

It is also important to see in Proverbs 31, which describes the role of a wife in Israel's agricultural economy, that even her limited role made provision for development of every potential of personhood. It's also revealing to study the lives of women like Deborah and Esther, who as religious and political leaders guided their people as proficiently as any man. For study: Proverbs 31, other references above. See also (*Sex,* p. 100; *Headship,* p. 685; *Women in the Church,* p. 625).

"Knowing good and evil:" 5. This was a direct lie by the serpent. Adam and Eve were already in God's likeness. Their coming to know evil intimately by sinning crushed God's moral likeness. God understands evil, but by personal experience "knows" only good. "We can only tell whether something is good for us by trying it" is an ancient satanic lie, designed to wreck human lives.

Psychological impact of sin: 7–13. Moral and psychological changes accompanied the first act of sin. Adam and Eve were crushed by guilt and shame (7). They hid from God, afraid of One who had only love for them (8–10). Striking out at each other, they accused and excused (12–13, cf. Rom. 2:15). Such relationships, ripped out of the original pattern of harmony, are still a most obvious and terrible evidence of the reality of sin. Man has been robbed by sin of inner peace, stripped of his fellowship with God, and of deep and easy relationship with others.

Sin: Old Testament

Unlike the NT, the OT has no dominant word for sin. Instead there are multiplied terms which describe offense, perversity, wickedness, violent acts, injustice, and so on. These, however, may be grouped as follows: (1) Some words imply deviation from the right way, or missing the mark. (2) Some imply conscious rebellion, unfaithfulness to a commitment. (3) Some imply a state of sin, a quality of character. Thus we may struggle to do right, but find ourselves falling short. We may know the good, but perversely turn from it. We find within a strange alienation in our relationship to God and with other men. Tainted, individuals in society find themselves trapped in a web of selfishness and injustice.

The OT affirms that all are tainted by sin, our common racial heritage from Adam and Eve. Still, man in the OT is viewed as personally responsible for his choices. There are no excuses: men and nations are to accept responsibility for their actions. But this fact is not meant to bring despair. Facing reality is seen as the first step in redemption, for recognition of the fact of sin is intended to turn man's attention to God. In God's unfailing love and commitment to mankind, hope is found. *For study:* sin's impact: Psalm 14, Isaiah 1, 59; penitence: Psalms 15, 32, 51, 102.

Additional impact of sin: 14–20. Sin's psychological impact was immediate and obvious. Others are now explained. It is best to take God's words here as explanation rather than curse. God outlines the necessary consequences which will flow from Adam and Eve's actions. The serpent's form will change (14) and the final doom of Satan will come from one born of Eden's human race (15). Physical changes will quicken the woman's menstrual cycle (16a), and the partnership of man and woman will be twisted into an ugly struggle for domination (16b). The environment will be affected and work, rather than the joy of ministering to a responsive creation, will become a struggle against unruly nature (17–19). The creation will groan, until a day comes when the curse can be removed (Rom. 8:18–21).

How do the consequences described in Genesis 3 find expression in your own life? Which consequences seem most serious to you?

Redemption prefigured (21–24). Many take God's action in providing animal skins to cover Adam and Eve to prefigure sacrificial atonement, recognized in Moses' day as man's avenue of approach to God. Note that banishment from the Garden was intended as a blessing. Endless life while still in the grip of sin would be no good gift.

Thus Genesis 3 traces even mankind's misery due to sin to a personal origin, this time not in God's action but in the moral choice of our first parents.

Chapters 4, 5. The Personal Origins of Death

God warned Adam about the tree, "when you eat of it you will surely die" (2:17). More than physical death was meant. The NT explains the death sentence [see *Death,* p. 612]. Here Genesis 4 illustrates the dark shadow death will cast.

Genesis 5 gives a geneological record from Adam's son Seth to Noah.

Cain and Abel: 4:1–16. Several themes are found in this tragic story. But its primary purpose is to demonstrate the impact of "death" on human experience. One of Adam's sons becomes angry with his brother. Cain coldly lures his brother out into a field for premeditated murder (8). The meaning of "death" begins to be unveiled.

Cainite civilization: 4:17–24. Cain and one of his sisters establish a settlement in a distant land. Capabilities God gave man are expressed in the resultant civilization, which moves quickly beyond survival levels to division of labor, taming of animals, and the development of a culture which features the musical arts and has the technical competence for metallurgy. Yet the murky pall of man's inner deadness lies over the land, illustrated in Lamech, who breaks God's pattern for marriage by taking two wives, and who excuses murder as repayment for an injury. Today, too, man masters the physical universe. But can we master the principle of death that shrouds our own personality?

Other themes. Cain's anger was kindled when God accepted Abel's animal sacrifice, but would not accept his offering of vegetables. God's statement to Cain, "if you do what is right" (7) makes it clear that Cain knew animal sacrifice was required. Cain appears to realize he merits execution, but is protected (15, 16). The chapter ends with a ray of hope as a new line learns to "call on the name of the Lord" (26).

Hebrew genealogies. In the seventeenth century, Bishop Ussher used OT genealogies to compute a date of 4004 B.C. for creation. He failed to grasp how the Hebrews kept or used genealogies. Generally these records traced roots, or claims to a land, and thus personal identity. This use is common to many non-Western cultures. Hebrew genealogies usually included only the famous. Incomplete genealogies are thus not "inaccurate," but simply reflect cultural patterns (cf. Gen. 10, 11; Matt. 1; Luke 3).

Length of age. Some dismiss the story of ages stretching hundreds of years; others offer explanations. In fact, Middle East traditions tell of an era before a great Flood when ages were extended [see *Archaeological Insights*]. In context, the deep cover of water vapor clouds described in Genesis 1 and 2 may have dampened cosmic radiation, which is associated with aging. Or racial vigor may well have been greater near man's origin in creation. At any rate, the principle of death is further illustrated here in the progressive shortening of man's time on earth.

Archaeological Insights

A mere 150 years ago Bible students had limited insight into Bible backgrounds. Now scientific archaeology, pioneered by Petrie in 1890 and refined by W. F. Albright and others after the 1920s, has provided a flood of data. For instance, from a 1974–76 excavation at ancient Ebla in Syria scholars gained some 15,000 clay tablets from about 2300 B.C. These include epic accounts of Creation and the Flood, literary and school texts, administrative records, trade invoices, poems, letters, and legal records. Yet of some 6,000 sites identified in Palestine alone, only about 200 have been explored, and only 28 excavated extensively. The same proportion holds true throughout the Bible lands area!

Values of archaeology. Some have suggested that archaeology "proves the Bible." Archaeology has corroborated Scripture's outline of history and many of its specific statements. Some rationalistic attacks, such as the challenge to Mosaic authorship on the grounds that writing did not exist in Moses' day, have been decisively refuted. Archaeology also gives us much insight into the cultural context from which our Scriptures sprang. Strikingly, over and over again we see the Bible's towering uniqueness within its culture! For instance, there are similarities between the Mosaic Law and the earlier Code of Hammurabi. But the OT in contrast to it reflects God's viewpoint by placing greater value on persons than on property. Many archaeological discoveries relate to the stories in early Genesis.

Creation. In the mid-1800s, the library of the Assyrian emperor Ashurbanipal at Nineveh yielded the ENUMA ELISH. This story, on clay tablets, explained origins by telling of two living masses of uncreated liquids, male (Apsu) and female (Tiamat). Their mating produced a brood of unruly gods, which Apsu determined to destroy. But one of the gods killed Apsu, and another his raging mate. Then from Tiamat's carcass the physical universe was shaped, while mankind crawled from the rotting blood of one of the rebellious gods, Kingu.

Suffering and death. The MYTH OF ADAPTA is an attempt to explain the origins of human suffering. Three tablets telling the story were found at Nineveh, and a fourth adding to the tale was later discovered in Egyptian archives at Amarna, which date to the fourteenth century B.C. This myth features a tree of life, as does Genesis 3. But in the myth the hero, Adapta, fails to win blessedness not because of sin but because of his obedience to his creator, Ea, who crassly deceives him.

Pre-Flood age length. Inscriptions dating between 2250 and 2000 B.C. give a *Sumerian King List,* first published in 1908. Eight kings are said to have ruled before "the Flood swept over (the earth)." The shortest reign is given as 18,600 years, the longest as 43,200.

The Flood. Stories of a great flood are common to most parts of the world. In the Fertile Crescent, the tale is the Assyrio-Babylonic *Epic of Gilgamesh.* The hero builds a boat five times the size of Noah's ark to escape a catastrophe originated by the gods. In the epic the motive for the Flood is the irritation of the gods at the noisiness of antlike men.

After the Flood the gods repent as they gather greedily to smell the fragrance of the sacrifice offered by the hero, Utnapishtim.

Implications. There are striking similarities between these ancient stories and Genesis. But there are more striking differences. Only Genesis is monotheistic. Only in Genesis is God both moral and loving, and distinct from the material creation. Only in Genesis is man a special creation. Attempts to explain Genesis as a variation of the cultural myths cannot explain the radical differences in basic perspective.

Another explanation is suggested when we accept the basic historical accuracy of the biblical account. Then parallel traditions are understandable as corruptions of a common tradition, rooted in actual events. However one explains the similarities, the differences in moral perspective and vision of God lifts the biblical account far above other ancient writings. Throughout our study of the OT we will draw on archaeological insights to gain a better understanding of, and deeper appreciation for, the message of our Bible.

Chapters 6–9. The Personal Origins of Judgment

The creatures God shaped to reflect his image have now been warped by sin. Adam and Eve have set the course for the race, and events have demonstrated the death they brought (ch. 3–5). Yet all human suffering so far described has come as a natural consequence of human choices. Where God has intervened, it has been to rescue and preserve.

Now however Genesis introduces another OT theme. If the suffering which comes as a natural consequence from sin fails to bring men to repentance, God will act in judgment. As a moral being, committed in his very nature to righteousness, God will not permit sin to exist unchecked.

The Bible speaks often of God as judge. Read Genesis 6–9 for what it reveals of him. Then explore further in Psalms 7, 50 and Isaiah 2.

Moral necessity: 6:1–8. After multiplied generations, wickedness dominates. This condition, with "every inclination of the thoughts of [man's] heart only evil all the time" (5), does not stimulate God to outraged anger. The text speaks of God's grief, and says "his heart . . . filled with pain" (6). God does not enjoy judging. He cares for us too much. God's judgments flow from moral necessity.

The obscure reference to the "sons of god" who had children by the "daughters of men" (2, 4) is much debated. Some note that the phrase is used elsewhere of angels, and identify the "sons" here with fallen angels (demons). Others interpret the phrases to

Noah's Ark

mean intermingling of the lines of Seth and Cain, with gradual abandonment of the knowledge of God. The point of the passage should not be lost in such dispute. Wickedness did permeate the pre-Flood culture, and God finally determines to judge.

Noah: 6:8–10. The single exception in this era of moral depravity is Noah, who "walked with God." Neither inner sin nor corrupt society determined his individual choice. We too remain responsible moral agents.

The Flood foretold: 6:11–22. God explains the moral basis of the coming Flood to Noah. The earth is corrupt, and full of wickedness (11, 13). The words chosen emphasize matured evil. Sin is institutionalized in Noah's society. God must purge the cancerous civilization, and man will be given a new start in Noah's family. The NT says, "By faith Noah, when warned about things not yet seen, in holy fear built an ark to save his family" (Heb. 11:7).

The proportions of the ark reflect modern shipbuilding specifications. The family was given some 120 years (3) to build the 450 × 75 × 45 foot vessel. These vast dimensions were required to provide space to preserve breeding stock of air-breathing animals, and to store provisions. Note that the pairs of animals are said to be of every "kind." The Hebrew word cannot be identified with any zoological terms, such as "species," so there is no way to estimate how many pairs were involved.

What Was the Flood?

Few biblical events have stirred more interest. Is the story a myth, or is it historical? Was the Flood universal, or local? When did it happen? How does it fit into the historic or prehistoric record? We know that:

1. No other story is so widely repeated in the traditions of ancient peoples all over the globe as that of a judgmental flood.

2. Detailed tradition from the Mesopotamian valley, where Scripture locates Noah, has revealed striking supportive evidence *(Enumi Elish)*.

3. Some argue the Flood was world-wide (universal), with "all the high mountains under the entire heavens" (Gen. 7:19) covered to a depth of 20 feet (7:20). Others argue this is phenomenological language, implying only that the high ground in the writer's part of the world was inundated. Local Flood proponents argue that God's purpose, to judge a civilization which was likely localized in the great valleys of the Fertile Crescent, could be accomplished without universality.

4. Universalists see the Flood as a great catastrophe, with continental changes. The water vapor canopy of Genesis 2 fell to earth; quakes released subterranean waters on which the continents floated. The great weight of released waters resculptured the surface of the globe, thrusting up mountain ranges and depressing sea beds. This view is well presented in *The Genesis Flood,* by Whitcombe and Morris.

5. Local Flood proponents argue that a catastrophic Flood would leave different evidence in the fossil record and rock strata. They interpret the words of Genesis 7 phenomenologically.

6. Neither group has solid evidence for dating the Flood, though suggestions range from 10 to 60 thousand years ago.

7. The NT treats the Flood as historical (Matt. 24:36 f; I Peter 3:18 f). Both the Old and New Testaments see the Flood as evidence that God will judge mankind. Those who scoff and insist that "ever since our fathers died, everything goes on as it has since the beginning of creation" are warned by the fact that the ancient world was "deluged and destroyed." The present world, too, is being "kept for the day of judgment and the destruction of ungodly men" (2 Peter 3:3–7).

Rescue of animals: 7:1–10. The animals that entered the ark included one pair of unclean animals (generally predators and scavengers) and seven pair of clean (animals usable for food).

The Flood described: 7:11–24. When all entered the great boat, God sealed the doors. Generally the ark has been visualized as rectangular, with openings high at the top for ventilation, shaped to maintain itself upright in tossing seas (see illustration, p. 38).

Rains and subterranean fountains are said to be the source of the flood waters (8:2). The text is explicit that "every living thing that moved on the earth perished" (21), repeating "everything on dry land that had the breath of life in its nostrils died" (22) and "every living thing on the face of the earth was wiped out" (23). Whether universal or local in scope, Genesis emphasizes the fact that the Flood did accomplish God's stated purpose of judgment.

Chronology: 7–8. If we assume the Hebrew calendar, which took April (Abib) as the first month, but do not consider its thirty-day months, we can gain a picture of the sequence of events and the time Genesis says the Flood consumed.

Ark built	6:3,14	
Animals enter	7:10	10 May
Flood begins	7:11	17 May
Waters increase	7:12	26 June
Waters prevail on inundated earth	7:24	
Ark touches ground in mountains	8:4	13 October
Waters recede, mountain tops seen	8:4	1 January
Windows opened, birds sent out	8:6	10 February
Dove sent	8:10	17 February
Dove sent again	8:13	24 February
Ark door opened, Noah sees land	8:13	1 April
Land completely dry, exit the ark	8:14	27 May

Noah's worship, 8:18–22. The survivors express thanks by sacrificial offerings. God makes a decision to never again bring such destruction on the whole race.

God's Covenant, 9:1–17. God's determination not to destroy the earth by flood again is revealed to Noah in the form of a covenant (see *Covenant,* p. 51). This is best understood as a promise which reveals God's firm intention. The Noahic covenant is made with all mankind and the animal creation as well. While the earth remains, such mass destruction will not take place.

A number of features of this passage are fascinating. Animal life is given to man for food (3). Was the pre-Flood culture vegetarian? The death penalty is established for those who shed human blood, "for in the image of God has God made man" (17). Is capital punishment essential to justice? The rainbow is established as a sign or reminder of God's covenant (17). Was the rainbow unknown to the canopied pre-Flood world described in Genesis 2? Was its significance to remind of God's oath when the strange phenomenon of rain might bring Noah's family terror?

Many questions are suggested by unexplained details in early Genesis, which does imply a different structure to the world before the Flood. But these questions are unanswerable: we simply do not have enough data. What is clear in the Genesis account is the major Bible teachings about origins. We live in a personal universe. And the Person who created us is a moral being, who will judge—or save.

Prophetic curse: 9:18–28. Ancient peoples thought curses caused future events. In contrast, OT curses are predictive, generally based on an observed characteristic which is expected to shape future generations (cf. Jacob's blessing of his sons, each with what is "appropriate to him," Gen. 49:28). Here Ham's immoral actions are projected and the future of one of his sons, Canaan, described. Archaeological research has shown the Canaanites became a sexually and religiously degraded people.

Chapters 10, 11. From Noah to Abraham

The origins have been described. Now Genesis uses two genealogical documents to link Abraham, and thus the people of Israel, to the beginnings. More importantly, the link is established between the God of the beginnings, and the God who spoke to Abraham and through Moses.

Origin of languages: 11:1–8. One brief story is included in these two listings. Noah's descendants were instructed to "fill the earth" (9:1). Instead, they chose to build a unified culture and constructed a "tower" as symbol and seal of their common identity (4). Many believe this was a ziggurat: a vast construction of clay bricks, on which southern Babylonian peoples housed the shrines of their city's patron gods. Thus the tower probably signified more than disobedience. It demonstrates the quick return of the generations after the Flood to paganism. Genesis tells how God confused the languages of these people, making unity impossible and causing different language groups to spread out from the central plains.

Table of nations: Genesis 10. This list of peoples is the oldest known ethnographic document. It is significantly different from the genealogy of chapter 11. Here the Hebrew words ("sons of") showing relationship are not in causitive form, indicating that parenthood is not in view. Instead the table records colonies or tribal groups which became peoples. Much research has shown the table of nations speaks accurately about peoples and nations which existed many centuries before the writing of our Bible. This passage also describes Nimrod (8–11) as the world's first dictator.

Shem to Abraham: Genesis 11. As does the genealogical list of Genesis 5, this list identifies ten ancestors. This number and the obvious abbreviation of the list are characteristic of Bible genealogies. The chief men highlighted would be easily memorized, and the list would serve to confirm the roots of the people of Israel, as well as the claim that the workings of Israel's God can be traced back to Creation.

Part Two: Revelation of Purpose in Origins

Genesis is divided into two sections. Chapters 1–11 explain the origins of the universe and mankind in the creative acts of one

God. In the context of Creation, the origins of human suffering, sin, death, and of hope, are also explained. In addition, God reveals himself in these early Genesis chapters. We see him as a powerful, yet very personal and loving God, who deals in mercy but will not draw back from judgment. In these first chapters the foundation is laid for our concept of God, and for our understanding of the human condition.

These first Genesis chapters sketch God's dealings with mankind as a whole from Creation to Abraham, a period of time which must have extended over many thousands of years. The second section, Genesis 12–50, concentrates on less than two centuries, and only four generations. This emphasis is significant. God no longer deals with the whole race, but with a single family, that of Abraham. Through this family he intends to ultimately bring salvation to all. Beginning with Genesis 12, the 905 succeeding chapters of our OT concentrate on the chosen people, Israel, through whom God's purposes will be worked out.

The heart of this second part of Genesis, and the OT itself, is the covenant God makes with Abraham, committing him to a unique relationship with man, and embodying promises which reveal the purposes he will be working out through salvation history.

Times of the Patriarchs

In the days of Abraham (c. 2000 B.C.) a number of mature civilizations touched on the land of the Bible. Abraham himself was born in lower Mesopotamia (present day Iraq). Ur, his city, had been the center of a strong state. In Abraham's day it had libraries, sewers, two-storied air conditioned dwellings, running water in many homes. There was an active business section, and well developed legal and educational systems.

In Egypt, Pharaohs had ruled the land along the Nile for nearly a millennium, and the great pyramids at which tourists wonder today had rested on the sands for centuries. Hittites in Asia Minor and Hurrians maintained vigorous northern cultures.

Established trade routes linked these civilizations, and many of the well-traveled roads passed through Palestine, then the land of Canaanites and Amorites. Gold, silver, copper, woolen cloth, tin, and clothing of various types as well as other commodities were carried by the traders whose caravans stitched the ancient world together. Towns which the Bible says Abraham visited lie along these trade routes, in a zone where rainfall remains high enough today to support the flocks he traveled with.

Thus it would be a mistake to visualize Abraham as a primitive.

Days of the Patriarchs

His times were cultured, his people wealthy, his civilization governed by customs which had matured over centuries.

Yet the patriarchal period also became a time of change. There were pressures of newer peoples on the old. There was competition for power, bringing shifting alliances and coalitions of kings. Cities were sacked and destroyed; populations shifted and thinned. Through it all the patriarchs were called by God to wander as nomads in a land where Canaanite peoples had been settled for nearly a millennium.

Historicity. A good deal is known of the customs and the practices of peoples in the second millennium B.C. The most important source of information, but not the only one, is some 20,000 clay tablets which were found between 1925–31 in the Hurrian town of Nuzi. The find dates to within a few hundred years of the patriarchs, and reflects a society and customs which had changed significantly by 1000 B.C. In the Nuzi tablets, illustrations of adoption processes, regulations about transfer of real estate, relationships between slave women and their mistresses, and many other aspects of daily life parallel and illustrate the Genesis stories of the patriarchs. These discoveries show how naturally the Genesis account fits into the

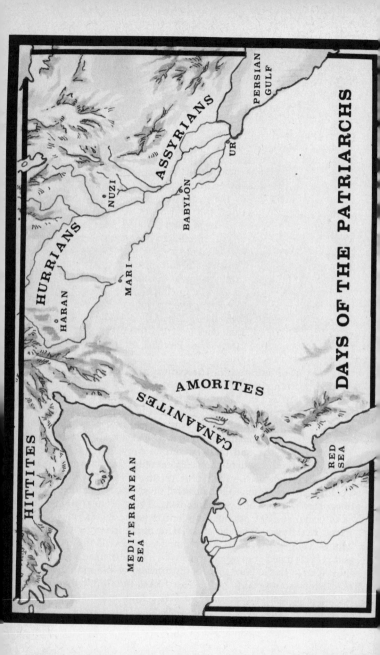

cultural setting. Multiplied links with the world of the second millennium B.C. demonstrate conclusively the historical basis of the Bible's record of events.

Religion. Abraham undoubtedly worshiped idols in his home city of Ur. The city's chief god, Nanna, lived atop the great clay-brick Ziggurat in a temple that overlooked the city he was supposed to own, and to govern through the city's priest/king. Multitudes of other gods and goddesses filled the imagination of Abraham's fellow citizens. These worshiped their idols and sought supernatural guidance from diviners, who used magic to discover the will of the gods or to manipulate them for their clients. Pagan sacrifices, thought of as meals for the gods, were offered out of fear or in an attempt to bribe deities. But in it all there was no hope. Few people in Mesopotamia thought there was an afterlife. They believed, with the Epic of Gilgamesh, that "when the gods created mankind, they allotted to mankind Death, but Life they withheld in their hands." Abraham was a cultured man, and the chosen people were selected out of a great civilization. But, as Joshua reminds Israel, "Long ago your forefathers, including Terah, the father of Abraham and Nahor, lived beyond the River and worshiped other gods" (Josh. 24:2). Then God spoke to Abraham, and led him out of spiritual darkness, that through him all mankind might rediscover light.

Chapter 12. The Call of Abraham

Call and covenant: 1–9. God revealed himself to the 75-year-old Abraham, commanding him to leave his country, people, and relations, to travel to a land God would reveal. This was Abraham's first test of faith: to abandon all that provides human beings with a sense of security, and trust his fate to the faithfulness of God.

Here too is the first biblical statement of the covenant, the promise made by God to Abraham and his descendants, which became the foundation of the OT believers' hope and sense of identity. From this point, God will be known as the "God of Abraham": the One who spoke to the first father, and gave him great and precious promises. The basic covenant elements given in Genesis 12 are:

* I will make you into a great nation (2)	Childless Abraham is to father a host of descendants.
* I will bless you (2)	God will work in Abraham's life and do him good.

* I will make your name great (2)	Abraham will be respected and revered as a source of blessing.
* I will bless those who bless you, curse those who curse you (3)	Individuals and nations will be dealt with by God on the basis of their reaction to Abraham's seed.
* I will give you this land for your offspring (7)	Canaan (now called Palestine) is given to Abraham's descendants.

This covenant is no bargain, contingent on Abraham's future behavior. The covenant is a statement of God's purposes, expressed as firm "I will's." It's important to realize that the covenant commitments will be expanded and explained, both in Scripture (cf. Gen. 15, 17; Jer. 30–31; Heb. 7–10) and in Israel's history. This early covenant is the very core of God's Old Testament revelation, and the key to our grasp of Scripture's view of history.

Read the Covenant promises (2, 3, 7). What ways can you see them worked out in history? Which seems most important to you?

Abraham stumbles: 10–20. As if to demonstrate the fact that God's commitments are not contingent on Abraham's works, the text immediately records two incidents. Abraham's faith fails when famine strikes Canaan, and he leaves the land for Egypt. In Egypt he fears because of his wife's beauty, and asks her to lie about their relationship. The fear may have been well based. A papyrus from the twelfth century B.C. tells the Tale of the Two Brothers, in which a Pharaoh once secured a beautiful woman to be his wife even though she already had a husband. The covenant rests on God's faithfulness, not Abraham's.

Abraham

Today Christian, Muslim, and Jew alike revere Abraham as founder of their faith, and trace their religious heritage back to this man who abandoned his home and comforts to follow his vision of God. When Abraham was born in Mesopotamia, Europe was populated by roaming tribal groups without written language or national boundary. Before the founding of Rome 1,400 years were to pass. China's first dynasty, the Hsia, was just taking form. It is to be a thousand years before any surviving Chinese literature will be delicately brushed on paper by yellowed scribes.

As a man, Abraham was a product of his times. Judged by the standards of his day, he was a moral man who carefully followed established customs (cf. Gen. 16; 21:12–21). At times he went beyond what convention would have required (cf. Gen. 13,14). But the Bible does not hold up Abraham

Excavations at Ur, home of Abraham

Mosque of the Patriarchs where Abraham purchased a cave in which to bury Sarah (Gen. 29:9–19). Later he was buried here (Gen. 25:9). Eventually Isaac, Rebekah and Leah were also buried here (Gen. 49:31–33)

as some sort of idealized hero. He is portrayed honestly, his faults and sins starkly recorded (cf. Gen. 12:10–20; 20). Thus the NT identifies Abraham as one of the "wicked" who, like the rest of us, desperately need forgiveness and redemption.

Yet two things set Abraham apart. First, God chose to reveal himself to Abraham, and to enter into a covenant relationship with him. Second, Abraham responded to God's self-revelation with a faith that led to radical changes in his life. Whenever God spoke to him, Abraham's faith produced obedience. He followed the word of his God, gripped by the sure confidence that what God had spoken would take place.

The NT focuses on three pivotal events in Abraham's life which illustrate this faith. (1) When called by God to leave his homeland and travel for months to a foreign land, Abraham obeyed and went. (2) When told by God that he and his wife, Sarah, would have a son, though he was long past age and his 90-year-old wife was barren, Abraham believed God. (3) When tested with a command to sacrifice his son, Isaac, through whose offspring God promised the Covenant would be fulfilled, Abraham prepared to obey. He reasoned that God could raise the dead—and would, if necessary, to keep his promises!

Abraham was merely a man. But the biblical record shows that he was a man whose life was anchored in God, and one who believed his promises.

When we read the record, we are deeply aware of Abraham's humanity. His thoughts and his actions were patterned by a culture whose morality at times shocks or disturbs us. But Abraham held fiercely to hope in God. You and I, too, are culture bound. We, too, are marred by weaknesses as well as blessed with strengths. And we, too, can be lifted beyond ourselves by Abraham's kind of confident faith in God. *For study:* Romans 4; Hebrews 11.

Chapter 13. Abraham and Lot

As the herds and flocks of Abraham and his nephew, Lot, increased, their numbers strained the land's capacity for grazing. Archaeology has shown that in the Middle Bronze Age, c. 2000–1500 B.C., Palestine had many verdant valleys. Many different peoples lived in valley settlements: Amorites (14:13) and Hittites (23:3) as well as Canaanites. Nomadic troops, like Abraham's, used the sparsely covered higher ground. Now Abraham gives Lot his choice, and the younger man chooses the broad Jordan valley, "well watered, like the garden of the Lord, like the land of Egypt toward Zoar" (10). Lot settled just outside the walls of a city called Sodom.

After this God again promises Abraham "and your offspring" the whole land "forever" (15). For a childless man in his 80s, whose name means "father," this might seem mockery. But Abraham believed God.

📖 What values may have motivated Lot's choice? What is shown of Abraham's values? What here can you apply to your own choices?

Chapter 14. Abraham Rescues Lot

A coalition of raiding kings comes from the east to war against a local coalition of city states. The Mari tablets indicate such an incident could only have taken place in this period of Palestine's history, for it was an age of coalitions. Archaeologists have even traced a string of Middle Bronze Age settlements along the route that Genesis indicates the invaders took and have named it King's Highway.

In the battle Sodom and Gomorrah were sacked. Lot and his possessions were taken with the other booty. Abraham mounted a rescue expedition, attacking the larger force at night (15). The fact Abraham was able to command some 318 "trained men in his household" (14) indicates his wealth and the size of his retinue.

Melchizedek, King of Salem (Jerusalem): 18–20. OT names identify as well as label. This one means "righteous ruler," and the man is identified as a "priest of God most high." The fact he blesses Abraham is significant. In the ancient world blessings were given by superiors. Abraham's tithe also explicitly affirms Melchizedek's superiority.

The OT tells us no more about Melchizedek, though the NT returns to this story to help explain Christ's priesthood (Heb. 7). In context, however, we note something important. God has chosen Abraham. But he has not abandoned others! Whoever shares Abraham's faith in God, as did Melchizedek and Job (who also probably dates from this age) finds a meaningful relationship with the Lord.

📖 Abraham refused to accept wealth offered by a grateful King of Sodom. What were his reasons?

Chapter 15. The Promise Confirmed by Oath

Abraham's heir: 1–7. According to customs attested in the Nuzi tablets, property in Abraham's culture must be inherited by family. As a childless man, Abraham normally would adopt a household servant or freedman. Here Abraham identifies his choice of Eliezer of Damascus, "since I remain childless." God repeats the promise of Genesis 12. Abraham's own son will be heir, and his offspring beyond counting. Here appears the OT's first clear statement of the nature of saving faith: "Abraham believed the Lord, and he credited it to him as righteousness" (v. 6) [See *Faith*, p. 562].

Covenant cut: 8–21. God's promise is now confirmed by a formal oath (see *Covenant*, p. 51). Note (1) the slain animals mark this as the most binding of oaths. (2) Only God passes between the animal parts. Normally both parties to a covenant would pass through, thus binding each to responsibilities that must be fulfilled. Here God binds himself alone, without condition, to fulfill his promise. (3) The focus here is on possession of the land, one of the Genesis 12 "I wills." God reveals that a 400-year captivity in Egypt lies in the future. Not every generation will possess the land. Thus the benefits of the promise need not be experienced by each generation for the Covenant to remain valid.

Faith would be important to Abraham's descendents, as the fulfillment of the promises was delayed for four centuries. How does this parallel Abraham's own faith experience with God? Are you, too, sometimes called on to have faith "in spite of"?

Chapter 16. Ishmael's Birth

The Nuzi tablets show it was common in Abraham's time for a barren woman to seek a child from her husband by one of her slave women. Sarah finally took this culturally accepted course. According to custom, if Sarah should later have a son, he would become heir. We have confirming information that each action reported in this chapter was sanctioned in every detail by contemporary custom. But the course was taken without God's direction, and led to much conflict within the household (4–6). It is of note that Ishmael is the father of the Arabs, with whom Israel still experiences conflict today.

Chapter 17. The Covenant Expanded

Thirteen years pass, and God again appears to explain more of his covenant purposes.

Relationship stressed: 1–8. Two aspects of the covenant are stressed. Abraham is to father many peoples, and thus his name is changed to Abraham, meaning "father of multitudes." Also, stress is laid on the relationship to be enjoyed by Abraham's descendants with God: the covenant is to be everlasting, and means that the Lord will "be your God and the God of your descendants after you."

Circumcision: 9–14. Circumcision has been misunderstood by some as a condition of the covenant. But the covenant is made with Abraham and his descendants as a class. Circumcision has to do with the membership of the individual in the class. Circumcision (removal of the flap of skin which covers the tip of the penis) was intended as a "sign of the covenant between you and me." Circumcision identified the individual with the people of God, and one uncircumcised was considered "cut off from the people" and thus outside the Covenant relationship (14).

Covenant

The idea of covenant played a vital role in OT times. In essence, a covenant was a solemn promise, made binding by an oath. The covenant concept was applied to a wide range of situations. It would govern alliances between families or nations (cf. Gen. 14:13; 21:27,32; 31:44; Josh. 9:6 f), and also serve as a constitution or definition of the relationship between an overlord and subjects. The form of this later type of covenant is well known from the archaeologists' discovery of Hittite suzerainty treaties, and matches in form the Mosaic (Law) covenant which we find in Exodus. The Abrahamic covenant is notable because it does *not* take this form.

Suzerainty treaties defined relationships by specifying required behaviors and giving the consequences of performing or failing to perform those duties. In such covenants as the one God makes with Abraham, and in later expansions of the basic Abrahamic covenant, God binds only himself! He does not lay conditions on Abraham.

The NT explains the purpose of this unique unconditional divine commitment. "When God made his promise to Abraham, since there was no one greater for him to swear by, he swore by himself, saying, 'I will surely bless you and give you many descendants.' And so after waiting patiently, Abraham received what was promised.

"Men swear by someone greater than themselves, and the oath confirms what is said and puts an end to all argument. Because God wanted to make the unchangeable nature of his purpose very clear to the heirs of what was promised, he confirmed it with an oath. God did this so that, by two unchangeable things . . . we who have fled to take hold of the hope offered to us may be greatly encouraged" (Heb. 6:13–18).

Forever now Abraham's descendants could look back at God's promise, confirmed by covenant-oath, and be encouraged. Israel often would fall short, and some generations would turn from God in angry rebellion. But God would never turn away from his people. God, who cannot lie, will perform what he has promised. In the framework of unconditional covenant, Israel's relationship with God would be forever secure.

For study: Psalms 105, 106.

Sarah to have a son: 15–22. The covenant relationship is to be transmitted through a son of Abraham's wife, whose name is now changed to Sarah ("princess"). God would bring life from a dead womb.

Household circumcised: 23–27. Abraham immediately obeys.

Circumcision symbolized identity with the people of God. What are signs today of your identity with God's people?

Chapters 18, 19. Sodom and Gomorrah

These chapters focus on God's judgment of cities in Abraham's day where, as in the days of the Flood, sin dominated in the society. They also give us further insights into the relationship of Abraham and God.

Sodom's sin. The depravity of the city is illustrated by the attempted homosexual rape of two visitors to Abraham's nephew, Lot, by the whole male population. The KJV selected the terms "sodomy" and "sodomist" to describe homosexuality, and to identify male cult prostitution. For God's attitude toward homosexuality see Leviticus 18:23–30.

Angelic appearance. These chapters contain the first clear indication that God's angels (lit., "messengers") might appear in human form and interact with men. The visitors first fix the time that Sarah will bear the promised child. They then tell Abraham of God's intent to judge the sin of Sodom and Gomorrah (see *Angels*, p. 370).

Abraham's prayer. Abraham's dialogue with God in chapter 18 is the first extended prayer recorded in Scripture (see *Prayer*, p. 216). In reading, note Abraham's concern that the righteous might be destroyed by God with the wicked. He asks God to spare the cities for 50, then 45, and finally for 10 righteous. Only one who might be considered even slightly righteous was found—Lot. God did not spare the wicked for Lot's sake, but he did save Lot and his family. We need not fear that God's sense of justice and mercy is less developed than our own!

Archaeological insights. Archaeologists believe Sodom and Gomorrah rested on a plain now covered by the waters of the south end of the Dead Sea. Geologic evidence indicates that the once rich valley area was stricken by an earthquake which, associated with the release of billows of natural gas, and with bitumen, caused the fiery doom described in Genesis. The judgment came through completely natural means; the timing was miraculous.

What does the account indicate about God's nature? Lot shows gross imperfections, yet God delivered him. Why?

Chapter 20. Abraham's Weakness Persists

Fear replaced faith as Abraham again lied about Sarah.

Chapter 21. Isaac Born

God is faithful to his promise, and Sarah bears a son. She is 90; Abraham 100. This child of miracle, symbolically resurrected as his life comes from a dead womb, will carry on the covenant line.

When Isaac was about two (8), Sarah insisted Ishmael and Hagar be expelled. Abraham was greatly disturbed: he loved his son, Ishmael, and such an act is specifically condemned in the legal documents of Abraham's day. God commanded Abraham to cut Ishmael off that there might be no misunderstanding: "it is through Isaac that your offspring will be reckoned" (12). Clear title to the covenant rights were to be guarded. Ishmael was not abandoned, for God promised to care for him and make him a great people too.

The treaty at Beersheba (22–32) illustrates again a typical covenant.

Chapter 22. Abraham's Final Great Act of Faith

Abraham often failed as a man and as a believer. Yet when God commanded, he acted with an obedience which proved the depth of his faith. Now God calls Abraham to sacrifice "your son, your only son, Isaac, whom you love" (2). Abraham did not question, even though the act went against God's nature. The Scripture says Abraham rose "early the next morning" to journey to the place designated for the sacrifice.

Abraham's statement to his servants when they reach the mount of sacrifice is revealing: "I and the boy will go over there. We will worship and then we will come back to you" (5). The NT picks up his statement, and explains that Abraham was so sure God would be faithful to his covenant oath that, if necessary, he would raise Isaac from the dead (Heb. 11:17–19).

God did not require Isaac's life. But one day God would offer up the life of his own Son as a sacrifice for us all (Rom. 8:32).

The experience demonstrated to all (perhaps especially to Isaac)

Abraham's conviction that God is a trustworthy Person, who will
always keep his word. In Isaac's hearing God then reconfirmed
the covenant promises (15–18).

Imagine yourself to be Abraham on the three-day journey
to the mountain God has designated for the sacrifice. What
might you have thought and felt? What might you have remembered to give you encouragement? Then read what the Book of
James says of the living nature of Abraham's faith (2:14–24).

Chapter 23. Sarah's Death

When Sarah died, Abraham purchased a grave site near Hebron.
Archaeological research has shown that the Hittites of Anatolia
did maintain a settlement here at this time, and the bargaining
process recorded in the chapter matches Hittite law and custom
in detail. Again we appreciate the fact that our Genesis text is
accurate. No invention of a later date could possibly match ancient
customs so exactly, even to the use of obscure technical terms.

Ephron the Hittite's offer to give Abraham the land was not a
true offer, but part of established bargaining process. The final
price paid was exorbitant. The Hittites did not want Abraham
to obtain the property, perhaps because he might thus claim citizen
rights among them. But Abraham saw the land as belonging to
his descendants. His family resting place must be in the Promised
Land.

Chapter 24. Isaac's Bride

Again archaeological finds illustrate the period. We know of
parents who sent great distances back to their homeland for brides
for their sons.

The incident also reveals Abraham's confidence in God's providential care. "Providence" is not a biblical term, but it does express
a biblical concept: that God continues to supervise events. Abraham
expresses confidence in God's providential care when he tells the
servant who is to be sent to seek Isaac's bride, "The Lord, the
God of heaven . . . he will send his angel before you so that
you can get a wife for my son from there" (7).

Some commentators tend to spiritualize this and other OT incidents, claiming to see "deeper spiritual significance" beyond the
straightforward narrative. For instance, this story is supposed to
prefigure God the Father (Abraham) sending the Holy Spirit (the
servant) to prepare the Church as a Bride (Rebekah) for Jesus

(Isaac). Such reading of later revelation into the text without specific warrant is, at best, questionable. It may lead us to miss the true significance of the narrative to salvation history, and to miss the valid application which may be made to our lives.

Here the significance is that of all later Genesis: Israel's title deed to her identity and to the land depended on God having made an historical covenant with the forefathers. The Genesis stories guarantee the genealogical claim to covenant relationship with God.

📖 The NT says that events "happened to them [OT people] for examples" (1 Cor. 10:11). What truths about God and relationship with God can you see exemplified in this story?

Chapter 25. The Next Generation

Abraham's death: 1–11. Little is told of Abraham's final 38 years, or his second family. Why? Because Genesis is the history of the covenant, and the covenant is transmitted through Isaac.

Ishmael's descendants: 12–18. The principle of selection is at work here. Ishmael is not in the covenant: he receives only six lines.

Jacob and Esau: 19–26. Genesis now returns to the covenant line, and introduces the twin sons of Isaac and Rebekah. Before birth she is told by the Lord, "the older will serve the younger" (23). Custom demanded the older son be heir. Romans tells us this departure was to demonstrate that God's purposes in the covenant depend on his sovereign choice: not on the works, or on the customs, of men (9:9–13).

Birthright despised: 27–34. We see something of the difference in personalities between the two sons, and of parental favoritism. One incident reveals much of Esau's lack of concern for relationship with God. Once, when hungry, Esau sold his brother his "birthright" for a plate of stew. The "birthright" was his claim, as oldest son, to the covenant promise. To despise it was a significant revelation of Esau's lack of spiritual values.

Chapter 26. Isaac's Weaknesses and Strengths

Faith and fear: 1–18. When a famine (drought) comes, God confirms the covenant to Isaac and commands him to stay in the land. Isaac obeys, but fear leads him to lie, as did Abraham (Ch. 20).

Isaac avoids conflict: 19–35. Isaac backs off from conflict over water rights, especially significant in times of drought. God again reassures Isaac and affirms the covenant.

📖 Develop a psychological profile of Isaac from this chapter. How are his faith and his weaknesses related? What weaknesses of your own are opportunities to exercise faith?

Chapters 27, 28. Jacob Steals Isaac's Blessing

Remember when reading these chapters that God had earlier revealed his choice of Jacob as inheritor of the covenant line (25:23). The deceit and family conflict portrayed resulted from unnecessary scheming.

Isaac blesses Jacob: 27:1–40. Jacob's name means "he grasps the heel," or figuratively, "deceiver." The aged and nearly blind Isaac is tricked into giving Jacob his blessing. Culturally this involved acknowledging Jacob as heir, and as the one through whom the covenant line would run. When Isaac learns he has been deceived he does not withdraw the blessing but confirms it—"he will be blessed" (33).

Esau's anger: 27:41–28:9. Esau is overheard plotting to kill Jacob after Isaac's death. To hide him from Esau's fury Rebekah sends Jacob to her brother for a bride.

Jacob's dream: 28:10–32. On the journey God appears to Jacob to confirm the covenant to him. God has now appeared to each of the three patriarchs, affirming transmission of the covenant line through Isaac and Jacob.

📖 Genesis 24 shows Abraham's confidence in providence. This passage shows another generation taking action without regard to God's providential care. What do the two experiences suggest to you about how to go about solving your own personal problems?

Chapters 29–31. Jacob's Twenty Years with Laban

For the next twenty years, Jacob stayed in northwest Mesopotamia with his mother's brother. There he married two of his uncle Laban's daughters, and there eleven of Jacob's twelve sons were born.

Working for a bride. It was common in that culture for a slave to work a number of years for his master before being given a wife. There is no parallel from archaeology of a free man, a relative at that, being bound to such service.

Laban's character. Jacob finally met his match in the wily and deceptive Laban, who "changed Jacob's wages" time after time (see 29:21–25; 26–28; 30:37,38).

Household gods. When Jacob finally fled with his family and flocks, Rachel stole her father's household gods. Archaeological discoveries suggest this may not have been a religious action. It may have been an attempt by Rachel to gain a claim to her father's possessions for her own children.

Marriage customs. The picture we see of polygamy (the practice of taking more than one wife) is not uncommon for patriarchal times. The use of the slave women, Bilha and Zilpah, as secondary wives, was also a recognized Middle Eastern practice. It should be noted that the servant women were not "taken" by Jacob, but were thrust on him by his wives in a competition between them to provide their husband the greater number of sons.

The Nuzi tablets show that while polygamy was sanctioned in the society, the jealousy and conflict it might bring to a household was well recognized. Many marriage contracts specifically prohibit the man from taking other wives, and provide penalties if he should.

The OT records history as it happened. It does not follow that it promotes or approves of the practices described. God's original intention that marriage be a monogamous, lifetime relationship, remains clear. The tensions this passage reveals illustrate an advantage of remaining faithful to the biblical ideal.

Make a list of lessons you believe God was teaching Jacob through his experiences. How can you apply these lessons to your own life?

Chapters 32–35. Jacob Returns to Canaan

Jacob gripped by fear: 32:1–12. To return means that Jacob must meet his brother, Esau, who has sworn to kill him. Terrified, Jacob turns to God and appeals to him on the basis of the covenant relationship and promises (9–12).

Jacob prepares gifts: 13–21. A series of flocks and herds is prepared and sent on ahead as gifts (bribes?) to Esau.

Jacob's name changed to Israel: 22–31. Jacob had wrestled with God in prayer. Now this is acted out in a midnight struggle with a supernatural messenger. That night Jacob's name is changed to Israel, which means "he struggles with God."

Jacob's new name will become the name of the covenant people, for of all the patriarchs only in the case of Jacob/Israel are all the sons in the covenant line (see genealogical chart, p. 58).

The Covenant Line in Genesis

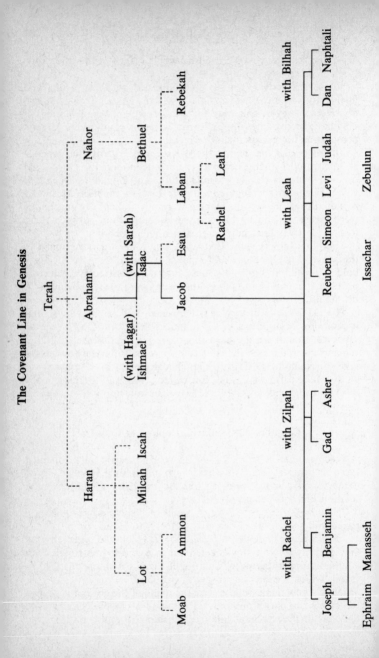

Jacob meets Esau: Chapter 33. When the two brothers finally meet, Jacob learns that Esau is no longer angry. The reason? Esau has become wealthy and leads his clan. He had never cared about relationship with God, so the loss of the covenant seems meaningless.

Conflict at Shechem: Chapter 34. The dangers of nomadic life in ancient Canaan are illustrated in this story of rape and multiple murder. According to the customs of the day, Shechem behaved much more honorably than did Jacob's sons. All parties in this tragic story show the impact of sin on individuals and on society, and remind us that commitment to God is essential.

Return to Bethel: Chapter 35:1–7. Events at Shechem revealed the family's need for complete commitment to God. Jacob is directed to Bethel. There he insists his family destroy the idols and other symbols of pagan superstition they carried. Apparently Jacob had failed to instruct his wives and family in the worship of God while they stayed with Laban.

Covenant again confirmed: 8–15.

Rachel and Isaac die: 16–29. Jacob's favorite wife dies giving birth to his last son, Benjamin.

Chapter 26. Esau's Genealogy

Esau's family, and the peoples who descended from him, are listed and then dismissed. Esau had gained more of this world's goods than he had imagined possible (cf. 6, 7). Satisfied, he passes off the stage of history. Only Jacob/Israel will be remembered and honored through history for his deeper concern for the spiritual than the material.

Chapter 37. Joseph Introduced

Background. All 12 of the sons of Jacob/Israel are in the covenant line, and from this point the OT will often use "children of Israel" or "Israelite" to designate the covenant people. But the rest of Genesis focuses on one son of Jacob, Joseph. Why?

God had told Abraham that his family would reside in Egypt for 400 years before being given the Promised Land (Gen. 15:13). God providentially uses Joseph to move the whole family to Egypt. His story illustrates the way God can work through circumstances, and even through the evil actions of human beings, to accomplish good.

Joseph. Joseph is the only person from the patriarchal period of whom no obvious faults or sins are reported. He was the open favorite of his father, Jacob, which stimulated the jealousy of his brothers. Joseph was not sensitive to their feelings, but he clearly did not deserve their hatred. When his brothers had sold Joseph into slavery in Egypt, he showed himself to be a highly principled individual. His sense of morality certainly exceeded that of his family and forebearers! Because of his spotless character some have suggested that Joseph is a "type" of Christ, and should be considered the "messianic patriarch" [see *Interpreting Symbolic Language,* p. 61].

It is better to see Joseph as he was: a real human being, seeking to live his faith in a difficult time, pressed by injustice and yet faithful to God. In Joseph's story we also see the faithfulness of God, who redeems Joseph's sufferings by using them for the deliverance of his family, and who brings Joseph personal blessing as well.

Joseph's youth: 1–11. Hated by his brothers because of their father's favoritism, Joseph deepens the antagonism when he tells of dreams which suggest the family will one day "bow down" to him (6–10).

Joseph sold as a slave: 12–36. When Jacob sends Joseph to his brothers in the fields, they plot to murder him. Only the eldest, Reuben, hopes to rescue him. Finally the young Joseph, probably then in his teens, is sold to traveling merchants, who resell him as a slave to a high government official in Egypt.

Chapter 38. Judah and Tamar

This story interrupts the flow of the Joseph story. The insight into the morality of Joseph's brother highlights by contrast Joseph's own moral choices in Egypt. The practice of levirite marriage, in which the bride of a son who dies is given to his brother as a wife, is well attested from Nuzi. It is also known in later Mosaic law (Deut. 25:5–10). The relationship between Judah and Tamar, and the "double standard" applied, illustrates sin's distortion of the man-woman relationship.

Chapters 39, 40. Joseph's Years of Testing

In Potiphar's household: 39:1–18. Joseph demonstrated administrative genius and the Lord "gave him success in everything he did" (4). But Joseph's good looks attract his master's wife, who campaigns incessantly to seduce him. Joseph refuses to "do such a wicked thing and sin against God" (9). Finally the spurned wife accuses Joseph of rape, and he is imprisoned.

"This Hebrew": 14. The term "Hebrew" is applied here to Joseph. In early Babylon "habiru" are mentioned as mercenary soldiers and marauders. The Nuzi tablets mention them as foreign contract workers. In Egyptian texts they appear as 'Apiru or 'Aperu. Thus when first applied to Abraham in Genesis 14:13, "Hebrew" likely meant "immigrant" or "wanderer." Here it is used by Potiphar's wife as an epithet with strong racial overtones: "this foreigner!" Only later did "Hebrew" come to be used of the people of Israel as an ethnic group.

In prison: 39:19–40:23. In prison Joseph's talents gain him a position as sort of trustee-administrator of the prison system. There too he has the opportunity to interpret the prophetic dreams of two members of Pharaoh's personal staff. The interpretations are accurate for, as Joseph says, "Do not interpretations belong to God?"

Interpreting Symbolic Language

There are recognized incidents in Scripture of the use of symbols, types, allegories, similes, and metaphors. While there are differences in the meanings of these terms, they are closely related. In each a person or historical event is taken to be a visible picture of a yet hidden spiritual reality. The rule for interpreting historical facts or events symbolically is simple: do so only if Scripture itself clearly states they are symbolic.

The Bible does so with a few elements from OT history. The tabernacle is said to represent invisible heavenly realities. A rock from which water came and the manna God provided for food in the desert are said to represent Christ. Abraham's unwilling expulsion of Ishmael is said to figuratively represent rejection of the law covenant in favor of grace as a basis for relationship with God.

These uses of the OT by NT writers are infrequent. They do not give us license to take any event or person in the OT and ascribe to it some "deeper spiritual significance." We can study the narrative and find applications to our own experience. But we must understand the Bible message in the plain sense of its words. We must concentrate on the unfolding history of God's great plan of salvation.

For study: 1 Corinthians 10:1–4; Galatians 4:22–24; Hebrews 9:1–10. What principles can you develop from these passages?

In what ways did the injustices help prepare Joseph for his greater role in life? How might Joseph have grown in skills, knowledge, character, etc? How would you apply Joseph's experience in counseling persons who are victims of injustice today—

Life in Egypt

or would you? What might be helpful to you to guide your actions should you suffer injustice?

Chapter 41. Joseph Becomes Ruler in Egypt

When Pharaoh is troubled by nightmares, his chief cupbearer recalls Joseph, who had interpreted his dreams in prison. Pharaoh's dream is also prophetic, and is interpreted by Joseph.

Dreams. In the ancient world different kinds of dreams were recognized. (1) Dreams might be revelations from gods. (2) Dreams might be symptoms of the dreamer's health. (3) Dreams might foretell coming events.

In Egypt

Many scholars believe Joseph lived during the Hyksos period in Egyptian history (c. 1780–1580). Others place him earlier in the Middle Kingdom

(c. 2160–1580). For a discussion of the dating of the sojourn in Egypt and the time of the Exodus, see p. 69 of this handbook and the chart on p. 71.

There are no recovered Egyptian records which specifically name Joseph. But archaeological discoveries match many of the biblical details and show the historical accuracy of Joseph's story. "Chief cup bearer" and "chief butler," and Joseph's designation to be "in charge of the palace" are all specific titles attested by archaeology. The ceremony by which Pharaoh made Joseph vizier (41:42, 43) fits details shown in Egyptian art and records.

There are also records of famines in Egypt extending up to seven years, and documents which show that frontier officials at times of famine beyond Egypt allowed strangers to cross the borders "in order to sustain them and their herds in the domain of Pharaoh, the good sun of every land."

Of note too: one papyrus from this period contains a list of prisoners at Thebes, with complete details on each individual, showing how highly organized the Egyptian penal system was. Another list names 79 servants in one Egyptian household, 40 of whom had Semitic names. Other documents show that such foreigners did rise to positions of importance in government as well as in private service.

Archaeologists have also shown that the office of "superintendent of granaries" existed in Egypt. Although the title is not mentioned, it is clear that Joseph took on that responsibility. Details of how Pharaoh ordered Joseph to be honored (41:43) have also been authenticated.

A century ago many tried to cast doubt on the biblical account as the invention of a much later time. They have been decisively refuted by such details, which show intimate acquaintance with all levels of Egyptian society, including the inner workings of the royal court. We see again that we can trust the historical reliability of the Bible.

The OT refers to dreams primarily when they are a medium through which God speaks to an individual (cf. Gen. 20:3, 31:10, 11, 24; Num. 12:6; Job 33:14–18). However dreams in the OT were at times predictive, as is Pharaoh's dream here (cf. Dan. 2:1–45, 7:1–28). The OT does warn that dreams must be evaluated with care. (Jer. 23:28), and never are dreams to be given greater weight than God's written revelation (Deut. 13:1–4).

Chapters 42–45. The Family Reunited

When famine comes to Egypt her storehouses are filled. But Palestine too is affected by the great drought, and Jacob sends his sons to Egypt to buy grain. The story of their reception and ultimate reconciliation with Joseph is one of the most dramatic— and in some ways most puzzling—in Scripture. The story is told simply, but the motive for Joseph's behavior is not explained. This narrative should be read in a single sitting as a drama. Only afterward should we return to meditate on questions the story suggests. What did Joseph discover about his brothers through his strange actions? What changes in his brothers is suggested by their attitude toward Benjamin, who is Joseph's younger brother and also his father's favorite? What does 45:4–11 reveal about Joseph's attitude toward his brothers, and his understanding of his Egyptian experiences?

Chapter 46. Jacob comes to Egypt

Now Jacob sets out for Egypt with all his family: 70 persons, listed here in this chapter. God's final words to a patriarch are recorded here, and they are words of reassurance and promise (3, 4). The 70 who enter Egypt, protected within the borders of this mighty empire from the strife that will rage over Palestine in the next few centuries, will become a great multitude.

Chapter 47. Israel Given Land in Egypt

Goshen: 1–11. Family members are introduced to Pharaoh and given a district in which to live. The area, Goshen, contains excellent land, but is distant from the Nile districts which the Egyptians prefer.

Joseph's stewardship: 13–31. The basis for taxation in Egypt was the theory that Pharaoh owned the land. This chapter tells the story of Joseph's purchase of the land for grain during the great famine.

Chapter 48. Manasseh and Ephraim

Joseph had two sons named Manasseh and Ephraim. Now Jacob adopts these two as his own. Through the rest of the narrative they will be considered his. Thus the 12 tribes become 13.

Chapter 49. Jacob's Final Blessing

This blessing by Jacob of his sons is prophetic, like that of Noah (see p. 40). It is also an analysis by the father of the strengths and weaknesses of his children.

Of special note is the prophecy that a world ruler will come from Judah (8–10). Jesus is from the line of Judah.

The blessing given Joseph reflects his stability, even when bitter enemies attacked,

A view of the Great Sphinx of Egypt

The ruins of Tanis, one of the treasure cities built by Joseph. Statue is Rameses II, probably Pharaoh of the Exodus

"because of the hand of the Mighty One of Jacob,
    because of the Shepherd, the Rock of Israel,
because of your father's God, who helps you,
    because of the Almighty, who blesses you" (24, 25).

As Jacob realized, Joseph's steadfastness can only be explained by God's hand in his life.

Shortly after giving this blessing, Jacob died. In accordance with his earlier instructions (cf. Gen. 47:29, 30), his body was taken back to Palestine and laid to rest with Abraham, Sarah, and his two wives.

Chapter 50. The Death of Joseph

The Book of Genesis closes with the report of Jacob's burial and the death of Joseph. Thus the age of the patriarchs closes.

For centuries the children of Israel, as strangers in a foreign land and later as slaves, would pass these stories on from generation to generation. In their retelling, the final words of Joseph to his brothers would find expression over and over again: "God will surely come to your aid and take you up out of this land to the land he promised on oath to Abraham, Isaac, and Jacob" (24).

The patriarchs were gone. But the covenant promises given them would never pass away, for they had been spoken by the Living God!

If you were one of the later generations born in Egypt, which of these stories would be most important to you? Why?

What seems to you to be the most important messages for Christians today from Genesis 1–11? From Genesis 12–50? Make a list from memory; then read quickly through Genesis, adding to your list as you read.

EXODUS
The History of Deliverance

Exodus is the second of the five OT books ascribed to Moses. It picks up the story of God's covenant people some 430 years after their entry into Egypt. Genesis lays the foundation for understanding ourselves and our universe as creations of a personal God. Exodus lays the foundation for understanding salvation, in this same God's mighty acts undertaken to win the freedom of his people. In the eyes of God's Old Testament people, the events recorded in this book will seem even more significant than creation. Again and again the thoughts and the songs of Israel will return to the time of Exodus.

Major themes and events. The Book of Exodus is approximately one half narrative, giving an historical report of Israel's deliverance from slavery. The other half outlines a system of law by which God sought to shape the delivered slaves into a strong and holy nation.

In Exodus we come upon a number of important themes which are foundational to the faith and life style of God's OT people. These include: (1) God's mighty acts. A series of judgmental miracles, by which God intervenes in space and time, breaks the power that holds Israel in slavery. (2) Passover. This annual feast, in remembrance of departure from Egypt, will mark the beginning of each new year for Israel for all time. (3) Law covenant. After being led to freedom, Israel is given God's Law in the form of a suzerainty covenant. God's earlier covenant commitment to Abraham is not changed or denied. Instead a new element is introduced. Israel is given the conditions on which each generation can live in harmony with God. (4) Law itself. The content of the law is designed to lead Israel to a life of practical holiness. It is also intended to shape a community in which the needs of each individual will be lovingly met. By the time of Jesus, the true meaning of law will be lost. It will be viewed by most then as a means of salvation. But the function of law, and the beauty of God's gift in it, shine brilliantly in Exodus. (5) Worship. The final chapters of Exodus establish a priesthood and sacrificial system. Here provision is made for reestablishing fellowship with God when the law is broken. Here too provision is made for the worship of God.

Each of these themes is woven through the rest of the OT, and reflected time and time again in the New. The study of Exodus is basic to our understanding of the message of the Bible as a whole.

Outline

Our outline of Exodus reflects the division of the book into narrative and legal sections, and focuses on the basic themes.

God revealed in Exodus. As revelation, the Bible records the unveiling of God. Mankind has known of God as Creator and moral judge through ancient traditions of Creation and the Flood. The patriarchs knew God as a covenant-making God, who established a special relationship with the family of Abraham, Isaac, and Jacob. Now, to a people living in slavery, God is about to reveal more of his character and person.

As we read this key OT book, we too are thrilled as the hidden God steps out of obscurity and into revelation's light. In Exodus the central revelations include:

(1) God as ever present. For silent centuries Israel has looked to the past, and reminded herself that once, long ago, God spoke. Now God shows himself as present with his people! (See *Yahweh,* p. 75).

(2) God of miracles. God's mighty acts of judgment against Egypt on Israel's behalf show for all time that God is willing

and able to intervene in history. He can act in our world of space and time (see *Miracles,* OT, p. 79).

(3) God as Savior. Enslavement in Egypt serves in the OT as an illustration of man in need of deliverance. God acts decisively to break the shackles that bind the helpless. Here Exodus states central truth related to the OT's teaching on salvation (see *Salvation,* OT, p. 574).

(4) God as faithful. God's actions in Exodus are clearly stated to be based on his covenant promises. From this point on, Israel will praise God as faithful and trustworthy; one whose word cannot be broken.

(5) God as holy. God's own moral character is revealed in the law he gives. The things he includes provide unique insight into the person who calls us to a holy life (see *Holiness,* OT, p. 101).

As you read Exodus, you'll want to be sensitive to God's self-revelation. Seeing him in Exodus will deepen your appreciation of the person who is our Lord.

The Date of the Exodus

Before the time of Solomon (c. 970 B.C.) it is impossible to correlate biblical events with known chronologies of Egypt or other ancient empires. Inscriptional evidence simply does not exist. This is not surprising, as Egyptian monarchs did not record defeats. Surely they would not advertise the loss of a chariot army pursuing runaway slaves! Silence in the records of Egypt has led to speculation, and to the development of two theories. One dates the Exodus about 1450 B.C. (the early date). The other dates the Exodus about 1290 B.C. (the late date). Neither date can be advanced with absolute certainty.

The late date. Proponents of this date argue that the biblical events fit better with what is known of the general historical and political situation around 1300 years before Christ. In this view, Israel left Egypt during the reign of Rameses II, and was in Canaan by 1220, when Hebrews are mentioned in an inscription on what is known as Merneptah's Stele. A good summary of the reasoning for this date can be found in R. Alan Cole, *Exodus,* published by InterVarsity Press.

The early date. Proponents of this date also argue that it fits well with the known history of Egypt and Canaan. However, they also point to a number of Old and New Testament references. Exodus 12:40, 41 gives the time Israel was in Egypt as 430 years "to the very day." Genesis 15:13 reports God's statement to Abra-

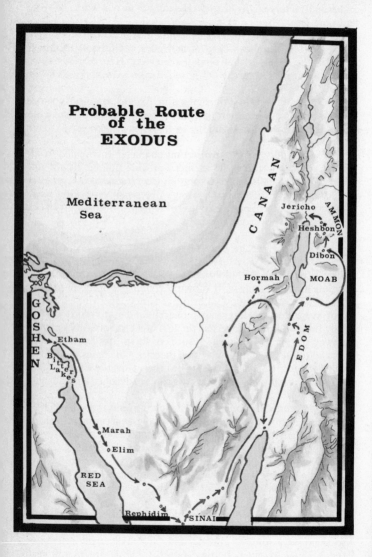

ham that his descendants will spend 400 years in a strange land. Acts 7:6, 7 also gives 400 years as the time in the land of bondage. First Kings 6:1 gives 480 years after the Exodus as the date of the beginning of the Temple (c. 966 B.C.). Proponents also insist that 400 years is the minimum time required for the amazing growth of the family from the handful who entered Egypt to well over 2,000,000 (cf. Exod. 12:37). For a good discussion of the early date point of view, see Leon Wood, *A Survey of Israel's History*, published by Zondervan. The chart below provides an early date chronology, from the patriarchs to the time of the judges.

Chronology from Abraham to Judges

The Patriarchs

Abraham		
born	c. 2166	
enter Canaan	c. 2091	
Isaac born	c. 2066	
Jacob born	c. 2006	
Joseph born	c. 1915	
sold to Egypt	c. 1898	Sensusert II
made vizier	c. 1885	
family to Egypt	c. 1859	Sensusert III

In Egypt

made slaves	c. 1730	Hyksos rule established c. 1730

Exodus Era

Moses born	c. 1526	Thutmose I
to Midian	c. 1486	Thutmose III
The Exodus	c. 1446	Amenhotep II
Conquest of Canaan	c. 1406–1399	
Judges Period Begins	c. 1390	

There are differences of opinion about the chronology above. But there is complete agreement that the events recorded in Exodus are some of the most significant and exciting in the entire OT.

I. The Story of Deliverance:

Chapter 1. Oppression in Egypt

Israel multiplies: 1–7. The family of Israel settled in a fertile district in the western delta of the Nile river, in what was known as Lower Egypt. There, not far from present-day Cairo, the first great burst of her population explosion took place. The Bible says the people "multiplied greatly" and came to fill the district. The first period of unrestricted growth would have been under the twelfth Dynasty just after Israel's immigration around 1859 B.C.

Israel enslaved: 8–14. Around 1730 B.C. Asiatic newcomers took over the leadership of Lower Egypt, establishing a new dynasty. These rulers, known as the Hyksos, adopted Egyptian ways. Although relatively few in number they dominated the administration. By 1680 they had replaced the old ruling line in Upper Egypt as well.

It is against this background we understand the ascension of a "new king" who comes to power in Egypt and makes Israel slaves (8). The oppression was initially motivated by fear. As a minority the Hyksos were actually outnumbered by Israel (9). There seemed to the Hyksos to be a possibility that the Israelites would form an allegiance with remnants of the old dynasty in Upper Egypt and destroy them (10). So the Israelites were put to work as slave labor on public projects. But even with oppression their explosive growth in numbers was not halted (12). Their multiplication intensified the rulers' fears, and led to more and more ruthless treatment (13).

Genocide: 13–22. Finally an Egyptian ruler determined to end the threat by killing each Hebrew boy at birth. When this did not succeed, the Egyptians as a people were commanded to drown any male Jewish child they found in the Nile!

Again history gives us insight into this command. After the Hyksos were driven out of Egypt the eighteenth dynasty was established. Thutmose I would have been ruler about the time of Moses' birth and author of the command designed to wipe out Israel. Thutmose was a conqueror, who concentrated on enlarging the frontiers of Egypt. His armies were on foreign campaigns during much of the year. As foreigners, Israel posed a potential threat at home when he was on campaign—a threat that multiplied daily with Israel's accelerated birth rate.

The Egyptian people seem to have welcomed the order. When Moses was born his parents fearfully hid the child to save his life.

What national characteristics or attitudes would you expect in the Israelites after some 300 years of oppression? What attitudes might you expect in the Egyptians? As you read on in Exodus, observe the behavior of the Israelites to see if your predictions were on target.

Chapters 2–4. Moses: The Deliverer Prepared

Moses' birth: 2:1–10. Moses is hidden at home for three months, and then concealed along the shoreline of the Nile in a floating basket. It's possible the daughter of Pharaoh who finds him is Hatshepsut, only living child of Thutmose I. Later this dynamic woman declared herself ruler of Egypt, and took most of the royal titles. As adopted son of this woman (10), Moses would have known every advantage. Moses' own mother is chosen by Pharaoh's daughter to care for him (8, 9). The truths he learns from his parents later lead Moses to identify himself with the God of Israel.

Moses' choice: 2:11–15. As a mature adult, Moses kills a taskmaster who is beating one of Moses' "own people" (11). Later he learns this attack has been observed (12–14). Moses flees just in time, for "when Pharaoh heard this, he tried to kill Moses" (15).

History adds interesting insights. As a woman, Hatshepsut could not take the throne in her own right. So she married a brother, born to one of her father's lesser wives. On his death, the throne passed to one of his younger brothers, who was then about 10. Hatshepsut seized the throne and ruled for another 22 years. After her death the long suppressed and bitter king, Thutmose III, ordered every mention of Hatshepsut obliterated. Throughout Egypt her statues were defaced and her name chiseled from stone inscriptions. Undoubtedly Thutmose, who went on to become the greatest ruler in Egyptian history, would have hated Moses, and welcomed any excuse to kill him.

Moses

Moses is one of history's most amazing characters. He was brought up as a son in Egypt's royal family, "educated in all the wisdom of the Egyptians and powerful in speech and action" (Acts 7:22). Yet he retained his identity with the covenant people. His choice must have been a traumatic one. Moses could be one with the wealthy and powerful, or one with the oppressed. Confident in God, Moses took his stand with the people of Israel.

We cannot tell what dreams the young Moses had of freedom for his people. We do know something of the high ideals he had for brotherhood among the enslaved, rooted in their family relationship with God (Exod. 2:14). When his commitment to his oppressed brothers exploded in violence, Moses was forced to flee Egypt. He was 40 years old.

Moses traveled to Midian. That land was broad, with undefined borders. It included within its vast desert landscapes, Mount Sinai, and much of the wilderness through which Israel would later wander. For 40 more years of his life Moses lived as a humble shepherd with the nomadic Midianites. Finally, at 80, his dream of freeing Israel was long dead (cf. Exod. 3:11). Then God spoke to Moses and announced the emancipation of his people!

The final four decades of Moses' life were dedicated to the work that has assured his place in history. Constantly under pressure, confronting enemies without and rebelliousness within Israel, Moses' flaming faith never failed. Though often discouraged, he was a model of faithfulness for every succeeding generation (Heb. 3:2). The law given through him has shaped the lives of the covenant people for millennia. And the five books of the OT ascribed to him have been revered above all others by the Jewish people.

📖 Explore the following passages for insight into Moses the man. From them develop a personality and character sketch. Which of the qualities do you want God to nurture in your own personality? Exod. 4:1–17; 15:1–18; 17:1–7; 33:12–17; Num. 12:1–13; 14:1–19.

Exile in Midian: 2:16–25. Although Moses feels himself to be an alien in a foreign land (22), he reconciles himself to his fate. He marries and has a son, and settles into the routine of nomadic life, unaware that God is soon to act on his covenant promises.

The burning bush: 3:1–22. God now appears to Moses as he is tending his flocks near Mount Horeb, the Semitic name for what we know as Mount Sinai. Drawn nearer to a flaming bush, Moses is warned to stop and remove his sandals, for "the place where you are standing is holy ground" (5). This is the first use of the word "holy" in the Bible (see *Holiness,* OT, p. 101).

God announces to Moses that he is the Lord's chosen instrument to deliver Israel. Now in the recorded dialogue, a new element of revelation is introduced: God tells Moses that from then on he intends to be known as Yahweh, or Jehovah (see *Jehovah/Yahweh,* p. 75). Moses expects Israel to ask the name of the God who sent him when he returns to Egypt. The question is equivalent to asking, "What new revelation of God do you have to share?" The name Yahweh, and all it implies of God's vital, living involvement with his covenant people, is the heart of the new revelation.

One additional element is introduced in this key chapter. God tells Moses that Israel will believe and respond to his message. Pharaoh will reject. God will then stretch out his hand to perform "wonders." This word expresses the OT way of viewing what we today would call "miracles" (see *Miracles, OT,* p. 79).

Verses 21–22 promise that the Israelites will ask silver and gold, and leave with Egypt's wealth. Later Mosaic Law will establish a similar principle for God's people: one who has served as a slave shall not be set free without compensation (Deut. 15:12–18).

Authenticating signs: 4:1–17. In spite of God's call, Moses hangs back. Earlier Moses has objected that he is too insignificant (3:11). God answers that he himself will be with Moses, and show himself in wonders (3:12, 20). Now Moses worries that he will not be believed (4:1). God provides him with authenticating signs (4:3–5, 6, 7, 8, 9). Moses pleads that he is not an accomplished speaker (4:10). God answers that he will help Moses speak, and instruct him in what to say. Still Moses begs to be excused (13). But God has called Moses, not another. Moses is too conscious of his inadequacies. He will soon discover the superabundant abilities of God.

As a special sign of grace, God promises Moses that his brother, Aaron, will be permitted to assist him (14–16).

Have you ever felt inadequate? How does God's response to Moses help you see the role he can play in your own life?

Moses returns to Egypt: 4:18–31. On the journey Moses circumcises his son (see p. 51), and is met by his brother Aaron. When the message is delivered to the elders of Israel, and the authenticating signs shown, the people believe and worship.

Chapters 5–11. The Ten Plagues

The confrontation between Moses and Pharaoh, which escalated from judgmental plague to more intense plague, had distinct purposes. The OT gives three goals for the series of miracles: (1) The mighty acts would help Israel "know that I am the Lord your God, who brought you out from under the yoke of the Egyptians" (Exod. 6:7). God will be forever identified by the deliverance of his people. (2) The Egyptians will know that "I am the Lord" (Exod. 7:5). In his first meeting with Moses, Pharaoh asks contemptuously, "Who is the Lord, that I should obey him" (5:2)? God provided an unmistakable answer. (3) The plagues were a "judgment on all the gods of Egypt" (Exod. 12:12). The pantheon of the oppressors was powerless before the God of the slaves!

Jehovah/Jahweh

Four Hebrew consonants form the name of God which, from the Exodus on, dominates the OT. As vowels were not included in written Hebrew, JHWH has been variously pronounced, as Jehovah, or as Jahweh.

What is important is not the pronunciation, but the meaning of the name, and the revelation of God it contains. The name is a form of the verb "to be," and thus translated in the KJV and other versions as "I

AM." While this translation is correct, it misses the impact of the original. For centuries, God had been known by Israel as one who spoke to the forefathers in the distant past. Or he was worshiped as one who would act in the future to redeem his covenant promises. But now, God says, Israel is to experience him in a present-tense way. From this point forward, God is to be known as "the one who is always present!"

The people in Egypt would soon experience God's presence through his mighty acts of judgment on the oppressors. For decades Israel would experience his daily supply of manna, and see him as present in a cloudy fiery pillar that guided Israel through the wilderness years. The lesson would be clear. Never again is Israel to relegate God to the past or the future only. From now on, they are to experience God as one who is present, fully involved in each day of their lives. The people of God are to live in the sure confidence that the living God is present in each today!

For study: Psalms 16, 118, 139.

What does it say to you personally that God wants you to know him as one who is always present?

Many OT peoples looked back on the events described in these chapters, and responded in different ways. Which best expresses your own response to the realization that God does act on behalf of his own? (Deut. 4:34; 7:19; Josh, 24:5; 1 Sam. 4:8; Ps. 78:43–51; 135: 8, 9; Jer. 32:21)

Pharaoh's hard heart. Many have thought they sensed a moral contradiction in the Exodus description of Pharaoh's response to God. Some Exodus verses speak of Pharaoh's heart hardening (cf.: 14, 22), others of God hardening Pharaoh's heart (cf 7:3), and others of Pharaoh hardening his own heart (cf. 8:15). Who was responsible for Pharaoh's actions?

This question simply was not asked by the Hebrews. In OT thought, God is involved in everything, without diminishing in any way an individual's responsibility for his choices.

For us, it's helpful to note one contrast. The elders of Israel reacted to God's self-revelation with belief, and worshiped (4:31). Pharaoh refused to believe and rejected (5:2). Yet in both cases the initiating cause is the same: God's revelation of himself. The response to revelation is the choice of those who receive the revelation. God did not force the will of Israelite or Pharaoh. Yet in a real sense his self-revelation caused both responses. In the same way that heat from the sun causes wax to melt and clay to harden, God's revelation of himself causes different responses in different individuals. Today as well some melt to him and believe. And others harden.

Oppression intensified (5:1–21). By the late date framework, Amenhotep II is 22 years old, in the fourth year of his reign, when Moses comes. Commanded in the name of the Lord to let Israel go into the desert to worship, the proud youth sneers. In the ancient world, gods were measured by the wealth and power of the people who worshiped them. A god of slaves merits only ridicule.

Pharaoh increases Israel's work load. Usually they are given straw to mix with clay, as decomposing straw releases chemicals which strengthens the bricks. Now Israel must find its own straw! The Israelites, bludgeoned by their taskmasters and their work doubled, lose heart and turn against Moses (19–21). Moses turns to God (22–23). Apparently all expected that following the course God lays out will be easy!

Deliverance promised: 6:1–27. God answers Moses' prayer with a promise. The Lord is the God of Abraham, Isaac, and Jacob. He will be faithful to the covenant he made with the fathers (2–5) [*Note.* In most English versions the name Jahweh is represented in capitals, LORD]. Moses relays the divine reply. But the Israelites are too discouraged to listen. Sent to Pharaoh, Moses wonders how the king can be expected to listen when God's own people will not hear.

The chapter also lists the clans which have sprung from the original sons of Israel. The genealogy is important. It shows the slaves' claim to covenant relationship with God.

Evidence rejected: 6:28–7:13. Moses and Aaron are sent to Pharaoh, but warned he will not listen. It will take multiplied judgments to bring him to his knees. Moses' authenticating signs (the staff which became a serpent, the hand which became leprous) are duplicated by Egyptian magicians (6–13), and Pharaoh ignores God's messengers.

In ancient times highly complex systems of magic were developed to manipulate supernatural powers. Usually magic was associated with religion. In Egypt magic was the providence of the gods Thoth and Isis, and was taught in temple schools. The OT recognizes the existence of occult powers (cf. Deut. 18:10–14). It is impossible however to tell if occult agencies or trickery were used by Pharaoh's magicians to duplicate Moses' signs.

Plague on the Nile: 7:14–24. The sacred Nile enriched Egypt's fields by its annual flood. This stream, the lifeline of Egypt, God has now polluted at Moses' word. It rots, stinking of spilled blood. Everywhere in Egypt fish die, and noxious odors drive the people from its shores. Pharaoh is unmoved. He simply withdraws from the river to his palace.

Plagues of frogs: 8:1–15. At Moses' word frogs swarm out of the waters and fill Egypt. The magicians bring up more frogs— an action which hardly helps! At a time set by Pharaoh, the frogs die, leaving rotting heaps under the tropic sun. Frogs were a fertility symbol, associated with the goddess Hequt. The goddess associated with new life has been defeated, and the stink of death marks God's victory.

Plague of gnats: 8:16–19. The exact insect named here is uncertain. Now the magicians admit the swarming billions are the work of God.

Plague of flies: 8:20–30. With this plague, God introduces a clear distinction between his people and the Egyptians. The land of Goshen is exempt from this and subsequent blows.

Pharaoh begs relief and offers a compromise. But when the insect swarms have disappeared, he goes back on his word (30–32). We can sense something of Pharaoh's anger and his struggle with fear and pride. It is hard for this man of power to face the reality of God's sovereignty.

Plague on livestock: 9:1–7. Two elements of these miracles are stressed in this chapter: the sickness that strikes the beasts do so at an appointed time. And the livestock of the Israelites are exempt (see *Miracles, OT,* p. 79). Pharaoh continues unyielding.

Plague of boils: 9:8–12.

Plague of hail: 9:13–33. Each plague has provided an opportunity for Pharaoh to repent (15). God has allowed the unrepentant Pharaoh to retain life and power, for Pharaoh has demonstrated both God's power and mercy. Here we see another evidence of mercy. This blow, like the others, is announced ahead of time. The officials of Egypt who have come to believe in the Lord hurry to get their slaves and livestock indoors. Those who ignore his word suffer the consequences as a devastating hailstorm pummels Egypt.

Finally Pharaoh admits he has sinned and is in the wrong. But when Moses prays, and the hail ceases, Pharaoh and his closest advisors again harden against the Lord.

Plague of locusts: 10:1–20. At the threat of locusts, the swarming disaster of the ancient world, even Pharaoh's officials urge him to give in. Pharaoh tries to bargain, but loses his temper and swears never to release Israel. The clouds of locusts that appear strip the land of every green thing, forcing Pharaoh to appeal to Moses and to God. But still Pharaoh will not release Egypt's slaves.

Plague of darkness: 10:21–29. Now, without the usual warning, God strikes the land of Egypt with three days of total darkness– darkness so deep the Egyptians fear to move (23). Even now Pharaoh seeks to bargain. Finally he drives Moses away with the threat that if Moses dares appear before him again, he will die.

📖 Pharaoh is an important example of the struggle of pride with belief. Reread Exodus 7–10 and record your impressions of Pharaoh's thoughts, motives, and feelings during each incident. What do these passages teach you about pride? How can you apply what you see to your present situation and relationships?

The final plague: 11:1–10. Moses angrily reacts to Pharaoh's death threat, pronouncing God's judgment. The firstborn son of every Egyptian household and animals will die. Pharaoh's officials will beg Israel to leave. Even this revelation only hardens Pharaoh. He will not free the slaves.

Each plague struck against a specific god or goddess of the Egyptians. This final judgment is a blow against the whole pantheon. Egyptian religion was obsessed with life. The pyramids are monuments to rulers who expected their gods to welcome them to eternal life. But all their gods together are unable to protect them from the death dealt by the God of their slaves!

Chapter 13. The Passover

Preparation: 1–13. The Jewish community is told to prepare for departure. But first the blood of a sacrificial lamb is to be sprinkled on the doorposts of the Hebrew homes. Inside, families are to hurriedly eat the roasted meat, standing, and dressed for a journey. On the appointed night God will judge Egypt's gods (12) by striking down the firstborn of his people's oppressors. Seeing blood on the doorposts, the messenger of death will pass over the Israelites.

Miracles, OT

Today a "miracle" is viewed by most people as a "violation of a law of nature." As such, miracles are greeted with skepticism, for laws of nature are considered unbreakable. Most argue that such laws should be binding even on God, if indeed he exists.

The OT perspective is dramatically different. God is the Creator of the universe. He is unquestioned Lord of nature: not in bondage to it, but its master. OT miracles are viewed in this framework of faith.

The three OT words for what we call miracles are helpful. They mean (1) sign, or omen, (2) a creation, or novelty, and (3) something difficult, or wonderful. Thus the OT sees miracles as purposive acts by God, marked off as out of the ordinary flow of events and thus a wonder or "mighty act."

The plagues on Egypt are excellent examples. Most of the blows against Egypt involved phenomena that were natural for the land and the time: hail, frogs, locusts, and so on. Even the means to remove them, like the east wind that drove the locusts to sea, were natural. But the intensity of each plague, its preannouncement, its timing, and the distinction made between Goshen and the land of Egypt, mark each off as the handiwork of God. The mighty acts were performed within the framework provided by nature, but they were so unusual in intensity and in timing that God's involvement is unmistakable.

Miracles were not a normal aspect of everyday OT life. They are not normal features of daily life today. Instead miracles were special in OT times, limited to God's purposes at moments of deep religious crisis, or when some new revelation was to be given. Israel looked back on her times of miracles not as evidence of some claim of the believer on God, but as a demonstration of the fact that God is able, and willing, to act for his people. Jehovah, the God who is always present, may not show his presence in supernatural acts. But he is here, beside us.

For study: Joshua 6:1–21; 1 Kings 17:17–24; 18:20–40; 2 Kings 19:20–37; Daniel 3:1–30 (see also *Miracles, NT,* p. 476).

Festival of remembrance: 14–28. The Lord institutes an annual feast by which each new generation is to relive the redemption experience. The Israelites now move to obey the Lord, and make preparations.

The Exodus begins: 31–42. The death angel strikes. And before dawn Pharaoh and his people fearfully urge Israel to leave. After 430 years, Israel is about to return to the land given them by covenant oath, bearing the wealth of the Egyptians (39).

Passover regulations: 43–51. The Passover is for Israel only.

What in the chapter indicates that the Passover is to be important in Israel's relationship with God? Why do you believe God so underscores this event? What is important for you to remember in your own relationship with God? How do you remember, or relive, it?

Passover

Passover has been called Israel's "Festival of Freedom." With the first month of each year (Abib, later called Nisan, corresponding with April), preparations for the celebration begin. The house is cleansed of leaven, the lamb for the sacrifice purchased, the special foods prepared. Then on paschal night the Passover meal is shared. The youngest son asks, "What does this mean?" And the answer comes: "With a mighty hand the Lord brought us out of Egypt, out of the land of slavery." Passover is a festival of remembrance; the annual reliving of redemption history.

Why was Israel given the Passover? It was part of God's plan for training each new generation: for building identity with the covenant people and their intimate link with God (see *Education,* OT, p. 124). It was a constant reminder of God as redeemer. It was a graphic expression of the fact that relationship with God is a life-and-death issue. It was another visualization of the importance of sacrifice to salvation [see *Atonement,* OT, p. 99]. And it established God's claim to the firstborn of Israel, who were spared when God struck Egypt.

The festival of freedom taught and retaught the lessons of the Exodus. Later the prophets would recall these lessons and urge Israel not to fear her enemies (cf. Isa. 10:24, 26 ff), or would call on Israel to ask in faith, "Where is the Lord, who brought us up from the land of Egypt?" (Jer. 2:6 f). The festival of freedom celebrated and affirmed Israel's redemptive relationship with God.

It is this festival to which Jesus went during his last week on earth. At the Last Supper, he shared the paschal meal with his disciples. Then he, as the true lamb of God, went out to offer himself as the redeeming sacrifice for Israel and all mankind.

For study: Psalm 77; Deuteronomy 16; 2 Kings 23; Numbers 9.

Chapters 13–15. Across the Red Sea

Passover reviewed: 13:1–16. The firstborn son and firstborn of Israel's cattle are consecrated to the Lord. Each is to be redeemed at a money price or, in the case of ceremonially clean animals, sacrificed.

Route of the Exodus: 13:17–22. The "Red Sea" of our English versions is actually a "reed sea." The exact body of water meant is unknown, as are locations mentioned in the text. We do know that the path Israel took avoided the normal military highway to Canaan (17). And we know that God marked out the path, for here is introduced the cloudy/fiery column which will guide Israel's journeys for nearly four decades. A likely route across the sea and on to Sinai is shown on the map on page 70.

Pharaoh pursues: 14:1–14. Pharaoh realizes he has lost his slave labor force. A crack chariot army is marshaled to recapture Israel. When the Israelites hear they are terrified. They forget all God's miracles, and berate Moses for not leaving them in slavery.

The reaction of Israel is significant, and the theme is repeated over and over in the next four chapters. Although God acts to provide for his people, in each emergency they grow less grateful and more rebellious.

📖 Have your reactions in a difficult situation ever paralleled
Israel's (14:10–12)? What might have released the Israelites
from their terror and bitterness? What is there in your relationship
with God that might bring you freedom from fear and bitterness?

The sea opens: 14:15–31. This wonder bears the mark of many
OT miracles: timing, and intensification of natural means (the east
wind, v. 21). The waters rise on either side of the dry path Israel
takes. When the Egyptians rush into the sea bed, the waters flow
back and the entire army is destroyed. Israel sees the bodies of
their oppressors washed up on the shore, and the realization of
freedom fills them with joy. Again, Israel honors God, and trusts
both him and Moses.

Song of victory: 15:1–23.

📖 Examine 14:15–31 carefully. What lessons was God teaching
his people? Examine 15:1–23. What lessons did Israel learn?
What might be a key verse from these chapters for you to memorize
and apply?

Chapters 15–18. Across the Desert

The journal of Israel's journey from the Red Sea to Sinai contains a number of significant features. The passage should be read
as a whole. While reading, watch for the following:

Manna: 16:1–34. When food supplies run out, God provides
Israel with food in the form of "manna." The food appears each
morning except on the Sabbath. It is in the form of seeds, and
tastes like honey wafers. For forty years Israel will be completely
dependent on God to provide her food. He will always be faithful.

Declining faith. The OT speaks of these days as Israel's "childhood" (cf. Hos. 11:1–4). The journal of the journey to Sinai shows
a "permissive" approach to child rearing. Over and over in these
chapters, as Israel comes to a point of crisis, God meets her needs.
But his gracious approach results in neither faith nor gratitude!
Only three days from the Red Sea the people grumble over
bitter waters. God makes the water sweet (15:23–25). Thirty days
later the Israelites mutter against Moses, accusing him of intending
to starve them in the wilderness (16:3). God provides manna and
quail (16:11–15). Israel then disobeys Moses' instructions for gathering the manna (16:20). Again in need of water, the grumbling
escalates. The people are now almost to the point of stoning Moses
(17:1–4)! There is no trust in God or gratitude to him. There is
no growth in character or holiness.

It is against this background that we need in part to understand the introduction to law.

📖 Look over these chapters. What things which you associate with "law" were absent from Israel's experience (for instance, discipline, clear standards, etc.)? How does this help to explain the importance to Israel of the introduction of law?

Authority shared: Exodus 18. Moses regularly judged the people and settled disputes. This involved teaching: the application and explanation of what Moses knew of God's will (15, 16). Moses is rebuked by his father-in-law for undertaking this task alone. God-fearing men should be appointed over tens, fifties, hundreds, and thousands. They will handle lesser disputes; only the most difficult will come to Moses. This report is interesting in two areas.

(1) It is evidence that the principles governing godly behavior were known to Israel before the full Mosaic code was given. While the written law would expand and clarify God's will, morality was known before it. What would the law then do? In its special covenant form it would provide basis on which God could act to discipline his people. And the covenant would also clarify the consequences of the choices Israel would have to make. The next chapters will help us understand better the OT role of law.

(2) The organization of the people of Israel is unclear at this time. The text mentions heads of clans (Exod. 6:14) and elders (Exod. 4:29). Now another structure is imposed by Moses. Soon God's own ordering of the nation will supersede these systems.

Chapter 19. Law Covenant

Now Israel arrives at Sinai. Here a cloud-shrouded, quaking mountain terrifies the people. The billowing smoke and flame that obscure the mountain top cows them. They are ready for the covenant of law.

The Law Covenant. Alone among OT covenants, this matches in form the Hittite suzerainty covenant. In such a covenant, a superior states the conditions of the relationship, and the inferior agrees. Common features of this type of covenant are:

(1) Preamble, which identifies the author   Exodus 20:1
     and gives his titles.
(2) Historical prologue, which recounts   Exodus 19:4, 5
     the deeds of the king on behalf of his
     vassals.

(3) Stipulations, stating the principles on   Exodus 20:2–17
which relationship between the parties   21:1–23:19
is to be based.

(4) Pronouncement of blessings and curs-   Exodus 23:20–33
ings associated with keeping, breaking
the covenant conditions.

(5) Oath of acceptance by the vassals.   Exodus 24:1–8

Contrasting Covenant. It is important to realize that the Mosaic
covenant is distinctively different from the Abrahamic and other
OT "covenants of promise." Law states what Israel is to do: the
other covenants state what God will do. Law is a conditional covenant, expressing what God will do *if* Israel behaves in one way
or another. The other covenants are unconditional, with their promises guaranteed by immutable oath (see *Covenant, OT.,* p. 51).
The law covenant is said in the OT to be temporary, to be replaced
by a New Covenant that is "not like" it, for the New will be
another unconditional expansion of the foundational promises to
Abraham (cf. Jer. 31:31–34). It is important to understand the
differences between the law covenant and the Abrahamic and other
OT covenants of promise if we are to understand the position
the NT takes on law (see *Law, NT.,* p. 617 and *New Covenant,
NT,* p. 653).

Existential Covenant. The covenants of promise point to the future, and give God's commitment to accomplish certain purposes
in human history. The law covenant does not look to the future,
but to each generation's "now." It tells God's people how to live
to experience the present blessing of God, and warns them against
sins which will bring judgment. Thus each generation renewed
the Mosaic covenant, binding themselves afresh to keep its statues
(cf. Deut. 29:12. Josh. 24:15 f). Even today individual Jews at
age 12 make their "bar mitzvah," becoming a "son of the commandment" and oath bound to law.

II. Design for a Holy Community

The first half of Exodus tells the story of Israel's release from
slavery in Egypt. This deliverance was accomplished only by God's
personal intervention in history. Through Moses, Jehovah entered
into deadly confrontation with Pharaoh and Egypt's gods, and
his mighty acts demonstrate the power of this God of slaves. Forever now, reminded by the annual passover Festival of Freedom,

Israel will have an historic anchor for her faith. God has brought his people up, out of Egypt!

But the freed people are a rabble. They are unbelieving, unresponsive, ungrateful, and completely undisciplined. God now must weld this mob of people into a nation—a nation capable of taking the Promised Land and holding it. They are a nation which, even more importantly, will be recognized as his people by their holy life style. In the second half of Exodus we are given an overview of the law through which God will guide his people toward life as a holy community.

Chapter 20. The Ten Commandments

These commands given to Israel by God are brief statements of principle. They reveal God's own moral character and embody the values he seeks to inculcate in us. There are two groups of commands. One speaks of relationship with God. The other speaks of relationships between persons. The commands are:

Relationship with God

1. No gods before me
2. No idols
3. Do not take my name in vain
4. Keep Sabbath holy

Relationships with others

5. Honor father and mother
6. Do not murder
7. Do not commit adultery
8. Do not steal
9. Do not give false testimony
10. Do not covet

These commandments lay the moral foundation of the holy community and help us grasp the significance of personal relationships in biblical thought. Each deserves comment.

1. *No other gods: 3.* God demands exclusive allegiance. No other is to exist for the believer (cf. Deut. 5:6, 7).

2. *No idols: 4–6.* Other peoples carved or hewed idols to bow down to. Israel's relationship is with an invisible God, and she is to respond to his word and Spirit (cf. Deut. 5:8–10). For a commentary, see Isa. 40:18–31.

3. *Do not take my name in vain: 7.* The command is not related to swearing. God revealed himself in his name as "one who is always present" (see *Jahweh/Jehovah,* p. 75). To take the name "in vain" means to consider it meaningless or empty, and thus to deny the reality of God's presence and power.

4. *Keep Sabbath holy: 8–11.* The day of rest is both in honor

of the Lord (cf. 16:23) and for the benefit of God's people (cf. 16:29). To observe the Sabbath involves remembering the Lord.

5. *Honor father and mother: 12.* Respect for parents and the integrity of the family is seen as basic to a holy and healthy community.

6. *Do not murder: 13.* The right of others to life is protected by this commandment. Any action which might rob another of his life is included in this prohibition against murder.

7. *Do not commit adultery: 14.* The value of faithfulness in personal commitments is stressed in this command, which views sex not as an "animal function," but in the context of deep, lifetime partnership between man and woman (see *Sex,* p. 100).

8. *Do not steal: 15.* Respect for persons extends to their property. Others are not to be "used" for our gain.

9. *Do not give false testimony: 16.* An individual's reputation is to be as carefully guarded as his life or property.

10. *Do not covet: 17.* Only if we do not set our hearts on the material possessions another has can we truly care about him. In God's value system, persons are always of greater worth than things.

Jesus said that the entire law can be summed up in love for God and for neighbor (Mark 12:28 f). How does each commandment relate to love? In which area do the commandments most clearly point out an area in which God wants you to grow in your relationship with him or with another person?

Chapters 21–24. Case Law Illustrations

Immediately following the Ten Commandments comes a passage which has been labeled the "covenant code." It is a compilation of case law—a collection of incidents which illustrate, and serve as precedents, for applying the basic law principles. The code pictures life in the land that God will provide, and shows that the whole life of the community was governed by God—political, social, and economic as well as religious. These illustrations show the great emphasis on the value of persons, rather than the value of property. This emphasis is in sharp contrast to the other law codes of that time.

Personal rights: 21:2–35. The rights of servants and accidental injury are discussed.

Civil laws on misuse of property: 22:1–17. Seduction of a virgin is included, because the act involves robbery of the father of the bride price he should have received (16).

Law, OT

The word for law, *Torah*, has several meanings. In the OT it usually refers to the whole divine revelation, with special emphasis on the first five books of Moses. It is also used of the OT codes which guided Hebrew life. By the time of Jesus, to most "law" included the mass of human traditions that had grown up to "explain" the OT. To us today, law usually is thought of as the Ten Commandments.

The word itself means "instruction." It is used of a parent's instruction of a child (cf. Prov. 1:8; 6:20) as well as of God's instruction of his people.

OT law is codified in several major passages. These are (a) The Ten Commandments, Exodus 20; (b) The Covenant Code, Exodus 21–23; (c) The Deuteronomic Code, Deuteronomy 12–26; (d) The Code of Holiness, Leviticus 17–27; (e) The Priestly Code, Leviticus 27.

OT law regulates every aspect of Israel's life. The moral law of the decalogue states enduring principles. Covenant and Deuteronomic codes give instruction about a broad range of daily social relationships, from administration of justice, to training children, to care of the poor. The Code of Holiness and Priestly Code deal primarily with religious matters. Thus many have divided the law's content into three divisions: moral, civil, and ceremonial.

The law has several functions. The first is to reveal the Lawgiver. The kind of person God is is shown in the values embodied in the law. The second is to reveal sin, by clearly expressing the standards that God establishes for his people. The third is to guide the choice of individuals and the believing community toward holiness.

The OT never suggests that the Mosaic covenant is a way of salvation, or a replacement for covenant relationship with God. Only God's present blessing or punishment are governed by law.

However, the OT is clear that a person who lives by faith in covenant relationships with God will, from love, choose to obey the law. To the true believer, the way of Law will be a joy and not a burden.

Yet law, for all its benefits and beauty, was never able to produce in men the holiness to which it points (Rom. 7:7–13; Gal. 2:19–22). God will never change his commitment to righteousness. But the OT law will pass away, for it is not his final solution to creation of a righteous community. For that solution history must wait for a New Covenant, instituted in Christ's death, and a new community formed of those in whom the Spirit of God will dwell.

How did the true believer feel about God's instructions for living conveyed in the Law? You can see in Psalm 119:9–16, 33–56.

Serious sins: 22:18–31. Unrelated but serious sins.
Humanitarian laws: 23:1–9. Protection for the poor and aliens.
Religious regulations: 23:10–19. Sabbath and annual festivals.
Covenant promise: 23:20–23. Obedience will bring many blessings.

Covenant accepted: 24:1–18. Israel now responds to the pronouncement of God's law. "Everything the Lord has said we will do," is their response and commitment (7). This commitment is made afresh by each new Israelite generation (see p. 84).

📖   Select four laws from Exodus 21–23 which you believe express in practice one or more of the ten basic commandments. How would you put their teaching into practice today?

Chapters 25–27. The Tabernacle Design

The key verse for this passage is 25:9: "Make this tabernacle and all its furnishings exactly like the pattern I will show you." God gives Moses detailed instructions for the construction of a worship tent, the Tabernacle. The details contained here are repeated in later chapters of Exodus as the divine blueprint is followed. For discussion see Exodus 35 following.

Chapters 28–31. Priestly Garments

The priesthood was charged with serving at the tabernacle and leading the worship of God. Detailed instructions for the preparation of priestly garments is given, and later repeated. See discussion at Exodus 39. (For *OT Priesthood,* see p. 103.)

Chapters 32–34. Interlude: The Golden Calf

Moses received the blueprints for the Tabernacle and the pattern for the priests' garments, on Mount Sinai. The people waited below.

Rebellion: 32:1–6. When Moses does not return, the people break their promise to obey God (Exod. 24). They make an idol in the shape of a "golden calf" (literally, a young bull). A weak Aaron gives in to their demands.

Moses' prayer: 32:7–24. Moses turns God's anger, but when he sees the idolatry and orgy associated with it, his own temper flares and he breaks the stone tablets on which God has written the Ten Commandments.

Judgment: 32:25 f. The Levites rally at Moses' call and kill the idolators. The next day a plague strikes all the rest who have sinned. No longer will Israel sin with impunity! Law has provided a standard, and with it a basis for judgment.

Fellowship restored: 33. God promises to keep his covenant, and promises Moses his presence.

Significance. The author includes this interlude here for a reason.

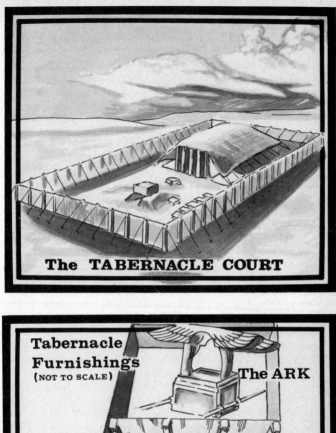

The TABERNACLE COURT

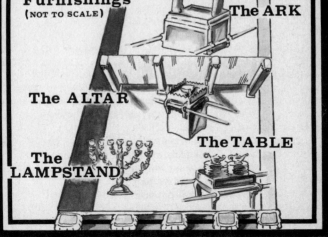

Tabernacle Furnishings (NOT TO SCALE)

The ARK

The ALTAR

The TABLE

The LAMPSTAND

(1) The events immediately illustrate the difference that law introduces into God's dealings with Israel. Faults which were passed over before have now become sin, and will be judged (cf. Rom. 7:7, 8). (2) It demonstrates the desperate need that exists for the tabernacle and priesthood systems. The priests will offer sacrifices to cover the sins of Israel. At the tabernacle, approached only by way of the altar of sacrifice, God will meet his erring people and accept their sacrifices.

New stone tablets: 34. Moses returns to the mountain and is given tablets to replace those he broke. When Moses returns, his face is radiant from being in God's presence.

These chapters contain several dialogues between Moses and God. What is revealed in them about the quality of Moses' relationship with the Lord? What about his "spiritual life" would you like to develop more fully in your own?

Chapters 35–40. The Tabernacle Constructed

The worship system of the OT focused around the tabernacle, until it was superseded by the temple (see *Temple,* p. 190). These Exodus chapters report the construction and dedication of this focus of OT relationship with God.

Tabernacle materials: 35:4–36:38 (Ch. *26*). Materials to make the tabernacle included gems, precious metals, and a variety of skins and linens. All are provided by individuals "whose heart moved (them)" (35:21). All are shaped to God's design by skilled craftsmen.

What does carrying out God's plan for your own life require? Can you see principles in this section to apply to your own life?

Tabernacle furnishing: 37:1–29 (Ch. *25*). The furnishings as well as the structure of the tabernacle are said in the NT to represent spiritual realities beyond themselves (Heb. 8:5). The furnishings described here are: *The Ark.* The top of this small chest was covered by the arching wings of golden angels. It is the only item in the holy of holies, the inmost room of the tabernacle. Here once a year, on the day of atonement [see *Atonement,* p. 99] blood was sprinkled by the high priest to represent the covering of Israel's sin. All other furnishings were placed in the outer room of the tabernacle. *The Table.* Here fresh baked loaves of bread were displayed daily in grateful acknowledgment of God as supplier of his people. *The Lampstand.* This seven-branched, or seven-wicked, oil lamp provided light in the windowless tabernacle. It served as an appropriate statement that God alone is guide to his people.

The Altar of Incense. Here incense made to a special formula denied to all other uses was burned. The worship of God is to be offered exclusively to him.

The OT calls the tabernacle the "tent of meeting." The term captures the significance of this portable worship structure in the experience of God's people. Law had brought knowledge of sin, and with it guilt. God's people thus needed an avenue through which they might approach God for forgiveness. The tabernacle, with its sacrifices and its priesthood, was that place of meeting, where a sinning human being might come to meet a holy God.

The tabernacle was also a constant reminder of the presence of God among his people. During the Exodus, a cloudy, fiery pillar stood over the tabernacle. The tent of meeting itself was placed in the center of the Israelite camp. God, known now through his revelation as Jahweh, the one always present, was to be visibly at the center of the life of his people Israel.

In addition to its immediate historical significance, the tabernacle was designed to harmonize with truths which would be made known in later revelations. We find this significance in the outer court as well as the tabernacle structure. There was only one entry to the tabernacle court, even as there is only one avenue of approach to God. Entering the door, the worshiper immediately was confronted by the bronze altar of sacrifice. Again the lesson is clear. Approach to God must be through sacrifice, by the atoning blood on the altar.

Within the tabernacle itself, other truths are reflected. Perhaps central is one stressed in the NT, yet a little known feature of the crucifixion story. Within the tabernacle a heavy curtain was hung, separating the outer room where the priests ministered from the inner "holy of holies." The High Priest only, and he but once a year on the Day of Atonement, was allowed to enter this holiest place. He came on that day with blood to sprinkle on the "mercy seat," the lid of the ark. A veil was also a feature of the temple, and served the same function there—to make it plain that the way into the holiest, where God's presence dwells, was not open to man.

But at the moment of Christ's death on the cross, the "curtain of the temple was torn in two from top to bottom" (Matt. 27:51). The message is clear. By Christ's death, the once closed way to God is opened for mankind; his sacrifice has won full forgiveness. Now, the writer to the Hebrews says, we come with confidence to the throne of grace, entering the presence of God without doubt or hesitation (4:16). What the tabernacle promised, is ours in Christ today.

The tabernacle court: 38:1–31 (Ch. 27). The tabernacle itself was to be placed in an enclosed courtyard with only one entrance. As one entered by the door, the first sight looking toward the tent of meeting was the bronze altar of sacrifice, and then, further on, a huge bronze basin at which the priests washed. The message was clear. God could be approached in only one way, a way which involved sacrifice.

The chapter includes an accounting of the weight and cost of the materials used in construction.

The priestly garments: 39:1–30 (Ch. 28, 29). The same care in workmanship, materials, and design is displayed in preparing the sacred garments the priests will use in leading worship as in preparing the tabernacle.

Tabernacle inspected and set up: 39:32–40:33. The tent of meeting is set up on the first day of the first month, just a year after leaving Egypt. Israel's second passover festival will be celebrated in freedom, under the law, and possessed of a place for sacrifice and worship.

The glory of the Lord: 40:34–38. The Book of Exodus, which begins in slavery, ends now as the glory of God fills the tabernacle. The slaves who, before, had only known of God by tradition passed on over the centuries now know him in an unmistakable, experiential way. And they know that God, as Jahweh, is with them!

Rethink the Exodus, and compare it to your own journey from a time when you knew of God by hearing to coming to know him experientially, and personally. How was your experience like that of Israel? How was your experience different?

LEVITICUS
The Way of Holiness

This is the third of the five OT books ascribed to Moses. It records God's instructions, given at Sinai, for worship by his people. For dating, see the discussion on pages 69 and 71.

Major themes. The book focuses on worship, and one value is to help us understand the nature of the worship portrayed in the OT. The key is found in the words that are repeated in the book: (1) *Holy.* This word is used 87 times in Leviticus, and helps us realize that worship involves far more than ritual. There is a necessary moral component in our worship of God. (2) *Sacrifice.* If we count its synonyms, "offering" and "oblation," sacrifice is mentioned approximately 300 times in this 27-chapter book! (3) *Atonement.* This word appears 49 times. As we study Leviticus, and come to understand the way these elements functioned in the worship system of Israel, we better understand our own relationship with God.

An outline of the Book of Leviticus should emphasize these themes, and one other structural feature. Two groups of people are addressed alternately: the people as a whole, and the priests. Major themes and the structure of Leviticus are both reflected in the outline below.

Outline

Chapters 1–6. Offerings to Be Made

The first chapters of Leviticus explain offerings and sacrifices to be made at the tabernacle (see *Atonement*, p. 99). Each offering is to be burned at the tabernacle altar. In most cases sacrifice of an animal is required.

Voluntary offerings: 1:1–2:16. The offerings described here are voluntary offerings, expressing dedication or thanksgiving to God. Chapter 1 contains regulations concerning the animals used in dedicatory offerings. Each animal is to be unblemished, signifying total commitment. The offerer lays his hands on the head of the animal, identifying himself with it. This act is repeated in most OT animal sacrifices, and is a vivid acting out of the concept of substitution. The animal is to die as a substitute, representative of the worshiper.

The grain offerings, described in chapter 2, all require personal labor in preparation. God is not to be offered that which costs us nothing.

Can our offerings be an affront to God rather than a gift? What misuse of offerings by Israel serves as a warning concerning our own attitude in worship? See Isaiah 1:11–17; Malachi 1:6–14. Can you list several principles relating to worship from these passages?

Peace offerings: 3:1–17. These are thanksgiving offerings. They too are voluntary, but differ from the offerings of chapter 1 and 2 in that only certain parts of the sacrificed animal are burned. The rest is to be eaten by the offerer and his family, honoring God as provider of the feast.

Sin offerings: 4:1–5:19. The sin offering is a required offering, to be made by any Israelite who discovers he has "sinned unwittingly."

One group of OT words for "sin" pictures it as a falling short of a goal, and implies sins of unintentional rather than rebellious character. Even our best intentions will not protect us, for as fallen persons we often fail (see *Sin, OT,* p. 33). But we remain responsible for our actions. So God, in his grace, provides a remedy for the unintentional as well as intentional sin.

The sin offerings which assert guilt also speak of forgiveness. Forgiveness is available to all, for even the poorest individual can bring an offering for sin. Those unable to afford two doves are even permitted to bring a less costly flour offering.

The message is clear. We can accept responsibility for all our actions. We can confess what we do wrong as sin, for acknowledgment of sin brings us to God for forgiveness (5:13).

Exodus 5:1 speaks of an intentional sin, but one of omission. *Restitution: 6:1-7.* This passage introduces a new dimension. If a sin involves injury to another person, by stealing, cheating, finding lost property and lying about it, and so on, the individual must make restitution. He is to return what has been taken in full, and add one fifth of the value! This must be done before he can bring a guilt or sin offering to the Lord. Restitution precedes confession and forgiveness! Relationships with our brothers and sisters is vital in relationship to God.

Guilt

Today "guilt" is usually viewed as an emotion. Most who are troubled by a nagging sense of condemnation or worthlessness will identify it as "guilt feelings." But in the OT, guilt is objective and real, not a feeling.

In Scripture several concepts are invariably linked. These are sin, personal responsibility, and punishment. Together they comprise what Scripture identifies as guilt. When we speak biblically of guilt we make a very important statement: when an individual commits an act of sin, he is responsible and deserves punishment.

Why does the Bible communicate such a negative message? Because God loves us. Both the Old and New Testaments make it clear that God takes no pleasure in punishing. No, the OT's announcement of guilt is God's invitation to face reality, acknowledge our sin, and seek forgiveness.

For study: Ezekiel 18:1-32; Psalm 38:1-22.

Forgiveness, OT

Several OT words speak of forgiveness. Their meanings include "to cover over, pardon," "to lift up, bear," "to pardon," and "to take away, hide." None imply leniency, as though sin can be lightly dismissed as unimportant. Instead, each word affirms a decisive action by God in which he deals with our guilt and sin.

The whole OT sacrificial system emphasizes the serious nature of guilt, and the fact that sin must be brought to God for him to deal with. But the OT does not explain the basis on which a holy God can dismiss sin and still remain true to righteousness. The later prophets do envision a day when a Servant of the Lord will come and himself serve as a sacrificial lamb, to bear mankind's punishment (Isa. 53). But most of the OT simply affirms forgiveness as good news. God is known as a forgiving God. When we who fail turn to him, he *will* restore the broken relationship, forgiving the sin that has brought us condemnation. The revelation of *how* awaits the NT.

What hope do we have of forgiveness? Psalm 103 shows the hope that's God's OT people had, rooted in who God himself is.

Chapters 6–10. Instructions to the Priests Regarding Offerings

The people have been given instructions concerning offerings. Now supplementary instructions are given to the priests, who serve at the altar.

Making the offerings: 6:1–7:21. The details here may seem dull at first glance, but they are significant. The altar fire will be kindled by God himself (9:24). The priests are to keep the fire burning at all times (6:13). God shows himself always ready to accept any who approach.

Morning and evening dedicatory sacrifices are to be made for the whole nation. The community as well as individuals are to be wholly dedicated to God.

In this section we learn that the priests are to be supported by a share of the offerings. Portions of the meat and cereal will feed their families. Hides will be sold to meet cash needs (7:1–10). This also means that priests will always be in touch with the spiritual tone of Israel. If the offerings slacken, the priests, who are wholly dependent on these contributions, will know! And they will recall Israel to commitment.

Read these chapters carefully. If you were a priest, which of your duties would have greatest significance for you? Why?

Aaron's sons ordained: 8:1–36. OT priests are to be taken only from the family of Aaron, who is of the tribe of Levi. No descendant of Aaron can be ordained a priest unless he is without physical blemish and has reached the age of 30. This ministry is considered too important to be placed in the hands of the young!

The chapter tells how Aaron and his sons are dressed in priestly clothing (see Exodus 28–31), and that a sin offering is made for them. OT priests, chosen from among men, share the weaknesses of their brothers. They share the need for forgiveness.

Sacrificial system instituted: 9:1–24. Now the leaders of the people bring sacrifices. Aaron and his sons follow the instructions given by Moses, and make their first sacrifices at the tabernacle altar. All this they do in the "prescribed way" (9:16), on an altar lit by God himself to indicate his acceptance of their sacrifices.

Imagine yourself a witness on that first day. What would you have thought and felt, standing in that great gathering?

Importance of obedience: 10:1–20. The sacrificial system speaks in every detail of forgiveness, so vital to one's fellowship with God. Thus the meaning of each sacrifice has to be guarded, and God's instructions must be strictly observed. When two of Aaron's sons, Nadab and Abihu, reject God's word, and offer incense in a fire which is not kindled from the altar, they themselves are consumed in a flaring flame. God explains to Aaron and his other sons: "You must distinguish between the holy and the profane, between the unclean and the clean, and you must teach the Israelites the decrees the Lord has given them through Moses" (10, 11). Priests are charged with teaching others God's commands. For priests to ignore and reject them is too serious a failure to overlook. Privilege brings great responsibility.

Yet that same day, when Eleazar and Ithamar inadvertently burn all of an offering of which they are to save part for food, this unintentional error is forgiven. God does not demand the impossible or absolute perfection. But he will not permit rebellion.

Chapters 11–15. Ritual Cleanness

This section of Leviticus deals with ritual cleanness and uncleanness. It's important to realize that here the OT speaks of cultic and not moral issues. This "uncleanness" is not to be equated with "dirty," or with "evil." Many things which are necessary aspects of life, such as caring for a dead body or giving birth, were "unclean" in this ritual sense. A person who was ritually unclean was not permitted to take part in Israel's worship.

Ritual cleanness and uncleanness set Israel apart from all other peoples, and emphasized approach to God as a unique and special experience.

Clean and unclean food: 11:1–47. Some have tried to explain these regulations on sanitary grounds. But the root of ritual cleanness and uncleanness is religious, not hygienic. On the prohibited list of unclean foods are scavenger animals, and many animals prominent in pagan worship and witchcraft. The ground these and other similar regulations rests on is this: "consecrate yourselves, and be holy, for I am holy" (44, RSV). Israel is to live out her consecration to God in everyday life as well as in special times of worship. Diet regulations serve as a daily reminder of separation.

Motherhood: 12:1–8. Women who give birth are ceremonially unclean. Again, this uncleanness has no moral connotations. Nor does it suggest that there is anything sinful about the sexual act or birth.

This passage introduces an important aspect of the OT teaching on ritual uncleanness: cleansing. An individual who is ritually unclean must be cleansed before he is restored to fellowship. Washing is part of most purification rites. Cleansing of direct uncleanness (see 15:1–32) requires sacrificial blood. Metal vessels which become unclean are purified with fire (Num. 31:22 f).

God always provides a way for the excluded to return to him.

Infectious skin diseases: 13:1–46. The chapter does not deal with leprosy. When this word appears in English versions, it is a mistranslation. Instead it covers a variety of skin diseases: infections (2), ulcers (7, 8), boils (19), scabs (30), and general eczema (38–40). A person with any of these symptoms is to appear before a priest to be judged clean or unclean. Anyone judged infected is sent outside the camp boundaries until healed. This regulation did protect Israel from plagues and some infectious diseases. But the primary emphasis is again cultic. A diseased person is not qualified to approach God.

Later the prophets use the image of disease to communicate the seriousness of Israel's sin. An Israelite, familiar from childhood with the laws of ritual cleanness, would immediately understand the prophet's message as he describes God's people this way: "your whole heart (is) afflicted. From the sole of your foot to the top of your head there is no soundness—only wounds and welts and open sores" (Isa. 1:5,6). Such a people, infected by sin and morally diseased, could never hope to approach God or be accepted by him.

Contaminated objects: 13:47–59. Objects as well as persons can be ritually unclean. Here molds and fungus on clothing or buildings are discussed.

Cleansing from infectious disease: 14:1–57. When disease symptoms disappear, a priest is to be called. If his examination shows a state of health, purification ceremonies are prescribed. Sacrificial blood, as well as washings, are central in these ceremonies.

Bodily discharges: 15:1–32. Here too it is important to remember that ritual uncleanness, not "dirtiness," is in view. These include both emission of male semen and menstrual discharge.

There are obvious health implications to these regulations. Yet the religious significance is central.

This chapter introduces another aspect of the laws related to ritual uncleanness. A person may become unclean directly, as in the case of his own skin disease. But uncleanness is also transmitted by touch. A person or object touched by anything unclean itself becomes ritually unclean.

Purification rites for direct uncleanness typically last seven days, and involve sacrifice. Uncleanness contracted by touch lasts only until evening, and only requires washing by water.

Rules of ritual cleanness and uncleanness are not given in the NT. In a striking incident, the apostle Peter was taught that these and other aspects of Jewish life style were not rooted in eternal moral principles. You can read about his experience in Acts 10:9–23.

What do you see as basic differences between these laws of ritual cleanness and the moral regulations given in the OT?

Chapters 16, 17. The Day of Atonement

The service of atonement: 16:1–34. At the heart of the Book of Leviticus beats the theme of atonement. Each year, the tenth day of the seventh month, a special sacrifice of atonement is to be made. Sacrifices ordained in the first seven chapters dealt with unintentional sins. Chapter 16 stresses the fact that on the Day of Atonement the sin offering is (a) for all the people (17), and that it is (b) for "the uncleanness and rebellion of the Israelites, whatever their sins have been" (16). Three more times in chapter 16 the sacrifice of the Day of Atonement is said to be for "all their sins" (21), "all your sins" (30), and "all the sins of the Israelites" (34).

A unique feature of the service of the Day of Atonement is the scapegoat. The sins of the people are symbolically laid on the goat, which is taken outside the camp and released in the wilderness. The picture is clear: Israel's sins are gone, taken away.

The blood of atonement: 17:1–15. Chapter 16 is addressed to the priests; this chapter is to all the people. The most significant statement is found in verse 11: "The life of the flesh is in the blood," the Lord tells his people, "and I have given it (the blood) to you to make atonement for yourselves upon the altar." Sin must be paid for by a life. But God shows he will accept a substitute for the sinner.

Atonement, OT

The Hebrew word means "to cover," or "wipe away." It is intimately related to reconciliation. The message of atonement which God communicated to his people through the OT sacrifices was that he would wipe away their sin. Atonement, like many biblical terms, witnesses to several realities. The realities affirmed by atonement are: Fellowship with God is ruptured by sin. God calls for judgment of sin and sinner. Sacrifice provides forgiveness and restoration.

The Day of Atonement, and other atoning sacrifices, had deep personal meaning to the spiritually sensitive Israelite. Repetition of the sacrifices remind him of the need for continual cleansing. The sacrifice itself brought him a deep sense of release and acceptance.

Yet the OT sacrifices could never really take away sins. All they could do was to picture the way that God had planned, before the beginning of time, to restore his sin-cursed children. One day Jesus Christ would enter the world, to take our sins upon himself. Then the reconciliation the OT sacrifices promised would be fully accomplished, and the believer would find perfect forgiveness and release.

For study. Hebrews 10:1–23.

Chapters 18–22. Holiness

In a strict sense, chapters 17–27 are all included in the Leviticus holiness code. But the dietary laws, and regulations concerning ritual uncleanness, are dismissed in later revelation. The call to moral purity remains a vital part of relationship with God.

Every moral issue discussed here is relational. Even more important, each rests on an intimate relationship between God and the people he calls to holiness. No less than thirty times in these five chapters does God state, in explanation of his commands, "I am the Lord," "I am the Lord your God," or "I am the Lord who makes you holy." God's own character is the source of the commands. Relationship with God makes holiness necessary. And experience of God as "our" God is the motivation for holiness.

Sexual restrictions: 18:1–29. This chapter defines different forms of incest, each of which is prohibited to God's people. Other regulations also protect the integrity of the family (18) and community (20).

Homosexual relationships like relations with beasts are identified as detestable perversions which defile (22, 23).

Sex

God is the inventor of sex. He designed every sensation associated with intercourse as a gift which he desires us to enjoy.

But pleasurable sensation is never an end in itself. Foods have flavor, but the function of food is to fuel life. Neither taste nor sexual pleasure is an end in itself. Biblically, sex is the seal of commitment. In the context of a lifetime commitment between a man and a woman, sex is enriching and fulfilling, as well as a source of intense pleasure. Out of this context, the fullfillment is lost.

In the OT the relationship between the Lord and Israel is often pictured as marriage, and idolatry is equated with adultery. In each case there is unfaithfulness to one who deserves our sole commitment.

While it's wrong to use sex (and thus another person) simply to experience the physical sensations, it is equally wrong to think of sex as something "dirty," or to view pleasure in marital relations as somehow "unspiritual." God intends us to give and to receive sexual pleasure within the marriage context. A person who rejects sex, as well as one who is unfaithful, distorts this loving gift of our good God.

For study: Proverbs 5:1–20; 7:10–27; Song of Songs 4:1–7. What are your feelings about sex today? Do you feel comfortable with a passage like Song 4:1–7? Do the Proverbs passages make sense? How do you think you developed your sexual attitudes?

Holiness, OT

The root meaning of the OT word translated "holy" is "to separate," or to "set apart." This idea is reflected in the charge to the priests: "you must distinguish between the holy and profane" (Lev. 10:10). But OT separation is not a negative concept: distinguishing is for the purpose of learning how to actively devote one's life to God.

Holiness is also seen in the OT to be rooted in the essential nature of God. Again and again Israel is told, "be holy, for I am holy." Holiness is never seen as a human quality, or even as an abstract idea. Always holiness is a term that affirms a unique relationship with God. Thus places (like Sinai) and things (like the Tabernacle, and its worship vessels) are holy because they belong to the Lord.

The reality of holiness through relationship underlay Israel's call to "be holy, for I am holy." Because the community and the individual believer have a personal relationship with God, each has been made holy. The life Israel is called to live is not supposed to *make* her holy: instead it is because Israel *is* holy through relationship with God that her life is to be different.

In the OT this unique set-apart relationship to God is to be evidenced in many ways. Worship and laws of ritual cleanness as well as morality, are associated with holiness. Every aspect of Israel's life is to be different from the nations around her, because of God.

Israel's Code of Holiness has a moral dimension. In other religions of the time, holiness was a ritual thing. Any morality associated with the religions of Canaan was depraved, involving prostitution and infant sacrifice. Thus the OT emphasis on morality as an aspect of holiness is striking. Because of relationship with God the Israelite is to be truthful (19:11), honest (19:36), fair to servants (19:13), loving toward neighbors (19:16–18) and kind to strangers (19:33,34). He is to care for the poor (19:10,15) and the handicapped (19:14,32), as well as to be sexually pure (18:1–30).

In summary, the OT teaching on holiness does not deal with man's nature, or even man's actions apart from relationship with God. Instead the OT reveals a God who is holy and who, because of his personal relationship with Israel, sets her apart as holy, and calls her to live out her holiness in every aspect of her life.

For study: Isaiah 6:1–8; Leviticus 18, 19. See *Holiness, NT,* p. 778.

Jot down your definition of what most people believe "holiness" to be. How do these definitions differ from the OT concept?

What is the importance of seeing "separation" as a positive, action commitment rather than negative withdrawal?

Various relationships: 19:1–37. This chapter reflects a variety of issues, many dealt with in Exodus 20–23, and touches on family, neighborhood, business, and other relationships.

Which of these commands do you think would witness most strikingly to surrounding nations about relationship with God?

Penalties: 20:1–22. The moral principles expressed in Leviticus are more than good advice to Israel. These are the commands of Israel's God. God is not indifferent to the choices Israel will make: the Lord says his people "must not" live according to the customs of other nations (23). Thus the chapter spells out specific consequences of disobedience to certain moral laws. Some consequences are brought about by God's action; in other cases punishment is the responsibility of the believing community.

Morality for the priests: 21:1–22:16. These commands for the priests and their families show several areas in which a higher moral standard is required of them than of the average Israelite. For instance, priests are not to marry a divorced or widowed woman, even though this is permitted under the law for others.

There are several important insights which this gives us. First, the priests have a special and higher moral responsibility because of their special relationship to God. While all Israel is set apart to the Lord, the priests are doubly set apart. They approached God more closely in the tabernacle service, and they are responsible to teach his laws to others. With intimacy and responsibility comes a call to a greater holiness.

Second, the very fact that a higher morality than that expressed in the general law exists, is significant. In OT times and in Jesus' day, some religious persons distorted law, attempting to use it as a ladder to climb to achieve holiness. They thought if they could keep the law they would *become* holy. But they were wrong. They were wrong because holiness comes from relationship with God (see *Holiness, OT,* p. 101), not from keeping the law. Keeping the law was an expression of a relationship which already exists with God, not a way to establish that relationship.

They were also wrong because the religious person who misused law tended to see it as a *perfect standard.* But if the law expressed moral perfection, there would have been no "higher" requirements for priests! Thus in the body of OT law itself, evidence exists that God does not intend law to picture perfection. Another truth emerges: the more intimate our growing relationship with the Lord, the more perfectly we will grasp and reflect his moral character.

For further study, see the following: *Holiness, NT,* p. 778; *Law, OT,* p. 87, and *Law, NT,* p. 617.

Priesthood, OT

Three institutions dominate the life of Israel as she developed within the Promised Land. These are expressed in the persons of prophets, priests, and the king. Of the three, two originate in the Exodus period. Moses is the prototype prophet. Aaron is the prototype Levitical priest.

What was the role of priesthood in Israel, and what are we to learn from this institution?

The word "priest" appears more than 700 times in the OT. While the root meaning of the word itself is uncertain, the role of priest is carefully explained. The priest was to represent the people before God, and to represent God to the people.

As a representative of the people of Israel, priests appeared before the Lord to make sacrifices and offerings. As God's representative, the ministry of the priests was more complex. They were to instruct in the law (Deut. 33:8-10; Hos. 4:1-10), to give judgment on legal issues (Deut. 33:7-11), and to discover the will of God, using the Ephod (I Sam. 23:6-12). The priests also watched over matters of ritual cleanness associated with disease (Lev. 13-15).

There were several orders of OT priests. At the top of the hierarchy was the high priest, who alone could enter the inmost chamber of the tabernacle or temple. He officiated on the Day of Atonement. The second level included the sons of Aaron, who were the hereditary priests. These served at the temple altar and officiated at regular sacrifices. There was also a priestly role for the rest of the tribe of Levi (of which Aaron's family was a part). Although the Levites never served the altar, they did carry the parts of the portable tabernacle during the wilderness years. In David's time they provided worship music, and later served as wandering law teachers in time of revival. Like the priests, the Levites were supported by the offerings and tithes given by the people to God.

After the Babylonian exile there was a change in the teaching function. Men like Ezra dedicated themselves to study and teach the Scriptures. By Jesus' time, a class of rabbis (teachers) was set apart as students and teachers of the Bible and Jewish traditions. By then the priests focused entirely on ceremonial matters.

The great institutional significance of the priesthood was mediatorial. In the priests who stood daily at the tabernacle or temple, making the prescribed sacrifices to the Lord, the average Israelite had living evidence that a way of approach to God was open and available to him.

For study: See passages noted above, and *Priesthood, NT.* p. 749.

Chapters 23–25. Worship Calendar

Israel's year included many festivals and holy days. These were intended by God to provide times of rest and refreshment. They also provided an annual review of Israel's redemption history. As such, the festivals were a vital part of the education of each new generation, as well as a constant reminder to all of Israel's role as a holy nation, set apart to God. Several of the feasts also have prophetic significance, prefiguring events which only become clear in Christ and later revelation.

The Sabbath: 23:1–3. One day in seven is to be set apart for rest and for sacred assembly.

Passover and unleavened bread: 23:4–8. The Passover festival is described in Exodus 12. The feast was held on the fourteenth day of the first month of the religious year. The fifteenth began a one week period during which bread without yeast was to be eaten, as a reminder of Israel's hurried departure from Egypt. By the time of Christ these two feasts had merged, and Passover was considered the "first day of unleavened bread" (Mark 14:12).

Firstfruits: 23:9–14. When the grain ripened, a bundle of newly cut stalks was harvested and brought to the Lord as an expression of thanks for the greater harvest to follow. The NT speaks of Jesus' resurrection as a "firstfruits." The meaning is that in his resurrection, Jesus stands as a promise of the multitudes who will be resurrected after him (1 Cor. 15:20–23).

Feast of Weeks: 23:15–22. Fifty days after the firstfruits were offered, another festival was ordained. Later the day became fixed on the calendar. In the NT this is called the Day of Pentecost.

Feast of Trumpets: 23:23–25. The seventh month was especially significant in the OT worship calendar. Its first day was marked by the blowing of trumpets, and set apart as a day of rest and assembly. This also is Rosh HaShannah, the first day of the civil year.

Day of Atonement: 23:26–32. Fasting and prayer were ordained for this solemn sacrifice (Lev. 16, 17). It too is in the seventh month.

Feast of Tabernacles: 23:33–44. Beginning the fifteenth of this month all of Israel was to live outdoors, in shelters made of palm branches or the boughs of other trees. The family did not work on these days, but were to relive the time of travel through the wilderness to the land they now possessed. The contrast between this joyful family experience and the solemnity of the Day of Atonement was a vivid lesson concerning the joys of redemption.

Some Christian fellowships keep a liturgical year, with a similar calendar. What might its advantages be for your family?

Israel's Religious Calendar

Month		Special Festival Dates
April (Nisan)	14th	Passover
	15th–21st	Unleavened Bread
May (Iyyar)		
June (Sivan)	6th	Weeks (Pentecost)
July (Tammuz)		
August (Ab)		
September (Elul)		
October (Tishri)	1st*	Trumpets
		*Also Rosh Hashanna, the first day of the civil year
	10th	Day of Atonement
	15th–21st	Tabernacles
November (Heshvan)		
December (Kislev)		
January (Tabeth)		
February (Shebat)		
March (Adar)		

By the time of Jesus, two additional festivals had been added. One is Hanukkah (the Feast of Lights), which honors the victories of Judas Maccabeus in 167 B.C. (see *Between the Testaments*, p. 436). This feast falls on December 25th. The other is Purim, which commemorates the deliverance of the Jews through the intercession of Queen Esther. Purim falls on March 14th.

Blasphemer stoned: 24:1–23. A historical interlude tells of blasphemy and its immediate punishment.

The Year of Jubilee: 25:1–56. Israel's religious cycle extended over spans of years as well as within calendar years. Every seventh year the land is to be given a rest. God promises that the harvest of the sixth year will be so great that the land will not need to be worked the seventh.

With this surprising vision of a Sabbath for the land, a totally unique concept is introduced. Every fiftieth year in Canaan is to be a year of Jubilee, or release. When Israel did enter Canaan, each family was allotted land. The land itself could not be transferred, although its harvest potential could be sold in advance.

When the year of Jubilee arrived, all land reverted to its original owner. In other cultures, as in our own, sources of wealth can be sold and, once sold, are lost forever. As a result, some become wealthy, and others poor. But in Israel, Jubilee provided for a unique preservation of capital. In God's plan, land, the source of wealth in OT times, would always be retained by the family.

Other laws associated with the Jubilee principle also protected God's people who became poor. If a Hebrew found it necessary to sell his services to pay his debts, he was not to be treated as a slave. And in the year of Jubilee he would be freed. Additional evidence of God's concern for the needy is shown in that no Jew was to loan money to a fellow Jew at interest. And every sabbatical year, personal debts were to be canceled.

If Israel had followed these laws of Jubilee, an ideal society, without poverty, would have resulted. But never in her history was the Sabbatical year or the Year of Jubilee observed.

Chapters 26, 27. Additional Instructions

Promises and Warnings: 26:1–48. God is to be honored. This is the heart and soul of Israel's worship and her life of holiness. Here the people are given pictures of the blessings associated with obedience (3–13) and the consequences of disobedience (14–39). But whatever discipline God may impose, he will not abandon his people.

Vows and tithes: 27:1–34. Verses 1–25 discuss voluntary offerings. A person who wishes to express gratitude to God may do so in a variety of ways. One feature of these vows is important to note. Vows are always made publicly, with the whole community as witness and participant in the individual's commitment.

The last verses review tithes and offerings required of all who enjoy the unique blessing of being God's own.

NUMBERS
The Wilderness Years

Numbers is fourth of the five books ascribed to Moses. The English title is taken from the census chapters (4 and 26). The Hebrew title for the book is "In the Wilderness."

The content of Numbers is drawn from the thirty-eight years Israel spent in the wilderness, from preparation to leave Mount Sinai to the plains outside of Canaan. For its date, see pages 69, 71.

Numbers is organized in loose chronological order. But the content is not in strict time sequence. After a narrative portion the author often inserts material from other times which is related to his subject. Thus, it's impossible from Numbers to develop a strict sequence of events. In fact, surprisingly little is told of the thirty-eight years Israel spent in the wilderness. Only isolated, but significant, events are included.

The historic value of Numbers is found in its picture of the impact of Mosaic law and the dramatic change law introduces in the way God deals with his people. Also important is the record of Israel's response to law and to God's discipline. Again and again Numbers illustrates the importance of obedience, and the tragedy which follows disobedience. The NT frequently refers to Numbers to demonstrate the importance of obeying the Lord.

Our outline of Numbers reflects the broad chronological structure and the high points emphasized within each time period.

Outline

Chapters 1–4. Organizing the People

The census: 1:1–54. One month after completing the tabernacle, a census is taken of men over twenty, able to serve in the army. The Egyptians had well developed plans for taking census. Moses organizes the process along their lines. The result shows 603,550 meaning the total population is between two and two and a half million.

Some commentators have argued that this is unrealistic and thought that an error in transcribing shifted a figure from David's time to the Exodus. But this number is given in a number of OT texts (Exod. 12:37; 38:26; Num. 1:46; 2:32; 11:21 and 26:51).

The family of Levi is not included in the military census (47).

The camp arranged: 2:1–34. Moses now assigns places to the tribes where their tents will be set up on the journey.

This order was once criticized as "artificial," and thought to be the invention of priests from a later era, ignorant of the actual events. Recent archaeological studies have shown that the square design of the encampment was used by the Egyptians in the time of Rameses II. It is the later Assyrians who used a round pattern.

The Levites assigned ministries: 3:1–4:49. At the time the Lord struck down the Egyptians and passed over Israel, he claimed the firstborn of his people, to be his in a special way. Now the firstborn of the whole people are carefully counted and matched to males a month in age and over in the tribe of Levi. The Lord claims the Levites for special service as representatives of the firstborn.

Chapter 4 records the assignments of the clans of the tribe of Levi. There is work for every Levite between the ages of thirty and fifty.

Chapters 5–9. Culminating worship

The events in these chapters are not in chronological sequence. They report what led up to the first anniversary celebration of Passover, celebrated at Sinai two weeks before the census. But the reported order of the events is significant. It demonstrates the purity of the camp as Israel joins in a culminating time of worship on the plains before Mount Sinai.

Camp purified: 5:1–31. The rules for ritual cleanness given in Leviticus are observed. All who are unclean are sent outside the boundaries of the camp (1–4).

The chapter also deals with a question raised by earlier moral legislation. How can a person who commits secret sin be found out, and the purity of the community protected? The chapter outlines a procedure used when a person is suspected of adultery. The person who lies under oath will be judged by God in an evident way; the person who is innocent will be just as clearly absolved.

Nazarite vows: 5:1–21. Regulations for a special vow of separation and personal dedication are given.

Benediction: 6:22–27. Here are words familiar in our churches today, with which the priests were to bless the people of God.

Dedication offerings: 7:1–89. Leaders of each tribal group present rich offerings on the twelve days following dedication of the tabernacle.

Lamp lit: 8:1–4. The design of the tabernacle lampstand is reviewed. It is set up in such a way that its light is always cast forward. Just so, God will light the path of his people. If they turn aside, or back, they will walk in darkness.

Levites dedicated: 8:5–23. The members of this tribe, specially set aside to serve God, go through special cleansing ceremonies before they can begin their ministry.

Passover kept: 9:1–14. On the first anniversary of leaving Egypt the people keep the Passover. Even those ritually unclean are permitted to take part in this redemption celebration. In fact, all of Israel is required to participate. Throughout history each Jew is expected to annually relive and affirm God's salvation.

The guiding cloud: 9:15–23. Now, as Israel is about to move on, the writer focuses on the cloudy fiery pillar, suspended over the tabernacle. If the cloud rises, Israel is to break camp and follow. If the cloud settles, Israel is to camp. They are to go only where God leads, and only when he determines it is time.

Chapters 10–12. The Journey

As Israel sets out on her journey from Sinai, it becomes clear that there has been no real change in the people. On the way to Sinai they murmured and complained rebelliously (Exod. 16–18). The law given at Sinai has not modified their character; they continue in that sinful course. What changes is God's response to Israel's behavior! Now God acts to discipline whenever Israel sins. This is absolutely necessary if Israel is to become a holy people and be able to take the Promised Land of Canaan.

Silver trumpets: 10:1–10. A blast on silver trumpets will call Israel to assembly and to war—and call on God for help.

Departure from Sinai: 10:11–36. Israel leaves the Sinai encampment, traveling in marching order (14–28). Moses' father-in-law is invited to come, but returns to his own land.

Rebellion: 11:1–3. Complaint against God is judged immediately as the Lord's anger flames at the edge of the camp. Prayer averts a greater disaster. The disciplining of Israel has begun.

The Angry God: 11:4–35. Now the people crave meat and yearn for the foods they ate before their redemption from Egypt. Frustrated, Moses turns to God and complains. These people are too great a burden for him to bear! In spite of the Lord's anger against the people, he pauses to give support to his faithful servant. Special spiritual enablement is provided to seventy of Israel's elders. They will help Moses with the burden of leadership.

But now God turns to the people. They demand meat? They will have it—so much meat they will loath what they have yearned for! God brings great flocks of quail that provide the meat demanded. But with meat comes a plague that strikes down thousands.

Israel has rejected God's provision, and treated him as if his name is empty of power (see the *Second Commandment,* p. 85). They have not responded as a holy community, and God's anger is aroused.

God's Anger

The OT speaks often about God's anger. There are eight Hebrew words that express this concept. Some are descriptive, and picture heavy breathing or foaming lips. Others mean indignation, rage, fury, burning, vexation, and pouring out of anger, or outbreaks of wrath. Both the emotion of anger and its expression are portrayed in these OT terms.

Many find it disturbing that words like these are used to describe God. But while human anger is often an unjustified reaction of the sin nature, God's anger is always rooted in his holiness and his love. God *is* angry with his people Israel—when they forsake his covenant and break his laws. He is angry with nations that institutionalize wickedness, and war on others. But only because God cares so deeply for human beings is he disturbed when men are oppressed, or when sin leads them away from him and the good he desires for them.

We too need to see God's anger, including the most drastic of the disciplines he brings on his people, from the perspective of covenant love. Like a good parent, who acts out of deep love for his children, God will not permit his own to continue on in dangerous and wrong paths. If God did not love us deeply, he would hardly care enough to be angry when we sin. Even the wrath of God testifies to how important you and I are to him.

For study: Amos 4:1–5:16; Psalm 94; Matthew 23:13–36. What seem to be the primary causes of divine anger?

In chapter 11 we see Moses complains *to* the Lord, while the people complain *about* the Lord. What is the difference, and why does God respond so differently to Moses and to Israel? Sometimes our prayers too are grumbling complaints. Are there prayers that it is good for God *not* to answer? What do you learn about prayer from this chapter? How can you apply what you learn in your own prayer life?

Miriam and Aaron dissatisfied: 12:1–16. The brother and sister of Moses are jealous of his preeminence. They speak against him, and so they too merit God's anger, and receive his discipline.

Chapters 13, 14. Israel's Disobedience

We come now to the turning point in this generation's experience. Israel is led by God to the border of Canaan. Here the people are commanded to enter the land, and take it from the inhabitants. But the people are terrified at the prospect of war, and refuse to obey. The NT returns to this event often, to illustrate the hard-heartedness of God's people, and to demonstrate the relationship between faith and obedience (Heb. 3, 4). Only when trust in God is expressed in obedience to God can the believer find rest.

Scouts sent out: 13:1–25. A representative from each tribe is selected to explore the promised land and bring a report. The twelve penetrate into the central highlands, and after forty days return with samples of the land's rich produce.

Scouts Report: 13:26–33. All twelve agree that the land is rich. But ten of the scouts fearfully talk about the power of the giant inhabitants. They discount God, who won their freedom from Egypt by acts of power; they insist "we cannot attack these people, for they are stronger than we" (31).

Rebellion! 14:1–10. All night long the agitated Israelites discuss and grumble. By morning they are agreed. They will choose a new leader and return to Egypt! When Moses and Aaron, supported by the scouts Joshua and Caleb, beg the people to remember the Lord, the "whole assembly" talks of stoning them!

Moses' intercession: 14:11–25. The people are suddenly cowed as the cloudy pillar above the tabernacle flames. God is angry enough to strike down the whole nation, and begin afresh with Moses! Moses' prayer of intercession is a model for all times. Moses

can say nothing good about Israel. But he can plead the character
of God! God announces his decision. Israel will be spared. But
not one of the rebels who treated God with contempt will live to
enter the Promised Land. God cites ten incidents of rebellion in
verse 22. These are recorded in Exodus 14:11–12; 15:23–24; 16:2;
16:20; 16:27; 17:1–3; 32:1–10; Numbers 11:1; 11:4; and 14:2

Death Sentence: 14:26–38. God now announces the fate of his
rebellious people. Not one person over twenty years of age (29)
who witnessed God's miracles in Egypt, and then treated him with
contempt, will survive forty years of wandering in the desert.

To emphasize the sentence, the scouts who stimulated the rebellion by their fearful advice are immediately struck down by a
plague.

Disobedience compounded: 14:39–45. Frightened at the judgment
which Moses announces, the people decide to invade Canaan after
all. But this is simply another act of disobedience! God has told
them to turn back to the wilderness.

The attack fails, and a stricken, cowed Israel retreats into the
desert.

What relationship do you see between faith and obedience?
How would Israel have responded if they truly did trust
God and counted on his presence? Can you see parallels or contrasts
with this event in your personal journey of faith?

Chapters 15–19. Years of Wandering

Little is told in Scripture of the years spent in the wilderness
waiting until the designated forty have passed. The events reported
in these chapters are not arranged chronologically.

Supplementary offerings: 15:1–41. Moses gives instructions for
offerings "after you enter the land I am giving you as a home"
(1). Moses is told to speak these instructions to the people. In
spite of defeat and disobedience, God will keep his promise to
the covenant people.

Korah's rebellion: 16:1–50. Korah, a Levite, insolently challenges
Moses' authority. He asks, "Why do you set yourself above the
Lord's assembly" (3)? But it is God who has given Moses and
Aaron authority.

Korah and his followers are told to present themselves before
the tabernacle, bringing incense to offer the Lord. Moses tells Israel
to move away from the tents of the rebel families. Suddenly fire
lashes out to destroy those bringing the unauthorized offerings.
At the same instant, the earth quakes. The ground opens to swallow
the possessions and the families of the rebels (28–35).

Amazingly, the very next day the congregation accuses Moses of having "killed the Lord's people" (41). Only the leader's intervention stops a resulting plague that strikes down 14,700 of the people.

No wonder the later Scripture speaks of this generation as stiff-necked and unyielding, as well as unbelieving.

Aaron's budding staff: 17:1–13. To demonstrate once for all that it is God who has chosen Aaron's family for the priesthood, a wooden staff is brought by each tribe to the tent of meeting (tabernacle). The next morning Aaron's staff has sprouted, and actually produced fruit. The staff is placed in the tabernacle, as a witness to God's calling. Finally now the people are frightened—but of the tabernacle, not of disobedience!

Priestly duties: 19:1–32. The tabernacle is not to be feared. But, as holy to the Lord, it is to be treated with respect. Regulations for priests and Levites are reviewed, and the offerings which will support them are reaffirmed.

Cleansing: 19:1–22. Israel has known death intimately since God's judgments have struck the people. Here regulations for purification from ritual uncleanness (see Leviticus 11–15) after touching a dead body are developed. This instruction is necessary. As Israel journeys, a whole generation will die in the desert.

Chapters 20, 21. Warfare

The people of Israel now come to Kadesh, on the edge of Moabite territory. The forty years have almost passed, for in this chapter we read of Aaron's death which took place in the fifth month of the fortieth year (20:23–29; 33:38). The old generation has nearly passed away. But there is still a tendency to rebel. There is still discipline to face, but the new generation will learn to obey. And they will enter the Promised Land. Even this is now a prelude to victory rather than defeat.

Moses' failure at Kadesh: 20:1–13. On returning to Kadesh, Israel finds the springs dry. The same old complaints and grumbling are heard. God tells Moses to speak to the rock he struck years before to produce water (Exod. 17). But Moses disobeys! Angrily he strikes the rock, and speaks as if his own effort plays a part in supplying the waters that now gush out (cf. 27:12–14; Deut. 32:38–52). This fails to honor God, or display trust. Moses is told he will not enter Canaan.

Confrontation with Edom: 20:14–20. An ancient, well-known route known as the Kings' Highway stretched from Kadesh to Canaan, crossing the land of Edom.

The Edomites are descendants of Esau, the brother of the patriarch Jacob (see Gen. 25 f). Existence of a monarchy at this time (14) is evidence of an established culture.

Moses asks permission to travel the established highway to Canaan, promising not to stray off it into the land. The request is rejected, and Edom sets a powerful army across the roadway. Israel turns away. Later they are told by God to honor the family relationship, in spite of this treatment (Deut. 23:7,8).

Aaron dies: 21:22–29. The high priesthood passes to his son.

The Bronze Serpent: 21:1–9. Harried by a minor Canaanite people, Israel destroys their cities. But even victory does not satisfy. The people complain against Moses, grumbling about the desert and the food God has supplied. In judgment the Lord sends venomous snakes. Finally the people exhibit repentance (7)! Moses makes a bronze snake and lifts it up on a pole in the center of the camp. All who are bitten can travel to the center of camp, look at the bronze serpent, and live.

Christ refers to this incident in John 3:14–15. There is nothing medically significant in looking at the serpent. Only trust in God's word will bring a person to the bronze image. Only trust in God's word will draw a person to Christ.

Journey to Moab: 21:10–35. After a long southern detour to avoid Edom, Israel turns north again. Moab has also been avoided by God's command (Deut. 2:9). But now, to reach Canaan, Israel must cross the land of the Amorites. Request for free passage is made and refused. Israel destroys the Amorite army and occupies their cities. The neighboring land of Bashan is also overrun, giving Israel possession of Transjordan, the lands east of the Jordan river.

A policy of total destruction of the enemy is established by God (see *War*, p. 125).

Chapters 22–25. Balaam

Israel is now camped on the plains below Moab, just across the Jordan river from Canaan. Although Moab is not threatened, the king and people are terrified. So Balak, the king of Moab, sends for a soothsayer. The Hebrew here is specific: Balaam is not a "prophet" *(navi')* but a "trafficer in magic" *(hakkisim)*. Barak intends to have this individual, known for supernatural powers, curse Israel. He believes the curse will weaken Israel's power.

The summons: 22:1–20. Barak's invitation is rejected, for God tells Balaam not to go. Another embassy is sent. Balaam receives permission to go, but is warned to say only what God commands. Balaam was already determined to gain the wealth promised by Balak.

Balaam's donkey: 22:1–20. To convince Balaam he must speak only what God commands, an angel is sent to confront Balaam along the way. Balaam's life is preserved only because the donkey avoids the angel, who stands with drawn sword blocking the way.

Balaam's first oracle: 23:1–12. Balaam directs the king to make sacrifices, promising to tell him whatever the Lord reveals in response. The message is disappointing. God refuses to curse Israel and instead actually blesses them.

William Albright, the best known of biblical archaeologists, has discovered that the poetic structure of Balaam's oracles is ancient, appropriate to the thirteenth century B.C.

The second oracle: 23:13–26. Balak is determined to try again. The company moves to another vantage point, from which a different part of the Israelite camp can be seen. But again the message is one of blessing. Balaam is forced to report:

> "The Lord their God is with them . . .
> There is no sorcery against Jacob,
>   no divination against Israel" (21, 23).

The third oracle: 23:27–24:14. They move to yet another location. Seven altars and sacrifices are prepared. Balak still hopes God will permit Balaam to curse Israel. But again the seer is forced to announce a blessing, one going back to the Abrahamic Covenant (Gen. 12:3):

> "May those who bless you be blessed,
>   and those who curse you be cursed" (9)!

The furious Balak banishes Balaam to his home.

The fourth and fifth oracles: 24:15–25. Before Balaam leaves he is forced to pronounce the coming destruction of Moab at the hands of Israel, and to announce Israel's ultimate ascendancy.

Balaam's advice: 25:1–18. Balaam has been unable to curse God's people. But after returning home, he devises a plan he believes will strip Israel of God's protection (cf. Rev. 2:14). He will entice Israel to sin!

Following Balaam's plan, Balak enlists the Midianites. They send women to entice Israelites to join in sacrifices to their gods—sacri-

fices which involve sexual intercourse as part of the worship. Again
God is forced to anger. The leaders are commanded to execute
the idolators, and a plague brings the number of the dead to 24,000.

Balaam's plan was to pollute Israel so that God would be forced
to curse his people. Instead God destroyed the guilty (cf. Deut.
4:3, 4), and spared the others, thus purifying his people and preserving their holy character.

Examine Balaam's relationship with God as shown in these
chapters. How does that relationship contrast with the relationship of Moses with the Lord?

The NT speaks three times in warning against Balaam-like
behavior. Second Peter 2:15 warns against the *way* of Balaam
(seeking wealth through religion). Jude 11 warns against the *error*
of Balaam (choosing profit rather than obedience). Revelation 2:14
warns against the *doctrine* of Balaam (the sanction of immorality
by religion). How does each find expression in these chapters?
What does each warn against in contemporary society? In your
own life?

Chapters 26–31. The New Generation

The second census: 26:1–65. The original generation has been
replaced during the years of wandering. There has been no loss
of strength. Men of military age still number over 600,000.

This census is taken as a basis for distribution of land in Canaan.
The larger tribes will receive a larger portion, and all parcels will
be distributed by lot (52–56).

Female inheritance: 27:1–10. The five daughters of Zelophehad
demand the right to inherit in their father's name, since he left
no sons. This request is honored, and the principle becomes a
part of Israel's inheritance law.

Joshua commissioned: 27:12–23. As Moses' life draws to a close,
he is deeply concerned about a successor. God tells Moses to commission Joshua to lead the people when he is gone.

Offerings, festivals and *vows reviewed: 28:1–30:16.* This is all material repeated from Leviticus. The repetition underlines how important faithfulness to God's design for worship will be to the
community of Israel.

Vengeance on Midian: 31:1–54. Midianites had taken the lead
in carrying out Balaam's plot to corrupt Israel. Now Moses is
commanded to attack that people. All in the area are wiped out,
including Balaam. And not a single Israelite soldier is lost (49)!

This time, while the Midianites are killed, their property is saved and divided among the soldiers and the community, with a proper share to the priesthood.

A new attitude is shown in the soldiers' voluntary offering of all the gold in their share, as atonement and as thanks for the victory. This is a new generation, and the people are beginning to show themselves ready to respond to the God who calls them to cross the Jordan, and take the land of promise.

Note. Incidents all along the journey, from slavery to the borders of freedom, have taught a number of lessons about life as a redeemed people. These lessons are shown, and the Exodus journey reviewed, on the chart on page 118.

Chapters 32–36. Victory Preview

Transjordan tribes: 32:1–42. Two of the tribes of Israel are impressed with the richness of the land east of Jordan. It seems ideal for their large flocks and herds. They ask it as their inheritance, but promise to lead the armies that cross the Jordan, and stay until the promised land has been occupied and divided.

The request is granted, and the lands of the Amorites are theirs.

Journey reviewed: 33:1–56. The stages of the journey from Egypt to the plains of Moab are listed. Most of the places have not been identified by archaeologists.

Boundaries established: 34:1–29. The inheritance in Canaan is carefully outlined, and the process of distribution reviewed (see map on page 145).

Levitical cities: 35:1–8. The Levites have been set apart to serve God. They will not be given a tribal land in Canaan. Instead, they are to be given towns and pastureland within the inheritance of the other tribes (cf. Lev. 25:32–34; Josh. 21). One value of this plan: no tribe will be without communities of those who are called to teach and witness to God's Law.

Cities of Refuge: 35:1–33. The structure of Israel as a nation made no provision for a federal police or justice system. The citizens in each community were responsible to God and to each other to punish offense against the divine Law, which governed civil as well as religious life. In this system, murder was to be avenged by the community. Often the lead would be taken by relatives of the murdered individual, called the "avenger of blood."

God has announced the death penalty for murder (cf. Gen. 9:6; Ex. 21:12). But now a clear distinction is made between manslaughter (accidental killing without hostility) and premeditated murder (hostility motivated killing). Here too provision is made to protect the individual who kills another accidentally.

Moses establishes the principle of refuge. He commands that six Levitical cities in Canaan be set aside as places to which one who has killed accidentally can flee. The killer is permitted to live in the confines of that city until the death of the high priest. Then he is free to return to his own property, protected from any vengeance.

Does this chapter provide any insights into the much debated capital punishment question? What do you conclude?

Female inheritance regulated: 36:1–13. The daughters of Zelophe-had (ch. 27) are instructed to marry within their clans, so that when their land passes to their children it will remain part of the tribal inheritance.

Understanding Redemption
(Exodus through Numbers)

Scripture	Events	Message	Key Word
Exod. 1–4	Enslaved in Egypt	Man needs redemption	Helplessness
Exod. 5–11	God's judgments on Egypt	God acts to redeem	Jahweh/Jehovah
Exod. 12–15	Release from slavery	Redemption comes through death	Passover
Exod. 15–19	Journey to Sinai	The redeemed must be godly	Rebelliousness
Exod. 20–24	Commandments and case law	Godliness requires love for God and man	Law
Exod. 25–40	Sacrificial and tabernacle systems instituted	Sins can be forgiven	Tabernacle
Lev. 1–10	Offerings and sacrifices ordained	Forgiveness involves blood sacrifice	Sacrifice
Lev. 11–22	Ritual cleanness, atonement and moral instruction	God's people are set apart to him	Holiness
Lev. 23–27	Worship calendar and Jubilee year	God's people are to worship and celebrate	Worship
Num. 1–9	Camp organized	The community of faith is to be orderly	Order
Num. 10–20	Refusal to enter Canaan, 38 years in the wilderness	Disobedience to God brings disaster	Disobedience
Num. 21–36	Journey toward Canaan	Obedience of a new generation brings victory	Obedience

DEUTERONOMY
The Book of Covenant Life

This is the fifth and last OT book ascribed to Moses. With Genesis, Exodus, Leviticus and Numbers, it completes what we call the Penteteuch, and what the Jewish people call the Law of Moses. For a discussion of the date of the Pentateuch, see pages 69 and 71.

This book contains three sermons by Moses to Israel. When Moses preached them, the Israelites were gathered on the plains just east of the Jordan river across from the Promised Land. Moses has led God's people out of slavery in Egypt, brought them to Mount Sinai to receive the law, and has been with them through four decades of wilderness wanderings. The years in the wilderness were a judgment by God on the first generation's rebelliousness. Now a new, obedient generation is poised and ready, after forty long years, to possess the land of Canaan which God promised to their forefathers. The story of the deliverance from slavery and the journey to Canaan is told in Exodus and Numbers.

Distinctives of Deuteronomy. Several features set Deuteronomy apart. The book is essentially a sermon, or exhortation. In it Moses urges Israel to choose a life of obedience to the law which God has given. Here we see a strong emphasis on personal relationship, as Israel is urged to love God, to hear him when he speaks, and to keep or do his words. Each of these emphases is expressed in phrases which are repeated often in Deuteronomy.

Theologically, Deuteronomy presents the Lord as God of the covenant, and God of history. And a new stress is placed on relationship. Here the phrase "Jahweh *our* God" ("the LORD our God") is introduced and repeated. God's people are never to approach law as a legalistic kind of thing, but are always to see the law covenant from the perspective of a personal relationship which already exists between God and his covenant people.

Covenant form. The Book of Deuteronomy would have been recognized by its first readers as a relational book. Its form closely follows the pattern of certain types of covenants well known in OT times—of treaties made between a ruler and his subject. This treaty form was well defined, and the content of Deuteronomy fits the form well. There was an important message for Israel in the form—a message we need to understand as we read this book.

Deuteronomy deals with the life of a people who are already redeemed, not with salvation. The people of Israel already have a faith relationship with God (see *Covenant*, p. 51 and *Law*, OT, p. 87). Thus the question dealt with in Deuteronomy is one of how God's OT people are to live out the relationship which God has already acted to establish. The questions of life and death raised in Deuteronomy are not questions about eternal life or eternal loss, but questions of life and death on earth, in the land to which God has brought his people.

The well-known format of this kind of treaty included:

Historical Prologue	Introducing the relationship which the ruler has with the subjects
Basic Stipulations	Stating general principles that govern behavior
Detailed Stipulations	Explaining certain specific regulations to be followed
Document Clause	Requiring ratification by the subjects
Blessings	Explaining the benefits to be provided under the treaty
Cursings	Warning of the punishments to come if the treaty is broken
Recapitulation	Reviewing and summarizing the treaty

This form does correspond closely with the content of Deuteronomy. The passages that fit the treaty form are: Prologue (1:6–3:29); Basic Stipulations (5:1–11:32); Detailed Stipulations (12:1–26:19); Document Clause (27:1–26); Blessings (28:1–14); Curses (28:15–68); and Recapitulation (29:1–30:10).

With this understanding, provided by archaeological discoveries, we can understand Deuteronomy as would an Israelite of Moses' day.

Duplicated material. Approximately 50 percent of the material in Deuteronomy is new. Yet much of its content parallels teachings already given in other books of the Pentateuch. Several extensive parallels between Exodus and Deuteronomy serve to illustrate.

Exodus 21:1–11	parallels	Deuteronomy 15:12–18
Exodus 21:12–14	parallels	Deuteronomy 19:1–13
Exodus 22:21–24	parallels	Deuteronomy 24:17–22
Exodus 22:29	parallels	Deuteronomy 15:19–23
Exodus 22:31	parallels	Deuteronomy 14:3–21
Exodus 23:2–8	parallels	Deuteronomy 16:18–20

Exodus 23:10 f	parallels	Deuteronomy 15:1–11
Exodus 23:14–17	parallels	Deuteronomy 16:1–17
Exodus 23:19a	parallels	Deuteronomy 26:2–10

In general, the Deuteronomy material tends to be longer than the Exodus parallels. Usually this is because the sermon or exhortation style stresses application. Exodus tends to simply state rather than explain the same statutes.

Outline of Deuteronomy. The treaty form of the book gives it clear organization and unity. But our outline needs to note one other feature. This book is a collection of three sermons by Moses to the people of Israel. Our outline stresses both the sermon structure and the treaty form explained earlier.

I. MOSES' FIRST SERMON: WHAT GOD HAS DONE FOR US		1:1–4:43
1. God's Actions Reviewed	1:1–3:29	
2. Israel's Allegiance Required	4:1–43	
II. MOSES' SECOND SERMON: LIFE UNDER THE COVENANT OF LAW		4:44–26:68
1. Principles of Covenant Life	5:1–11:32	
2. Details of Covenant Life	12:1–26:19	
3. Covenant Ratification Required	27:1–26	
4. Blessings and Cursings	28:1–68	
III. MOSES' THIRD SERMON: A CALL TO COMMITMENT		29:1–30:20
1. Exhortation to Commitment	29:1–15	
2. Warnings to Be Heeded	29:16–28	
3. Forgiveness Assured	30:1–10	
4. Appeal to Choose Life	30:11–20	
IV. THE LAST DAYS OF MOSES		31:1–34:12

Values today. Christ often returned to Deuteronomy to find a principle which he applied to his own life or to his hearers. In the same way, many basic principles of life lived in close relationship with God here in Deuteronomy can enrich our Christian experience. While we no longer live under the law covenant, nor is our life with God governed by the treaty (see *Law, NT,* p. 617), the deep expressions of love, and the obedience that love motivates, are the same for us today. There are many lessons here—about who God is, about our relationships with him and others, and particularly about the need for full commitment to the Lord which can greatly enrich our lives.

Moses' First Sermon: What God Has Done for Us

Introduction: 1:1–5. This brief editorial insert tells us that it is the eleventh month of the fortieth year after leaving Egypt (3) that Moses gathers the people of Israel to hear his final words. He now expounds the law (5), as an impassioned preacher.

The plains on which Israel stands to listen are only eleven days' journey from Mount Horeb (the name Deuteronomy gives Mount Sinai). The unbelief of the first generation has stretched an eleven-day hike into forty years!

Chapters 1–3. God's Acts Reviewed

The treaty form on which Deuteronomy is patterned begins with a historical review of relationships between ruler and subjects. Here Moses recreates a series of incidents which sum up God's experiences with the generation he brought out of Egypt.

The call to possession: 1:6–25. After the law was given on Sinai, God called Israel to move toward Canaan, to take possession of the land God promised the forefathers. The camp was organized and the scouts sent out to view the Promised Land. The report of the scouts was unanimous: "it is a good land the Lord our God has given us" (25).

Rebellion recalled: 1:26–46. But Israel failed to trust God, even though he "carried you as a father carries his son" (31). They rebelled and refused to enter the land.

Desert wanderings: 2:1–24. The years spent wandering were punishment for sin. Still God guarded his people. For the entire time "the Lord your God has been with you, and you have not lacked anything" (7).

Victories recalled: 2:26–3:20. Then Israel again approached Canaan. This time Israel did fight, and the Lord gave total victory over the nations who chose to be their enemies. The Lord even gave the lands east of Jordan to two tribes as their possession: it was his action that gave victory, and he gave the land.

About "total destruction" of the enemy (3:3–6), [see *War*, p. 125].

Joshua commissioned: 3:21–29. Moses too disobeyed God and will not be permitted to enter Canaan. But God has appointed Joshua as the leader who "will lead this people across and will cause them to inherit" (28). The promise made of old will be kept, now.

Read these chapters, noting each incident which Moses relates. Why did he select each to emphasize? If you were using this sacred history in a sermon, as Moses did, what application or exhortation might you now add, to bring its lessons home?

Chapter 4. Israel's Allegiance Required

In a deeply moving chapter, Moses applies the lessons of recent history, and makes an impassioned plea for allegiance to God. This is to be expressed by obedience (1–14), by rejecting idolatry (15–31), and by always remembering who the Lord is (32–40).

Deuteronomy 4:32–40 merits memorization and meditation. If you are ever discouraged, turn to these words of Moses. Let them direct your thoughts to the Lord, who "is God in heaven above and on earth below."

Verses 41–43 are an historical insert, reporting establishment on the east side of Jordan of cities of refuge (Numbers 35).

Moses' Second Sermon: Life under the Covenant of Law

The historic prologue to the treaty has been stated in Moses' first sermon. Now Deuteronomy moves, in the second sermon, to examine the life to which God calls his people. Woven into Moses' exhortation is a distinctive exposition of the love bond between the Lord and his people. Only love will move them to become a holy community. After a historic note (4:44–49) the text quickly moves to the sermon.

Chapters 5:1–11:32. Principles of Covenant Life

Covenant life is a life of allegiance. This is revealed as the basic principles that underlie Mosaic Law are lifted up and explained.

The Commandments: 5:1–32. The Ten Commandments, first given at Sinai, are repeated for the new generation. These lay the foundation for life under the Mosaic covenant.

The commandments are in two sections. The first (commands 1–4) speak of relationship with God. Israel is to guard her allegiance to the Lord by acknowledging his identity, nature, name, and day. The second (commands 5–10) speak of relationship with others. In a holy community, each is to care for others by respecting life, person, property, and reputation. Both Jesus and the NT epistles point out that these commands can be summed up in love (Matt. 22:34–40; Rom. 13:8–10; Gal. 5:13,14). For more on the commandments, see pp. 85–87.

The chapter ends as it begins, with an urgent appeal to Israel to hear, to learn, and to be "sure to follow" (1) the law God has given. If Israel does stay with the life style of love marked out by law, they will "live and prosper and prolong your days in the land that you will possess" (33). Each succeeding generation will be given this choice—and this promise.

Love for God: 6:1–25. Many see this chapter as an exposition of the first commandment. It includes warnings against forgetting God when prosperity comes (10–12), against the dangers of serving idols, and against testing God (13–19). He is Lord, and is to be honored and obeyed (13–19). Two themes in the chapter are special. First, Israel is called to "love the LORD your God with all your heart and all your soul and with all your strength" (4). Only love can motivate full allegiance. Second, much attention is paid to the training of children (1–2, 6–9, 20–25). Both law, and God's motivation in giving is ("so that we might always prosper and be kept alive," 24), are to be taught. The commands of God can never be understood apart from the deep love that is to motivate each party to covenant relationship.

Education, OT

Deuteronomy 6 insists that children be taught, and shows how the Lord's commands can be "impressed upon" the next generation. How was religious training provided, when there were no Sunday schools or similar training agencies?

OT education was life-oriented. Trades were learned by apprenticeship. Religious training was similar, for the goal of OT education was not a knowledgable individual, but a godly one.

The festivals and holy days that marked Israel's year (see pp. 104–106) and reviewed Israel's history of relationship with God were part of the educational process. So were symbols of faith in the home (Deut. 6:8,9), memorization of Scripture, and patterns of Sabbath keeping. But the heart of the process was the relationship of children to adults.

Hebrew children were to grow up in the context of a holy community, among adults who loved God and had taken his commandments to heart (6:6). Thus the whole community, and especially the parents, would model the godly life into which the children were expected to grow.

These same adults were to talk about the commandments they live, not in a special "school" room, separated from the realities of daily life, but "when you sit at home and when you walk along the road and when you lie down and when you get up" (6:7).

Living within a community of adults who love God, who live his Word, and who take time to share that word with children, each new generation would come to know the Lord in a personal way.

📖 In what ways does religious training given children today differ from the OT pattern? How are the differences significant?

📖 What has been the most significant influence in your own growth in faith? How was that influence like or unlike the OT pattern? What purpose did close and loving friends serve?

Love as total allegiance: 7:1–26. Moses explains that total allegiance to God will involve being his instrument in war against the peoples of Canaan. These are to be totally destroyed (1–6). They need not be feared—even though they seem stronger—for "the Lord your God, who is among you, is a great and awesome God" (21). With the command to destroy the enemy and their worship centers is a promise of the blessings that full allegiance to God will bring.

War

"Thou shalt not kill." Does the commandment, which affirms the sanctity of human life, permit war? Or is God's call of his people to war, seen here in Deuteronomy 7, a moral contradiction?

The word. The term translated "kill" in the King James is correctly rendered "murder" in the NIV. The Hebrew term, *rasah,* speaks of private killing. It does not refer to the execution of lawbreakers (cf Deut. 13:5, 9) or of killing in warfare. Thus arguments against capital punishment or for pacifism cannot rightly rest on an extension of this commandment, but must be supported some other way.

Warfare. The Bible presents God as Lord of history. As such he both redeems and judges. The armies of Assyria and Babylon as well as the army of Israel are called God's instrument in the Bible, in each case called out by him to punish some evil. A modern parallel would be the use of war to destroy Nazi Germany, and thus put Hitler's evil to rest. As an instrument of God's judgment or wickedness, the OT sees war as both moral and necessary.

Total destruction. The conquest of Canaan described in the OT does raise a question beyond that raised by normal war. Here the OT portrays God as urging Israel to pitiless destruction of an entire culture, and to kill men, women, and children. How can this be? To understand, we need to know something of Canaanite culture. It was morally depraved, with a religion that featured cult prostitution and child sacrifice. Its continued existence would be a snare to God's people, whom the Lord determined to protect from the Canaanite depravity. Yet even here we can see God's grace in action. In Abraham's day, some 400 years earlier, God would not permit the Canaanites to be dispossessed, for the "iniquity had not

yet come to full measure" (Gen. 15:16). Only when their commitment to
evil was complete did God act to judge. Now, as Israel approaches, wickedness in Canaan has achieved its full development. God, using Israel as
his instrument of punishment, does not draw back.

For study: on war as judgment, Isaiah 8, Habakkuk 1. On destruction
of the Canaanites, Deuteronomy 20:1–20; 21:10–14; 23:10–14; 25:17–19.

Love as remembrance: 8:1–20. Once in the land, Israel will have
the prosperity promised in God's covenant. Then they will need
to recall the years in the wilderness, remembering both God's discipline and his supply. Wealth must not lead to pride or self-reliance.
It must stimulate remembrance of God, thanksgiving and obedience.

Love as choice: 9:1–10:11. Why has God loved Israel? Deuteronomy 7 introduces both the question and a warning. Israel may
try to explain her relationship with God by some supposed merit
in the people (7:7). But actually, God simply chose to love Israel.
And he delivered the people from Egypt because he is faithful to
his commitments.

Chapter 9 suggests another reason Israel might later grasp for
as explanation. Possessing the law, they might say, "The Lord
brought me here to possess the land because of my righteousness"
(4). This is exactly the attitude of the Jews of the apostle Paul's
day (see Rom. 2:17–29)! Again Moses rejects this explanation,
and as evidence of Israel's unrighteousness recalls the incident of
the golden calf (Exod. 32). Only Moses' intercessory prayer turned
aside God's anger (23–29). The real explanation is found solely
in God's character: in his free choice to love Abraham's descendants, and in his faithfulness to that commitment.

How does God's love for Israel in spite of her behavior
help you understand the nature of his commitment to you?
Can you write out a brief description of a relationship in
which you have remained faithful to a commitment, in spite
of hurts and the other person's failures?

Love as fear of God: 10:12–22. Moses now applies his message.
How are the people of the Lord to respond to his great love?
Moses' answer is to fear the Lord, walk in his ways, love him,
and serve him in complete commitment (12). (See *Fear of God*,
p. 127).

Love as obedience: 11:1–32. Moses has demonstrated from history
the reality of God's love for his people (Deut. 9). Now he calls
on Israel to return that love, and shows how love for God finds
practical expression. This generation has witnessed God's acts on

Israel's behalf (1–7). Now they are to "observe all the commands" of the law Moses has given. Faithful obedience will bring great blessings, as the Lord enriches Canaan (8–15). But Israel must not turn away from the Lord to worship other gods (16–21). Thus Moses sets two ways before Israel: a way of blessing, if they love God and walk in his ways; and a way of discipline, if a generation should turn its back on God and move away in disobedience.

How does love for God find expression in your own life? Jot down a list of the choices you have made because you love him. How has your love grown over time?

Details of Covenant Life

The broad principles of covenant life have been laid out. Now the treaty form Moses has chosen requires that he list detailed stipulations. Many themes already introduced in Exodus and Leviticus are included in these chapters. In general Moses expands on the selected laws. The material is drawn from each of the types of codes given in the law.

Chapters 12–16. Worship in Covenant Life

A center of worship: 12:1–32. Canaanite worship featured many places of worship, often on hilltops or in groves of trees. Moses instructs Israel that God is not to be worshiped in that pagan way. Instead the Lord will choose a central location in the Promised Land, and only there may sacrifices and offerings be made. Not until David, some 500 years later, was that place selected: Jerusalem, the site of Abraham's ancient offering of Isaac (Gen. 22).

Fear of God

There are a number of OT words for fear, with meanings that encompass "dread," "terror," "wonderful," "stupendous," and "awe." The OT emphasis is not, however, on the emotion aroused. The focus is on the object feared, and on how fear functions in our life.

Because God "comes in awesome majesty," and "is beyond our reach, and exalted in power, in his justice and great righteousness . . ." (Job 37:22,23), it is right for men to hold him in reverence and awe. Fear of God, a respect appropriate to who he is, is a great treasure (Isa. 11:3; 33:6). The person who maintains a healthy sense of who God is will avoid evil (Prov. 16:6), listen to God's voice (1 Sam. 12:14), and keep the Lord's commandments. Thus the OT presents the fear of God as a reverence appropriate to relationship with our great God; a wholly good and healthy thing.

The OT also contrasts fear of God with fear of men. What other persons think or do should not dominate an individual's thoughts. This kind of fear "lays a snare" (Prov. 29:25), for mere men are not to be lord over our conscience or choices.

The OT also seems to suggest that a person who lacks fear of the Lord will have no protection against wickedness, and may be gripped by dreadful hallucinations (cf. Prov. 10:24; 28:1). Only one who knows how great God is, and who has a personal relationship with him, is freed by his fear of God from the terror of the unknown future, which robs life of peace and of joy.

Judgments on idolators: 13:1–18. The command to worship God only is essential to covenant life. It is so vital that the entire community must take personal responsibility for obedience. Any prophet or spiritualist who tries to lead others to worship other gods is to be executed. No matter how close a relationship with a person who urges idolatry, even if "your closest friend secretly entices you" (6), that person must be delivered up to judgment.

Rules of evidence under the law require at least two witnesses to any crime, so individuals were protected from false accusations.

Clean and unclean foods: 14:1–21. Regulations from Leviticus are repeated here.

Tithes: 14:21–28. Establishment of a worship center may make it difficult for distant families to follow some laws given in the wilderness. Moses explains modifications for the settled life in the land. He again affirms how tithes are to be used. They will support the Levites, who serve God at the temple and are landless. OT giving supported those who served God.

Love, OT

Some have argued that the OT presents a primitive, legalistic image of God, and thus deserves to be supplanted by the NT, which presents a more enlightened and loving deity. However, Deuteronomy makes it clear that love infused the OT as well as the New. Both testaments picture a relationship between God and man which is rich in mutual love.

God's love. Over and over the OT stresses the fact that God has acted out of love in establishing his relationship with Israel. He loved the forefathers, and has a changeless covenant commitment to care for the descendants. This love was not earned by Israel. God made a free, spontaneous, and sovereign choice to love them. Even the punishments which God at times is forced to bring on his people are acts of love, the discipline of a father who will do whatever is necessary to guide his children to blessing and righteousness. Law too is a love gift, designed to point Israel toward blessing, and to teach her how to truly love both God and her fellow men.

Man's response. The OT makes it clear that what God seeks from human beings is not some terror-ridden observance of impersonal standards. Instead, when God is known as redeemer, and trusted as faithful to his covenants, people will respond with a wholehearted love, expressed naturally as joyful obedience. As does the NT, the OT links love for God with obedience to him (cf. John 14:15–21).

For study: God's OT love: Deuteronomy 4:32–38; 7:7–9; Hosea 11:1–11. Man's response of love: Deuteronomy 6:4; 10:12–22; Psalm 118.

Care of the needy: 15:1–18. God's release of Israel from slavery provides the basis for his call to Israel to cancel personal debts every seventh year (1–6), to freely lend to the poor (7–11), and to release those bound to service each Jubilee year (12–18). Those who have experienced oppression are not to begrudge release to others, but are to share what God has so liberally given to them (see Leviticus 25, p. 105).

Three annual pilgrimages: 16:1–17). Three of the annual festivals which enrich Israel's worship cycle (see p. 104) require that God's people leave their homes and gather at the central sanctuary.

Chapters 16–18. Leadership of the Covenant Community

Several different kinds of leaders emerged during Israel's history. Here Moses looks ahead and gives regulations as to how different leaders will function.

Judges: 16:18–17:7. These seem to have been leaders of local councils of elders, to exist in "each of your tribes in every town" (18). They settle local differences, and are to decide justly, without perverting justice, showing partiality, or taking bribes (19).

Whenever an accusation is made, the judges are to investigate carefully (4). The testimony of at least two witnesses is required for proof (6). God's law is the standard by which judgment is to be made (2).

Priests and Levites: 17:8–13. These served as a court of appeals to which more difficult cases could be brought. This court was to sit at the sanctuary location (Deut. 12), and its verdict must be accepted.

The King: 17:14–20. Moses here predicts a future time when Israel will demand a king. When that happens, the people are to anoint one whom God selects. The passage describes a number of additional safeguards king and people are to follow. Later Solomon's failure to live by this passage caused his personal decline (see 1 Kings 11).

When a king took the throne, Moses ordained that he should be given a personal copy of God's law. Israel's king ruled under the overarching authority of the Great King, God himself. Like his brothers, the king was to accept his place as a subject of Jahweh.

Priests and Levites: 18:1–8. How the Levites will be organized once Israel is in the land is discussed.

The Prophet: 18:9–22. This individual, vital to covenant life, is now introduced, and his role explained (see *Prophet, OT* , p. 130).

What personal qualities would be required in a leader who functioned in the covenant community? Why would these be needed?

In what ways is the leadership system described here strong? What is required of the community for the system to work well?

The Prophet, OT

The third key institution in OT covenant life, with the priesthood and monarchy, was the office of prophet. Unlike the others, a prophet did not inherit his position. God called each prophet individually.

The root meaning of the word "prophet" in the Hebrew is uncertain. However there is no doubt about how the word is used in its over 300 OT occurrences. A prophet was a spokesman, a person who communicated another's message. Thus the second time the word occurs in the OT, God tells Moses that Aaron will be a mouth for Moses, and speak his words to Pharaoh, serving him as a prophet serves God (Exod. 4:10–17).

The OT speaks of large groups of false prophets (cf. 1 Kings 22:6; Jer. 5:31). But God's call to a prophetic ministry was an individual and usually lonely calling. The phrase, "sons of the prophets," which appears seven times in the OT, does not suggest either a group or a training school for prophets, but describes those who gathered around a prophet to learn from him or assist him.

Deuteronomy 18 is the key to understanding the OT prophet. Here Moses warns against the detestable practices of the Canaanites, who looked for supernatural guidance from diviners, sorcerers, witches, spiritualists, and mediums (9–13). These are abominations, forbidden to God's people.

But God will not leave Israel without special guidance. He will send prophets to carry his messages to particular generations.

Israel was responsible to recognize the true prophet and distinguish the false. A true prophet will be an Israelite (18), speak only in Jahweh's name (20), and the events he foretells will actually happen (22).

Today we distinguish between writing prophets (those who penned the prophetic books in our OT) and speaking prophets (those whose ministries are described in narrative OT passages). Both however had the same basic mission: they were spokesmen, conveyers of God's word to his people, Israel. Each spoke, first of all, to his own generation, with a message shaped to his own day. To understand a prophet's message we must first understand what his words meant to those to whom he spoke.

Looking through the OT, we see that prophets might confront or counsel kings (cf. 2 Sam. 7:1–17; 12:1–10). They might confront the nation, to call them back to God in times of apostasy (1 Kings 18:16–45; Amos 6:8–17). They would command, invite, denounce, warn. Tragically, the history of Israel shows few of the OT prophets were heeded in their own times and many were killed.

Women, as well as men, were called to the work of a prophet (cf. Judg. 4:4–6; 2 Kings 22:14–22; 2 Chron. 34:22–26).

Chapter 19. Cities of Refuge

Regulations concerning unintentional killing are repeated (1–14), and rules of evidence for legal cases are laid down (13–21).

Chapter 20. Rules of War

When Israel goes to war, a priest is to encourage the army to trust the Lord (1–4). Officers are to release anyone newly married or with an undedicated house, or one who is fearful (5–9). Cities that are attacked are to be given an opportunity to surrender (10–15), and trees around a besieged city are not to be cut down (19–20). But the peoples of Canaan are to be destroyed completely, "Otherwise they will teach you to follow all the detestable things they do in worshiping their gods, and you will sin against the Lord your God" (18).

Chapters 21–24. Miscellaneous Laws

One major theme of these chapters is marriage practices and violations. These regulations (22:13–30; 24:1–5) are primarily concerned with purity and with faithfulness. This is particularly important for Israel, surrounded as it was by licentious pagan cultures. It is vital, for the family is not only essential to the health of the society, it is also the primary communicator of faith (cf. Deut. 6:4–8; 11:16–22).

Divorce and Remarriage, OT

Deuteronomy contains the basic OT teaching on divorce, which is allowed to God's covenant people. Divorce is not permitted only to a man who rapes a virgin and then marries her. Remarriage is denied only to priests, or to those who would remarry a first spouse after an intervening marriage (22:28, 29; 24:1–4).

While divorce is permitted and to some extent regulated, the OT discourages it. God, who is uniquely faithful, hates divorce, as an act of unfaithfulness to a couple's marriage covenant (Mal. 2:16). Yet divorce is specifically provided for in the law.

Jesus explains this permission as something granted by God because "your hearts were hard" (Matt. 19:8), not because God's ideal had been lowered. Our Lord's point is that sin still has a grip on man, and the marriage relationship, like every other, is subject to shattering alienation. There are times when a marriage is so distorted by the sin of one or both partners that divorce is better for the persons involved, and thus is permitted to them as a gift of grace.

In the case of divorce, remarriage was not simply allowed; it was expected.

Various additional legal instructions are found in these chapters. Israel is told how to deal with unsolved murders (21:1–9), local disputes (25:1–17), and other potential problems.

Chapter 26. Liturgical Instruction

A liturgy is provided for the celebration of firstfruits (see p. 104), and for the paying of the third year tithe (see 14:28, 29). Use these liturgies as a pattern to develop a family liturgy you can use on one of our holy days.

Chapter 27. Covenant Ratification

The Law covenant was no unconditional announcement of what God is committed to perform. Instead, it is a treaty, defining relationships between the Lord as ruler, and the Israelites as subjects. The first generation accepted the covenant of law at Sinai. Now the second generation is given instructions for a ceremony of covenant renewal. Particularly important is the response of Amen ["so be it"] that the people are to make as each stipulation is stated in the ceremony. This constitutes the voluntary commitment of that generation to the covenant of law, by which a generation existentially "became" (9) God's people.

A similar ceremony of renewal was later held for the third generation, as reported in Joshua 24 (see p. 146).

Chapter 28. Blessings and Cursings

Following the treaty format (see p. 120), Moses now lists the blessings and the curses associated with keeping or breaking the covenant. During Israel's centuries in Canaan (Palestine), each blessing and each curse was experienced by different generations. God is faithful to his word; both to his promises of good, and his warnings about the consequences which will most certainly follow sin.

Moses' Third Sermon:

Chapters 28–30. A Call to Commitment

This brief, final sermon recapitulates the covenant established between God and his people, and records Moses' impassioned plea to Israel to obey God and so to choose life.

Exhortation to commitment: 29:1–15. Based on all God has done, Israel is urged to commit herself to covenant life.

Warnings to be heeded: 29:16–29. No individual dare make a merely verbal commitment. Commitment must be from the heart, or judgment will surely follow.

Forgiveness promised: 30:1–10. Even should Israel be scattered in judgment, God will accept his people when they return to him with their whole hearts. And he will restore all the lost blessings.

Appeal to choose life: 30:11–20. The choice Israel always has before her is the choice between life and death. Eternal life is not in view here, or in other sections of Deuteronomy. What is at stake is the experience of blessings during this life, on the land God gives his people. It is not difficult to find the way to blessing. All Israel need do is to love God, to listen to his voice, and to cling only to him (20).

Chapters 31–34. The Last Days of Moses

The Book of Deuteronomy, and the Pentateuch, closes with a description of Moses' final days and of his death.

Joshua presented: 31:1–8. Moses has been told earlier that Joshua will succeed him as leader. Now Joshua is officially presented to Israel.

Covenant readings ordained: 31:9–13. Every seven years the law which Moses has written down (9) is to be publicly read in solemn ceremony at the Feast of Tabernacles.

Rebellion predicted: 31:14–29. Moses has no illusions about Israel. He predicts that whatever commitments the people now make, their children will turn to the gods of the land, abandon the Lord, and become corrupt. Because they will do evil, disaster will follow.

The Song of Moses: 31:30–47. The song which Moses now teaches to Israel has an important purpose. It will serve as a testimony, and as a witness against the people (31:19). The law itself might seem long and complicated. But poetry, set to music, will be learned and passed on as folk song from generation to generation. In Moses' song, God will continue to warn against wickedness. Any who turn to evil pathways will not be able to plead ignorance.

Moses' prophetic blessing: 33:1–29. Having suffered with Israel for forty years, Moses is well acquainted with distinctive tribal traits. As prototype prophet (18:15; 34:10), Moses is able to look ahead and share information God revealed to him. A similar type of blessing before death is found in Genesis 9 and 49 (see p. 49).

Moses' death: 34:1–12. Deuteronomy closes with a sensitive report of Moses' death. God leads him, alone, into the mountains overlooking Canaan. Peering together across the Jordan, God shows Moses the Promised Land. Moses dies there, and God buries his faithful servant in a secret grave.

Moses is gone. But a new leader is about to bring Israel into her heritage.

JOSHUA
The Book of Conquest

The Book of Joshua continues the sacred history of Israel, begun by Moses. God has rescued his covenant people from slavery in Egypt. He has shaped them, through forty years of discipline in the wilderness. Now an obedient people are ready to conquer Canaan, promised centuries before to Abraham (cf. Gen. 12, 15, 17) as a possession for his descendants.

The book has a significant role in salvation history. It demonstrates, in the conquest and division of Canaan, the great truth that God is well able to perform whatever he promises his people (21:45).

Authorship. The author of Joshua is unknown, but speaks as an eyewitness of the events he describes (cf. 5:6; 6:25). He was close enough to Joshua to hear of that leader's private encounters with God (cf. 1:1–9; 3:7; etc.). Some have suggested that the author is Phinehas, son and successor of the high priest of Joshua's time. Phinehas is the last individual mentioned in the book, and a prominent leader (cf. Num. 25:7–13; 31:6–8; Josh. 22:10–34; 24:33).

Phinehas is one of the little known personalities of the Bible. Yet he played a significant role in his own time. Study the passages listed just above. What qualities made him a man God could use?

Joshua. The dominant figure in this book is Joshua, Moses' successor as leader of Israel. He was recognized early as a military leader (Exod. 17:8–16). This may suggest he served before the Exodus as an officer in the Egyptian army. Military rolls show that Egypt's officer corps included many different nationalities. Josephus, the first century Jewish historian, transmits a tradition that Joshua once led an Egyptian army against the Ethiopians. While this is probably not true it shows a long tradition existed about Joshua's background.

Joshua is closely associated with Moses in the Exodus history (cf. Exod. 24:13; 32:17; 33:11). He was one of only two adults who left Egypt who lived to enter Canaan. He won the privilege by his total faithfulness to the Lord (Num. 14:6–9; 26:65; 32:11; Deut. 1:34–40).

What qualities of Joshua are important to develop in believers today? How do they find expression in your life?

Two qualities mark this OT hero. He was a brilliant military leader. And he was a strong, stable spiritual influence. As strategist Joshua constructed a campaign that first cut Canaan in half. Then in lightning moves that featured night marches and unexpected attacks, he destroyed the forces of the south and the north in turn. The strategy is still studied in military academies today.

As a spiritual leader, Joshua set an example of obedience to the Lord, and moved others to personal commitment. During his life Israel remained faithful to God.

Dating. What was the century of the Exodus and conquest? External evidence (data gathered in archaeological digs, from inscriptions and other historical sources) seems to some to support an early date (1450–1400 B.C.), and to others a late date (1250–1200 B.C.). This kind of data has been appealed to by individuals on each side. However, internal evidence (specific dates and the structure of history given in the Bible) unquestionably requires the early date. To accept the late date would demand much reconstruction of the OT version of Israel's history. (For a careful discussion of the evidence, see Leon J. Wood, *A Survey of Israel's History,* Zondervan, p. 83–109.) If we accept the picture given in the OT, it was spring of 1406 B.C. when Joshua led Israel across the Jordan.

Canaan. In 1406 B.C., Canaan held mixed peoples, settled in independent city states. The cities were walled; the people warlike. In many ways the Canaanites were more advanced than Israel. Cities were well designed and constructed. Drainage systems were used. The people were skilled in metal work and pottery making. Extensive trade was conducted with many foreign peoples.

The whole area had long been a province of Egypt. But Pharaoh Amenhotep III (1417–1379) had no interest in his Asian territories. Archaeologists have recovered messages (the Amarna tablets) begging for Egyptian help against the "Habiru." These date from after the time of conquest, and are all cities not listed in Joshua as destroyed or controlled by Israel. But Egypt was not roused to a strong foreign policy for nearly a century, till Seti I (1316–1304). Undoubtedly Israel's conquest required an era when the great powers of the world were passive.

The religion of Canaan emphasized fertility and sex. In some locations evidence of child sacrifice has been found. Ritual prostitution was common. Deuteronomy 18:9–13 lists some of the detestable religious practices for which God decreed the Canaanites must be destroyed and not simply defeated.

Outline. The Book of Joshua is essentially historical narrative. Like other OT books, material is selected to fit the author's theme.

Thus the story of Jericho and Ai is given 85 verses, while defeat of northern and southern halves of Canaan are given only 90! The outline shows the process of Conquest, and the author's emphases.

Outline

Chapter 1. The Commander Prepared

Victory promised: 1–9. On Moses' death, God meets with Joshua. God will be with the new leader; no enemy will stand against Israel (5, 9). Joshua is to count on this promise and "be strong and very courageous; be careful to obey" (7).

📖 God's promise "I will never leave you or forsake you" was also given to all Israel (Deut. 31:6). The NT teaches this is also God's commitment to you and me (Heb. 13:5). What difficulties do you have that, because God is with you, you can meet with courage?

Advance announced: 10–18. Joshua does not hesitate. Israel is commanded to prepare to cross the Jordan. The people promise to obey the new leader, "only may the Lord your God be with you as he was with Moses" (17).

Chapters 2–5. Israel Prepared

Rahab and the spies: 2:1–24. Joshua sends spies to examine Jericho. This walled city controls the passes into central Canaan. The spies are discovered, but are hidden by a woman named Rahab. Rahab tells of the demoralization of the Canaanites, who fear Israel's God. She wins a promise that her family will be spared when Israel destroys Jericho, and helps the spies escape over the city wall.

📖 James 2:25 points to Rahab to illustrate the difference between mere "belief" and saving faith. What knowledge did all the people of Jericho have about God? How did their response differ from that of Rahab? How would you define the difference between their belief, and Rahab's faith?

Jordan crossed: 3:1–17. God now demonstrates conclusively that

he is with Joshua. Joshua has priests, carrying the ark of God
(see Exod. 37), lead the people into the Jordan.

In this spring of 1406 B.C. the Jordan is in flood (3:15; 4:18).
Yet when the feet of the priests touch the stream, the waters stop
and "pile up in a heap" as far as the town Adam (16). Adam is
el Damish, where in modern times (1906 and 1927) rock slides
have cut off the flow of the Jordan river. Yet the text stresses
miraculous aspects. The waters stop "as soon as the priests who
carried the ark" touch the river (15). And Israel does not wallow
through a sea of mud, but crosses on "dry land" (17).

Memorial established: 4:1–24. Joshua immediately shifts the focus
from himself to the Lord. Twelve stones from the place the priests
stood in the middle of the Jordan are carried to Israel's first camp
in Canaan, at Gilgal. The stones are set up as a memorial—a
sign to future generations, who can bring their children to see
the stones and tell the story of what the Lord has done.

When the people are all across, the priests move to the Canaan
shore. Immediately the Jordan returns to flood stage (18). Joshua
is now held in awe by Israel (14), and there is new evidence of
God's power to feed the fear of the peoples of the land (24).

Israel circumcised: 5:1–12. Gilgal lies in the valley between the
Jordan and Jericho. It now becomes the base of operations for
conquest. But first three important events take place. The men
of Israel are circumcised, a rite apparently neglected in the desert
(see Gen. 17). The Passover Feast is kept on the fortieth anniversary
of the first passover, held in Egypt (see Exod. 12). And the manna
which God has supplied as food for the wilderness journey ceases,
as Israel eats the produce of Canaan (see Exod. 16:14–22). The
new era has begun, and a deeper faith relationship with God is
developing.

Chapters 5:13–9:27. The Central Campaign

Rugged highlands overlook the Dead Sea and Jordan valley.
Several passes lead up through the mountainous ridge into the
heart of Palestine. These passes were controlled in Joshua's day
by the walled city of Jericho, where there was also a vital fresh
water supply. Today too Jericho is watered by the ancient springs—
an agricultural oasis in a barren region of Israel.

Militarily, Joshua and Israel had to conquer this strong point,
and quickly establish control of the passes at their top as well as
bottom. Delay could have been fatal to the conquest.

There is also a spiritual necessity facing Israel. The people must

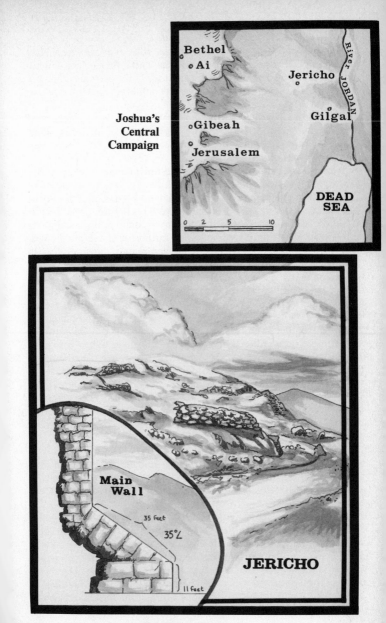

The Walls of Jericho

realize that it is the Lord who brings them victory. And they must learn the importance of obedience. These themes are emphasized as the author of Joshua tells the story of the central campaign, during which the military objectives are achieved, and the spiritual lessons are dramatically underlined.

The map on page 139 shows the location of the cities mentioned in these chapters, and shows the topography of the area. Page 141 gives more information on Jericho itself, and on the modern dispute surrounding it.

Strange Command: 5:13–6:5. Jericho must be taken quickly. But the city is shut up, prepared for a siege. Joshua goes to reconnoiter, but is met by a figure with a sword who claims that he is the true commander of the Lord's army. This figure gives Joshua strange orders—orders which from any human vantage point are ridiculous. Yet Joshua recognizes the authority of the divine messenger and prepares to carry out his commands, however foolish Joshua may appear to the people he leads.

Jericho taken: 6:1–27. The people follow the strange orders which Joshua relays. For six days they march in complete silence around the walls of Jericho, and return to camp. The seventh day they circle the city seven times. When the last circuit is completed, as a signal trumpet sounds, Israel shouts . . . and the walls of the city tumble outward! All except those who have taken refuge in Rahab's house are destroyed, while all silver, gold, and bronze objects are set aside for the Lord's treasury.

Imagine yourself a close observer of the Israelites and the inhabitants of Jericho. How would you expect their attitudes to shift each of the six preliminary days? Do you ever see (or feel yourself) with similar attitudes today? What lessons does God teach us from this story of the taking of Jericho?

Achan and Ai: 7:1–26. Not everyone obeyed the command to surrender Jericho's spoil. When Joshua sends a few thousand men up one of the passes to take the small settlement of Ai, Israel is defeated, and thirty-six men are killed! It is clear that God has withheld victory.

The defeat is potentially pivotal. Much depends on fear immobilizing the Canaanite peoples. A shaken Joshua turns immediately to God (6–9); God commands Joshua to gather the whole people. Defeat has come because of disobedience: the sin must be purged before Israel will be able to stand against her enemies (13).

Achan is identified from all the tribes, clans, and families of Israel, and confesses his sin. He has taken from Jericho a Babylonian robe, with silver and gold, in direct disobedience to God.

The hiding place, "in his tent, with the silver underneath" (21, 22) makes it clear the whole family is involved, and thus share Achan's responsibility. Achan and his family are condemned to death, and all his possessions are burned.

The twin lessons of Jericho and Ai are particularly vital in this initial stage of the conquest. Obedience will bring continued victory. Disobedience will bring defeat.

Jericho

Jericho is a focus of the debate between those who hold to an early date of the Exodus (1450–1400) and those who argue a late date (1250–1200). John Garstang first excavated old Jericho (1930–36). The mound revealed massive destruction which Garstang dated to the reign of Amenhotep III (1417–1379) by pottery and scarab evidence. Doubt grew when other Palestinian cities showed layers of destruction dating some 200 years later. Kathleen Kenyon returned to Jericho (1952–1958). She disagreed with Garstang and fixed a date for the massive devastation at 1550, with later destruction about 1325. Her dates fit neither of the Exodus theories!

The debate between Garstang and Kenyon followers continues today. Proponents of the late date theory use Jericho to attack the early date, even though Kenyon's conclusions do not support their own dating, and in fact portray Jericho as a minor settlement in Joshua's time. Early date proponents support Garstang's basic conclusions, and point to additional archaeological evidence. In this sharp debate the early date should be accepted. (1) It best fits the OT picture of a strong, walled fortress city blocking Israel's entrance to central Canaan. (2) The archaeological evidence is open to interpretation, as the existence of the debate demonstrates. In such cases the interpretation which fits the picture given by the OT of Israel's history should be accepted.

What was Jericho then like in Joshua's day? It was a city built to withstand siege. Its walls made assault impossible. Behind a stone base 11 feet high, a smooth stone slope angled up at 35 degrees for 35 feet, to join massive main walls. Attackers would have difficulty scrambling up the slope, and would have no footing on which to rest ladders.

Jericho's walls enclosed eight acres. This was not a large city for Canaan, though it was typical. Other walled cities Israel would take ranged from 14 acres at Megiddo, to 200 acres at Hazor. Yet none would be as important to Israel as Jericho. Jericho demonstrated conclusively that God would fight for his people as he had promised, and that no walls could prevail against the Lord. To Israel, Jericho stood as a vital lesson in faith.

Ai taken: 8:1–29. With sin purged, God sends the Israelites to take Ai. Joshua's classic strategy lures the enemy away from the city, and then sets an ambush (3–8). The city is taken and destroyed. It is possible that the fighting men of Bethel were involved in

this battle. Joshua 12:9 identifies Ai as "near Bethel," and implies
Bethel might have been taken early in the campaign.

Reading of the Law: 8:30–35. Moses has commanded that when
Israel enters Canaan, the law is to be written on plastered stones,
erected atop Mount Ebal (Deut. 27:1–26). Now the people stand
between the peaks of 3080 foot Mount Ebal and 2891 foot Mount
Gerazim, and hear the words of Moses' law read to them.

The Gibeonite deception: 9:1–27. Gibeon is the major city of a
minority people in Canaan, the Hivites. The other peoples unite
to resist Israel (1, 2), but the Gibeonites are convinced resistance
is futile: they have been told "how the Lord . . . commanded
his servant Moses to give (Israel) the whole land and to wipe
out all its inhabitants" (24). Now they send a delegation to Joshua
dressed in worn clothes and carrying molded bread. Though they
are only a day's march from Gilgal (10:7), they pretend to have
come a great distance, and urge a quick treaty. The leaders fail
to inquire of the Lord (14), and hurriedly swear an oath of peace.
When the deception is discovered, Joshua feels committed by the
oath Israel has sworn in God's name.

God's Will, OT

How did Joshua pick Achan from all the people of Israel? How might
the leaders have "inquired of the Lord" before making their treaty with
the Gibeonites?

The foremost source of knowledge of God's will in OT times was his
written revelation. But such decisions simply could not be made on the
basis of the written Word. Thus Israel was given additional helps. Prophets
were sometimes sent as special messengers (see *Prophet,* p. 130). Infrequently
angel messengers were received (cf. Josh. 5:14 f). But a basic tool for learning God's will in OT times was the Urim and Thummin (cf. Num. 27:21;
I Sam. 14:41; 28:6; Ezra 2:63). These were most likely two stones, placed
in a pouch in the front of the high priest's ephod (Exod. 28:16; 30). If
the high priest reached into the pocket and drew out Urim, the answer
was negative. If he drew out Thummin, the answer was positive.

Use of Urim and Thummin disappears after the Babylonian captivity.
But their existence in Joshua's time suggests a procedure Israel might have
followed with Gibeon, but did not.

The OT stress on obedience makes it clear that the Lord does want
his people to know his will. Our way of discovering God's will today
differs from the ways of the OT people. But we can be just as sure that
the Lord wants us to bring our significant decisions to him, and walk in
the path he will mark out (see *Wisdom,* p. 265).

Joshua consigns the Gibeonites to menial work. They still live
in Canaan some 400 years later, in David's time.

What events of this period would you associate with each of these lessons? Ignore appearances. Remember what God has done. Fear disobedience. When in doubt, ask God. Obedience brings victory. Which of these lessons from sacred history do you believe God wants you to apply in your life now?

Chapters 10–12. Northern and Southern Campaigns

Northern and southern Canaan have now been separated by Israeli forces. In a series of battles Joshua crushes the southern coalition, and then turns to demolish the north. Not every city in Canaan is destroyed in Joshua's campaign. Each tribe is left with enemies to mop up. But all effective opposition is crushed.

Little is told of these campaigns. The author is very selective in what he reports, choosing events that demonstrate God's involvement. This is in keeping with the theme verse of Joshua: "The Lord handed their enemies over to them. Not one of all the Lord's good promises to the house of Israel failed; every one was fulfilled" (21:44, 45).

Southern region subdued: 10:1–43. The angry Canaanites lay siege to Gibeon, to punish them for their treaty with Israel. An all night march brings Joshua and his army to the rescue. The enemy forces are caught in the open and destroyed. God's actions for Israel are stressed in the report. He sends hailstones to strike the enemy (11). And, in a unique miracle, God answers Joshua's prayer and prolongs daylight (13–14) so that destruction of the enemy can be complete. "Surely the Lord was fighting for Israel" (14).

Northern kings defeated: 11:1–12:24. A northern coalition is formed, led by Hazor, a city of some 40,000 people. The united army is huge, and also has war chariots, the tanks of the biblical world. But again it is Joshua who launches the sudden attack (7). The enemy army is destroyed, and their cities are taken. Only Hazor is burned. Israelites will populate the other towns. But the war of extermination is conducted as God has commanded (see *War,* p. 125).

Chapter 12 lists the kings and the peoples that Israel has conquered west of the Jordan. With all possibility of effective opposition removed, the people can go about distributing the land.

Chapters 13–24. The Land Divided

Organized resistance is destroyed. So Israel now divides the land among her tribes by lot. Great care is taken to record the geographical boundaries of each tribe's inheritance.

Principle of continuing conquest: 13:1–7. The land allotted still contains Canaanite settlements. Now each tribe is to be responsible to expand its own territory, trusting the Lord's promise that he will fight for them (6). Later, reasons are given for this principle: the Canaanites are left to test the faith of Israel (Judg. 2:22), to keep Israel familiar with war (Judg. 3:2), and to keep the cultivated lands from reverting to wilderness.

Land east of Jordan divided: 13:9–32.

Land west of Jordan divided: 14:1–19:51. Fascinating insights are nestled among the careful geographical notations.

Caleb, with Joshua, is the only person from Egyptian days to survive the wilderness journey (Num. 14:20–25). Now he asks for hill country around Hebron which is held by the Anakim. He immediately goes up and drives them out (14:6–15).

The Ephraimites complain they are not given enough land. Joshua tells them to take what they need from the Canaanites. But the people of Ephraim hesitate: "all the Canaanites who live in the plain have iron chariots" (17:12–19).

Contrast the attitudes revealed in 14:6–15 and 17:12–19. Predict what the future will hold for Israel if Caleb's attitude prevails. If the Ephraimites attitude prevails. In what ways do these two attitudes find expression in your own life?

Levitical towns and cities of refuge: 20:1–21:45. The tribe of Levi has been set apart to serve God, and is supported by the Lord's offerings. Now cities and pastureland scattered within the lands of the other tribes are provided for Levi, and a number of the towns are designated as cities of refuge (cf. Exod. 13:1–15; Num. 3:40–51; 13:8–32; 35:1–8).

Eastern tribes return home: 22:1–34. The battle for Canaan, which is covered so briefly in the Book of Joshua, has taken seven years! Now, at last, the men whose families have settled on the east side of Jordan can return home (2–4). But on the way they pause to erect an imposing altar near the Jordan! This appears to the others as apostasy, for Mosaic law requires that sacrifices be made only at the tabernacle, by Aaronic priests. Phinehas heads a fact-finding mission, which discovers that the easterners have not really turned away from God. Instead, the altar, constructed on the same design as the altar of sacrifice, is intended as a witness to the unity of all Israel, demonstrating that the eastern peoples share a common heritage and Lord with those of the west. The explanation is accepted, and civil war is averted.

Joshua's farewell: 23:1–16. About 1390 B.C. Joshua, now nearly 110 (24:29), calls the leaders of the tribes together. He exhorts

Palestine Divided

them to follow the Lord "without turning to the left or to the right" (6). He reminds them of the victories won: "one of you routs a thousand, because the Lord your God fights for you, just as he promised. So be very careful to love the Lord your God" (10, 11). As long as this generation of leaders lives, Israel will serve God (24:31; Judg. 2:6, 7).

Covenant renewed: 24:1–27. Joshua's final public act is to lead the people and the new generation represented, in a ceremony of covenant renewal. This important act of personal commitment bound the individual and the community to be faithful to God, and recognized the Lord's right to discipline and to bless according to the Mosaic law (see Exod. 19, Deut. 27).

The various strata of Jericho as seen in an archaeological dig

JUDGES
The Book of Defeat

After the conquest, Israel quickly adapts to a settled life in Canaan. But her spiritual motivation and commitment are soon lost. The unknown author of Judges selects stories out of the extended period from the conquest to the establishment of a monarchy to show the political, social, and moral deterioration which accompanies apostasy.

The judges. The book takes its name from charismatic leaders whom God sent to his people. The judges were military leaders who led the struggle against various oppressors (2:16) and then sought to dissuade the Israelites from return to idol worship (2:17).

No judge shows the high moral character and religious motivation of Moses and Joshua. In an era of moral decay, even the leaders were not the best examples. Scripture faithfully records their sins and failures.

Structure. The book has three distinct sections. An introduction describes reasons for the decline. An historical section treats a number of judges in chronological sequence. An epilogue examines three incidents, which show the depths to which God's people have sunk in their abandonment of covenant life (cf. Deut. 5–11; Exod. 21–24).

Outline

I. The Times Explained	1:1–3:6
II. Stories of the Judges	3:7–16:31
III. Portraits of Decay	17:1–21:25

Date. Dates of the events described in Exodus are hotly disputed. The difficulty is magnified if the years each judge is said to have ruled is added to the years of the others. The resulting figure (410 years) is too long a span for any dating system.

But adding these dates gives little useful information. (1) In this period there was no central government. A judge's influence was usually only regional. (2) The oppressors lived on different borders (see map, p. 150). We conclude that the activities of both enemies and judges often overlapped. Because of this feature of the days of the judges, it is impossible to construct an accurate internal chronology, or to say with certainty when a particular judge lived.

However, working with the early date system explained in the introductions to Exodus (p. 69) and Joshua (p. 136), we can assume that the time of the judges stretches from the death of Joshua, about 1390, to the anointing of King Saul, about 1050 B.C.. This fits well with 1 Kings 6:1, which says 480 years passed between the Exodus and King Solomon's dedication of the temple in his fourth year.

Chapter 1:1–3:6. The Times Explained

The days of the judges were so disastrous that it is necessary to explain how God's chosen people could be so crushed. The answer given is: sin. God proved himself faithful in the conquest. Now Israel proves herself unfaithful, and her suffering is deserved.

Incomplete obedience: 1:1–2:4. The Israelis continue to win victories over the remaining Canaanites (1:1–6). But enemies settled in plains areas have war chariots, and the tribes hesitate to attack (19). Doubt is the first hesitant step toward decline.

Other Canaanite communities are subdued, but not destroyed. Instead the conquered are set to forced labor (28–33). This is a direct violation of God's command through Moses (Deut. 20:16–18). The Canaanites were supposed to be driven out, lest they pollute the faith and morality of Israel.

God confronts Israel with her acts of disobedience (2:1–2). He will no longer guarantee victory to his rebellious people.

Idolatry and intermarriage: 2:6–3:5. The author continues his preliminary explanations of the causes of Israel's decline. The generation that follows Joshua, without personal experience of what God has done for his covenant people, are enticed into pagan worship of the Canaanites' Baals and Ashtoreths.

"Baal" designates Canaanite male deities in general, and often is associated with the place name (as Baal-peor, Num. 25:3). The word means "master," or "owner," and reflects the beliefs of ancient peoples that each locality had its own deity. Baal was also designated the most important god of the Canaanites. Because the Baals were thought to control the fertility of the land, sexual promiscuity was early associated with Baal worship.

"Ashtoreth" designates the ancient mother-goddess of the asiatics. In Canaan too she was a fertility goddess, modeled with exaggerated breasts, and worshiped in earthy cult rituals.

The disobedience of Israel to God's demand for a holy war

left the Canaanites in the land, and tempted numbered generations to participate in their false religion and moral depravity. For some 800 years, until the Babylonian captivity, God's people struggled with the temptation to worship the gods of the Canaanites among whom they lived.

Like idol worship, intermarriage is forbidden in Mosaic law. Yet now "they took their daughters in marriage and gave their own daughters to their sons, and served the gods" (3:5–6).

With the causes of this dark age of Israel's history explained, the author is ready to tell his stories of the individual judges.

One supposed moral contradiction in Scripture focuses on the divine command to destroy and drive out the Canaanite peoples. This God of the OT has been attacked as brutal and nationalistic, most unlike the God revealed in Jesus. What insight does Judges 1:1–3:6 provide on the necessity for, and morality of, this command?

Chapters 3:7–16:31. Stories of the Judges

The dreary picture of apostasy and oppression is brightened only by the stories of the judges God sent Israel as deliverers. A strict pattern is followed in each story; a cycle of events that is repeated over and over during the dark centuries.

Sin	The Israelis turn to worship idols, and desert the way of life marked in the law.
Servitude	Neighboring nations oppress the Israelis, who are drained of ability to resist.
Supplication	Under intense oppression, the people confess their sin and return to God.
Salvation	God hears the prayer, and empowers a deliverer who drives away the oppressors.
Silence	A period of rest follows, during which the judge keeps the people faithful to God.

These repeated cycles take place as the territory of the twelve tribes shrinks rather than grows. The map on page 150 shows the area of Canaan actually occupied by Israel, the oppressing nations, and the place where each judge lived.

Othniel: 3:7–11. The brief report clearly shows the deadly cycle that characterizes the times of the judges. Sin (7) leads to servitude (8), to supplication (9), followed by salvation (9, 10) and silence (11). The oppressors here are Mesopotamians, from the distant north.

Israel, Her Early Enemies, and the Seats of the Judges

The Twelve Judges

	Name	Reference	Oppressor	Years of Oppression	and Subsequent rule
1.	Othniel	3:7–11	Mesopotamians	8	40
2.	Ehud	3:12–30	Moabites	18	80
3.	Shamgar	3:31			
4.	Deborah, Barak	4–5	Canaanites	20	40
5.	Gideon	6–8	Midianites	7	40
6.	Tola	10:1,2			23
7.	Jair	10:3–5			22
8.	Jephthah	10:6–12:7	Ammonites	18	6
9.	Ibzan	12:8–10			7
10.	Elon	12:11–12			10
11.	Abdon	12:13–15			8
12.	Samson	13–16	Philistines	40	20

Ehud: 3:12–30. The Moabite oppressors are neighbors, just across the Dead Sea, and south of the eastern tribes. Ehud uses deceit to assassinate the Moabite, and then an uprising cuts off the army that occupies southern Israel.

The text speaks of 80 years of subsequent peace (30). This may well have been due to the return to the area of Egypt as a dominant power, under Seti I and Ramses III (1316–1238). While the cycles reported in Judges were certainly affected by the activity of great powers like the Egyptians and Hittites, the writer of the sacred history ignores them. His focus is completely on the life of God's people within the Promised Land.

Deborah and Barak: 4:1–5:31. Resurgent Canaanites have built a new power base at Hazor. Now oppression comes from within the land, from enemies Israel should have driven out over a century before. The deliverer is a woman, Deborah, widely recognized as a prophetess (4:4). She also serves as a judge, in settling disputes (5). She provides the spiritual leadership, while Barak provides military leadership, under her guidance. A great victory is won when the Canaanite chariot army is mired down in the overflow of the Kishon river (5:21), about 90 miles north of Bethel, where Deborah holds court.

Deborah's song (5:2–31) is recognized as one of the most beautiful poems ever written in any language.

Gideon: 6:1–9:57. The history of only three judges is given extensive treatment by the author. Gideon is one of these, suggesting there are significant spiritual lessons taught in his story, and that these chapters deserve careful study.

The oppressors are several eastern peoples, led by the Midianites. They overrun Israel at harvest time, stripping the country of its grain and cattle. The overwhelmed Israelis simply desert their homes at these times, to hide in mountain caves (6:1–6).

Gideon is the youngest member of an insignificant family in the minor tribe of Manasseh. He is stunned when told by an angel that he is chosen to deliver Israel (6:1–24). Gideon destroys the community worship center, dedicated to Baal and Asherah (see p. 148). The angry reaction of his neighbors shows how completely Israel is polluted by idolatry (6:28–35). Unable to see himself as a deliverer, Gideon proposes his famous series of tests with a wool fleece (6:36–40).

Empowered by God's Spirit, Gideon does assemble an army to battle the Midianite host. God step by step reduces his outnumbered army from 32,000 to 300 (7:7, 8). In this Gideon continues to trust God. His faith is strengthened when he overhears a dream told in the Midianite camp (7:9–14). That night Gideon divides his force of 300. They approach the Midianite encampment. At its edge, all blow trumpets and smash clay pots that contain burning torches. The Midianites awaken to terror, strike out against each other, and flee (7:15–25).

After victory, the Israelites urge Gideon to become their king, and credit him with the victory (8:22). Gideon refuses. Only God should be recognized as Israel's monarch (8:22). For the rest of Gideon's life the people refrain from Baal worship.

But Gideon's story does not end here. Later he names one of his sons Abimelech. The name means "My father is king!" This Abimelech, after Gideon's death, murders his brothers and sets himself up as king, with the aid of the citizens of the city of Shechem. Within three years this association, based on murder and greed, breaks down. Abimelech is killed attempting to put down the rebellion.

Use the outline of events above as framework for a biographical study of Gideon. What environmental forces influenced his early character? What do his responses to God tell of Gideon's strengths? His weaknesses? Of the people of Israel at that time? What are God's motives for limiting Gideon's army? How does Gideon change over time? After careful exploration make three lists: What do I learn here about my own relationship with God? What is there in Gideon for me to emulate? What is there in Gideon for me to avoid?

Tola and Jair: 10:1–5. These two judges may have been contemporaries, for they lived on opposite sides of the Jordan.

Jephthah: 10:12–15. This is the second judge given extensive treatment in the book. Jephthah was an illegitimate son, driven from his home by his legitimate brothers. He won a military reputation by leading a band of adventurers outside Israel's settled area (11:1–3). When, after eighteen years of oppression by the Ammonites Israel returns to God, Jephthah is begged to return and lead the battle for liberation. Under Jephthah the Israelites not only free their own land; they invade Ammon and crush the Ammonite power decisively.

The account records an important document; the message Jephthah sends to the King of Ammon, arguing that the land in dispute belongs to Israel because it was given to her by God 300 years before, during the Exodus. The document helps in dating the period, and shows that in spite of her worship of Canaanite gods, Israel remembers the stories of the Lord's deliverance.

Israel's sin during this time is apparently not a sin of ignorance. How does this help put Judges 10:6–16 in perspective?

Jephthah makes a vow when going out to battle. If victorious he will give to God or sacrifice as a burnt offering "whatever comes out of the door of my house to meet me when I return in triumph" (11:29). To Jephthah's shocked dismay the first to meet him is his only daughter (11:34). Jephthah keeps his vow. He does not offer his daughter as a human sacrifice, as some have concluded. This is strictly forbidden by God's Law (Lev. 18:21; 20:2–5; Deut. 12:31; 18:10). Instead the girl is dedicated to lifetime service at the tabernacle, and never marries (see 11:37–39, and compare Exod. 38:8; 1 Sam. 2:22; Luke 2:36–37).

Ibsan, Elon, and Abdon: 12:8–15. These minor judges may also have been contemporaries.

Samson: 13:1–16:31. Samson is given more space in the biblical record than any other judge. He is also undoubtedly the least qualified morally for leadership—the only judge whose rule did not bring some relief from the oppressors.

The story of Samson introduces us to the Philistines, who will be Israel's dominant enemy through the days of Saul and David. The Philistines were members of a wave of "Sea Peoples" from the Aegean that swept the eastern Mediteranean about 1200 B.C. They not only attacked Palestine, but also Egypt to the south, and the Hittite empire to the north.

The Philistines settled on the narrow coastal plain in southwest Palestine, incorporated the Canaanites already there, and established five principal cities, which are mentioned often in the Bible (Ashkelon, Gaza, Ashdod, Gath, and Ekron). Earlier in the times of the judges the Philistines were occupied by warfare with Egypt under Ramses III. It's possible that in Samson's day the Philistines guarded Egypt's interests in Canaan, for she claimed control over Palestine then. One reason for the dominance of the Philistines was the superiority they maintained in weaponry. They controlled the smelting of iron and kept Israel from having a single ironsmith (1 Sam. 17:7).

Samson is set apart from birth for his divinely appointed mission (13:3–24). And he is endowed with amazing strength. But he is a slave to his physical appetites, and betrays his calling. His lack of religious and patriotic motivation is revealed in the selfish focus of his personal vendetta with the Philistines. The writer focuses on Samson's feats of strength (ch. 14, 15), and on his early and dramatic death (ch. 15).

Read these chapters on Samson first as exciting story telling. Then do a careful biographical study of this most puzzling of the judges. Develop your own questions and insights as you work. The ideas suggested for the study of Gideon (p. 152) will help. Then list lessons you believe God wants to teach you from Samson's life.

Chapters 17–21. Portraits of Decay

Judges concludes with a series of tales from earlier days in the times of the judges. Each story explores the impact of Israel's apostasy, not on the nation as a whole, but on the individuals who lived in what was to have been a "holy" land.

An additional recurring theme is, "In those days Israel had no king." The community has refused responsibility for disciplining its members to covenant life. The next stage in history will see emergence of a monarchy, in which one person is responsible to command obedience.

Micah's idols: 17:1–13. An Ephraimite named Micah steals 28 pounds of silver from his mother. Frightened when he overhears her curse the thief, he returns it. The mother dedicates the silver "to the Lord" to be made into an idol! Micah sets up the idol in the family shrine, and makes one of his sons a priest. Later he enlists a young Levite as priest, thrilled because he thinks "the Lord will be good to me, since this Levite has become my priest" (13).

The story illustrates the utter corruption of Israel's faith by the religious views of the Canaanites. Under the law (1) idols were forbidden, (2) only the family of Aaron was to serve in the priesthood, (3) sacrifices could be made only at the tabernacle, (4) the Levites were to teach the law, not violate it, and (5) blessing came from obedience, not ritual observance. The religious decline is portrayed first, for society crumbles as knowledge of God is corrupted.

The theft: 18:1–32. Scouts from the small tribe of Dan pass Micah's house in search of land to settle. Later they return with their army, steal Micah's household gods, and offer the Levite a position as priest to their whole tribe. The Levite gladly agrees (20). When Micah complains, the Danites threaten to kill him and his family. The Danites then attack a "peaceful and unsuspecting" city in violation of the law's rules of warfare (Deut. 20:10f.).

Immorality: 19:1–30. Another Levite is traveling with his concubine (secondary wife). He refuses to stay in Jerusalem, still occupied by Jebusites, to go on to an Israelite town (13–15). When he is finally offered hospitality, the house is surrounded by citizens who demand the Levite be surrendered for homosexual rape (22). To avoid violence the Levite's host gives them his concubine. They assault her till dawn, when she dies. The Levite returns home, cuts the woman's body in pieces, and sends it throughout Israel to call the tribes together.

The most shocking aspect of the story is that the Levite and his host, who feel themselves morally superior to their brutal neighbors, are totally unfeeling in their treatment of the concubine.

Civil war: 20:1–21:25. The perpetrators of the assault of the concubine are members of the tribe of Benjamin. When the gathered tribes demand surrender of the criminals, the Benjamites refuse. This brings on a destructive civil war in which the Benjamites are nearly wiped out, with heavy losses to the united tribes. When only 600 men of Benjamin remain the other tribes relent, lest one of the 12 families of Israel be destroyed.

Here the Book of Judges ends. Israel entered Palestine a strong, disciplined, and obedient people, held close to God by the example of committed leaders.

Judges shows both political and spiritual decline, as the moral and spiritual values on which Israel's life was to be based are deserted along with that faith in God on which morality must ultimately rest.

RUTH
The Book of Quiet Faith

The story of Ruth takes place in the days of the judges (1:1). It was probably written down during David's rule, unless the genealogy (4:13–21) is a later addition. As Ruth is King David's great grandmother, the events quite possibly took place in the time of Gideon.

Some have clouded the message of this OT gem by forcing typological interpretations on every detail of the story. The book is significant. But its value is found by understanding it in the context of its times, not by reading NT truths into its narrative.

Significance. Ruth provides important balance to the dreary picture of decline drawn in Judges 17–21. Here we see that there are still pockets of faith in Israel; that in spite of general apostasy, some still live out God's Law. The conversion of Ruth the Moabitess to the God of Israel shows what might have been, had all Israel wholly followed the Lord. For us, the story of Ruth is a welcome reminder that a godly life is possible, even when one lives in a sin-saturated society.

The book tells a single story, with beautiful simplicity and unity.

The choice: 1:1–5. When a famine strikes Israel, the family of Elimelech and Naomi move to Moab. There, in violation of Mosaic law, their two sons marry Moabite women. There too the father and sons die.

Return to Bethlehem: 1:6–22. When Naomi hears that the Lord is again blessing Israel, she decides to return. One daughter-in-law, Ruth, refuses to be left behind. Ruth makes a firm commitment: "your people will be my people, and your God my God" (16).

Meeting Boaz: 2:1–19. The two women have no means of support. So Ruth goes into the fields during the harvest season to glean.

Mosaic law requires that the poor be permitted to follow the harvesters and gather grain that falls to the ground when the sheaves are gathered up (Deut. 24:19–21).

Boaz notices the young woman. Knowing of her faithfulness to Naomi and good reputation (11–12), he tells her to return to his fields and promises her protection (9). Privately Boaz tells his workers to leave some stalks in the fields for her to find.

Naomi's plan: 2:20–3:18. Naomi urges Ruth to return to Boaz'

fields. Her grim warning is a reminder of the moral condition of
Israel: "in someone else's field you might be harmed."

But Naomi has another reason. Boaz is a relative of her family,
and thus a potential "kinsman-redeemer." This phrase refers to
a provision of OT law especially for women whose husbands die
and leave them childless. To preserve the family line and the
family land, a relative is permitted to marry the widow. The first
boy will be counted as son of the dead husband, and the line
will thus be preserved.

Ruth's request in 3:10 is no invitation to an immoral relationship;
it is an appeal to Boaz to marry her and perform the duty of a
kinsman-redeemer.

Marriage of Boaz and Ruth: 4:1–21. Boaz is willing. But there
is a nearer relative, who has prior claim. When the nearer relation
realizes that taking over the land of the deceased (2–4) will also
mean marrying Ruth, he surrenders his claim to Boaz (5, 6). This
transaction, witnessed by the city elders, is concluded by taking
off a sandal and passing it to Boaz. Archaelogy has corroborated
this way of concluding a contract.

Boaz immediately announces his intention to take Ruth as his
wife and guard the land for her offspring.

The first son of Ruth and Boaz, Obed, is raised by Naomi as
her own. He becomes the grandfather of David, Israel's greatest
king.

How do the values seen in Ruth and Boaz contrast with
the values of others in their society? What can you learn
about living a quiet and godly life today in your own community,
from this picture of faith in a time of apostasy and decline?

1 SAMUEL
The Origin of the Monarchy

This important OT book tells the story of two men: Samuel, Israel's last judge, and Saul, Israel's first king. It is an important book historically for it marks the origin of monarchy: the passing of one era, and the beginning of another. Soon another king, David, will unify the disorganized tribes and lead them to greatness and glory.

The author of 1 Samuel is unknown, although Hebrew tradition suggests Samuel penned this book which carries his name.

Dating. Saul's reign began about 1050 B.C. Samuel, who had sons old enough to serve as traveling judges when Saul was anointed (1 Sam. 8:1, 2), must have been born prior to 1100 B.C. This makes him a contemporary of Samson, for the Philistine forty-year oppression described in Judges 13–16 was not broken till the battle of Mizpah, about 1055 (1 Sam. 7). It was not unusual for more than one judge to function in Israel at the same time, in different tribes.

Samuel. This last of the judges was also the greatest. He is also identified as a prophet (1 Sam. 3:20), and functioned as a priest (1 Sam. 9:12, 13; 13:8–13). His own character was exemplary as he remained uncorrupted by his power (1 Sam. 12:2–4). Toward the end of his life Samuel stimulated the revival which led to the breaking of Philistine domination (1 Sam. 7:2–6).

Saul. Saul is a tragic OT figure. He was a humble and attractive youth. But under the pressure of leadership, his character dissolves. Each test reveals deepening flaws, and Saul ends his life in the grip of jealousy and depression. Saul stands as a grim reminder to us, to maintain a close relationship with the Lord as we face pressures in our own lives.

David. This young shepherd, slayer of Goliath, also has a role in this book. He meets Saul, who is both drawn to him and moved to a jealous hatred. The book takes us to the death of Saul: the reign of David as king is picked up in 2 Samuel.

Value. First Samuel is important for anyone who wishes to understand the OT. It is a source of many familiar Bible stories. Most important, it is a book of living illustrations of great truths which span both Testaments. Here we see God's faithfulness, explore the results of failure to trust God, and catch a vision of the cost—and rewards—of commitment. Here, in vivid portraits of OT believers, we find many lessons for our own lives.

The book of 1 Samuel can be outlined around the events in the lives of the men it features.

Outline

Chapters 1–3. Samuel's Early Life

Hannah's vow fulfilled: 1:1–29. The tabernacle worship center (see pp. 91, 92) has been preserved, and is located at Shiloh. One of the priests who serves there when his shift is on duty (4) is named Elkanah. He is called an Ephraimite because he lives in one of the Levitical towns (Joshua 21) located in Ephraim's tribal territory (cf. 1 Chron. 6:33–35). During one of his times of service, Elkanah's childless wife, Hannah, vows to dedicate her first child to the Lord if only God opens her womb (11).

This prayer is answered. Hannah has a son, who is named Samuel ("heard by God"). When Samuel is weaned at three, he is brought to Shiloh to the resident high priest, Eli. There Samuel is to serve the Lord at the tabernacle "his whole life."

Hannah's praise: 2:1–11. Hannah's prayer at the dedication of her son is a beautiful example of praise and thanksgiving.

Hannah's prayer helps us understand praise. She (1) speaks directly to God, (2) expresses appreciation for his character (3) and for his actions. Study Hannah's prayer. Then write your own prayer of praise, building on these three elements.

Eli's sons: 2:12–26. Eli himself is a righteous man. But his two sons, who carry on the worship rituals, are "wicked men" who lack personal relationship with God (12). Their immorality is a known scandal, as is their contempt for the worship regulations they are supposed to follow. Eli's great failure is his unwillingness to judge or discipline his family. Young Samuel's character stands in marked contrast to these adults among whom he grows up.

Judgment prophesied: 2:27–36. A prophet ("man of God") is
sent to Eli to announce God's judgment, because "you honor your
sons more than me" (29). A curse is placed on Eli's line. God
will raise up a man who will be faithful to all that is in God's
heart and mind (35).

Samuel's call: 3:1–19. The prophet's message is confirmed when
the Lord speaks directly to Samuel. Such direct revelation is rare
during the time of the judges (1), in contrast to the times of Moses
and Joshua.

As Samuel matures he is widely recognized as a prophet, for
the Lord "let none of his words fall to the ground" (e.g., that
which Samuel foretells happens, and thus he is authenticated by
God). This, and the contrast between Samuel's character and that
of Eli's sons, are the source of the great influence which this last
of the judges is to have in Israel.

How much importance can we attach to family influence
in the development of character? How much is a result of
the life-shaping choices an individual makes for himself or herself?
What answers to these questions are suggested in 1 Samuel 1–3?

Chapters 4–6. Defeat at Aphek

The ark taken in battle: 4:1–11. For some twenty years the Philistines (see p. 153) have exerted pressure on the Israelites and other
peoples of Canaan from their coastal lands. The battle that takes
place at Aphek is critical, for it opens even more Israeli lands to
the Philistines. Archaeological excavations show that eventually
Philistine occupation forces even penetrated beyond the mountains
of Palestine, to the Jordan plain.

The battle is fought in two phases. After an initial defeat, the
Israelites send to Shiloh for the ark of God. This portable wooden
chest, overlaid with gold, symbolizes the very presence of God
(see p. 90). It is supposed to stay in the tabernacle, but now is
superstitiously brought to the battleground. In the second phase
of the battle Israel suffers a crushing defeat and the ark of God
is captured.

Judgment on Eli's house: 4:12–22. Eli's two evil sons die in the
battle. When Eli hears, he falls and breaks his neck. The death
of this man, who has led Israel for forty years, with the capture
of the ark, completely demoralizes the Israelites (21, 22) and ends
organized resistance to the Philistines.

Judgment on the Philistines: 5:1–7:1. The people of the ancient
world credited victories to the superiority of their gods over the

gods of the enemy. The Philistines make this mistake, and view
the Lord as a defeated enemy. They place the ark in the temple
of their chief god, Dagon, as a trophy. The next day the idol
has fallen on its face before the ark. They prop up Dagon, but
when another night has passed he is found fallen again, with hands
and head broken off.

Now the people suffer a plague of tumors. The ark is moved
from Ashdod to Gath, and the epidemic breaks out there as well!
In panic the Philistines return the ark to the Israelites.

What concepts of God did the Philistines appear to have?
What might they have learned about him from events in
these chapters?

Chapter 7. Mizpah

The action in this chapter takes place some twenty years after
the defeat of Aphek (2). In these two decades, Samuel has become
Israel's acknowledged leader. He has also moved the people to a
fresh commitment to God (3, 4). When all Israel gathers at Mizpah
for fasting and commitment, the Philistines attack, seeking to break
up what they view as a dangerous unity movement in the subjugated
people. The Philistines are fought and defeated, as the Lord battles
for Israel as in olden times (10–12). The victory drives the Philistines out of Hebrew territory, and they are never able to occupy
Israel's land again (13).

Samuel has proven himself an effective leader, and has restored
a sense of national identity and pride.

Chapter 8. Demand for a King

When Samuel is old, the elders of Israel come to him and demand
a king. Two reasons are given. Samuel's sons lack his integrity,
for they accept bribes (3). And Israel wants to be like "all the
other nations" (5).

Samuel takes this as a personal affront, but it is really a rejection
of God, Israel's true ruler (7). Samuel tries to warn Israel of the
disadvantages of an absolute ruler (10–18), but the people will
not listen. They demand a king, and the Lord tells Samuel to do
as they ask (19, 20).

Some have looked at the motive of the people (19, 20) and concluded it was not God's intention to set up a monarchy at this
time (see *Kingship in Israel,* p. 162).

Chapters 9–12. Saul Anointed King

Saul divinely selected: 9:1–10:13. Saul meets Samuel while searching for lost donkeys. God identifies him to the prophet as the chosen king (9:16, 17). The humble Saul is stunned when Samuel honors him, and then anoints him with oil (9:18–10:1). The detailed prediction of what will happen on Saul's way home is important: it confirms to Saul that Samuel does speak for God in this call to the kingship (10:2–13).

Saul proclaimed and confirmed: 10:14, 15. Saul is presented to the people by Samuel as God's choice for king. When the Ammonites besiege Jabesh Gilead, Saul calls Israel out, and falls on the enemy camp at dawn (11:1–11). The total victory won firmly establishes Saul in his office. Even those who held back are now committed to loyalty (11:12–15).

Samuel's farewell speech: 12:1–25. Samuel is now ready to withdraw completely from leadership. In a last great oration he warns Israel against turning from God. He also calls for a destructive storm, to demonstrate that their motives in asking for a king were sinful (16–19). However, Samuel reassures Israel: the Lord will not desert them, and Samuel himself will continue to serve by praying for the welfare of the nation.

Samuel's farewell highlights one danger of success, and the danger of depending on a successful leader rather than on the Lord. How might what Samuel says apply to us in our churches today?

Kingship in Israel

The three dominant institutions during OT times are expressed in the persons of prophet (see p. 130), priest (see p. 103) and king (see p. 162).

Exodus 19:4, 5 introduces the kingship of God over his own people. Israel's insistence on a human king to lead them into battle is thus a rejection by that generation of God (1 Sam. 8:7; 10:17–19). Yet the OT predicts a monarchy, and carefully regulates the institution so that it might be an expression of the divine kingship (see Deut. 17:14–20). Under the Law the king is to be chosen by God, a brother Israelite, and is not to accumulate a standing army, wives, or personal wealth. Like any other Jew, the king is to subject himself to the law. He is to have a personal copy of the written word to study, meditate on, and obey. In essence, the godly king will recognize the fact that he is only a representative of Israel's true King. Godly rulers like David and Hezekiah did exhibit personal failings. But they also remained responsive to God; subject both to his written words, and to messages communicated by the prophets.

The kingship existed in Israel only between Saul and the Babylonian captivity (1050–586 B.C.). Like the other forms of government under which God's OT people lived at various times, it was successful when king and people were committed to God. But it was a failure when the Lord was abandoned. No social structure, or form of government, can ever guarantee utopia. Personal commitment to the Lord by leaders and people is necessary for the experience of God's blessing.

For Reading: Psalm 93, 103; 1 Samuel 12; Deuteronomy 17:14–20.

Chapters 13–15. Saul Rejected As King

Saul ruled in Israel for 42 years (13:1). His reign brought few changes in the life style of the average Israelite. Saul's capital was his home at Gibeah; excavations there have unearthed a simple fortress residence. Saul's military garrison included only 3,000 men. The rest of the male population served as a militia, and was called out in time of need. Thus there was little initial impact of the monarchy, except to identify Israel's chief military leader. Even in this limited role, Saul soon demonstrated serious flaws, which led to his rejection by God.

Fear: 13:1–22. Early in Saul's reign a skirmish with the Philistines at Geba leads to a major invasion. The Israelis are terrified at the size of the forces that come against them. Saul is at Gilgal, sent there by Samuel with instructions to wait for him seven days. Then the aged prophet/priest will come to pray for victory.

As the days pass the forces with Saul dwindle, for his army deserts him. On the seventh day a desperate Saul determines to offer up the sacrifice himself, an act forbidden anyone who is not a priest. Samuel appears just as the sacrifice is finished. Furious, he tells Saul that God will not permit a son of his to inherit the throne.

Ironically, the 600 men who remain with Saul are twice the number Gideon had to defeat an even larger army of Amalekites!

Humanly speaking, Saul's fears are understandable. Not only are the Philistines numerically superior, they also have iron weapons. Only Saul and Jonathan his son are so equipped in Israel.

Battle won: 14:1–52. Later Jonathan attacks a Philistine detachment, killing twenty of them. The surprise, and an earthquake sent by God, terrifies the Philistines. Saul notices the Philistines army is fleeing, and hurries to attack them.

Now Saul foolishly commands his army not to stop fighting to eat. Jonathan, who has not heard the order, takes a little honey from a honey tree. Only the insistence of his men keeps Saul from putting his son to death for this violation. Saul, who knowingly violated God's command, was willing to execute his own son for unknowing disobedience! No wonder this man of flawed character was rejected by God.

Final rejection: 15:1–35. God's rejection of Saul is confirmed as the king again disobeys. Sent to destroy an ancient enemy, Saul permits the people to keep the best of the cattle for themselves, and destroys only what is worthless. Samuel confronts Saul and announces God's judgment. Saul, who before excused his disobedience by fear of the enemy (13:11, 12) now says weakly "I was afraid of [my] people" (24)! This is the last meeting of Saul and Samuel, although the old prophet grieves for the man who had shown such promise, and for all that might have been (17–19, 35).

Saul is a person who should be carefully studied as a warning to all believers. From the following critical passages, develop a personality study of Saul at each stage of his life. The key passages are: 13:5–15; 15:1–33; 9:2 with 17:1–11; 18:6–30; 22:9–19; 24:2–20 with 26:2; 28:5–10, 17–19. What seems to you to be Saul's basic flaw, and how can you guard against its appearance in your life? What else do you learn from your study of Saul?

Chapters 16–20. Saul and David

David secretly anointed: 16:1–13. Samuel is now sent to Bethlehem to make a sacrifice, with the hidden purpose of anointing another to replace Saul on the throne (1). God's choice will be of a man whose heart is in tune with the Lord. The youngest son of a man named Jesse is selected, and David is anointed with oil in a private family ceremony. Even his brothers apparently do not grasp the significance of Samuel's act (13, cf. 17:28).

David court musician: 16:14–23. Saul's emotional instability now expresses itself in deep depressions (14, 15). David is recommended to help him, and comes to Gibeah to play his harp. This brings Saul some relief (23). David is liked and given the honor of serving as one of Saul's armor bearers.

David defeats Goliath: 17:1–58. The Philistines again assemble an invasion army. But now they send a giant warrior, over nine feet tall, with a challenge to single combat. Such a contest is not common, but is known in the ancient world.

David, apparently still too young to serve, now visits the army with food from home for his brothers. He is shocked that no one will face this pagan who defies "the army of the living God" (27).

When someone reports David's reaction, he is called before Saul. There David volunteers to fight Goliath himself. Saul, a head taller than any Israelite, and war leader, should have taken up Goliath's challenge. Instead he holds back and lets a youth who cannot fit in his armor fight Israel's battles (38, 39). David's faith in God is well founded. He kills the giant with his shepherd's sling, and the demoralized Philistines flee.

Saul's request for information about David (55–58) need not imply that 16:14–23 is out of sequence. When David was merely a favorite harpist his lineage was unimportant. Now that he is a hero, the king is concerned about his genealogy.

Saul's jealousy and fear: 18:1–30. David is rewarded with a military position. For a decade David carries out all his duties so successfully that he advances rapidly (5). However, Saul becomes jealous of David's success and popularity (18, 19). Recognizing that the Lord is with David, Saul begins to fear him (12–16, 28, 29). These emotions harden to implacable enmity. David's friendship with Jonathan also begins.

Saul's plot against David: 19:1–23. Earlier Saul threw his spear at David in a fit of anger (18:10–12), and plotted to have David killed in battle by the Philistines (18:24, 25). Now, despite his promises to Jonathan (4–6), Saul determines to kill David, who has become his son-in-law. David, after some ten years in Saul's court, is forced to flee for his life (14–21). But he and Jonathan are now close friends.

This chapter contains a disputed description of Saul who, in pursuit of David, moved to join a group gathered around Samuel "prophesying" (18–24). Some take this to refer to an ecstatic, trancelike state, known in the pagan religions of Greek and Roman times. There is no real evidence of such an expression of OT faith. It is best to understand this and the only parallel passages (Num. 11:24–30; 1 Sam. 10:5–10) as praise and worship, rather than mindless esctasy. Only Saul seems to have acted strangely (24), and the fit of night-long depression is in character for him.

David and Jonathan: 20:1–42. Back in Gibeah, Jonathan angrily confronts his father. Finally he realizes that Saul is determined to kill David. Jonathan, a truly admirable individual, carries a promised warning to David. The two swear everlasting friendship in the Lord's name, and each makes a commitment to care for the other's descendants (42) whichever of them survives.

These few chapters contain some of the most significant and beautiful verses in the Bible. Two worth committing to memory are 16:7 and 17:45–47.

Jonathan is another admirable character in the OT, whose life is an example. A careful study of this son of Saul is recommended.

David is a truly charismatic individual. All whose lives he touches respond strongly to him, in one way or another. To gain insight into the personality of this man God used so significantly, examine the response of those around him, as portrayed in chapters 16–20. What do they tell us about David? About ourselves?

Chapters 21–30. David a Fugitive

David now faces a jolting change in status. For a decade he has been a respected military hero. Suddenly he is a lone fugitive. The story of his outlaw years, and his many struggles to survive, are told in these chapters of 1 Samuel. Many of David's emotions during this time of intense personal pressure, and David's maturing relationships with God, are communicated in his psalms.

David and the Priests: 21:1–9; 22:1–23. David flees, weaponless and hungry, to Nob, where the tabernacle rests. There Ahimelech, the priest, helps David with food. He also turns over Goliath's sword, which is kept at the tabernacle as a trophy. Later an Edomite, Doeg, informs Saul that the priest has helped his enemy. In spite of Ahimelech's protests of innocence, Saul puts him and 85 other priests, with their families, to death.

Psalm 52 and possibly 53 were written by David out of this tragic experience.

David flees to Gath: 21:10–15. David has only two choices. He can find a hiding place in Israel, or leave the country. At first David goes to Philistia, where he is recognized. Afraid for his life, David pretends madness. Psalms 56 and 34 flow from this experience, and reveal David's inner torment.

David at Adullam: 22:1–5. David returns to Israel and hides in a cave about fifteen miles from his Bethlehem home. He is joined by his family, and by others alienated by Saul's increasingly erratic behavior. Psalm 142 shares his thoughts at this time.

David saves Keilah, and is betrayed: 23:1–29. When the Philistines raid an Israelite town, David and his men hurry to the rescue. But Saul immediately raises his army to attack the town. Before he can arrive, David leaves the city. Jonathan comes to "help him find strength in God" (16). But David is betrayed by the Ziphites, who offer to lead the king to his young enemy. David's emotions at this betrayal are shared in Psalm 54.

David twice spares Saul's life: 24:1–26:25. Now Saul dedicates himself to hunting David down. On two occasions David has the opportunity to kill Saul—but will not. God has made Saul king. David will not lift his hand against God's anointed, even though his own life is threatened. The story of David and Abigail (25:1–44) shows how much David and his band needed food during these days of pursuit, and David's care that they not act as outlaws.

Even though David made the godly choice in refusing to touch Saul, he is deeply discouraged, as Psalm 57 reveals.

David's despair: 27:1–12; 29:1–30:30. Deeply despondent, and convinced that Saul will destroy him if he remains in Israel, David leads his men back to Philistia. There he enlists as a mercenary soldier with Achish, the king of Gath. He is given the town of Ziglag.

David and his men raid Israel's old enemies (27:6–8), but mislead Achish, who believes that they are raiding southern Israel. In fact, David distributes some of the loot from his raids to Judean towns (30:26–31), building good will toward the day when Saul will die and David will become king.

When war again threatens between Israel and the Philistines, the rulers of the other plains cities will not trust David among their forces. He is sent back to Ziglag, where he discovers his own town has been raided and stripped by Amalekites (30:1, 2). David pursues, and thus is far away when the decisive battle between Israel and the Philistines is fought.

Saul's last days: 28:1–25; 31:1–13. The loss of David as a military leader has seriously affected Israel. Abner, identified as captain of Saul's army, is never seen in battle. Jonathan and David were Saul's field commanders.

Now, as the Philistines assemble to fight against Israel, Saul looks desperately for help. Samuel has died, but Saul goes to a spiritualist and demands she contact the dead prophet. The woman is amazed when Samuel actually does appear (12–14)! Samuel announces that Saul and his three sons will be killed in the battle the next day, and that Israel will be defeated.

In that battle, Saul is struck by an enemy arrow and wounded. To avoid being taken alive, Saul falls on his own sword, and dies. The tragic rule of Saul has ended at last.

Read the historical account in 1 Samuel. With each incident, read and meditate on the Psalm which David has written out of that situation. What do you learn about expressing feelings to God? What do you learn about the relationship between testing and faith? Try writing a psalm expressing your feelings now.

2 SAMUEL/1 CHRONICLES
The Books of David the King

Two OT books provide parallel accounts of the rule of David, who becomes king on the death of Saul. This is a critical time in the history of Israel and in the unfolding of God's plan, and so is given extensive space in the Scriptures.

Historical significance. The years of David complete Israel's transition from a loose tribal structure, under which God's people lived in the days of the judges, to a monarchy. A number of important aspects of the transition are accomplished under David's leadership:

* Transition from government by judges to an established monarchy.
* Transition from a loose confederation of tribes to a united nation.
* Transition from anarchy to a strong central government.
* Transition from bronze age poverty to iron age economy and wealth.
* Transition from a subject people to conquerors. David expanded Israel's territory some ten times!
* Transition from decentralized worship to centralized worship, with one city as both political and religious capital.

Theological significance. The era of David is important for adding new revelation concerning God's plan. David is given a promise that his line will culminate in a person who will rule Israel forever (see *Davidic Covenant,* p. 177). This promise is fulfilled in Jesus, who is of David's family through both Mary and Joseph. It is Jesus who, as King of kings and Lord of lords, will establish God's rule through the whole earth.

The Psalms. Another heritage from this era is found in the Psalms. While the book was codified at a later date, many of the psalms are from David's time, and were written by the king himself. As the superscriptions of the Psalms show, most were intended for public worship. This includes some of the most revealing and humbling of those written by David, out of his personal experience (cf. 52, 34). One of David's great contributions when his rule was established was to organize worship and to train the Israelites in the worship of God. His psalms stand today as a great resource

The Era of Transition

JUDGES 13–16		1 CHRONICLES	
	1 SAMUEL	2 SAMUEL	

1–7

SAMUEL

CH 1   CH 25

SAUL

CH 8   CH 31

KING OF JUDAH

KING OF UNIFIED ISRAEL

DAVID

CH 16   1 KINGS 2

c. 1100 B.C.   c. 1050 B.C.   c. 1010 B.C.   c. 1003 B.C.   c. 970 B.C.

for believers, still showing us how to bring all we are to God in prayer and praise.

History of the transition in overview. While the transitions described above were accomplished during the decades of David's rule, the process was begun earlier, and encompassed the lives of Samuel and Saul as well as David. The chart on this page shows the overlap of these men, their times, and the Bible passages that tell their stories.

The Chronicles. The basic history of the time of David, and of other kings during the era of monarchy, is contained in 2 Samuel and the two books of Kings. Why then do we have a second and parallel account in the Chronicles? The answer is in the perspective from which the Chronicles are written. They are not so much a history as a divine commentary on Israel's history. That is, the Chronicles look at historical events and evaluate them in the light of God's character and his purposes.

It is common to suggest that Samuel and the Kings reflect a

prophetic viewpoint, while the Chronicles reflect a *priestly* view.
It is more helpful to note that the Chronicles were written much
later than the basic historical books, directed to Israelites who
were then captives in Babylon (after 586 B.C.). The message of
the Chronicles, in genealogy (1 Chron. 1–10) and historical review,
is to demonstrate that God remains faithful to his purposes. Men
will fail him and themselves. But, the Chronicles argue, even in
the most dangerous of times, God is in full control of history.
This message is important for us too. We too need to be reminded
that even in our greatest tragedies, God is working out his good
purposes in Jesus Christ, David's descendant, and our eternal King.

Outline. Our outline of the two books of David the king is best
structured around his experiences, as reported in sequence in 2
Samuel. The distinct emphases of 1 Chronicles can be easily seen
below.

Outline

I. Historical Prelude			1 Chron. 1–10
II. David's Triumphs as King	2 Sam. 1–10		1 Chron. 11–19
A. Rule over Judah		1–4	
B. Rule over United Israel		6–10	11–19
III. David's Troubles	2 Sam. 11–20		1 Chron. 20:1–3
A. With Himself		11, 12	20:1–3
B. With His Family		13–18	—
C. With His State		19–20	—
IV. Appendix: Six Incidents	2 Sam. 21–24		1 Chron. 21–22

As this outline demonstrates, Chronicles does not attempt to
record every event of David's rule. Some of his greatest sins, and
many of his personal tragedies, are passed over in silence. The
reason for this is not a lack of compassion, or lack of concern
over David's failings. The reason is, again, found in the divine
perspective and emphasis: what Chronicles explores are those
events which have significance in relation to God's unfolding purpose and plan.

1 Chronicles 1–10. Historical Prelude

The writer of the Chronicles takes great care to provide genealogical information. OT genealogies were important. They established
identity, and especially they demonstrated the right of Abraham's
children to inherit the covenant promises made to him by God
(see *Covenant, OT,* p. 51). Much of the material in these genealogies

is found in other OT passages. However, the reaffirmation of identity these genealogies provide was important to a people who languished in Babylonian captivity. A summary of the ten chapters indicates what the Chroniclers felt was important to reaffirm.

This section ends with the divine evaluation of Saul. "Saul died because he was unfaithful to the Lord" (13). With his death, the kingdom is turned over by God to David (14).

This first section of 1 Chronicles does not fit here historically; it was not written at this time. But it does fit here in the writer's mind. To the Chronicler, the beginning of David's reign is the great divide in Israel's history. From David on, nothing will be the same.

2 Samuel 1–4. David Rules over Judah

Initially David is recognized as king only by his own tribe of Judah. The others remain loyal to Saul's remaining son, Ish-Bosheth. The coalition of northern tribes, however, is held together only by Abner, the commander of Saul's army. It is seven years before David's partial rule is consolidated, and he is king of a united Israel.

Report of Saul's Death: 1:1–27. An Amalekite brings Saul's crown and armband to David. He expects a reward, and tells a tale of striking the death blow himself (9, 10). But David mourns for Saul and Jonathan. Then he has the Amalekite executed for his confession that he killed God's anointed ruler of Israel.

The lament for Saul and Jonathan communicates David's surprising appreciation for the feats of his old persecutor (19–27).

David anointed King of Judah: 2:1–7. The tribe from which David springs now recognizes him as king.

War between David and Saul's family: 2:1–3:5. Abner, Saul's army commander, apparently holds off Ish-Bosheth's coronation for some years (cf. 2 Sam. 2:10 with 5:5). A long war simmers, with David growing stronger while his rival is weakened.

Second Samuel 2:9 speaks of "all Israel." This is a significant turning point in history. From now on "Israel" will often be used to identify all the tribes north of Judah's territory (see map, p. 184). Along this line rivalry will grow, and ultimately the nation will be partitioned into two often hostile kingdoms.

During these years of strife between David and Ish-Bosheth a blood feud develops between Abner and David's commander, Joab.

Abner turns to David: 3:6–39. Ish-Bosheth accuses Abner of having sexual relations with one of Saul's concubines. This is the same in that culture as a charge of treason. The angry Abner determines to bring all Israel over to David. Abner completes his compact with David. But on the way home he is assassinated by Joab. David mourns publicly, making it clear he does not condone the murder. All know that without Abner to prop up the throne, the weak Ish-Bosheth is doomed.

Ish-Bosheth murdered: 4:1–12. Now two of Ish-Bosheth's captains seek to win David's favor. They murder their king, and bring his head to David. In OT times it is normal to reward bringers of good news. The two surely expect a reward for opening David's way to Israel's throne. Instead an angry David executes the two for killing "an innocent man in his own house and on his own bed" (4:11).

Amid the plotting and bloodshed, David alone seems to have kept perspective and acted morally.

2 Samuel 5–10; 1 Chronicles 11–19

The history of David's early, active years is told in both 2 Samuel and 1 Chronicles. The key to events in David's reign lists the events, shows the Bible passages which describe them, and gives in parentheses the page in this handbook on which they are discussed.

David crowned: 2 Samuel 5: 1–5; 1 Chronicles 11:1–3. It is 1003 B.C. Finally David is acknowledged as king of a united Israel. He will rule for 33 years.

David takes Jerusalem: 2 Samuel 5:6–9; 1 Chronicles 11:4–9. The city of Jerusalem has been Jebusite territory since before the Exodus (Josh. 18:16, 28). It lies along the dividing line between Judah and Israel. It becomes his capital, and is neither of the rival north or south. By taking it from an enemy, David avoids any show of favoritism. It is mountainous, easily defended, and has a good water supply.

The Jebusites jeer when David attacks, shouting that blind and lame men could hold their city. David urges his men on to take the citadel, and to destroy the "lame and blind" defenders!

Jerusalem is destined to become more than the capital city of a short-lived empire. It will become the Holy City, the center of worship for the Jews, and the city of the death, and resurrection, of Jesus (see *Jerusalem Temple*, p. 190).

David's military organization: I Chronicles 11:10–12:40. Little is known of the structure of David's army. This passage lists his "mighty men," and does give some hint as to David's

Key to Events in David's Reign

David Crowned (173)
2 Sam. 5:1–5
I Chron. 11:1–3

David Takes Jerusalem (173)
2 Sam. 5:6–9
I Chron. 11:4–9

David's Military Organization (173)
I Chron. 11:10–12:40

David Defeats the Philistines (174)
2 Sam. 5:10–25
I Chron. 14:1–17

The Ark Comes to Jerusalem (174)
2 Sam. 6:1–11
I Chron. 13:1–14;
15:1–18

David Leads in Worship (175)
2 Sam. 6:12–23
I Chron. 15:19–16:6

David's Psalm of Praise (175)
I Chron. 16:7–43

God's Covenant with David (175)
2 Sam. 7:1–29
I Chron. 17:1–27

David's Military Victories (177)
2 Sam. 8:1–14
I Chron. 18:1–13

David's Civil Government (179)
2 Sam. 8:15–18
I Chron. 18:14–17

David and Mephibosheth (179)
2 Sam. 9:1–13

Victory over the Ammonites (179)
2 Sam. 10:1–19
I Chron. 19:1–19

military command structure. The 600 men who joined David in his fugitive years seem to have formed the core of his military forces. It is clear that leadership in the army is based in large part on personal merit and prowess in battle.

We are told later, after David has expanded the borders of his kingdom, that he kept a standing army of 24,000, serving in monthly rotations (1 Chron. 27:1–15). This meant Israel had 288,000 trained men who could be called out to battle at any time.

David forged his mighty men into a military organization which surrounding peoples were never able to defeat.

David defeats the Philistines: 2 Samuel 5:10–25; 1 Chronicles 14:1–17. The Philistines now attack Israel in force, hoping to catch David and kill him. Both 2 Samuel and Chronicles carefully report David's attitude going into battle. He "inquires of God" (see *Knowing God's Will,* p. 142), and is careful to follow the Lord's directions. The Philistines are defeated. Second Samuel 21:15–22 and 23:13, 14, which relate incidents out of historical sequence, expand on the record of this early conflict. The war with Philistia involves a series of battles, and ultimately leads to an invasion by David of Philistine territory. The victories won are decisive, and only skirmishes are later fought with this ancient enemy.

It is also significant that David's victory over the Philistines breaks their monopoly on iron, and makes this metal available for equipping David's army.

The ark is brought to Jerusalem: 2 Samuel 6:1–11; 1 Chronicles 15:19–16:6. Years before, in Samuel's youth, the ark of God had been captured by the Philistines in the battle of Aphek (I Sam. 4–6). It was returned to Israel, but has rested for seventy years at Kirjathjearim. David now determines to bring the ark to Jerusalem. Israel's capital will also be its worship center. Deuteronomy foretold that one day God would choose a place as "a dwelling place for his name" (26:2, 3). Now, through David, his choice is expressed.

David brings 30,000 warriors to escort the ark to Jerusalem. But they put it on a cart for transport. On the way, when one of David's men reaches out to steady the ark, he is struck dead. David is both angry and afraid, and leaves the ark when the incident happens.

David is angry, but the incident has underlined the holiness and majesty of God. A sense of God's holiness is greatly needed. Saul treated the ark with contempt, and even executed members of the priesthood (1 Sam. 29:9–21). This incident, and the example of commitment which David provides, begins a recovery of fear of the Lord (see *Fear of God,* p. 127).

David now discovers regulations in the law of Moses instructing how the ark is to be moved (Num. 1:47–52). Reassured, David assembles priests and Levites, and joyfully brings the ark to Jerusalem. First Chronicles 15 details David's careful preparations to continue the journey, and his explanation of why God's anger broke out earlier (11–15).

Later in his rule, David will turn his organizational genius to the reorganization of Israel's worship system, and he will prepare for the construction of a temple which his son Solomon will build (1 Chron. 23–26).

David leads in worship: 2 Samuel 6:12–23; 1 Chronicles 15:19–16:6. As David brings the ark into Jerusalem, he is caught up in worship. Dressed as the other worshipers, without robes of royalty or warrior's armor, David dances and praises God in the streets (1 Chron. 15:27–29). His wife Michal, Saul's daughter, watches contemptuously. She apparently despises David as a religious fanatic. But David is not thinking of the impressions of observers. David's heart is filled with praise to his God (see *Worship, OT,* p. 176).

David's Psalm of praise: 1 Chronicles 16:7–43. Chronicles records a psalm which David gives to Asaph, the worship leader, the day the ark is brought to Jerusalem. Its words recall who God is, and tell of what he has done for Israel. The central theme is the goodness, the glory, the greatness, and the majesty due God's name.

Michal may have despised David's enthusiasm. But his joyful dancing before the Lord on that occasion was no mindless abandon. It was part of a wholehearted worship, which involved David's emotions and his intellect, and would continue to find expression in the king's commitment to do the will of his God.

How does the worship with which you are familiar compare or contrast with that of David, as seen in his celebration and his psalm? Why is Michal's attitude wrong? What warnings do we see in this passage that help us not to be critical of the ways in which others express their praise of God?

God's Covenant with David: 2 Samuel 7:1–29; 1 Chronicles 17:1–27. David has had a cedar palace built as his residence (1 Chron. 14:1–7). Now he is troubled. Why should he live in a palace, when the ark of God is covered only by a tent? So David determines to build God a temple. When he inquires, the prophet Nathan is enthusiastic. But that night God gives Nathan a message for David.

David is not to build God a house; instead God will build David's "house." This is a reference to the line, or family, of David. The right to Israel's throne will pass from generation to generation of David's descendants, forever. And God will be with them. No king who abandons God will escape discipline. But God will never reject the line of David, as he did the line of Saul (1 Sam. 15). This promise to David is known as the Davidic covenant (see p. 177), and when later generations speak of the "sure mercies of David," they are referring to God's commitment never to reject him or his line.

Worship, OT

Worship was significant to God's OT people. At the very beginning Moses asked Pharaoh to let Israel go, that they might serve *('abad)* God. This concept, often expressed in the OT, included ritual worship. But it involves far more; especially a life of obedience to God.

Ritual worship. The OT law specifies how God is to be worshiped in sacrifice, when annual worship festivals are to be held, and that a Sabbath day of rest be kept. Over time, Israel's public worship developed around these three regulated elements of religious life. In David's time, and at other times of revival, music played an increasingly important role in public worship. Later psalms were written to be sung at special times, as our Christmas music. The psalms of ascent (120–134) were sung by the people as they journeyed to Jerusalem for the Feast of Tabernacles. The Hallel psalms, 113–118, were sung at Passover. Psalm 148 is for the beginning of Passover, 136 for its end.

Private and family worship. Little detail is given in the OT of family worship practices. More is known of the pattern in later Judaism, which included prayers, memorization of Scripture, family keeping of festival practices, and talking often of God's words, as the law requires (Deut. 6:7, 8). Many symbols of faith were also found in homes (6:9). We do read in the OT of the prayer life of many OT saints, and many moving personal prayers are recorded for us.

Response to God. It is a mistake to try to understand OT worship by observing either the emotions or the practices of God's people. This is because, essentially, worship is a response to God as he initiates relationship by self-revelation. David's prayer on the occasion of bringing the ark to Jerusalem illustrates this. He was deeply affected emotionally. But his psalm of thanks (1 Chron. 16:7–36) does not focus on himself or on his emotions. The psalm focuses on the Lord. David speaks directly to God. He praises God for who he is, and for how he has acted for his people. Thus the heart and center of true worship, however that worship may be expressed— in ritual, in dancing, or in quiet privacy—is the person of the Lord himself.

True and false worship. True worship in Israel involved personal response to God in his great, historical revelation. False worship might be bowing down to an idol or a god of surrounding peoples. But it might also be careful observance of prescribed ritual—without that heart response to God which will always find expression not only in ritual but also in daily obedience to the Lord.

For study: Deuteronomy 10:12 f; 1 Chronicles 16:7–36; 1 Samuel 2; worship psalms.

David's prayer of response (2 Sam. 7:18–29; 1 Chron. 17:16–27) reveals a touching sense of wonder and humility, and expresses that complete confidence in the faithfulness of God which helped to make David an obedient and godly man.

Study David's prayer. What can you learn here that you can apply to your own prayer life?

David's military victories: 2 Samuel 8:1–14; 1 Chronicles 18:1–17. David has taken most of the territory the Philistines possessed along Israel's coasts. Now, in a series of wars which are not described in any detail, his armies defeat other surrounding nations. David's normal practice seems to be to make these states subject to Israel. He demands annual payment of tribute, but does not occupy the countries. However, David does push the borders of Israel out, to encompass more of the land promised to Israel than has ever been previously occupied. Not even Joshua came so near to full possession of the Promised Land.

Davidic Covenant

The Davidic Covenant (2 Sam. 7; 1 Chron. 17) is one of the OT covenants of promise (see *Covenant,* p. 51). Like the other promise covenants, this one announces what God will do. God's commitment to the announced course of action in no way depends on any subsequent human actions. Nor will God take back his covenant oath if his people are disobedient.

Like the other covenants in the OT, this one is prophetic, focusing on the end of history, when a ruler from David's line will be established "on the throne of his kingdom forever" (7:13, 16). Like other OT prophecies (see *Understanding the Prophets,* p. 276 f), this predictive promise has immediate as well as distant application. The immediate application is to Solomon and the other descendants of David who will occupy the Jerusalem throne during the centuries of the monarchy. The distant application is to a single descendant from David's line, in whom the promise will find its fulfillment. This individual, who by right of ancestry will have a claim to David's throne, will be more than a mortal man, for his reign will continue into eternity's "forever."

It is because of this promise to David that Luke and Matthew take such care in tracing the genealogy of Jesus. For Jesus Christ, who is of

David's family, will at the end of time, when all God's promises are kept in their fullest sense, reign over the universe forever and ever.

For study: Psalm 89; 1 Chronicles 22: 9, 10; Isaiah 42:1, 6: 55:3, 4

David

David not only shaped his own time. He also transformed Israel's sense of her identity and of God's purpose in his people.

Accomplishments. David was unmatched as a war leader, winning victories over all Israel's enemies, and expanding her territory ten times beyond that occupied in the days of the judges. As an administrator, David established efficient tax, worship, and military structures. His impact on Israel's worship life is reflected in the psalms, and seen in the fact that, centuries later, Hezekiah used David's rituals when reinstituting temple worship (2 Kings 19:34).

Personal Qualities. Three serious sins committed by David during his forty year reign are recorded in the OT. These are never excused. But David's readiness to confess his faults publicly, and openly seek God's forgiveness, set him apart from Saul. A number of passages in the OT express God's evaluation of David as a person whose heart was in tune with the Lord (cf 1 Kings 2:33; 3:6; 8:66). David, like each of us, was vulnerable to temptation. He did fail, especially in the governing of his own family. It is not his sinlessness, but his great love for God and his quick readiness to respond to God's word, even words of rebuke, that make him a man of faith.

Impact on Israel. David made a great and lasting impression on the people of the OT. The conviction that God had made a commitment to David, to maintain his throne, was a source of hope to future generations in the darkest of times (2 Kings 8:19; 2 Chron. 21:7). The prophets often return to this theme, speaking of the sure future of David's house, throne, city, and especially of a future seed who will come from David's line to rescue God's people.

New Testament impact. David is also an important figure in the NT. But the NT focus of attention is Jesus, who is the long awaited heir of David and who supplants him as his "greater son." Jesus' genealogy is carefully traced back to David through Joseph, his "father of record" (Matt. 1), and through Mary (Luke 3). The NT focus is on the fact that in Jesus all the promises to David will be at last fulfilled. Thus Christ is presented as superior to that great OT King who, in his human nature, was the forefather of our Lord.

An example to follow. David's life deserves careful study, not simply for the dramatic content of the stories told, but also as an example—and in some cases warning—for our own relationship with God.

Check a concordance for references to David outside the books of Samuel and Kings. What view of David do they express? What seems to you to be the emphasis of the OT and NT in referring to David—his personal qualities or relationship to the Messiah?

David's civil government: 2 Samuel 8:15–18; 1 Chronicles 18:14–17. David organizes a powerful military machine, and reorganizes Israel's worship. He also establishes a central governmental system for the collection of taxes, storage of supplies, and supervision of agriculture. Little is known of the various administrators' duties, although the offices are identified here and in 1 Chronicles 27:16–31. It was a monumental task to impose this kind of structure on a people unused to any kind of government control, and all in a single generation. The fact that David is able to design and build such a system is a testimony to the many gifts of this warrior, worshiper, and unmatched administrator.

David and Mephibosheth: 2 Samuel 9:1–13. David is clearly established as ruler of a country he has made powerful. Now he searches for any descendants of his friend Jonathan. One man has survived, who is crippled from childhood. David restores Saul's land to him, and shows him great kindness. Normally any change of dynasty meant the new ruler would attempt to kill surviving members of the royal family, to forestall any later challenge to the throne. David shows how different he is from those rulers who neither trust God nor care for other human beings.

What bonds of relationship do we build with our own Christian friends? Explore 1 Chronicles 20, 23:14–18, and this passage. What can you learn here that will help you see how to develop David-Jonathan relationships with those in your church and community?

Victory over the Ammonites: 2 Samuel 10:1–19; 1 Chronicles 19:1–19. The record of David's conquest in this section of the sacred history concludes with the report of war with the Ammonites. The war is not initiated by David. It stems from a tragic misinterpretation of David's expression of sympathy on the death of the Ammonite king. The ruler had been friendly to David, but the son and new king sees David's delegation as spies. In the war that results, the Ammonites enlist a mercenary army of Arameans. David defeats the combined powers, and then immediately invades Aramea, to prevent future coalitions forming against him. The lesson is learned: "the Arameans were afraid to help the Ammonites anymore" (10:19).

2 Samuel 11–20. David's Troubles

David was a remarkable and successful leader, who left his imprint on secular and sacred history. David was also a spiritually sensitive man, who truly loved God and desired to obey him. But

David, like the rest of us, was a sinner, and knew what it means to fail personally. Second Samuel now reports David's personal troubles and failings. But these are not mentioned in 1 Chronicles! Why? Because Chronicles records history from *God's* perspective. While David's sins were real, and are recorded as historical events in 2 Samuel, they are also *forgiven* sins. It is another indication of God's great grace that they are omitted in Chronicles. Scripture says "our sins and iniquities he remembers no more" (Jer. 31:34). David's sins are not discussed in the history reported from the divine viewpoint, because God has dismissed them, and in his sight they are gone!

David and Bathsheba: 2 Samuel 11–12. David's most notorious sin involves his adultery with Bathsheba, and later arrangement for the death of her husband, Uriah, in battle. This action is even more despicable because Uriah is one of his old companions (cf. 1 Chron. 11:41). David then marries the pregnant widow.

Nathan the prophet is sent to confront David. Their meeting is one of the most vivid dramas of the Bible. David immediately confesses his sin and humbles himself before the Lord. Because the sin is known publicly, David makes an open confession through a psalm delivered to the director of music for public use (Psalm 51). Possibly Psalm 32 also expresses David's feelings at this time of disobedience and humiliation.

David shows no outward remorse until his sin is identified and condemned by Nathan. But what was going on within him? Study Psalms 32 and 51. Can you relate their elements to any experience of your own, when you strayed from righteousness?

Amnon and Tamar: 2 Samuel 13. David, like others in his day, has many wives. Many of his problems stem from conflicts which develop within his household, between half-brothers and half-sisters. One son, Amnon, rapes his half-sister, Tamar. Tamar's brother, Absalom, arranges to kill Amnon in revenge. David neither punishes Absalom for the murder nor forgives him, but permits him to live in exile.

Absalom's revolt: 2 Samuel 14–18. Absalom flees the country after the murder. Three years later David permits him to return. But David will not see the young man.

In the next four years Absalom sets out to win the loyalty of the northern tribes (Israel) away from his father (ch. 15). He even wins the support of some of David's oldest associates! Finally Absalom is ready for open rebellion.

David is forced to flee Jerusalem. The aging king, deserted by the people he has loved and led so well, and stripped of all that men call glory, hurries into the gathering darkness (15:13–37). On that bitter journey he is even cursed by a distant relative of Saul's named Shimei. David will not permit his men to punish Shimei: it may be that God is speaking and has turned from David because of his sins (16:1–13). David's feelings at this time are expressed in Psalms 3 and 4.

Not all of David's old friends have turned against him. He succeeds in placing an advisor in Absalom's camp, who delays pursuit until David can raise an army from loyal Judah (16:15–17:29). By the time Absalom has gathered a larger army and pursues his father, David's commanders are ready. The supporters of Absalom are defeated and the young man is killed (18:1–18). David mourns deeply for his son. Finally Joab, his commander, confronts the king and insists that he go and express appreciation to his loyal supporters, before his tears over his dead son make the victory seem a defeat (19:1–8).

Sheba's Rebellion: 2 Samuel 19:9–20:26. The civil war is not ended. The loyal men of Judah are furious with the Israelite tribes. And the northerners are ashamed, desperately eager to demonstrate their loyalty. On the way back to Jerusalem they quarrel over the honor of escorting David to his throne. When a "troublemaker" named Sheba shouts, in effect, "Let's go home!" the Israelites desert David again! It takes no civil war to reestablish David now. Joab, his military commander, simply follows Sheba and sees to it he is killed (ch. 20).

The kingdom has been preserved. But the uneasy antagonism that exists between the north and south has been intensified. In another generation that antagonism will harden into permanent enmity.

2 Samuel 21–24; 1 Chronicles 21–29. Appendix

We now read of six incidents which are not recorded in chronological order. Chronicles gives the greatest emphasis to David's work in shaping Israel's worship and preparing for the building of the great temple at Jerusalem.

Gibeonites avenged: 2 Samuel 21:1–14. Centuries before this time, Joshua made a solemn covenant in God's name with the Gibeonites (see Josh. 9). Saul violated this treaty. When three years of famine cripples Israel, David seeks the reason. He discovers that God has brought the famine on account of Saul's attack on the Gibeonites. David asks the Gibeonites to set compensation. They demand nothing less than the right to execute seven of Saul's male descendants, for Saul is the one "who plotted against us and destroyed us" (3).

Philistine wars reviewed: 2 Samuel 21:15–22, 1 Chronicles 20: 4–8. See the discussion of David's military might on page 173.

The note which says Elhanan killed Goliath (2 Sam. 21:19) is an obvious transcription error. First Chronicles 20:5 tells us that he killed "Lahmi the brother of Goliath."

David's praise for deliverance: 2 Samuel 22:1–51; 23:1–7. David's regret, expressed as a lament at the death of Jonathan and Saul, was honest (2 Sam. 1). But so is the great joy David experienced at his release from persecution and the opportunity to fulfill his destiny as king of a united people. The psalms of praise recorded here tell David's feelings as success comes to him as king. The second psalm, written later, continues the theme, and is the final testimony of Israel's great shepherd king.

Read these psalms carefully. How is David's joy related to confidence that he has lived to please God, and done righteousness? Are we right to think of our good actions as a basis for confidence in our own relationship with God?

David's mighty men: 2 Samuel 23:8–39. See pages 173–174.

David counts his people: 2 Samuel 24:1–25; 1 Chronicles 21:1–30. Sometime during his reign, David takes a census. This is viewed even by David's military commanders as a sin, possibly because the act suggests confidence in numbers rather than the Lord. At this time, possibly in the midpoint of his rule, 1,300,000 fighting men are available. The high proportion of them in Judah (500,000) makes it clear that the tribe of Simeon and part of Dan, are also included in "Judah," just as a number of northern tribes are called "Israel" (see map, p. 184).

God judges this sin, but gives David a choice of national punishments. The plague which David chooses is stopped just outside Jerusalem. There David builds an altar and offers sacrifices.

This place will become the site of Solomon's temple and all other temples built in Jerusalem. It is the same place where Abraham was about to offer up Isaac (Gen. 22). It is the place that prophecy says a rebuilt temple will stand in Messiah's day (Ezek. 40–48).

David prepares for building the temple: 1 Chronicles 23:1–29:20. David is not permitted to build the temple himself (see 2 Sam. 7; 1 Chron. 17). But he spends his later years preparing for this culminating expression of his love for God. David designs the structure, prepares building materials, and assembles millions of dollars worth of gold and silver. He assembles 3,750 tons of gold alone (ch. 22)! In addition David takes a census of Levites and Aaronic priests, and begins to organize and train them for work at the temple (ch. 23). This is necessary because tasks assigned the Levites in the law relate to transportation of a portable worship center. Now, with a central worship structure being built, the ministry of the Levites must be rethought. Roles for singers (ch. 25), gate-keepers and treasurers (26), and others, are created and their job descriptions developed.

David will not be allowed to build the great edifice he plans. But his last days are happily filled with its details, and in gathering the resources to create a structure which will honor the Lord.

What do these last chapters reveal of David's heart and his motives? How would you evaluate the life and career of this great man?

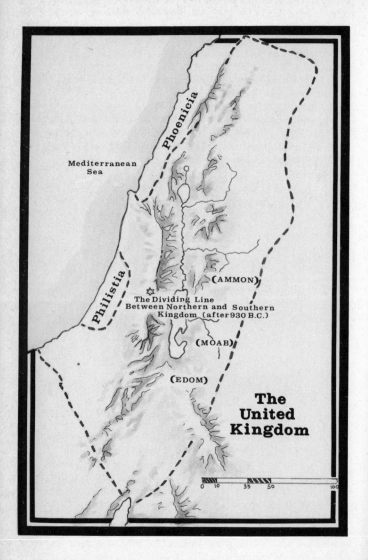

Phoenicia

Mediterranean
Sea

Philistia

(AMMON)

The Dividing Line
Between Northern and Southern
Kingdom (after 930 B.C.)

(MOAB)

(EDOM)

**The
United
Kingdom**

0 10   35   50   100

1 KINGS/2 CHRONICLES 1–20
The United and Divided Kingdoms

The two books of Kings and the second book of Chronicles tell the story of the monarchy, from David's death to the Babylonian captivity. First Kings spans some 120 years. The first 40 of these saw the great era of Israel's prosperity under the rule of David's son, Solomon. After the death of Solomon the nation splits into two rival states, Israel and Judah. First Kings, and the parallel account in 2 Chronicles 1–20, records the glory, and tells the reasons for the tragic division. They also describe the spiritual direction taken by the two halves of the divided land.

The Chronicles. Chronicles provides a parallel account of the basic history given in the books of Kings. They are a divine commentary on the events which both report, and often reflect a different perspective (see p. 169).

Dating. We can speak with certainty by the time of Solomon about dates. Solomon rules a united Palestine between 970 and 930 B.C.

Outline. The Book of 1 Kings falls naturally into two equal sections, paralleled by the 2 Chronicles account. A detailed list of the kings of the North and South is given on page 193.

Outline

I. Solomon's
   United Kingdom   1 Kings 1–11   2 Chronicles 1–9
II. The Divided
   Kingdom   1 Kings 12–22 2 Chronicles 11–20

Solomon. The dominant person in 1 Kings is Solomon. He shared his father's genius for organization and went beyond him in diplomacy. Spiritually Solomon began in his father's tradition, with a true dedication to the Lord. But his later life saw him fall away, led by his foreign wives to worship their gods and goddesses. Two OT books are ascribed to Solomon. The "Song of Songs" is a beautiful and natural love story (p. 274). The other, "Ecclesiastes" (p. 269), records Solomon's inner struggle to find meaning in life apart from God. This most brilliant of men can only conclude, "Emptiness. All is emptiness." In spite of his wealth, power, and ability to satisfy his every desire, Solomon finds life without a vital relationship with God is meaningless. Many of the Proverbs are also ascribed to Solomon (p. 264).

1 Kings 1–11/2 Chronicles 1–9. Solomon and the United Kingdom

World situation. During the nearly eight decades of David and Solomon, the great world powers that normally dominated Palestine were in eclipse. Egypt to the south, and the Hittite empire to the north, had been seriously damaged by wars with the Sea Peoples, of whom the Philistines were a branch (see p. 153). Assyria was weak, and Babylon had not yet begun to expand toward empire. David left Solomon a strong, dominating military. Solomon never had to use his forces for war; no powers then existing could seriously threaten him.

Solomon did know trade rivalries. But he also developed close ties with the Phoenicians of Tyre as trading partners, and built a network of treaties with the nations around him.

Archaeological discoveries. The OT pictures Israel during Solomon's era as a vigorous, wealthy nation, aggressively pushing for new trade routes and engaging in a number of ambitious building projects. Archaeology has confirmed and deepened these impressions. Excavations at Megiddo (1925 to 1939) revealed construction features like those described for the temple (1 Kings 7:12). Sites of great storage cities, trading ports, and copper smelting furnaces from Solomon's time have been found and examined.

Wealth. The years of Solomon saw a great influx of wealth into Palestine. Israel controlled many trade routes vital to the ancient world: horses were purchased in Egypt and resold at great profit in the north. Solomon engaged in joint ventures with Hiram of Tyre to develop a trading fleet, which searched the Mediterranean and Africa for exotic goods, and sold them the copper and bronze produced by Solomon's mines and refined in his furnaces.

The land of Palestine also produced rich agricultural harvests of olives, grain, flax, grapes, and figs.

Second Chronicles 9:13 gives Solomon's income, exclusive of trade revenue and taxes, at 25 tons of gold annually!

Because of this tremendous income and the natural wealth of the land, Solomon's government grew into a weighty bureaucracy. His ambitious building projects demanded more money than was available. So Solomon laid heavy taxes on his people. At his death the wealthy land was near bankruptcy, and the people cried out desperately for relief from the oppressive taxation.

Map. The map on page 184 shows the extent of the united kingdom, won by David and maintained by his son Solomon. Never before or since has so much of the Promised Land been occupied by God's people.

1 Kings 1, 2. Solomon Made King

Competition for the throne: 1:1–27. David is old and feeble. But still he hesitates to confirm the succession of Solomon, which he has promised to do. Another son, Adonijah, invites key supporters to a feast, intending to make himself king. Other advisors warn David. Unless he acts, both he and Solomon will likely be killed!

David makes Solomon co-regent: 1:28–53. David acts with his old decisiveness. He has Zadok the priest and Nathan the prophet escort Solomon to the springs at Gihon, where David had first won the city (2 Sam. 5:6–9). All Jerusalem breaks out in spontaneous demonstration. When the news is brought to Adonijah, his supporters slip away, and Adonijah begs Solomon for his life. The request is granted—so long as this brother of Solomon keeps his place.

David's charge to Solomon: 2:1–12. After a time of co-rule, David is near death. He gives his final instructions to his son. "Show yourself a man," David commands, and underlines the need to keep all of God's commandments wholeheartedly (2–4). David also instructs Solomon to deal with several of his old enemies (5–9).

Solomon's control established: 2:13–46. After David dies Adonijah maneuvers for another try at the throne. He asks through Solomon's mother to marry one of David's concubines—a girl who cared for David in his last months (1–4). By custom a king's concubines are part of the inheritance of his heir (cf 2 Sam. 16:21). Such a marriage would provide basis for a later claim to Solomon's throne by the popular (1 Kings 2:15) Adonijah. Solomon immediately puts Adonijah to death for treason. There is no indication Solomon harmed other brothers.

Solomon finds ways to deal with his father's enemies. For background on these actions, see 2 Samuel 2, 3 (Joab) and 2 Samuel 16 (Shimei).

1 Kings 3–4/2 Chronicles 1. Prayer for Wisdom

Request for wisdom: 1 Kings 3:1–19; 2 Chronicles 1:1–13. Solomon acts quickly as king. He strengthens his relations with other states and marries a daughter of Pharaoh as part of an alliance with Egypt. Solomon also shows love for God, first by obedience, and second by his worship. God then appears to Solomon and instructs him to request whatever he wishes. Solomon asks only that God's promise to David (see *Davidic Covenant,* p. 177) be kept, and that Solomon be given the wisdom and knowledge needed to "lead this great people of yours," and to distinguish between right and wrong (1 Kings 3:10). This request pleases God. Solomon is promised wisdom, and also granted riches and honor.

Wisdom demonstrated: 1 Kings 3:16–28. Kings records the difficult decision Solomon faces when two women claim the same child. His wise decision helps establish Solomon in the eyes of his people.

Solomon's administration: 1 Kings 4:1–19. Solomon expands the governmental structure developed by David (cf 2 Sam. 8:15–18).

Solomon's finances: 1 Kings 4:20–27; 2 Chronicles 1:14–17. Solomon's rule is a time of security for the people of Israel. During his reign, trade brings great wealth into Jerusalem and supports Solomon's growing court.

Solomon's intellectual achievements: 1 Kings 4:29–34. Solomon's knowledge and his wisdom are "greater than the wisdom of all the men of the East." With all his other activities, Solomon finds time to add thousands of proverbs and over a thousand songs to the literary heritage of Israel. He also becomes a botanist, cataloging all kinds of plant life, and a zoologist, researching the habits and characteristics of animals, birds, and reptiles.

These early chapters dealing with Solomon's first years give us a picture of an extremely gifted man. How many advantages (including personal gifts, heritage, etc.) can you find in exploring these chapters? Which do you consider most important?

1 Kings 5–7/2 Chronicles 2–4. Construction of the Temple

The great achievement of Solomon's reign is construction of the temple of Jerusalem (see *The Jerusalem Temple,* pp. 190, 191). These chapters tell of its construction, and the massive effort required. There are 30,000 laborers conscripted just to cut timber, and another 150,000 needed for other tasks. The temple is built of stone, paneled with cedar, and overlaid with gold. The gold alone, figured at the old price of $35 an ounce, is worth almost three billion dollars ($2,780,000,000)! The temple is twice the size of the portable tabernacle: 90 feet long and 30 wide. Its design and furnishings are the same, reproducing the divinely ordained

Solomon's Temple

plan that carries so much spiritual meaning (see *Tabernacle,* pp. 90–92). The temple is enclosed by two courts. The first contains the bronze altar on which sacrifices are made, and the laver of washing. The larger outer walls enclose a number of elegant buildings. Here is Solomon's own palace, which takes thirteen years to build. Also this splendid district includes a "House of the Forest of Lebanon" (1 Kings 10:17, RSV; Isa. 22:8), a hall of pillars, and a hall of judgment, in which is Solomon's golden throne (1 Kings 10:18–20). Here Israel will now come to worship and keep the annual festivals, for here is Israel's true treasure: not the gold, but God.

The Jerusalem Temple

In the ancient world, deities were attached to locations. Temples were normally built as a residence for the local god. Solomon realized this notion did not apply to Israel's God: "The heavens, even the highest heaven, cannot contain you. How much less this temple I have built!" (1 Kings 8:27). The OT temple was not built to house God, but as a place of meeting between God and man. Here men could approach the Holy One of Israel through sacrifice. The temple then was not for God, but for man—a marked pathway to salvation for the penitent sinner (1 Kings 8:27–30).

There was to be only one place of sacrifice and worship in Israel. This was to demonstrate the unity of God, and the one way of access to him for a unified people. God graciously "put his presence" there in a special way, to let his people know that their prayers were heard, and that God was keeping his covenant promise to be with them.

Solomon's temple. The structure built by Solomon was the first raised on the temple site in Jerusalem. It remained there until it was destroyed at the beginning of the Babylonian captivity (c. 586 B.C.). Ezekiel portrays the glory of the Lord (e.g., his presence) being withdrawn from the temple in chapters 8–11, before both temple and city were burned.

Zerubbabel's temple. When God's people straggled back from Babylon, a second temple was built on the same site. It was far less glorious than Solomon's, but vital as a sign of God's presence with the restored people, and as a place for sacrifice. A strong motive for rebuilding was the conviction that the promised Deliverer would one day stand in a completed temple. Messiah could not come until the temple stood.

Herod's temple. Herod rebuilt Zerubbabel's temple on a magnificent scale. According to the Gospels this temple took 46 years to complete. It is the temple in which Jesus spoke, and on whose courts he walked. Herod's temple was destroyed by the Romans in A.D. 70, and no Jewish temple has stood in Jerusalem since that date.

Ezekiel's temple. The prophet Ezekiel, writing during the Captivity, foretells a temple yet to be built. Its dimensions and plan are described in great detail, and its limits extend to the whole top of the temple mountain. The temple of Ezekiel is associated with the Messiah (see *Messiah,* p. 255). It is from here the Savior is to rule. As Ezekiel puts it, it is "the place of my throne, and the place for the soles of my feet. This is where I will live among the Israelites forever" (43:7).

For Study: 1 Kings 5–7; Ezekiel 40–48; Haggai 2:1–9; Ezra 5–6.

---

1 Kings 8:1–9:9/2 Chronicles 5–7. The Temple Dedicated

The ark brought to the temple: 1 Kings 8:1–12; 2 Chronicles 5:1–14. The ark was constructed in the days of Moses, and is the historic focus of God's presence with his people (see p. 90). With the Ark in place in the Temple, God's glory visibly fills it.

Solomon's sermon: 1 Kings 8:12–21; 2 Chronicles 6:1–11. Solomon briefly recounts to the people how he has completed the temple, which God told David his son Solomon would build.

Solomon's prayer of dedication: 1 Kings 8:22–61; 2 Chronicles 5:12–42. Solomon's prayer of dedication is a model OT petition. In it the king affirms who God is, and bases his requests on promises made and principles laid down in the written law. The prayer concludes with a blessing on Israel, and a call to the people to commitment. Solomon exhorts them, for "your hearts must be fully committed to the Lord our God, to live by his decrees and obey his commands . . ." (1 Kings 8:61).

Read Solomon's prayer carefully. What does it reveal about Solomon? What does it tell of his concept of who God is?

Two weeks of worship: 1 Kings 8:62–66; 2 Chronicles 7:1–10. The prayer of Solomon is accepted. The whole congregation sees flame fall from heaven to kindle the altar of sacrifice. This is another link with the tabernacle, for miraculous fire also fell at its dedication in the wilderness (Lev. 9:24; cf. Judg. 6:21).

God's response to Solomon's prayer: 1 Kings 9:1–9; 2 Chronicles 7:11–22. This is the second time God appears to Solomon. God tells the young king that his prayer has been heard. God has consecrated the temple by his very presence. But Solomon is exhorted to "walk before me in integrity of heart and uprightness" (9:4). God warns that if his people fail to observe the law, and turn aside to worship other gods, they will be stripped of their glory and become objects of ridicule, scattered throughout the world.

1 Kings 9:1–11/2 Chronicles 8–9. Summary of Solomon's Rule

Solomon's many projects: 1 Kings 9:10–28; 2 Chronicles 8:1–18. The first twenty years of Solomon's rule are productive and active. He starts ambitious building projects. He keeps the annual festivals prescribed by the law. He reaches out in varied trading ventures. Solomon also puts the descendants of the Canaanites who are left in the land to slave labor. In all his projects Solomon is a great success. During these years Solomon's reputation spreads worldwide.

The Queen of Sheba: 1 Kings 10:1–13; 2 Chronicles 9:1–12. "Sheba" is a land at the southern tip of Arabia, known today as Yemen. The queen's 1200-mile journey is not undertaken just from curiosity. She comes to Jerusalem to negotiate trade issues with Solomon and is successful (cf. 1 Kings 10:13).

📖 Read the account in either 1 Kings or 2 Chronicles. What is the most significant impact of Solomon on foreign nations as long as he remains faithful to God?

Solomon's splendor; 1 Kings 10:14–29; 2 Chronicles 9:13–28. A summary is given of the wealth that flows into Israel from Solomon's various ventures. However, Solomon "accumulates chariots and horses" (10:26), which is strictly forbidden to Israel's kings (Deut. 17:14–20). This is the first indication that in his later years Solomon will drift away from his early commitment to God.

Solomon's wives: 1 Kings 11:1–13. The law concerning kings also forbids multiple wives. And the general law strictly prohibits taking foreign wives. But Solomon makes many political alliances, and these involve marriages between royal houses. However wise this course seems, it leads Solomon into serious trouble and involves him in direct disobedience to the Lord.

Solomon's love for God is gradually replaced by his love for his foreign women. As he grows older "his wives turn his heart after their gods" (4). Now the Lord appears to Solomon a third time, but this time to announce judgment!

It is during this later part of his life, when he has wandered from his spiritual foundations, that Solomon writes Ecclesiastes (p. 269).

Enemies arise: 1 Kings 11:14–40. Now the days of unmixed blessing are past. Hadad, of the royal family of Edom, and Rezon, who will launch a dynasty in Syria, begin movements which will lead to the rebellion of these subject lands. One of Solomon's own officials, Jeroboam, rebels against the king. This ambitious and talented young man is told by the prophet Ahijah (see *Prophet, OT,* p. 130) that on Solomon's death he will become king over the northern tribes. Solomon tries unsuccessfully to kill Jeroboam, who flees to Egypt.

In these rising external and internal enemies, the seed for years of agonizing strife for Solomon's successors has begun to grow.

Solomon's death: 1 Kings 11:41–43; 2 Chronicles 9:29–31. After forty years as king, the book is closed on Solomon's reign. He is buried in Jerusalem, the city of his father, David.

Solomon began his reign well. Trace the causes of his decline, and indicators along the way. What lessons can you learn for your own life from Solomon?

1 Kings 12–22/2 Chronicles 10–20. The Divided Kingdom

On the death of Solomon in 970 B.C. the Hebrew nation was divided into Northern and Southern kingdoms, called Israel and Judah. This division was never healed, but continued until Assyria carried the ten Northern tribes into capivity in 722 B.C. The Southern kingdom survived until 586 B.C. Then the Babylonians deported its citizens.

The story of the two lands is told in the last half of 1 Kings, in 2 Kings, and the rest of 2 Chronicles. Chronicles does not comment on the history of the Northern Kingdom, which apostasized under its first king. These historical books can best be outlined by the reigns of the various kings, listed here with their dates.

JUDAH		ISRAEL	
Rehoboam	930–913	Jeroboam I	930–909
Abijah	913–910	Nadab	909–908
Asa	910–869	Baasha	908–886
Jehosphaphat, coregency	872–869	Elah	886–885
Jehosphaphat, total reign	872–848	Zimri	885
Jehoram, coregency	853–848	Tibni	885–880
Jehoram, total reign	853–841	Omri	880–874
Ahaziah	841	Ahab	874–853
Athaliah	841–835	Ahaziah	853–852
Joash	835–796	Joram	852–841
Amaziah	796–767	Jehu	841–814
Azariah, overlap	792–767	Jehoahaz	814–798
Azariah, total reign	792–740	Jehoash	798–782
Jotham, coregency	750–740	Jeroboam II, coregency	793–782
Jotham, official reign	750–735	Jeroboam II, total reign	793–753
Jotham, total years	750–732	Zachariah	753
Ahaz, overlap with Jotham	735–732	Shallum	752
Ahaz, official years	732–715	Menahem	752–742
Hezekiah	715–686	Pekah	752–732
Manasseh, coregency	697–686	Pekahiah	742–740
Manasseh, total reign	697–642	Hoshea	732–723
Amon	642–640		
Josiah	640–609		
Jehoahaz	609		
Jehoiakim	609–598		
Jehoiachin	589–597		
Zedekiah	597–586		

1 Kings 12:1–24/2 Chronicles 10:1–11:4. Israel Rebels

On Solomon's death, the Northern tribes demand that his son
lighten the taxes and the forced labor levies which Solomon imposed. Rehoboam threatens to make the load even heavier. Israel
immediately rebels. Only the intervention of the prophet Shemaiah
prevents civil war between Israel and the still faithful Judah.

1 Kings 12:25–14:20. Jeroboam I of Israel (930–909 B.C.)

False worship system: 12:25–33. Solomon's old enemy Jeroboam
is made king of Israel. He must now break the strands which
link his new nation to Judah. Most serious is the common faith
of Judah and Israel, for all Israelites are to come to Jerusalem
(the capital of Judah!) for worship and sacrifice. Jeroboam devises
a false worship system which imitates the system given by God.
He sets up two worship centers, at Bethel and Dan. There he
places golden calves, on which the worshiper is to imagine the
invisible Jahweh standing. Jeroboam consecrates a new priesthood
and institutes festivals which mimic the OT festivals but are held
in different months. This apostasy sets the spiritual direction of
the Northern Kingdom.

Judgment announced: 1 Kings 13:1–6. An unnamed prophet is
sent from Judah to the Bethel worship center to confront Jeroboam
(see *Prophet, OT,* p. 130). He announces that one day a king of
Judah, to be named Josiah, will defile this worship center and
burn the bones of the false priests who serve it on its altar. As a
sign that this is truly God's word, the altar will crack and spill
its ashes—and immediately does so.

Obedience demanded: 1 Kings 13:7–34. The prophet who carries
the message to Jeroboam is himself killed by a lion before he can
return to Judah. His death comes because of his disobedience to
a command of God. The message is clear. If Jeroboam persists
in disobedience, his own judgment is certain. But Jeroboam will
not turn and continues the false system which directly violates
Mosaic law.

Jeroboam I as King: 1 Kings 14:1–20. Secular sources tell us
that Jeroboam lost much territory during his twenty-two-year reign.
In Syria an Aramean state is established under Rezon; Moab is
lost in the east, and Israel is invaded by Egypt under Shishak.
But most serious is the fact that Jeroboam leads Israel into the
detestable practices of the nations the Lord had driven out of Palestine (9).

1 Kings 14:21–31/2 Chronicles 11:5–12:16. Rehoboam of Judah (930–913 B.C.)

Rehoboam has border skirmishes with Jeroboam of Israel during his seventeen-year reign. But his nation grows stronger, as those who are faithful to the law and the Jerusalem temple migrate to the tribal areas of Judah and Benjamin (see map, p. 184). Rehoboam does not remain faithful (2 Chron. 11:15–16). Still, when Judah is threatened by Shishak of Egypt, Rehoboam and his officials repent and turn to God. Judah is not occupied but becomes a vassal state. The treasures of gold that Solomon has gathered are surrendered to the Egyptians.

Other sources tell us about Shishak's invasion. Egyptian records list some 150 cities in Palestine overrun in this campaign. Many of the cities listed are in Israel. But none of the cities of central Judah are included. God did provide the deliverance he promised (2 Chron. 12:7–8).

Rehoboam fortifies a number of Judah's cities (2 Chron. 11: 5–9). These are located in the south, and suggest his major enemies were the Philistines and Egyptians rather than Israel.

1 Kings 15:1–8/2 Chronicles 13:1–14:1. Abijah of Judah (913–910 B.C.)

Abijah's brief reign is not marked by a return to piety. But it is marked by a significant victory over an invasion force from Israel.

Read Abijah's oration to Jeroboam before the battle (2 Chron. 13:4–12). It identifies the basic distinction that is maintained between Judah and Israel throughout their joint history.

1 Kings 15:9–24/2 Chronicles 14:2–16:4. Asa of Judah (910–869 B.C.)

Asa is one of only eight kings of Judah who are said to have been good in God's eyes. Not one king of Israel is so praised. Each of them "did evil."

Some thirty years after Shishak, Asa defeats another Egyptian army, under a commander called Serah. Asa's attitude of humble dependence on God is shown in his prayer recorded in 2 Chronicles 14:11, 12. After the victory an encouraging message from the prophet Azariah motivates Asa to purge the land of idolatrous worship centers and repair the temple altar at Jerusalem. He then

leads a great revival worship service (2 Chron. 15:10–15) which
causes additional thousands to move to Judah from Israel for freedom to worship God according to his law.

Asa's forty-year reign does not end as well as it begins. War
threatens with Israel. Without inquiring of the Lord, Asa makes
a treaty with Benhadad of Aram (Syria), who attacks Israel. This
removes the pressure from the Judean border. But in spite of the
success of the strategy, the prophet Hanani rebukes the king. He
has failed to trust the Lord and has relied on a pagan nation!
The furious Asa does not repent but imprisons the prophet (16:7–
10).

On balance, however, Asa was one of Judah's more godly kings.

1 Kings 15:25–31. Nadab of Israel (909–909 B.C.)

Nadab is the son of Jeroboam. As the prophet Ahijah has foretold, (1 Kings 14), he is assassinated. His killer destroys Jeroboam's
whole family.

1 Kings 15:33–16:7. Baasha of Israel (908–886 B.C.)

Baasha has replaced Jeroboam's dynasty. But he follows the
apostate system set up by that king. Little is told of Baasha's twenty-
four-year reign. However, he is the king against whom Asa stirs
up Benhadad I, so he did threaten Judah with war.

1 Kings 16:8–20. Elah and Zimri of Israel (886–885 B.C.)

Two minor kings are mentioned, each of whom takes the throne
by murder, and each of whom is killed for the throne he stole.

1 Kings 16:21–28. Omri of Israel (885–874 B.C.)

A civil war between supporters of Tibni and Omri is settled
after some five years by the death of Tibni. Omri "did evil . . .
and sinned more than all those before him" (16:25).

Little is said of Omri in the OT. But other records of that era
give us a picture of his significant reign. The Arameans under
Benhadad I were putting on pressure from the east. Assyria was
expanding, and during Omri's time Ashurnasirpal II (883–859 B.C.)
occupied the lands above Israel even to the Mediterranean Sea.
Omri rebuilt Israel's strength during this critical period. He established a new capitol at Samaria (1 Kings 16:24), built to be a

defensive stronghold. Excavation has shown the high quality of its construction. From the Moabite Stone, a monument found in 1898, we know that "Omri, King of Israel" conquered Moab and imposed tribute. The marriage of his son Ahab to Jezebel, a Phoenician princess, shows he made an important alliance with that coastal power. Final evidence of the resurgence of Israel under this vigorous though evil king is found in inscriptions from several Assyrian rulers, which over a century later still identify Israel as the "land of Omri."

1 Kings 16:29–22:40. Ahab, King of Israel (874–853 B.C.)

No king of Israel or of Judah is given so much space in the OT as Ahab. This is due to the significant religious struggle that developed during his reign.

Jezebel, Ahab's Phoenician wife, was not satisfied with that coexistence of pagan worship with worship of Jehovah which to a great extent marked the history of both Israel and Judah. She introduced the Baal cult of her people (Baal–Melqart), and sought to have it completely replace the faith of Israel. Like other Canaanite religions, this cult was morally degrading and included religious prostitution.

God sent the prophet Elijah to Israel, to confront the king and to stand against the new pagan religion. While it is impossible to know the full impact of Elijah's ministry, there is no doubt he did stem the tide of apostasy.

The biblical record focuses on the religious conflict. But from OT hints and other historical sources we can reconstruct other elements of Ahab's long rule. In general, he was a capable leader. He continued to build (cf. 1 Kings 22:39). Twice he defeated the Aramean forces of Benhadad II. He also joined a coalition of kings who temporarily stopped the advance of the Assyrians under Shalmaneser II at Qarqar in 853 B.C. Ahab also made an alliance with Jehoshaphat of Judah, maintaining the peace that had existed between the two nations since the time of Omri.

The story told in the OT rightly focuses on the struggle between the two faiths in Israel, and on their representatives.

Ahab as King: 1 Kings 16:29–34. The basic evaluation of Ahab is that "he did more evil in the eyes of the Lord than any of those before him" (30).

Elijah and the famine: 1 Kings 17:1–24. Elijah is called to confront Ahab and announce a severe drought in Israel. God cares for the prophet during the terrible three-year famine that settles on the land. Elijah is fed by ravens (17:1–6), and then miracles support him during his stay with the widow of Zerephath (17:7–24).

📖 The stories in chapter 17 are told to every Sunday school child. What truths do you think God was teaching his OT people through the record of these events? What is he teaching you?

Elijah reappears: 1 Kings 18:1–15. Elijah now returns to Israel. He meets a devout believer who is one of Ahab's administrators. This man's fear, and the fact he has been forced to hide a number of prophets because Jezebel "was killing off the prophets of the Lord," gives us some insight into the fierce battle between religious faiths going on at that time, and the persecution of true believers.

On Mount Carmel: 1 Kings 18:16–46. Elijah confronts Ahab and the people of Israel. The people must choose whom they will worship. In a contest held on Mount Carmel, the 450 prophets of Baal call on their impotent god all day. When Elijah prays, fire falls from heaven to consume a water-soaked sacrifice. The people kill the prophets of Baal, and a great rain comes to break the drought. The OT law calls for the execution of false prophets.

Archaeologists have located wells below Mount Carmel which do not go dry, even in droughts.

Elijah's fear: 1 Kings 19:1–9. The furious queen, Jezebel, grimly promises to kill Elijah. Strangely, Elijah is suddenly terrified and flees, aided by God.

God appears to Elijah: 19:9–21. Finally God speaks to Elijah, who has fallen into deep depression. Gently God tells his prophet that there are still 7,000 in Israel who have not bowed to Baal. And God gives Elijah a companion who will become his successor.

📖 Fear and depression may come at surprising times. How does God respond when this happens? What in God's attitude toward Elijah might you want to recall the next time you feel fearful or depressed?

Ben-Hadad attacks Samaria: 1 Kings 20:1–43. The Arameans, with a coalition of kings, attacks Samaria. An unnamed prophet comes to Ahab and promises victory, evidence from Jahweh that "I am the Lord" (13). The inferior Israeli forces drive back the enemy. The next year Israel wins another victory, and Ben-Hadad is taken. When Ahab sets Ben-Hadad free, a prophet appears to condemn this act. Rather than being thankful for the victory, Ahab is "sullen and angry" (43) over the rebuke.

📖 Trace the way in which God has dealt with Ahab (16:29–20:43). What evidences are there of God's patience and his willingness to be gracious? How does Ahab respond to God? What does this tell us about Ahab's character?

Naboth's vineyard: 1 Kings 21:1–29. Ahab decides he wants a vineyard that belongs to a man named Naboth. Naboth will not sell, for family inheritances of land are not to be transferred (4). Jezebel bribes two men to accuse Naboth of treason and blasphemy, and he is executed. The moral character of the king and queen, and of their religion, is clearly revealed in this terrible incident.

Elijah finds Ahab at Naboth's vineyard. He announces God's judgment on this king who has had so many chances to turn to the Lord. Dogs will eat Jezebel's body in the streets, and Ahab's line will be destroyed. Now Ahab repents (27). God graciously extends the time before the judgment will come.

Micaiah prophesies against Ahab: 1 Kings 22:1–39. Ahab makes a treaty with Judah against the Aramaeans. False prophets promise victory, but Jehoshaphat of Judah insists on asking "a prophet of the Lord." Micaiah is called by Ahab, and at first gives a sarcastic response (15). The tone is unmistakable, and Ahab angrily demands to know what God really says (16). Micaiah tells him. Israel will lose the battle, and Ahab will be killed.

Micaiah also reveals that "a lying spirit from the Lord" has deceived Ahab's prophets. The OT teaching on angels and fallen angels makes it clear that even Satan is subject to God (see *Satan* p. 245 and *Angels,* p. 370). The implication in I Kings is that a fallen angel (e.g., a "lying spirit") volunteers to deceive Ahab's prophets, and is permitted to do so by the Lord.

Micaiah's words are from the Lord. In the battle Ahab is killed, and thus the reign of one of the most evil men produced in Israel comes to an end.

1 Kings 22:41–50/2 Chronicles 17:1–21:3. Jehoshaphat of Judah (872–848 B.C.)

Jehoshaphat is the second good king of Judah. He battles the penetration of Baal worship in Judah, and sends Levites on itinerant preaching missions to communicate God's law to all. His own faith is shown when Judah is invaded by enemies.

Jehoshaphat builds a strong army and fortifies many cities. He also revises the legal/judicial system, to fit that ordained in the Mosaic law (cf. 2 Chron. 19:4–11 with Deut. 16:18; 19:12; 21:18 f; 22:13 f).

His primary errors are to make alliances with Israel, none of which prospered. He even marries his son Jehoram to one of Ahab's daughters, who is as evil as her mother Jezebel.

Jehoshaphat's piety: 2 Chronicles 17:1–19. Jehoshaphat's whole-hearted commitment to God is expressed in his purification of Judah. He builds a strong military force, and the peoples around fear to make war on him (10, 11).

Micaiah's prophecy: 2 Chronicles 18:1–19:3. Chronicles retells the story related in I Kings 22, from Jehoshaphat's point of view. The outcome: Israel is defeated, and Ahab killed. But we are also told that Jehoshaphat is rebuked by a prophet named Jehu. The rebuke is a warning for us today as well: "Should you help the wicked and love those who hate the Lord?"

Jehoshaphat's revival efforts: 2 Chronicles 19:4–20:34. Jehosha-phat's efforts to teach and enforce the law bring him strong com-mendation. His trust in God is also honored. When the Moabites and Ammonites attack, Jehoshaphat does not trust his army but turns to God. God fights the battle for Judah, causing the allies to turn against each other. The enemy army is destroyed and Judah does not lose a man.

Jehoshaphat does not succeed in turning Judah to wholehearted commitment to the Lord. But he does remain faithful to God during his twenty-five-year rule.

1 Kings 22:51–53. Ahaziah of Israel (853–852 B.C.)

The son of Ahab succeeds him, but rules only two years.

The time of the divided kingdom saw extensive prophetic activity. Read through 1 Kings 12–22, and make a list of all the prophets mentioned. Then record whom they were sent to, and the nature of their missions. How were their messages received? From these chapters, what can you conclude about the nature and role of prophetic ministry in OT times?

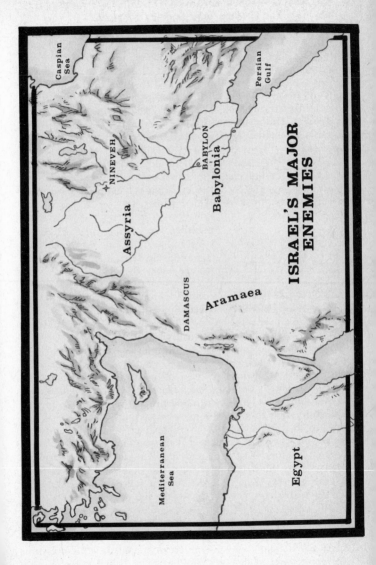

2 KINGS/2 CHRONICLES 21–36
The Divided and Surviving Kingdoms

These books continue the story of the monarchy, begun in 1 Kings and 2 Chronicles 1–20. The Hebrew nation has been broken into a northern kingdom called Israel, and a southern kingdom called Judah. The basic history is contained in Kings, while Chronicles provides a much later commentary on the rulers of Judah (see p. 169 f).

The dates of the kings of Israel and Judah are known, and shown on the chart found on page 193. The books of 2 Kings and Chronicles can be outlined by the reigns of the kings they record. However, there are two major divisions to 2 Kings:

Outline

I. To Israel's Captivity   2 Kings 1–17
II. The Surviving Kingdom   2 Kings 18–25

The prophets. First Kings and 2 Chronicles are dominated by stories of rulers and the prophets God sent to them. These were the "speaking prophets," so called because they delivered their messages verbally and did not write them down.

Now we come to the times of the prophets who wrote our OT books. To understand their writings we need to see them, and grasp their message, in the context of their own times. The chart on page 203 shows both the kings and the prophets of this era, with the approximate dates of their prophetic ministries. In the commentary that follows, the ministry of these prophets will be related to their time. You can turn to their books and see why their messages were important in their own day.

Foreign enemies: This is also an era increasingly dominated by foreign powers who shape the history of Israel and Judah. The map and identity key to these foreign powers, on pages 201 and 203, will orient you to the significant peoples and to their kings.

Increasingly now the old enemies, like Moab and Philistia, which lay next to Palestine, are swallowed up by great world empires. Assyria and Babylon, with Egypt, are dominant. It is the pressure of the great powers, and their rise to empire, which leads first to the fall of Israel and then of Judah. The Bible presents these powers as instruments God uses to purge his people of idolatry.

The Writing Prophets and Their Times

Israel	Prophets		Judah
			885 B.C.
Omri (885–874)			Asa (910–869)
	←Obadiah?		
Ahab (874–853)			Jehoshaphat (872–848)
			—
Ahaziah (853–852)			Jehoram (853–841)
Joram (852–841)			Ahaziah (841)
			Athaliah (841–835)
Jehu (841–814)			Joash (835–796)
	Joel	→	
Jehoahaz (814–798)			
Jehoash (798–782)			Amaziah (796–767)
Jeroboam II (793–753)			
	←Jonah?		Azariah (792–740)
	←Amos		Jothan (750–735)
Zachariah (753)			
Shallum (752)			
			Ahaz (735–715)
Menahem (752–742)			
	←Hosea	Micah →	
Pekah (752–732)			
			Hezekiah (715–686)
Pekahiah (742–740)	Isaiah	→	
Hoshea (732–723)			Manasseh (697–642)
Captivity			Amon (642–640)
Assyria			Josiah (640–609)
722 B.C.			
	Nahum	→	
	Habakkuk	→	
	Zephaniah	→	Jehoahaz (609)
			Jehoiakim (609–598)
	Jeremiah	→	Jehoiachin (598–597)
	Ezekiel	→	Zedekiah (597–586)

Israel's Major Enemies

Aramaea. These originally nomadic peoples formed a number of small states east of Israel. During the times of Ben-Hadad I and Ben-Hadad II (c. 900–841 B.C.), a large kingdom-state that encompassed most of Syria was formed. Israel and Judah alternately fought Aramea and, when under a common threat from Assyria, formed common alliance with her. This OT state is identified at times by its capital, Damascus.

In 802 B.C. Damascus was taken by the Assyrians under Adad-Nirari III and Aramean power was broken. When Assyrian influence ebbed, Jeroboam II of Israel took Damascus. Another leader of whom we read in the Bible, Rezin (c. 740–732 B.C.), won independence, but never restored Aramaean power.

Assyria. This ancient Mesopotamian people had a long imperial history. In the time of the conquest and judges, Assyria was one of the great world powers, with Egypt and the Hittites and the Mittani. When its power expanded west under Tiglath-pileser (1116–1976 B.C.), Assyria came into direct contact with the states of Palestine.

Shalmaneser fought a coalition of Aramaean and Hebrew kings at Qarqar in 805 B.C., and placed the Palestinians under tribute. Adad-nirari III (810–782 B.C.) attacked Damascus, enabling Joash to take back land occupied earlier by Hazael of Damascus. Tiglath-pileser III (745–727 B.C.) successfully expanded Assyrian power to dominate both Aramaea and Israel. His son, Shalmaneser V (727–722 B.C.), took Samaria after a three-year siege, and transported the people of Israel to the area of the upper Euphrates river. The final victory is also claimed in secular records by Sargon II (722–705 B.C.), who co-commanded the Assyrian armies there.

Babylon. Babylon is the city of Chaldea which gave its name to the Babylonian empire of the Bible. The city has an ancient history, going back even before the famous Hammurabi (1792–1750 B.C.). It struggled to become a competing power to the dominant Assyria from 722 B.C. onward. Various bids for independence and power failed until 627 B.C. when Nabopolassar succeeded. By 605 B.C. Babylonian armies were in the west, and Nebuchadnezzar defeated Assyria's Egyptian allies at Carchemish. At this time Babylon established authority over Judah and all Palestine. Three years later Judah rebelled. So in 598 Nebuchadnezzar marched to Palestine. He captured Jerusalem on 15/16 March, 597 B.C. In a series of deportations the people of the Southern Kingdom were carried back to Babylon as captives—God's final punishment of his unfaithful people.

2 Kings 1:1–8:15. Joram King of Israel (852–841 B.C.)

Joram has a brief, twelve-year rule. Most of the space in these chapters is devoted to a description of the ministry of Elisha.

Elisha. The prophet Elisha succeeds Elijah. He ministers to the people and kings of Israel for some fifty years. Like Elijah, Elisha withstands the spread of the cult of Baal-Melqart, introduced into Israel by Jezebel, the mother of King Joram.

Elisha prayed for a "double portion" of Elijah's spirit as enablement for his ministry. The OT reports just twice as many miracles of Elisha as of Elijah. Elisha's miracles tend to reflect compassion, showing something perhaps of this prophet's character. Most, if not all, of the miracles reported here happened during Joram's reign.

Joram's rule. Joram's era is a time of war and foreign pressures. He invades the Moabites (3:4–27) but fails to restore them to a vassal state. The Aramaeans continue to harass Israel, finally bringing Samaria itself under siege (6:24–7:20). Joram continues the religious policies of his parents, and is a devotee of Baal (2 Kings 3:13, cf. 10:19–28). The report of removing an altar set up by his father does not imply a religious change of heart (cf. 3:1–3).

Death of Ahaziah: 2 Kings 1:1–18. Ahaziah, king after Ahab, has injured himself in a fall. The messengers he sends to Philistia to inquire of Baal-Zebub are intercepted by Elijah and sent back. The angry prophet announces Ahaziah's doom, and when he dies, his brother Joram takes the throne.

Elijah taken up: 2 Kings 2:1–18. Elijah is taken directly into heaven by the Lord, in a chariot of fire that appears as a whirlwind. Only one other person is said to have been so taken by God (Enoch, Gen. 5:23, 24).

Elisha asks for a "double portion" of Elijah's spirit. This is a request to be Elijah's successor, for the heir and oldest son in a family is traditionally given a double portion of the family wealth as his inheritance. The request is granted (2:10–12). Returning from the desolate area where Elijah was translated, Elisha carries Elijah's cloak and parts the waters of the Jordan (13–14). This is a sign to other prophets that Elisha is Elijah's successor (cf. 8).

Two miracles: 2 Kings 2:19–25. Elisha's first two miracles set the tone of his ministry. When the people of Jericho appeal to him, Elisha purifies their waters. This is Elisha's ministry of mercy. But when a number of youths (not "children" as in the King

James) jeer at him and thus at God, challenging him to "go up" into heaven as Elijah is supposed to have done, Elisha curses them. Two bears appear and maul 42 of the scoffers. This is Elisha's ministry of standing up for God's honor and in judgment of sin.

Moab revolts: 3:1–27. Moab has ceased to pay the tribute imposed in the time of Omri. So Joram, with Jehoshaphat of Judah, invades. The invasion force tries to cross the desert to surprise the enemy. After seven days they run out of water and are near death. Elisha, honoring the godly king Jehoshaphat, seeks God's guidance. The water needed is provided, and victory over Moab's army follows. However, the combined forces retreat after the king of Moab sacrifices his son. This reaction to human sacrifice is not explained in the OT text or by archaeological finds.

An inscription on what is known as the Moabite Stone tallies with the biblical account. It tells us that in spite of this military victory, the Moabites were not returned to tributary status.

Ministries of mercy: 2 Kings 4:1–6:7. A number of wonders performed by Elisha are now reported (see *Miracles, OT,* p. 79). It is likely but not certain these all take place during Joram's reign.

The mercy miracles are: saving a widow from her creditors (4:1–7), restoring a Shunammite woman's son to life (4:8–37), saving a company of prophets from poisoned food (4:38–41), multiplying food to feed the hungry (4:42–44); healing an enemy general of leprosy (5:1–27), and recovering a borrowed axhead (6:1–7).

Read the accounts of these miracles. What impression do you have of Elisha as a person? What would his miracles have told the people about the nature and the character of God?

Read the story of Naaman (2 Kings 5). The reaction of each key individual in this story tells us both about the nature of faith/unbelief and about values. Study each, and list what you learn of their faith and values. The five are: (1) the young captive girl from Israel, (2) the general, Naaman, (3) the king of Israel, (4) the prophet Elisha, and (5) the prophet's servant, Gehazi.

Ministries of national import: 2 Kings 6:8–8:15. In the period of conflict with Aramaea, Elisha plays a vital role. He often warns the king of Israel of Ben-Hadad's plans (6:9, 10). Finally Ben-Hadad sends a raiding party to take Elisha. Instead the party is deluded and led to Samaria.

Later Samaria is besieged by Ben-Hadad, and its people begin to starve. The king of Israel sees this disaster as God's work (6:33) but does not repent. Instead he determines to kill Elisha in revenge

(6:31)! But the stunned king hears Elisha promise that the next day God will lift the siege and flood the city with food.

That night the enemy army is stricken with terror. The men flee mindlessly, leaving food, riches, horses and mules behind. The prophet's words have come true.

Read this story in 6:24–7:20. If you had to teach a lesson or preach a sermon on this passage, what would you stress? Why?

Elijah's ministry takes him to the land of the enemy, to Damascus (8:7–15). There he weeps as he tells Hazael, who will become a great enemy of God's people, that he is to succeed the ill Ben-Hadad.

2 Kings 8:16–23/2 Chronicles 21:4–20. Jehoram of Judah (851–841 B.C.)

Jehoram's eight-year reign is short and brutal. He has married Jezebel's equally wicked daughter, Athaliah. Now Jehoram follows their religious and moral example. He kills his six brothers to be rid of potential rivals, the only king of Judah to do so. Both Edom and the city of Libna successfully rebel against Judah's authority, and the Philistines, who had feared the godly Jehoshaphat a few years earlier, attack Judah and capture the king's family. Jehoram is cursed by God with a lingering, painful, and fatal disease. When Jehoram dies there is only relief in Judah: no one mourns.

2 Kings 8:25–29/2 Chronicles 22:1–9. Ahaziah of Judah (841 B.C.)

Jehoram's only remaining son rules just one year. He follows his father's example, encouraged in "doing wrong" by his mother Athaliah. He is killed while visiting Joram of Israel.

2 Kings 9:1–10:36. Jehu of Israel (841–814 B.C.)

Jehu is charged by God with the task of wiping out the house of Ahab. He does so, and establishes a dynasty that lasts 89 years. Politically Jehu's 28 years are tormented ones, as outside enemies constantly pummel his land. Both Assyria and Aramaea, under Hazael, invade and subjugate the crumbling Israel.

Jehu's call by God: 9:1–13. Elisha sends a prophet to anoint Jehu, a military commander, as king of Israel. Jehu is told to destroy Ahab's family in vengeance for all the followers of the Lord Jezebel has murdered.

Jehu obeys: 9:14–29. Jehu responds immediately and leads his troops against Joram. He personally kills Joram, and his men mortally wound Ahaziah of Judah.

Jezebel killed: 9:30–37. Jezebel is thrown from a window to her death. Later, when men are sent to bury the body, they find that wild dogs have eaten her body, just as Elijah prophesied (1 Kings 21:23).

Ahab's children destroyed: 10:1–17. All members of the royal house are killed, as are 42 members of Judah's royal family.

Priests of Baal destroyed: 9:18–35. Jezebel and Ahab have established the cult of Baal-Malqart in Israel. Jehu sees this foreign sect, introduced by the dynasty he has destroyed, as a threat. He does not oppose the religion openly. Instead he assembles all its priests and leaders to the principal temple of Baal for sacrifice. There he has the cult leaders killed, and then destroys its idols and worship centers throughout Israel.

But Jehu keeps the false religious system established by Jeroboam I (1 Kings 12). As a result God begins to "reduce the size of Israel" (10:32). During the 28 years of Jehu's rule neither the king nor the people know peace.

2 Kings 11:1–3/2 Chronicles 22:1–12. Athaliah of Judah (841–835 B.C.)

Athaliah shows herself to truly be the daughter of the cruel and vindictive Jezebel. When her son King Azariah is killed, she acts immediately to kill her grandchildren and seize power for herself! No one seems able to withstand the queen mother, and for some six years she holds the throne for herself.

2 Kings 11:1–12:21/2 Chronicles 23:1–24:27. Joash of Judah (835–796 B.C.)

Althaliah has not destroyed all her grandchildren. One, Joash, is snatched up and hidden in the Jerusalem temple. He is hidden there until he reaches the age of seven. Then the high priest, Jehoiada, plans with the Levites and the military to restore this rightful descendant of David to the throne of Judah.

Athaliah hears them rejoicing and comes to investigate. She is killed there, just outside the temple, executed at last for her crimes. Jehoiada leads in a service of covenant renewal (see pp. 85, 124), in which all the people again promise to be the Lord's. Immediately the crowds destroy the altars and worship centers of Baal, to great rejoicing.

Jehoiada the priest is the young king's chief advisor. During Jehoiada's life, Joash follows the Lord. During this period the great Jerusalem Temple is restored and repaired, financed by contributions from the people.

Jehoiada's death brings a change in Joash. He turns from God to worship idols. Zechariah, the son of Jehoiada, is sent by God to warn Joash. But the king does not respond to God's word. Instead he actually orders the death of this son of his old friend and protector.

God permits the Aramaeans under Hazael to overcome Judah's superior forces. Joash is wounded, and then assassinated in bed by those who are against the apostasy of their king.

> **Joel**
>
> A plague of locusts launches the prophet Joel's vision of the future. He warns of the danger of judgment in the form of an invasion by a northern army. He speaks of revival: a time of renewal when God's spirit is poured out. His call to return to God may have been issued during the early years of Joash. See pages 385–388.

2 Kings 13:1–9. Jehoahaz of Israel (814–798 B.C.)

Jehoahaz succeeds his father Jehu on Israel's throne. He continues in the religious policies established by Jeroboam (1 Kings 12), but he does turn to God for relief from the neighboring Aramaeans. The king's prayers are answered. The "deliverer" mentioned in verse 5 is the Assyrian conqueror Adad-Nirari III, who crushes the power of Damascus in 803 B.C. This is one of many incidents in which a foreign army is used by God to discipline or deliver his people.

2 Kings 13:10–25. Jehoash of Israel (798–782 B.C.)

Jehoash follows the religious pattern of all the kings of Israel. But there is a military resurgence toward the end of his sixteen-year rule.

Elisha suffers his final illness in the days of Jehoash. The king is honestly concerned about the prophet's coming death, for Jehoash views Elisha as his kingdom's greatest resource: "the chariots and horsemen of Israel" (14). Toward the end of his reign, Jehoash defeats the Aramaeans. Hazael dies, and this keys a number of military victories. Jehoash is able to push the Damascus power back and to retake a number of Israel's border towns.

2 Kings 14:1–21/2 Chronicles 25:1–28. Amaziah of Judah (796–767 B.C.)

Amaziah begins well. He obeys the written word and the messages of the prophets, and wins a victory over the Edomites. But then Amaziah turns to idolatry. Judah is defeated by Israel, and the king taken captive. The treasures are taken from Jerusalem, and one wall of the city is torn down. This is the ultimate humiliation, for unwalled cities are viewed with contempt as defenseless. It's likely that Amaziah is kept in Samaria as captive for some years, for his son Uzziah (Azariah) becomes co-regent about the time of the defeat.

2 Kings 14:23–28. Jeroboam II of Israel (793–753 B.C.)

Only a few verses in the OT are devoted to Jeroboam II. Yet his forty-one year rule is remarkable. Israel began a resurgence under Jehoash. Her power keeps on growing under Jeroboam, until Israel becomes the leading eastern Mediterranean state.

During this period Assyria is particularly weak. There are pressures from a people called the Urartu; there is internal strife; and Assyria has a series of weak rulers. Just before Jeroboam II, Assyria had mauled the Aramaeans and weakened this enemy of Israel. Now the Assyrians are unable to move against the growing power of Israel.

Jeroboam II fills the power vacuum. He recovers all the Transjordan, and expands Israel to the limits of Solomon's days (cf. 2 Kings 14:25 with 1 Kings 8:65). He also takes Damascus and Hamath, which had belonged to Judah in David's time.

The time of Jeroboam II is a time of great prosperity. The wealth, and the luxury of the

> **Jonah**
>
> About this time, Jonah is sent to Nineveh, the capital of Assyria. He is to warn the people of God's judgment. Nineveh repents and is saved, to the prophet's frustration. Within decades, a revived Assyria will carry Jonah's fellow Israelites into captivity. See pages 399–404.

> **Amos**
>
> Amos condemns the Israel of Jeroboam II as an unjust society. He warns the materialistic people to return to God and to justice. Nineveh had repented under the preaching of Jonah. Now God's people have had the opportunity to repent. The prophet's message and ministry are discussed on p. 389.

rich, as well as the lack of concern of that society for the poor, are graphically portrayed in the Book of the prophet Amos. But the king and the people continue to do evil, nor will they turn away from the false religious system instituted by the first Jeroboam (1 Kings 12).

2 Kings 15:1–6/2 Chronicles 26:1–23. Uzziah (Azariah) of Judah (792–740 B.C.)

Uzziah, called Azariah in 2 Kings, rules for some 52 years in Jerusalem. For the first 24 he is co-regent with his father, Amaziah. Uzziah is a contemporary of Jeroboam II, and during this time Judah too knows a great resurgence of prosperity.

Uzziah reorganizes his army, extends his territory, and after the death of Jeroboam II surpasses Israel in influence. Assyrian records dating to Uzziah's forty-eighth year identify him (Ariau of Yaudi) as the chief of a coalition of kings organized to defend against her.

Uzziah is a godly king. But his successes bring character change. "After Uzziah became powerful, his pride led to his downfall" (2 Chron. 26:16). The king is struck with leprosy and lives in isolation until his death.

The year Uzziah dies Isaiah, who becomes one of the greatest of the prophets, receives his call from God to a ministry that will span many decades.

2 Kings 15:8–16. Zechariah and Shallum of Israel (753, 752 B.C.)

In quick succession these two take the throne, and are assassinated.

2 Kings 15:17–22. Menahem of Israel (752–742 B.C.)

Menahem represents the seventh ruling family in the north. He was one of Jeroboam II's administrators, in Tirzah. He assassinates Shallum and claims the throne. But now Assyria is strong again. The great Tiglath-pileser III puts down Babylonian and Urartu threats in the north and south, and then turns west to the Mediterranean world. Menahem is forced to buy off the threatening Assyri-

> **Hosea**
> Hosea rebukes Israel for its unfaithfulness to God, and announces that she will now be treated without pity by the Lord. For a picture of the sins that cause the rejection, see pages 378–384.

ans. He continues to rule, but as a vassal king under the Assyrian overlord.

2 Kings 15:23–31. Pekahiah and Pekah of Israel (752–732 B.C.)

The last confusing years of Israel saw internal strife as well as war. Pekah, one of Menahem's officials, sets up a rival kingdom across the Jordan at Gilead. A dozen years later Pekah crosses the Jordan with fifty men and kills Pekahiah. He is probably supported by an anti-Assyrian party, incensed at the heavy taxes levied to pay off that power. He rules eight years as sole king.

Pekah forms an alliance with Rezin of Damascus and rebels against Assyria. The two attack Judah, but Ahaz appeals to Assyria for help. Tiglath-pileser II returns, devastates Damascus, and executes Rezin. Before Israel is attacked, Pekah is assassinated and the killer, Hoshea, confirmed by Assyria as vassal ruler. But Assyria strips away much of Israel's territory. Galilee and the Transjordan become Assyrian provinces, and Israel is reduced to the hills west of the Jordan.

2 Kings 15:32–38/2 Chronicles 27:1–9. Jotham of Judah (750–735 B.C.)

It is difficult to sort out the dates of this king of Judah. While he is still co-regent with his father Uzziah, he makes his own son Ahaz his co-regent. Thus Judah has three overlapping kings living at the same time. We do know that Jotham is the fourth of Judah's godly kings, and that God keeps his nation strong and free.

2 Kings 16/2 Chronicles 28. Ahaz of Judah (735–715 B.C.)

When Ahaz becomes sole ruler on the death of his godly father, he turns his back on the Lord. He follows the most detestable of the pagan religious practices. God acts in quick judgment. Judah is defeated on every side, and many of her people are taken captive. Ahaz is desperate and appeals to Assyria, thus surrendering any claim to independence, and Judah becomes a vassal state.

What lessons should Judah and Israel have drawn from the king's actions and military reverses? How do you explain his strange behavior? What lessons can you learn from this king?

2 Kings 17. Hoshea, and Israel's Exile (732–723 B.C.)

When Tiglath-pileser dies, Hoshea rebels against his son. A treaty is made with Egypt, and tribute withheld. This is foolish, for Egypt is in a particularly weakened state.

Shalmaneser V (727–722) does not hesitate, and returns with his armies. Hoshea crumbles. He rushes to meet the Assyrian with his tribute money. He is taken captive, and Israel is invaded. It takes three years (724–722), but Samaria finally falls, and the history of Israel ends.

Exile. Assyria's policy is to take defeated people from their lands and resettle them. This is designed to shatter nationalistic feeling and prevent future rebellions. People from many nations are brought in to settle Israel's vacated lands.

The "ten lost tribes." Israel's exile has stimulated much speculation about the fate of the ten "lost" tribes. Wild theories have suggested that the British, or the American Indians, are descended from these "lost" peoples. But the tribes are not lost! The original division of the land into two kingdoms saw many peoples from Israel move south to Judah. These were those who refused to accept the false worship system instituted by Jeroboam I, and who came to Judah for the freedom to worship the Lord (1 Kings 12:27; cf. 2 Chron. 11:13–17). Thus representatives from all the families of Israel are included in the "two" tribes of Judah, and none of God's people have been "lost."

Some have suggested, because Assyrian records list only 27,290 deportees, that most of the Israelites stayed in the land. It is best to understand this number as those taken when Samaria fell, and to realize that the others would have been moved during the siege of the capital. The OT record itself seems to suggest that most if not all the Israelites were taken (cf. 2 Kings 17:20).

Historical impact. The people of Israel were replaced by others from a number of regions of the Assyrian empire (17:24). These people brought their own gods and cults, but also added worship of Jahweh, who was viewed as a local deity who should be worshiped to avoid his displeasure. This thinking was typical of the time.

The imported peoples' worship of God was always mixed with the worship of pagan deities as well (17:33). In NT times their descendants are the familiar "Samaritans" of the Gospels, who were held in contempt by the Pharisees and other orthodox Jews.

Read the 2 Kings 17 summary of the reasons for Israel's judgment (17:7–23). Compare this with the warnings given in the Scripture when the law was first instituted (Deut. 28:15–68).

2 Kings 18–20/2 Chronicles 29–32. Hezekiah of Judah. (715–686 B.C.)

Hezekiah is co-regent with his father Ahaz when the northern kingdom falls to Assyria. He assumes full control some four years before his father's death.

Hezekiah proves to be one of Judah's most godly kings. He reopens the temple, reinstitutes the festivals ordained in the law, and purges the land of its places for idol worship.

> **Micah**
> Micah prophecies before and after the fall of Israel. He speaks to confront Israel and Judah with their sin, and to explain the Assyrian invasion as God's judgment. He undoubtedly helps stimulate the revival under King Hezekiah. See pages 405–409.

Unlike his father, Hezekiah is anti-Assyrian. But he wisely holds back from open hostilities until after the death of Sargon II in 705. However, his successor invades Judah in 701. When the fortified city of Lachish is taken by Sennacherib, Hezekiah submits. But the Assyrians seem determined to destroy Jerusalem. When a delegation jeers at the land and its God, Hezekiah brings the matter to the Lord with great faith. Jerusalem is spared.

A number of events in Hezekiah's times are reported in detail in 2 Kings and 2 Chronicles, and in chapters 37 through 39 of Isaiah.

Evaluation of Hezekiah: 2 Kings 18:1–8; 2 Chronicles 29:1–11. Hezekiah is praised as one who does "right in the eyes of the Lord" (18:3). The first month of the first year of his reign he opens the temple and proclaims his intention to be faithful to the Lord (29:10)

Hezekiah's revival in depth: 2 Chronicles 29:12–31:21. The book of 2 Chronicles gives details of Hezekiah's steps

> **Isaiah**
> Much of the wide-ranging ministry of Isaiah takes place in Hezekiah's time, and the prophet is a familiar figure at court. Isaiah directs his words to Judah, and deals with the difficult religious, social, international, and theological issues that are raised by events in these troubling times. See pages 282–312.

toward religious revival. He gathers the Levites and reassigns them to the duties first planned by David (29:25). They cleanse and purify the temple, and once again make offerings there. Hezekiah sends couriers to all Judah and Israel, inviting them to come and keep Passover.

After a full week of celebration and offerings, the people spread out through the land, smashing the hillside shrines and worship centers that remain.

For the first time in decades, the people bring their tithes and offerings, so the priests and Levites are able to dedicate themselves to serving God.

Israel deported: 2 Kings 18:9–12. In Hezekiah's fourth year Israel is invaded by the Assyrians. In the sixth Samaria is taken, and the people of the neighboring northern kingdom are deported and sent into exile (see p. 222).

Sennacherib threatens Jerusalem: 2 Kings 18:13–37; 2 Chronicles 32:1–19. Eight years later, in Hezekiah's fourteenth year, Sennacherib of Assyria takes Judah's fortified cities. Hezekiah strips the temple and his treasury to pay Assyria a ransom of eleven tons of silver and one ton of gold. But a delegation comes to the Holy City, ridicules Hezekiah's faith and his god, and demands surrender and deportation. These taunts, and other letters which ridicule God, speak of him as though he were one of the empty deities of pagan peoples.

Hezekiah's prayer: 2 Kings 19:1–19. Hezekiah is shaken, in part by the affront to God and the disgraceful ridicule. He spreads the letters out before the Lord in the temple, and asks the Lord to intervene for his own glory (see *Prayer, OT,* p. 216).

Study the report of this incident in 2 Kings 18 and 19. What pressures are on Hezekiah? How does his faith hold up under pressure? Can you describe his emotions? What do you learn about the meaning of faith and prayer that you can apply in your own life?

God's answer: 2 Kings 19:20–37; 2 Chronicles 32:20–23. Isaiah brings God's word to Hezekiah. The Lord has heard his prayer. Judah will survive, and the king of Assyria will not see a single arrow released against Jerusalem.

That night 185,000 men in the Assyrian army die! Sennacherib returns to his capital of Nineveh, where he is assassinated by two of his sons.

The Assyrian records of this invasion claim conquest of 46 strong cities in Judah, and the capture of 200,000 persons. They make no claim to the capture of Jerusalem, saying only that the king shut Hezekiah in that city "like a bird in a cage." Sennacherib makes no mention of the disaster which struck his army. But no ancient conqueror raised monuments to his defeats. However, the Greek historian Herodotus tells of Sennacherib's army being attacked by field mice, which ate their weapons and forced a withdrawal. It may be that rats and mice, the plague-carriers of Europe as well as of the East, were the instruments God used to deliver his people. Cf. Isaiah 36, 37.

Prayer, OT

The OT records many prayers offered to God by his people. A survey of them helps us discern a number of basic prayer principles which infuse this most intimate of experiences with God.

First, although rituals are often associated with OT prayer, the Bible makes a clear distinction between empty formality and true heart worship (cf. Isa. 29:13; 5:21–24). There is such a thing as meaningless prayer.

Second, access to God in prayer is an outcome of covenant relationship. The OT saint comes to God with confidence because God has chosen to commit himself to a relationship with his people (see *Covenant, OT,* p. 51). Prayer then is an outgrowth of personal relationship and an expression of personal relationship.

Third, appeals in prayer are based either on promises already made in God's Word, or on the revealed character of the Lord. The basis for confidence in prayer is not what the believer has done or will do, but instead rests on the foundation of who God himself is.

Fourth, God hears every kind of petition. Prayers offered for the nation and those that are the heart cries of burdened individuals are alike the concern of Israel's God. The certainty that God truly does care is an important dimension in true prayer.

Fifth, OT prayer recognizes God as One who is not limited or bound by circumstances. No matter how grim the situation, God can intervene, through natural processes or by setting aside "natural law" (see *Miracles, OT,* p. 79). Because God's power is unlimited, the believer can have unlimited confidence in him.

Sixth, God is sovereign. No believer has the right to command him, or the wisdom to counsel him. Prayer in the OT is not an effort to manipulate or an attempt to tell God what he must do. Instead, prayer is an expression of the believer's submission to God and his confidence that God's purposes and plans are best.

Seventh, the believer can be totally honest with God in prayer. There is no need to pretend—to mask emotions.

Eighth, OT prayer is intimately linked with thanksgiving and praise. These are offered when prayers are answered, but also often accompany the prayers themselves. For thanksgiving is appropriate in the unique relationship we have with the Lord, which permits us to talk with him.

For Study. Examine the following OT prayers and see how the various principles above find expression: Genesis 18:16–33; 24:39–45; Exodus 32:5–14; Numbers 11:4–17; 1 Samuel 1:9–17; 2:1–10; 2 Samuel 7:18–29; 12:13–

23; 1 Kings 8:22–53; 2 Kings 19:14–19; 2 Chronicles 20:5–12; Ezra 9:6–15; Nehemiah 1:4–11.

Hezekiah's illness: 2 Kings 20:1–11; Isaiah 38. Near death, Hezekiah prays emotionally for healing. Isaiah announces God's reprieve. Hezekiah's thoughts and feelings at this time are recorded in Isaiah 38.

Envoys from Babylon: 2 Kings 20:11–21; Isaiah 39. The king of Babylon sends Hezekiah congratulations on his recovery. At this time Babylon is a distant and insignificant power. Foolishly Hezekiah shows the envoys all his wealth and his armory. Isaiah angrily rebukes him: the day is coming when the Babylonians will carry away the wealth Hezekiah has displayed, and Judah's people as well.

Hezekiah's accomplishments: 2 Chronicles 32:24–33. Hezekiah's age is a time of prosperity and building in Judah, and he continues in lifelong devotion to the Lord.

2 Kings 21:1–27/2 Chronicles 33:1–20. Manasseh of Judah (697–642 B.C.)

Manasseh succeeds his father, Hezekiah, and rules for fifty-five years. The first eleven are as co-regent with his father. He is one of Israel's most evil kings. He practices sorcery and witchcraft, burns his sons in idol worship, and brings idols within the Jerusalem temple itself. And he leads his people into practices more evil than the Canaanites God's people replaced! It is probable that Isaiah is one of the prophets killed at his order.

The whole people's eager plunge into evil brings judgment. All of Judah will soon be led captive, as was Israel. As for Manasseh, he is taken captive by the Assyrians. The OT describes his humiliation. He is chained, and a metal hook set in his lips, by which he is led away. This practice is shown in Assyrian inscriptions.

The Assyrian ruler of that time is unnamed, but is probably Esarhaddon. Chronicles says Manasseh was taken to Babylon, and Esarhaddon rebuilt that city after its destruction by his father.

Chronicles tells us of Manasseh's repentance and his conversion while in captivity. He is released and returns to Judah. There he spends the final four or five years of his rule attempting to recall Judah to serve the Lord (33:15–17). But he cannot undo the impact of forty-five years of evil example.

Manasseh dies, a vivid personal illustration of God's grace.

Manasseh illustrates several principles expressed by the prophet Ezekiel in chapter 18 of his book. Read Ezekiel 18 and see if you can relate its teachings to the life of this wicked king. Be sure you relate the chapter to Manasseh's heritage from his father as well.

2 Kings 21:19–26/2 Chronicles 33:21–25. Amon of Judah (642–640 B.C.)

Amon is not touched by his father's experience. He does evil and is assassinated by his own officials in his second year.

2 Kings 22:1–23:20/2 Chronicles 34, 35. Josiah of Judah (640–609 B.C.)

Josiah is the last good king of Judah. He is crowned when he is only 8, and rules in Jerusalem for 31 years.

The power of Assyria slips during Josiah's three decades. During the later years of his rule, Babylon suddenly surges to unexpected dominance. But Josiah's 30 years are a time of peace.

Josiah's time is also one of reform. Josiah's grandfather, Manasseh, had apparently destroyed all copies of the law of Moses that he could locate.

> **Habakkuk**
> Concerned about the evil that still characterizes Judah in spite of Josiah's reforms, the prophet cries out to Israel's holy God. God shows the prophet he will not tolerate evil. God is doing a striking thing: he is raising up the Chaldeans (Babylon). They will scourge his sinning people. See page 412.

Josiah experiences a personal conversion at age 16 (2 Chron. 34:3), and at 20 attempts to purge Judah of false worship. During refurbishing of the temple a copy of the lost law is found.

Josiah's early reforms: 2 Chronicles 34:1–13. Josiah begins by destroying pagan idols and worship centers. The burning of the bones of the dead on the altar defiles them so they can never be used again.

Book of the law found: 2 Kings 22:3–20; 2 Chronicles 34:14–33. Lost copies of the

> **Nahum**
> Nahum's message is one of judgment on Nineveh, the capital of Assyria. The message means more than the doom of an old enemy. It is a warning to Judah, that her punishment too must surely come. See page 410.

Mosaic law are located when the Temple is repaired. The first reading reveals how short Judah has fallen of obedience, and the fact that God is committed by his word to punish Judah's wickedness (see Deut. 28). Josiah sends to Huldah the prophetess, to inquire about what God will do. The response is encouraging. Judgment must come, but because Josiah has been responsive to God, the destruction will be delayed until after his death.

Total dedication: 2 Kings 23:1–28; 2 Chronicles 35:1–19. Guided by the Scriptures, Josiah sets about his reformation with fresh zeal. Again God's people keep the Passover. Again the Levites are called back to temple service. Josiah redoubles his efforts to destroy local shrines, and even goes into the territory of Israel to desecrate the altar at Bethel, thus fulfilling prophecy (1 Kings 13:1–3). And the king leads all the people in a ceremony of covenant renewal (see pages 84, 132).

Josiah's death: 2 Kings 25:29–30; 2 Chronicles 35:20–27. In the world outside of Judah great changes are taking place. The Babylonians have begun to replace Assyria, defeating them in a series of great battles. A decisive battle seems to be coming.

In 609 B.C. Pharaoh Necho II of Egypt hurries north with an army to support the Assyrians, in a desperate attempt to keep Babylonia from becoming the dominant world power. Josiah attempts to stop the Egyptians at Megiddo and is killed in the battle. The struggle with Egypt is futile, for the Assyrians are crushed. Judah has lost her last godly king. And Babylon, God's instrument of discipline for sinning Judah, will soon be the unquestioned master of the world.

Josiah's reform reproduces other reform efforts of godly kings. Compare his efforts (2 Chron. 34, 35) with the reform of Hezekiah (2 Chron. 29–31). What common elements mark the revivals? What can you learn about a personal return to God after straying?

Look again at the reforms of Josiah and Hezekiah. What are the sins that each must deal with? What does this tell you about the nature of drift away from God, and what modern dangers might exist?

2 Kings 23:31–35/2 Chronicles 36:1–4. Jehoahaz of Judah (609 B.C.)

Jehoahaz rules in Jerusalem for only three months. He is taken by Pharaoh-Necho to Egypt, and dies in captivity.

2 Kings 23:36–24:7/2 Chronicles 36:5–8. Jehoiakim of Judah (609–598 B.C.)

Jekoiakim is also a son of Josiah. But like his deposed brother Jehoahaz he is evil. And Jehoiakim is a foolish and ineffective ruler. Jehoiakim foolishly misuses his kingdom's resources. Though pressed between Egypt and Babylon, he raises taxes and labor levies to build himself a new palace, which leads Jeremiah to suggest he should be "buried with the burial of an ass" (Jer. 22:19, RSV).

The political issue is settled when Egypt and Babylon meet at Carchemish in 605 B.C. The Babylonian victory assures her king, Nebuchadnezzar, of unquestioned world dominance.

Judah is soon invaded. Jehoiakim submits, but within three years he rebels, rejecting the warnings of God's prophets.

> **Zephaniah**
> This prophet's ministry, like that of Jeremiah, begins in the time of Josiah, and spans the rule of several kings. His burden is to warn Judah that punishment for her sins must surely come and cannot be avoided. See page 417.

Jehoiakim is the king who tears up the first draft of Jeremiah's written prophecies (Jer. 36:23). It is during his reign that Daniel and his friends are deported to Babylon. And it is from this first invasion and deportation that the seventy years of the Babylonian captivity will be numbered.

2 Kings 24:8–17/2 Chronicles 36:9–10. Jehoiachin of Judah (598–587 B.C.)

After just three months as king in Jerusalem, the city is besieged and Jehoiachin taken captive to Babylon. At this time a much larger group of captives is deported, along with all the treasures left in the temple and the royal treasury.

2 Kings 24:18–25/2 Chronicles 36:11–23. Zedekiah of Judah (597–586 B.C.)

Despite the desperate political situation, this king too is committed to evil. He is particularly set against the messages of God through Jeremiah, who constantly urges the king and people to be subject to Babylon. Zedekiah comes very close to killing the great prophet for his "unpatriotic" views.

During Zedekiah's rule Ezekiel is transported in a vision from Babylon to the Jerusalem temple. He sees the sins that infest the holy place, and he describes the gradual withdrawal of the glory of God from the place where he established his presence in the days of Solomon (cf. Ezek. 8–11; 2 Chron. 7:1–4).

Zedekiah has been placed on his throne by Nebuchadnezzar, and given his name by that conqueror. He is the third son of Josiah to rule. Like his brothers, the new king refuses to follow God's guidance or to honor the Lord. Still, Zedekiah is more shrewd than his predecessor. When a coalition is formed by Edom, Moab, Ammon, and Phoenicia against Babylon (Jer. 27:1–3), Zedekiah holds back. The urgings of the anti-Babylonian party and even the promises of false prophets that God has already broken Babylon's yoke fails to move Zekediah to rebel.

> **Jeremiah**
>
> Jeremiah's long ministry extends from Josiah's day past the extinction of Judah. His call is first to warn Judah to submit to Babylon, and then afterward to encourage, with the promise that God will bring his people back to the land and one day make a new covenant with his people. See pages 313–335.

But some five years later, a new Pharaoh makes the king a promise of support. Encouraged by the aid committed by Psammethichus II, Zekediah rebels. Early in 588 B.C. Nebuchadnezzar marches west. The Babylonians have little difficulty in disposing of Egypt. After an interrupted siege, Jerusalem is taken. Zedekiah's children are killed and he is blinded. The remaining treasures of the temple are raped, and the city and temple burned. Now most of the remaining population are taken captive to join their brothers in Babylon.

> **Ezekiel**
>
> While Jeremiah prophesies in Judah, Ezekiel speaks in Babylon to the captives. The two prophets have the same message. Judah must submit. The exile is God's punishment, and he will not relent until his people are purged. See pages 339–360.

The era of the kingdom has ended as did the era of the judges— in sin, in misery, and in defeat.

THE BABYLONIAN CAPTIVITY

The deportation of the people of Judah by Nebuchadnezzar initiated a seventy-year period of captivity in Babylon. This was a time of judgment for God's people. Like other disciplines God has chosen to use, the captivity had a purifying impact and helps shape the course of future history.

In the land. The final deportation in 586 B.C. stripped Judah of most of its population, leaving only a handful of "the poor of the land" (2 Kings 25:12) in the southern kingdom. Babylon did not follow the Assyrian policy of intermixing populations, so no foreign peoples were imported to replace the exiles. The story of those who are left behind is told by Jeremiah, who stayed with them when given a choice by the Babylonians (see Jer. 40–44).

Nebuchadnezzar took away the king, and appointed a governor named Gedaliah, who established his seat in Mizpeh. Archaeology has shown that most of the cities of Judah, as well as Jerusalem, had been devastated by Nebuchadnezzar.

In just two months Gedaliah is murdered by a member of the royal family who fled Judah earlier. The murderer takes hostages and flees. Johanan, Gedaliah's military commander, pursues the killers and retakes the hostages, but the murderers escape. The population is now terrified at the prospect of Nebuchadnezzar's reaction.

Jeremiah is asked for a word from God. When the message comes some ten days later it is a warning against turning toward Egypt—and a promise that if the people stay in Judah there will be no reprisals. But the prophet's word is rejected, and Jeremiah is accused of lying! The people make offerings to their pagan gods and goddesses, and seek refuge in Egypt.

The remaining people gather and migrate to a district in Egypt's eastern delta. Jeremiah goes with them, continuing his warnings. For a time the company stays together. Then gradually they scatter. Because of their disobedience, none of these people or their descendants will return to the Promised Land.

Archaeological research provides insights into these scattered communities. Particularly significant are papyri dating to the fifth century B.C. The Elephantine papyri, which take their name from the island colony of their origin, tell of a group of Jews living

The City of Babylon

on the Nile some 500 miles from the Mediterranean. The Aramaic writings speak of a temple to Jahweh, and include orders from Persian overlords to keep Passover. But they also speak of worship of at least three other deities, so these Jews' worship of the Lord was not pure. Around 405 B.C. the papyri record correspondence between these Egyptian Jews and those who have returned to Jerusalem from Babylon. Sanballat, governor in the days of Nehemiah, is mentioned in the letters, as is the high priest named in Nehemiah 12.

The captives. There were three staged deportations of captives to Babylon. The first group was taken in 605 B.C. This group included choice individuals taken for special training. Among them were Daniel and the three friends we read of in the Book of Daniel.

A second group of captives was taken in 597 B.C. It is difficult to ascertain how many were in this group. A specific number is mentioned in 2 Kings 24:15, 16, but it is clear that these are members of special classes. Jeremiah lists a smaller number arriving in Babylon (52:28–30). Albright explains this by a high mortality rate on the long desert trek to Babylon.

The final deportation came in 586 B.C. This was probably the largest group taken, as it included all but the "poor" who remained. It has been estimated that probably some 70,000 altogether arrived in Babylon.

While the captivity was a punishment, it was not marked by any unusual suffering. Archaeology tells us that the urbanized Babylonians recognized three levels of citizens. *Awelin* were free men of the upper classes. *Wardu* were slaves. *Mushkenu* were free men of lower classes. It's likely the Jewish captives were settled and became members of this third class.

We know from archaeological discoveries and from the OT that the Jews had many privileges. They were taken to several settlements, the best known being a district called Tel-abib by the river (actually a canal) Chebar. There they worked on the king's building projects, or entered business as merchants. Babylonian records show Jewish names on records of business transactions, and at least one successful trading house was owned and operated by Jews.

Babylonian records also tell us that King Jehoiachin was released from prison and given court apartments. There are even records of the food and oil ordered for him and his five sons, and his servants.

The typical exile may well have owned his own home and raised garden crops (Jer. 29:4,7; Ezek. 8:1; 12:1–7). The land on which they lived was irrigated and fertile, and many even in the early days sent money back to Jerusalem. By the time a return was possible, many decided to stay in Babylon, unwilling to trade their prosperity for the privilege of pioneering the now deserted land God had given their fathers.

We also know from Jeremiah and Ezekiel that there was considerable self-government permitted. The Jewish community had its own elders, and priests and prophets played leading roles.

Yet with all these privileges, Babylon was still a punishment from God. The Book of Lamentations shares with us the agony that many of the godly felt in a foreign land, where in spite of personal prosperity true believers realized they simply did not belong.

Babylon. Nebuchadnezzar the Great led the armies that had overrun the West and taken Judah. He began his conquests in 605 B.C., and ruled for some 43 years. As a conqueror none could withstand him. As a builder, few could equal him.

The city Babylon became a great city under Nebuchadnezzar, and he later boasted that his building efforts had made it great. He built a third wall around the city, which written records from his day describe:

A great wall which like a mountain cannot be moved I made of mortar and brick. . . . Its foundations upon the bosom of the abyss I placed down deeply . . . its top I raised mountain high. I triplicated the city wall in order to strengthen it, I caused a great protecting wall to run at the foot of the wall of burnt brick. . . .

Nebuchadnezzar's building efforts included temples, streets, an entire district of the city, and the great terraced mountain that he raised and covered with hanging gardens. The Greeks were so impressed by this man-made mountain of greenery that they listed it among the seven wonders of the ancient world. And all of this is described by Nebuchadnezzar with great boasting:

Huge cedars from Lebanon, their forests with my clean hands I cut down. With radiant gold I overlaid them, with jewels I adorned them . . . the side chapels of the shrine of Nebo, the cedar beams of their roofs I adorned with lustrous silver. Giant bulls I made of bronze work and clothed them with white marble. I adorned them with jewels and placed them upon the threshold of the gate of the shrine. . . .

Nebuchadnezzar's accomplishments were great. But so was his pride, as the Book of Daniel attests.

Nebuchadnezzar was succeeded by a series of rulers who were never able to match his greatness. Amel-marduk ruled only two years. He was assassinated by his brother-in-law, Nergal-shar-usur, in 560 B.C. This man was an official under Nebuchadnezzar in 586 B.C. (cf. Jer. 29:3, 13). Nabonidus (556–539 B.C.) took the throne from Nergal-shar-usur's young son. Belshazzar, Nabonidus's son, was his co-regent for some ten years, and ruled from Babylon while his father lived in Tema.

Daniel lived through the rule of all of these kings of Babylon. Early in the reign of Nebuchadnezzar he won a post which made him one of the king's closest advisors. He had served in some administrative post for 63 years when the Persians replaced the Babylonian rulers. Then, past 80, he was still valued enough to become one of the three principal administrators under Cyrus who governed the 120 provinces of that great empire.

Impact of the captivity. It was during the days of captivity that the Hebrew people began to be called Jews, after Judah. But there were other, far-reaching results of the exile.

(1) *Idolatry.* The Jews had always been susceptible to idol worship. Over and over this sin had entrapped the people in Palestine, to lead king and commoner away from dedication to the Lord. But after the captivity, idolatry no longer is attractive to Israel. In fact, later attempts to force Israel to worship idols is resisted to the death. So the captivity does purify God's people of this besetting sin of the pre-Exile people.

(2) *The synagogue.* The captivity also seems to be the source of a new institution, the synagogue. The word simply means "gathering," and the belief is that without the temple as a focus for the nation's worship, smaller groups of Jews began to assemble for worship and study of the written Word.

There is little documentary evidence, but it seems likely that the passion for personal and group study which finds expression in the synagogue originates in this period (see Ezra 7:10). Thus a study of the Word began to take precedence over the worship rituals which dominated Hebrew life in the days of the temple. When the temple was rebuilt, ritual and study continued side by side.

(3) *The scribes.* The OT speaks of "Ezra the scribe" as a man who "devoted himself to the study and observance of the Law of the Lord, and to teaching its decrees and laws in Israel" (7:10). While of the priestly line, Ezra's authority clearly rests on his ability to interpret and instruct in the law.

One reason for such interpreters is found in the fact that the

Jewish people now speak Aramaic, while the OT is written in Hebrew. Thus a translator as well as interpreter became necessary. Parts of both Ezra and Daniel are written in Aramaic rather than Hebrew.

Gradually the importance of these interpreters was magnified. Their writings were collected, and their explanations of the Law came to have the same weight as the Scriptures. These are the "traditions" which Jesus condemns in his confrontations with the Pharisees.

By NT times the connection between the scribe and the priesthood no longer exists, and anyone who was schooled in the law and religious wisdom could win recognition as a "rabbi" (teacher).

(4) *Times of the Gentiles.* Descendants of David continued among the people of Israel. But never again has any actually sat upon the throne of a free Israel. Throughout Bible times the Jews were subject to some foreign power, whether Babylon, Persia, Rome, or some other. This period of gentile domination is spoken of in the prophets who wrote during and after the Exile. The times will come to an end when the promised Messiah returns to lift Israel to the place God intends, at the head of all the nations.

(5) *The remnant.* The captivity and return establishes another OT principle: that of the remnant. Isaiah and others speak of the remnant as a message of hope for captive Israel. No matter how the nation is judged and purged, there will always be a core of the faithful remaining to carry on the nation's identity and to fulfill her destiny.

The remnant principle is illustrated in several ways in the Captivity. First, it insists that sinners will be purged. This happened in the land, as many were casualties of the warfare that swept over Judah. Many others died on their way to Babylon. But not all the unfaithful died. Some left the land to go to Egypt, and were lost from the stage of history. Others chose to remain in Babylon when the time came to return, selling their birthright for the possessions they had gained in that pagan land. These too were purged— but by prosperity.

When the call comes to return, it is only those moved by God who choose to leave. Thus the purified and religiously motivated turn toward Jerusalem, to establish a presence in the land of promise that testifies to their belief in God's faithfulness to his covenant promises.

Two views of the wall decorations from the palace of Babylon now in the Berlin Museum.

THE RETURN FROM CAPTIVITY

Jeremiah the prophet identified a period of seventy years during which the Jews would be kept in captivity, away from their land and their heritage (25:11–12; 29:10). The return Jeremiah promised was accomplished on time. But it required a change in world leadership, which God brought about at his intended time.

The Persian Empire. Babylon had replaced Assyria as dominant world power—a feat accomplished under brilliant military leadership. Babylon itself fell to another brilliant conqueror, Cyrus the Great. The rise of Cyrus was spectacular. Coming from a minor district in the east, Cyrus took the province of Persia. By 550 B.C. he had added the larger Media. He then crushed King Croesus and added Lydia to his territories. In 539 Babylon itself fell. The city surrendered without a fight, and welcomed Cyrus as a deliverer. Now Cyrus simply placed himself and his officials atop the Babylonian administrative system, and then controlled more land than anyone before him. From the Aegean Sea to India, the east was his.

The Medo-Persians retained control of the empire all during the extended time of the Jewish return to their land.

Cambyses (530–522) succeeded his father Cyrus, and added Egypt to the empire. Darius Hytaspes (522–486) was the next ruler. He was a military commander, but showed much skill in reorganizing the empire. He attempted to move into Europe, but was thrown back by the Greeks at the battle of Marathon in 490 B.C. Darius was succeeded by Xerxes. He invaded Greece and burned Athens, but he too was at last thrown back. This Xerxes, called Ahasuerus in the Bible, is the person who makes the Jewish girl Esther his queen.

The final Persian ruler of this period who overlaps the Bible record is Artaxerxes (465–425).

The OT books that tell the story of the return fit into this extended period of time during which the Persian empire has replaced the Babylonian, and prior to its own fall before a victorious Alexander the Great of Macedon.

Dates of the return. The deportation to Babylon came in stages, with different groups of Jews taken there in 605, 597, and 586 B.C. The return also took place in stages. A pioneer group headed

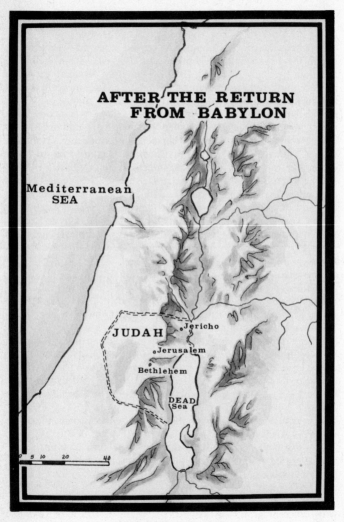

Judah after the Exile

home in 538 B.C., a second group came some eighty years later in 458, and a final group in 444 B.C.

The return was possible because Cyrus reversed the policy of the Assyrians and Babylonians, and encouraged ethnic groups to go back to their homelands. In the first year of his rule in Babylon, Cyrus, possibly influenced by Daniel, issued the edict that freed the Jews to return. The edict ordered them to rebuild the temple at Jerusalem, and ordered that all costs be paid from the Persian treasury! In addition, all the gold and silver vessels used in worship were released as well. Thus it is likely that the first group of 42,360 pilgrims turned toward their homeland in 538 or 537 B.C.

The temple foundations were quickly laid by this group. But opposition from the Samaritans (see p. 524) and flagging zeal left the structure incomplete for over a decade. The building was completed then, urged on by the prophets Haggai and Zechariah.

The second return came 58 years after the temple was completed. The leader at this time was Ezra, a Babylonian official who was also a devoted student of the Word of God. Ezra's great contribution and his mission was to strengthen the people in the land spiritually.

A third return took place under Nehemiah, in 444 B.C. Nehemiah's mission was to rebuild the walls of the city, and to lead another spiritual reformation. This mission accomplished, Nehemiah spent most of the rest of his life in the land and served as Persian governor of the province in which the Jews lived.

The Book of Malachi concludes the OT record, and reveals conditions in the land some decades after Nehemiah.

EZRA
The First Book of Return

Ezra and its companion book, Nehemiah, continue the history of God's OT people after the age of the Captivity (see pp. 229–231). They pick up the report from the final verses of the Chronicles, which report that seventy years after the captives were taken away, in the first year of the Persian conqueror Cyrus, "the Lord moved the heart of Cyrus the king of Persia to make a proclamation throughout his realm and to put it in writing:

> The Lord, the God of Heaven, has given me all the kingdoms of the earth and he has appointed me to build a temple for him at Jerusalem in Judah. Anyone of his people among you—may the Lord his God be with him, and let him go up" (2 Chron. 36:29–23).

Cyrus. Cyrus, the Persian conqueror who ordered the return, was not necessarily a believer. It was his policy to return ethnic groups to their homelands. His other decrees show he spoke with equal respect of other people's gods. But the Lord surely used Cyrus to accomplish his own purposes, as he did other pagan rulers.

For background on Persian rulers and on the various stages of the return to Palestine, see pages 229–231.

Authorship. Parts of both Ezra and Nehemiah are written as first person reports of the two men. Other parts are in the third person, descriptions of their actions. There are a number of documents quoted in Aramaic, the diplomatic language of the day. And there are lists which would have been on file in the temple archives. While we cannot tell who organized all these sources into the books we have today, Ezra and Nehemiah are accurate reports of the times they discuss and were probably completed shortly after 430 B.C.

Ezra. Ezra was a priest, of the line of Zadok. Thus one of his priestly tasks was to teach the law of God. Ezra committed himself to this mission while in Babylon (7:10). Ezra also held a position of influence in the Persian court (7:21–26). It's likely this dedicated individual initiated the Bible study movement which undergirded the synagogue and found later expression in the rabbi (teacher) of Jesus' day.

Date and outline. The first group returned the first year of Cyrus (538 B.C.). Ezra's group came the seventh year of Xerxes (458 B.C.). The book tells the story of these two groups and thus can be outlined as The First Return (ch. 1–6) and The Second Return (ch. 7–10).

Chapter 1–6. The First Return

The return commanded: 1:1–11. In Cyrus' first year the decree permitting the return of the Jews is issued. This may be due in part to Daniel's influence (cf. Dan. 10:1). The prophecy mentioned in 1:1 was made by Jeremiah, identifying the length of time the Jews would be captive in Babylon. The seventy-year period was fixed in order that the land might "enjoy its Sabbath rests" (2 Chron. 36:21). OT Law said that every seventh year the land was not to be planted. The Hebrews would live from the extra harvest granted the sixth year. But for 490 years this commandment had been ignored. So God gave the land its rest, by removing his people to Babylon!

Cyrus also permitted other peoples to return home and to bring their idols. The Jews were permitted to bring gold and silver articles used in the temple worship, plus freewill offerings from those Jews who chose to stay in Babylon.

The list of exiles: 2:1–70. Genealogical records were carefully maintained in OT times. These records of family lines were kept in the rebuilt temple and available to the author of Ezra.

The altar and temple foundations: 3:1–13. As soon as the people are settled, they assemble at Jerusalem. Immediately there is antagonism and pressure from the people around them (3). These peoples are descendants of foreigners imported into the old Northern Kingdom by the Assyrians, nearly two centuries before. But the altar is built and sacrifices resumed "in accordance with what is written" (4). Work is also begun on foundations of a new temple.

Opposition begins: 4:1–4. When the semipagan peoples around Judah claim that they worship the Lord, and should help build the temple, they are rejected. They are not descendants of Abraham, and thus are not part of the covenant people (see p. 51). Angered, these mixed peoples begin a campaign of rumor and threat which succeeds in halting the building project.

The pattern of opposition explained: 4:6–23. Here the writer jumps ahead of his story, to give illustrations of opposition from later decades. The illustrations are carefully dated and refer to building the city and its walls rather than the temple. The author's purpose is to show that God's people experienced only antagonism and fierce resistance from these surrounding peoples, whose descendants are known in the NT as the Samaritans.

Prophetic encouragement: 4:24–5:17. Verse 24 brings us back to the early years of the return and tells us that under the pressure of opposition work on the temple stopped. It is some 15 years later, in 520 B.C., when new leaders (Zerubbabel and Joshua) resume construction. They are aided by the preaching of two dynamic prophets, Haggai and Zechariah.

The construction project is challenged by the governor of the Persian satrapy (district) of which Judah is a part: Abarnahara. A search of the Persian archives shows that the Jews do have authority to build the temple, and a new decree orders that temple costs are to be paid from the district treasury (6:3–10). King Darius is aware that there has been opposition. So the decree adds a penalty to be exacted from anyone who "lifts a hand to change this decree or destroy the temple in Jerusalem" (6:11,12).

> **Haggai and Zechariah**
> These two prophets lived and ministered among the people who returned. Haggai's messages can be dated to the very day they were given (see pages 419–421) and focused on completion of the temple. Zechariah also urged its completion. But his written prophecies are on the broader theme of God's plan for his people during the times that Gentiles will have political authority in Palestine (see pages 419–431).

With this encouragement, the temple is finished in four years. It is dedicated with great rejoicing and again a great Passover is celebrated in the land (6:13–23).

Chapters 7–10. The Second Return

Fifty-eight years after completion of the Temple, another group of Jews comes from Persia. This group is led by Ezra the scribe.

Ezra's mission: 7:1–28. Ezra is a "teacher, well versed in the law of Moses" (6). He is given privileges by Artaxerxes which indicate he was a trusted official in the Persian court. This mission of Ezra, defined by the Persian king, is to appoint magistrates and judges to administer justice to all the people of Trans-Euphrates: according to "the law of your God and the law of the king" (26). This gives Ezra judicial as well as religious authority, and makes the OT law the "law of the land" in Judah.

Ezra's companions: 8:1–14. The genealogies of those who accompany Ezra are recorded.

The journey home: 8:15–36. Ezra is carrying much wealth, but he is ashamed to ask for military protection. Instead he calls for prayer and fasting, and then sets out, trusting God for protection against enemies and bandits.

Intermarriage: 9:1–15. Ezra finds that even priests and Levites have intermarried with the pagan peoples around Judah. This is a violation of OT law, for the covenant people are to keep their line unmixed and avoid entanglements which will lead to unfaithfulness to the Lord. Appalled, Ezra weeps and prays, humbling himself before God.

Study Ezra's prayer. Why is the command not to marry given? What do you learn about repentance from this model OT prayer?

Confession and cleansing: 10:1–44. Ezra's broken-heartedness sparks a revival in others, who join him in weeping and confession. Out of this grows a determination to deal with the matter according to God's law. The whole nation assembles at Jerusalem, Public confession of sin is made, and the foreign wives are divorced.

NEHEMIAH
The Second Book of Return

Nehemiah continues the story of the Jews who return to Judah after the Babylonian captivity. The story of the first two groups to reach the land is told in the Book of Ezra.

Date. The third return of a small group accompanying Nehemiah takes place in the twentieth year of Artaxerxes (444 B.C.). For a general history of the times and of the Persian period, see pages 229–231.

Authorship. Much of the book is clearly a first person report by Nehemiah. The final contents were probably compiled by someone else some time after 430 B.C.

Nehemiah. Nehemiah was a court official in Persia. The office of "Cupbearer" is not simply domestic. It is also administrative and marks the individual holding it a person of great trust and influence. Nehemiah's administrative skills, and his personal power as a motivator are shown in his organization of the work of rebuilding Jerusalem's walls. He was also a man of deep commitment to God, with a personality strong enough to influence the lives of those who lived in Judah toward godliness.

Outline. The Book of Nehemiah can be outlined by the three main accomplishments of Nehemiah in his two terms as governor.

Outline

Chapter 1–6. The Walls Rebuilt

Nehemiah's prayer: 1:1–11. Nehemiah is cupbearer to Artaxerxes in Susa when a brother brings news of the Jewish settlement in Judah. The news is discouraging. The small colony is in trouble, the walls of Jerusalem still broken down. Ezra 4:6–23 reports the intrigue against the Jews which led to a royal command not to rebuild that city. This has disgraced the Judeans and left them helpless in case of an attack. Nehemiah mourns, fasts, and prays.

What is the relationship between prayer and human responsibility? What can you determine from Nehemiah's prayer (5–11)?

Nehemiah comes to Jerusalem: 2:1–10. Nehemiah is given a leave of absence from the Persian court. Letters to the governors of the Trans-Euphrates province, and his military escort, establish Nehemiah's status.

Nehemiah 2:10 and 2:19 identify the Jews' chief enemies. Archaeologists have discovered written and inscriptional evidence about these individuals. Sanballat enjoyed a long life and continued as governor in Samaria after Nehemiah's day. Tobiah the Ammonite is from a family which remained politically important from the fifth through the second century B.C. Geshem is of the ruling family of an extensive Arab kingdom, which included northern Arabia, the Sinai, and part of the Nile delta. In Nehemiah's day this kingdom was subject to the Persians, but its own king was permitted to serve as a Persian governor.

The shattered walls inspected: 2:11–20. Nehemiah quietly inspects the tumble of ruins where the city walls had stood before the Babylonian attack. When his plans are made, Nehemiah urges the priests and local officials to commit themselves to rebuilding. For the first time he tells them of his letters and his commission, and of the answer to prayer that brought him to them.

The work organized: 3:1–32. Each community in Judah is given a specific portion of the walls to build. This means that no gap will be left through which enemies might attack. The danger of attack does exist!

Opposition grows: 4:1–23. The peoples around Judah are hostile and oppose building of Jerusalem's walls. They first count on ridicule. But when the walls reach half their height, the enemy coalition is ready to kill the workmen and thus end the project (8–12)!

Nehemiah encourages the people to rely on the Lord, and arms them. From that point on half stand guard while the others work.

Read the description of the effort in 4:10–23. What would be the workers' morale? What impact would you normally expect from such pressures? What was Nehemiah's role in maintaining the effort?

Caring for the poor: 5:1–19. Work on the walls is threatened when it brings special hardship on the poor, who cannot afford to leave their fields to work on the central city. This is caused in part by heavy taxes levied by the Persian government.

Archaeologists have recovered large jars from this period, marked with seals that identify Judah and Jerusalem, and a sign which identifies them as "belonging to the king." Similar sealed jars have been found in Egypt. Evidently these large jars were issued and then used locally to collect portions of the harvest as taxes.

Many in Judah have been forced to mortgage their property to pay their taxes. Others have loaned money at high interest and then foreclosed if the poor could not repay on time. Nehemiah deals with the issue quickly, and during his first governorship requires that foreclosed lands be returned, and money loaned without interest. He sets the example himself, both by making no interest loans and by remitting taxes due to support the local governor. He pays his own expenses.

The plot against Nehemiah: 6:1–14. The three enemies realize that Nehemiah is the key to the Jewish resurgence. They attempt to neutralize him. But Nehemiah avoids their traps, ignores their threats, and refuses to hide when threatened by assassination.

The wall completed: 6:15–19. The wall is completed in a stunning 52 days. This evidence of God's blessing encourages the Jews and is a terrific blow to the self-confidence of their enemies.

Chapters 7–10. The Covenant Renewed

As governor, Nehemiah quickly sets the land in order, taking a number of civil and religious steps.

Security measures instituted: 7:1–4. Guards for the wall are appointed, and the city gates closed at night.

Genealogies consulted: 7:5–73. Nehemiah registers the present population, matching their family lines with the genealogies of those who returned in the first year of Cyrus.

Reading God's Law: 8:1–18. In the fall of 444 B.C., shortly after completing the walls, Nehemiah calls all the people together to hear Ezra read and interpret the OT.

Ezra may have read a portion of the Hebrew text, and then waited as Levites he has trained explain that portion to the Aramaic-speaking population gathered in smaller groups (7). Or it may be that the task of reading and interpreting was done in shifts by the Levites listed. Interpretation is necessary. Hebrew is no longer the common language. Aramaic, the old diplomatic language, is spoken by all and is the common tongue across Persia.

When the passage of the law which explains the Feast of Tabernacles (see Leviticus 23) is read, the people realize the festival is to be held that very month. Enthusiastically they prepare for it and keep the seven-day festival the fifteenth through the twenty-second,

and the Sabbath that follows it the twenty-fourth. Each day more
of the Scriptures are read to the joyful people.

Confession of sins: 9:1–37. The religious revival stimulated by
finishing the walls and by reading the law simply will not stop.
On the twenty-fourth the reading of Scripture continues, but now
the people are moved to a great confession of sins. This wave of
confession is expressed in a liturgy of worship, recorded in 5–37.

The liturgy of confession recorded here involves identification
by the worshipers with their fathers and their failures, and
includes affirmation of God's righteousness in his dealings with
them. If you were to write a liturgy of confession for your local
church, or for the church in your country, what would you include
today?

Covenant renewal: 9:38–10:39. The people now enter into a solemn covenant, swearing to be God's people and to serve him.
The principle of covenant renewal, by which a generation makes
a personal commitment to God and acknowledges the authority
of his law, is a repeated and important OT tradition (see Deut.
29 and Josh. 24).

This particular occasion is unique, however, in that special oaths
are taken, which reveal the areas in which this generation has
strayed from the law. No longer will God's people intermarry
with pagans, or buy and sell on the Sabbath. And they promise
to support the priests and Levites who should minister at the temple
with their tithes and offerings. This is a bold commitment in view
of the general poverty and heavy Persian taxation.

Jerusalem settled: 11:1–36. The people have been scattered in
smaller communities. Now, partly as a security measure, Nehemiah
moves a tenth of the population to Jerusalem.

Priests and Levites: 12:1–26. The genealogies of worship leaders
is given special attention, to assure their right to serve the Lord.

Dedication of the city walls: 12:27–47. Great choirs are formed
and the new walls dedicated with great celebration. Nehemiah
then takes steps to make sure that the people follow through on
their commitments (10:28–39).

Chapter 13. Sins Purged

It is not known how long Nehemiah stays in Judah before returning to Susa (cf. 1:6). The walls were built in 444 B.C. Nehemiah
returns to Susa and then is released to come back to Jerusalem
in 431 B.C.

Nehemiah is shaken to find the solemn commitments the people

made have not been kept. One priest has made apartments for
Tobiah, the Jews' enemy, in the temple storerooms (4,5)! The support promised to the Levites has been withdrawn (10), and the
Sabbath is not being kept (15–18). And the people are again inter-
marrying with the pagans around them (23–28). Nehemiah corrects
these failures.

But after Nehemiah's death, the people sink again into the same
patterns of disobedience. We know this, for the last of the writing
prophets, Malachi, paints a similar picture of decline, showing
how deeply the sins Nehemiah struggled to correct are ingrained
in the character of God's people.

ESTHER
The Book of Providential Care

The Book of Esther is set in the era of Persian empire (see pages 229–231). While a small group of Jews is established in Judah, most Jews live outside the Promised Land. Most live in major population centers, like Babylon, where they prosper.

The story told in Esther is about an orphaned Jewish girl who lives with her uncle, Mordecai, a minor official in the Persian court of Xerxes the Great at Susa (Shushan). The book reports a series of incidents which lead to Esther becoming queen, just in time to abort a plot which would have wiped out the Jewish people.

The action takes place between the third and twelfth years of Xerxes (483–471 B.C.). The feast mentioned in Esther 1:3 is the feast Herodotus the Greek historian identifies as one held to discuss plans for a military invasion of Greece. Esther 2:6 tells us that the search for a new queen began that year, but Esther was chosen in the seventh. This fits Herodotus, who says Xerxes spent four years gathering his armies and then campaigned in Greece.

In Herodotus, Xerxes' wife is identified as Amestris. This may have been a secondary wife, or Vashti, now deposed as queen but still a wife. This woman accompanied the king, but was disposed of after she brutally mutilated one of Xerxes' mistresses.

The Persian records which have been recovered to date do not mention Esther or Mordecai. But the Book of Esther contains many detailed descriptions of practices and customs which archaeology has shown are historically accurate. Also the author uses many technical Persian governmental terms. The author of Esther is unknown but many believe it was Mordecai himself.

Esther's Story

Queen Vashti deposed: 1:1–22. Vashti refuses to obey Xerxes' command to appear at the great feast he gives his third year. The queen is removed, in part to affirm the authority of husbands over their wives and to prevent stirrings of "women's liberation" in Persia (17–20)!

Esther made queen: 2:1–18. A search for a new queen is begun immediately. Following defeat by the Greeks in the west several years later Xerxes chooses Esther, the adopted daughter of a minor court official named Mordecai.

Mordecai discovers a conspiracy: 2:19–23. Subsequently Mordecai overhears a plot to assassinate Xerxes and gets word to the king through Esther. The report is investigated and the two plotters hung.

Haman's plot: 3:1–15. Haman is a high court official who becomes furious when he thinks Mordecai fails to show him sufficient respect. So he determines to wipe out Mordecai's whole race in revenge!

Haman complains about the Jews to Xerxes. He is given permission to write his own decree and stamp it with Xerxes' signet ring. Haman sets a date on which anyone is permitted to kill Jews, and to make sure their enemies will act, he authorizes plunder of Jewish goods. His goal is nothing less than their total extermination.

Esther's help: 4:1–5:18. Mordecai appeals to Esther to speak to the king. Because of prejudice against the Jews, Mordecai had earlier counseled Esther not to reveal her race. Now she fears but does go to the king. Esther invites Xerxes and Haman to a meal in her rooms.

Providence

The Book of Esther records a message Mordecai sends to Esther the queen after an unlikely set of circumstances has made her consort of the Persian emperor Xerxes. "If you remain silent at this time, relief and deliverance for the Jews will arise from another place . . . and who knows but that you have come to royal position for such a time as this?"

The doctrine of providence affirms that God is in sovereign charge of all events. The incidents described in Esther, the timing of events and their sequencing, all fall together to bring about the deliverance of God's people. As a true believer, Mordecai does not know for sure the purpose behind the events in which he has participated, but he is sure that "relief and deliverance" will "arise" for God's people.

The doctrine of providence which Mordecai illustrates affirms (1) that God's control is all-inclusive. Nothing happens merely by chance, or is the result of "fate." (2) Providence does not mean that God violates any individual's freedom of choice. Each person in the Esther story acts in harmony with his own character, values, and beliefs, without any divine coercion. Providence however affirms that God is able to blend these free choices into his overarching plan, without in any way infringing on human freedom. (3) Providence also involves God working through and within the framework of natural cause and effect, in distinction to miracle (see *Miracles, OT,* p. 79).

The doctrine of Providence is not stated explicitly in the Bible. It is taught in the OT's picture of a sovereign God, however, and is often illustrated in sacred history.

For study: Explore how the events described in Esther worked together to bring about the deliverance that God has promised to his people.

Haman's rage: 5:9–14. In spite of the published decree, Mordecai ignores Haman, showing neither fear nor respect. Grimly Haman raises a high gallows, intending to ask Xerxes the next day for permission to hang Mordecai.

Mordecai honored: 6:1–14. That night Xerxes cannot sleep. He has servants read the records of his reign, and when they come to the conspiracy earlier uncovered by Mordecai, the king asks how Mordecai has been honored. When told nothing has been done for him, Xerxes resolves to correct the oversight. The next day, before Haman can ask for Mordecai's life, the king orders him to lead a horse carrying Mordecai, dressed in royal robes, through the streets of the capital. Crushed, Haman completes the hateful task and rushes home.

Haman hanged: 7:1–10. At the evening banquet, Queen Esther reveals that she is Jewish, and that Haman has ordered the slaughter of her and all her people. One of the king's servants then volunteers the information that Haman has built a gallows on which to hang Mordecai, "who spoke up to help the king." The furious Xerxes orders Haman hanged there instead.

The edict modified: 8:1–9:17. According to the laws of the Persians, a royal decree once published could not be revoked (see Dan. 6:12). So Xerxes gives Mordecai his seal and permission to write any decree that will correct the situation. Mordecai does this by simply giving Jews the right to protect themselves from attack on the date Haman has set. The Jews organize, and on the appointed date kill the individuals who had planned to kill them. The decree does not permit any victims to be plundered, so the motives of the defenders will not be greed. This amazing deliverance causes the peoples of the empire to stand in awe of the Jews and of Mordecai.

Purim celebrated: 9:18–10:3. This great deliverance came to be celebrated yearly, and took its place with the festivals ordained in the Mosaic law in the life of God's people. Purim is known and kept today, on March 13 and 14, with great rejoicing.

Mordecai went on to become Xerxes' leading official, and was able to provide much support for other Jews all of his life.

JOB
The Book of Human Suffering

Job is the first of five OT "poetical" books. It is probably the oldest book in the Bible and raises an age-old question: Why do the righteous suffer? The Book of Job provides a unique answer to this question, one which is often misunderstood. But the message of Job is vital for anyone who tries to do right and finds that despite his best efforts, problems or suffering follow.

Date. The literary form of Job is similar to documents which go back to the first part of second century B.C. In the dialogue section of the book the poetry (see Hebrew poetry, p. 252) is in the most difficult and archaic Hebrew. Even the name, Job (literally *'iyyob*), is a common second century name, well attested in other documents. This, plus failure to mention covenant or law, places Job in the time of the patriarchs, probably between 2100 and 1700 B.C.

Concept of God. Job is distinctively non-Israelite in character. Yet its place in the OT canon was never challenged by the Jews. As a non-Israelite book, it plays an important role in the history of revelation. Its contents show us truths about God available to mankind through tradition before Moses penned the first five OT books around 1400 B.C. Exploring Job, we see that while knowledge of God was incomplete, Job and his friends surely knew enough to have a faith relationship with him, and to live moral lives.

A summary of ideas about God found in Job show that he was viewed as personal and transcendent, beyond nature, but the master of the world he has made. God is also the Creator of men, who permits freedom of choice and thus makes men morally responsible. He is a moral being, and so acts as judge, and will punish evil and reward those who do right. God is also gracious. He can be approached through sacrifice. And he forgives the sinner who turns to him in repentance. Yet, however much is known of God, he does not meet us face to face. Ultimately God remains hidden, a Mystery.

Outline

I. Prologue: Satan's Test   1:1–2:10
II. Dialogue with Friends   2:11–31:40

Chapters 1, 2. Prologue: Satan's Test

Job is a man of wealth and piety. In God's own words, Job is "blameless and upright; a man who fears God and shuns evil" (1:1).

But the main characters in these two chapters are the Lord and Satan. The two enter into a contest, with Job as the battleground. Satan insists he will move Job to "curse [God] to your face" if only the Lord removes the protection he maintains around Job. The Lord does so, and permits Satan to test Job. In a series of disasters whose timing and nature label them as supernatural, Job's wealth is stripped away, his children killed, and his body is covered with agonizing boils.

In spite of his suffering, Job does not curse God. The test ends at 2:10 with this summary; "in all this, Job did not sin in what he said." Satan failed to accomplish what he said he would achieve.

Satan

Old and New Testaments agree that Satan is a personal being, not a "force" or "evil influence." The OT indicates that Satan was created by God as a ruling angel called Lucifer, with great powers. But pride led Lucifer to rebel against God (cf. Isa. 14:12–14; Ezek. 28:12–15). Warped now by sin, Lucifer is transformed into Satan, which means "enemy" or "adversary." He leads other angels into rebellion (see *Angels,* p. 370) and together they form a spiritual army struggling to thwart God's plans and to corrupt his people.

Various names given to Satan in Scripture reveal his character. He is called "destroyer" (Rev. 9:11 margin), "the evil one" (Matt. 13:19, 38), "deceiver" (Rev. 12:9 RSV), the "father of lies," "murderer" (John 8:44), "tempter" (I Thess. 3:5), and the "ancient serpent" (Rev. 12:9), which is a reference to the role that Satan played in the fall of humankind (Gen. 3).

Satan is not omnipotent or omnipresent, nor does he have other attributes of God. But Satan is a powerful being who directs "his angels" (Matt. 25:41), the demons of the NT, in the struggle against God. Satan is also called the ruler of this world, for he has succeeded in building into human society his own warped values and principles of relationship (cf. John 12:31; Eph. 2:2,3; Col. 1:13; I John 2:15–17).

In spite of Satan's powers and his influence (see *Satan and the Believer,* p. 801), Satan is a limited being, who operates only within a framework permitted by God. His ultimate fate is assured. Jesus announced that "eternal fire" has been prepared for "the devil and his angels" (Matt. 25:41), and Revelation graphically portrays his prophesied doom (Rev. 20:7–14).

The first chapter refers to angels as "sons of God." This is a common OT phrase, indicating direct creation or causation by God. The fact that all angels good and evil were required to present themselves at God's command shows that even those who have rebelled against God cannot deny his ultimate authority.

The prologue of Job raises many questions. How would you respond? (1) God initiates the test by pointing Job out (1:8). Is God just "using" this good man? (2) Is this world nothing but a gameboard for a contest between God and Satan? (3) Job may not have uttered a word against God during the time encompassed in these chapters. But what was Job thinking?

Chapter 3–31. Job's Dialogue with Friends

Three of Job's friends hear of his tragedy and come to offer comfort. Stunned by his misery, they sit with him in silence for a week. This section of the book is a report of the dialogue which follows as the four men struggle to understand Job's suffering. In the dialogue Job's fears, frustration, and his suppressed resentment are expressed.

Job complains: 3:1–26. Job breaks the silence to complain. He might better have died at birth than live to experience such anguish.

Eliphaz condemns: 4:1–5:27. Eliphaz gently reminds Job that the innocent individual does not suffer. It is sinners whom God punishes. Since God is punishing Job, Job ought to turn to God quickly, for when he does God will restore him.

Job shares his terror: 6:1–7:21. Job protests that he cannot be undergoing punishment, for he has done nothing wrong. He then expresses the terror his unexplained suffering is causing. Job simply cannot understand why God lets this happen.

Bildad rebukes Job: 8:1–22. Bildad is upset by Job's protestations of innocence. Is Job actually suggesting that God is unjust? So Bildad reminds Job of all the fathers have said about God. The Lord simply does not punish the upright person.

Job cries to God: 9:1–10:22. Job cannot defend himself against this attack, for he too believes what Bildad says it true. But how can Job answer? Job is sure he has done nothing wrong, but God keeps on whipping him! Looking up, Job addresses God and cries out his innocence. If Job is wrong, let God speak up and prove it.

Zophar challenges Job's "pride": 11:1–22. Job now is frightening his friends. So Zophar attacks Job, condemns his boasting, and insists that there must be some secret sin which God knows even if Job's friends do not. Zophar concludes with an appeal. If Job will only get his heart right with God, God will accept Job.

Job insists on his innocence: 12:1–14:22. Now Job expressly states what he has before implied. Job knows as much about God as his friends. Job knows God's attributes. But Job also *knows* that he is right! So his friends are being unfair, to side with God!

Again Job appeals to God. He insists his treatment is unfair, protests his frailty, and weeps over his loss of hope.

Eliphaz angrily attacks: 15:1–35. Job's self-defense has forced his friends into a difficult position. He has challenged their whole concept of God and their basis for understanding God's actions. Eliphaz now attacks Job, reminding him of truths they both accept. It is the wicked who suffer. It is the proud whom God brings low. The implication is clear. To suffer as Job has, he simply must be wicked!

Job's position hardens: 16:1–17:16. Job bitterly complains about the "comfort" offered by his friends. He again states the facts as he knows them. God is against him. It is not because of any fault of Job's. Job's only hope is to die.

Bildad applies more pressure: 18:1–21. Now Bildad takes up the attack. It's futile for Job to try to justify himself. The friends *know* it is the wicked who know calamity. They are the ones who see their families die. The wicked dash toward death in terror.

Job cries out: 19:1–29. The pressure on Job is unbearable. Crushed by God, with relatives and friends turning against him, Job begs for pity. And he accuses his friends of fearing to take his side.

Zophar condemns Job: 20:1–29. The appeal for pity falls on deaf ears. Zophar sternly tells Job to stop defending himself. He falls back on common knowledge about God and notes that while the wicked may prosper for a time, they suffer in the end. Again Zophar illustrates by naming events that have happened to Job. Zophar's accusation is clear. All the years that prosperity seemed to indicate God's blessing, there must have been some hidden wickedness in Job. Now the depth of Job's suffering has revealed to all the extent of the hidden wickedness!

Job's defense: 21:1–34. Up to this point Job has agreed with the basic premise of the argument his friends have used against him. But now Job openly attacks the view of God which all have held. Job points to evidence that doesn't fit the accepted picture. Some people who are known to be wicked do prosper. Some who

appear good do suffer. Faith may insist they'll be punished and
rewarded in the end. But when? Job charges that the case the
friends have built, based on their idea of God and how he acts
in the world, is a tissue of lies!

Eliphaz continues his attack: 22:1–30. If Job is so righteous,
why does God reprove him? Eliphaz insists that deep in Job's
heart sin must always have been hidden. Perhaps men could not
see Job's wickedness. But God saw! Eliphaz ends with an appeal.
Turn and be saved. Hidden sins too can be forgiven.

Faith and Reason

Job provides insights into the classic tension which exists between faith
and reason. Which has priority? How much can we depend on reason?
And when should we reject reason in favor of faith?

Job and his friends share a concept of God as a righteous judge, who
punishes the wicked and rewards the good. All four reason from this concept
to explain what happens in their world. Thus when Job suddenly loses
his health, his family, and his wealth, reason leads all four to a seemingly
logical conclusion:

> God punishes only the wicked.
> Job is being punished.
> Therefore Job is wicked.

But Job knows that he is *not* wicked. He has lived a good and a moral
life. But Job cannot convince his friends! Their reasoning leads them to
only one acceptable conclusion.

Even worse, Job has no explanation for what is happening to him. His
reasoning is locked into the same pattern as that of his friends. So Job's
inner anguish is multipled. God seems to be acting unfairly, against his
very nature! Under the pressure placed on him by his friends, Job finally
attacks their major premise. Perhaps God doesn't punish the wicked and
bless the good. Job even goes so far as to point to wicked men who prosper,
and good folks who suffer. This seems to Job's friends to be an attack
on God himself, and they react by condemning the sufferer even more
strongly.

As the Book of Job develops, we see problems with the approach taken
by Job and his friends, and gain insights into faith/reason relationships.

First, the reasoning of Job and his friends was faulty because they lacked
sufficient information about God's motives and actions (see Elihu's contribution, p. 249 f). We must always remain humble in our claims to "know"
or to be "right." Because human knowledge *is* incomplete, conclusions
reached by reasoning from what we know must always be open to question.

Second, "faith" does not require blind agreement to common ideas about
God. Job's experience forced him to challenge the concept of God held
in his day, while Job's friends rejected any evidence he presented. They
felt they were defending God, but really were defending their ideas about

God. Job's honest questioning was later praised by God; the friends' "blind faith" required forgiveness (42:7)!

Third, our faith is to be placed in God himself, not in our understanding of him. We are invited to reason. And privileged to trust!

Job refuses to bend: 23:1–24:25. Job wishes aloud that he could talk with God. The Lord would be forced to agree that Job is innocent. Job categorically denies doing wrong. And Job again challenges God's ways. Sin does exist in the world, and God does not immediately punish those who murder, steal, commit adultery, or cause the poor to suffer.

Bildad affirms "faith": 25:1–6. Bildad will not respond to Job's argument, nor join him in his questioning. Instead Bildad simply insists that God must be right, and that man has no right to question.

Job restates his position: 26:1–27:12. The argument has gone around and around, with nothing resolved. Job sarcastically thanks his friends for their "comfort." And he insists that he will not lie, even to protect God's honor! Job has not sinned. And God is treating him unfairly.

Zophar's final argument: 27:13–28:28. [*Note.* Zophar's name is not in the text. But the speech picks up his argument from 20:29. Thus most scholars suppose either Zophar's name was omitted from the text, or that Job parodies his position. That position is the same as that of the other friends.] God is God. And he does judge the wicked.

Job's final statement: 29:1–31:40. The final statement is made by Job. He has not done wrong. He is clean and blameless. And thus Job has nothing more to say.

Read Job's speeches. Jot down words that tell how he feels under his pressures. What seems to cause him the greatest anguish?

Read the speeches of one of Job's three friends. Is he supportive or helpful to Job? What is his attitude toward Job? Why does he feel and act as he does?

From this section of Job can you outline any principles for relating to friends of your own who might be going through difficult times? See if you can develop a list of dos and don'ts. Why must you avoid condemning or judging?

Chapters 32–37. Elihu's Contribution

Job and his friends are frustrated because they see no way out of their dilemma. All four are bound by the circular logic of their understanding of God. God brings suffering only on the wicked. Job is undergoing suffering caused by God. Thus Job is wicked. But then a young observer named Elihu breaks the grip of the logic that has trapped Job and his friends.

Elihu does this by pointing out that God may use suffering to instruct as well as to punish (33:19–30)! As soon as this new reason for suffering is suggested, the bondage of false logic is broken, and each of the four is free to confess that he does not *know* why God has permitted Job to undergo this experience. It is now possible to accept Job's testimony, and still to honor God as one who does right!

Suffering, OT

The OT uses some twelve Hebrew words for suffering, anguish, pain, distress, and torment. The concept includes mental anguish as well as physical pain.

Many in OT times assumed that all suffering is punitive, a punishment brought on an individual by God for personal sins or wickedness. This idea is derived in part from the discipline introduced by God in the Mosaic law. In that law God commits himself to bless obedience and to punish disobedience. But while the suffering of an individual *may* be punishment, it does not follow that suffering *must* be punishment.

Some suffering is a natural consequence of human choices, such as hunger following laziness. God is a moral being and has structured the universe in such a way that natural consequences follow most of the good or evil choices we make. Also the OT suggests that God often has our good in mind when he permits us to suffer! Suffering is not equivalent to punishment!

Ultimately, however, the root source of human suffering is sin. When man fell, forces were unleashed which have warped society and which have an impact on the innocent as well as the guilty. Every human life, wrapped up as it is in a network of relationships with others who are also sinful, is subject to pain, to suffering, and to death. Suffering is thus the lot of the innocent and godly as well as the guilty and wicked.

For study: Genesis 3, 4; Deuteronomy 28:15–68; Habakkuk 2:4–20. See also *Suffering, NT,* page 780.

Elihu does rebuke Job. Calling God unfair is hardly a valid solution to the problem of suffering (34:10)! Twin themes dominate Elihu's discourse. The physical universe demonstrates that God's wisdom and understanding far surpass man's. Why then should we expect to understand his ways of working in human lives? Since we are confident that God's character is marked by "an abundant righteousness he will not violate" (37:23), when we cannot understand we are simply to trust him. This is perhaps the most significant message of Job.

Chapters 38–41. The Lord Speaks

Now God speaks to Job. But God does not explain his servant's suffering! Instead God first reveals his omnipotence and wisdom, demonstrated in the creation (ch. 38, 39). When Job is invited to present his case, the awed sufferer simply covers his mouth. Then God emphasizes human frailty. Man is impotent even before the creatures that populate the earth. How then can any man expect to stand before the Creator of these awesome beasts (40:10–41:34)?

The Lord is God, Job is merely a man.

Chapter 42. Epilogue

God's revelation of himself seems inadequate to those who demand to know the reason for all things. But it is enough for Job. The sufferer now accepts his position as a creature and bows before the Creator. Having seen the Lord, Job makes no claim to righteousness, but simply submits to the Lord.

Job is told to pray for his three friends, who have not spoken rightly about God, as Job has (7). Job's health is restored, his wealth is doubled, and his household blessed with many more children.

Several verses in Job suggest that God had a special purpose in his servant's suffering, that was designed for Job's benefit. What conclusions can you draw from the following: Job 3:25; 42:6?

The OT does not explain why the righteous suffer. But the NT adds to our information about God's purposes. See *Suffering, NT*, p. 780 and explore 1 Peter 3:13–18. Can you apply this in Job's case?

The NT book of James looks back at Job and tells us that the epilogue is added to reassure us about God and his intentions toward us. Look at James 5:11 and think how you might teach the Book of Job to communicate the truth James stresses.

Finally, think about the lesson of trust which Job stresses. We cannot and do not know the reasons for what happens to us. What then is the believer's response to be? How should we relate to others when disaster strikes them? How should we respond to our own suffering?

PSALMS
The Book of Praises

The Hebrews called this collection of 150 psalms the "book of praises." It is the second of three OT books designated as poetical: Job, Psalms, and Proverbs. These three were also called "books of truth."

Hebrew poetry. English poetry relies on rhyme and rhythm for its impact. Thus it is difficult to translate into another language. But Hebrew poetry can be easily translated, for its major feature is not rhyme but parallelism. The balance of thought is vital to Hebrew poetry, not the balance of sounds or rhythm.

The basic unit of Hebrew poetry is the verse, in which the first line states a theme, and one or more following lines in some way develop that thought. This is what is meant by "parallelism": the balancing of thoughts by following lines. Among the various types of parallelism three are basic:

(1) Synonymous parallelism repeats the thought of the first line.

> "Our mouths were filled with laughter,
> our tongues with songs of joy" (Ps. 126:2).

(2) Antithetical parallelism emphasizes the thought of the first line by contrasting it with an opposite.

> "A kind man benefits himself,
> but a cruel man brings himself harm" (Prov. 11:17).

(3) Synthetic parallelism uses the second line to fill in or complete the thought of the first.

> "I will lie down and sleep in peace,
> for you alone, O Lord, make me dwell in safety" (Ps. 4:8).

It is important to keep this parallelism in mind when reading or trying to interpret the Psalms and other OT poetry.

Date, structure, and authorship. The Psalms were written over an extended period of time (probably 1000–400 B.C.) by different authors, and several times new groups of Psalms were added to the basic collection.

Seventy-three of the Psalms were written by David. A number were contributed by the Levitical singing clans of Asaph and Korah. Forty-nine are anonymous.

The 150 Psalms are organized into five books, which represent four collections added to the first worship book. Book I (Psalms 1–41) is Davidic, compiled before his death. The collection is largely personal psalms which reflect David's own experiences. Book II (Psalms 42–72) was probably added in the days of Solomon. Books III and IV (73–89, 90–106) are collections from the days of the exile, while the final book (V, 107–150), is strongly liturgical and probably was organized around the time of Ezra the scribe after the return from Babylonian captivity. It is likely that many psalms were used by the Hebrew people before their official compilation in these books.

Superscriptions. Many psalms are identified by music type and aim, author, and occasion for writing (cf. Ps. 60). The NIV, unlike other translations, gives the English meaning of all the Hebrew phrases.

The exact purpose of the term "Selah," which occurs 71 times within the body of 39 different psalms, simply is not known. The word means "to lift up" and is probably some kind of pause mark or musical signal.

Contents. A number of repeated themes have been noted in the psalms, and some psalms may be classified by their content. Types of psalms which have been identified are:

(1) Praise psalms, which focus on the person of God and praise him by describing his nature and qualities. Illustrations are 33, 103, 139.

(2) Historical psalms, which review God's dealings with his people. Illustrations are 68, 78, 105, 106.

(3) Relational psalms, which explore the personal relationship between God and the believer. Illustrations are 8, 16, 20, 23, 55.

(4) Imprecatory psalms, which call on God to overthrow the wicked. Illustrations are 35, 69, 109, 137.

(5) Penitential psalms, in which the psalmist expresses sorrow over his own failures. Illustrations are 6, 32, 51, 102, 130, 143.

(6) Messianic psalms, which refer in some sense to the Savior who will come from David's line. A number of such psalms can be identified by NT references to them. Psalms identified as messianic in the NT are: 2, 8, 16, 22, 40, 45, 69, 72, 89, 102, 109, 110, 132. Others also have messianic elements.

(7) Liturgical psalms, which were used at specific times of the year or on specific occasions. Most psalms had some public use.

Special liturgical psalms may be illustrated by 30, 92, 120–134.

Distinctive values and uses of Psalms. Though used in public worship, this collection of prayers and praises is essentially a model for every believer's devotional life. While some psalms instruct, as a whole the psalter is intended to help each of us see how to praise God and pray to him. Of particular note is the ways the inner life and emotions of the psalmists are shared freely and completely with God. Thus Psalms is one of the most intimate and relational books of the Bible. And for each emotional need expressed by the worshiper, Psalms points us to an attribute of the Lord. He is an anchor when we are buffeted, a comfort when we feel abandoned, and an encouragement when support is desperately required.

Book I (Psalms 1–41)

Psalm 1. The godly person is likened to a well-watered tree, while the ungodly are like dry chaff, blown away by winds.

Psalm 2. This messianic psalm shows the futility of rebellion against God (1–6), and affirms the certainty of God's ultimate rule, to be established by his coming Son (7–12).

Psalm 3. David experiences abandonment when he flees during Absalom's rebellion (1–2, cf. 2 Sam. 15, 16), his hope is restored by thoughts of God (3–4), and he knows a peace which frees him to rest (5–8).

Psalm 4. David's experience when crushed by troubles (1–2) shows that prayer brings confidence (3), restored faith (4–5), and a present experience of peace (6–8).

Psalm 5. This prayer asks blessings for the godly (1–3, 7–8, 11–12), alternating with calls for judgment on the guilty (4–6, 9–10).

Psalm 6. A prayer for mercy, uttered while in deep distress.

Psalm 7. A psalm on the theme of righteousness. David reminds God he has lived righteously and calls for deliverance from wicked and violent enemies.

Psalm 8. How awesome God is, whose greatness is shown in creation, and who stoops to care for man!

Psalm 9. In this praise psalm David honors God for his intervention in history on behalf of the righteous, and calls on him to continue to judge wicked nations.

Psalm 10. A prayer in a time of trouble, this psalm explores the ways and motives of the wicked (2–11), and calls on God the King to arise and defend the oppressed (12–18).

Psalm 11. This very personal expression of confidence in God comes when life's "foundations are being destroyed."

Psalm 12. We can be confident in God's commitment to protect the righteous from those who lie about and malign them.

Psalm 13. A brief prayer when feeling alone and abandoned.

Psalm 14. Here is the "fool" (morally distorted) who denies God's existence and the depravity which follows rejection of relationship with the Lord. The psalm is quoted in Romans 3:10 f.

Psalm 15. A brief outline of the character of the man who lives in close relationship with the Lord.

Psalm 16. This beautiful psalm expresses satisfaction with personal relationship to God. God alone is the source of all good (1–4), the one who assigns our place in life (5–6), and the one who guides us by his presence (7–8). The final verses (9–11) express David's expectation of resurrection, and are also messianic references to Christ (cf. Acts. 2:24–31; 13:35–37).

Psalm 17. An expression of devotion to God and confidence in him.

Psalm 18. Shout out joy and love! David's feelings when delivered from Saul and his other enemies. In graphic language David portrays God coming to aid his trusting servant.

Psalm 19. Here is a measured statement of God's revelation of himself in nature (1–6) and in the written word (7–14).

Psalm 20. A public prayer for Israel's leader (1–5), expressing trust in the Lord rather than military power (6–9).

Psalm 21. Rejoicing in the Lord and in his strength.

Psalm 22. This messianic psalm focuses on the sufferings of Christ (1–18) and the exaltation that follows (19–31). Many NT passages quote or refer to this psalm, which prefigures the crucifixion of Jesus (see Matt. 27:35–46; John 19:23–25; Heb. 2:12).

Messiah

The word itself simply means "anointed." It refers to the consecration of individuals or objects to special service. OT kings were set apart by anointing. Because God promised a great deliverer from David's kingly line, the name "Messiah" was applied to the Savior.

Through the ministry of various prophets, an increasing body of knowledge about the ideal King which God would someday send to Israel began to develop. He was to be born of a virgin, and called Immanuel, which means "with us is God!" (Isa. 7:14). He was identified by Isaiah as Wonderful Counselor, Mighty God, Everlasting Father, and Prince of Peace, and his promised rule will never end, for he "will reign on David's throne and over his kingdom" forever (Isa. 9:6–7). Literature from the centuries between completion of the OT and Jesus' birth show us Jewish interpreters understood that when Messiah appeared, Israel's enemies would be judged by him in righteousness. One of Messiah's tasks was also understood to be the raising of the righteous dead.

Today, from the perspective provided by the birth of Christ and the NT revelation, much can be seen in the OT that points to Jesus. Much can be understood that was not grasped before the Incarnation. So it is important when interpreting messianic passages to remember that most carry a double meaning, with a message that expresses the experience or thoughts of the writers, as well as a message about the day when Christ would come, or come again.

□□ Study Psalm 22 and the NT passages which refer to it (see above). What can you see now that might have been hidden to OT saints, but which events in Jesus' life make clear?

Psalm 23. This famous Shepherd Psalm likens God to a good shepherd, who guides and supports the believer through his life.

Psalm 24. The writer affirms God's sovereignty and expresses joy in his rule as King of Glory.

Psalm 25. This appeal for help is also an expression of trust. David asks God to show him the Lord's ways (4–7), confident that one who follows the Lord will find release (8–15). This prayer is offered despite David's present loneliness and anguish (16–22).

Psalm 26. David appeals for vindication by God, deserved because of his trusting, obedient heart.

Psalm 27. A prayer of confidence in God, on whose person David's whole being is concentrated.

Psalm 28. God is appealed to as rock, strength, and shield, who will deliver us from the fate deserved by the wicked.

Psalm 29. Here is a psalm of pure praise, exalting in God's power over nature.

Psalm 30. Praise is given answered prayer, after being healed.

Psalm 31. In a psalm of commitment David leads the believer to surrender his situation to God, and rely completely on him. Verse 5 of this great psalm of commitment was quoted by Christ on the cross.

Psalm 32. Confession of sin, and God's subsequent forgiveness, brings joy. David shares his inner anguish at unconfessed sin (3–5) and the great release which comes when transgressions are brought to the Lord (6–11).

Psalm 33. This public call to praise God (1–5) reminds us of the many benefits of a close relationship with the Lord (6–22).

Psalm 34. Protection granted at a time when David acted unwisely stimulated this teaching psalm on the benefits of relationship with God.

Psalm 35. An imprecation on David's enemies, who are malicious and evil. The tone of this psalm is one of wounded suffering rather than anger.

Psalm 36. The wicked (1–4) are held up and contrasted with God's loving faithfulness (5–12).

Psalm 37. David exhorts patience and trust when pressures come. The theme "wait for the Lord" is repeated, with warnings against hasty action. This is an important psalm for anyone wronged by others.

Psalm 38. David appeals to God when he feels crushed and deserted under divine discipline.

Psalm 39. An expression of feelings of an individual under discipline.

Psalm 40. Remembrance of salvation (1–5) leads to willing commitment to God (6–10) and an appeal to God for support (11–17).

Psalm 41. Sums up David's lifelong experience with God and praises the Lord for his mercy and faithfulness.

Book II (Psalms 42–72)

Psalm 42. Here is a psalm of encouragement for times of spiritual depression when God seems very far away.

Psalm 43. This plea for vindication is uttered, like Psalm 42, at a time of great discouragement.

Psalm 44. After a historical review of the principles of God's dealings with Israel under the Mosaic covenant, this psalm calls on God to restore his people and redeem them.

Psalm 45. This messianic psalm (cf. Heb. 1:8,9) dwells on the noble theme of God's rule (1–9), and pictures those who share the glory as the king's bride (10–17).

Psalm 46. God is his people's mighty fortress!

Psalm 47. A praise psalm, exalting God as ruler of the nations.

Psalm 48. God is great (1–7), and life in his land satisfying (8–14).

Psalm 49. Peace comes when our hearts trust in God, not in riches.

Psalm 50. All gather to hear God speak (1–6). He encourages his people to honor him, which is more important to him than sacrifice (7–15), and he warns the wicked (16–23).

Psalm 51. David's great penitential psalm was written after his adultery with Bathsheba (2 Sam. 11, 12). Confession of his sin (1–6) brings forgiveness and cleansing (7–9), renewing David's ability to once again serve the Lord (10–19).

Psalm 52. Disturbed by a great evil (1 Sam. 21, 22), David reminds himself of the fate of the wicked (1–7) and destiny of the godly (8–9).

Psalm 53. Another psalm like 14 which describes the "fool" (morally lacking individual) who denies God.

Psalm 54. Here is a cry for help uttered when those David aided turned against him (2 Sam. 2, 3).

Psalm 55. This is a deeply emotional expression of David's fear and anguish, magnified by the pain of his betrayal by those who were long-time friends. The situation described in the psalm fits the time of Absalom's rebellion (2 Sam. 15–17).

Psalm 56. Another psalm affirming trust in days of fear.

Psalm 57. David is confident in God's faithfulness, even when he is forced to hide from King Saul (1 Sam. 22, 24).

Psalm 58. A call for judgment on unjust judges and rulers.

Psalm 59. This deliverance psalm likens the wicked who persecute God's people to snarling dogs that prowl the city at night.

Psalm 60. Praise is given to God, who has led the forces of David to victory over foreign enemies.

Psalm 61. David takes refuge in God and relies on the Lord's promises to support his throne.

Psalm 62. Rest can be ours in God, for he is strong and loving.

Psalm 63. Close personal relationship with God brings the believer to the place of praise and joy.

Psalm 64. A prayer for protection from conspiracy.

Psalm 65. God is honored for his rich provision in nature.

Psalm 66. An exalting expression of praise for God's works on behalf of his people.

Psalm 67. This simple expression of praise looks forward to a time when all peoples will know and praise the Lord.

Psalm 68. This long psalm of praise extols God as father and savior, and looks forward to a time when all the earth will gather to worship the Lord at his sanctuary.

Psalm 69. This messianic psalm is quoted in Acts 1:16–20. It is a quiet sharing of David's personal distress and disappointments, mixed with frequent expressions of trust in God.

Psalm 70. An urgent prayer for speedy deliverance.

Psalm 71. A stately confession of faith in God as sovereign Lord.

Psalm 72. This strong messianic psalm looks forward to the day Messiah will rule over the whole earth. Like the prophets, this psalm emphasizes his endless, universal rule, portrays a time of justice for the oppressed and needy, and prosperity for all.

Book III (Psalms 73–89)

Psalm 73. This unique psalm traces the experience of the poet, who feels envy at the prosperity of the wicked (1–12) and frustration at his own lot (13–16). He finds release by comparing the end of the wicked (18–20) with the blessings of his present and future fellowship with God (21–28).

Psalm 74. In exile, God's people call on him to note the desecration of the sanctuary and to remember his covenant promises.

Psalm 75. Praise to God as righteous judge.

Psalm 76. Exaltation of God as majestic.

Psalm 77. This deeply introspective psalm shares feelings and thoughts while in distress, and explains how hope was restored by recalling God's miracle works for his people.

Psalm 78. This teaching psalm, directed to future generations (1–8), recalls Israel's history and relationship with God (9–64) up to the time of David (65–72).

Psalm 79. A call for God to act and deliver shamed Israel, which has been carried into capitivity and has seen Jerusalem in ruins.

Psalm 80. The exiles' prayer for restoration to the land.

Psalm 81. A divine promise of restoration for Israel . . . when God's people put away their idols and submit to him.

Psalm 82. A psalm directed to rulers, reminding them that they exercise authority as God's representatives (which is the meaning of the phrase "gods" here).

Psalm 83. The psalmist calls on God to overthrow national enemies who seek to destroy Israel.

Psalm 84. The blessings of worship and nearness to God are expressed in this psalm about service in God's temple.

Psalm 85. A prayer for revival and restoration.

Psalm 86. God's abounding love meets David's deepest needs (1–10) as he chooses to commit himself fully to God's truth (11–17).

Psalm 87. The glories of the holy city are extolled.

Psalm 88. This anguished cry for help to a God who does not seem to hear mirrors the experience of many believers.

Psalm 89. This praise psalm magnifies God's faithfulness (1–8), his rule (9–13), and his righteousness (14–18), each of which is expressed in the Davidic covenant (19–37, see p. 177). Based on God's character and covenant, the psalmist calls for Israel's restoration (38–52). This messianic psalm is quoted in Acts 2:30.

Psalm 90. The only psalm attributed to Moses, this meditates on human frailty (1–12) and on dependency on the Lord (13–17).

Psalm 91. Security is found in the shadow of the Almighty.

Psalm 92. A psalm for liturgical use on the Sabbath, it proclaims that "it is good to praise the Lord."

Psalm 93. God reigns.

Psalm 94. God is praised as avenger of evil, who sees all and who judges the wicked, while supporting those who take refuge in him.

Psalm 95. A call to rejoice, worship, and hear God's voice.

Psalm 96. How to worship God, ascribing glory to his name.

Psalm 97. God reigns, idols are empty, and those who worship the Lord are guarded from the wicked.

Psalm 98. This song of salvation is a jubilant shout of joy!

Psalm 99. Exalt the Lord.

Psalm 100. A brief psalm of praise.

Psalm 101. God's love and justice find reflection in the worshiper's relationship with others.

Psalm 102. This messianic psalm is quoted in Hebrews 1:10–12. The psalm records the prayer of an unnamed person, who is greatly afflicted and pours out his heart to the Lord.

Psalm 103. Praise is offered to God for the gracious way he relates to David, and for God's great love for all who fear him.

Psalm 104. All nature displays the glory of God.

Psalm 105. History calls to mind God's strength and all he has done for his people. Praise the Lord!

Faith and Feelings

The psalms are filled wth expressions of emotion. Despair, anger, anguish, loneliness, and fear are expressed along with gratitude, wonder, peace and sheer joy.

The free and open expression of emotions found in the psalms helps us understand the relationship between faith and feelings. In the superscriptions telling experiences which stimulated various psalms, we see that events are bound to cause both the "positive" and "negative" feelings with which each of us is so familiar. Human frailty guarantees we will each be subject to the whole range of pleasant and unpleasant emotions.

But the psalms provide a unique perspective on our emotions. While feelings have subjective reality, they are not the ultimate reality! Our feelings can and do change. Through relationship with God we can move from fear to trust, from alienation to comfort, from envy and jealousy to joy. Many of the psalms actually trace the process by which feelings are transformed and brought into harmony with reality.

What can we say of the relationship between faith and feelings? First, all human beings will experience at one time or another most of the emotions of which mankind is capable.

Second, God, who fully loves and accepts us, also accepts our feelings. We are free to share them with him in prayer and express them without hesitation or fear.

Third, while feelings will surge, at times our feelings may not be appropriate. By consciously relating ourselves and our situation to God, we will change our perspective on the situation. As a result, our feelings as well may change to reflect a release and joy that are found through faith.

Fourth, we are never to judge the strength or validity of our faith by our feelings. Instead we are to let God shape our feelings as we relate to him. We cannot change our own feelings simply by willing them to be different. But as we focus on who God is, and the meaning of our relationship with him, God will graciously work in our emotional life as well as in our understanding, and shape us to his image.

For study. Examine several psalms which show the impact of relationship with God on changing an individual's feelings. Psalms to explore include 73, 77, and 116.

Look through the psalms quickly, and jot down all the feeling words which you can locate. What do you conclude from the range of feelings expressed? How freely can you express your emotions to God? Make a list of psalms which have proved especially helpful to you.

Psalm 106. Again the history of the Exodus period is retold, as basis for confidence that God will deliver again.

Book V (Psalms 107–150)

Psalm 107. A psalm of redemption—from wandering (4–9), prison (10–16), rebelliousness (17–22), and distress (23–32).

Psalm 108. Praise to God, who has made Israel his own.

Psalm 109. This messianic psalm describes Judas (see Acts 1:16–20). David's description of his own anguish (22–29) reflects Jesus' feelings at the time of the crucifixion.

Psalm 110. This messianic psalm speaks of Jesus' exaltation and his present priesthood (see Matt. 22:43–45; Acts 2:33–35; Heb. 1:13; 5:6–10; 6:20; 7:24).

Psalm 111. Praise is due God for the steadfastness of his works.

Psalm 112. The blessings of those who trust God are proclaimed.

Psalm 113. God is praised as an exalted person, who yet stoops to lift up the poor and seat them with princes.

Psalm 114. This brief historic psalm praises God as earth shaker.

Psalm 115. A call to Israel to trust God.

Psalm 116. Deliverance from death stimulates praise and personal commitment to the Lord.

Psalm 117. A two verse psalm of praise.

Psalm 118. Here is a great affirmation of God as he whose "love endures forever."

Psalm 119. The longest of the psalms, this is an acrostic poem, in which the first letter of each verse in each section begins with a different letter of the Hebrew alphabet. The word of God, and its impact in the life of the believer, is the subject of this great work of poetry.

Psalms 120 through 134 are liturgical psalms, probably sung by the people of Israel as they journeyed to Jerusalem for the three annual feasts which the law established as national festivals.

Psalm 120. God saves the godly in their distress.

Psalm 121. Our help is in the Lord, who neither slumbers nor sleeps.

Psalm 122. Prayer for the peace of Jerusalem.

Psalm 123. A plea for mercy.

Psalm 124. The Lord's help has won Israel's victories.

Psalm 125. Those who trust God are truly secure.

Psalm 126. God's deliverance from captivity filled his people with laughter and joy.

Psalm 127. Joy can be found in God's gift of family.

Psalm 128. A right relationship with God brings blessings.

Psalm 129. God has freed the oppressed and will bless them.

Psalm 130. Praise for forgiveness and redemption.

Psalm 131. Humility and trust bring hope.

Psalm 132. This messianic psalm (see Acts 2:30) rejoices in the Lord's choice of David and God's promises to him.

Psalm 133. Unity is a great blessing.

Psalm 134. Praise from those who minister in God's sanctuary.

Psalm 135. The greatness of God, and his superiority to all idols, is shown by his mighty acts in history.

Psalm 136. This great praise psalm repeats "His love endures forever," as a response by worshipers to statements about God.

Psalm 137. Weeping marks the life of the exiles in Babylon, for they are cut off from the land promised to Israel by the Lord.

Psalm 138. God is praised by David for his love and faithfulness.

Psalm 139. God is exalted as one who is omniscient (1–12) and who has known the psalmist intimately from before his birth (13–24).

Psalm 140. A cry for rescue from the wicked and from oppressors.

Psalm 141. The psalmist needs protection against hasty choices which might lead him into sin.

Psalm 142. Praise for the freedom to express needs to God.

Psalm 143. A cry for deliverance and guidance.

Psalm 144. A joyful call to God, who is strong to deliver, with praise for expected blessings that will follow God's answer.

Psalm 145. Pure praise, offered to God for his many wonderful attributes and qualities.

Psalm 146. We trust ourselves to God, not men.

Psalm 147. Praise to God, who "delights in those who fear him."

Psalm 148. Praise to God offered by the entire universe.

Psalm 149. Praise to God offered by his saints.

Psalm 150. Praise to God offered by everything that has breath!

Look through the psalms in Book V (107–150). List all the reasons found for praising God. List also all the ways in which believers express their praise. Which of these psalms provides a helpful pattern for your own worship? Use your selected psalm daily for a month, to focus your worship and praise.

PROVERBS
The Book of Wise Sayings

This collection of sayings is designed to guide the reader's daily choices. The sayings cover many topics touching on such varied subjects as interpersonal relationships and attitudes toward work. They also probe values with evaluations of wealth and poverty. The insights shared in the proverbs have been valued by many over the ages.

Date and authorship. Most of the proverbs are attributed to Solomon (970–930 B.C.). Archaeological discoveries have shown this type of literature was common in the ancient world. These have blunted critics who once insisted the book must come from a later time. While Solomon wrote most of the proverbs, others were added to his basic collection (10–22) at various times. It's probable the book took its present form in the days of Hezekiah (715–686 B.C.), as suggested by 25:1.

Outline. This collection of unrelated sayings is difficult to outline. Most thus break the Book into units according to authorship or the time added to the basic collection.

Outline

Using the Proverbs. Proverbs can be used by believers in several helpful ways. Read until stopped by a significant thought and then memorize it. Read a chapter, seeking one principle to apply during the day or week. Or gather insights on a single topic. For instance, what should our attitude be toward work (see 10:4, 5; 12:24; 13:4; 14:23; 18:9)? What are the implications of setting our heart on gaining wealth (10:2, 16; 11:4, 16, 18, 28, 16:8, etc)? How much of poverty is the "fault" of the poor, and what should be our attitude toward them (13:8, 23; 14:20, 31; 16:19, 17:5; 19:1, 20:4,

17, etc)? Selecting topics touched on by proverbs, and then the organizing insights the book shares can be a very helpful personal study project.

Theological note of caution. One thing must be kept in mind when studying and applying the book of Proverbs. The proverbs state general principles, which have universal application to all men in all societies. Thus the proverbs describe patterns God has built into humanity and into providence. But the proverbs are *not* a collection of God's covenant commitments to his people. Thus the general principles will not hold true in every case. There will be exceptions.

Chapters 1–9. In Praise of Wisdom

The purpose of Proverbs: 1:1–7. Solomon has written Proverbs and begun this collection to help the reader "acquire a disciplined and prudent life, doing what is right and just and fair" (v. 3, see *Wisdom, OT*).

The benefits of wisdom: 1:8–4:27. Warnings and exhortations describe the dangers of rejecting the wisdom offered, and tell the benefits of accepting it. Solomon promises that the reader who hears and applies will prolong his life and win a good name with God and man. He need only pay close attention, and not swerve to the right or left of the righteous path the proverbs mark out. Relationship with God is critical for God is to be trusted in making life's choices, not our own understanding. As God is acknowledged, and his ways are followed, "he will make your paths straight."

Wisdom, OT

OT words that relate to wisdom range from those which speak of skill and reasoning ability to those which emphasize understanding. The skillful artisan is "wise" and the ruler "wise" if he rules well.

But in OT thought the dominant aspect of wisdom is moral. The goal of instruction such as is given in the Proverbs or other wisdom literature is neither knowledge nor skill, but holiness. To the OT believer, one is wise if he makes morally correct choices, and thus lives a life that is pleasing to God.

This cannot be overemphasized, for it marks a distinct difference between Proverbs and other similar ancient literature. The author of the Egyptian *Proverbs of Amenemope* was concerned that the scribes he wrote to instruct did their jobs well. Solomon and the other OT wisdom writers were concerned that believers make godly choices. Thus in Proverbs we see a constant contrast between the wise and the "fool," which is appropriate as the Hebrew word for "fool" identifies one who is morally lacking.

It is important to keep this focus in mind in reading Proverbs. The instruction given is not designed to help the reader *know* more, for wisdom is not identified with either knowledge or intelligence. OT instruction focuses on the volition or will, for true wisdom can only be discerned in the choices a person actually makes in daily life.

Warning against adultery and other folly: 5:1–7:27. The danger of choices motivated by lust is treated extensively in these chapters. Also stressed are the dangers of laziness (6:1–11) and the characteristics of the villain (6:12–19).

Praise of wisdom: 8:1–36. Solomon praises wisdom. Much debate has developed over 12–31, which pictures wisdom as a woman and speaks as if she has separate identity as a person. To some this is merely a literary device. Others argue that there is a relationship between "wisdom" and the NT "Logos," or Word, of John 1. There "Word" is a title for Christ. However, no NT passage refers to Christ as "wisdom," or refers to this proverb, so it is best to take Solomon's language as a picturesque way of dramatizing the way of wisdom to which Solomon calls his people.

Wisdom versus folly: 9:1–18. The two ways of life are contrasted, with both Wisdom and Folly personified as women.

Chapters 10:1–22:16. Solomon's Proverbs

The OT tells us that Solomon wrote more than 3,000 proverbs (cf. 2 Chron. 9:1–24). The text indicates these are a few of the wise sayings he recorded. The sayings are couplets, using the literary device of contrast (see Hebrew poetry, antithetical parallelism, p. 252). These proverbs range over many topics, without special organization.

Chapters 22:17–24:16. Collected Sayings

No author of these "sayings of the wise" is indicated. These are longer sayings than the ones preceeding them and tend to use synonymous parallelism (p. 252). Like Solomon's short sayings, these describe wise and foolish conduct.

Chapter 24:23–34. More Collected Sayings

A brief addition to the "sayings of the wise."

Chapter 25–29. More Proverbs of Solomon

In the days of Hezekiah's revival, his scribes apparently worked from written sources which contained many of Solomon's sayings. The scribes edited them and included a number in an addition to the OT scroll which contained the Proverbs.

These proverbs are also couplets, like Solomon's first collection (10–22). They tend to teach by synonym rather than contrast.

Chapter 30. Sayings of Agur

Agur and the others mentioned in verse 1 are unknown. The first section (2–9) is personal, sharing the writer's awe of God and his own sense of inadequacy. The rest (10–33) contain wisdom sayings which focus on nature rather than moral instruction.

Chapter 31. Sayings of King Lemuel

Like Agur, Lemuel cannot be identified. The first section (1–9) contains his mother's advice to him, warning against strong drink. The second section is an acrostic, in which each verse begins with a different Hebrew letter. This famous poem (10–31) contains the OT's description of a wife who earns praise for her noble character.

Woman's Role, OT

It's popular with some to portray the woman's role in biblical times as one of slavery or drudgery, and to picture women as oppressed in a male-dominated society. While women in the agrarian society of the OT were limited in occupational opportunities, it would be a mistake to misunderstand the significant and fulfilling place women had in that day.

Proverbs 31 gives us a description of a women's life, centered around the home and family. But that life was not limiting! The wife had many areas of freedom and responsibility (13), and her counsel was heard with respect (26). She also made independent business decisions (13, 16, 18, 24), and had discretionary funds to use in helping the poor (20). Her life was active and full (17), and involved management of time and employees (15). As a person who made a significant contribution to her family unit, she was appreciated at home (11, 28) and respected in the community (31). As a result she was secure and confident (25). The many challenges facing her gave her opportunities to use to the fullest every capacity and potential that God has given to all human beings.

It would be a mistake to idealize OT times or the role of the woman in similar societies. But it is important to realize that a woman in such a society had both family (with the context of intimate relationships a family provides) and a career, with the potential of personal fulfillment that a career today implies. It is also important to realize that men in a culture like that of the OT for the most part shared the woman's opportunities, for a man's work involved just the same kind of activities (labor, buying and selling, supervising others, and so on) as hers. For each, personal fulfillment came as personal potential was stretched and developed by meaningful work and by participating in family life.

ECCLESIASTES
The Book of Philosophical Reasoning

Ecclesiastes is like no other OT book. It is also unique among writings recovered from the biblical world. The Hebrew title, *Qoheleth,* means "assembly speaker." As literature the book is clearly philosophical discourse.

Date and author. Traditionally the book was held to have been written by Solomon toward the end of his rule, when his foreign wives had turned his heart from God (c. 740–730 B.C.). This view is strongly criticized by some. However, linguistic studies in the 1950s demonstrated characteristics and word choices which distinctly fit Solomon's time and his activities. There is no reason to doubt that the author, who claims to be a king in Jerusalem whose wisdom surpasses all preceding wise men (1:12–14), is anyone other than Solomon.

Theological difficulties. There are many apparent contradictions between statements in Ecclesiastes and the teachings of other OT books—for instance, the suggestion that "the dead know nothing; they have no further reward" (9:5). This has been used to teach the doctrine of soul sleep, and the notion that death brings dissolution of the individual's personality. How can we answer such difficulties?

—By noting what Solomon himself says in Ecclesiastes. Seven times he states he "communed with my own heart" (KJV), and twenty-nine times he says that his reasoning is based on "what is done under the sun."

The point is clear and vital. In his old age Solomon set himself the task of determining life's meaning using only his ability to reason from information gained by experience and observation! He rigorously ruled out revelation as a source of information, and thus makes no mention of the covenants, the law, or the Lord's miraculous interventions in the history of Israel (see *Reason and Revelation,* p. 270).

Thus this book is not communication of truth from God, but an inspired report of Solomon's reasoning. We can no more treat the content of this book as a revelation of truth than we can treat as true the statements of Satan in Genesis 3. In such cases inspiration guarantees a true report of what is said, but not the truth of the statement.

Value of Ecclesiastes. What then is the value of this unique OT book? It is not meant for us to use as a source of information. Instead it is meant to communicate in compelling and deeply moving tones a message needed by all mankind. Apart from the perspective on life God's Word provides, life truly is meaningless and empty.

Reason and Revelation

The twentieth century existentialist argues powerfully that, to any reasonable man, life is meaningless and the only attitude which fits the facts of human existence is one of despair. Does an application of pure reason lead to despair?

The answer has to be developed by careful definition of the differing roles of reason and revelation, as these terms are often used philosophically. "Reason" involves making deductions about the meaning of life and other ultimate issues, using only information available through observation and experience. The Bible makes it clear that this source of information is simply inadequate to provide a basis for valid analysis! While certain truths about God are revealed in nature—particularly his existence and power— no understanding of God's motives or his plans can be known through natural sources. Thus no matter how accurate the reasoning processes, the end result of a "reasoning" approach to discerning life's meaning will fail, through lack of relevant data.

For this reason the Bible affirms the necessity of special revelation; the communication of information to man by God through some method other than nature (see *Inspiration of Scripture,* p. 729). On the basis of information shared by God through revelation about his thoughts, plans, actions, and dealings with mankind, the questions philosophers ask about life's meaning *can* be answered! And the answers will bring joy, not despair.

What happens when the greatest intellect reasons accurately from the data available to mankind through observation and experience? How would questions of meaning then be answered? In Ecclesiastes, Solomon limits himself to these sources and applies his great intellect to the ultimate questions about life. His conclusions? Life is meaningless and empty. Apart from truths shared with us by God, it is impossible to make sense of human existence.

What then can we say about reason and revelation? (1) Reason is capable of deducing from Creation a limited body of knowledge about God. (2) Reason cannot deduce all that human beings need to know to discern life's meaning, for experience and observation do not provide enough data from which to draw valid conclusions. (3) God, knowing our need and loving us deeply, has provided through revelation what we need to know to understand the meaning of our lives, and to find personal relationship with him. Because God did speak, we have the best of reasons to hope!

For study. See Psalm 19; Romans 1:18–20; 1 Corinthians 2; and *Inspiration of Scripture,* p. 729.

Outline. Ecclesiastes contains a number of brief discourses, which first present a series of proofs of Solomon's theme, and then follow with a series of deductions from his conclusion. The book can be outlined simply.

Outline

I.	Prologue	1:1–11
II.	Theme Proven	1:12–6:12
III.	Deductions from Theme	7:1–12:8
IV.	Epilogue	12:9–14

Chapter 1:1–11. Prologue

Solomon boldly states the theme he will demonstrate. "Meaningless! Meaningless!" This is how the NIV correctly translates the word the KJV renders "vanity."

Chapters 1:12–6:12. Theme Proven

In a series of brief discourses, Solomon shares the reasoning by which he arrived at the conclusion that life is meaningless.

Knowledge disappoints: 1:12–18. Solomon's own experience proves to him that knowledge and learning bring only grief. A less intelligent person might not have realized how meaningless life is!

Pleasures are empty: 2:1–11. Solomon's position made it possible for him to taste sensual pleasures, accomplish great projects, and gather the world's luxuries and delights. Although he denies himself nothing, he finds that all are meaningless.

Contrasts are irrelevant: 2:12–17. While ultimate meaning escapes us, isn't it possible that one man's life might be more meaningful than another's? No, for even distinctions between the wise and the fool are irrelevant, as death overtakes both. In death no distinctions count.

Work too is meaningless: 2:17–26. Solomon's great accomplishments cannot give his life meaning. The good things of life can be accepted and enjoyed, but will not give meaning to a man's existence.

Life's cycles do not reveal meaning: 3:1–15. Life is organized in a pattern of repeated cycles. Yet observation of the cycles does not lead to an understanding of beginnings or endings. Only a grasp of origins or destiny might reveal life meaning.

Injustice demonstrates meaninglessness: 3:16–22. The existence of injustice is a demonstrable fact of life. There may be judgment after death. But from all that man can observe, a human being dies just like an animal. There is no evidence that the spirit of one rises up to God, and the other dissipates into dust.

Oppression, toil, and friendlessness: 4:1–16. Human suffering and ambition also give evidence of meaninglessness. While two are better than one, relationships with other beings as transient as we ourselves cannot provide life with any ultimate sense of meaning or purpose.

Religion is mystery: 5:1–7. The existence of God is evident to Solomon from the creation. But beyond that, little can be said by those limited to earth of a God who is in heaven (2). Standing in awe of Mystery cannot provide life with a sense of meaning.

Riches are meaningless: 5:8–6:2. However rich a person may be, he never seems to have enough, even though one can only consume a little, however much he has. Possessions cannot make life meaningful.

Man's meaningless destiny: 6:3–12. Whatever the future holds for a newborn infant, its days will be without meaning. Solomon's despairing conclusion is that a child might better die stillborn than live to discover the meaninglessness of life!

Existence of God

The Bible does not attempt to prove that God exists. Instead it simply affirms, presenting God as a self-revealed reality.

Even Ecclesiastes, the only OT book which adopts the approach of reasoning from human observation and experience, does not argue for God's existence. The fact of God seems so evident the writer speaks to him as a "given."

How would Solomon arrive by reason at the conclusion God exists? While there is no statement of his reasoning, two of the classic "proofs" for God may be implied in Ecclesiastes. Solomon seems struck by recurring patterns in life (3:1–15). One classic proof is the argument from design, which reasons that where there are regularities there must be a Designer, for "chance" fails to exhibit this characteristic. Solomon also calls God the Creator (12:1). Another classic proof argues from cause and effect, insisting that the chain of cause and effect which links all events must logically extend back to a First Cause, who is God.

Whatever reasoning Solomon found compelling, Romans 1:18–20 states that evidence of God's existence is planted in his creation. Honest examination of the universe does lead to the conclusion Solomon reached: that God must exist, whether or not he is known.

Yet while Ecclesiastes speaks confidently of God as a being who exists, it says little about him. Even the word used for "God" is a general term and not the personal name Jahweh, given to reveal his essential nature (see *Jehovah/Jahweh*, p. 75). We need to know more about God than reason can tell us. We need to know him by revelation (see *Reason and Revelation*, p. 270).

Chapters 7:1–12:8. Deductions

Solomon has demonstrated that no meaning or purpose to human life can be discerned by an examination of human experience. Still, Solomon concludes that some ways are better than others. He proceeds from his discoveries to suggest rules for the best life possible to us under the circumstances.

Some ways that are to be preferred: 7:1–12.
A fatalistic attitude is to be adopted: 7:13, 14.
Extremes are to be avoided: 7:15–22.
Wisdom is preferable to folly: 7:23–8:1.
One must submit to authorities: 8:2–10.
Be God-fearing: 8:11–13.
Enjoy life's good things: 8:14, 15: Even though they cannot make your life meaningful.
Death awaits all: 9:1–12: So enjoy life while you can.
Follow wisdom's ways: 9:13–10:20.
Prepare for the future: 11:1–6. Though you cannot control it.
Enjoy your youth: 11:7–12:8. For old age and death soon come. Then all will be proven to be utterly meaningless.

Chapter 12:9–14. Epilogue

Now, at the end of his report, Solomon looks back over the wasted years of his life during which he turned from God's commandments and lost his grip on those realities which give life its meaning (see p. 269). His final words point back to his youth, and invite us to fear God and obey his commandments.

Read through the first six chapters of Ecclesiastes. How does the writer seem to feel about his life? Would he have felt the same way if he had not had a chance to experience all the things that most persons value?

From your own experience, which of the things that Solomon discusses have you looked to for meaning? Have you been disappointed?

SONG OF SONGS
The Book of Romantic Love

The Song of Songs (or Solomon) is a unique OT book. It makes no theological statements. It contains no explicit revelations. Instead it appears to be an extended proverb in the wisdom tradition, speaking of the beauty of love between a man and a woman. Its eroticism caused this lyric love poem to be challenged by some pre-Christian rabbis. But it continued to be given a place in the Hebrew canon, because its author was thought to be Solomon, and because it had long been read during the Passover season.

Date and authorship. Solomon is named in the book as author of Song of Songs (1:1). This would date it between 970 and 930 B.C. The traditional date has been challenged, but there are no compelling reasons to reject it in favor of suggested alternatives.

Interpretations. The greatest debate continues to focus on how we are to understand and interpret the Song of Songs. Is it simply a lyric love poem, or does it have a "message"? If it is simply what it appears to be, why is it included in the Scriptures? Among the approaches suggested for interpreting the Song, three have gained strong support historically.

(1) Allegorical. Many Jewish rabbis saw the Song as an allegory of God's relationship with Israel. Early Christian interpreters took this same approach, but applied it to the relationship between Christ and the Church. With this approach a phrase like "black but comely" in 1:5 was taken to mean black with sin, but made beautiful by conversion, and the comment "between my breasts" in 2:12 was taken as a reference to the Old and New Testaments.

The primary problem with such interpretation is that there is no objective way to check interpretive flights of fancy for literal meanings are deemed to be irrelevant.

Some versions of the Bible reflect an allegorical approach to this book in the chapter headings, as: 1–3, The mutual love of Christ and the Church; 4, The graces of the Church; 5, Christ's love to it; 6–7, The Church professes her faith and desire; 8, The Church's love to Christ.

(2) Typical. In the twelfth century A.D. a tradition began which held Song to be what it seems, a love poem, but with typical meaning, meant to help us understand the relationship of Christ and the Church. This view is held by many today. But there is no

indication in Song of Songs or other passages of Scripture to suggest
a type is intended (see *Symbolic Language,* p. 61).

(3) Literal. Those who see Song of Songs as a celebration of
love as God intended it to be experienced by a man and woman,
have held different views about the book's structure. To some it
seems just a collection of love poems. To others it tells a unified
story. The great scholar Franz Delitzsch suggested it is a drama,
telling the story of King Solomon falling in love with a girl from
one of Israel's northern villages. He meets her while traveling incog-
nito, returns to the capital, and later returns in splendor to carry
her back to Jerusalem.

This dramatic view is reflected in the NIV, which marks out
the alternating speeches of the beloved (the bride) and lover (Solomon), and infrequent refrains spoken or sung by a chorus of her
friends. The structure fits the Hebrew text, and the determination
of who is speaking is made by the gender (male, female) of the
Hebrew pronouns.

The story. Because of its poetic and dramatic nature, it is not
possible to outline Song of Songs effectively. However the following
generally accepted structure helps fit together the story told in
the book.

> 1:1–2:7. The bride longs for her bridegroom. They meet and
> praise each other.
>
> 2:8–3:11. As their love grows, the bride praises the groom,
> using figures from nature.
>
> 4:1–5:1. The lover comes and praises the bride.
>
> 5:2–6:3. The lover has gone away and the bride expresses
> her longing for him.
>
> 6:4–8:14. The lover returns, the marriage is consummated
> (7:1–8:4), and the happiness of the couple is cele-
> brated.

Read through Song of Songs. Which of the approaches to
its interpretation seem to you to best fit the contents? Why
do you believe God included this book in the canon of Scripture
(see *Sex,* p. 100)?

UNDERSTANDING THE PROPHETS

The OT is divided into four major sections: the Law (the first five books), History (Joshua through Esther), the Poets (Job through Song of Songs), and the Prophets. The books of the Prophets fall into two categories: the Major Prophets, and the Minor Prophets, so called because their writings are relatively brief.

The Major Prophets	The Minor Prophets	
Isaiah	Hosea	Nahum
Jeremiah/Lamentations	Joel	Habakkuk
Ezekiel	Amos	Zephaniah
Daniel	Obadiah	Haggai
	Jonah	Zechariah
	Micah	Malachi

There has been much debate over how the writings of the prophets should be understood. Do the prophets speak symbolically? Do their words figuratively describe the experience of the church today? Or is their language to be taken literally and understood to describe events many of which are still future? Before reading the prophets, these and other questions need to be answered.

The Prophets. The prophets were men and women who received a special word from God, to communicate to others (cf. 2 Sam. 24:11; 1 Chron. 17:3; 1 Kings 12:22). In most cases this involved a life-long call to minister to God's people (cf. Isa. 6; Jer. 1; Ezek. 1, 2; Amos 7:14, 15). The prophets spoke boldly to kings and to common people. They warned, they encouraged, they gave instructions, they comforted (see *The OT Prophet,* p. 130). Many prophets left no writings. But the prophetic books in our OT are writings which contain God's message to the people of each prophet's day, and to God's people across the centuries.

A Contemporary Message. Each of the prophets spoke directly to the conditions of his own day. Yet we find certain common themes in most of the OT prophetic books.

* The prophets speak out strongly against distortion of the law and of the worship rituals instituted by God (cf. Isa. 1:11–15; Amos 5:21–25). Simply going through the motions (worship without heart commitment to God) is strictly condemned.

* The prophets also speak out against moral and social evils. Personal sins, and the oppression and injustice which mar society, are strongly condemned (cf. Isa. 1:16–17; Amos 2:6–8).

* The prophets foretell God's coming judgments, due because of Israel's and Judah's sins. They often speak of specific foreign nations God will use to punish his erring people (cf. Isa. 22:6–16).

* The prophets also reassure God's people. In spite of failures, and the discipline that sin brings, God's people will not be abandoned. As Isaiah reports, "For a brief moment I forsook you, but with great compassion I will gather you" (54:7).

In their own time, then, the prophets cried out against sin, calling for personal and national commitment to God. Few prophets saw their contemporaries respond, although there were short times of revival (cf. 2 Kings 18, 22–23). Yet even when God's people rushed after evil, and the judgment came, the prophet's message provided a basis for hope. When God's people return to the Lord, he will restore them.

You and I gain much from reading these messages given to a people who lived over 2500 years ago. We see a unique revelation of God, who continues to be concerned about holiness and justice. We see a God whose commitment to his people cannot be shaken even by their sins, and who continues to offer fellowship if we return to him, to walk in his ways of holiness and love.

A View of History. Much in the writings of the prophets stretches out beyond their own day, to envisioning the far future. Thus it's important to know how the prophets viewed history, and what they themselves thought their utterances meant.

The basic framework for the prophets, as for all OT believers, was the covenant (see *Covenant,* p. 51). This expressed God's personal commitment to his people, found in specific promises recorded in the OT. These promises concern the descendants of Abraham through Isaac and Jacob and include, with the promise of special relationship to the Lord, the promise of a homeland in Canaan. Thus the prophets looked at history, and at their own writings, in a very literal way. God had spoken in history past; God continued to act in history present; God would act in history future. God would keep the promises he had made to his chosen people.

When the prophets spoke of future events, they did not introduce something *new* into Israel's faith. Instead they saw themselves as channels through whom God explained more fully how he intends to keep the promises he made Israel of old.

The conviction that God does act in space and time, in this

world, is basic to the thought of the prophets, as is the firm belief that the God who spoke in past ages will act in the future.

The prophets did not fully understand the future that was pictured in their writings. But they never doubted that their visions came from God, or that their words would one day find literal and historical fulfillment.

Principles of Interpreting the Prophets. Most Protestant believers have adopted an approach to interpreting the Bible which treats the Scriptures with respect. This approach bases interpretation on a literal and historical understanding of the biblical documents. Several principles of interpretation are generally accepted. These principles are: (1) study the meaning of individual words and how they were used in the day they were written; (2) study the grammar and how different parts of speech expressed thoughts; (3) study the context, and see how words and sentences fit into paragraphs, and into the intent of the entire book. Especially study the flow of thought [the "argument"] of the material just before and after verses and paragraphs. And (4), be aware of the literary mold. A prose narrative will not have the same implications as a piece of poetry or drama.

To understand prophecy, several procedures need to be added to these general interpretive principles. These procedures are simply steps to take to make sure we understand the context of a section of prophetic literature, and can be summed up in four questions to ask in prophetic study. They are: (1) Is the passage didactic teaching, focused on the prophet's own time, or is it predictive, focused on the near or distant future? (2) Is a prediction conditional or unconditional? That is, will what is foretold happen "unless" the people to whom the prophet speaks repent, or act in some specific way? Or will what is foretold happen no matter what the hearers do? (3) Has a prediction been fulfilled, or is it still to be fulfilled? For instance, prophecies about Jesus' death reported in Isaiah 53 have been fulfilled. They were future in Isaiah's day, but to us are past. Other predictions may be unfulfilled, and thus be future to us as well as to the people of the prophet's time. (4) Does the prediction have a "multiple fulfillment"? This final question points up a special difficulty in interpreting prophecy. A single passage may refer to an event that will happen in the prophet's own day *and also* to another event which will happen at a much later time. Often when a prophetic warning is given about an enemy army which will soon invade Judah or Israel, the prophet seems to speak both of Assyrians or Babylonians, and of a distant day at the end of history, when another great army will assemble against

God's own. Likewise a passage in the prophets may have a "double reference," in which the writer shifts from one object to another without warning. For instance, many believe that when Ezekiel is speaking of the fate of a particular King of Tyre in chapter 28, he shifts in midpassage to speak of the nature and fate of Satan.

The need to ask these four questions helps us see why it's not easy to interpret prophecy. And why it is best not to be too positive in our attempts to fit the details of prophetic passages together into a particular system. The Bible does give a broad picture of the future in OT and NT prophecy. But the prophets themselves were forced to search their own writings "intently," and with the greatest care, trying to find out "the times and circumstances" of their fulfillment (I Pet. 1:10, 11).

A Special Problem. One of the great debates about understanding the OT focuses on how prophecy should be interpreted. If the normal principles of literal and historical interpretation are applied to prophecy, and the four guiding questions asked and carefully answered, a consistent outline of the future *does* emerge from the OT prophets. But some have been disturbed by this picture of the future and argued that prophecy cannot be taken literally. Some adopt an open "spiritualizing" approach (see *Symbolic Language,* p. 61). Others suggest a "modified literalism" or opt for a different approach to interpreting prophecy based on an "expanded theological principle." The issue in this disagreement is Israel. Does the OT mean *racial* Israel when it speaks of the future of Abraham's descendants? Or should we apply OT prophecies and promises directly to Christians? Does God intend to work out in history the fulfillment of OT promises about a land for and the conversion of a Jewish nation and people? Or is the "land" really "spiritual blessings," and the converts those who come to Christ in the Christian era?

Four prophetic systems have been developed in the past 200 years, each of which takes a different approach to OT prophecy:

Prophetic System	Interpretive Approach	View of Israel
A-Millenial	Spiritualize	No future for Israel, as a nation or as a special people. OT prophecies are fulfilled in the Church.
Post-Millenial	Spiritualize	The people of Israel will be saved, but a national destiny is unthinkable.

Prophetic System	Interpretive Approach	View of Israel
Covenant, Pre-Millenial	Modified Literalism	Israel will be converted and restored, but without special prominence.
Pre-Millenial	Literalism	Israel will be converted and restored as a nation, and the OT promises to Israel will be fulfilled.

Understandably, the approach to interpretation which each group takes is the one which supports its prophetic system (see Prophetic Systems, p. 812). This is the danger with systems: they may lead us to approach the Bible in ways that seem to support our preferred conclusions! Thus it is very important in our attempt to understand prophecy to choose our approach to interpreting rather than to decide which prophetic system we may prefer!

Reasons for Literal Interpretation. There are a number of reasons why the normal, or literal/historical approach should be used in seeking to understand the predictive messages of the OT prophets.

First, that method is in harmony with the prophets' own view of history and of the covenant. If we are to understand the OT as the people of OT times did, we need to adopt their viewpoint.

Second, we should be guided in our understanding of unfulfilled prophecy by the pattern of fulfilled prophecy. Here we have much clear evidence, particularly in OT references to the future coming, life, death, and resurrection of Jesus. Strikingly, these OT prophecies were all fulfilled *literally.* Even references which could not have been understood before the events took place (such as "he was assigned a grave with the wicked, and with the rich in his death," Isa. 53:9), were fulfilled in literal fashion, as Christ was brought out to a public execution ground and then laid in the garden tomb of the wealthy Joseph of Arimathea. Because the prophecies which have been fulfilled in history have been fulfilled literally, we should take the literal as the intended sense of the Bible's predictive material. Certainly we have no warrant from fulfilled prophecy to take the words of the prophets figuratively, or to modify our approach to biblical interpretation because we like or dislike a particular prophetic system.

One word of warning. "Literal" does not imply "plain" or "clear." Prophetic materials often leave out details and normally fail to specify times and sequences of events. Too often those who claim to take a literal approach to prophecy develop highly detailed and complete pictures of the future. True, the main themes in predictive materials are boldly sketched in the OT and confirmed in the NT. But no one can be sure of how the details will work out in history until the events themselves unfold.

Third, the literal approach is in greatest harmony with the way the NT interprets unfulfilled prophecy (cf. Rom. 11). It has been argued that the NT supports nonliteral interpretation (cf. Gal. 4:21–31). But in this passage Paul says "these things *may* be taken figuratively." His point is that OT events may be *applied* figuratively. Paul does not suggest that events, much less the words of prophecy, should be interpreted in any other way than literally and historically.

Summary of Principles for Understanding the Prophets. We can safely conclude that there are basic principles which will guide us to study the OT prophetic books with understanding. These are:

(1) The OT prophets had a message for the people of their own day. We should listen carefully to that message, to see what God reveals of himself and of the values and commitments he calls his people to live out in every society.

(2) The OT prophets had a philosophy of history. They believed that the God who in times past had given Israel her great covenant promises acted in their own day in harmony with his covenants. They were convinced that God would act in the future to faithfully fulfill every promise he had made.

(3) The OT prophets viewed their own writings, including their predictions, as divine amplifications of covenant promises. They expected their words to be literally fulfilled in future history.

(4) If we are to treat the OT with respect, we need to approach the OT predictive writings and seek to understand them as the prophets understood them: as pictures of events that would come to pass, even though each detail of when and how could not be comprehended.

As we read the prophets today, and take their predictions in a literal and historical sense, we will not understand every detail. We will not come to any neatly packaged system, telling what will happen in the 1980s or 1990s. But we will see the main outlines of a world and a society envisioned by the prophets of old: a world redeemed and a society reshaped by God at the end of time, when all his marvelous promises will come true at last.

ISAIAH
The Promise of Salvation

The Book of Isaiah is one of the most significant in the OT. The NT alludes to it over 250 times, and quotes it at least 50 times. God gradually unfolded his revelation during OT times. This great eighth century prophet significantly added to his people's knowledge of God, their awareness of the coming Messiah (see *Messiah,* p. 255), and to the OT's vision of the time of covenant fulfillment (see *Covenant,* p. 51).

Historical Setting. Isaiah lived in Judah and spoke to the people of the southern kingdom during critical decades (he wrote about 739–681 B.C.). His ministry spanned the rule of Uzziah, Jotham, Ahaz, and Hezekiah. Tradition says Isaiah as an old man was martyred by evil King Manasseh.

These were years during which Assyria was expanding toward world empire (see p. 204). Great pressure was placed on Judah. This danger, with the preaching of the prophets Isaiah and Micah, helped to stimulate a return to God led by godly King Hezekiah (715–686 B.C.). The great messages of Isaiah condemning Judah's sin and social injustice show how greatly reformation was needed in Isaiah's day.

But the revival was brief and superficial. Thus many of Isaiah's messages look beyond his own time, to a future in which Judah will follow her sister Israel into exile.

Despite the dangers of Isaiah's own time and despite his awareness that God will one day punish Judah, his final messages emphasize hope and confidence. God will bring his people back to the land and to intimate relationship with himself. Sin will be punished. God will send a Servant to redeem his people, and he will rule over an everlasting kingdom.

Isaiah the Man. Little is known of Isaiah. He is often mentioned in Kings and Chronicles, and his name occurs several times in his own book. But his family background and social status remains a mystery. The fact that his great personal vision of God took place in the temple (Isa. 6) suggests he may have been a priest, as only priests were to enter the holy place. Isaiah was an intimate of King Hezekiah—probably a sort of court preacher. His mastery of Hebrew is as rich and great as Shakespeare's grasp of English, and shows he was a highly educated man. Most significantly, Isaiah responded totally to the Lord, and faithfully communicated God's message for his time, and ours.

Were There Two Isaiahs? In the eighteenth century German scholars began to argue that Isaiah was not the work of one person, but of two or more. They argued from the different themes and the different language found in the first half of the book (Isa. 1–35) and in the final section (Isa. 40–66). The dominant reason for the division of Isaiah, however, was the belief that the later chapters view history from a time beyond the Babylonian captivity, some 100 years after Isaiah lived.

Conservatives generally reject the two-Isaiah theory. They note that both parts are quoted in the NT and ascribed to Isaiah. They also argue that any great writer will use different words and styles for different subjects and forms, and note that Isaiah uses sermons, poetry, and prose. Why shouldn't one person, writing in different forms and on different topics, and writing over a fifty-year span, show great variety in vocabulary and style? Most importantly, however, those who hold to the unity of Isaiah are supernaturalists, who do not find it strange that God might speak through a prophet of a time different than his own. The notion that the later chapters of Isaiah view history from a time beyond the Babylonian captivity holds no difficulty for a supernaturalist.

When we add to this the fact that no early tradition for multiple authorship exists, and that no early manuscript of Isaiah or any other document before or after Christ supports the eighteenth century suggestion, there seems no compelling reason to think all of Isaiah was not written by the man who lived in Hezekiah's day, and whose name is found as author in both halves of this great prophetic book.

Isaiah's View of God. One of the most exalted of Isaiah's themes is the prophet's portrait of the Lord. Isaiah uses a number of names for God, each of which reflects some attribute or majestic aspect of God's character. Each of these names is enfleshed by rich and graphic description. Significant names for God used by Isaiah, and passages which help us sense their meaning, are: The Holy One of Israel (5:15–16), Sovereign Lord (8:13–15), God the Judge (11:3–5; 24), God, Our Salvation (26:1–4, 12–13), Everlasting God (44:6–8), the Living God (40:11; 41:10, 13), Lord of Glory (60:1–3).

We can come to know God in a deeper way if we meditate on the names used in Isaiah, and on the passages in which he fills the names with fresh meaning.

Isaiah's Messianic Emphasis. In the NT John says that Isaiah "saw Jesus' glory and spoke about him" (John 12:41). Many passages in this OT book speak of the coming Savior. Most of them focus on fulfillment of the Davidic covenant's promise of a ruler. Key chapters on this theme, and their emphases, are: Isaiah 7 (a child born of a virgin will be Immanuel—"with us is God!"); Isaiah 11 (a descendant from David's line will reassemble God's people and establish a righteous kingdom) and Isaiah 53 (an individual identified as God's Servant will die for the sins of others and thus bring salvation). Many other references in Isaiah flesh out this picture of God's incarnation as a human being, come to suffer for his people and to rule over them forever.

Isaiah's Servant Theme. A major messianic theme explored in Isaiah is found in what are called the "Servant Songs" (42:1–9; 49:1–6; 50:4–16; 42:13–53:12). Israel, chosen by God for a servant role (41:8–9), has failed to be an agent of God's grace. So God will send a Servant to pick up the shambles of the unfinished task. This Servant will redeem Israel and all mankind. Isaiah beautifully portrays the Servant's desire to serve God, his humility, the great personal cost of his obedience, and his suffering and death.

Jewish scholars long before Jesus' birth recognized the Servant as the promised Messiah. But they were deeply puzzled at the contrast between the suffering servant and the triumphant ruler whom Isaiah also describes. This uncertainty can be understood by comparing the two lines of messianic teaching in Isaiah.

Isaiah's Visions of Christ

As Servant, He . . .	As Sovereign Lord, He . . .
*will be obedient (50:4, 5)	*will enforce obedience (11:3, 4)
*will suffer injustice (53:7–9)	*will blot out injustice (41:4, 5)
*will not raise his voice (42:2)	*will exercise power (40:10)
*will not reject the worthless (42:3)	*will judge the earth (41:14, 15)
*will be rejected by Israel (50:6)	*will be welcomed by Israel (44:3, 6)
*will be mocked and spit on (53:3)	*will win the allegiance of all mankind (49:6)
*will die (53:9)	*will establish an endless kingdom (9:7)

These apparent conflicts could not be resolved until, as history unfolded, it became clear that God intended two comings of the Savior: the first through incarnation, to suffer and die for humankind, and the second as triumphant resurrected Lord, to establish a glorious rule at the end of time. Only after the coming of Christ could the prophet's contradictory portrait of Israel's Messiah be understood.

Isaiah's Vision of the Future. Along with vivid images of God and the Messiah, one other picture filled the vision of this great OT prophet. This is a vision of history's end, when God's great promises to Israel will be fulfilled. Then sin and injustice will be removed, and God's righteous, peaceable kingdom will become a reality on earth. This recurrent vision has several clear elements. The people of Israel will be returned to Palestine (11:10–12; 14:1, 2; 27:12, 13; 43:5, 6; 49:10–12). Palestine itself will be transformed and become a fertile land (30:23–26; 35:1–10; 62:4, 5; 65:21–25). In that day Jerusalem will be the center of the restored earth (4:2–6; 52:1–12; 60:1–12; 62:1–7). There will be great blessings poured out on converted Israel (12:1–6; 25:1–12; 26:1–19; 54:6–10), and also on the gentile nations, which will also find faith (2:1–4; 11:3, 4, 9, 10; 25:6–9; 60:1–12). Isaiah's great and confident picture of the end reveals the power of hope in a time when Judah's very existence as a nation was threatened. Whatever dangers may exist, God will turn history to his own ends and bring the promised blessings to his people.

Value of Isaiah Today. Isaiah's towering work moves us today to awe and worship. Here we see a majestic portrait of God and are helped to grow in our relationship with him. Here too we see an unfolding of God's purposes and join with Isaiah in a confident hope for a future that God will surely bring to pass. Here too we bow before our Savior, revealed so clearly as suffering Servant on ancient pages, confidently penned centuries before the birth of our Lord.

Outline

How should we study Isaiah for greatest value? Here are several approaches which are especially enriching: * Read through Isaiah, to underline verses and phrases which reveal God's person and his character. Use these as a focus for praise and worship. * Read, list, and memorize verses which express God's heart and his values. * Study the Servant Songs (see above) to deepen your appreciation for Christ, and to understand your own calling to serve God and others.

The Holy One of Israel (1–6)

This first section is a collection of three sermons from Isaiah's early ministry, with a description of his call by God. The messages boldly confront the people of Judah, whose superficial religion revolts Israel's Holy God. The prophet's meeting with this Holy One has changed his own life. Now he lifts up God to his listeners as holy, eager for God's Word to purify them and bring about a national repentance and renewal.

Chapter 1. Indictment (First Sermon)

The whole universe is the courtroom! God, the prosecutor, cries out in mingled anger and anguish. His people, his children, have rebelled. They have spurned him and his holiness (2–4). Note here that Isaiah uses "Israel" in the sense of descendant of the patriarch Israel, rather than as the northern kingdom of Israel.

In spite of God's attempts to turn his people through discipline (5–9), they have failed to return to him. Even their worship is a repulsive thing, a trampling of God's courts to bring meaningless offerings (10–14)! Until God's people turn from their sin and learn to seek justice, their worship will be detestable to God (15–17).

Now the indictment becomes a plea. God promises cleansing if only his people will respond to his call to holiness (18, 19). But if they continue to rebel, destruction will surely come (19, 20).

God calls on Israel to see herself and her corruption through his eyes (21–24) and warns that if his people will not repent he will act as the Mighty One of Israel, to purge every impurity (24–26). When he has at last redeemed his people, they will be flooded with shame, and realize why those who forsake God must perish (27–31).

From Isaiah 1, what would you identify as "unholiness"? Can you write a description of what God might call a holy life for a believer today?

Chapters 2–4. Judgment Described (Second Sermon)

Isaiah looks ahead to the last days (2:1) and sees the judgments through which the Lord will finally purify his people. Three themes are emphasized in this description of the distant future.

Holiness Restored; 2:1–5. God's temple dominates the skyline of a purified Jerusalem (see *Jerusalem Temple,* p. 190). There, where he is again exalted in holiness, the peoples of the whole world will eagerly assemble to learn his ways (2–3). Then the world will know peace.

The Day of the Lord; 2:1–4:1. This phrase, with "that day," is used some 45 times by Isaiah. In each case it seems to mark out a time of judgment as history reaches a climax (cf. 13:9–13; 24:1–23; 32:1–20; 63:1–6). Now Isaiah describes the dark night of intense suffering which precedes the dawning of holiness.

Isaiah envisions an era of material prosperity but moral bankruptcy (2:8–9). He warns the people of that time to hide from the splendor of the Lord, who is about to humble the proud (2:10–18). In the day that God acts to judge the arrogant, the earth itself will shake and the lands shatter (2:19–22). In the collapse of that time men will turn against each other, snarling among the ruins of a fallen Jerusalem (3:1–9). God will act then to guard the godly (3:10), but the wicked will experience death and disaster, for it is God himself who enters into judgment with his unholy people (3:11–15). The women, too, so haughty in their rich clothing, will be stripped and destitute (3:16–4:1). Thus judgment will shatter every human illusion.

The Names of God

In the first few chapters of Isaiah several names are used to identify and describe God. He is called the "Holy One of Israel" (1:4), "Lord Almighty" (1:9), "Mighty One of Israel" (1:24), and "God of Jacob" (2:3). Throughout Isaiah other names are added: "Sovereign Lord" (28:16), "everlasting God" (40:28), "Redeemer" (41:14), "Savior" (43:3), and many others.

What is the significance of such names, and why are they found in the OT?

To the people of OT times, names were very significant. Unlike names today (such as Tom or Ellen), OT names are revelations of the essence or character of the person or thing named. This is especially true of the names ascribed to God. Understanding the importance of names helps us gain fresh insight into the OT.

When Isaiah calls God the "Holy One of Israel" he is alerting us to the fact that the passage expresses something important about God's nature as a holy Person. If we want to understand holiness, we might study those passages in which God is given this special name. Thus also the name "Lord Almighty" or the "Mighty God" underlines God's commitment of his own power to carry out the actions described. We can gain much insight into the nature and attributes of God by letting the names by which OT writers call him, guide us to a closer look at the context in which they are found. And to a deeper understanding of the wonderful Person we worship. See also *Jehovah/Jahweh*, p. 75.

The Branch of the Lord; 4:2–6. After the Judgment has passed, Isaiah promises that a "Branch of the Lord" will be "beautiful and glorious" (4:2). Many prophets use this term, Branch, to identify Messiah (cf. Jer. 23:5, 6; Zech. 3:8; 6:12) The word emphasizes his origin in David's line and his title to the promised Davidic dynasty. Here Isaiah describes the inauguration of that kingdom. The sinners among Israel have been purged in the preceding judgment; the holy survivors assemble in the shelter of the Lord's glory, which covers the holy city as a radiant canopy.

In this second sermon, then, Isaiah begins with a picture of holiness restored, describes a dreadful but purifying judgment, and concludes with a vision of a Jerusalem under Messiah's protection.

Chapter 5. Judgment Vindicated (Third Sermon)

The Vineyard; 5:1–7. The sermon begins with a striking illustration. God, like a careful gardener, has planted good stock in a fertile field. He has carefully and lovingly tended his vines, eager that they bear fruit. But when they matured they bore only bitter grapes.

Isaiah applies this illustration. The people of Israel and Judah are the garden in which God delighted. In spite of his loving care, they have borne the bitter fruit of injustice and oppression. Surely God is justified in the judgment which will uproot his unfruitful people!

Woes; 5:8–30. A flood of woes will come upon this people whose sins Isaiah now recounts. Their drunkenness, greed, arrogance, deceit, and oppression of the innocent (6–23) will cause God's anger to burn against them, until he strikes them down (24–25). Then God will call out distant nations, who will rush to war against the land and will seize his people as though they were some wild animal's prey (26–30).

One charge in Isaiah 5 is that God's people "call evil good and good evil," and "put darkness for light and light for darkness." What is the nature of this sin? How is it committed in our day?

Page 278 gives several principles and key questions to ask when studying predictive passages in the prophets. Apply these to both Isaiah 2:6–3:23 and to Isaiah 5:9–30. How do the passages differ? Do you believe they speak of the same time? Why, or why not?

Chapter 6. Isaiah's Call

God appeared to Isaiah in 739 B.C., the year King Uzziah died. According to tradition, this may have been the actual year in which, across the Mediterranean, Rome was founded along the river Tiber.

Isaiah's call came before his three sermons were preached. The sermons are reported first in his book to help us understand the society in which Isaiah lived and the impact of his vision of God as "holy, holy, holy" (4). Seeing God, Isaiah also sees himself and realizes in horror that he is a sinful man living in a corrupt society (5, cf. Job 42:4–6). But God has not shown Isaiah himself to condemn him. God's purpose is to cleanse. Isaiah is symbolically cleansed and his guilt set aside with fire from the altar of sacrifice (6–7; see *Atonement, OT,* p. 99). Forgiven now, Isaiah volunteers when God asks for a messenger and is commissioned for his prophetic ministry (8).

Isaiah's mission is to speak to a people who will refuse to respond (9, 10). In fact the prophet's call to repent will harden Israel's heart (cf. "Pharaoh's Hard Heart," p. 76). The people will remain hardened until, a century after Isaiah's death, the land lies ruined and the people are dragged away into exile.

How does a person's vision of God affect his or her life? Might Isaiah's conversion experience offer a model or pattern for today? How?

Isaiah and the Dead Sea Scrolls

Isaiah wrote his great work of prophecy some 700 years before the birth of Christ. Across the generations his work was loved and carefully studied, especially by a group of Jewish believers who formed a small community at Qumran. That community ended in 68 A.D., but not until its members carefully hid their precious writings. The scrolls lay in a cave near the

Dead Sea, preserved in Palestine's dry heat for fourteen centuries. Then, in 1947, they were accidentally found by a young Bedouin.

Among the scrolls were copies of Habakkuk and Isaiah, with fragments of Daniel and other OT books. Some of the biblical scrolls were copied as early as 160 years before Christ!

What is so significant about the find? The earliest text of the Hebrew OT which scholars possessed before the Dead Sea discovery dates from around A.D. 1100. These could now be compared with texts more than a millenium older!

Many textual critics had challenged the accuracy of the OT. They claimed that all sorts of changes had been introduced across the centuries. But the scrolls gave witness to the fact that the text of our OT has been preserved across the milleniums essentially unchanged! When we read the words of Isaiah, or any of the other OT prophets, we can be confident. We are reading translations of the very words that God's spokesmen carefully brushed on those first scrolls, preserving for all time the living messages of God.

The Book of Immanuel (Chapters 7–12)

This section of Isaiah takes its name from the prophecy of 7:14. It contains messages from the early years, during which Isaiah confronted evil King Ahaz (732–715 B.C.). These were years of constant crisis for Judah. Aram and the northern kingdom, Israel, pressured Ahaz to join a coalition against the rising power of Assyria. When they threatened to attack him, Ahaz actually appealed to Assyria for help, against Isaiah's counsel. After Judah's army was crushed by the coalition, Tiglath–Pileser swept down to destroy both Aram (Syria, whose capital was Damascus) and Israel (whose capital was Samaria). But then he turned on Ahaz and "afflicted him instead of strengthening him" (2 Chron. 28:20). The bitter Ahaz closed the temple, stole its treasures, and offered sacrifices to the gods of Syria rather than to the Lord. It is against this historical background that we read the "book of Immanuel."

Chapter 7. Immanuel!

A Word of Hope; 7:1–9. When Aram and Israel signed their alliance, Ahaz of Judah was shaken (1–2). Isaiah is sent to reassure the king: the enemies' threats will come to nothing. Ahaz must only remain calm and trust. God's messenger predicts the ruin of both powers (3–9). The reference in verse 8 to "sixty-five years" is best taken as a reference to Rezin of Aram's age: before his sixty-fifth year the destruction will come. And it did!

Unbelief; 7:10–25. Isaiah commands Ahaz to specify some miraculous sign from God to authenticate his message (10). Ahaz refuses to obey (11)! Angry now, Isaiah unveils God's ultimate sign to mankind. One day a virgin will bear a child, who will be Immanuel, which means "With us is *God!*" (7:14).

Then Isaiah points to another child, one he is carrying in his arms (cf. 7:3). Before his son Shear-Jashub is old enough to know right from wrong, the land of the two enemy kings will be a waste and Assyria will turn on Judah (15–17).

Thus Ahaz is clearly told how quickly the enemies he fears will be gone. By Rezin's sixty-fifth year and Shear-Jashub's early childhood, this prophecy came true! The enemy were crushed and the message of the coming birth of one who is God authenticated!

Virgin Birth? Does Isaiah 7:14 really foretell a virgin birth? One recent translation renders the Hebrew word "young woman," and some scholars argue that no supernatural birth is implied. But the Hebrew word is never used in the OT of a married woman: "unmarried girl" would be an accurate translation. More significantly, when Hebrew scholars translated the OT into Greek some two centuries before Christ, they chose a Greek work, *parthenos,* which does specifically indicate a virgin. The conclusive evidence is found in Matthew 1:23. There the word selected by the inspired writer is "virgin." Thus there is no doubt that, over 700 years before the event, the OT does prophesy the miraculous birth of our Lord.

Destruction; 7:18–25. God will turn the Assyrian scourge against Judah once her enemies have been destroyed. Ahaz' unbelief merely mirrors the deep unbelief of the whole people.

Chapter 8. Assyria, God's Instrument

Destruction Certain; 8:1–10. Isaiah gives a third sign to his nation. Before witnesses he writes a name which means "Quick to the Plunder, Swift to the Spoil." Nine months later his wife (a prophetess) bears a son who is given that name (3). Judgment hastens, and the capitals of Aram and Israel will be destroyed before the child is a year old (4)! Then the army of Assyria will overflow, flooding into Judah, and no strategy will save her.

Accept the Judgment; 8:11–22. God warns Isaiah not to react when this message raises charges of treason and conspiracy. He is to fear God, not man, for only the Lord is worthy of trust (12–17). Thus Isaiah remains faithful and stands with his family as a sign to Judah.

As for the people, they creep off in terror to consult mediums and spiritualists, but will not turn back to God and his law (19–22).

Chapter 9:1–7. A Child, A Son

Isaiah interrupts his portrait of judgment to include one of the brightest and most brilliant of messianic prophecies. In spite of dark despair, a light will dawn (2)! The great hope is centered on one who is both "born a child" (a reference to Jesus' human nature) and "a son" when given (a reference to Jesus' deity). The names given the child clearly identify him as God (6b). Of note is the phrase "Everlasting Father," which may be translated "Father of Eternity," e.g., originator of the ages (cf. Heb. 1:10–12). This child is to be the Messiah, destined to rule forever on David's throne (7).

How significant are these titles? See *Names of God,* p. 287. What in this passage would lead you to believe Isaiah speaks of Jesus?

Chapters 9, 10. God's Anger

The prophet now returns to the theme of judgment, to show how completely God's anger will scorch the land (9:8–21). Again God gives specifics, naming the sins that have aroused him to judge (10:1–4). Assyria will serve as the "rod of my anger" (10:5), the agency he uses to carry out his judgment (see *War,* p. 125).

But Assyria will overstep herself. In willful pride, Assyria will cause more harm than God intended. As a result Assyria will herself be punished by God (10:5–19).

At the end of this sermon Isaiah includes a recurrent theme. God will leave survivors to Israel and Judah; a remnant who has relied on the Lord (10:20–23: *See* Isa. 4:2–6). Even when the Assyrians come and Judah suffers under her yoke, believers are not to despair. In the end God will crush Assyria and free his sad but wiser people (24–34).

Chapters 11, 12. Messiah's Just Rule

The "book of Immanuel" closes with a beautiful description of the just rule of the Messiah, and of the kingdom he will establish.

Justice, OT

The OT word "justice" is the word often translated "right" or "righteous." Sadly, the idea of a "righteous" person seems out of style today, possibly because it wrongly calls to mind a stiff, forbidding individual who is quick to condemn us if we fall below his rigid standards.

But this is not the OT picture at all! In the Bible justice and righteousness are positive, dynamic, and compassionate traits. When Isaiah and the other prophets cried out against injustice, they expressed anger at the cold insensitivity of the wealthy who oppressed the poor, the businessmen who short-weighted the widow, the judges who accepted bribes, and landowners who cheated workers of their wages. The call for justice is a call to share God's own deep concern for the poor and oppressed.

The law set up rules for a just, moral society in which the needs of all can be met and the rights of every man respected. But God's OT people turned aside from this vision, seeking wealth and personal power over their countrymen. The prophets were ignored, as men loved themselves and not others, valuing money more than the good of their fellows.

In the prophets, judgment is pronounced on injustice. And in the prophets a new day for mankind is revealed. When God steps into history, the dream of justice will be fulfilled, and as Davidic king, Messiah will "with justice give decisions for the poor of the earth" (Isa. 11:4).

For study: Job 31:13–23; Isa. 1:21–26; Amos 5:1–15; Lev. 19:9–19.

God through the prophet calls us today to a life committed to doing justice. What might that involve for you and me?

A Branch (cf. Isa. 4:2–6) will spring from David's family tree who, filled by God's Spirit, will bring justice to the bloodstained earth (11:1–5). Even nature will respond to him, and jungle killers become tame (11:6–9, cf. Rom. 8:19–23 and *The New Heavens and Earth,* p. 311). In the day of Messiah's kingdom Israel's exiles will be regathered, returning to a land which has at last become a land of rest (11:10–16). In that day God's people will finally recognize him and find the joy that is always available to those who drink deeply of waters drawn from the well of salvation (12:1–6).

Read the praises expressed in Isaiah 12. Which of these words can you express to God, because they reflect your personal experience of his blessing?

Isaiah is a book rich in words which bear memorization. From these chapters you might memorize 11:1–3 and 12:1–3.

Oracles of Judgment (13:1–24:23)

This third section of Isaiah contains a collection of brief messages of woe or judgment. These are prophetic pronouncements, directed against nations around Israel. Each of these Gentile powers has been an enemy to God's people. Each has gone beyond the limits of God's intention for discipline. Each will be punished by God for its treatment of his people (cf. Gen. 12:3).

The Oracles	
Isa. 13:1–14:23	Against Babylon
Isa. 14:24–27	Against Assyria
Isa. 14:28–32	Against Philistia
Isa. 15–16	Against Moab
Isa. 17	Against Damascus
Isa. 18	Against Cush
Isa. 19	Against Egypt
Isa. 20	Against Egypt and Cush
Isa. 21:1–10	Against Babylon
Isa. 21:11–12	Against Edom
Isa. 21:13–17	Against Arabia
Isa. 22	About Jerusalem
Isa. 23	About Tyre
Isa. 24	Portrait of judgments

Chapters 13:1–14:23. Against Babylon

The first oracle in this collection of woes announces God's coming judgment on Babylon. Assyria is the great enemy of Isaiah's time: the dominance of Babylon lies far in the future. Yet Isaiah describes the terror of those who will be threatened by Babylonian armies a century later (13:1–8), and sees that desolation as a shadow of the judgment to come at history's end (13:9–16). Most striking is the statement that Babylon will fall to the Medes (13:17–19), and the prophet's description of the ruins of the great city as they can be seen in our own day (13:20–22).

There are two special aspects of this oracle which have drawn attention. Isaiah speaks of Judah's release from Babylonian captivity and describes her fall to the Medes. This has been taken by some scholars as evidence that this section is a later insertion in the book written after the events. Those who believe that God can and does predict the future (see *Fulfilled Prophecy,* p. 305), find this argument unconvincing. As God says later through Isaiah, "I foretold the former things long ago, my mouth announced them and I made them known; then suddenly I acted, and they came to pass" (Isa. 48:3).

The second issue relates to a taunt launched by the freed captives against the King of Babylon (14:3–23). Many believe that 14:12–17 is actually a description of Satan's original sin and his fall from heaven (cf. Luke 10:18). The emerging pride expressed in the "I will" statements of verses 13 and 14 may be the Scripture's revelation of sin's introduction into the universe!

Make your own decision about the interpretation of Isaiah 14:11–15. Be guided by the steps outlined for the study of prophecy on page 278. Whatever you decide, the application of this passage is clear. Every arrogance which exalts itself against God, in Satan, in kings, or in you and me, will fall under judgment!

Chapter 14:24–32. Against Assyria and Philistia

Sure judgment is determined for these two nations, long enemies of God's people. The oracle against the Philistines is dated the year King Ahaz died (715 B.C.).

Chapters 15, 16. Against Moab

Isaiah utters a soon-to-be-fulfilled prophecy of destruction against Moab (cf. 16:13). The tone of sadness at the fate of this neighbor is in stark contrast to the note of triumph over Babylon's fall (cf. 15:1–9; 16:1–12 with 14:5–11). Moab's judgment is deserved (16:6, 7), but God takes no pleasure in it.

Chapter 17. Against Damascus

In this announcement of the doom of the capital of Aram (1–3), the author's focus quickly shifts. The fall of Damascus will mark the beginning of Judah's decline as well (4–8). The decline will not come because of Assyria's great power, but because Judah has "forgotten God your Savior; you have not remembered the Rock, your fortress" (19).

Chapter 18. Against Cush

The land of Cush is Ethiopia. Before it became independent, around 1,000 B.C., it was a part of the Egyptian empire. The two lands are associated in Isaiah 18–20. The prophet announces that even this distant and aggressive nation will one day be humbled, and bring tribute to the Lord Almighty at Mount Zion.

Chapter 19. Against Egypt

Historically Egypt stands as the lasting symbol of Israel's long bondage. In Isaiah's day it appeared to some as a possible ally against the Assyrians. The prophecy begins by describing internal events which will drain Egypt of power, making her people weak and helpless (1–15). But this prophecy, as many in the OT, shifts from the near to the distant view of future history. The shift is marked by appearance of the phrase "that day" (16, 18, 19, 21, 23, 24; see p. 287, "The Day of the Lord").

The picture given here of the distant future is striking (16–25). At first the Egyptians will be terrified of God and his people (16–17). But God's intention is to bring a great healing to that ancient land. Egypt will come to know and worship the Lord (19–22), and in the end a great highway will link Egypt and her deadly enemy Assyria. The two peoples will travel it, not to make war, but to worship the Lord together (23–25).

Chapter 20. Against Cush and Egypt

This dated prophecy foretells the imminent defeat of Egypt and Cush (see Ch. 18 above). Isaiah the prophet has acted out their fate, walking "stripped and barefoot" (2) in Judah. Now God announces that the Egyptians will be led away in just this condition by Assyria. Thus the hopes of all those who rely on Egyptian alliance will be crushed. Nothing can substitute for trust in God!

Chapter 21. Against Babylon, Edom, and Arabia

The first prophecy looks beyond the captivity and tells of the fall of the city of Babylon to the Medes (1–10). Two brief woes follow.

Chapter 22. About Jerusalem

The people of Judah have refused to listen to Isaiah's call to a life of justice and his threats of judgment. Now, in the valley, Isaiah experiences a vision in which he sees the destruction of this people. In the vision Isaiah is gripped by and shares God's own bitter sorrow (1–4). He sees the landscape around Jerusalem covered by enemy armies, but even then the people trust in their weapons and in great underground reservoirs, hewn to store water against such a siege (5–11). God calls, but the people ignore him (12–13).

Isaiah is sent to a high official, Shebna, to tell him the reservoirs in which he trusts are nothing but graves (15–19). The Lord will depose this man and replace him with another (20–25).

Chapter 23. About Tyre

Tyre was a powerful coastal Phoenician city-state, resting on an offshore Mediterranean island, protected by its great fleet. The prophet looks forward to the day when Tyre's vast wealth is drained and her fleets crushed by the Babylonians, a "people that is now (when Isaiah writes) of no account" (13). See also Ezekiel 26.

Chapter 24. Portrait of Judgments

This section of Isaiah ends with a summary of the impact of the oracles of judgment. A time is coming when the Lord will judge and devastate the earth. Yet, despite the punishments, in the end the Lord will reign, and Jerusalem will be glorious.

The Sure Purpose of God (25–35)

This fourth and final section in part one of Isaiah affirms the great purposes to which God is committed for the future. Isaiah gives us two looks at the distant future and the blessings it holds (24–27; 32–35), to put the tragedies to be experienced in the immediate future (28–31) in perspective. The failure of any single generation of God's people on their millennium's long march through salvation history will not detour the sure progress of the ages toward God's promised time of fulfillment.

Chapters 25–27. Songs of "That Day"

The prophets, when speaking of history's end and of the Day of the Lord (see Isa. 2–4), normally stress the judgments God will bring upon the world. But in this section Isaiah the prophet lifts up the joy to follow the purgings of "that day."

Joy for All Peoples; 25:1–12. When the strongholds of the foreign powers are broken down, never to be rebuilt (2), all peoples will join in a great feast, prepared by the Lord Almighty (6). Then all tears will be wiped away, for death will be swallowed up forever (8).

Experiencing the Blessings of God's Way; 26:1–11. Praises will be sung in Judah in that day (1–6) by a people who have learned at last to love God and to live by his righteous laws (7–11).

The Just Raised; 25:13–21. Israel failed in her mission to bring the blessings of salvation to the whole earth (16–18). But God himself has acted to put her failures behind her, lost in a forgotten past. Joining in that salvation heritage, Judah's "dead will live" and, awakening from the dust, shout for joy!

The Fruitful Vine; 27:1–6. In his early ministry Isaiah indicted Judah as a vineyard gone bad, producing only bitter grapes. Now he sees God's people replanted in that land, guarded by God, filling all the world with choice fruit (cf, Isa. 5:1–7).

Retribution; 29:7–13. The day of joy will come after God has repaid those nations who persecuted his people.

Chapters 28–31. Principles of Judgment

The blessings of the last days are to be preceded by God's judgment. Now Isaiah outlines principles related to judgment.

Woe to God's Befuddled People; 28:1–15. Priests and prophets among Israel, like drunkards (7), will be unable to grasp the meaning of God's Word. They will miss its message of grace and (as did the Pharisees of Jesus' day) take the law as a system of rules by which to win salvation (13). Finally it will be Gentiles, speakers of foreign tongues, who by their faith in Jesus the Messiah point out, "This is the resting place" (12).

A Place of Safety; 28:16–29. In another great messianic prophecy Isaiah speaks of a precious cornerstone God will lay in Zion as the foundation of his kingdom (16–17). When the scourging judgment of that day sweeps down, those who trust him will never be put to shame (16). In a striking simile, the prophet explains the time of judgment in terms an agricultural people will understand: judgment is God's wise preparation of the ground for a rich harvest to follow (23–29).

Woe to Jerusalem and Her Conquerors; 29:1–24. Jerusalem will be encircled and crushed (1–4), but her conquerors will be destroyed (5–10). Discipline is due because God's people "come near to me with their mouth and honor me with their lips, but their hearts are far from me" (13). In the judgment, all who have an eye for evil will be cut down (14–21). Then the remnant will acknowledge the holiness of the God of Israel (22–24).

Resurrection, Old Testament

The OT emphasizes the blessings of living on earth in obedient, intimate relationship with the Lord. In most cases, the "salvation" spoken of in the OT is deliverance from some present enemy or trouble. Yet it would be a mistake to conclude that the OT is a stranger to the doctrine of resurrection, or that OT saints enjoyed no such hope. In fact, saints who "died in faith" did look forward to a better country, to a city God would one day found (Heb. 11:8–16,19).

Many OT references may allude to the possibility of resurrection (cf. Gen. 5:22–24, Deut. 32:39; 2 Kings 2:11,12). Other statements, whose meaning may not be perfectly clear, still make sense only in the context of a belief in resurrection (cf. Job 19:25–27; Ps. 16:9–11).

When we reach the prophets, we see this belief expressed clearly and confidently. One day death will be defeated (Isa. 25:8), and "your dead will live" as their bodies rise when "the earth gives birth to her dead" (Isa. 26:19). Daniel is very explicit. Those who "sleep in the dust of the earth will awake: some to everlasting life, others to shame and everlasting contempt" (Dan. 12:2, 3).

When reading the OT, with its emphasis on God's blessings in this life, and with its majestic prophetic view of a cleansed and purified earth, it is good to remember that God does not forget the trusting individual. The saints of old will join us, sharing with us in the resurrection won for us all by Christ Jesus. See *The Resurrection of Jesus*, p. 492).

Woe to Those Who Reject Trust in God; 30:1–31:9. God's people obstinately seek help from foreign nations (30:1–5). But an alliance with Egypt is utterly useless (30:6–11). Worse, it is a rejection of God (30:12–14), who has announced that deliverance comes through repentance, and quiet trust in him (30:15–18).

The poetic warnings are interrupted by a great passage of promise: God will bind up the wounds he inflicts: Jerusalem will weep no more (30:19–26). Grace, not judgment, is nearest to God's heart!

But judgment must come first. So Isaiah returns to this theme, with a description of God approaching his people. The Lord is aflame with anger (30:27–33). There is no help for those who will not rely on God (31).

This section of Isaiah contains many truths that can be applied to our lives. While an interpretation of the passage must relate it to Israel, the principles dealing with judgment and the believer's source of hope can be applied to our own experience. What lesson for living in this passage touches you most closely in your present situation?

Chapters 32–35. Joy Follows Judgment

This first half of the book of Isaiah ends with a series of descriptions of the Kingdom that will follow the judgments.

A Kingdom of Righteousness; 32:1–20. Isaiah calls on all to look to the "coming" king who will "reign in righteousness" (1). The thoughts and actions of the scoundrels who now plague the land will be no more (3–8). The complacent women of Jerusalem, who feel secure in an unjust society, will tremble as Judah falls (9–14). But one day God's Spirit will be poured out. Then prosperity and justice will canopy a land of peaceful dwellings, which knows true security (14–20).

The Kingdom for a Righteous Remnant; 33:1–24. Isaiah returns to a familiar prophetic theme. The brunt of the judgment will fall selectively, on the ungodly. Those who walk in righteousness will survive to enter God's peaceable kingdom. The chapter begins with a description of the judgment (1–12) and turns to the promise that those who "walk righteously" will dwell among the coming consuming fires and live to see the king in all his beauty (13–24).

Destruction of Enemy Armies; 34:1–17. The armies of the nations will be totally destroyed and God's people regathered.

Kingdom Joy for the Redeemed; 35:1–10. This is one of the most beautiful chapters in the OT. It describes the renewed land which the redeemed of the Lord will inherit, when God's promises are fulfilled.

Verses worth memorizing in this fourth "book" of Isaiah include Isa. 25:1,9; 26:3–4; 29:13; 30:15; 32:1–2; 33:5–6, 15–16; 35:3–4.

Chapters 36–39. Historical Interlude: Events of Hezekiah's Reign

Hezekiah is one of Judah's few godly kings. His thirty-year reign was marked by a definite, but superficial, revival. Isaiah was one of his counselors. Background, and a commentary on these events, is found on pages 214–217 (2 Kings 18–20; 2 Chron. 29–32). But why are two events of Hezekiah's reign repeated here, among the great visions of the OT's premier prophet?

Sennacherib's Invasion; 36, 37. When Sennacherib's Assyrian army invades Judah and threatens Jerusalem, Hezekiah turns to God. Isaiah brings God's promise of deliverance; the king and his people are simply to trust. God will act! This is a recurrent theme in Isaiah's earlier prophecies, as recorded in chapters 1–35. Now this promise is put to the test, and God does act. His people are delivered! This historic event gave testimony to the reliability of Isaiah's ministry and should have stimulated Judah to obedience.

Hezekiah's Recovery; 38, 39. A year later Hezekiah falls ill. He prays for recovery from his terminal illness. God hears and fifteen years are added to his life. When he recovers he receives a delegation from Babylon, come with congratulations. Hezekiah shows them his treasures and the defenses of Jerusalem. Rebuked by Isaiah, Hezekiah objects: "But Babylon is so far away!" (39:3). The point is that Isaiah's earlier prophecies have often spoken of Babylon as the future enemy and persecutor of God's people! Even godly king Hezekiah has not truly heard and understood God's words to Judah through Isaiah!

These two historical narratives demonstrate (1) the faithfulness of God to his word through Isaiah, and (2) the insensitivity of God's people to the message of repentance and warning which Isaiah has delivered.

📖 Read through these narrative chapters. Then reread the first thirty-five chapters of Isaiah at one sitting. In your Bible mark messages of Isaiah which the historic events of 36–39 illustrate and authenticate.

Chapters 40–66. Visions of Splendor

The second half of Isaiah, sometimes called Second Isaiah or Deutero-Isaiah (see page 283), launches us into a fresh and joy-filled world. The tone becomes one of optimism and celebration. Here the prophet seems to look back on judgment: the prospect of onrushing terror is gone. The message of the prophet in the two sections is essentially the same. But the difference is real. Now Isaiah focuses on the kingdom that will arise from the ashes of judgment, not on the judgment through which the kingdom will come. It is as if before we looked toward a distant kingdom through a more real and closer cataclysm, now we look back, with the kingdom at hand, at the judgments fast receding into the past.

Chapters 40–48. Beyond the Exile

The second half of Isaiah, like the first, may be divided into four sections, or books. The first of these is the Book of Comfort: a comfort that comes as Judah passes through her exile, and returns to the promised land.

Chapter 40. Comfort!

God speaks tenderly to Jerusalem. Her Sovereign Lord is coming, eager to "gather the lambs in his arms" and carry them close to his heart (1–11). The chapter continues with an exalted description of God's great power and wisdom (12–24). This one, enthroned above the circle of the earth, cannot be compared with any competing power, or with the universe itself (25–26). It is he, Israel's Sovereign Lord, who lifts up the weary and who renews the strength of those who find hope in him!

Isaiah 40 contains several incomparably great expressions of encouragement for believers of all the ages. Read them and meditate on this great God of ours. He has not forgotten you but is available now to renew your strength and to lift you up when you stumble.

Chapter 41. Israel's Helper

God, the master of history (1–7), has chosen the descendants of Abraham as his servants. A good master, God will not desert them (8–10). Those who rage against Israel will ultimately be disgraced, for God himself will help his people (11–20). In contrast to dumb idols, God is able to tell what the future holds (21–24). When the future is transformed into history, unveiling what God revealed beforehand, all will shout, "He was right!" (25–29).

Chapter 42:1–13. The Lord's Servant

My Servant; 42:1–9. The servant theme is an important one in Isaiah (see *Servanthood, OT,* p. 306). Here the servant in view is Messiah. Verses 1–3 emphasize the gentleness of Messiah. The "bruised reed" is a cracked shepherd's flute, and the "smouldering wick" a carbon-clogged bit of flax, used in an olive oil lamp. Each is worthless, fit only to discard. But the worthless of this world are precious to Messiah, whose mission is revealed in Christ to be one of redeeming the lost and worthless. To free the captives God will make this servant a "covenant for the people" (see *New Covenant, OT,* p. 330, *New Covenant, NT,* p. 653).

Praises to the Lord; 42:10–13. The work of Messiah will bring the peoples of the earth a new song: praise to the Lord.

Chapters 42:14–43:28. Israel's Unfaithfulness

The Unfaithful Servant; 42:14–25. The Messianic servant stands in contrast with Israel, the servant who has failed. Even when foretold judgments overwhelmed Israel with violence, God's people did not understand or take God's discipline to heart.

The Faithful Savior; 43:1–13. Now the words of comfort echo again. Israel is not to fear. The unfaithful servant will be redeemed by her faithful Savior. "I am the Lord," God reassures, and "no one can deliver out of my hand."

Mercy and Unfaithfulness in Contrast; 43:14–28. Israel has not called on the Lord, but nevertheless he will have mercy on her. He will blot out his people's transgressions.

Chapter 44:1–23. The Lord vs. Idols

The living God has chosen, formed, and given birth to Israel. He is her only source of help (1–5). How foolish then to turn from the Rock, who can protect his people (6–8), to worship dumb, blind, and hollow idols.

Isaiah's graphic description in this chapter is the OT's most scathing denunciation of the foolishness of idolatry. An artisan cuts down a tree, burns some for warmth, more to bake his bread, and from the rest carves an idol for worship, begging it, "Save me; you are my god!" How glorious God stands in contrast to idols: the God who formed all peoples against the gods that people form!

What empty things do people today count on to save them from troubles or dangers? Why is it as foolish today to trust something other than God?

Chapters 44:24–45:25. Jerusalem Restored

Cyrus Called by Name; 44:24–45:13. God announces that "Jerusalem shall be inhabited" and names Cyrus, who overcame Babylon, as his anointed instrument. The decree spoken of in this chapter was issued in 538 B.C., some 200 years after Isaiah's time. This mission is performed by Cyrus "though you do not acknowledge me" (45:4).

This chapter thus focuses on a theme often stated by the prophets and related to the biblical view of history. Nations and empires are raised up by God to accomplish his purposes. All are like clay in the hands of a potter: none is able to command the Maker of all. Thus God will "raise up Cyrus in my righteousness . . . He will rebuild my city and set my exiles free" (45:13).

An Everlasting Salvation; 45:14–25. In the end all peoples will turn to God. They will confess in new-found faith, "In the Lord alone are righteousness and strength" (24).

Chapter 46. The Gods of Babylon

The Lord speaks of the idols who serve Babylon for gods, so different from the one who sustains Israel (1–7). The rebels of Isaiah's day are to remember there is none like God, who "makes known the end from the beginning, and whose purposes will surely stand" (8–13). (See *Fulfilled Prophecy,* p. 305).

Chapter 47. Fall of Babylon

Isaiah has named Cyrus as the one who will overthrow Israel's great future enemy (44:24–45:13). Now the proud city, which her citizens thought would continue forever, is swept away by disaster.

Chapter 48. Israel Freed

Israel's Stubbornness; 48:1–11. In the past God has foretold events and spoken of yet future judgments. But Israel refuses to respond to him: God's people are as stiffnecked as though their sinews were cast in iron. Isaiah's fresh burst of prophecy contains a revelation of plans hidden earlier from God's people.

Israel Freed; 48:12–22. Among the new messages is the promise of deliverance from Babylon through God's chosen ally (Cyrus). The day will come when Israel's captives leave Babylon with shouts of joy (12–22).

Chapters 49–55. The Servant of the Lord

This is the second "book" or section of this half of Isaiah. It concentrates on one known as the "Servant of the Lord." It is clear from the context, and was recognized by the Hebrew people before Jesus' birth, that the suffering servant of Isaiah portrays the Messiah. Yet all puzzled over how the suffering and gentle individual portrayed here could be the great king of other Isaiah passages. Today we clearly recognize Jesus' character and his mission on earth from these beautiful portraits of the Lord's Servant (see *Servanthood, OT,* p. 306).

Chapter 49. The Servant and Israel

The Servant's Mission; 49:1–7. Isaiah has shown that the people of Israel were called to be God's servants (42:8 f). But Israel failed to complete her mission. Now a new Servant, an individual named before his birth (1), will be formed in his mother's womb to regather Jacob and Israel to their Lord (5–6) and to light the way of the Gentiles to God. When the despised Servant accomplishes his mission, he will be recognized and worshiped (7).

The Restoration of Israel; 49:8–21. The Servant himself is said to be a Covenant (see *New Covenant, NT.* p. 653), and to win release of the captives (8–13). Zion will never be forsaken (14–20), though now bereaved. The exiles will return and live!

The Humbling of the Gentiles; 49:22–26. The Gentiles will be humbled, and all mankind will then know that the Lord is the Redeemer of Israel.

Chapter 50. The Servant's Obedience

Israel's Transgression; 50:1–3. Israel's disobedience has led to her shame, like a woman divorced because of her sins.

The Servant's Obedience Assures He Will Not Suffer Disgrace; 50:4–9. The ministry of the Servant to sustain the weary is successful because he learns from God (4–5). He is obedient, and does not draw back even though he is mocked, beaten, and spit on (6–7). In his suffering he is fully vindicated by God, whatever men say about him (8–9).

Fulfilled Prophecy

Isaiah affirms it: "I am God, and there is none like me. I make known the end from the beginning, from ancient times what is still to come" (Isa. 46:9, 10). God can announce beforehand because he has the power to bring his purposes to pass. This, says Isaiah, is one thing which sets God apart from idols (41:21–24; 45:20–21; 46:8–11; 48:5–7).

This affirmation ushers us into the realm of prophecy: predictions made before the events they foretell happen.

Antisupernaturalists have challenged the idea of fulfilled prophecy. Celsus, in the second century A.D., denied that Daniel could have written during the Babylonian era. His detailed description of succeeding world kingdoms, including the conquests of Alexander the Great, either prove the supernatural origin of the prophet's words or were written after the events occurred! Eighteenth century critics also denied that Isaiah wrote chapters 40–66 of his book. How could he have known beforehand that Babylon would fall to Media-Persia? Especially, how could he have named, a hundred years before the man's birth, the very individual who would decree the rebuilding of Jerusalem (Cyrus: see Isa. 44:24–28)?

But there are fulfilled prophecies which cannot be denied simply by changing their date of writing. The youngest book in the OT was written hundreds of years before Christ. The dozens of prophecies which focus on the person of Jesus unquestionably were written long before the events described! Yet the OT foretells Jesus' birth of David's line (Isa. 9:6–7; 11:1), birth by a virgin (Isa. 7:14) in Bethlehem (Mic. 5:2). It tells of his early life in Galilee (Isa. 9:1–2) at Nazareth (Isa. 11:1). The OT tells of Jesus' rejection by his people (Isa. 6:10; 53:1), his triumphal entry into Jerusalem (Zech. 9:9), his betrayal by a friend (Zech. 11:12–13), his death with criminals (Isa. 53:9, 12) and burial with the rich (Isa. 53:9), all reported in the Gospels as history. Even the details of his death were foretold: the lots cast for his clothing (Ps. 22:18), vinegar offered him to drink (Ps. 69:21), his dying words (Ps. 22:1; 31:5), and the fact that while no bone would be broken (Ps. 34:20) his side would be pierced (Zech. 12:10; Ps. 22:16).

This stunning array of fulfilled prophecies—and there are many more—communicates to us the same assurance that Isaiah's words communicated to the Hebrew people long before Christ or the critics. God *is* in charge of history! What he promises, he will perform, for his words are reliable and sure. What God's word foretells does, in a literal and historical way, actually come to pass!

The Servant an Object of Faith; 50:1–11. Trust in the Lord and obedience to the Word of the Servant mark the life to which believers are called.

Chapter 51. Everlasting Salvation

God had determined everlasting salvation for his people. Those who have his words in their heart need not fear (1–8). A vision of God's actions in the past to deliver (9–11) will comfort God's people until he arises to defend them (12–16).

Servanthood, OT

Isaiah identifies two OT servants: Israel and the promised Messiah. Israel is a servant who failed. Messiah is the successful servant, a pattern to all who seek to live in close, obedient relationship to God.

What do we learn about a servant life style from the example set by the OT's coming Deliverer? First we learn that God calls and shapes his servants. He is personally committed to them (44:1, 2). In response, the servant is to commit totally to obedience. Gifted by God's Spirit, he adopts a gentle and quiet spirit and so works toward the birth of justice. He meets resistance but is not discouraged. He does not fail, but succeeds in carrying out the purposes for which he is called (Isa. 42:1–4). Throughout his life he meets obstacles with quiet reliance on the Lord who leads him (Isa. 42:6).

This picture of servanthood does not seem particularly attractive. One writer has summarized from Isaiah what servanthood meant to Jesus and what it may imply for us when we follow in his steps: "The Servant was chosen by the Lord (42:1; 49:1) and endued with the Spirit (42:1). He was taught by the Lord (50:4), and found his strength in him (49:2, 5). It was the Lord's will that he should suffer (53:10); He was weak, unimpressive, and scorned by men (52:14; 53:1-3, 7-9), meek (42:2), gentle (42:3), and uncomplaining (50:6; 53:7). Despite his innocence (53:9), he was subjected to constant suffering (50:6, 53:3, 8-10), so as to be reduced to near-despair (49:4). But his trust was in the Lord (49:4; 50:7-9); he obeyed him (50:4-5), and persevered (50:7), until he was victorious (42:4; 50:8, 9)." [Robert T. France]

This remains God's pathway to a fruitful life for you and me; a path first walked by Jesus who points out our way.

Chapter 52:1-12. Jerusalem Redeemed

God foretells Israel's captivity, and her redemption. Those who blasphemed God's name will come to know him then (1-6). Then even the feet of those who bring the good news that "Your God reigns!" will be beautiful, as all burst together into songs of joy.

Chapters 52:13-53:12. The Suffering Servant

This passage has long been recognized as one of the clearest and most explicit OT representations of Christ. In this passage his suffering and death are prophetically described, and the meaning of his death is interpreted (see *The Death of Christ, OT*). This passage was understood by Jewish rabbis before Christ's birth to be a messianic passage. Later the passage was reinterpreted and applied to Israel which, as a people, was supposed to suffer vicariously for all mankind. This interpretation is contradicted by the whole tone of Isaiah, which insists again and again that Israel's suffering must be understood as a judgment brought from God. The sin and disobedience of God's OT people means that she needs redemption as does the rest of the world (cf. Isa. 2-4; 9:10:14; 51:17-52:6, etc.).

The Death of Christ, OT

The Bible is a Book of gradually unfolding, or progressive, revelation. Many truths expressed in the OT are only fully explained in the New, with their true significance illuminated. This is the case with the meaning of the strange death of Jesus the Messiah. And yet the OT does speak about that death.

The institutions God established in Israel are clearly linked to Christ's death. The blood on the altar of sacrifice was understood by God's OT people to provide atonement (Lev. 17:11). Forgiveness was mediated to the believing sinner by blood sacrifice. The annual passover festival, with its passover lamb, was a yearly reminder that safety and substitution are linked (cf. Exod. 12:21–29). Thus when Jesus spoke of himself, and was announced as the Lamb of God who takes away the sin of the world (cf. John 1:29), the meaning of the crucifixion was linked to the familiar OT symbols.

But the clearest OT exposition of the death of Christ and its meaning is found in Isaiah 53. Here the suffering servant of the Lord is likened to a passover lamb at slaughter (7). He goes to his death, to be pierced for our transgressions (5). His wounds bring us healing and peace (5), for God has chosen to take our iniquity from us and lay them on his bent shoulders (6). He is cut off from life for the transgression of humanity, though he himself is completely innocent (8, 9). His suffering is that of a guilt offering, spread on the true altar. Through it he will bring us life as God's own children (10). He will die, but he will see the result of his suffering and be satisfied. He will carry our iniquities and thus justify us (11), for in his death he will bear our sins (12). Looking back into this OT passage, we can know the meaning of Jesus' death.

📖 Explore Isaiah 52:12–53:12. Underline each phrase which clearly refers to Jesus. Then write out several paragraphs explaining what an OT believer might have known about the Messiah before Jesus was born.

Chapter 54. Glory Ahead

Hard on the description of the Servant's sufferings (Isa. 53) comes God's call to Israel to rejoice in the coming glory. Barren Israel is invited to burst into song (1–3). Past shame will be forgotten as God, with deep compassion, recalls her to an endless relationship (4–8). Once God swore to Noah the waters of judgment would never again flood the earth. Now he promises that Jerusalem will know endless peace and be established in righteousness (11–15). God, the one who forged the weapons that have struck Israel, promises that no weapon will again prevail against his redeemed and restored people.

Chapter 55. Invitation to the Thirsty

Now all are invited to come to the Lord, to experience fully and freely the complete satisfaction he provides (1–2). God's people will be endowed with splendor (3–5), through the deliverer promised in the Davidic covenant (see p. 177).

Even now the Lord can be found! The wicked are invited to

turn to him, assured of his free pardon (6–7). Man will not be able to comprehend this gracious way, but man's ways are not God's ways. Yet his words of promise and blessing will surely be accomplished, and in that day the very hills will burst into song and share Israel's joy (9–13).

The Need for Redemption (Isaiah 56–59)
Chapters 56, 57. The Sins of God's People

In an extended passage Isaiah reviews the sins of God's people. It is these which have invited judgment and which have led a loving God to send his suffering Servant to provide redemption. The indictment closes with a promise: God will comfort and revive the contrite, and heal them. But there will be no peace for the wicked.

Chapter 58. Empty Ritual

The worship of Israel has not been an expression of piety but part of her rebellion. The rituals and fastings of Mosaic religion are meaningless as long as the people exploit workers and forge chains of injustice. True religion can never be separated from compassion and social justice.

Chapter 59. Separated from God

As in the Garden of Eden (Gen. 3), sin has widened the gap of separation between man and God. The bloodstained hands of God's people cannot be held out to him, for he turns away from wickedness. At the heart of all Israel's failings is rebellion against the Lord and turning their backs on his ways (1–15).

Thus God himself will come to bring righteousness and salvation. He will come in judgment but also with redemption for those who repent of their sins (15b–20). Afterward God's Spirit will rest on his people, and on their children, forever and ever (21).

The Restoration of Mankind (Isaiah 60–66)

The Book of Isaiah closes with an exalted vision of the distant future. When God's purposes are finally achieved in history, all will be set right. Then the blessings God has yearned to pour out on humanity will flood the heavens and the earth.

Chapter 60. The Glory Unveiled

Isaiah sees the dark clouds that cover the earth burned away by the light of God's glory (1–3). All will lift their dulled eyes to look around in amazement, as their hearts throb with joy (4–7). The whole world will gather at Jerusalem to adorn the temple of the Lord and the holy city (8–14). Now that long forsaken spot will be the pride of mankind and mother of a righteousness that fills the earth (15–22).

Chapter 61. The Ruins Rebuilt

Jesus quoted part of this chapter (v. 1) when he announced himself as Messiah (see Luke 4:16–20). The prophet promises that through him the oil of gladness will cleanse away the ashes of mourning when the devastated city of God is restored (1–6). Shame and disgrace will be replaced with pride, as righteousness supersedes the injustice which once plagued the holy land (7–8). Then the people of God will delight in him and be a beacon of righteousness to all nations (9–11). So the promise of redemption will be truly fulfilled.

Chapter 62. Zion's New Name

As a bride takes the name of her husband, so Zion, the holy city, will take a new name to reflect her consummated union with the Lord (1–5). God will establish Jerusalem as the praise of the earth (6–10), when the Savior comes to claim the city as his reward (11–12).

Chapters 63, 64. Vengeance and Redemption

Again these two themes are linked in an extended prophetic message. The garments of the Redeemer will be stained with blood from the terrible judgments he metes out on the earth (63:1–6). But when the necessary judgments are past, it is God's kindness and his mercy which will be celebrated (63:7–10).

Isaiah now returns to the perspective of an exiled Israel, suffering in the days of her rejection. Yearning for her Redeemer, Israel can look to history for evidence of God's faithfulness through the ages (63:11–19). So Isaiah speaks with longing of the day God will come to release Israel from her current sufferings (64:1–7), even though he realizes that the sins of God's people have led to her desolation and that judgment must precede blessing.

Chapter 65. Renewed Heavens and Earth

Judgment must precede the time of blessing, but only because God's obstinate people would not respond when he held out his hands to them in invitation (1–7). But judgment will not bring complete destruction: not all will be killed when the terror comes (8–12). Those who are the true servants of God will survive to enter a new earth (13–16) where man's lifespan is multiplied, and all is marked by unbroken peace (17–25).

Chapter 66. Judgment and Hope

Isaiah closes his book of prophecy by restating his message of judgment and hope. What pleases the Lord? Not ritual worship but the humble and contrite spirit of a person who responds to God's word. Those who choose their own way find only judgment (1–4). Those who are faithful to God will triumph. Like a woman whose birth pains precede the joy of delivery, so the pangs of judgment foretell a joy which will comfort Jerusalem (5–11). God promises that he will comfort his people and that their hearts will rejoice (12–16).

In the end God's people will be regathered from throughout the world, and the new heavens and earth which he shapes will endure (for verse 24, see Daniel 12:1, 2).

The New Heavens and Earth

One of the most fascinating of the prophets' visions in the OT is that of the "new heavens and new earth" (Isa. 51:6; 66:22). Does this refer to the transformation of our present world, or the literal creation of a new universe?

The OT does speak of a transformation. Human lifespan will be extended (Isa. 65:20), and meat-eating animals refashioned to eat only vegetation (Isa. 11:6–9; 65:25). Changes in rainfall and the heat of the sun will multiply the fertility of the land (Isa. 32:23–26). All these themes are mentioned in passing; all are hints about a universal renewal we can only imagine (cf. Rom. 8:18–22).

In the NT replacement of the physical universe is clearly taught. John sees a "new heaven and new earth, for the first heaven and the first earth has passed away" (Rev. 21:1). The apostle Peter graphically describes their destruction in a fiery burst of divine judgment: "the present heavens and earth are reserved for fire" (2 Pet. 3:7). Then, when the Day of the Lord has come, "the heavens will disappear with a roar; the elements will be destroyed by fire, and the earth and everything in it will be burned up" (2 Pet. 3:10).

What does God really have in mind? The details may not be clear, but something new and wonderful is part of his revealed plan.

JEREMIAH
The Book of Judgment Executed

Jeremiah's forty-year ministry spanned the final days of Judah's existence as an independent kingdom. He shared in the last great revival under Josiah (640–609 B.C.), then struggled with an unresponsive people as Judah rushed toward destruction under a series of apostate leaders. Jeremiah's call to Judah to submit to Babylon as a discipline from God was considered unpatriotic by Jeremiah's contemporaries, and his life was often in danger. Yet he lived to see his warnings fulfilled when the holy city and temple were razed. Jeremiah's prophecies of doom are lightened by two notes. The first is the promise that the captivity of her people will last only seventy years. The second is the announcement that the Lord will one day make a new covenant with his people, to replace the Mosaic code which they have been unable to keep.

Historical Background. Jeremiah lived in a time of international unheaval. Assyria had long dominated the Eastern World but was now challenged by a suddenly emerging Babylon and shaken by internal rebellions. At first this meant reduced pressure on the Palestinian states, so Josiah's time was marked by political as well as religious revival. But Nineveh, capital of Assyria, fell in 612 B.C., and a series of military campaigns soon established Babylonian ascendancy. When Egypt attempted to support the last Assyrian armies, Josiah made a vain attempt to delay Pharaoh Necho's column. His forces were brushed aside and Josiah was fatally wounded. Four years later, in 605 B.C., the massed might of Egypt was destroyed at Carchemish, and Babylon was master of the world.

The kings who succeeded Josiah were bent on the old evil ways which had so often led God's people away from the Lord. Jeremiah saw God's hand in the rise of Babylon, and warned the king and people of his homeland that the long threatened judgment of God was to be executed by this foreign power. His warnings to submit to Babylon were ignored, and Judah was gradually crushed in a series of invasions and deportations. Finally the few stragglers left in the land fled to Egypt, taking along the aged prophet whose words they continued to ignore.

Most of Jeremiah's prophecies are associated with the historical events outlined above. The chart on the next page shows the events that chronicle Jeremiah's long life and ministry.

Chronology of Jeremiah

686	MANASSEH sole ruler of Judah.		
648	JOSIAH born	652–648	Jeremiah born
642	AMON succeeds Manasseh		
640	JOSIAH succeeds Amon		
633	JOSIAH turns to the Lord		
	Ashurbanipal of Assyria dies		
628	JOSIAH begins reforms	627	Jeremiah called to be a
626	Nabopolassar becomes king of Babylon		prophet. Jeremiah 1–10 mes-
621	Book of the Law found in Temple		sages given during the Josian
			time of reform.
612	Nineveh, capital of Assyria, is destroyed		
	by Babylon		
609	JOSIAH killed		
	JEHOAHAZ rules for 3 months		
	JEHOIAKIM succeeds Jehoahaz		
605	Babylon defeats Egypt at Carchemish		Jeremiah 20–39 messages given
	Nebuchadnezzar becomes king of Babylon		during rules of evil kings Je-
	Daniel taken with other hostages to Baby-		hoiakim and Zedekiah.
	lon (1st deportation)		
604	Nebuchadnezzar returns to Palestine for		
	tribute		
601	Egypt invaded, Babylon thrown back		
598	JEHOIACHIN succeeds Jehoiakim. He is		
	taken in the 2nd deportation 22 April, 597.		
	He rules from December 598 to 16 March		
	597		
597	ZEDEKIAH succeeds as king in Judah		
588	Babylon begins siege of Jerusalem January	587	Jeremiah imprisoned for trea-
	15		son. Jeremiah 40–52 reports
586	Jerusalem falls and her destruction begins		the fall, and contains messages
	on August 14. Zedekiah has already fled.		of judgment on the enemy na-
	Now the third and final deportation takes		tions.
	place. October 7 the Babylonian governor		
	is assassinated and the Jews flee to Egypt,		
	taking Jeremiah with them.		

Note: See pages 220–221 for a review of the history of this period.

Jeremiah the Man. Jeremiah is often called the weeping prophet. His later life was marked by the hostility of the people to whom he ministered and by the trauma of seeing his homeland, gripped by internal wickedness, slowly crushed by its external enemy. He expresses his sorrows openly and refuses to hide his feelings, making his writings some of the most emotional of the OT.

Jeremiah was born of a priestly family during the reign of Manasseh, who murdered many pious men. Shortly after Josiah began his reforms, Jeremiah was called by God to be a prophet. God promised Jeremiah special protection from those who would hate him, and also promised that he would live to see his words vindicated. Little is known of Jeremiah's relationship with Josiah; some of his despairing messages would hardly stimulate reform. More details are given of his conflict with the evil rulers who followed this last godly king.

After flames destroyed Jerusalem and Solomon's glorious temple, Jeremiah stayed to serve the remnant of Judah that escaped deportation. He was taken with them when, disobeying God's commands through the aged prophet, they fled to Egypt.

The Covenant Announced. The great contribution of this prophet to the OT vision of things to come is found in his announcement of a new covenant. This covenant is one day to be made with Judah and is to replace the Mosaic or law covenant. The NT tells us that the new covenant was made and sealed at Calvary, on Christ's cross (see *New Covenant, OT,* p. 330 and *New Covenant, NT,* p. 653).

Outline. It's difficult to outline the contents of this anthology of Jeremiah's prophecies. Commentators seldom agree on the chronological background of specific sermons. Yet the dominant theme of national sinfulness and looming judgment echo again and again through the poetic oracles of the sorrowing prophet.

A loose outline of the book might reflect five divisions, the first two autobiographical, and the others biographical.

Outline

I.	Jeremiah's Mission	1–10
II.	The Broken Covenant	11–20
III.	Judgment Nears	21–29
IV.	New Covenant Promises	30–39
V.	Jerusalem Fallen	40–51
	Historical Appendix	52

The prophecies in these sections do not necessarily come in the same time period. A chart of the historical background against which each oracle might be studied is found below.

Historical Background of Jeremiah's Oracles

Josiah's Reign		Zedekiah's Reign	
2:1–3:5	Judah's Sinful Heart	21	Advice for the King
3:6–6:30	Jerusalem to be Destroyed	24	Zedekiah Abandoned
7:1–10:25	Ruin and Exile	27	Judah Must Submit
11–13	The Broken Covenant	28	God's Iron Yoke
18:1–20:18	The Potter	29	To the Exiles
Jehoiakim's Reign		30–33	The New Covenant
14–15	Prayers Are Fruitless	34	Judah's Broken Covenant
16–17	Jeremiah's Celibacy		
22	The King Rejected	37–39	Jerusalem's Fall
23	False Prophets Charged	49	The Nations Warned

I. Jeremiah's Mission (1–10)
Chapter 1. Jeremiah's Call

Jeremiah, whose name means "the Lord lifts up" or "The Lord establishes," is a young man when God calls him to prophesy to a hardened Judah. God himself has designed Jeremiah's ministry: he has been set apart from before birth to become a prophet to the nations (v. 4, see *Predestination/Election, OT,* p. 317). God will put words in the prophet's mouth, and he is to speak what God commands (6–10). His words will uproot nations, for many must be destroyed before rebuilding and planting can begin (10).

Jeremiah is given two visions at this time. One is of an almond branch, the first of the trees to bud in the spring. Jeremiah's messages will blossom to an early fulfillment (11, 12). The other is of a boiling cauldron, symbolizing disasters to be poured out on Judah from the north (13–16). Twenty-three years later the northern enemy of this prophecy is identified as Nebuchadnezzar (Jeremiah 25).

But now the young Jeremiah is warned to prepare himself. He will have to stand against hatred and opposition from his own people. Jeremiah is not to be terrified. God has fortified his prophet: kings, priests, and people will not prevail against him.

How would you feel if you were commissioned to share a message from God, and knew that everyone would be openly antagonistic? What in this chapter on Jeremiah's call might have encouraged him in just this situation?

Chapter 2:1–3:5. Judah's Sinful Heart

First Love Forsaken; 1:1–13. Like Isaiah (ch. 1), Jeremiah begins with an indictment. Israel loved God when he brought her into the land (2:1–4). How has God failed, that she defiles the land with idols (5–7)? All . . . priests, teachers of law, secular rulers, and prophets, have abandoned the LORD. (8)

Even pagan peoples remain true to their national gods, worthless though they are. The appalling fact is that Israel has abandoned the source of living water (see John 4:10–14; Rev. 21:6) and carved idols which, like some cracked cistern, will never hold the waters that can meet their spiritual needs (12, 13).

God Rejected; 2:14–30. Judah's present depressed condition is a direct result of abandoning God (14–19). Her rejection was conscious and willful: "I will not serve you" (20). Judah's love for foreign gods became a dominating passion (21–25). Yet now when Judah is threatened, her people dare to call on God (26–27)! Sarcastically, the prophet asks if none of the gods Israel has made for herself will come to her aid (28–31).

Punishment Assured; 2:31–3:5. A divorced couple is prohibited in the Mosaic law from remarrying if either has married another (Deut. 24:1–4). Israel has been a harlot bride (2:31–37): can God simply welcome her back, after she had prostituted herself with a host of lovers (idols)? No, her brazen actions show the falseness of her present cajoling pleas for mercy (3:1–5).

It is no wonder that little is found in the historical books of a relationship between Jeremiah and Josiah. The prophet's stern look at Judah's heart must have been unwelcome to the king, who was struggling to bring a religious reformation (2 Chron. 34, 35).

Predestination/Election, OT

These philosophical Greek terms find no exact parallel in the OT. However, the Lord's announcement to Jeremiah that "before I formed you in the womb . . . I set you apart" (1:5) raises the same theological questions.

The concept of election in the OT is expressed in the verb *bahar,* "choose." God chose Abraham and his descendants to receive his covenant promises (see *Covenant,* p. 51). The OT stresses the fact that this choice did not rest on Israel's merit or righteousness (Deut. 4:37; 7:6–8; 9:4–6). In fact, the choice was made despite God's awareness of Israel's rebellious character (Deut. 9:7–13). Even when she rejects him, God's love for Israel is such that he will not cast her out (Hosea 11:1–11; Jer. 33:1–26).

But the call of Israel did not guarantee salvation to any individual Jew. The wicked would be judged; those with a personal trust in God would be guarded even in the judgments that fell upon the nation (cf. Isa. 10:20–23; Ezek. 18:19–32). This point is often made in the NT (Rom. 9:6–13; 11:7–10; Heb. 4:2–7).

Israel is called to a ministry for God: to a holiness that will glorify him (Ps. 33:12; 135:4; Ex. 32:9–14; Isa. 43:24; 48:9–11; 63:12–14) and to other missions. Yet God's purposes for Israel do not affect the clear impact of the OT's testimony: it is God as Sovereign Lord who exercised his own free choice and acted to establish the covenant relationship with this people.

Does the notion of God's sovereign call extend to individuals as well as the nation? Isolated OT cases like that of Jeremiah (1:4, 5) and Jacob (Gen. 25:23) do not provide a clear answer (see *Predestination/Election, NT,* p. 619).

Chapters 3:6–6:30. Jerusalem to be Destroyed

The protestations of loyalty won from Judah during Josiah's reform echo, hollow and empty, as the prophet strips away the facade of repentance and pronounces God's judgment on a corrupt society.

Faithless Israel; 3:6–4:4. The northern and southern kingdoms, like sisters, have pursued adultery (idolatry) on every hill and in every grove. The northern kingdom, Israel, has been divorced (sent into exile). Yet Judah has not heeded the warning. Her faithless behavior is thus even worse than Israel's (3:5–11).

Still, God calls out to individuals to return to him. They must acknowledge guilt and turn fully to him. Only one from a town, or two from a clan, will respond. But the remnant of believing individuals who do turn will be regathered and restored. It is too late for the corrupt society to respond as a whole (3:14–4:4).

Judgment on Judah and Jerusalem; 4:5–31. The judgment to strike this sinful society has been determined, and as Jeremiah speaks it is taking shape in the north. His vision of a mourning, ruined land, shrouded by a darkened heavens, moves Jeremiah to weep in anguish (18, 19). But the future is fixed: the Lord has pronounced a sentence of devastation.

None Righteous; 5:1–31. Jeremiah searches desperately through the streets of Jerusalem for one righteous person (cf. Gen. 18:16–33). But there is none to be found. Judgment on such a nation and people is a moral necessity (1–9)! Like a ravaged grape arbor, or a woods consumed by a forest fire, Judah will crumble (10–17). Yet even the coming cataclysm will not destroy all. When at last God's people, captives in a foreign land, pause to ask "Why?" they will recall Jeremiah's message. The judgment has come because Judah forsook the Lord to serve foreign gods (18–25), and as a result slipped into a life of wickedness and evil (26–31).

Jerusalem Besieged; 6:1–30. Now Jeremiah describes the holy city under siege (1–8). The mission of the assaulting armies is to destroy the whole society (see 11–15). But the enemy is supposed to preserve a remnant (9). Judah has rejected the testimony of history, the law, and the prophets (16–20): only armies coming to destroy her will awaken her to reality (22–26).

Sadly, Jeremiah reflects. He hoped that the fire of his prophetic message would purge the impurities from Judah, as a refiner's fire purges metal ore. But the fiery word of God has only demonstrated conclusively that the people of Judah are totally corrupt; they are hardened rebels all (27–30).

A repeated note in these chapters is found in the words of hope and repentance spoken to individuals. What do you see in these chapters of the relationship between an individual and his society? What is your own responsibility to God in the society in which you live?

Chapters 7:1–10:25. Ruin and Exile

Jeremiah is sent by God to the temple gates to announce the certain approach of ruin and exile. In this message he confronts the false theology of his day: a blind superstition which argues that because God has chosen Zion for his dwelling (1 Kings 9:3), he is bound to protect the temple and those who live in its shadow. The result is a shallow, cultic faith, which emphasizes ritual and ignores the moral aspect of covenant relationship with God. Boldly the prophet stands before the people and calls this distorted faith a lie. His messages reveal the weakness of the Josian revival. The people have adopted a form of religious behavior without taking the whole Word of God to heart (cf. 2 Tim. 3:5).

True Worship; 7:1–29. The prophet stands at the temple gate to warn Judah. This people cannot oppress their fellows, steal, murder, commit perjury and bow down to idols, and then come to stand before the Lord in his house! God's commandments for holy living are as much a part of his law as regulations dealing with sacrifice and worship! True religion requires walking in God's ways, which this rebellious people will not do.

If Jeremiah were to speak to the church today, what do you believe his message might be? Would he have similar things to say to us, or would his message be different?

Valley of Slaughter; 7:30–8:3. The dead carcasses of these men and women, who fill the temple with dumb idols, will fill the valley below the temple site and lie unburied on the ground.

Sin and Punishment; 8:4–9:25. The reasons why judgment must strike God's people are carefully explained. Foolish in its claim to "wisdom," Judah rejects God's Word and turns away when the Lord speaks to his people (8:4–13). Instead of the peace they hope for there will be only terror: Judah is doomed to perish (13–

17). The prospect is so vividly clear to Jeremiah that he again cries out in anguish: "since my people are crushed, I am crushed" (8:21). Yet at the same time Jeremiah is repelled by the corruption all around him and wishes he could leave this tainted land, filled with spiritual and moral adulterers (8:18–9:6). As the law has warned, the faithless people of God will be torn from the land and scattered among the nations (9:16; cf. Deut. 28:49–68). The punishment is fixed: wailing and death will soon fill this land (9:17–25).

Study Deuteronomy 28:49–68. Compare it with this passage and what you know of the history of the Hebrew people. In what ways has the pattern foretold 1400 years before Christ found expression in the experience of the Jews? See *Babylonian Captivity*, p. 222–228.

God and Idols; 10:1–23. Jeremiah echoes Isaiah's scornful condemnation of idolatry (Isa. 44:6–28). Judah has turned from the Maker of the heavens and earth to bow down to images no more powerful than a scarecrow in a melon patch (1–16)! The sickness of the land is incurable: now it must endure God's cauterizing judgments (17–22).

This great sermon denouncing Judah's sins ends with Jeremiah's prayer. Bring judgment, yes. But only to correct, not in anger. Then Jeremiah begs God to pour out his wrath on the nations who will crush the people of God beyond God's intended measure (23–25).

II. The Broken Covenant (11–20)
Chapters 11–13. The Covenant Broken

The discovery of the lost Book of the Law when the temple is being repaired in 621 B.C. during the Josian revival provides the context for Jeremiah's preaching about the broken covenant.

The Message; 11:1–17. Jeremiah is sent through Judah to teach that obedience to law is vital to the covenant relationship of each generation with the Lord (see *Law, OT,* p. 87). But his listeners simply whisper together and turn away, to keep on worshiping their idols (1–13). There's no use even praying for such a people (14)! Because of their evil deeds, God has decreed disaster (15–17).

Jeremiah Threatened; 11:18–23. Jeremiah's message on the broken covenant rouses such hatred that his life is threatened.

Prosperity of the Wicked; 12:1–4. Jeremiah knows that judgment will strike Judah in the end. But the plot against his life has shaken him. He turns to God, questioning God's justice in permitting the wicked to prosper even temporarily.

Prosperity of the Wicked

Believers of all ages have been troubled by the prosperity of the wicked and the question this raises about the fairness of God. How can God permit evil men to live at ease while the good suffer?

This question was posed by Job (21:4–21), caused anguish to the psalmist (73), and puzzled the prophets (Jer. 12:1–2; Hab. 2:12–17).

There seems to be no simple answer. But there are a number of Bible passages which deal with the question. The psalmist is released from depression when he recalls his relationship with God and sees the destiny of the wicked. He realizes that prosperity is dangerous to the evil: they walk then on "slippery ground" (73:17–21). Their life of ease lulls them into pleasant dreams; their riches insulate them from the basic issues of life and death and keep them from facing their need for a personal relationship with God.

Habakkuk gives yet another insight. God invites the prophet to look beneath the surface, to see the inner life of the wicked rich. With all his getting, such a person is never satisfied. His greed and his possessions simply fan a burning desire for more, and he is robbed of peace. The hostility his wickedness generates will cause all to turn on him if he falters. The wicked are not to be envied! God's judgmental processes are even now at work within!

The NT adds another note. Judgment withheld is an evidence of God's grace, to give every opportunity for repentance. Thus the wicked's prosperity is testimony to God's goodness (Rom. 2:4).

There is no simple answer to the question of why the wicked are permitted to prosper. But there is enough revealed in Scripture to free us to trust such situations into the hands of a gracious God who, for all his goodness, will not be mocked.

God's Answer; 12:5–17. Judgment will come, swift as a racing horse, like flames fanned by God's burning anger (5–13). The people will be uprooted, but the enemy will be uprooted in his turn, so that a remnant can return to relationship with God (14–17).

Five Warnings; 13:1–27. The certainty of coming judgment is reinforced by five warnings. The people who stubbornly reject God will become like a rotten linen belt (1–11), and be smashed like clay pots drained of wine (12–14). The arrogant are warned that the flock of the Lord will be taken captive (15–17), while young King Jehoiakim and the Queen Mother are told they will be stripped of their crowns (18–19). The northern army God sends will blow away the people of Judah like chaff swept up in a windstorm. This is a just penalty for all their wickedness (20–27).

Judgment of the Wicked

One responsibility which God accepts is that of Judge (Gen. 18:25; Ps. 96:10; Isa. 33:22). The basic moral necessity for judgment is clearly laid out in Scripture. It is rooted in the character of God as a righteous person, who by nature is adamantly opposed to evil. The prophet's conviction that God is too pure to bear the sight of evil (Hab. 1:13) is fully borne out in the OT (cf. Isa. 11:3–5).

It's important to realize that God's righteousness is not a cold, impersonal quality (see *Holiness, OT*, p. 101, and *Justice, OT*, p. 293). God's character is well expressed in his burning concern for the oppressed and in the anger heartless sins arouse. Judgment is sure for those who "sell the righteous for silver, and the needy for a pair of sandals," trampling "on the heads of the poor as upon the dust of the ground and denying justice to the oppressed" (Amos 2:6, 7). Thus all the prophets echo the same warnings. God's judgment will surely be poured out on those who turn to wickedness and evil.

The OT and NT reveal several aspects of God's judgment:

(1) *There is societal judgment.* Any society which institutionalizes oppression will not survive (Jer. 5:7–9, see 18:7–9).

(2) *There is internal judgment.* The individual who chooses the ways of wickedness will never find rest or satisfaction (Hab. 2).

(3) *There is eschatological judgment on mankind.* The prophets speak of a cataclysmic disaster to sweep the whole world at history's end, and view this as an act of judgment (Isa. 13:6–16).

(4) *There is eschatological judgment on individuals.* God will not execute judgment on all of the wicked in this life (see *Prosperity of the Wicked*). But resurrection lies ahead, when final judgment will be made (see Dan. 12:2).

Chapters 14–15. Prayers Are Fruitless

Drought; 14:1–12. When a drought strikes Judah (1–6), the people beg God to send water, but ignore their sins (7–9). God makes a stern reply. Judah will be punished for her sins. Jeremiah is not to pray for this people (10–12). This theme, that Judah's sins have at last brought her beyond the help of prayer, is sounded often in Jeremiah (cf. 7:16; 11:14).

False Prophets; 14:13–15:2. Jeremiah's unpopular warnings are ignored. False prophets, whom God has not sent, tell lies in the Lord's name. They contradict the message of judgment and promise that no famine or sword will touch Judah (13–16). Jeremiah is told to confront them! He is to announce a disaster so sure that even if Moses and Samuel should pray for Judah, God would not listen (14:17–15:2).

God's people are destined for death, the sword, starvation, and captivity.

Four Destroyers; 15:3–21. Graphically, the prophet now exposes the fate that awaits his people (3–14). But then, in an iron captivity, Judah will finally turn to God. Then God's words will sustain her, as if they were food (15–18). Then at last a remnant will listen to the message Jeremiah has so urgently proclaimed: it is not prayer, but repentance and obedience that will deliver God's people and cause him to save them (19–21, cf. Jer. 7:16–26).

Chapters 16–17. Jeremiah's Celibacy

God called on Jeremiah to act out many of his warnings, as well as to preach. This obligation caused the faithful prophet to wander among his people, cut off from social relationships, as a lonely and condemning spectre who was increasingly despised.

Signs of Disaster; 16:1–18. To communicate the grim reality of the approaching disaster, Jeremiah is told not to marry and have children. Children born in his day will only die of deadly diseases and lie unburied in the streets (1–4). Also, the prophet is not to mourn the death of friends, for God has no compassion left for Judah. Nor is he to take part in any feasting (5–9). Instead, Jeremiah is told to speak words that condemn, and hold up the sin and faithlessness of God's people (10–13). A distant generation will know God's blessing once again (14–15). But for this people there is only death (16–18): disaster is assured.

Judah's Sin; 16:19–17:4. The evil engraved on the hearts of sinful Judah will inevitably bring the judgment deserved.

Psalms of Trust; 17:5–18. The wickedness of man's incurable heart can only be healed by trust in God (5–10). This beautiful psalm concludes with an appeal by Jeremiah for vindication (14–18). He has not run from his heartbreaking and lonely task. He has served as God's shepherd to a wayward people. May God soon bring on the terrors and vindicate the prophet's ridiculed words!

Keeping the Sabbath; 17:19–27. Despite the personal anguish Jeremiah feels, he faithfully obeys when God sets him at the gates of Jerusalem on the Sabbath, to confront those who break the sabbath law and work on the holy day. Again he announces doom.

Jeremiah 17:5–18 contains several expressive verses which show the nature of a Jeremiahlike faith in God. Which of the expressions do you feel were particularly meaningful to Jeremiah? Which are particularly meaningful to you?

Chapters 18–20. The Potter

The Potter's Wheel; 18:1–17. Jeremiah's next series of messages is stimulated when he is sent to watch a potter at work. This artisan used two wheel-shaped stones, linked by a common shaft. The lower wheel was turned by the potter's feet, and his hands shaped a soft mound of clay resting on the rotating upper wheel. At times a defect would appear and the clay could not be worked properly. Then the potter squeezed the clay into a lump and began again. God will deal with his people as the potter deals with unmanageable clay (1–7); they will be crushed so he can begin again to shape them toward the holiness his nature requires him to demand.

In the message that follows God reveals an important biblical principle. When he announces judgment on any nation, that judgment is conditional. If its people repent and change their ways, judgment will be withheld. In the same way, national blessing is contingent on moral behavior (7–10). Despite this offer, God's people will not repent (11–17).

Jeremiah Abused; 18:18–23. For decades Jeremiah has warned of impending judgment and nothing has happened. Now the people ridicule him, either attacking or ignoring his messages.

The Broken Jar; 19:1–13. Despite the ridicule, Jeremiah is told to gather some priests and elders and bring them, with a clay jar, to the Valley of Slaughter (7:30 f). As the leaders watch Jeremiah breaks the jar. This is what the Lord will do to their nation and city.

Jeremiah Beaten and Placed in Stocks; 19:14–20:6. Again Jeremiah stands in the temple court and preaches disaster. Pashhur, the official responsible to keep order in the courtyard, has Jeremiah beaten and restrained! The "stocks" in which the prophet is placed are a wooden scaffolding, to which a prisoner is tied in a cramped position. Jeremiah is released the next morning. When he is, he has a word from the Lord for Pashhur. This official, who tried to gag God's prophet, will experience terror on every side and be dragged away to die, a captive in a foreign land.

Jeremiah Depressed; 20:7–18. The strain of his lonely ministry tells on the prophet, and the constant stream of derision throws him into deep depression. He feels betrayed by the Lord, whose delay in fulfilling the prophet's words of doom have led to the ridicule. Yet Jeremiah can't stop speaking God's messages (9–10).

And awareness of God's presence does enable Jeremiah to go on (11–13). Still, the sorrowing prophet often finds himself wishing he had never been born (14–18)!

III. Judgment Nears (21–29)

As this series of messages is delivered, Jeremiah is no longer ridiculed. The crushing weight of Babylon is now felt in Palestine. As new armies approach, the terror that Jeremiah has so long foretold begins to grip the hearts of the inhabitants of Judah.

Chapter 21. Advice for the King

As Nebuchadnezzar mounts an attack against Judah's fortified border cities, Zedekiah sends representatives to Jeremiah. Will the Lord miraculously deliver his people, as in the past (1, 2)? Jeremiah only repeats his message of doom. The God who once fought for his people will now fight against them (3–7). Jeremiah carries this demoralizing message to all the citizens of Jerusalem. Those who flee the city and surrender to the Babylonians will live. Those who stay behind her walls will die (8–11). To the king Jeremiah offers the law's age-old advice: "Do justice." But the king will not listen. The city will die (11–14).

Chapter 22. The King Rejected

Jeremiah stands in the king's palace to deliver a word of condemnation. The same themes are repeated: Do justice. Keep the covenant, or the palace will become a ruin (1–10). Three kings are discussed by name. Shallum (11–17), who forced the poor to labor on his luxurious home, will die in his present captivity. Jehoiakim (18–23), who refused to heed God's voice, will have the donkey's burial he deserves. Jehoiachin (24–30), to whom the prophet is speaking, will die in captivity, and none of his family ever again sit on David's throne (see the history on pages 220, 221).

[□] How might the appearance of the Babylonian army affect Jeremiah's feelings? Will it have any special impact on his behavior? What lessons can you learn from Jeremiah's courage and faithfulness?

Chapter 23. False Prophets Charged

The Branch; 23:1–8. Jeremiah warns those who are Israel's shepherds (a term that applies to both political and spiritual leaders), who are responsible to guide the people. They will be punished for their evil. In the future God himself will provide a "righteous branch" to rule Israel wisely and to save her.

The term "branch" is used by the prophets as a title for the Messiah, the promised Savior (see Isa. 4:2). This is Jeremiah's first emphatic statement of the future hope of Israel in a divine/human redeemer.

Lying Prophets; 23:9–24. God now turns to the prophets and priests who are spiritually (10–12) and morally (13–14) corrupt. Their messages of false hope are lies, wishful thinking, or simply a repetition of others' words (15–17). God has not sent these men.

Recognizing False Prophets

Both OT and NT warn against false prophets. These are individuals who claim to communicate God's message, but who are not sent by him. OT and NT agree on the characteristics of a false prophet, and how one can be recognized. It may be hard to judge from appearances, but close examination reveals unmistakable signs in words and life style which are not in harmony with God's Word.

These signs are carefully spelled out in both OT and NT.

Doctrinal Signs	Jeremiah	Peter	Jude
introduce destructive heresies, denying the Sovereign Lord who bought them	23:13	2:11	
Personality Signs			
bold, arrogant	23:10b	2:10	16
despise authority		2:10	3
follow corrupt desires of the sinful nature	23:14	2:10	4, 19
love profit to be gained		2:15	12
Ministry Sign			
appeals to "lustful desires of the human nature,"	23:14b	2:17	16
promising "freedom" to the depraved	23:18,19		

A person whose life, personality, and ministry reflect the characteristics of the false prophet of Jeremiah's day will be recognized, and rejected, by those who live by God's Word.

Delusion; 23:25–40. The prophets who fill Jerusalem with lies and lead the people astray are lost to reality: they live in a world of delusion (25–32). They are no longer to claim that what they say is an "oracle of the Lord" (33–40).

Chapter 24. Zedekiah Abandoned

It is after the second deportation, of 598 B.C. Jeremiah passes the temple and sees two baskets of figs. One is ripe and succulent, the other shriveled and spoiled. God tells Jeremiah that the good figs represent the exiles. God will watch over his people in Babylon, give them a heart to know him, and bring them back to the land. But Zedekiah and those in Jerusalem will be treated like rotted fruit. They will be rejected and destroyed.

Chapter 25. Nebuchadnezzar, God's Servant

Babylon Identified As the Agent of God's Judgment; 25:1–10. This prophecy is dated 605 B.C. This is the year that Nebuchadnezzar defeats the Egyptians at Carchemish and becomes king of Babylon. Thus it is much earlier than the other messages in this section. It is an important message for the prophet. Now, at last, the words of doom Jeremiah has spoken to his heedless countrymen are about to be fulfilled! Now Jeremiah can reveal that it is Nebuchadnezzar God has chosen to be the instrument of judgment on his evil people.

Seventy-Year Captivity; 25:11–14. The prophet also reveals the length of time the Hebrew people will be held captive in Babylon. They will serve there for 70 years. After the 70 years have passed, a transformed remnant will return to the Promised Land (see *Babylonian Captivity*, pp. 222–228).

The Cup of Wrath; 25:15–38. Strong drink is a common symbol of God's wrath (cf. Isa. 51:17, 22; Jer. 13:12; 49:12; Zech. 12:2). This symbolic cup is now held out to Judah and the nations of the world, as Jeremiah looks beyond the captivity to a day when all evildoers will be punished. See "Day of the Lord" (see Isa. 2–4).

Chapter 26. Jeremiah's Life Threatened

It is the early reign of Jehoiakim (609 B.C.). Jeremiah stands in the court of the temple and passionately announces his prophecy of desolation (1–6). Furious, priests and prophets demand that Jeremiah be put to death for the unpatriotic message (7–9). Jeremiah survives (10–19). But the danger is real. Uriah, another prophet of the Lord, has been executed for daring to give the same message (Jer. 26:20–26).

Chapter 27. Judah Must Submit

Early in Zedekiah's reign (in 593 B.C.), Jeremiah sends a word from the Lord to surrounding nations, to the king, and to the populace. Those who submit to Nebuchadnezzar will survive. Those who resist will be crushed and taken into exile. The hopeful words of Judah's false prophets, who predict the return of temple wealth taken by Nebuchadnezzar in 598 B.C.., are lies. In truth even the massive pillars that stand before the temple will be moved from Jerusalem to Babylon, and with them all Judah's people.

Chapter 28. God's Iron Yoke

Jeremiah again acts out his prophecies. He appears at the temple wearing a yoke, to symbolize submission to Babylon. Hananiah confronts Jeremiah and announces in God's name that Babylon's yoke will be broken within two years. He claims the captives taken by Nebuchadnezzar will be returned, with all the temple booty. Hananiah then takes the wooden yoke Jeremiah wears and breaks it (1–10). Shortly after God speaks to Jeremiah and sends him to Hananiah. This man is persuading God's people to trust lies! Hananiah will soon die and God will forge an unbreakable yoke of iron to fit the shoulders of his sinning people. Within two months Hananiah is dead (11–17).

Chapter 29. Letter to the Exiles

The conflict between Jeremiah and those who wishfully expect return of the captives grows more intense. Jeremiah sends a letter to those who survived the long trek to Babylon. They must adjust to their captivity, for 70 years will pass before anyone returns (4–14). Jerusalem and the homeland will be destroyed (15–23).

The response is all too predictable. The exiles send a letter to the acting high priest in Jerusalem, reporting Jeremiah's unpatriotic words. Why should such a madman, pretending to be a prophet, not be imprisoned (24–28)? Confronted by one of the priests, Jeremiah is moved by the Lord to pronounce the doom of Shemaiah, the author of the Babylonian captives' reply.

II. New Covenant Promises
Chapter 30–33. The New Covenant

The prophets in Jerusalem and among the exiles offered false hope to God's people. Jeremiah, in contrast, urged Judah to accept the reality of present judgment and to wait submissively for 70 years of discipline to pass. Among the litany of Jeremiah's grim warnings of disaster are three chapters which contain one of the OT's most significant revelations of hope for all mankind.

The Restoration of Israel; 30:1–31:22. The repeated phrase "that day" (30:7,8) immediately indicates that the restoration of which the prophet now speaks takes place at history's end (See Isa. 2–4). Then the promised Davidic Ruler, the Messiah, will save God's people (30:2–10). He will bring them back from the lands where they have been scattered as a judgment for their sin (30:11–17). The restored community of Israel will then truly be the Lord's people (30:18–24). The relationship expressed in the age-old Abrahamic covenant (31:3) will be experienced at last, as the remnant of Israel is gathered from the ends of the earth (31:1–9) by the very One who has scattered them (31:10–11). Then the promise will be fulfilled, and Israel will experience joy in the bounty of the Lord (31:12–14). Present weeping will be stilled when, after the discipline, true repentance is known at last (31:15–22).

Righteousness Within; 31:23–40. After the return described in these chapters, the land of Judah will again be addressed as "righteous dwelling" (23). There is an explanation for this moral transformation. The Lord announces he will "make a new covenant with the house of Israel." The new covenant will not be like the Mosaic (law) covenant, which generation after generation of Israel broke. No, the new covenant will write God's law on hearts, not stone tablets. In its day "they will all know me, from the least of them to the greatest" (31–34). By two striking oaths, God affirms unconditional commitment to his special relationship with Israel (35–37). When the new covenant is in force, Jerusalem will be established, never to be overthrown (38–40).

The Prophet Purchases a Field; 32:1–44. Now Jeremiah returns to the present. It is the tenth year of Zedekiah, and Jerusalem is surrounded by a Babylonian army. The prophet is confined by the king. His warnings about the city's fall are bad for the defenders' morale! As the king is arguing with Jeremiah, a relative appears and asks Jeremiah to buy a plot of land in occupied territory. Jeremiah makes the purchase, witnessed by all in the palace courtyard. He seals the deeds in a jar, where they will be protected for decades. Years from now the deed will be good, for the lands of Judah again will be bought and sold (1–15).

But Jeremiah asks for further explanation (16–25). God explains. The purchase is a sign of trust in God's faithfulness. As Jeremiah's words of judgment have come true, so will the prophet's promises of restoration. This message is important. Even Judah's terrible sins have not turned God from his covenant commitment to Israel.

The New Covenant, OT

A "covenant" in OT terminology is an agreement, spelling out the relationship between two parties. Typically both parties to a covenant have responsibilities which must be fulfilled.

There are two kinds of OT covenants between God and man. One is a "covenant of promise": an unconditional statement by God of his intention to accomplish purposes announced in the covenant oath (see *Covenant, OT,* p. 51). The basic covenant of promise was made to Abraham (cf. Gen. 12, 15, 17). God promised to be the God of his descendants through Isaac and Jacob, to bless them, and to give them the land of Palestine. This basic statement is expanded in promises given to David. The Abrahamic blessing will come through a king descended from David, who will sit on the throne of Israel forever (see *Davidic Covenant,* p. 177).

The OT also features one conditional covenant, known as the Mosaic or the law covenant (see p. 87). This covenant defined the moral, worship, and social regulations which were to guide the daily life of God's OT people. If a particular generation obeyed this law, God promised blessing. If they disobeyed, he promised judgment (see Deut. 28). It is important to note that however a particular generation of Israel might behave, their sins did not affect God's gracious and unconditional commitments expressed in the promise covenants (see Gal. 3:15–18).

Like the Davidic covenant, the new covenant that Jeremiah announces is an expansion or explanation of the earlier Abrahamic promises. It tells how God will work in history to fulfill his oath. Jeremiah's prophecy looks forward to a time when God will deal with the inner life of human beings, and with their personal relationship with the Lord. This new covenant will work on principles that are "not like" those underlying the Mosaic or law covenant (Jer. 31:32). The new will not give men a law written on stone, but will instead transform human beings from within, inscribing holiness on their hearts and minds. Then, when each individual knows the Lord in a personal and intimate way, and has his sins forgiven, a new day of righteousness will dawn for mankind.

Jeremiah's words do not constitute the new covenant. They simply look forward to a day when it will be made with mankind. Today we look back to Jesus and realize that Jeremiah's promise of something new has been kept! For the new covenant was written, 2,000 years ago, in the blood that Jesus poured out for us on Calvary's cross (see *New Covenant, NT.* p. 653).

Restoration Reaffirmed; 33:1–26. Still in confinement (32:1, 2), Jeremiah is told by God of a restored Judah to stand where there is now only death and desolation (1–13). The full restoration of which the prophet speaks will not come after 70 years. It awaits the appearance of Messiah, identified as the "righteous Branch from David's line" (15).

This covenant of promise is unbreakable and immutable, for

God will never retract his unconditional oath (19–22). The point which the Lord makes through Jeremiah is important to our understanding of the OT. The Babylonian disaster, or any disaster which may befall God's people in history, does not change God's unshakable purpose. He will keep his covenant with the descendants of Abraham, Isaac, and Jacob (23–26).

Thus the new covenant is foretold in the context of unmistakable assurances that the Abrahamic and Davidic covenants are still in force, never to be set aside.

Chapter 34. Judah's Broken Covenant

Jeremiah tells Zedekiah that he will be taken captive but will live to die peacefully in Babylon (1–7). This promise may have been made by God in response to a movement to free Jews who were enslaved by their fellow Hebrews. The law provided that servitude should last only for six years and then freedom be granted. The king led the people to return to this practice, and to make a solemn covenant of blood (see *Covenant, OT*, p. 51) in the temple itself, before the Lord. But the people changed their minds and forced their fellow-countrymen back into service (8–16)! Judah violated this covenant just as they violated their covenant relationship with God and will be delivered up to those who seek their lives.

Chapter 35. The Recabites' Example

Jeremiah invites to the temple a family which remained faithful to the command of a distant ancestor. He sets bowls of wine before each of the men of the family and bids them to drink. They refuse, remaining true to a command given generations ago! God commends the Recabites and promises to bless them for their faithfulness. What a contrast they make to the people of Judah, who have ignored and disobeyed the word of the Living God!

Chapter 36. The Burned Scroll

Jeremiah is restricted and not allowed to go to the temple. God commands him to record all the prophecies he has spoken concerning Judah. So Jeremiah dictates them to his secretary, Baruch. Jeremiah then sends Baruch out to read the prophetic words he himself cannot deliver (1–7). The words are reported to the king. When he hears them, the furious Jehoiakim cuts the scroll apart and burns it (8–26). He orders the arrest of both Jeremiah and

Baruch. But the words of the first scroll are quickly rewritten, and "many similar words are added."

Chapters 37–39. Jerusalem's Fall

As the grip of the Babylonians around Jerusalem tightens, terror heightens the tensions within its walls. A clique of officials determined to resist Babylon have effectively taken over authority. King Zedekiah, who wavers fearfully between resistance and surrender, is too frightened to exercise his supposed authority. In this deteriorating situation, Jeremiah's life is in great danger.

Jeremiah Imprisoned; 37:1–21. Jeremiah's continual urgings to surrender to the Babylonians made him very unpopular. When the siege is temporarily lifted and Jeremiah attempts to go out, he is arrested and accused of deserting to the enemy. He is beaten and locked in a cell controlled by one of the most vicious of his enemies. Zedekiah intervenes and Jeremiah is moved to a cell where his life will not be in danger.

Jeremiah Placed in an Empty Cistern; 38:1–13. The resistance leaders demand that Jeremiah be killed, for his messages discourage the soldiers and the people of Jerusalem. The cowardly Zedekiah fears to oppose them and Jeremiah is turned over. The aged prophet is lowered into a now empty cistern, where water was stored for the siege. Now he sinks into the muck at its dark bottom and is left to die.

Another official of the king, Ebed-Melech, gets permission from Zedekiah to take a troop of men and rescue Jeremiah. His quick action saves the prophet's life, and Jeremiah is returned to confinement in the courtyard of the royal guard.

Questioned by Zedekiah; 38:14–28. Jeremiah is questioned by the crumbling king and repeats the familiar words that God has given him. Jeremiah remains confined until the city falls.

Jerusalem Falls; 39:1–18. After a long siege Jerusalem's wall is breeched and resistance crumbles. Zedekiah flees but is captured near Jericho. The king, who has rebelled against his Babylonian overlords and against the word of his God, sees his children and advisors executed. Then his own eyes are put out.

Jeremiah is found in his prison by the Babylonians. When he is recognized, he is treated with respect. One special note is found in verses 15–18. Ebed-Melech, the court official who defended Jeremiah and once acted boldly to save his life (38:7–13), is promised safety when the city falls. God rescues this man, who maintained trust in the Lord in Judah's time of greatest apostasy.

The Fall of Jerusalem

V. Jerusalem Fallen (40–52)
Chapters 40–43. Flight to Egypt

After Jerusalem is destroyed, only a few of the poor are left in Palestine. They are given land to farm, and Gedaliah is appointed governor of this last remnant. Jeremiah elects to remain.

Gedaliah Assassinated; 40:7–41:15. Gedaliah reassures the few who remain that they will be safe under Babylonian rule. But almost immediately Gedaliah is assassinated! The killers escape.

Flight to Egypt; 41:16–43:13. The Jews who remain are terrified of the Babylonian's response to this new act of rebellion. They beg Jeremiah to pray to God for direction and promise to obey his word. But when the prophet tells them to remain, and not to fear, and especially warns them against a flight to Egypt, Jeremiah is accused of lying! Again God's word is directly disobeyed and the frightened company heads south.

Chapter 44. In Egypt

When Jeremiah speaks out to condemn the idolatry the survivors practice, and to threaten further disaster (1–14), the whole assembly tells Jeremiah openly that they plan to continue their worship of idols! They will listen to no more words from God (15–18). A final word of judgment is announced. These people will perish in Egypt and never return to the land. The Pharaoh with whom they think they have found shelter will be destroyed by Nebuchadnezzar, just as Zedekiah was destroyed (19–30).

📖 A story of this last group of Jews and their flight to Egypt is particularly important. What makes their rejection of Jeremiah's words so striking? What does their behavior tell you about the true spiritual state of God's people in the last days of the southern kingdom?

Chapter 45. Promise to Baruch

Jeremiah's secretary is told not to expect any reward, but promised that his life will be spared.

Chapters 46–48. Against Foreign Nations

Jeremiah records a series of prophecies against Judah's enemies. God's people have undergone discipline. Surely pagan nations will not escape. Egypt (46:1–28), the Philistines (47:1–7), Moab (48:1–

47), Ammon (49:1–6), Edom (49:7–22), Damascus (49:23–27), Kedar, Hazor, and Elam (49:28–39) are all warned. A similar section of words against the nations is found in Isaiah 13–24.

Chapters 50, 51. Against Babylon

This extended oracle looks toward the time when Babylon will be destroyed in her turn. Of special note are the promise of a true revival to take place among the captives (50:4, 5), and the description of Babylon's destiny: "desert creatures and hyenas will live there, and there the owl will dwell. It will never again be inhabited or lived in from generation to generation" (50:39, 40).

Chapter 52. Jerusalem Revisited

In an appendix, the Book of Jeremiah provides another description of the fall of Jerusalem and the razing of the temple. The number of deportees given here (28–30) seems to represent adult males or heads of families, while the figures given in 2 Kings 23:31 and 24:18 represent a count of the total number of persons involved.

The book closes with an account of Jehoiachin's release from prison and his privileged place in the court at Babylon, a happening independently attested by Babylonian records.

And so the passionate Book of Jeremiah ends with a dry recitation of facts. But how appropriate this is. The words the great prophet uttered about Jerusalem have passed from the realm of vision into history. The historic record of Jerusalem's fall stands before us today as a testimony to the trustworthiness of the prophetic word.

LAMENTATIONS
Dirge for Lost Jerusalem

These five somber poems were commonly read aloud by the Hebrew people in mid-July, on the date set to commemorate the fall of Jerusalem. Poems reflecting this same dark mood are not uncommon in the ancient Near East, and have a long literary tradition. This set of poems was originally untitled.

Date. It is clear from the content of these poems that they were written after the destruction of Jerusalem, by a person who speaks as an eye-witness. Thus they probably were authored within a decade of Judah's desolation in 587 B.C., and accurately reflect the crushing sense of loss felt by the exiles.

Authorship. No author is named in these poems. Jewish tradition agrees that Jeremiah was the author. The deeply emotional expressions, with reflection of the judgment themes found in Jeremiah, indicate that this tradition is probably correct. Style and content do show that a single author wrote these anonymous words.

If Jeremiah is the author, he likely left the group that fled to Egypt and found his way to Babylon—a most arduous journey for the aged and sorrowing prophet.

Structure and Outline. The book is composed of five poems. Each is written in a highly sophisticated style. Each line or segment of a particular poem begins with a different, consecutive letter of the twenty-two-letter Hebrew alphabet. The third poem is made up of groups of three single lines, each of which begins with the same Hebrew letter. Such alphabetical poems are called acrostics.

Outline

Value. The fall of Jerusalem and the loss of the Promised Land shocked the Jewish people. Jeremiah's theology of sovereignty, justice, judgment, and morality, reflected in these laments, was fully vindicated. Reading these poems, we can sense the impact of the national disaster which shattered the false hopes of the people, and demanded they face the reality of their sins. The poems also reflect the response of the spiritually sensitive, who begin to turn to God in the place of their exile (see *Impact of the Captivity,* p. 226).

At times you and I know tragedy. We find ourselves deep in the anguished mood expressed in Lamentations. How good at such times to realize that God intends to bring us good, even through the pain. Often suffering is God's pathway to healing.

Chapter 1. Jerusalem in Mourning

Deserted Jerusalem is slumped in ruins, like a widow who has lost all her children (1–7). At last her sins have been exposed, and she is despised by all (8–11). Though she stretches out her hands piteously, no one comes near to comfort her, and her enemies delight in the torment the Lord has brought upon her (12–22).

Chapter 2. Jerusalem in Ruin

The fierce anger of the Lord has caused the ruin of Jerusalem (1–9). Her condemned people faint, caught in the grip of famine (10–13). All the lying visions of the false prophets, who promised perpetual security, are now seen to be illusions. The Lord has done what he has planned (14–17)! In deep anguish the poet weeps for those who once peopled Jerusalem: "no one escaped or survived; those I cared for and reared, my enemy has destroyed" (18–22).

Chapter 3. Call for Renewal

The experience of the afflicted is described with overflowing anguish (1–21). Yet hope is found in God's past faithfulness to Israel and in the very fact that the exiles survived the destruction of Judah with their lives. How can they complain? All that has happened is a punishment for sin (22–39). Perhaps, if the exiles examine their past carefully, and lift up hearts and hands to God in heaven . . . (40–42)? All the tears and terrors now experienced are a consequence of their own sins (43–54). But Jerusalem's outcasts can call on the Lord to redeem and to punish her enemies (55–66).

Chapter 4. Restitution to Come

Fondly the poet recalls the past, as picture after picture of better days is cast against the raw horror of Jerusalem's destruction (1–

12). Again the poet confesses that all this has come about because of sin, and particularly the sins of the priests and the prophets who were charged by God with the care of his flock (13–20). One day joy will be restored in Jerusalem, and her enemies will suffer in turn (21–22).

Chapter 5. A Cry for Relief

The collection of dirges ends with a poem in which the writer expresses the exiles' cry to the Lord for mercy (1–10). Sin has worked its sure consequences and the joy has left his people's hearts (11–18). At last a true cry of repentance is expressed, as the poet expresses the prayer of the people. "Restore us to yourself, O Lord, that we may return" (19–22).

EZEKIEL
Words to the Exiles

In the final years before the destruction of Jerusalem by the Babylonians in 586 B.C., Jeremiah ministered God's word to the people in Judea. During this same period Ezekiel communicated the same basic message as Jeremiah to the community of Jews already in Babylonian exile. Like Jeremiah, Ezekiel proclaimed the ruin of the homeland and destruction of the great temple Solomon had built (see *Jerusalem Temple,* p. 190). But after the promised devastation occurred, Ezekiel's words surged with hope. Judgment would pass, and in God's good time he would bring a faithful remnant back to the Promised Land.

Historical Background. After centuries of domination, the Assyrian empire was suddenly overthrown by the rising power of Babylon. Under her great king, Nebuchadnezzar, Babylon crushed the last Assyrian armies and humbled the power of Egypt. Babylon became master of the ancient Near East.

In Palestine, Jeremiah announced the unpopular message that Nebuchadnezzar was God's chosen instrument to punish the sin of the Hebrew people. Both Israel, the northern kingdom which fell to Assyria in 722 B.C. and Judah, the surviving southern half of David's once proud Jewish state, had been warned. Prophets were sent by God to each people. They condemned the sins of religious idolatry, moral wickedness, and social injustice. Time after time these messengers attempted to call God's chosen people back to their Lord, to a life of holiness under his Law. But the prophets were ignored or persecuted. The people of each kingdom plunged eagerly into the pursuit of evil.

For twenty-three years before Nebuchadnezzar was crowned as Babylon's king, Jeremiah warned Judah that the long-promised judgments were about to fall. Even when the Babylonian armies appeared, the people of Judah refused to submit. Judah's resistance was slowly crushed in a series of invasions, followed by deportation of the Judean aristocracy and skilled workmen. But the rebellious nation was not subdued until the countryside was razed. Jerusalem was torn down stone by stone, and the magnificent temple built by Solomon was burned. The prophets' words were fulfilled.

Ezekiel was taken to Babylon among the second group of exiles in 587 B.C. There he ministered to his fellow captives, affirming

Jeremiah's message of judgment until Jerusalem fell in 586 B.C. Then he offered words of hope, making the promise that restoration would come, in God's own time (see *The Babylonian Captivity*, pp. 220–228).

Date and Authorship. Dates given within the book tell us that its prophecies came to Ezekiel between July of 593 B.C. and April of 571 B.C. (Ezek. 1:1, 2 and 29:17). A number of other dates for his messages are given by the author, who speaks in the first person throughout the book. Ezekiel is identified as a member of one of Judah's aristocratic priestly families (1:1, 2), called to act as a prophet.

Ezekiel the Man. Nothing is known of Ezekiel beyond what is contained in this OT book. But the picture given in Ezekiel of life among the exiles in Babylon has been strikingly attested by archaeology. The book provides a background against which we can come to know the prophet well. We sense his social standing as he meets with the elders of the exiled community and the stress he must have known as he acts out his prophetic messages. Like Jeremiah, Ezekiel would have been viewed as an eccentric: a man with an unpopular message and an uncommon willingness to be totally obedient to the Lord.

In this great book of the OT we see a man who has become uniquely aware of God. He is visited by strange visions, then driven to communicate his revelations in a ponderous and repetitive way, seeking to drive home to his people truths God has made him responsible to share.

Theology of Ezekiel. Ezekiel shares the common understanding of God which pervades our OT. Yet he adds a new dimension to several of the themes of the OT prophets. Five dominant themes are repeated over and over in this book of messages to the exiles.

1. *God Is Transcendent.* This is no new truth. Ezekiel and the godly always recognized the fact that God cannot be confined to any location, or squeezed into doctrinal categories. Yet in Ezekiel's day the nation was convinced by the false prophets, of whom Jeremiah speaks, that God was bound: tied to the temple and to the land of promise.

In Babylon, Ezekiel receives a number of visions of God's glory. How thrilled the prophet must have been to experience what he had known intellectually! Our God is able to touch our lives and to reveal the glory of his presence wherever we may be!

2. *Israel Is Sinful.* There are many ways that persons try to justify themselves. This was true even of the exiles in Babylon. But Ezekiel is especially sensitive to the holiness of God. As a

result he is able to look back and to interpret Israel's history. He shows that inner wickedness has always found expression in the relationship of the nation with the Lord. He also describes the specific sin of idolatry which, as spiritual adultery, pollutes the worship which Judah even now claims she offers to the Lord.

3. *Judgment Is Certain*. Ezekiel insists that the threats of the prophets of past generations can no longer be ignored. The day of judgment on Judah is certain and has arrived!

4. *Individuals Are Responsible*. The law and the prophets stress the responsibility of the whole Israeli community to obey the Lord and live out his laws of love. While there are incidents reported in the Scriptures which show God's relationship with individuals, the overall OT emphasis has been on the responsibility of the community. In Ezekiel there is a shift in emphasis. What had been implicit in the Psalms and the earlier writings is now emphatically underlined: each individual will bear responsibility for his personal response to the Lord—and will be treated by the Lord accordingly.

5. *Restoration Is Ahead*. The vision of a holy community has not been set aside. Ezekiel too expects the appearance of the Davidic Messiah. Then the nation and people will be restored to the land. Then another, greater temple will be erected, where God will be truly worshiped and from which healing will flow to the world—and endless peace.

Structure and Outline. Ezekiel's writings, like those of Isaiah, contain initial messages of judgment, followed at a later date by words of comfort and hope. The contents can be divided into four sections. Within each section the separate prophetic messages are generally in chronological order.

Outline

I. Prophecy against Judah   1–24
II. Prophecy against Foreign Nations   25–32
III. Prophecies of Restoration   33–39
IV. Prophecy of the Rebuilt Temple   40–48

Value. The importance of Ezekiel's ministry to his contemporaries in Babylon is understood when we grasp the historical situation. But there is also value for us today. The prophet's words call us to a personal vision of the glory of God—a fresh sense of his transcendent presence as we struggle with the details of our daily lives. There is also an important message in the prophet's demand that each individual accept responsibility for his own choices. God does deal with societies and cultures. But within the community of mankind, each of us individually has the privilege of choosing a personal, responsive relationship with Ezekiel's God.

I. Prophecy against Judah (1–24)
Chapters 1:1–3:27. Ezekiel's Call

The Vision; 1:1–28. Ezekiel is thirty years old, just the age when a priest begins his ministry before the Lord. He has been in exile in Babylon since the second deportation some five years before, settled with his fellow countrymen in a district along one of the great irrigation canals [the "Kebar River"] that makes the land around the capital city so fertile (1, 2).

In his stunning vision a bright object rushes toward Ezekiel from the north. It is a great platform on wheels, borne by four "living creatures." Seated on a high sapphire throne under a sparkling canopy is a man-like figure, which burns like metal fire. Ezekiel realizes that he sees the glory of the Lord and falls face down before him.

The full implications of this vision, best translated in the NIV, cannot be understood. But several significant elements are clear. The four living creatures who serve God have faces representing created life, each face standing for its highest expression: man, wild animals (lion), domesticated animals (ox), and birds of the air (eagle). These same living creatures are seen in John's vision of heaven (Rev. 4). Often Revelation reverts to such OT symbols.

The figure of God is glimpsed by Ezekiel, so radiant he cannot be described, but bearing human form. This is far more than others have seen! Even Moses saw only God's back (Exod. 33:18–23); (cf. John 1:18). The point is that as God's word is increasingly revealed through the marching ages, the person of God is seen with increasing clarity! One day he will be fully seen, in a Man who is born of a virgin, who will come to show God's glory in a way that we can at last understand.

Ezekiel's Call; 2:1–10. Ezekiel is told to stand and is given his commission. God sends him as a prophet to the rebellious people of Israel. Ezekiel is to fearlessly speak God's words of mourning and lament. His countrymen may not respond, but they will realize God has sent a prophet among them.

Ezekiel is called "son of man" some 90 times in this book. Later the phrase will have messianic implications, as when Jesus applies it to himself (Matt. 8:20; 12:8, etc.). Here the phrase simply emphasizes Ezekiel's humanity.

Ezekiel's Mission; 3:1–27. Ezekiel eats a scroll on which God's words to rebellious Israel are written, symbolizing his full acceptance of message and mission (1–3). Ezekiel's countrymen are unyielding rebels. But Ezekiel is to speak the words of God, whatever their response (4–11). The vision over, Ezekiel sits stunned for seven days (12–15). Then God's word comes to Ezekiel again. He has been appointed a watchman to warn the wicked. The title "watchman" is often applied to true prophets (Isa. 55:10; Jer. 6:17; etc.). Their responsibility is to be sensitive to the word of God, to communicate it accurately, and thus to warn God's people of danger. As a watchman Ezekiel is not responsible for the response of others to his warning. But he is responsible to deliver it (16–21)! Each hearer will decide individually his own response to the Lord's word (22–27). This theme of individual responsibility, introduced here, is developed in the prophet's later messages (cf. Ezek. 18).

Ezekiel's call introduces two basic principles of ministry. The believer is called to faithfully share God's message with others. But each hearer is personally responsible to accept or reject. How can your relationship with others express each of these ministry principles? What might happen if one or both are misunderstood?

Chapters 4, 5. The Siege of Jerusalem

Ezekiel begins his prophetic ministry to the exiles by acting out four oracles which concern the fate of Jerusalem. The use of symbolic actions to illustrate a prophet's message is a common OT device (cf. 1 Kings 22:11; 2 Kings 13:17; Isa. 20:2–4; Jer. 19:1–10).

Siege Works; 4:1–3. Ezekiel builds toy siege works against a clay tablet which represents Jerusalem. This is a sign to the exiles of that city's coming fate.

Bearing Sin; 4:4–8. The prophet is told to lie on his side a fixed number of days, to represent the years of Israel's and Judah's rebelliousness. The span of years represented is debated but probably goes back to the founding of the northern kingdom, Israel, as a separate state (cf. pp 194 f). The punishment the people bear will be in proportion to their sins.

Starvation Rations; 4:9–17. For over a year Ezekiel lies on his side in obedience to the divine command. During this time he eats a daily ration of about eight ounces of food and a pint of water! His own diet reflects the desperate straits of Jerusalem under her siege.

Three Fates; 5:1–17. At the end of the enacted siege, Ezekiel shaves his beard and his head with a sword. The hair is divided into three parts, to show the fate of Jerusalem's inhabitants when the city falls. One third of the people will die of plague or famine during the siege. Another third will be killed by the sword outside her walls. The last third will be scattered, but pursued by God and killed. All this comes because of the idolatry and wickedness of God's people.

Chapter 6. Against the Mountains

Ezekiel announces to the mountains of Israel that destruction is about to visit them. The altars and idols built upon them will be torn down and defiled by the dead bodies of those who worshiped there (1–7). One day Judah's captives will turn to God and loathe themselves for such detestable practices (8–10). But now God stretches out his hand, to make the land a desolate waste (11–14).

Chapter 7. The End Has Come!

God's anger is unleashed, now! The long promised doom bursts upon Judah, and the Promised Land will be washed in crimson violence. The prophet's dramatic words convey a sense of God's own eagerness for the imminent judgment.

Chapter 8–11. God's Glory Departs

In September of 592 B.C., while the elders of the community in exile are gathered at Ezekiel's house, the prophet is carried in a vision to Jerusalem (8:1–3). What Ezekiel sees there strikes a death blow to those who count on the existence of the temple to protect Jerusalem, and explains fully why the judgments must come.

Idolatry in the Temple; 8:1–18. Ezekiel first notices the glory of God, expressed in the same form as the vision of chapter 1, in the temple. In view of the desecrations now pointed out, God's presence here is amazing! A wooden idol stands at the altar gate (5, 6). In a secret chamber seventy of Judah's leaders worship. They offer incense before wall carvings of loathsome beasts and reptiles from the cults of Egyptian, Canaanite, and Babylonian religions (7–13). Nearby, women participate in the nature cult of Tammuz, which involves fertility rites (14, 15). At the very door of the temple a group of men stand, their backs turned on God's presence within it, bowing in worship to the sun! God must act and purge his people from such detestable sins.

The Glory of God

"Glory" is a term used in association with God's revelation of his presence. God's glory appeared to Ezekiel as overwhelming brightness (1:14). At the dedication of the Jerusalem temple it appeared as a cloud (2 Chron. 5:13, 14; cf. Exod. 40:34 f). Thus God's presence was both revealed and concealed. Such OT revelations feature some physical manifestation, but a tangible expression of God's glory is necessary for a human being to perceive it. The NT comment, that we see "the glory of God in the face of Christ Jesus," builds on this concept (2 Cor. 4:4, 6). In Jesus God is present. In Jesus we come to know God. But there is still more for us to know of him! When Christ returns in "power and great glory" (Matt. 23:30), then the essential nature of God will have its full and glorious expression in our resurrected Lord.

Marked Out for Life; 9:1–11. The glory of the Lord now moves away from its resting place in the temple's inner room, called the "holy of holies." It moves to the temple door. Ezekiel hears instructions given. Every individual in Jerusalem who is grieved by these sins is to be marked, and when the city falls his life is to be preserved. The rest are to be slain.

The Glory Departs; 10:1–22. Burning coals from the throne are scattered over the city. The fires of judgments will supplant the radiant presence of God, for the glory leaves the temple. It rests momentarily above the outer gate of the temple compound. It is accompanied by the living creatures of Ezekiel 1, which the prophet realizes now are cherubim, an order of angel (see *Angels,* p. 370).

Judgment Certain; 11:1–15. Ezekiel is told to hurl God's word against the false prophets who promise Jerusalem peace. The ruling clique there considers the city a cooking pot (the source of sustenance) and themselves meat (the choice members of society). God will indeed make the city a cauldron. But the "meat" of the city are the righteous dead this clique of false prophets and leaders has persecuted! The persecutors will be driven out to die!

As Ezekiel speaks, a familiar aristocrat, Pelatiah, falls dead. Ezekiel is shaken. Will God destroy the whole remnant of Israel? The answer comes: your brothers—the true house of Israel—are with Ezekiel in the captivity (13–15).

Return Prophesied; 11:16–25. God promises through Ezekiel a regathering for the scattered (16, 17). Then a new heart will be

Pagan Worship in the Temple

given to God's people (18–21), and they will be purified (see *New Covenant, OT,* p. 330).

Now, as Ezekiel watches, the glory of the Lord mounts up and moves away from the city, coming to rest above the distant mountains. Ezekiel is returned to Babylon and there reports everything that God has shown him.

Chapter 12. Exile Symbolized

Again Ezekiel is called to act out prophetic messages. Daily he packs what he can carry on his shoulders and leaves his home: each night he slips in through a hole he has dug in the wall with his bare hands. So it will be for Jerusalem (1–16). As Ezekiel eats and drinks he trembles and shakes violently, to mirror the terror the inhabitants at home will feel (17–20). The popular sayings in Judah that dismiss the warnings of God's prophets as merely something for the distant future, with no meaning for today, will be silenced. The judgment will no longer delay (21–28).

Chapter 13. Against False Prophets

Prophets and prophetesses have promised Jerusalem peace in the Lord's name. But they lie! Their delusions and deceitful visions have cost the lives of many innocent people who trusted them. They are justly condemned (see *Recognizing False Prophets,* p. 326).

Chapter 14. Inner Idolatry

Some of Israel's elders come to Ezekiel to ask direction from God. The Lord reveals they have "idols in their hearts." It is not necessary to bow down before wood or stone objects to abandon the Lord (1–6)! God announces that anyone guilty of this inner idolatry who dares inquire of a prophet of the Lord will be immediately judged (7–11).

The Lord turns again to Jerusalem. Even if Noah, Daniel, and Job lived in that city, it would not be spared (12–23).

What do you think inner idolatry might involve today? Can you think of any reasons why Noah, Daniel, and Job might have been chosen by God for the illustration in verses 12–23?

Chapter 15. The Useless Vine

Isaiah pictured Israel as a vine that bore only bitter grapes (Chap. 5). Ezekiel picks up this image and points out that the stringy

wood of the grapevine is useless. Judah has not borne fruit: she
will be consigned to the fire.

Chapter 16. Faithless Jerusalem

Beautifully and emotionally, God speaks an allegory about his
long relationship with his people. They were born mongrels, thrown
out in a field to die. God rescued and cared for them. Later he
entered into a marriage contract (for so the covenant is viewed
here) and brought his bride wealth and beauty. But like a faithless
wife she turned into a prostitute, and even offered the gifts God
gave her to her lovers (idols). This harlot nation has proved to
be sister to Sodom and Samaria and must be punished. But God
says, "I will remember the covenant I made with you in the days
of your youth, and will establish an everlasting covenant with you"
(60).

Though God's people are faithless, God remains faithful to his
commitments and to his word (cf. Heb. 6:13–20).

Read Ezekiel 16 and imagine yourself one of the community
in exile to whom it first came. With what events in the
history of your people will you associate each element? What in
the allegory seems most convicting to you? What is most comforting? What impression of God's feelings does the allegory convey?

Chapter 17. Parable of the Eagles

Two eagles represent the great powers, Babylon and Egypt. A
vine represents Judah, now under the domination (and protection)
of Babylon. But the vine turns from the eagle which sustains it
to bend toward the second (1–10). The parable is explained by
Ezekiel. Judah's King Zedekiah is secretly breaking his oath of
allegiance to Nebuchadnezzar and has sent envoys to Egypt. God
will punish this oath-breaking (11–21). One day God himself will
take a shoot from the top of the most noble of trees and it will
grow to be splendid. It is likely Ezekiel did not understand this
final, messianic word picture (22–24).

Chapter 18. Individual Responsibility

The people of Judah exhibited a fatalistic attitude. They blamed
their misfortunes on the sins of their ancestors and shrugged. What
could they do about the past? Both Jeremiah (31:29) and Ezekiel
speak against this irresponsible attitude. True, past generations

did set the direction of the present. But judgment never comes *solely* because of others' actions. Judah willfully participates in the sins of the fathers, and her judgment is just.

It is against the background of an attitude of irresponsibility, which questions the justice of God, that Ezekiel speaks.

The Soul Who Sins Is the One Who Will Die; 18:1–4. This chapter is not about hell or punishment after death. The word translated "soul" in the OT does not refer to some immaterial part of man that survives physical death. The word means "self" and refers to an individual's life or person. Thus the passage says "the *person* who sins is the one who will die." Death here, in the context of Ezekiel, is physical death. God will save the righteous of his people alive when the nation is destroyed: the wicked are marked out for death (see Ezek. 9).

The Principle Illustrated: 18:5–20). Three examples are provided by the prophet. A righteous man who does right will live (5–9). A violent and wicked son of a righteous man will die for his own sins (10–13). The righteous son of a wicked father will live (14–18). Each individual will be judged on the basis of his own response to God and to God's laws, which call for justice between men.

The Possibility of Change; 18:21–32. No individual's fate is determined by his parent's behavior. Even his own sins need not bind him! God passionately desires that his people turn to him, and he takes no pleasure in the death of those who die. A wicked man can save his life by turning from his sin to righteousness.

Thus the message of personal responsibility Ezekiel brings to the people of Israel is also a message of hope. God will not reject anyone who turns to him, to walk in his ways.

Chapter 19. Lament for Princes

This dirge poem (see Lamentations) mourns the fate that sin has brought to the last of Judah's kings: Jehoahaz (2–4), Jehoiachin (5–9), and Zedekiah (10–14). The "lioness" and "mother" referred to in the poem is the nation.

Chapter 20:1–44. Record of Rebellion

Now without allegory (cf. Chap. 16, 23) Ezekiel reviews Israel's history and its witness to Israel's endless rebellion. In Egypt Israel took up with idols and would not surrender them (5–9). In the wilderness journey a pattern of rebellion against God's law was established (10–26). Brought into the Promised Land, Israel ran eagerly after the heathen Canaanite religions (27–29). The present judgment is necessary to purge the unclean people (30–38), after which a purified remnant will be returned (39–44).

Chapter 20:45–21:32. Song of the Sword

Ezekiel turns to face south where Judah lies (20:45–49). Babylon is identified as God's sword, to be used now against the Lord's own people. Parts of this chapter are poetry and are often called the "song of the sword."

Chapter 22. Sins of Jerusalem

Three oracles chronicle the sins of God's people. They are guilty of violence and social immorality (1–16). Jerusalem has nothing of moral value to offer God or man (17–22). She is completely corrupt throughout every social class, from the royal house to the people (23–29). Thus judgment will surely come (30, 31).

Chapter 23. The Two Sisters

A famous allegory portrays the twin nations of Israel and Judah. They are adulterous sisters, whose lewdness led them to pursue their lovers in every grove and tree. Despite seeing the fate of the first sister (Israel, carried captive in 722 B.C.), the other continues to sin.

Free Will/Human Responsibility, OT

There is no theological debate in the OT between "predestination" and "free will." No OT writer suggests that, since God is sovereign, he must choose an individual for salvation (see *Predestination, OT,* p. 317). No OT writer suggests that for a person to have "free will" his salvation must rest on his own completely free choice. But we do find a movement among God's OT people to deny personal responsibility.

In the days of Jeremiah and Ezekiel, such people argued that God deals only in national terms, with the whole community of Israel. They said that God's attitude toward them was based on what earlier generations had done. Thus when the prophets detailed the sins for which God would bring judgment, and called for repentance, these people simply shrugged and complained that it was all their forefathers' fault! It was unfair, but if they must suffer for what others had done, there was nothing they could do.

In this atmosphere the idea that any individual had personal responsibility, or that anything an individual could do made a difference, was simply rejected.

The later prophets, and particularly Ezekiel, speak out against this form of determinism. National repentance *could* change the course of history and stay the hand of judgment (Jer. 18:7–10). By the time of Ezekiel, the nation as a whole was committed to the pursuit of evil. So this prophet stresses another aspect of the message of personal responsibility. God does deal with individuals as well as the nation! If an individual in a corrupt society chooses righteousness, God will mark him out (9:3–6) and preserve his life. This preservation is based on the individual's personal response to God, not what his father has done (Ezek. 18:5–20). Even a wicked person can turn to God, begin to live righteously, and will be forgiven (18:21–23). The message of the prophets, then, stresses the fact that a person *is* responsible for his choices, and that if he chooses God, then God will exercise his power on the individual's behalf.

Looking ahead to the end times, the prophet says of the nation, "I will give you a new heart and put a new spirit in you" (Ezek. 36:26). And in chapter 18 Ezekiel reports God's exhortation: "Get yourselves a new heart and a new spirit" (18:31). The role God plays in the transformation of an individual is one of those hidden things we can safely leave to him. What is revealed in Scripture is that the philosophy of determinism, which suggests you and I are not responsible for our choices, is wrong! We *do* choose. And our loving God invites us to choose *him*.

Chapter 24. The Cooking Pot

Judgment Begins; 24:1–14. In a poetic allegory, Jerusalem is pictured as a cooking pot, and her inhabitants the meat stewed in it by the fires of judgment; fires so hot the very pot will melt into slag (3–12). Thus God will deal with Israel's lewdness (13, 14).

The prophecy comes on January 15, 588 B.C., the very date that Nebuchadnezzar begins the siege of the city in distant Judah.

Death of Ezekiel's Wife; 24:15–27. A few days later Ezekiel is warned that his wife, "the delight of your eyes," will die suddenly. The prophet is not to mourn or weep (15–18). Ezekiel explains his reaction to the wondering exiles. Their relatives in Judah will soon be cut off as well, and they too will sit crushed, wasting away as a result of their sin.

II. Against Foreign Nations (25–32)

Like Isaiah and Jeremiah, this prophet of the exile delivered words of judgment, hurled against Israel's foreign oppressors.

Chapter 25. Against Amon, Moab, Edom and Philistia

Short prophecies are uttered against Israel's near neighbors in a sequence beginning to the northeast of Israel and swinging southward around to Philistia in the southwest. Standing on the heights of Jerusalem, a person today can see each of these territories with the naked eye.

Chapters 26–28. Against Tyre

Tyre was a wealthy trading city in Ezekiel's day, lying just 100 miles from Jerusalem, and about 35 miles from the Sea of Galilee. It is built on a coastal island, connected by an artificial causeway to a twin city on the mainland. Tyre is deemed impregnable. Her fall will demonstrate that no worldly power is truly secure.

Tyre's Destruction Coming; 26:1–21. A month after the news of Jerusalem's fall reaches the exiles, God turns the prophet's words against Tyre. She too will fall to Nebuchadnezzar. The description of the siege foretells in detail the method of attack the Babylonian king actually used: he tore the city on land down to the bare rock, and put the rubble into the sea, building a land bridge for his armies. The site is doomed by the prophet to silent desolation: the modern city of Tyre is near by, and fishermen still spread their nets on the deserted rocky shore of the ancient location (13, 14).

The Shipwreck of Tyre; 27:1–36. The city is pictured allegorically as one of her own wealthy trading vessels. The description of the fittings of the ship (5–11) and the geographically organized directory of trading partners (10–25) provide history's best written source of information about ancient ships and trading.

Downfall of the Prince of Tyre; 28:1–10. Ezekiel now drops the use of allegory and speaks clearly of the contemporary prince (ruler) of Tyre, Ithobal II, who claimed deity. His pride will topple as he is brought down to a violent death.

Lament over the King of Tyre; 28:11–19. The shift in terms from "prince" to "king" as this passage begins, as well as the description of an original perfection, have led some to believe the description is of Satan before his fall and before man's creation. Others suggest the imagery speaks of unfallen man in the garden of Eden.

Prophecy against Sidon; 28:20–26. Judgments are announced against Sidon, a neighboring city long associated as a trading partner of Tyre.

Chapters 29–32. Prophecy against Egypt

At the time Ezekiel writes, Egypt is still a potential threat to Babylonian world domination. Because of this, some of Judah's last kings treacherously sought Egyptian support to rebel against Nebuchadnezzar. Seven messages are addressed to Egypt's Pharaoh.

The Sins of Egypt; 29:1–16. This message comes a year after the Jerusalem siege begins. Egypt's pride, and her failure to support Israel from its days of servitude, are condemned. Egypt will fall.

Egypt's Loot Promised Nebuchadnezzar; 29:17–21. The land of Egypt and its wealth is reserved as a reward for Babylon's king.

Lament for Egypt; 30:1–19. In this picture of the coming "Day of the Lord," judgment is predicted for Egypt. The lament, a somber poem, grimly describes that future scene.

Pharaoh's Arm Broken; 30:20–26. "Arm" is a common OT image to indicate strength or power.

The Great Tree Fallen; 31:1–18. An allegory portrays Egypt as a noble cedar tree, proud of its age and towering height. This pride will be brought low as the tree (nation) is toppled.

Lament for Pharaoh; 31:1–16. The dark day approaching this ruler and his nation is graphically described. The picture is of a funeral, at which the nations gather to chant the somber dirge.

Descent to Death; 31:17–32. The NIV translates it "the pit!" Other versions often keep the Hebrew term, "sheol." The word is best taken as the place of the dead, or the grave. This too is a funeral dirge, consigning the Egyptian armies to death, to lie among a great heap of slain from all nations.

III. Prophecies of Restoration (33–39)

Jerusalem has fallen. The destruction now requires interpretation in view of God's promises concerning Israel's future. Themes from Ezekiel's earlier messages are repeated. But the tone now is one of expectation rather than woe.

Chapter 33. Work of the Watchman

The Prophet's Duty; 1–9. It is the duty of a watchman to sound warnings in time of danger. This is the prophet's mission as well.

The Hearer's Duty; 10–20. God's invitation to repent, given by the prophets, lays the responsibility for response squarely on the shoulders of each individual. Those who turn to God will live (cf. *Human Responsibility,* p. 350).

Jerusalem's Fall Explained; 21–33. Israel's failure to respond to prophetic words of warning (31) is the reason why the crushing judgment has fallen on this generation.

Chapter 34. The Shepherds

The rulers of Israel were to guard her people against oppression. But they have fed off the flock rather than cared for God's lambs (1–10). God will take the role of Shepherd of his people on himself. He will bind up the injured and care for the sick (11–16). God will also judge between the good and evil of his flock, to save the weak (17–22). The promised king from David's line will be placed over God's flock (23–24), and in that day God's covenant of peace will be fulfilled. Israel will be showered with blessings (25–31).

Chapter 35. Against Edom

When Jerusalem fell, the neighboring Edomites joyfully joined in. They turned fugitives over to the Babylonians to be killed, and searched for loot in Judah's ruined towns. Because of this evil, God will desolate their land.

Chapter 36. Restoration

The mountains of Israel have witnessed her spiritual adultery, for idols and altars were set up on their peaks and in their groves. These same mountains are assured by the prophet that the future holds a complete renewal.

Enemies of the Mountains to Be Judged; 36:1–7. The peoples who plundered and ridiculed desolate Israel will suffer judgment.

Blessings to Come to the Mountains; 36:8–15. The now empty land will be repeopled and will again be cultivated and prosperous.

God's Holy Name; 36:16–21. Ezekiel introduces this theme for the first time. Israel's sins are so gross that God's name has been profaned by the pagans! He is forced to act in judgment to preserve that good name. But blessing too is associated with God's good name and will follow discipline.

God's Motivation and Purposes; 36:22–38. In this important passage, Ezekiel reveals God's motives for the coming restoration. The Lord's holiness will be demonstrated to all the nations, not only in the judgment, but in the restoration. Only God is able to take such sinners and transform them, so they at last respond to his Spirit and desire to keep his laws (22–27). Saved from their uncleanness, restored Israel's life in the land will be a constant testimony to the Lord. Remembrance of the past will be a testimony to Israel herself as to how great God's salvation truly is (28–32). When Israel's sins are cleansed, the land will be resettled (33–36) and the people multiplied (37–38). Then all will know that "I am the Lord!"

How does the explanation which God gives for Israel's ultimate salvation in 36:22–38 compare with your understanding of his purposes in our salvation today? How are they similar? How might they differ? Does the emphasis on benefits to God in bringing salvation detract from the teaching that salvation is rooted in God's love? Why, or why not?

Chapter 37. New Life for the Nation

The Dry Bones; 37:1–14. Ezekiel sees a valley full of dry bones—remains of the long dead. Ezekiel is told to prophesy toward them. As he does, the bones come together, are covered with flesh, but still lie dead on the valley floor. The prophet is then told to speak to "the breath" (NIV). This word in Hebrew means "breath, wind, or spirit." The appeal is to the Spirit to come and breathe life into the dead. As the prophet speaks, the dead come to life (1–10).

The vision is interpreted in verses 11 through 14. This is not a vision of individual resurrection. It is a vision of the regathering and spiritual restoration of the nation Israel. Now, some ten years after deportation, with Jerusalem destroyed, the exiles have lost hope. They believe they are cut off from their God and his covenant promises (11). But the foreign nations where God's people are scattered, likened metaphorically to graves, will surrender their dead: God will bring his people back to the Promised Land (12). There God will "put my Spirit in you and you will live" (14).

Because this restoration is associated with Messiah's rule (37:15–28) some believe the 1948 establishment of Israel as a nation is foretold in the reassembly of the bones and the flesh coming on the still dead bodies. They believe the "Spirit of life" will be breathed into Israel in a national conversion when Jesus comes.

A United People; 37:15–28. Two sticks represent the divided people of the northern and southern kingdoms, separated since 930 B.C. Gripping them in one hand, the prophet announces that God will again unite his people in one kingdom (15–23) which will be ruled over by "David my servant," a title for the promised Messiah (see *Davidic Covenant*, p. 177). Then at last a holy Israel will be the dwelling place of God. Forever.

Chapters 38, 39. Against Gog

These chapters contain an apocalytic vision of a great battle in the far future "last days." The events described fit the picture given by other prophets of a final great battle between the evil forces of the north and God's people (see Jer. 4:5–6:26; Joel 2:28–32; Zeph. 1:14–18; Isa. 29:5–8; Zech. 12:1–9; 14:1–15). While details are difficult to interpret with confidence, the main thrust of the prophecy is stated boldly and clearly.

The primary question concerns the identity of Gog, who rules Magog and is associated with Meshech and Tubal. Firm identification of Gog and Magog with Russia cannot be made on etymological grounds (that is, from the historic origins and use of the word). The same power is mentioned in Revelation 20 as leader of a coalition of nations. Many of these nations can be identified and are from widely scattered regions of the earth.

The three most common interpretations for this passage are that: (1) it describes an attack by Russia and its allies on the Middle East; (2) it describes a final catastrophic struggle with real but unidentifiable powers; and (3) it is a symbolic portrayal of the struggle between the church and the world, demonstrating that God comes to the aid of his people.

The chapters include seven oracles, each of which is introduced by "Thus says the Lord God."

The Armies Gather; 38:3–9. A great horde is gathered under the leadership of Gog to attack Israel, which feels secure. This gathering is stimulated by the Lord, not to judge Israel but to judge the nations (cf. 16, 17).

Gog's Intent; 38:10–13. Greed, and a desire for plunder, motivate this attack on an unsuspecting peace-loving people.

Invasion! 38:14–16. The great horde advances against Israel.

Massacre of Gog's Army; 38:17–23. As the enemy reach the borders of Israel, God acts. A great natural disaster strikes the invaders. The timing and focus of the disaster unmistakably mark it as a direct intervention by God.

God's Spirit, OT

The later prophets look forward to an age of the Spirit, when God's Spirit will be poured out on all flesh (cf. Ezek. 35:25–29; Isa. 44:3; Joel 2:28, 29). What did the OT believers understand of the Spirit, and what is the meaning of the term "spirit" in the OT?

The word translated "spirit," like the Greek term used in the NT, simply means "wind, breath, or spirit." It is a word associated with life, as when

God breathes the breath (spirit) of life into Adam, and man becomes a living being (Gen. 2:7). The breath, or spirit, is that active, life-giving force which animates all who move and breathe. Not every reference to spirit in the OT is a reference to God's Spirit.

When the OT speaks of the Spirit of God, or of God's Spirit, the Scriptures focus our attention on who God is as a vital, active, life-giving person. The OT does not state, and OT saints did not suspect, that God exists in Trinity, with God the Father, God the Son, and God the Holy Spirit as separate and yet equal persons. But they did know that the one the prophets spoke of as "the Spirit" is God.

In the OT it is God as Spirit who hovers, superintending the shaping of the universe (Gen. 1:2 f). It is God as Spirit who contends against man's sins and who finally acts to bring on the cataclysmic judgment of the Flood (Gen. 6:3).

The Spirit of God is also known in the OT as the one who provides power or skill or ability for special ministries, whether to artisans for construction of the wilderness Tabernacle (Exod. 28:3), to men for the leadership of God's people (Exod. 11:17–19), or to warriors for battle (Judg. 6:34; 11:29). It is the Spirit of the Lord who speaks through the prophets (2 Sam. 23:2).

In the OT the Spirit is associated with the person and mission of the Messiah. It is the Spirit who rests on Messiah to give him his wisdom and understanding (Isa. 11:2, 3; cf. Isa. 41). While it is the Holy Spirit who has been angered by Israel's sins (Isa. 63:10, 11), it is this same Spirit who will one day be poured out on all, to bring man purification and transformation from within. The new heart is a gift brought by the Spirit (Ezek. 37:14; Joel 2:28, 29).

When Jesus, in John 3, expresses surprise that Nicodemus does not understand his reference to the wind (Spirit) and being "born again," he is referring to the OT promises associated with the age of the Spirit. A ruler in Israel, versed as Nicodemus was in the Scriptures, should have understood new birth as the fulfillment of Jeremiah's new covenant promises, and a sign of the advent of the promised new age.

Destruction of the Invaders; 39:1–16. The prophet, in typical Hebrew fashion, returns to elaborate on the massacre. The devastation will leave the enemy troops strewn across the countryside bordering Israel. Their abandoned weapons will provide raw materials for Israel for seven years. Through it all, God's purposes will be fulfilled. He will keep his prophetic word (5, 8), he will vindicate his holy name (7), and all peoples will know that he is Lord (7).

Feast of the Beasts; 39:17–24. As the beasts gather to gorge on the bodies of the slain, Israel will realize that the Lord is still their God (22), while the nations of the world learn that a holy God does punish evil—in his own people, and in others (23, 24).

God's Goal for Israel; 39:25–29. In the end, history will testify to the faithfulness of God to his covenant promises. A purified people, regathered in their own land and to a true relationship with God, will know the full blessing of His Spirit in their lives (cf. Gen. 12:2–3, 7 and see *God's Spirit, OT,* p. 356).

IV. Prophecy of the Rebuilt Temple (40–48)

Nearly a dozen years after the utterance of his other prophecies, Ezekiel is given a culminating vision of the final, perfect kingdom to be established when God sets his presence among men, and the Spirit is at rest on the whole people. Highlighted in this vision is the temple, built on the site of earlier temples (see *Jerusalem Temple,* p. 190). There God will be worshiped and served in the golden age to come. This temple, the sacrifices offered there, and the territory to be occupied by each tribe of the restored Israel, are all described in careful detail.

This passage has raised a number of questions. Is the scene described by Ezekiel a prophecy which will be literally fulfilled? If not, why are such careful measurements taken and recorded, just as the measurements of the tabernacle were revealed to Moses by God in the wilderness (Exod. 25–28)? If literal fulfillment is expected, how can the restoration of animal sacrifices, which Ezekiel describes, be explained? Christ's one sacrifice on the cross won a completed salvation for all mankind (Heb. 10:14–18). Reinstitution of an OT sacrificial system seems to raise serious theological problems. The usual answer suggested, that the sacrifices in Ezekiel's temple are commemorative, seems to many to be inadequate.

What can we say with certainty? That to the people of Ezekiel's time this vision kindled hope. The promise of the temple rebuilt, more glorious than ever before, reinforced confidence that they had not been abandoned by God. Surely the temple that Ezekiel saw and described appeared real to him, and the believers of the OT expected a literal fulfillment of this vision at the end of time. Ezekiel is not attempting to disguise "spiritual truths" behind architectural symbols and measurements.

Chapters 40–43. The Temple

Detailed measurements are taken as Ezekiel is shown Jerusalem's rebuilt temple. The gates and courts are described (40:1–37) and also rooms for preparing sacrifice (40:38–43). The temple itself is

PLAN OF EZEKIEL'S TEMPLE

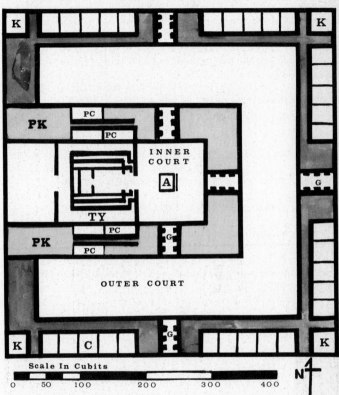

Scale In Cubits

0   50   100   200   300   400

N

Pavement

A: ALTAR
C: CHAMBER
K: KITCHEN
PC: PRIEST'S CHAMBER
PK: PRIEST'S KITCHEN
TY: TEMPLE YARD
G: GATEWAY

measured and described (40:48–41:26). In the temple are rooms set aside for the priests who serve there (42:1–20).

A most significant element of the vision involves the return of the glory of the Lord. Ezekiel 8–11 described the departure from the old temple of this visible expression of God's presence. Then the temple and the city were destroyed. The Lord was finally driven out of that temple by the gross sins of his people. Now, with the land purified and the people made holy, the glory returns to Jerusalem (43:1–12).

Finally the altar of the temple is carefully measured, and Ezekiel is told what sacrifices are to be offered there (42:13–27).

Chapter 44. Temple Duties

The duties of the priests and Levites who serve God at the restored temple are carefully detailed. The specific branch of the family of Aaron which is to serve as priests is identified.

Chapters 45, 46. The Temple District

A narrow strip of land running from the Mediterranean to the Jordan is set aside as a sacred district. Some of it is in the charge of the priests, and the rest in the charge of the prince (Messiah). Regular offerings are made, and the OT festivals (see p. 104) are celebrated (45:13–46:24).

Chapter 47. The River

Geographical changes are seen by Ezekiel. A great river full of life springs from the temple, flowing away in four branches.

Chapter 48. The Tribal Areas

The Book of Ezekiel closes with a new division of the land among the twelve tribes of Israel (cf. Josh. 13–20). As for the city to lie in the center of the regathered tribes, it too will have a new name: THE LORD IS THERE!

DANIEL
Visions of the Future

The Book of Daniel records the personal history and prophetic visions of an exiled Hebrew who won significant posts in the government of the Babylonian empire. Daniel's visions give a detailed picture of the political future of the Mediterranean world. They also include predictions concerning the more distant future.

Date and Authorship. The book purports to be a first person account, written by a youth taken from Judah in the deportation of 605 B.C. It includes many stories of Daniel's training and his rise to power in Babylon's administration. But most commentators concentrate on Daniel's detailed prophecies of the future.

It is the prophecies of Daniel which have given some commentators problems. Daniel predicts political history from Babylon to NT times, including the emergence of Rome as the dominant world power. These political prophecies were challenged as early as the third century, A.D. The philosopher Prophry argued that the book must have been written after the events it so clearly describes.

Critics during the past two centuries have also challenged the traditional dating of Daniel. Uncomfortable with the supernatural, they have argued that the book was written in the time of the Maccabees, at least 300 years after the dates given by the author in the book itself.

This late date is suggested despite the fact that it would make the author of Daniel a deceiver, and despite the fact that both Ezekiel (14:20) and Christ (Matt. 24:15) give testimony to the trustworthiness of the book, identifying the author as God's prophet.

Value of Archaeology. The arguments once advanced to support a Maccabean date for Daniel have been strikingly refuted by the science of biblical archaeology (see *Archaeological Insights,* pp. 36, 37). Three illustrations show the kind of contributions archaeology makes to OT studies and dating biblical documents.

(1) Historical error was alleged in conflict between dates given in Daniel 1:1 and Jeremiah 23:1, 9 and 46:2. Archaeological discoveries have shown that the Hebrews and Babylonians used a different system of counting to number years of rule. Daniel follows the Babylonian system; Jeremiah, in Judah, follows the Hebrew system.

(2) The term "Chaldean" is used by Daniel in a specialized sense, to designate a class of wise men and advisors. Discovery of Assyrian records show that Daniel's technical use is absolutely correct.

(3) Daniel portrays Belshazzar as ruler when Babylon falls. But cuneiform records show Nabonidus on the Babylonian throne. This was long held to be evidence that Daniel must have been written much later, for what contemporary would make such an obvious mistake? But further Babylonian records show Daniel is correct! Belshazzar was made co-regent with his father Nabonidus, who was in Syria when the city of Babylon fell.

These and many other similar details show the writer of Daniel had an intimate knowledge of the Babylonian court, of specialized terms, and of contemporary history. All this supports the traditional date of Daniel—the date given in the OT book itself. As for fulfilled prophecy, the supernaturalist finds nothing strange in the fact that the Lord, who gave Daniel his revelations, knew the course of history in advance (see *Fulfilled Prophecy*, p. 305).

Historical Background. Daniel was taken captive in 605 B.C. When he was led from Judah to Babylon he was probably in his teens. His last prophetic vision is dated in the third year of Cyrus, or 536 B.C. This is two years after Cyrus issued a decree freeing the Jews to return to their homeland and rebuild the temple (538 B.C.) For a review of events in Judea and in Babylon during the long life of this premier OT prophet, see *Babylonian Captivity*, p. 222–228 and "Historical Background" on Ezekiel, p. 339.

Daniel the Man. Daniel's name means "God is my judge." He stands in Scripture as one of the most admirable and upright of all OT personalities. From his youth Daniel "resolved not to defile himself" in the pagan land (1:8). He continued utterly faithful to God and faithful in his responsibilities to the government of the empire. Daniel stands today as a model of uprightness, and his experience shows that it is possible to live a godly and meaningful life under a totalitarian system hostile to God.

Structure and Outline. The Book of Daniel can be divided into two sections. The first (Chaps. 1–6) tells of Daniel's personal experiences against the background of life at the court of Babylon and Persia. These chapters are organized in chronological order. The second section (Chaps. 7–12) contains a series of visions given to Daniel, in which God opens the near and distant future to the prophet's gaze. The prophecies of Daniel are extremely detailed, and some are distinctive in their careful specification of time elements.

Outline

One other feature of this book is distinctive. It is written in two languages: Aramaic (2:4b–7:28) and Hebrew (1:1–2:4b and 8:1–12:13). As a result of archaeological discoveries it is now known that writers in ancient Mesopotamia did at times adopt such contrasting forms to increase the general impact.

Values. The book Daniel wrote, and the picture of the future he conveyed, gave added confidence to the people of his own day that God truly is in charge of history. The Book of Daniel is often the primary focus of those interested in the study of prophecy in the OT (see *OT Eschatology: The Future According to the Old Testament,* p. 372, 373). The testimony of Daniel's own life is significant, even to a person not entranced by his prophecy. The Lord God of Israel is shown to be greater than the idols of Israel's pagan conquerors. As you and I trust in this God, and remain faithful to his Word, we can expect him to be present with us, even as God so surely was with his servant Daniel.

I. Daniel's Life and Work (1–6)

The first half of Daniel features five events selected from the prophet's long life in Babylon. Each account has much of value for application to our lives today. There is also a report of an experience of his three Hebrew companions, which apparently took place when Daniel was away from the capital (Chap. 3).

Chapter 1. Daniel's Commitment

Nebuchadnezzar is one of the ancient world's most effective rulers. Among his practices is the selection of promising youths from subject nations for training as administrators of the empire. Daniel, with three friends, all members of noble families brought from Judah in 605 B.C., is selected for such training (1:3–7).

Daniel immediately rejects the diet provided for the students by the king, which apparently violates Jewish dietary laws. He wisely, and respectfully, asks for ten days in which he and his friends prove their restricted diet is healthy. They pass the test and are permitted to eat as they choose. God gives Daniel and his friends great ability and understanding. After three years of

training, when the graduates are questioned by Nebuchadnezzar
himself, Daniel and his friends surpass the rest (8–21).

How important was Daniel's initial, immediate act of commitment? How did Daniel remain committed and still not
offend the man who was placed over him? What can you learn
from this chapter about how to take a stand for your faith and
still not be offensive? Is there a stand God is calling you to take
now?

Chapter 2. Nebuchadnezzar's Dream

The Dream; 2:1–12. Ancient cultures found great significance
in dreams. Thus when Nebuchadnezzar has a strange dream it
troubles him deeply, and he calls his advisors to interpret it. Many
different disciplines, including magic and astrology, are represented
in his group of "wise men." The king demands the group not
only interpret the dream but first prove their interpretation is valid
by relating the dream itself! When the astrologers confess they
cannot, the furious ruler orders all the "wise men" of Babylon
executed.

Daniel's Prayers Answered; 2:13–23. Daniel and his friends are
among the class of wise men and so are also condemned! When
Daniel hears, he promises that God will tell the dream and its
meaning. As his three friends pray, Daniel is told the dream and
interpretation.

The Dream Interpreted; 2:23–45. Daniel tells Nebuchadnezzar
his dream. The king has seen a great statue, with a gold head,
silver chest and arms, a bronze belly and thighs, legs of iron and
feet of mixed iron and clay. A rock, not cut out with human
hands, shatters the statue, grinds it into dust, and then grows to
fill the whole earth.

God tells Daniel this statue represents succeeding kingdoms,
each inferior to the previous one. The rock represents a kingdom
which God will set up and which will never be destroyed (39–
45). Thus the dream is prophetic—a vision given the king by God,
telling what will happen to his empire in the future.

Daniel is honored by Nebuchadnezzar and made first administrator of the empire. Nebuchadnezzar also recognizes the greatness
of the Lord: "your God is the God of gods and the Lord of kings"
(47).

History's Vindication. This picture of the future is repeated in
another vision, with the interpretation given in even more detail
(see Daniel 7 and 8). These prophecies so clearly match the events

Daniel 2, 7, 8

	Babylon (605-538 B.C.)	Medo-Persia (538-331 B.C.)	Greece (331-146 B.C.)	Rome (146 B.C.—A.D. 476)
Daniel 2: 31-45 Dream image (603 B.C.)	Head of gold (2: 32, 37, 38)	Breast, arms of silver (2: 32, 39)	Belly, thighs of brass (2: 32, 39)	Legs of iron Feet of iron and clay (2: 33, 40, 41)
Daniel 7 First vision: Four Beasts (553 B.C.)	Lion (7:4)	Bear (7:5)	Leopard (7:6)	Strong Beast (7:7, 11, 19, 23)
Daniel 8 Second vision: Ram and goat (551 B.C.)		Ram (8:3, 4, 20)	Goat with one horn (8: 5-8, 21) Four horns (8: 8, 22) Little horn (8: 9-14)	

of world history in the centuries following that many have denied the Book of Daniel could have been written in the Babylonian era. They insist it must have been written after the events, in the second century B.C. (see p. 361). The chart on page 365 lists the world empires and their correlation with the king's dream and Daniel's later visions.

Daniel showed remarkable poise under pressure. This is clearly founded on his personal relationship with God and his concept of who God is. What can you see in the following verses which might help explain Daniel's reactions, and might also help you in personal pressure situations? Study these verses and jot down your insights: Daniel 2:14–16, 18, 19–23, 27, 28, 30.

Chapter 3. The Fiery Furnace

Daniel is unquestioned leader of the small group of Hebrews in the Babylonian administration. But when Daniel is absent, the other three (Shadrach, Meshach, and Abednego) prove their faith is not dependent on their leader. Nebuchadnezzar sets up a gold statue. At its dedication he commands all his officials to worship it. When the three refuse, the furious monarch orders them thrown into a blazing furnace. But then Nebuchadnezzar leaps to his feet in amazement! The three are not consumed and a fourth figure appears with them, walking in the white-hot center of the flames. To Nebuchadnezzar this fourth figure looks like a "son of the gods" (that is, a deity). Many believe this is a preincarnate appearance of Jesus.

Called out of the fires, the three Jews are examined. They are not burned, and their clothing is not even scorched. This second confrontation with the Hebrew's God deeply impresses Nebuchadnezzar. He commands bloody execution for anyone who dares say anything against the God of Shadrach, Meshach, and Abednego.

What is the attitude of the three in this test of their faith (3:16–18)? What is there here for you to apply to your life?

God clearly has begun to work in the life of this pagan ruler. How does Nebuchadnezzar's response to God's revelation compare with that of Pharaoh (cf. Exod. 8:1–15)? As you read in Daniel, be alert to what is happening within this ruler.

Chapter 4. Nebuchadnezzar's Madness

The Dream; 4:1–18. Near the end of his 43-year reign, Nebuchadnezzar has a second prophetic dream. He sees a great tree, which a heavenly messenger commands be cut down. The stump, bound with iron, remains in the field.

The Interpretation; 4:19–27. Daniel is upset when told the dream. Nebuchadnezzar is the tree, and the messenger an angel from God. The Lord has decreed that Nebuchadnezzar will be driven from human society, to live with the animals and eat grass like cattle for seven "times." In Daniel this word is used to indicate a year. Afterward, when the king acknowledges the rule of God, his kingdom will be returned and he will recover. Daniel urges repentance. God may relent.

The Fulfillment; 4:28–37. A year after the dream, Nebuchadnezzar is walking on the roof of his palace. Suddenly he is filled with pride at all his accomplishments. Immediately the king is struck with madness and rushes from the city into the fields. But at the end of the appointed time, "I, Nebuchadnezzar, raised my eyes toward heaven, and my sanity was restored" (v. 34).

The chapter closes with the converted monarch's expression of praise to God and acknowledgment of God's sovereign rule over all earthly kingdoms.

Some have viewed OT faith as "exclusive," as if God's choice of the Jewish people ruled out his care for other peoples and individuals. Nebuchadnezzar is one OT example of God's grace to a pagan. Study these passages and see if you can discern a pattern in God's relationships with other non-Jews in OT times. See Ruth 1:15–17; 2 Kings 5; Isaiah 49:5, 6 and Jonah 4.

Chapter 5. Belshazzar Found Wanting

Nebuchadnezzar died in 563 B.C. The events of this chapter take place in 539 B.C. Belshazzar is co-regent with his father, Nabonidus, a "son of Nebuchadnezzar" (v. 22) only in the sense of successor.

At a great banquet held in Babylon, a hand appears and writes unknown words on the wall. Daniel, still active in Babylon's administration, is called. He interprets the writing. It is God's announcement of doom on the ruler, who has been weighed and found wanting (22–29). That very night Belshazzar is killed and the kingdom passes into the hands of Cyrus the Persian.

Chapter 6. Daniel in the Lion's Den

Daniel is now over 80 years old. Cyrus has reorganized the empire into 120 districts, overseen by a counsel of three on which

Daniel serves. Darius, mentioned in this chapter, has been variously
identified with (1) another name for Cyrus, (2) a name for Cambyses, son of Cyrus, or (3) Gubaru, whom Cyrus appointed as
governor of Babylon after the city fell. The action probably takes
place around 536 B.C.

Daniel is resented by some of his subordinates but is so honest
and efficient they can find nothing with which to charge him. At
last they influence Darius to issue a written decree. No one can
make a request to any god or person other than the king for 30
days. But Daniel continues to pray openly at the window in his
home facing Jerusalem. He is charged and the frustrated ruler
has no choice but to condemn Daniel to the lion's den.

There Daniel is protected by angels. The next morning the agitated Darius, who has not wanted to carry out his binding decree,
takes Daniel from the den alive. Then the men who plotted against
Daniel are themselves thrown to the lions and are killed.

This chapter indicates that Daniel's faith in God was well
known by all. What do 6:5, 16, 19–20 and 25–28 suggest
about the impact of a faithful believer's testimony about the Lord?
How did Daniel's personal character relate to this testimony?

II. Daniel's Visions and Prophecies (7–12)

Daniel's visions of the future come shortly before the return
of the exiles to Judea, but after most of the period of captivity is
passed. The purpose of the visions is to reaffirm the commitment
of God to his people and his covenant. This is accomplished by
previewing world events between the captivity and the appearance
of the promised Messiah, who is to institute the glorious age of
covenant fulfillment foreseen by all the prophets.

There are four visions in these chapters. Two focus on coming
world empires, with emphasis on the fourth (Chap. 7, 8). One
focuses on time and, unique to OT prophecy, gives a time framework for eschatological fulfillment (Ch. 9). The final vision explores
more fully the cataclysmic events associated with establishment
of God's rule over the earth (Ch. 10–12).

It is helpful before reading these chapters to have some idea
of the course of the empires of which Daniel speaks.

Babylon. This world empire replaced the Assyrians. Under Nebuchadnezzar it established unquestioned superiority over vast territories (see p. 222–228). Nebuchadnezzar died in 562 B.C. and was
followed by weaker rulers. Babylon itself was taken over by the
Medes and Persians under Cyrus in 538 B.C.

Medo-Persia. Cyrus was a great and charismatic leader. Apart from reorganizing the administration of the Babylonian empire, he left it intact. His rule was significantly humanitarian, with vassal states permitted great freedom of religion and custom. He reversed the Babylonian policy of deportation and permitted captive peoples to return to their homelands. Under this new policy the Jews were freed to resettle in Palestine, and even granted funds from the royal treasury to finance the rebuilding of their temple.

For much of the Persian period Egypt was a part of this gigantic world empire. Aggressive political and trade policy by successive rulers expanded Persian influence and finally brought the empire into conflict with Greece. Persian invaders were thrown back in Europe, however, and increasing internal revolts, with the decline of central authority, prepared for the total collapse of the empire some two centuries after Cyrus.

Prophecies concerning this empire, which stood between 538 and 331 B.C., are found in Daniel 2:32, 39; 7:5; 8:3, 4, 20; 9:25 and 11:2.

Greece. The Persian invasions had convinced the Greek states that they must put an end to the Eastern menace. But it was not until Alexander the Great of Macedon that a serious invasion was mounted in 334 B.C. Alexander's outnumbered forces won against incredible odds, taking over the capital and empire in 331 B.C. On Alexander's early death in 323 B.C., the combined territories were divided between four of his generals. Seleucus I took most of Persia, Ptolemy took Egypt, Lysimachus much of Asia Minor, and Cassander took Macedonia and Greece. The passages in Daniel which refer to this first unified and then shattered empire are: Daniel 2:32, 29; 7:6; 8:5-8, 9-14, 21, 22; with 11:3-35.

Rome. The iron empire of Rome succeeded these world powers, effectively taking over the elements of the old Babylonian empire by 146 B.C. and welding it together with its own empire in Europe. Rome is represented in Daniel 2:33, 40, 41; 7:7, 11, 19, 23.

Chapter 7. Vision of the Four Beasts

The Vision; 7:1–14. In 553 B.C. Daniel is given a vision. He sees four beasts, one after the other. As one "horn" of the last beast uproots its other horns, God himself appears. ("Horn" in the OT is a symbol of a ruler or ruling power.) The final power is destroyed when one "like a son of man" is given authority over the earth. This is the first clear messianic use in the OT of "son of man." The worship offered to him indicates that he is recognized

as divine. This son of man now establishes a kingdom which will
never be destroyed.

The Interpretation; 7:15–28. The vision is explained to Daniel
by "one of those standing there," identified in 8:15 is the angel
Gabriel (see *Angels,* p. 370). The beasts are identified as world king-

---

Angels

The original words translated "angel" in both Old and New Testaments
mean literally, "messenger." These messengers are directly created beings
who do not reproduce or die (cf. Luke 20:34–37). Both Testaments present
them as an order of created life which differs from human beings, but
is like us in many ways. Angels are presented as superior to humans in
strength or power and knowledge (cf. 2 Pet. 2:11; 2 Sam. 14:17, 20; Ps.
2:7).

The Bible speaks of both good and evil angels. Like Adam and Eve,
angels were given freedom of choice. At the time of Satan's rebellion (see
Satan, p. 245), many remained true to God. But others joined the great
deceiver (cf. Matt. 25:41). Many identify the demons of the NT with these
evil, or fallen, angels (see *Demons,* p. 480).

The good angels, who remain faithful to God, are often shown in the
Bible ministering to God's saints (cf. Heb. 1:14). Angels are seen protecting,
guiding, instructing, and defending God's people. At one time of extreme
danger human eyes are opened to see an army of angels ringing the prophet
Elisha to protect him (2 Kings 6:7).

The Bible records appearances of angels. Many times they appeared in
the form of human beings (cf. Gen. 18:2; Heb. 13:2; Josh. 5:13). There is
no record of an angel appearing as a woman or a child. At other times
angels were seen as bright and shining beings of awesome aspect, as described by Daniel (10:5, 6) and the women at Jesus' tomb (Luke 24:4).

Some angels do not appear in human forms, such as the cherubim of
Ezekiel 1 and the seraphim of Isaiah 6. As directly created living beings,
who serve God and his purposes, these too are designated angels. Two
angels are given personal names in the OT—Gabriel and Michael (Dan.
19:13–11:1).

Of special note is the OT appearances of the "Angel of the Lord." This
title is often identified with God himself (cf. Gen. 31:11–13; 32:24–30;
Exod. 3:6). Some theologians believe the Angel of the Lord is God the
Son, appearing prior to the incarnation.

Despite multiple references in Scripture to angels, the focus of the Bible
is not on them. Nor does God seem concerned to satisfy our curiosity
about these beings. Scripture, and God's own concern, focuses instead on
the Lord's relationship with human beings. God the Son chose to become
a man, not an angel, and the wondrous message of the Word of God is
that "surely it is not angels he helps, but Abraham's descendants" (Heb.
2:16). In the end we will be lifted in Christ above the angels, to know
the fullness of God's grace.

doms. The "horn" from the last beast is a ruler who will directly oppose God and oppress his saints. He will seem to succeed for some three and one half years (v. 25). But then "the court will sit," and all power on earth will be given over to the saints. God's everlasting kingdom will be established.

It is clear that Daniel's teaching on events preceding the establishment of God's kingdom goes beyond earlier revelations. But they are in complete harmony with the pronouncement of all the OT prophets about God's plan for mankind (see *Old Testament Eschatology: The OT Picture of the Distant Future,* p. 372, 373).

Chapter 8. The Ram and the Goat

The Vision; 8:1–14. In 551 B.C. Daniel has another vision concerning these kingdoms. He sees a ram which overpowers the world. It is defeated by a goat with one great horn. At the height of its power the great horn is broken off, to be replaced by four horns. From one of these comes another horn, which sets itself up as "prince of the host" and desolates God's own sanctuary, causing sacrifices to cease.

The Interpretation; 8:15–27. Again the vision is interpreted by an angel. Its focus is "the appointed time of the end." The two-horned ram is specifically identified as Media-Persia (20), and the goat as "the king of Greece" (21). Just as Daniel foretold, this king, Alexander, did die suddenly and was replaced by four hellenic kingdoms that "emerge from his nation." But the angel goes on. A "stern-faced king" will emerge from one of these four empires and devastate God's people. Finally he will be destroyed, "but not by human power." The reference to 2,300 days is uncertain. Daniel is told this prophecy relates to the distant future (26).

Chapter 9. Prayer for Restoration

Daniel's Prayer; 9:1–19. Daniel discovers Jeremiah's promise that the captivity will last 70 years (Jer. 25:11–14). Now, in 538 B.C., the appointed years are almost complete. So Daniel pleads with God to act.

The Seventy "Sevens"; 9:20–27. The angel Gabriel appears as Daniel is praying, to give God's answer. Daniel is told that a set period of time is determined "for your people and your holy city to finish transgression, to put an end to sin, to atone for wickedness, to bring in everlasting righteousness, to seal up [e.g., fulfill] vision and prophecy, and to anoint the most holy" (24). This is a unique prophecy in that rather than being indefinite about time, the whole prophecy focuses on time and announces in advance a prophetic time framework.

Some have taken these figures in the literal sense Daniel clearly intended. The best interpretation, viewing each "time" as a year, and each "week" or "seven" as seven years, takes the "decree to restore Jerusalem" as that given by Artaxerxes to Ezra in 458 B.C. The first seven (49 years) takes us to 409 B.C., when Nehemiah and Ezra complete the task of walling in and populating the city. The next group of 62 sevens (434 years) brings us to A.D. 26, and the baptism of Jesus (e.g., the "anointing of the most holy") (cf. Matt. 4; Luke 4).

What about the last group of seven years? Daniel says that "after the sixty-two sevens the anointed one will be cut off and have nothing" (26). "Cut off" is used in the OT to indicate execution (cf. Lev. 7:20; Ps. 37:9; Prov. 2:22). This is "after" the anointing. Thus the text implies an indeterminate time gap between the sixty-ninth and seventieth week. The final seven-year span begins when an evil ruler comes and makes a seven-year treaty with God's people, which he will break at midpoint.

To those who take prophecy in a literal way, the picture of Jesus crucified stands out in bold relief. So does a fact not known to OT prophecy—that the Messiah will suffer and die, and that a great gap of time exists between the first coming of Jesus and his second coming. When this gap finally closes, the last week of Daniel, like the first sixty-nine, will see prophecy fulfilled as literally and strikingly as Daniel identified the empires of Greece and Rome.

What if the vision is not taken literally? Then no attempt is made to link the "decree to rebuild Jerusalem" (25) with any historic event. Normally the weeks of years are dismissed as a symbolic representation of the period between Christ's first advent and the second coming. Their meaning is simply considered obscure, and the words hide rather than unveil the mind of God.

Old Testament Eschatology:
The Old Testament Picture of the Distant Future

Many of the predictive passages of the OT deal with what was to the prophet and his contemporaries the near future. The coming death of a king, the quick destruction of an enemy, the number of years of Judah's captivity in Babylon—all these deal with events that were, to the prophets, relatively near at hand.

Another group of predictive passages deals specifically with the person of the Messiah. Scores of prophecies cover his birth, life, ministry, and death. All these events were hundreds of years future to the prophets who spoke them, but for us today these prophecies relate to the past. Looking back at Jesus, we can see how clearly and how specifically predictions about him have been fulfilled (see *Fulfilled Prophecy,* p. 305).

There is yet another group of predictions found in the OT. These, as the Lord told Daniel, concern "the distant future" (8:26). It is these predictions about the distant future and a time of the end which, together, compose what it known as OT Eschatology.

OT pictures of the end times are not easy to interpret. For one thing, the prophets do not give an outline of events in chronological order. Instead they tend to focus on one aspect of the end times and to highlight particular themes. Even the prophets themselves were uncertain about how God would ultimately fit together all that he revealed through them (1 Pet. 1:10, 11).

It is clear, however, that the prophets do predict a conclusion to history. The world will not stumble on endlessly, with nothing resolved and no purposes achieved. Instead the prophets sound a note of triumph. History will close with a great culmination. God will act to fulfill the promises made in the covenants (see *Covenant,* p. 51). Evil will be dealt with, holiness vindicated, and blessing ushered in.

What themes do the prophets return to when looking into the distant future? Nearly all highlight these aspects of the time of the end.

(1) *The Regathering of Israel.* At history's end God's OT people are in their land, regathered there by him for the final working out of God's purposes (Isa. 11:11, 12; 14:1–3; 27:12, 13; 43:1–8; 66:20–22; Jer. 16:14–16; 23:3–8; 30:10, 11; 31:8, 31–37; Ezek. 11:17–21; 20:33–38; 34:11–16; 39:25–29; Hosea 1:10, 11; Joel 3:17–21; Amos 9:11–15; Micah 4:4–7; Zeph. 3:14–20; Zech. 8:4–8).

(2) *World Conflict and Tribulation.* At history's end the nations of the world, under the leadership of a northern power, assemble to invade and crush the people of God. The time is also one of great suffering and tribulation, which comes as a judgment on God's people as well as the people of the world. Yet a remnant survives the great destruction (the nations: Ezek. 38, 39; Dan. 11:40; Joel 2:1–17; Isa. 30:31–33; the sufferings: Deut. 4:30, 31; Isa. 2:12, 19; 13:6, 9; 24:1,3,6, 19–21; 26:20–21; Jer. 30:7; Ezek. 13:5; 30:3; Dan. 9:27; 12:1; Joel 1:15; 2:1, 2, 11, 31; 3:14; Amos 5:18–20; Zeph. 1:14, 15, 18; Zech. 14:1; the survivors: Isa. 4:3, 4; 6:12, 13; 26:20; 65:13, 14; Jer. 15:11; 33:25, 26; Ezek. 14:22, 30:34–38; 37:21, 22; Hosea 3:5; Amos 9:11–15; Zech. 13:8, 9; Mal. 3:16, 17).

(3) *The Glorious Kingdom.* The final battle is resolved by God's own intervention, as his Messiah appears. With the power of evil crushed and holiness vindicated, a great spiritual conversion takes place among Jews and Gentiles, and the Messiah, a ruler sprung from David's line, establishes an endless kingdom (Isa. 2:1–4; 4:2–6; 9:6, 7; 11:1–13; 24:1–23; 32:1–5; 33:17–24; 35:1–10; 52:7–10; 60:1–61:6; 66:15–23; Jer. 22:1–8; 31:1–27; 33:14–26; Dan. 2:31–45; 7:1–28; 9:20–27; Mal. 3:1–5; 4:1–6; Ezek. 20:33–42; 34:20–31; Hosea 3:4, 5; Joel 2:28–3:2; 3:9–21; Amos 9:9–15; Obad. 15–21; Micah 4:1–5; Zech. 2:1–13; 14:1–21).

Chapters 10–12. Vision of the Last Days

An Angel Messenger; 10:1–11:1. Daniel's final vision comes in
536 B.C. He has fasted and prayed for three weeks when an angel
messenger appears to "explain to you what will happen to your
people in the future" (14). Thus the focus of this prophecy is clear.
It is about Israel and Israel's future.

A special insight is provided in this chapter into the realm of
angels. Both good and evil angels seem to be organized in ranks,
and active in national events as well as with individuals. The angel
overseeing Satan's affairs in the Persian kingdom blocked the passage of God's messenger to Daniel (12,13). It is not until an angel
of even higher rank came to open the way that God's messenger
was able to proceed (see *Angels,* p. 370).

Steps toward the End; 11:1–35. In earlier visions Daniel watched
as history marched toward the culminating time of the end. This
same pattern is seen in the information given Daniel by the angel
messenger. He is told much of the next few centuries before the
focus shifts to history's end.

Commentaries on Daniel (such as that by Leon Wood, Zondervan, 1973) show the detailed correspondence between events described here and the actual historical events. The time up to the
division of Alexander's kingdom (2–4), the history of the Ptolemys
and Seleucids (pp. 436, 437) up to 187 B.C. (5–20), and the reign
of Antiochus Epiphanes (21–35), are all described with complete
accuracy.

The Anti-Christ? 11:36–45. Many commentators believe these
verses now leap the gap between the second century B.C. and the
end times, propelled by a similarity in character and actions between Antiochus and the final ruler to exalt himself against God.
This later person's motives and actions are the opposite of Messiah's, and he has been called the "anti-Christ." This kind of time
leap is not unusual in OT prophecy (see *Understanding the Prophets,*
p. 276–281). Many elements of the description given in these ten
verses do not fit the history of Antiochus. And these elements
do fit other prophetic passages which describe the end (cf. Ezek.
38–39; Joel 3:2, 12; Zech. 14:2.)

The End; 12:1–4. With destruction of God's enemies there comes
a new beginning! Those who "sleep in the dust of the earth" will
awake, to either everlasting life or endless shame. All those who
have died in hope, looking toward the golden age to come, will
have a share in the fulfillment of God's promises.

Hell, OT

The King James Version of the Bible uses the word "hell" some 31 times in the OT. In each case the Hebrew word translated is *Sheol,* which simply means grave, or place of the dead. It does not imply hell as we think of it, as a place of punishment.

However Daniel 12 does touch on this doctrine, which is developed in the NT. Daniel speaks of a resurrection at the end when those who "sleep in the dust of the earth will awake." Some are aroused to everlasting life. But others are aroused to suffer "shame and everlasting contempt." The nature of this endless experience of shame is not explained. But it is clear that physical death does not end the existence of any individual human being. There is resurrection for all, and afterward there is a judgment (see *Hell, NT.* p. 531).

This is not the only OT reference to resurrection (cf. Job 14:11–14; 19:25–27; Ps. 16:10; 49:15; Isa. 25:8; 26:19; Hos. 13:14). It is, however, the first mention in the Bible of "everlasting life" (v. 2), something which is emphasized significantly in the NT.

The Last "Week"? 12:5–13. Daniel's book closes with a return to its most unique element: a prophetic treatment of specific periods of time (cf. 9:20–27). The three-and-one-half-year period spoken of immediately calls to mind the seven-year period of Daniel 9:27, to begin some time after the cutting off of Christ. Why does the passage also count days, with one figure extending 30 days beyond the three and a half years, and another extending 75 days beyond (11)? No one knows, for Daniel is told to close his book, and seal it until the time of the end comes (9).

As for Daniel, that 83-year-old who has lived so faithful a life in a pagan land is finally released. "You will rest," the angel tells him. "And then at the end of the days you will rise to receive your allotted inheritance" (13).

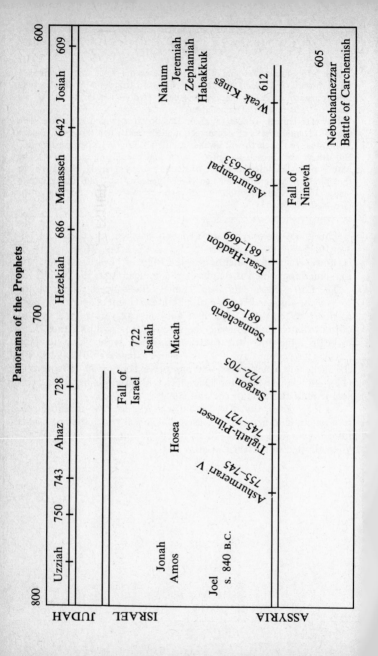

Panorama of the Prophets

JUDAH

| 800 | Uzziah | 750 | 743 | Ahaz | 728 | 700 Hezekiah | 686 | Manasseh | 642 | Josiah | 609 | 600 |

ISRAEL

Jonah
Amos
Joel
s. 840 B.C.

Hosea

Fall of Israel
722
Isaiah

Micah

Nahum
Jeremiah
Zephaniah
Habakkuk

ASSYRIA

Ashurbanipal 755–745
Tiglath-Pileser 745–727
Sargon 722–705
Sennacherib 681–699
Esar-Haddon 699–681
Ashurbanipal 669–633
Weak Kings

Fall of Nineveh
612

Nebuchadnezzar
Battle of Carchemish
605

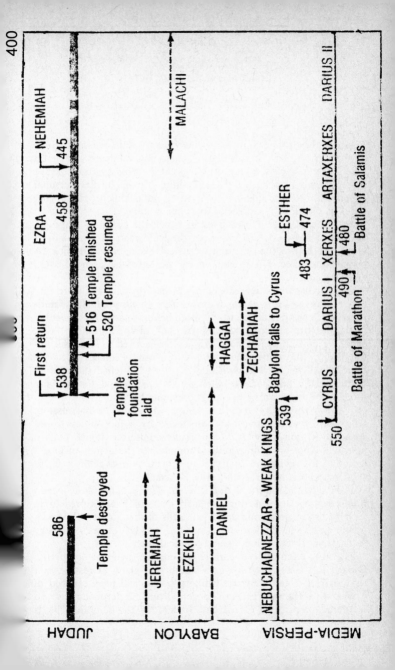

HOSEA
Book of the Faithless Wife

Hosea the prophet is called by God to a special mission. He is to share the Lord's anguish and then to communicate with great emotion the impact of unfaithfulness. Like God's people Israel, Hosea's own beloved wife deserts him. Moved by his personal experience, the prophet cries out to an unfaithful people, urging them to return to a God who loves them still.

Date and Author. Hosea lived in Israel, the northern kingdom. He ministered to its citizens from the later years of Jeroboam II until just before the Assyrians crushed his nation and took its people into exile. His preaching can be dated between 753 B.C. and 723 B.C.

Little is known of Hosea's family or background. His word pictures, however, feature images drawn from country life. He is familiar with the restless dove, the stubborn heifer, weary oxen, morning mists and the swirling, windblown chaff of the threshing floor. Sensitive and compassionate, this tender-hearted poet seems untouched by the materialism of his age, solidly anchored to the basic values in life. His own family tragedy softened rather than hardened the prophet. He shows deep compassion for straying Israel even as he warns her and condemns her sins.

It's easy to see why a man like Hosea was needed for his mission. Only a man whose love had been tested by unfaithfulness could speak with such integrity to spiritually adulterous Israel. Only a man who kept on loving could communicate the depths of God's love and his invitation to Israel to return, as a straying wife, to the One who is her true and only Husband.

Religious and Political Background. The prophet Amos, who ministered to Israel during the early years of Hosea's preaching, focused on the economic and social evils of that society. (For economic and social background see *Amos,* p. 389). Hosea's ministry focuses on Israel's religious and political sins.

The long reign of Jeroboam II was marked by great prosperity. During this time Assyria was a slumbering giant, at rest beyond the horizon. Nearby Syria's military power had been crushed in a war with Hamath-Luash. The opportunistic Jeroboam moved in to take control of Damascus. In his day the combined lands occupied by Israel and Judah almost reached the boundaries won centuries before by David's united land.

But Assyria began to awake under the aggressive rule of Tiglath-pileser III (called Pul in the Books of Kings). After Jeroboam's death, and for most of Hosea's ministry, Assyria was a growing threat to all the smaller states of Palestine.

The uncertain kings of Israel wavered. Their foreign policy vacillated between association with Assyria and Egypt. "Like a dove, silly and without sense" (7:11) Israel turned first toward one and then toward the other. But she would not turn to God.

Political life in Israel was marked by murders, intrigues, and other evils. "All their princes are rebels," Hosea charges (9:15), looking back some 250 years at Israel's 18 kings from 10 different families. Everyone of them had been unresponsive to God and to his law. These men, none from the chosen line of David, were "set up without my consent" (8:4). The people who follow such leaders are rebels at heart.

But it is the religious unfaithfulness of Israel which moves Hosea most deeply. God had brought his people into the land to supplant a corrupt civilization. That civilization rested its moral foundation on a religion that ascribed agricultural fertility to its local deities, called Baals ("lord," "owner," or "master"). This male god had a female consort, Astarte, or Asherah. The fertility of the land was thought to depend on sexual relations between the Baal and his consort. To encourage intercourse in their gods, the worshipers came together at shrines or groves, usually located on hills or other high places. There they attempted to stimulate their gods sexually. Cult prostitution, orgies, and other erotic practices were thus an integral part of Canaanite worship.

By the time of Hosea many of the beliefs and practices of Canaanite religions were actually integrated with worship of the Lord! Sacrifices were offered in local shrines, and usually the religious celebrations were marked by drunkenness and debauchery. In it all, the people actually supposed that they were worshiping Israel's God by the pagan rites.

Thus idolatry and sexual promiscuity were in fact closely linked in Hosea's day. No wonder his imagery portrays Israel as "playing the harlot" and being untrue to God, her true Husband. Idolatry and adultery were linked in practice. At heart both were unfaithful to a commitment which was to be lifelong and exclusive. Against this background we can understand something of the impact Hosea's words should have had on those of his own day.

Structure and Outline. The Book of Hosea is largely composed of sermons which Hosea must have spoken many times, in many different locations throughout the land of Israel, as he struggled for thirty years to turn Israel back to God. The first three chapters are introductory. They tell the story of the prophet and his own unfaithful wife, Gomer. In the context of his own continuing love for Gomer, the imagery of the messages and the deep love God expresses for Israel take on even more poignant meaning.

Outline

Chapter 1. Hosea's Unfaithful Wife

Gomer; 1:2, 3. Hosea is told to "take to yourself an adulterous wife." Some believe this statement is made in retrospect—that Hosea is told by God to marry Gomer, who later proves to be promiscuous. Others hold that, like Isaiah, Jeremiah and Ezekiel, Hosea is told in advance the personal cost of obedience to the Lord. The text seems to indicate Gomer is an adulteress when Hosea marries her. If so it is appropriate. God too knew the character of his OT people before he called them and chose to love them anyway!

Their Children; 1:4–9. The prophet and Gomer have three children. Each is named to communicate a message to Israel. The first is called Jezreel, name of the city where the founder of Jeroboam II's line (Jehu) took the throne by massacring his predecessor's family. The other children, "Unloved" and "Not My People," symbolize God's forced rejection of Israel.

God's Promise; 1:10,11. The message of a present rejection is immediately placed in perspective. God's commitment to his people is unchanged, even though Israel is unfaithful. In the end he will reunite the divided kingdoms and bless them under the promised messianic king (see *OT Eschatology,* pp. 372, 373 and *Davidic Covenant,* p. 177).

Chapter 2. Israel Disciplined And Restored

The kernel of the prophet's message is presented in this introductory chapter. His words about Israel help us to understand his feelings about his relationship with Gomer, even as his family tragedy helps us to understand the Lord's emotions as he watches his idolatrous people run from relationship with him.

Using the metaphor of adultery, God through the prophet shares the anguish and the anger he feels at Israel's spiritual adultery (1–5). He will act to discipline the harlot. Her lovers will leave her unsatisfied, and the blessings which God has provided will be removed, to be replaced by harsh disciplines (6–13). But God remains committed to Israel. He will tenderly draw her back to him, until at last she recognizes her true Husband and no longer mentions her old lovers (14–20). Then, planted anew in a bountiful and responsive land, Israel will be "My people" and, with deep love, they will confess "You are my God" (21–23).

Chapter 3. Hosea's Wife Returned

After the birth of their children, Hosea's wife deserted him. She lived with other men and apparently was at last forced to sell herself as a bondservant (1,2). Now God sends Hosea to her, and tells him to love her "as the Lord loves the Israelites." Hosea purchases Gomer from her master and brings her home. There she is forced to live a continent life "for many days." This disciplinary experience mirrors the years that Israel will be forced to live under foreign powers, without political independence (5). But then there is a full restoration of the relationship between Hosea and Gomer, just as there will be a full restoration of Israel when she at last seeks God and he sends the Davidic Messiah to be her king.

In what ways is God's commitment to faithfulness "no matter what" reflected in Hosea's relationship with Gomer? Why didn't Hosea divorce Gomer, since this was permitted under OT law (see *Divorce and Remarriage*, p. 131)? What do you think this prophet may suggest to us concerning difficulties that may occur in marriages today?

Chapters 4–8. Israel's Sins Denounced

Each OT prophet pointed out sins that warped relationship with God and called for judgment. No one could complain that God failed to make his ways plain to his people, or failed to express his horror at unrighteousness. Hosea too denounces, and thus defines, the actions which make Israel guilty before God.

Beginning in this section, "Ephraim" is used 31 times to refer to Israel. This is because Jeroboam I, the first king of the northern kingdom, was an Ephraimite. Gradually the name of the tribe from which he came was used for the nation and its people.

Charge against Israel; 4:1–19. Cursing, lying, murder, stealing and adultery have replaced faithfulness and love in Israel (1,2). Israel has ignored God's law to the point of practicing ritual prostitution at the sites where they commit idolatry (4–14). Like a stubborn heifer that God wants to lead to pasture, Ephraim jerks away and sets out to accomplish its own ruin (15–19).

Judgment against Israel; 5:1–15. Arrogant Israel, moved by the spirit of prostitution which grips its heart, will never locate God even if she stumbles after him (1–7). Thus a day of wrath is coming (8–12). Why, even when Israel recognizes her vulnerability, she turns not to God but to Assyria! God must wait until at last misery will drive his people to seek him.

Unrepentant Israel; 6:1–7:16. Israel's heart is revealed by her actions rather than her words. Despite verbal expressions of repentance (6:1–3), she consistently turns back to her sins. Such a "love" is as fleeting as a morning mist.

God does not seek words from Israel, or ritual sacrifices, but faithfulness to a covenant law which prohibits the murders and other shameful crimes which God witnesses in Ephraim (6:4–11). Deceit fills the land, tainting every class, from the common thieves who break into others' houses (7:1,2) to those who surround the throne with drunkenness and intrigue (7:3–8). From this people which turns for help to pagan nations, words of repentance mean less than nothing. Their actions are a daily testimony to their rebellion against God and to the fact that they have not repented (7:9–16).

The Whirlwind of Judgment; 8:1–14. God's judgment will roar down upon this land of broken covenants like a tornado. The religious and political evils which are practiced in Israel (2–6) have sold the people to devastating punishment. Now they must experience it in full. Israel has sown the wind. It will reap the whirlwind.

Chapters 9–10. Israel's Doom Announced

What is about to happen to Israel must be understood against the background of its people's sins. Judgment comes "because of all their wickedness" (9:15). God must now reject this generation which has rejected him and refused to respond. Israel's population will become wanderers among the nations. The people who rejected God as king, and came to worship calf-idols, will be taken to Assyria (10:6).

They have planted wickedness. They will reap evil. For all that is about to happen comes "because your wickedness is great" (10:15).

Chapter 11. Love Affirmed

Hosea keeps the intimacy of the family context but changes the image. He now reveals God's love focused on Israel as if the nation were a precious child. "It was I who taught Ephraim to walk," God laments. "But they did not realize that it was I who healed them" (3). God looks ahead. He sees the suffering that will come because his child rejects the ties of love with which he seeks to bind her, and is determined to turn away (5–7). We can sense the anguish the Lord feels as he cries out, "How can I give you up, Ephraim?" The discipline must come. But God will not surrender his people, "For I am God, and not man—" Instead God will bring his people back and "settle them in their homes" (11).

Grace, OT

One of the most significant relational words in the OT is *hesed*. The King James translates this Hebrew word "mercy." The ASV calls it "loving-kindness," the Berkeley, "covenant love," and the RSV usually adopts "steadfast love." It is a word which, perhaps better than others, reflects the meaning of the NT term, "grace."

Three concepts are closely linked with this strong, active word, which helps us understand God's relationship with his people. The first link is with God's original choice of the Hebrew people. "The Lord your God has chosen you out of all the peoples on the face of the earth to be his people, his treasured possession," Moses explains in Deuteronomy (7:6). Then Moses goes on to point out that God had no reason other than his love to motivate this choice: nothing in Israel's nature or character *deserved* love.

The second link is with God's covenant promises to Abraham and his descendants. God has freely given his word to his people and committed himself to keep the covenant. The covenant expresses a visible and verbal commitment. Thus commitment is closely associated with God's mercy, or grace.

The third linkage is with faithfulness, or persistence. Sacred history shows over and over again that the chosen people failed to respond to God's love. They turned away again and again, proving themselves to be stiff-necked, disobedient, idolatrous, materialistic, and oppressive. They ignored God's laws or turned their backs on them; they persecuted and killed the prophets God sent to them. But in spite of these affronts, God continued faithful to that relationship he had acted to initiate. Choice. Commitment. Persistence.

Each of these three elements is touchingly illustrated in the prophet Hosea. The wife God had chosen has proved unfaithful (Hosea 2:5). The children of the covenant, whom God brought up with such gentle love, did not recognize their father or know the one who healed them (11:3,4). Despite everything God, who does not react as a human being would to such rejection, continues to love. He promises, "I will bring them back, and settle them in their homes" (11:11).

To understand grace we must look not at ourselves, but at God.

Chapters 12–13. Discipline First

The themes emphasized throughout Hosea are found in this bold sermon of the prophet, who again confronts Israel with her sins. Twisting away from her relationship with God, Israel has turned from the Lord to make treaties with Assyria and Egypt (12:1–6). Her prosperous people love to defraud and show only contempt for the prophets God sends them (12:7–14). Once tentative, Israel has now thrown herself into frenzied pursuit of spiritual wickedness, even offering human sacrifice and kneeling to kiss the calf-idols (13:1–3).

But the great reality which Israel has forgotten will soon confront her. "I am the Lord your God," the prophet relays. The One who cared for Israel as she wandered on the burning sands of the wilderness can and will destroy her, and this without compassion. Now the people of Samaria must bear their guilt. They have rebelled against the only One who can redeem (13:4–16).

Chapter 14. Blessing Following

This generation will experience judgment as a result of their sins. But this does not mean God has rejected his people! The prophet calls on the exiles to "take words with you, and return to the Lord" (2). When the people appeal for forgiveness, God will heal their waywardness and love them freely (2,3). Then people and land will flourish again, and Ephraim will have nothing more to do with idolatry. God's grace will be revealed in the forgiven, healed, and holy land.

JOEL
A Vision of Judgment

A great cloud of locusts settles on Judah, stripping every green thing from the land. Joel understands this invasion to be a judgment from God—a discipline which calls for repentance. But the locust plague is something more for Joel. The prophet is suddenly moved to see in the insects' devastation another scene of complete destruction. He sees another army and a battle which will come in the days just before history's end.

Date and Author. Nothing is known of the author beyond his name: Joel, son of Pethuel. Unlike most prophets, Joel gives no date for his message (cf. Hosea 1:1; Amos 1:1). He does mention a still-standing Jerusalem. And the enemies he refers to are those Judah faced before her exile. But aside from the fact that such references place Joel before the Babylonian captivity, there is no sure way to fix his time. This is appropriate. For Joel's message is timeless, not dealing with any particular contemporary social or religious issue. Instead Joel deals with the very principle of divine judgment itself. Joel affirms that God will act in history and in the time of the end.

Locusts. Nine Hebrew words are translated "locust" in English versions. These may be different kinds of insects. More likely they are different common names or nicknames, or even names for the different stages of this grasshopper-like insect's life cycle.

Locusts were a terrifying reality to peoples of the ancient Middle East. At times they would multiply at an unbelievable rate, coming together in huge swarms so thick that they literally blotted out the sun. One swarm of desert locusts that crossed the Red Sea in 1899 was estimated to cover 2,000 square miles!

When such swarms land they eat all crops and green plants, leaving a brown and empty land behind. From the most ancient times locust swarms in the lands of the Bible were synonymous with destruction.

It is one of these swarms, darkening the skies and devastating the land of Judah, that stimulates Joel's preaching. He first utters a call to his people to repent. And then, suddenly, stunningly, he finds himself captured by an apocalyptic view of the coming Day of the Lord.

Features. Three features of this short book merit special note.

First, Joel's leap from a contemporary event to the distant future is not unusual. Many of the prophets linked and interwove the present and the distant future.

Second, Joel uses a term found often in eighth century prophets: "the Day of the Lord." In Isaiah this phrase is used to locate a passage in time. This phrase, or "that day," tells the reader of Isaiah that the prophet is speaking of history's end. But Joel relates the Day of the Lord to both his present and the distant future. In Joel the common element is judgment. Any time God acts to judge his people is, to this prophet, an expression of "that day."

Third, the theme of judgment is always tempered in Scripture by reminders of grace. Joel shows that grace operates in his own generation. When the people repent, the locusts are removed. When the last judgments are past, "afterward" Judah's fortunes will be restored and God's Spirit poured out. The great promise of the Spirit is quoted by Peter, as recorded in Acts 2, and there has been a wonderful but unexpected fulfillment.

Thus even God's OT portraits of judgment, however dark, are brightened by reminders of God's mercy. Even when you and I suffer under God's disciplining hand, we can be encouraged by the vision of grace shared so long ago by God's prophet, Joel.

Structure and Outline. The Book of Joel divides naturally into two sections. Each discusses judgment. But the first looks primarily at contemporary judgment, while the second looks ahead to judgment coming at history's end.

Outline

I. The Locust Plague   1:1–2:27
II. The Day of the Lord   2:28–3:21

Chapter 1:1–2:27. The Locust Plague

The Invasion; 1:1–12. The worst swarm of locusts in memory sweeps into Judah (1–4), stripping not only the leaves but even the bark from the trees (5–7). Despair grips the people as the crops they depend on for life are destroyed (8–12).

Call to Repentance; 1:13–20. Joel calls on the priests to declare a fast and gather the people to God's house to cry out to the Lord.

The Locust Army; 2:1–11. Joel powerfully announces that the locusts are a divine judgment—a contemporary expression of that

The Locust Invasion

final "day of the Lord," known to be "a day of darkness and gloom, a day of clouds and blackness" (2). The cloud of insects pours down the mountainside like a great army; the whirring of their wings sounds like the crackling of a consuming fire (5). The modern world is just as helpless before locust swarms as was the ancient: the army of judgment which the Lord himself leads against Judah (11) is invincible.

Return to God; 2:12–17. Jeremiah 18:7–10 teaches that God's announcements of judgment on a nation are conditional. If a nation or person turns from the sins which made judgment a necessity, God will relent. As the locusts swarm over his land Joel declares that even now it is not too late for Judah. "Return to me with all your heart," God pleads through the prophet, "that he may turn and have pity" (12,14).

The people respond. Priests and citizens of Judah join in a sacred assembly, begging the Lord to spare his people (15–17).

God's Answer; 2:18–27. God responds by driving the locusts from the land. Most swarms of locusts do not approach Israel from the north: however, some have been so recorded. The direction is significant. It is from the north that all Bible prophecy sees the enemy approach for the great battle at history's end.

The answer to Joel's generation is an affirmation of fruitfulness and a promise that Zion's people will yet rejoice in their God (21–24). Then God will repay for the years the locusts have devoured, and Joel's generation will know that there is a God in Israel. Those who are his people will never be put to shame (25–27).

Chapter 2:28–3:21. The Day of the Lord

The plague of locusts corresponds in several ways to a great battle to be fought at history's end. Many prophets speak of this battle (cf. Ezek. 38, 39, and *Old Testament Eschatology,* pp. 372, 373). The invaders swarm from the north in irresistible force, bringing devastation. God acts supernaturally to destroy the enemy and, in a great turning to God, his people are given the Lord's Spirit. The parallels, between the judgment and following blessing experienced in Joel's own day and in the "day of the Lord," launch Joel into what may be the first of the OT's extended written apocalyptic visions.

A Day of Salvation; 2:28–32. Joel begins with the great promise of the Spirit of God. The Spirit will be poured out on all people in the day of final wonders, when "everyone who calls on the name of the Lord will be saved." God's intention, even in the final cataclysmic judgment, is not to destroy but to heal.

This passage is quoted by Peter on the day of Pentecost. He explains the strange behavior of the disciples and their speaking with other tongues as due to that pouring out of the Spirit of which Joel speaks.

The Nations Judged; 3:1–8. The blessings are preceded by terrors. God will call all nations to the "Valley of 'the Lord Judges'" (2a). The people who oppressed Judah, and who even then gather against her, will be crushed.

God's People Blessed; 3:9–21. The gathering together of the nations to war against Judah is an indication that the Day of the Lord is near (9–14). There are other indications—cataclysmic changes in the heavens and the earth (15,16). Then God will act to establish his authority. A forgiven Israel will live peacefully in her land forever (17–21).

AMOS
Call for a Just Society

Amos, a simple shepherd, is sent as God's angry man to denounce the social and economic sins of Israel in a time of great prosperity. The prophet bluntly and plainly exposes the injustice which corrupts the nation in his day. In bold, stern tones, Amos announces God's judgment on a people who ignore both justice and compassion.

Date and Author. Amos lived during the reigns of Jeroboam II of Israel, and Uzziah of Judah. He is a simple farm worker, with no pretentions to the role of a prophet. But God gives Amos a message to communicate and calls him to the prophet's task. The preaching mission which took Amos from his home in Judah across the border into Israel probably took place around the year 760 B.C. Most believe Amos preached for only a few months, but there is no way to tell for sure.

The Man and His Mission. Amos appears in the OT as a blunt, honest, and straightforward man. His home is in Judah, about ten miles south of Jerusalem and six from Bethlehem. Most of the year he cares for his sheep, wandering with them over the rocky landscape. In season he works with the sycamore harvest. These trees provided food for the poor: their figlike fruit had to be punctured while green if it was to ripen and become edible. Amos' own poverty and simple life style would make this prophet well acquainted with the life of those who struggled to wrest a bare living from the land.

While carrying out his lonely duties in the fields of Judah, God speaks to Amos. He is given visions which impel him to cross into the neighboring northern kingdom. There Amos goes boldly to the centers where the idle rich gather, to confront them with God's condemnation of their sins and of their distorted values.

Social and Economic Background. The later reign of Jeroboam II was a time of exploding prosperity for Israel. The earlier destruction of the military power of Syria had enabled Jeroboam to expand his kingdom, even taking over the old capital of Aram, Damascus. Now Israel controlled the important trade routes which crisscrossed Palestine, linking the ancient world. Their multiplied revenues made Israel rich. But the wealth was distributed unequally. The old aristocracy of nobles and the new merchant class kept the wealth for themselves. They demanded luxury goods and residences, and the pattern of life in Israel began to change. More and more people left the country and drifted toward the towns and cities. For the first time towns of the northern kingdom became overpopulated.

The concentration of wealth stimulated economic corruption. Heavier and heavier taxes were laid on workers. The wealthy became land-hungry, forcing out the small farmers and building great estates. Many of the poor were forced to sell themselves and their families as bondservants, becoming no better than serfs on lands that had once been their own. Even the small merchants were corrupted, and it became common for them to use unjust weights to measure out purchases. The process of corruption was accelerated by failure of the justice system. Rather than acting to protect the poor, judges took bribes from the rich and so joined the oppressors! The old middle class began to disappear, and the society was increasingly divided into oppressed poor and the very rich.

In this situation the rich showed no sense of responsibility to the poor. Instead of showing compassionate concern, they seemed bent on depriving the poor of all rights and property. The heartlessness of the rich is well expressed in one angry charge hurled by Amos—these people are willing to "sell the needy for a pair of sandals" (2:6). Luxury footwear meant more to the wealthy of Amos' day than did the suffering of fellow human beings!

Hosea, who also preached in Israel in this age, also spoke out against these injustices. But Hosea's mission was to focus on the moral and religious corruption which also marked the unjust society (see *Religious and Political Background,* p. 378). It remained for Amos, God's angry man, to expose the economic and social sins that aroused the anger of God. For the God of Amos, the God of our OT and NT, is committed to compassion and cares deeply about the sufferings of the poor.

Structure and Outline. Like most of the OT prophets, Amos preached the words found in his book before they were written. The chapters contain a series of messages, linked by common themes.

Outline

Value. Amos is an important book for today. The NT emphasis on personal relationship with God and individual salvation does not alter God's concern for justice and holiness in a society. The God who cried out through Amos cries out today on behalf of the poor and the oppressed, and calls on you and me to "do justice!"

Chapters 1–2. Judgment on Transgressors

Amos' mission is to identify sins that call for judgment and to announce the doom about to fall on the transgressors. He begins his sermon by looking first at the nations around Israel. Loudly he pinpoints their offenses and then announces the punishment God will bring on them. How his hearers must have applauded as enemy after enemy was disposed of by the prophet's words!

But then, after a look at the sins of the sister kingdom, Judah, Amos turns on Israel. Brutally, with a list of concrete examples, the prophet exposes the practices which God must judge.

The Nations under Judgment; 1:2–2:5. The phrase, "for three transgressions, even for four,"means "for multiplied sins," or for sins practiced habitually.

The neighbors which come under God's judgment are Damascus (1:3–5), Gaza (1:6–8), Tyre (1:9,10), Edom (1:11,12), Ammon (1:13–15), Moab (2:1–3) and Judah (2:4,5). But after brief scrutiny, Amos turns to a concentrated exposition of the multiplied sins of Israel!

The Transgressions of Israel; 2:6–16. The detailed list of evils provided by Amos focuses on the sins of the wealthy and on a justice system which is bribe-hungry and corrupt. Human beings are sold for silver, and the poor are less valued than fashionable sandals (6–8). God did not drive out the peoples who inhabited Canaan so that his own people could corrupt the land (9–12)! Because of such sins God will crush Israel as surely as a heavily laden cart inexorably crushes whatever its wheels roll over. Nothing will save sinning Israel in that day (13–16).

Chapters 3–6. Sermons of Indictment

First Sermon: Judgment's Plan Revealed; 3:1–15. In this sermon Amos reminds his listeners that God reveals his plan through the prophets (7). Now Amos himself stands to speak out against the family which God brought up from Egypt.

It is because God chose Israel that he will judge her (2). The fact of privilege makes punishment for sin certain. This is illustrated by a series of cause/effect statements. Just as surely Israel's sin (cause) must be followed by judgment (effect: 3–6).

The nature of the punishment is revealed. Amos proclaims that this people who "do not know how to do right" will be overrun by an enemy (11). In that day the altars at Bethel, where God is worshiped with empty rites (see p. 194), will be destroyed. The mansions of the rich, with their ivory inlays, and the summer and winter homes of the wealthy will also be demolished (12–15).

Second Sermon: Refusal to Turn to God; 4:1–13. We can picture Amos, a stern figure dressed in rough clothing, as he stands at one of the worship centers of Bethel or Gilgal. Boldly he announces God's judgment on the sins of Israel.

Amos addresses the first words of this sermon to the wives of the wealthy. These women, who urge their husbands to keep on providing luxuries, are also guilty of oppressing the poor (1). God will drag them away, caught on the hooks of their captors (2,3). From such a people worship itself is nothing but sin, and the rich offerings the people bring (and then boast about) are an offense (4,5).

Amos then reviews God's dealings with Israel. Time and again disciplinary judgments struck Israel. They knew drought, disease, and military defeats. But the people remained unresponsive and would not turn to the Lord (6–12). Amos closes with a grim and final warning, "Prepare to meet your God, O Israel." The One to whom Israel might have turned for healing will overtake them— to judge.

Third Sermon: Call to Seek God; 5:1–6:14. This sermon begins with a lament for the fallen nation and what is about to happen (5:1–13). But Amos moves quickly to invitation: the people are urged to "seek God and live!" But it must be God himself they seek, not a religion of ritual, and they must confront him in all his awesome majesty (5:4–9). These are people who trample on the poor, who hate truth, who love their luxuries, and take bribes to deprive the oppressed of justice. For them to find God they must learn to seek good and not evil. If they will not commit themselves to justice, they can be assured that wailing and misery will come (5:14–17).

Passionately, Amos announces the coming day of the Lord; a "day of darkness, and not light." God, who loves justice, utterly hates the religious facade that masks oppression and inner idolatry with a thin coating of religion (5:18–27).

This people to whom Amos speaks feels complacent. They think

Amos at Bethel

their wealth makes them secure, as they rest on their ivory inlaid beds and eat the choicest foods. But they will be the first to go into exile (6:1–7)! The pride of this people, so abhorrent to the Lord God, will be smashed along with the kingdom when God stirs up a foreign land against them. In that day, God promises his sinning people, his nation of oppressors, the enemy whom God calls against them "will oppress you all the way" (6:8–14).

Chapters 7–9. Visions of Warning

These chapters relate five visions of judgment seen by the prophet. They also report the response of the men of Israel who heard the Lord's words . . . and expelled his prophet from the kingdom!

The Vision of the Locusts; 7:1–3. God shows Amos that he is preparing swarms of locusts to strip the land of its crops. At Amos' intercession the Lord relents. The judgment is averted. "This will not happen," the Lord promises.

The Vision of Fire; 7:4–6. God now shows Amos preparations he is making for a great fire to sweep Israel and devour the land. Again the prophet begs God to stop, and again God relents. But the judgment will not always be put off.

The Vision of the Plumbline; 7:7–9. Amos sees God standing beside a wall. He is holding a weight, tied to a line. This instrument is used by builders to tell if their walls are upright. God tells Amos that the time has come to go among his people and measure them. Israel is not upright, and God will spare her no longer.

Opposition to Amos; 7:10–17. Amos is a citizen of the southern kingdom, Judah. His mission to neighboring Israel is not appreciated! His announcements of judgment and promises that "Israel will surely go into exile" are viewed as an attempt to stimulate a conspiracy against Jeroboam! Amaziah, the priest in charge of the Bethel worship center, demands that Amos go home and stop prophesying against Israel "in the king's sanctuary and the temple of the kingdom"!

Amos answers. It is the Lord who called him to prophesy and the Lord who sent him to preach in Israel. Now the prophet turns on Amaziah. This man who has tried to silence the word of the Lord will die in a pagan country, his family killed, and his wife will become a prostitute in the city.

The Vision of Ripe Fruit; 8:1–14. The Lord shows Amos a basket of ripe fruit which represents Israel. The time is now ripe for judgment. God will no longer spare (1–3).

Amos again lists the sins of oppression which so anger God (4–6). God will not forget such wickedness. The oppressors will soon weep and mourn under the judgment of the Lord (7–14).

The Vision of Smashed Pillars; 9:1–10. Now God calls to Amos to witness a vision of judgment executed. The buildings shake, the leaders are dragged into exile, and the commoners are killed by the sword (1). Although the people flee in terror and scramble to find hiding places, they are hunted down. God's own eye is "fixed on them for evil and not for good" (2,3). The Lord's piercing gaze is fixed "on the sinful kingdom" and he will "destroy it from the face of the earth" (5–8). Even in this vision of judgment there is a glimpse of grace. The destruction will not be total. There will be survivors. Although the sinners of Israel will die, the good, like kernels of grain, will be shaken out and distributed among the nations. In time they will be gathered and returned.

The Poor and Oppressed

God designed a society for Israel which was to exist without poverty. There might be needy individuals. But each one was cared for in what was to truly be a just and a compassionate society.

We can read about the design of this OT community and God's provision for the poor in three books of the OT: Exodus (Ch. 22, 23); Leviticus (Ch. 19, 23) and Deuteronomy (Ch. 15, 24). A number of social institutions were set up by God to deal with poverty in a just and compassionate way.

First, each family was given property. This was to remain theirs across the generations. The property could not be sold, although its crops could be sold for a number of years in advance. But every fifty years the land reverted to its original owners. Thus each family in Israel had capital, which could never be lost. Second, each man in Israel was commanded to look with compassion on those in need. Farmers were to leave some of their crop in the fields for the needy to gather. A Hebrew was encouraged to lend to a brother freely, even though every seventh year all debts were canceled. If a person had such difficulties that he was forced to sell himself or his family into servitude, he was to be released when the seventh year came. And when freed he was even to be given a gift of money for his labor! Thirdly, the justice system in Israel was charged with responsibility for the poor. But judges were not to show partiality, either toward the rich or the poor. If Israel had lived by the holy laws that God gave, and if the hearts of the people had been open to their neighbors, then each man's needs would have been cared for and poverty erased.

There are many references to the poor in the OT, and a number of Hebrew terms identify them. Some words speak of a lack of material possessions and subjection to oppression or abuse. Others emphasize need and talk of the destitute. At times poverty is associated with laziness or slack planning. But far more often poverty is associated with oppression. It is only because God's people loved material things rather than their brothers that it was possible for poverty and misery to stalk the land.

Though men may turn against their brothers and lack compassion for the needy, God expresses special concern for them (Ps. 2:12; 34:6; 40:17; 72:4, 12; Isa. 49:13; Prov. 14:21; 14:31). Godliness is unquestionably linked in the OT with active concern for the poor.

Justice in the OT was both the concern of society and of the individual. How are we to apply the teachings of such books as Amos in our own day? To society? As individuals?

Chapter 9:11–15. A Vision of the Kingdom

Most of the prophets' messages conclude with a promise of Israel's ultimate blessing. Amos is no exception. The severe judgments of God on a sinning generation is not complete rejection of the whole people, or withdrawal of God's commitment to Abraham's children. Thus Amos closes with a vision of hope.

A day is coming when a ruler from David's line will be placed on David's throne (11). In that day many nations will bear the name of the Lord (12) and the earth will know unmatched prosperity (13). Then a regathered Israel will dwell in the promised land (14), never to be uprooted again (15).

Study the sections of Amos which speak out against social and economic injustice (2:6–8; 5:10–15; 6:1–7). In what ways does our society differ? In what ways is it similar?

God calls on his people to "do justice." What does this mean for the Christian today? What can or should the individual do about injustice? What can or should congregations do? What should the individual or church *not* do?

OBADIAH
Judgment on Edom

This brief, one-chapter book of judgment tells of Judah's coming victory over an enemy which should have been a friend.

Background. The Edomites were descendants of Esau, a brother of the patriarch Jacob (Israel). Esau's family settled south of the Dead Sea and became a prosperous nation. When Moses led the people of Israel out of Egypt toward Canaan some 400 years after Jacob and Esau, the Edomites refused Israel passage through their territory (Num. 20:14–20). Threatened by an Edomite army, Moses avoided battle and took the long route around Edomite territory.

In King David's time the Edomites fought Israel, were subdued, and became a subject people. The next few hundred years saw great hostility between the two peoples, and intermittent warfare. In the fifth century B.C. the Edomite kingdom was destroyed. About a hundred years before Christ the descendants of the Edomites, called Idumeans in the NT, were forced to accept Judaism. The best known of the Idumeans is Herod the Great, founder of the line of Herods so intimately linked with the time of Christ.

Date and Author. The book pronounces judgment on the Edomites for their role in supporting an attack on Jerusalem. Two possible dates are suggested by history. One places Obadiah shortly after 844 B.C., when the city was attacked by a Philistine/Arabian coalition (2 Chron. 21:16 f). The other places Obadiah shortly after the destruction of Jerusalem by the Babylonians in 587 B.C. The ninth century B.C. date is supported by (1) traditional placement of the book in the Hebrew canon, and (2) similarities of Jeremiah 49:7–22 to Obadiah 1–9. No conclusive evidence is available, however, and the name of the author, which means "worshiper of Jahweh," is a common one. Nothing beyond the name is known of Obadiah.

Value. The book underscores the belief of the prophets that God does make moral judgments and acts on them. It also looks forward, as do all the prophets, to a time of final blessing following "the day of the Lord" (see *Old Testament Eschatology,* p. 372, 373).

Obadiah

Disaster Awaits Edom; 1:1–9. The major city of Edom was Sela (Petra). This impregnable city is carved into solid rock and set deep in a canyon which can only be entered through a single, narrow, easily defended gap. God speaks to "you who live in the cleft of the rocks" and condemns their pride and false security (1–4). As Sovereign Lord, God promises that the city will be ransacked. The hidden treasure of Edom will be pillaged, and both warrior and citizen cut down (5–9).

Cause of the Disaster; 1:10–14. The disaster comes because of a promise made in God's Covenant with Abraham (cf. Gen. 12:3). It is this very covenant (the "birthright" Esau despised) which now becomes the basis for his descendant's doom (Gen. 25:27–34).

The judgment will fall because, despite the brother relationship between the two peoples, Edom stands aloof when foreigners attack Jerusalem. They take joy in the destruction of the people of Judah and join in the pillage. They even cut down Jewish fugitives who try to escape. It is this treatment of the Jewish people by the Edomites which cries out for judgment.

The Day of the Lord; 1:15–21. As with so many other prophets the focus of Obadiah's prophecy is the distant future. He looks forward to "the day of the Lord" as a time of vindication.

Some prophets stress the judgments that will fall on Israel when "that day" arrives (cf. Isa. 2–4). Others stress judgments which will fall on the pagan nations which are Israel's enemies (cf. Ezek. 38, 39). In this passage judgment is focused on Edom. Then this people will find their deeds returning on their own heads. As a result of God's intervention, "on Mount Zion there will be deliverance." The lands of Israel's enemies, including those of the Philistines to the west as well as Edom (Esau) in the south, will be occupied by God's people. Both these lands are granted to Israel in the Abrahamic covenant, and "the kingdom will be the Lord's."

JONAH
The Extent of God's Grace

This short book is unique among the minor prophets. It tells the story of one prophet's struggle with God as he resists his calling and tries to flee his mission. Jonah's story teaches us much, and it contained a distinctive message for his countrymen in the northern kingdom of Israel.

Author. The superscription of the book (1:1) identifies Jonah as the son of Amittai. Jonah has been traditionally accepted as the author, telling his own story in a third person narrative style.

Jonah, son of Amittai, is known from the historical book of 2 Kings. He ministered just before and in the early days of Israel's great king, Jeroboam II. It was the prophet's happy task to predict the victories which permitted Jeroboam to expand his country's borders and brought Israel to sudden prosperity. For the full impact of Jeroboam II on Israel see the "background" sections in Hosea (p. 378) and Amos (p. 389).

Date. If the book was written by Jonah, it would have been completed in the eighth century B.C. Some suggest 760 B.C. as a reasonable approximation. However, the dating of Jonah depends largely on whether it is taken as an historical narrative or, as some critics argue, a parable.

History or Parable? Pre-Christian Jewish writings regard the book as historical. References to Jonah by Christ seem also to treat it as history (Matt. 12:39 f; 16:4 f; Luke 11:29). For most of church history, scholars accepted the book as an authentic historical account.

In recent times some critics have argued that it is a parable, written sometime during the Persian period, after the Babylonian captivity. While a variety of arguments have been advanced to support this view, all have been answered adequately by those who view the book as history. The major point dividing the scholars seems to hinge on the supernatural: some cannot or will not accept the supernatural elements of the story. Those who reject the idea that God would or could "prepare a great fish to swallow Jonah" are unwilling to accept the book as history.

Interpreting Jonah. Even those who see Jonah as historical narrative tend to interpret it differently. Some have seen in it a picture of disobedient Israel, swallowed up in the Gentile sea. To them the book is "predictive history." Others teach Jonah as typology: they see Jesus or Israel foreshadowed by the prophet. On the one hand Jonah is either compared to Jesus (both had a mission) or contrasted with Jesus (Jonah was disobedient, Jesus obedient). On the other hand Jonah is compared to Israel, which like the prophet disobeyed, suffered exile (the fish), and will be restored.

None of the imaginative interpretations seem either necessary or justified to understand the impact of the Book of Jonah, or its lessons for you and me (see *Symbolic Language,* p. 61). The events of the prophet's life, and their meaning in the historical context, are clear. The timeless lessons from the prophet's experience with God can be just as easily applied if we take Jonah in the straightforward historical sense in which our Bible tells his story.

Structure and Outline. The book is a straightforward historical narrative: a story told by Jonah of his unwanted mission to Nineveh.

Outline

I. Jonah's Disobedience   1:1–17
II. Jonah's Prayer of Submission   2:1–10
III. Jonah's Mission to Nineveh   3:1–10
IV. Jonah's Motives . . . and Gods   4:1–10

Values. The fact of Nineveh's repentance under the reluctant preaching of Jonah carried a special message to Israel. Soon Amos and Hosea would carry God's message of judgment to the northern kingdom. Just as Nineveh had repented, and the judgment was withdrawn, so might God's people expect grace if they responded to the word of their God. The refusal of Israel to listen to God's prophets is even more shameful as they have the facts of Jonah's journey before them!

For you and me there is a special picture of grace as well. Jonah fought hard against God. But God did not reject him! Jonah was given a second chance to serve the Lord. How good to know that our past failures have not turned God against us. He is still willing and eager for us to find meaning for our lives by serving him.

Chapter 1. Jonah's Disobedience

The climactic incident described in the first chapter of Jonah has the prophet, hefted in the arms of his ship's pagan crew, thrown

Jonah

into a storm-tossed sea. What brought Jonah to this desperate condition?

The Story. Called to go to Nineveh and preach against it (2), Jonah flees. He takes a ship from Joppa bound for Tarshish, a port on the Spanish coast as far from Nineveh as the prophet can go. At sea a violent storm threatens to break up the ship. When the mariners cast lots to see if the storm may be caused by some sin, the lot falls to Jonah. Jonah tells them the only way the storm can be stopped is for them to throw him overboard. The unwilling sailors struggle to reach shore. Finally, as the sea grows even wilder, they beg God's forgiveness and do as the prophet has instructed. The raging waters calm. The men on ship recognize God's hand and worship him. Jonah is gone. But Jonah has not drowned. God has "provided a great fish to swallow Jonah." For three days and nights the prophet is in the belly of the fish.

The "Great Fish." The Hebrew word does not specify "whale" or any particular species. A number of commentaries on Jonah point to documented incidents of seamen swallowed by whales and list a number of survivors. Such stories are not necessary to "prove" the reliability of the biblical account. The unusual size of the fish, and its presence when Jonah is thrown overboard, is undoubtedly supervised by the Lord.

Which of these observations seems justified by the OT report? (1) Jonah's disobedience led pagans to worship God. (2) Jonah, even though he was disobedient, was used to lead pagans to worship God. (3) God's way of dealing with his disobedient servant led pagans to worship.

Chapter 2. Jonah's Prayer of Submission

The Prayer. This poetic section reveals Jonah's inner struggle and submission. In great danger, the prophet finally turns to the Lord. Later he writes, "When my life was ebbing away, I remembered you, Lord, and my prayer rose to you, to your holy temple" (7). Vowing to follow the Lord, Jonah determines never to act like one of those who forfeits the grace that could be his in God.

"Look Toward Your Temple." This phrase, repeated in vv. 4 and 7, is significant. Solomon had asked at the dedication of the temple: "When a prayer or plea is made by any of your people Israel—each one aware of his afflictions and pains, and spreading out his hands toward the temple—then hear from heaven, your dwelling place. Forgive, and deal with each man according to all

he does" (2 Chron. 6:29,30). The Lord does as he has promised. Jonah is forgiven and will be restored to his place of service.

Chapter 3. Jonah's Mission to Nineveh

The Story. God repeats Jonah's commission. This time Jonah obeys, traveling to this "very large city." It takes three days for Jonah to cover all its districts, standing on its street corners to deliver his message in just five Hebrew words. "Forty more days and Nineveh will be destroyed!"

Amazingly, the king and nobles lead the whole population in confession and repentance. The people turn from evil practices and humble themselves before the Lord. And God relents! Judgment does not come.

Nineveh. At the time, Nineveh with its suburbs housed some 600,000 inhabitants. During the reign of Adad-Nirari III (810–783 B.C.) the Assyrian religion was marked by a trend toward monotheism. This, with a great plague in the reign of Assurdan III (771–754 B.C.), may have prepared the way for the mass movement stimulated by Jonah's preaching.

The day would come when Assyria would destroy Jonah's people. But this generation of Assyrians responded to the word of the Lord and their civilization lived.

Which of these seems to best capture the meaning of Jonah for the people of his own homeland? (1) When a people responds to God's Word, God withholds judgment. (2) God's words of warning are meaningless. (3) God is gracious to pagan peoples as well as to the people of Israel. (For background see Jer. 18:7–10, and Jesus' statement in Matt. 12:39–42.)

Chapter 4. Jonah's Motives . . . and God's

The Story. Jonah is angry that his preaching has stimulated repentance. He complains to God, revealing his motive for fleeing in the first place. Jonah knows God is merciful (2). But he does not want mercy shown to this enemy of his people! Jonah wants Nineveh destroyed.

The disgruntled prophet finds a hillside east of the city and settles down to see what will happen. When the Lord makes a vine grow to shade the prophet from the sun, Jonah is very happy. But the next morning the plant dies. Now, as the day grows unusually hot and windy, the bitter prophet grows angry at the Lord.

God then speaks to Jonah. The prophet cared passionately about the vine. But he had closed his heart to the people who would have been destroyed with Nineveh. Jonah did not care about these people. But God did care!

Motivations. We can understand Jonah's feelings. As a patriot, he loved his own people and rightly feared the enemy who would one day devastate his homeland. But the Lord is God of the whole earth. His compassion reaches beyond Israel and Judah, to encompass all peoples. Yes, God will act to judge sins (see *Judgment of the Wicked,* p. 322). But God would far rather be gracious. How good to see here the love and grace of God extended to all mankind and to know that in the OT as well as the NT our God is shown to be full of compassion.

Which of these statements seem to you the "main message" of Jonah for us to apply today? (1) When I fail God is always willing to give me another chance. (2) I need to adopt God's attitude of love for those who are not of "my group" in order to be like him. (3) God will accept me in spite of unchristian attitudes, but will instruct me and help me change.

MICAH
Visions of Judgment and Restoration

Micah was a prophet of the southern kingdom, Judah. He was a contemporary of Isaiah and, in Israel, Hosea. Micah's visions encompass both sections of the divided nation. For each he sees impending judgment. And for each he sees bright days of holiness and blessing, which will follow the dark days of God's wrath.

Date and Author. Micah carefully identifies his time. He is a prophet called to share the visions which God gives him during the "reigns of Jotham, Ahaz, and Hezekiah" (742–687 B.C.). The events of these days are well known from Scripture and other sources. Thus we have a sharp and definite background in history against which to understand this prophet's ministry to the people of his day.

Micah the Man. Like Amos, Micah is a man deeply concerned with justice. He is sensitive to the fact that Judah and Israel have wandered from the good ways marked out in the law. And he is convinced that only a spiritual renewal, a return to God by individuals and by society, can save his nation.

Micah's life was not without conflict. But Micah was, superficially at least, a success. Looking back on Micah's day, one of Jeremiah's defenders spoke of Micah's messages of judgment and the king's response. The defender asks, "Did Hezekiah king of Judah or anyone else in Judah put him (Micah) to death? Did not Hezekiah fear the Lord and seek his favor? And did not the Lord relent, so that he did not bring the disaster he pronounced against them?" (Jer. 26:17–19). There *was* a revival in the days of Hezekiah. The king did hear the warnings of Micah and of his great contemporary Isaiah. The king led the people to turn to God, and judgment passed over the southern kingdom, while unrepentant Israel was crushed and taken captive to Assyria. It may well be true, as some have suggested, that the revival of Hezekiah's day was built on the preaching of this prophet and preacher of righteousness, and of personal relationship with God.

Historical background. When Micah began preaching, both Judah and Israel were experiencing the glow of political expansion and great material prosperity. (For a description see "background" sections in Amos, p. 378, and in Hosea, p. 389.) But with expansion came a great concentration of power in the capital cities of Jerusa-

lem and Samaria, and a host of social sins. The avaricious nobility
seized the land of the poor to build great personal estates. Widows
and others were evicted and oppressed, and the centralized power
was used to support the wealthy who defrauded the poor. No
wonder the prophet Micah was forced to take the theme of Amos
("do justice") as well as the theme of Hosea ("return to God").
But Micah is convinced of one thing. Only a religious revival can
stimulate true reform.

Was there really a national reformation in Hosea's day? Or does
the message recorded in his book show that Hezekiah's reformation
was superficial and failed to reach down and change the lives of
the common people? Of that we cannot be sure. But Hosea did
not depend simply on his own generation to turn to God. Hosea,
like the other OT prophets, looked beyond his own day and saw,
at history's end, a day of glory and righteousness approaching,
brought in by the hand of God. Then truly the revival Micah
yearned for will be real!

Micah and Isaiah. Many have commented on the similarities
in the messages of Micah and his great contemporary, Isaiah. This
is not surprising, as each spoke to the same generation, sharing
a common message of sin, repentance, and renewal. The following
chart lists parallels in thought and message between these two
great prophets.

Micah	Isaiah	Micah	Isaiah
1:9–16	10:28–32	4:7	9:7
2:1,2	5:8	4:10	39:6
2:6,11	30:10	5:2–4	7:14
2:12	10:20–23	5:6	14:25
3:5–7	29:9–12	6:6–8	58:6, 7
4:1	2:2	7:7	8:17
4:4	1:19	7:12	11:11

Structure and Outline. The book is generally considered to develop three themes, reflected in the outline below.

Outline

I.	Punishment Promised	1:1–2:13
II.	Kingdom Coming	3:1–5:15
III.	From Sin to Salvation	6:1–7:20

Within the framework provided by this outline, Micah deals with
all the themes of the major and minor prophets.

Chapter 1. Judgment Pronounced

The prophet describes God's awesome descent to the earth to judge Israel and Judah for their idolatry (2–7). Graphically the prophet describes the shame and weeping which that judgment bring (8–16).

Chapter 2. Disaster Planned

Micah contrasts man's plans and God's. The people of Judah and Israel lie awake nights, plotting how to defraud others of their homes. As soon as morning comes, they rush to carry out their evil designs (1–2). But God is planning too. His plan is for a disaster to strike all those who walk so proudly now. The rich will be ruined and their possessions taken by strangers who taunt and ridicule them (3–5).

Then Micah turns on those who try to silence his voice (6–7). These people do not want to hear the truth. They are eager for liars and deceivers to come and tell them what they want to hear (8–11). The chapter's closing verses relate the only good news that Micah can honestly share. Though there is no hope for this present civilization, a "remnant of Israel" will be brought together by God (12,13).

The promise of a remnant, survivors of God's great judgment, is common to all the prophets. But judgment will come from God before the time of blessing.

Chapter 3. Leaders Rebuked

The political leaders of Israel should have protected the innocent, but they "have forgotten justice" and they savage the flock they are charged to care for (1–4). The prophets, "who lead my people astray" with their promises of continued blessing, are also condemned (5–12). How different Micah's approach to ministry from that of those who "tell fortunes for money." It is because of them and their sins that Jerusalem will soon be nothing but a heap of rubble, and brush will grow on temple hill. But Micah remains true to his calling. He does have an impact on his generation. "As for me," he explains, "I am filled with power, with the Spirit of the Lord, and with justice and might, to declare to Jacob his transgression, to Israel his sin" (8). If only all were as true to their calling!

Chapter 4. Temple Mountain Established

Micah looks beyond the coming disaster and sees a new temple erected on its old site. It is a place of glory, and all peoples stream to it. These verses (1–3) are duplicated in Isaiah 2:2–4. It may be that Micah is quoting his contemporary, or Isaiah may quote Micah. The scene described by both prophets is one of universal peace under the rule of God's law, when "no one will make them afraid" (4).

God's ultimate plan is for an age of endless blessing (6–8). Judah will first writhe in agony, and her people will be carried away to Babylon (10). But after the judgment, the glory days will surely come.

Chapter 5. A Ruler from Bethlehem

The glory days are linked to appearance of the promised Davidic king (see *Davidic Covenant*, p. 177). Micah 5:2 is quoted in the NT as a prophecy of Jesus' birth: "You, Bethlehem of Ephrathah, though you are small among the clans of Judah, out of you will come for me one who will be ruler over Israel, whose origins are from old, from ancient times."

Israel will be abandoned until his time (3,4). But after the Assyrian invasion and exile among the nations (5b–9), the promised ruler will lead Israel to triumph. All that is unholy in Israel will be destroyed, and vengeance will be taken on pagan nations.

The references to destruction of horses and chariots in verse 10 relates to Deuteronomy 17:14–20. Kings were not to multiply military resources but to trust in God as their only real security.

Chapter 6. The Case against Israel

Micah uses a familiar prophetic device. He pictures a courtroom and God presenting his case. God has serious accusations to make against this people whom he has cared for and loved. He has not asked for their multiplied sacrifices and ritual, but "has shown you, O man, what is good. And what does the Lord require of you?" Micah goes on to ask. "To act justly and to love mercy, and to walk humbly with your God" (1–8). Guilty Israel, a nation of dishonest merchants, of violence, and of deceit, will be given over to ruin (9–16).

Chapter 7. Misery and Restoration

Micah shares the misery that God feels as he observes the wickedness of his people. The godly have been swept from the land, rulers demand gifts, and judges accept bribes. The only skill left to the hands of his people is a talent for doing evil! No neighbor can be relied on; no friend can be trusted. Even the family is shattered, as its members turn against one another (1–7). Such a nation must fall.

But Israel will rise! The people will bow under God's wrath until a day comes when he will lead them into the light (8–13). Then at last God will have his inheritance in his people, and they will praise him for his faithfulness to his promises to Abraham (see *Covenant, OT,* p. 51). And they will praise him for the forgiveness they enjoy.

Micah's closing image of a God who will "hurl all our iniquities into the depths of the sea" is a beautiful picture of the completeness of forgiveness. As his redeemed our sins too are forgiven . . . and gone.

NAHUM
Prophecy against Nineveh

Nahum's words are intended to comfort the people of Judah. They suffer now as subjects of mighty Assyria. But Nahum announces the destruction of the great capital city of the enemy.

Author and Date. The author is identified as Nahum, a man from the village of Elkosh. Nothing else is known beyond his short OT book.

We do know more about the prophet's time. From Nahum's statements we know he writes after the fall of Thebes to the Assyrians (668/667 B.C.). We know that Nineveh is still standing, resplendent in her grandeur as capital of an unchallenged world empire. And the picture of Judah's oppression by Nineveh (cf. 1:13,15; 2:2) fits the reign of Manasseh, but not that of later kings. Thus Nahum probably spoke his message between 667 and 655 B.C.

Judgment Theme. The theme is God's judgment on Assyria. This is not unique to Nahum. Isaiah especially speaks of Assyria's judgment (cf. Isa. 10:5–19; 14:24–27; 17:12–14; 18:4–6; 30:27–33; 31:5–9; 37:21–35). The Book of Nahum is an extended and detailed pronouncement of doom, intended to comfort the people of Judah who are suffering under the Assyrian yoke.

Chapter 1. God's Anger against Nineveh

The prophet begins with a vision of God. God is a "jealous and avenging God." Although slow to anger, the Lord will not leave the guilty unpunished. It is always important to link the fact of guilt with the concept of God's wrath (see *God's Anger*, p. 110). This Nahum does and goes on to describe the earth trembling as God comes burning with indignation, his wrath pouring out like fire before him (1–6).

Nahum balances his picture of an angry God with an affirmation that "God is good, a refuge in times of trouble" (7,8). It is only those who plot against the Lord and plan evil that he will cut down (9–11). Though Judah has suffered, God is about to turn against her oppressor. He will destroy Nineveh, filling Judah with joy (12–15).

Chapter 2. Nineveh to Fall

Nahum warns the city of Nineveh. An enemy advances against her—dashing against the city wall, throwing open the river gates. Looking ahead, Nahum sees the great palace of the king crumble and collapse. Nineveh's endless supply of gold and silver is stripped by her conquerors (1–10). This once fearsome den of lions will soon be torn down, for " 'I am against you,' declares the Lord Almighty" (11–13).

Chapter 3. Poetic Vision of Nineveh's Fall

In a final exalted poem, Nahum revisits his vision and describes Nineveh's fall. He sees the corpses of the people piled in the streets and the fires that blacken the skies. Nothing can stay the stroke or heal the deadly wound that God will give to this city of blood (1–19).

HABAKKUK
The Struggles of Faith

Habakkuk struggles with some of the most painful questions which face believers. Why does God permit evil among his people? How can God permit the more wicked to overcome those less evil than themselves? These questions emerge from Habakkuk's own experience. But they are questions that believers have faced across the ages. The answers Habakkuk finds, and his discovery of the necessity of personal faith, speak to all times and especially to our own.

Date and Author. Habakkuk is known only through his book in which he calls himself "the prophet." Two possible dates have been argued for his writing. One date assumes the book was written after Babylon came to power and threatened the freedom of Judah. This would place Habakkuk during the reign of evil King Jehoiakim (608–597 B.C.). The other earlier date builds on Habakkuk's reference to the rise of Babylon as so unexpected as to be unbelievable (1:6) and places the book in the days of Josiah (639–609 B.C.). For several reasons, the Josian date seems most likely.

Historical Background. Other prophets (Amos, Hosea, Micah, and Isaiah) saw injustice in their society and spoke out strongly against it. They condemned the sins of Judah and Israel, and announced that God would judge such wickedness. Habakkuk, looking at the same sins, is driven to puzzled despair. He cannot understand how God can permit the sins he sees among his people. Habakkuk's reaction makes special sense because, under Josiah, there has been a religious reformation. Habakkuk does not mention idolatry, which all the other prophets condemn. This no longer seems to be a problem, for Judah worships at a restored temple and holds the festivals ordained by the rediscovered law (see p. 218 for historical background). Yet for all the veneer of religion there has been no moral transformation. It is this, the failure of religious revival to transform the society of Judah and to cleanse it of oppression, which sends Habakkuk on his lonely quest seeking answers from God.

Theme. The theme of Habakkuk is simply his search for an answer to moral and theological questions raised by the existence of sin in the lives of God's people. The prophet is given answers which are objective and clear. But the objective answers are only half the struggle for this prophet. He must work through the meaning of God's answers for his own life and his own faith. He must find a personal response that will sustain him when the evil days come.

This book has great value for us today. We too need objective answers to theological questions. But we also need the grace that Habakkuk found, to apply God's answers in our own lives and finally come, as Habakkuk did, to experience the triumph of faith.

Chapter 1. The Prophet's Lament

In an unusual way Habakkuk alternates poetic laments with prophecy. The first chapter contains two laments. Each expresses a question which troubles Habakkuk deeply. The prophet's name means "wrestler." How appropriate this is, as Habakkuk wrestles with issues that have troubled saints through the ages.

The Complaint; 1:1–4. Habakkuk cries to God because of the injustice which pollutes his society. The wicked surround and overwhelm the good, so that the justice administered is perverted.

Habakkuk has been asking God to deal with the violence and wickedness. But God has been silent. And that silence implies tolerance of wrong! Habakkuk can no longer stand the doubt and anguish this situation creates. He must have an answer from God.

The Lord's Response; 1:5–11. God does answer and makes clear to the prophet that he is not tolerating Judah's injustice. "I am raising up the Babylonians," he tells the prophet. God is at work now, in the prophet's own day, though at this moment the message of a Babylonian invasion is so amazing "that you would not believe, even if you were told" (5). But God promises that this fierce and rapacious people will soon swoop down on many nations, bent on violence and conquest. Nothing will stop them: fortified cities will be overwhelmed, as earth is piled against their walls until the unconquerable armies simply pour up the earthen ramp and over the walls. But these are guilty men, God adds, "whose own strength is their god."

Habakkuk's Second Complaint; 1:12–17. The answer at first satisfies Habakkuk, who can accept the Babylonians as an instrument of God's judgment (12). But soon Habakkuk is troubled by a new question.

Habakkuk knows that God is "too pure to look on evil" and "can not tolerate wrong" (13). Why then does God remain silent when a wicked people like the Babylonians swallow up nations more virtuous than they? The march of history makes men seem nothing more than "fish in the sea, like sea creatures that have no ruler" (14). There is no testimony here to a God who stands in judgment over nations and peoples, and who is working out his purposes in history!

Jealous for the glory of God, Habakkuk wonders how God can remain silent while some treat others like fish to net and feast on. Won't their successes lead men away from God, to worship their own power?

Chapter 2. Principles of Judgment

Habakkuk is determined to have an answer to his questions. He finds an isolated spot to station himself. He will wait until God answers his complaint and resolves his doubts (1).

God does answer. God explains the hidden processes of judgment which are at work in the lives of the wicked. He has planted a testimony to the moral nature of the universe deep in each personality, and in the inner workings of society. When Habakkuk comes to understand these processes he will realize that God does not overlook or tolerate wrong. Habakkuk is told to write the principles revealed and communicate them to the people of Judah.

Never Satisfied; 2:4,5. Success does not bring the wicked person rest or satisfaction. Instead his gains make him desire more, never realizing that all his getting simply stokes the fires of his unrest. Such a person will never find satisfaction or peace.

Create Enemies; 2:6–8. Mistreatment of others creates enemies, who will turn on the wicked when they can. How different this is from relationships forged by compassion and love!

False Security; 2:9–11. The wicked use their gains to build a "nest on high." But the pain they cause others means that no matter how they try to protect themselves from disaster, they will never escape the fear of ruin . . . or its grim clutch.

Empty Future; 2:12–14. The monuments the murderers build to themselves are all founded on emptiness. The earth is destined to be "filled with the knowledge of the glory of the Lord." The future holds no lasting hope for the wicked.

Disgrace Certain; 2:15–17. The wicked exult in the shame of others. But they themselves will be exposed to disgrace. Their violence will turn back on them.

No Guidance or Escape; 2:18–20. That which the wicked worship, whether idols or their own power (1:11, 16), has no ability to guide them or to deliver. When terror comes, the wicked have no one and nothing to turn to.

All these are realities which are at work in individuals and in interpersonal relationships. If we could see into the inmost heart of the wicked, or see ahead into his near future, we would never suggest that God tolerates evil! Every success of the evil brings with it its own judgment.

Which of these principles of judgment have you seen demonstrated (1) in your own life, (b) in the life of a friend, or acquaintance, or (c) in the history of nations? Which of these seems to you to be the most devastating judgment?

Chapter 3. Habakkuk's Prayer

Habakkuk is intellectually satisfied. But now, in a prayer later set to music, Habakkuk examines his own fears and struggles to come to a triumphant faith.

Hurry! 3:2. Habakkuk's first reaction is an eager cry for God to bring on the purifying judgment. He is sure that God will remember mercy as the Babylonians strike his land.

Vision of Judgments; 3:3–15. But then God gives his prophet a vision of what judgment involves. Habakkuk looks back across sacred history. He sees God marching from Sinai to judge his sinning people at Kadesh (cf. Num. 13). The blinding brilliance of his coming, the burning plague and shaking mountains, seem to the prophet only to conceal God's elemental power (3–6). Then Habakkuk sees another scene. God, as judge, is visiting punishment on Israel at Midian (cf. Num. 25). The bursting fury shocks the prophet as he sees God, like some warrior, string his bow and nock his war arrows (7–9). Then suddenly Habakkuk is shown the overwhelming waters of judgment, rushing like some Genesis cataclysm (Gen. 6) to burst over the prophet and his people (10–15). Now Habakkuk must struggle to remember that judgment is ultimately intended "to save your people."

Habakkuk's Reaction; 3:16–19. Stunned, the prophet slumps, his legs trembling, crushed by the terror of his vision. He must wait patiently for the day of calamity, knowing now the misery it will bring. Yet, with all the material things in which men take joy gone, Habakkuk knows, "I will rejoice in the Lord, I will be joyful in God my Savior" (18).

Looking out, Habakkuk sees a deer picking its way along a sheer and dangerous cliff. And he realizes the great truth which lifts him to the pinnacle of faith. Whatever comes, "the Sovereign Lord is my strength; he makes my feet like the feet of a deer, he enables me to go on the heights" (19).

As a member of his society, Habakkuk will be caught up when the judgment falls on Judah. Often we too are caught when judgment falls because we are linked to others. What does Habakkuk conclude about the meaning of his faith in God for such times? How can this be significant to you?

ZEPHANIAH
The Prophet of Universal Judgment

Habakkuk looked deep within the personality of the wicked and saw processes of judgment at work. Zephaniah, a contemporary, looks ahead. There Zephaniah sees a day when God will act dramatically and history will prove that he is Judge of all.

Date and Author. Zephaniah is a descendant of godly King Hezekiah. He lives and prophesies in the reign of Josiah. Because the picture Zephaniah sketches of widespread idolatry in Judah fits best before the great religious revival, which Josiah led in 621 B.C., his book is usually dated in Josiah's earlier years.

Message. Zephaniah's message is simple. God is a God of judgment. God will act personally, intruding into history to judge all peoples and all nations in a great "Day of the Lord" at the time of the end. But Zephaniah is also convinced that God acts along history's way!

It is Judah's sin which concerns Zephaniah. He is convinced that her sins are so great that a judgment is inevitable. So Zephaniah addresses his preaching to individuals who may respond to God's invitation to mercy, as well as to the remnant that will survive the judgment which now looms dark over the horizon.

Structure and Outline. The universal judgment Zephaniah describes follows this pattern:

Outline

I.	Judgment on Judah	1:1–2:3
II.	Judgment on the Nations	2:4–15
III.	Jerusalem's Future	3:1–20
	A. Near Judgment	3:1–7
	B. Eternal Kingdom	3:8–20

No one escapes the sweeping view of the prophet, who sees all mankind as meriting the coming visitation of God.

Chapter 1:1–2:3. Judgment on Judah

Zephaniah begins with two warnings of universal judgment. Everything will be swept away when the judgment comes (1:2,3).

Those in Judah who think, "The Lord will do nothing, either good or bad," will be jolted from complacency when the day of wrath comes (1:4–13).

Zephaniah speaks of a "great day of the Lord." Like other prophets, his primary focus is on the final judgment which is to sweep the whole earth just before history's end (see *OT Eschatology*, pp. 372, 373). But Zephaniah, like others, also sees divine punishments that fall on a nation as a contemporary expression of that day. Now Zephaniah sees a day of judgment that is "near—near and coming quickly." This day "of trouble and ruin, of darkness and gloom, of clouds and blackness" will bring distress to all the people of Judah (1:14–18).

Because judgment is imminent, Zephaniah urges individuals who are responsive to God to "seek righteousness, seek humility." They will not escape the troubles that come when their nation falls, but "perhaps you will be sheltered on the day of the Lord's anger" (2:1–3).

Chapter 2:4–15. Judgment on the Nations

Now the prophet seems to lift his eyes and look beyond the borders of Judah. Turning full circle from west to north Zephaniah predicts judgment to strike Philistia (2:4–7), Moab and Ammon (2:8–11), Cush [Ethiopia] (12), and Assyria (13–15).

Chapter 3. Jerusalem's Future

Near Judgment; 3:1–7. The immediate future holds only woes for this city of rebels and oppressors. These unresponsive and faithless people will be punished by a God who is righteous and who does no wrong.

Eternal Kingdom; 3:8–20. At history's end another fate awaits the city. Then, when the whole world is bathed in the fire of God's anger, Jerusalem's people will be purified. "I will leave within you," God promises, "the meek and the humble." The survivors of the final judgment will be those who trust in the name of the Lord (8–13).

Then Jerusalem will sing! Then God will be with the city and her people. He will at last give the oppressed praise and honor among all the peoples of the earth (14–20).

HAGGAI
Rebuilding the Temple

Haggai is a man with a single message: Rebuild the temple! His exhortation is to a discouraged people. They have returned to the Promised Land after a generation of captivity in Babylon, only to struggle with fields that have reverted to wilderness. But now, after years of neglect, Haggai insists that rebuilding the temple is a necessary affirmation of faith and of expectation.

Date and Author. We do not know who wrote down the messages that Haggai gave. Little is known of the prophet himself, although Jewish tradition suggests he was a prophet/priest. Some suggest he is an old man when these words are spoken, and that he remembers the old temple of Solomon, destroyed in 587 B.C. (see *Jerusalem Temple,* p. 190).

Because each message of Haggai is carefully dated, we can place the preaching of his brief sermons to the very day!

Background. Haggai is one of three postexilic prophets who ministered to the people who returned from Babylonian captivity to reestablish a Jewish community in Palestine. For details see *Return from Captivity* (p. 229–231), and the historical books of Ezra (p. 232) and Nehemiah (p. 236).

The remnant that returned came with high hopes. They remembered a rich and fertile land. But the Babylonians had devastated Judea, and years of untended growth had pushed the small section of Judah in which they settled back toward wilderness.

The people scattered, settling on the old fields surrounding the ruins of Jerusalem, struggling to make their living from the land. They rebuilt their homes, planted crops, and cleared fields. But they seemed to make no progress. Droughts destroyed their crops and each year they seemed a little further behind financially.

It is to this discouraged people that Haggai comes with a fresh word from the Lord. Their difficulties are God's discipline and instruction. The people have failed to put God first and so lost the blessing which comes only from a life centered on God. Haggai challenges them to act now and rebuild the temple of the Lord on the old Jerusalem site. By this act of faith they will affirm the place God must again have in their hearts and in their lives.

The Significance of the Temple. Rebuilding the temple is important as a reaffirmation of faith. But Haggai sees an even more important reason why it must be begun. And begun now!

The earlier prophets outlined God's plan for the future (see *OT Eschatology,* pp. 372, 373). They saw a great war and world-wide divine judgment. They saw the appearance of the Messiah, the promised deliverer from David's line. And they saw an endless kingdom over which God would rule. In these prophecies of the future, the Jerusalem temple played a significant role. Ezekiel saw the glory of the Lord return to Jerusalem and settle into a temple built there to receive the Presence (43:1–5). Micah described the nations approaching a new temple, humbly eager to hear the word from God which would bring world peace (Micah 4:1–4). Isaiah had this same vision (Isa. 2:2–4). Surely then God's people must show their faith in the promised future and build a temple on Jerusalem's sacred hill! They must be ready for their Messiah when he comes!

None of the prophets, including Haggai, understood the time frame with which God was working, or how all the elements of his plan fit together (cf. 1 Pet. 1:10–12). But rebuilding the temple is a necessary act of faith and preparation. Israel must look forward to an imminent appearance of her Savior. That hope will give their lives perspective as they wait expectantly.

Structure and Outline. The Book of Haggai is composed of four short sermons given by the prophet and brief reports of the response of the people. The book can best be outlined by the dates on which these sermons were delivered.

Chapter 1. 29 August 520 B.C.

The Sermon; 1:1–11. Haggai confronts his people with the fact that they have neglected God, to concentrate each one on his own affairs. Haggai calls for the people to honor God by rebuilding the temple. He makes no promise of material blessings. But he does convey the Lord's message that blessing has been withheld because the people have failed to put God first.

The Response; 1:12–15. The leaders and the whole people recognize the voice of God in Haggai's words, and they obey. God stirs up enthusiasm for the project, and the whole community comes together to begin work on September 21st.

Chapter 2:1–9. 17 October 520 B.C.

Haggai's second message to the people is one of encouragement. Under the Mosaic law covenant (see v. 5), God committed himself to be with each generation that obeys him. These people have obeyed. Thus God announces through Haggai that he will keep his word: "I am with you, declares the Lord Almighty" (4).

But how can a people on the bare edge of poverty rebuild the temple? God announces through Haggai that he is owner of all the gold and silver of the world. God will meet the need, and "the glory of this present house will be greater than the glory of the former" (e.g., Solomon's temple). Ezra 6:8–12 tells us that God did meet the need. Although the governor of the Persian province opposes the rebuilding, he is commanded by the king himself to finance the whole project! Later, in the days of Herod the Great the temple was greatly expanded and was the recipient of fabulous gifts. By the time of Jesus it did surpass the temple of Solomon for glory.

Haggai also speaks in this sermon of God "shaking the heavens and the earth, and shaking the nations." This eschatological language is an affirmation that the end to history foreseen by the other prophets will indeed come.

Chapter 2:10–19. 18 December 520 B.C.

Haggai is sent to make a public inquiry of the priests concerning a point of Mosaic law. Under the law an object or person which is ceremonially unclean makes unclean whatever it touches. Under the law nothing which is holy can make any defiled thing clean.

Haggai applies the principle. This people is not to think that the presence of the temple makes them holy. They are defiled by sin. But God operates among them in grace. He will accept their gift of obedience, and "From this day on I will bless you."

Chapter 2:20–23. 18 December 520 B.C.

The same day Haggai receives a message from God to give to Zerubbabel. This individual is of the royal family. He is not king, for Judah is under the domination of Persia; it is a minor region in one of 120 administrative districts! But the words of Haggai look forward to a time when God will shake the nations. Then Zerubbabel (that is, the family of David), will again be established.

Thus Haggai's final words are a reaffirmation to Judah and to future generations of the great covenant of God with David (see p. 177). The time is coming when God will fulfill his promises. The future envisioned by all the prophets will become a reality.

ZECHARIAH
The Future of Israel

The Book of Zechariah is apocalyptic. Looking into the distant future, full of symbols, shapes, and of images glimpsed by the prophet, it has been called "obscure." Like other prophetic visions, many of the things it describes will only be understood when the words are fulfilled. Even so Zechariah's broad themes are clear. We can sense with the prophet the gathering of sinister forces and hear the thundering battles which seem for a time to portend the victory of evil over good. And we can sense the sudden joy as God intervenes to deliver Jerusalem and rejoice with him as the bitter mourning of her people is transformed to joy.

Date and Author. Zechariah is a contemporary of Haggai and speaks out of the same historical background (see p. 419). In fact, the first part of his book gives dates which overlap the dates given for Haggai's recorded sermons:

Haggai		*Zechariah*	
First Sermon	29 Aug. 520 B.C.		
Second Sermon	17 Oct. 520 B.C.	Sermon	17 Oct. 520 B.C.
Third/Fourth Sermon	18 Dec. 520 B.C.		
		Visions	15 Feb. 519 B.C.
		Sermon on Fasting	7 Dec. 518 B.C.

Chapter 1 gives Zechariah's genealogy. Most agree with the tradition which makes him a leading member of the priestly family mentioned in Nehemiah 12:4,16. But the name Zechariah is a common one in OT times.

Significance. The Book of Zechariah is one of the two key books of OT prediction which are primary sources for the symbolism of the last book of the NT, Revelation. Zechariah 9–14 is also the section of the OT most quoted when the gospel narratives relate the last days of Jesus on earth.

The focus of Zechariah's writings are clearly apocalyptic and in full harmony with the visions of the other OT prophets concerning the time of the end (see *OT Eschatology,* pp. 372, 373). The terms used are well established by earlier writings, and the bold pictures that Zechariah paints in vibrant terms are seen throughout the older Testament. The future Zechariah sees is the future God has revealed through a dozen others among his prophets.

Structure and Outline. The book is easily divided into major segments. Chapters 1–6 relate visions given to the prophet. Chapters 7–8 relate to questions about fasting. Chapters 8–14 contain two blocks of apocalyptic teaching, focusing on God's intervention in history at the time of the end.

Many critics have challenged the unity of this book. They have argued that changes in subject and focus, as well as a shift from prose to poetry, suggests that Zechariah did not write both major sections. It has often been said that the contents of these last chapters are disorganized collections of unrelated teachings. However, the section is not disorganized. As P. Lamarch has demonstrated, this section as well as the rest of the book is organized in a sophisticated literary form called *chiasmus*. This form balances progressions of thematic material. The chiasmic organization of the last section is illustrated below:

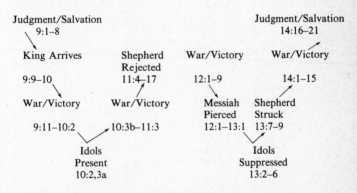

Because this book can best be understood by carefully tracing its structure, an analytical outline, adapted from J. Baldwin, is provided on page 424.

Chapter 1:1–6. A Call to Return

On the same day Haggai promises the people of Judah God's blessings because of their obedience (Hag. 2:19). Zechariah speaks to reinforce his message. The covenant promises are still in force, so Zechariah urges a wholehearted response to God, not a superficial response like the ones made by Judah during revivals before the exile. Then superficial response failed to avert judgment.

Analytical Outline
Part I

II. Eight Visions and Oracles (1:7–6:15)

Zechariah is shown eight visions. In them he is not a passive observer. He is actively involved and free to question the angel God has provided as a guide. The meaning of most of these visions is explained in their context. Their focus is God's intention for

Jerusalem and Judea as history moves on and as the end time comes. Many of these themes are picked up in Revelation.

Chapter 1:7–17. The First Vision: The False Security of the Nations

On February 15 of 519 B.C., God speaks to Zechariah in visions. In the first vision he sees four horsemen whom an angel identifies as watchers who patrol the whole earth (10). The four report to the angel of the Lord (see *Angels,* p. 370) that the world is at rest and peace.

This is not good news for Judea. Haggai proclaimed just a few months before that the nations must be shaken before Messiah comes and Jerusalem's peace is assured. But God reassures the prophet. God does care deeply ("is very jealous") for Jerusalem and Judah. And he is angry with the nations that have been their persecutors. God will return to Jerusalem with mercy, and goodness will overflow.

Chapter 1:18–21. The Second Vision: Retribution on the Nations

Zechariah sees four horns (representing the world powers that will hold political domination over Jerusalem). The horn symbolism is used in the same way in Daniel 7, 8, and 12.

Zechariah also sees four smiths or craftsmen. These are workmen, bearing heavy hammers or chisels, whose function it is to throw down the "horns of the nations" that have acted against Jerusalem. Thus each of these oppressors of God's people will be crushed as history marches toward its intended end.

Chapter 2. The Third Vision: God's Protection of Jerusalem

Now Zechariah sees a man with a measuring line. He is about to survey the city of Jerusalem. But Zechariah's angel guide sends another angel to hurry after this man with good news. Jerusalem will overflow beyond her walls. And walls will be unnecessary, for God himself will "be a wall of fire around it," and "I will be its glory within" (5). When at last God dwells among his people, "many nations will be joined with the Lord in that day and will become my people" (11).

Chapter 3. The Fourth Vision: The High Priest Reinstated

This vision and the next take place in the temple court. Zechariah sees the high priest, Joshua, dressed in filthy clothing, standing before the angel of the Lord (3). Satan stands by as accuser. But the angel calls on God to rebuke Satan, because God has chosen Jerusalem. None can lay any charge against God's chosen (cf. Rom. 8:33).

As Zechariah watches, the filthy clothing is removed and the high priest, Joshua, is dressed in rich garments (1–5). Symbolically cleansed of sin and clothed by God with righteousness (4), Joshua is charged to "walk in my ways" (the moral law) and "keep my requirements" (a term used in the OT of ritual duties of the priesthood). If Joshua does so, he will exercise sole religious authority and have access to God (6,7).

In the vision Joshua is specifically told that he and his associates are "men symbolic of things to come." Fulfillment looks ahead to the appearance of God's servant, the Branch (Messiah), identified in Isaiah 4:2 and 52:13–53:12. The stone placed before Joshua with seven "eyes" may be a stone cut with seven facets, or perhaps a stone from which flow seven springs. From these the water of life will pour on the day when the Lord "removes the sin of this land in a single day" (9).

The main thrust of this complicated vision is clear. A cleansed and renewed priesthood is symbolic of the coming Messiah, whose mission as God's servant will be to take away the sins of God's people "in a single day."

Chapter 4. The Fifth Vision: Supernatural Resources

Both Joshua the High Priest and Zerubbabel, representative of the royal line of David, are spoken to through this vision. It teaches dependence on God's Spirit, for he is the one through whom God's work is accomplished. In the vision the oil in the lampstand also speaks of God's Spirit.

It is clear from the chapter that many in Judah doubted that the temple, whose foundation was now laid, could be finished by the little group of some 50,000 who had returned from the exile. They must also have doubted that this tiny community, insignificant among the millions in the Persian empire of which they were a part, would one day reshape the world. But God promises that the temple will be finished by Zerubbabel (8), for the true resources to accomplish any work set by God are spiritual and do not rest on human abilities. "Not by might nor by power, but by my Spirit," the prophet reports. We are never to "despise the day of small things," for from them God can build the great!

Chapter 5:1–4. The Sixth Vision: Punishment of Evildoers

This vision features an open scroll, some ten yards by five. On it are written two of the commandments, representing the Mosaic law's teaching of duty to God and to neighbor. These words are called a "curse," for God has promised to punish all who refuse to obey. Now the words fly through the land, actively carrying out the Lord's judgment on sinners.

Chapter 5:5–11. The Seventh Vision: Purification of the Land

Zechariah sees wickedness personified, locked in a large container used to measure out grain. Powerless, wickedness is carried away to Babylon by two angels.

Earlier God's people had been carried captive to Babylon because of their wickedness. In the future God will separate his people from evil, and it is evil that is taken captive and sent far away from Jerusalem into exile.

Chapter 6. The Eighth Vision: Priest and King to Be One

The Four Chariots; 6:1–8. The angelic patrols that cover the earth (see 1:7–17) are mounted in war chariots and sent out to sweep over the earth. A report comes back that "those going north" have "given my Spirit rest in the land of the north" (8). In Bible prophecy the north represents the nations and power of evil (cf. Joel 2:20f, Ezek. 38, 39). The rest God's Spirit now enjoys there indicates that the enemy which north represents has been defeated.

Joshua's Crown; 6:9–15. Now, the enemy defeated, Zechariah is told to approach Joshua the high priest. He is to take gold and silver and shape a royal crown. The Hebrew word for "crown" is always used of a royal crown, never of a priest's headdress.

According to Zechariah 3:8 Joshua stands symbolically in these visions "for things to come," and especially for the promised Branch (Messiah). The picture is one of a union between the office of priest and that of king in a single individual. When he appears to "be a priest on his throne," the final and true temple of the Lord will be erected (11–13).

As for now, the royal crown Zechariah shapes is to be placed in the temple as a reminder of this prophecy and as a testimony to the coming one (14).

The arrival of gold and silver from afar will be God's proof

he is speaking through Zechariah. All God has promised for this
generation "will happen if you diligently obey the Lord your God"
(15).

III. Chapter 7, 8. Messages on Fasting

The Question; 7:1–3. The Hebrew text of verse 2 is difficult. It
is best understood as telling of a royal officer (a *regum meleck*)
named Bethel–Sharezer (cf. Jer. 39:3) who leads a delegation from
the large Hebrew community that still remains in the land of captivity. He comes to inquire of the priests and prophets. His question:
Now that the temple is nearly rebuilt, should they continue to
keep the holy days set aside by the exiles for fasting and mourning
the events associated with the fall of Jerusalem?

The First Sermon; 7:4–14. The delegation is not answered directly. Instead a word from God comes to Zechariah "to all the
people of the land and to the priests" (4). What is the purpose
of their fasting? Is it really for the Lord? Or is it an expression
of their own needs, like eating and drinking? Fasting must not
be motivated by self-interest but by concern for the glory of God
(4–17). Then, in a second word from God, Zechariah calls on
Israelis to recognize the basic issue facing them. God's real concern,
as shown in the history of Judah before her fall, is that his people
"administer true justice; show mercy and compassion to one another." What God wants is that they "do not oppress the widow
or the fatherless, the alien or the poor. In your hearts do not
think evil of one another" (9,10). The issue is not fasts, but the
willingness of this people to commit to a life that pleases God.

How do you think the teaching of this chapter applies to
us today? What besides questions of fasting might the chapter
be applied to?

Relevant Sayings; 8:1–8. A series of sayings of the Lord assures
his people that they are the objects of his love. The hard-heartedness
of their fathers (7:11–14) has not swayed the Lord from his commitment to Jerusalem and her people.

The Second Sermon; 8:9–17. Zechariah's second sermon looks
ahead and twice contrasts the future with the unhappy past. The
people are encouraged to finish the temple with the promise that
the poverty they have known (see "background" to Haggai, p.
419) will be turned to prosperity (9–13). Zechariah also contrasts
God's intentions. God had determined disaster for their unresponsive forefathers. He has determined blessing for them (14,15). Again

Zechariah urges the people to live godly lives in a just and loving community (16,17).

The Answer; 8:18,19. God looks ahead and promises a day when the fasts they find burdensome now will become "joyful and glad occasions, and happy festivals."

I. Conclusion to Part One (8:20–23)

Zechariah looks forward to the day when all nations will seek the Lord and come to Jerusalem to find him. In those days God's presence will be plain among his people.

V. Intervention of the Lord (9:1–11:17)
The Shepherd Rejected

The second part of the book (chapters 9 through 14) contains two groups of apocalyptic oracles. In these poetic sections the prophet describes events associated with the end times. His particular focus is on how God will intervene in history to bring about the time of blessing which all the OT prophets foresee. The first of these two sections describes the Good Shepherd sent to and rejected by Israel.

Jubilation in Jerusalem; 9:1–9. The marauding forces of the peoples who have oppressed Jerusalem will be crushed, and God will keep personal watch over his own.

The King Arrives; 9:9–10. Shouts of joy greet the promised king as he enters Jerusalem on a donkey, bringing salvation (9). This prophecy has been fulfilled in Jesus' triumphal entry (Matt. 21; John 12). The program of the king awaits Jesus' second coming: "He will proclaim peace to the nations. His rule will extend from sea to sea" (10).

Jubilation and Prosperity; 9:11–10:1. God appears to keep his blood covenant with his people. This marks the beginning of blessings. He "will appear over them . . . and the Lord will shield them" (14,15). Then "they will sparkle in his hand like jewels in a crown" (16).

Rebuke for Deceitful Leaders; 10:2,3a. In all the Prophets "shepherd" is a term applied to spiritual and political leaders. Because of the deceit of the leaders at this coming time, "my anger burns against the shepherds, and I will punish the leaders."

Jubilation and Restoration; 10:3b–11:3. The time of restoration is marked by God's own intervention. Then he himself "will care for his flock, the house of Judah" (10:3). God promises to redeem, restore, and return his scattered people, for "I had not rejected them, for I am the Lord their God" (10:6).

Fate of the Good Shepherd; 11:4–17. What happens when God comes to fulfill his promise? In a difficult allegory God speaks to a person yet unnamed (4) and tells him to pasture the flock "marked for slaughter." They are so marked by their own leaders, who think only of the profit they can gain by selling out their people (4–6).

But when the good shepherd comes to care for the flock, and "particularly for the oppressed of the flock," he is rejected! Though he rids them of false shepherds and seeks to guide them with grace (favor) and unity (union), he is detested by his sheep! The only pay they offer is "thirty pieces of silver." Strikingly, this price is the amount set in OT law as compensation to be paid for a dead slave (Exod. 21:32)! And the price of the good shepherd is thrown "into the house of the Lord to the potter" (13).

The Gospels present this passage as a prophecy about Jesus. He came, announcing himself as the Good Shepherd (John 10:11–18). But the flock he came to pasture detested him. The priests weighed out the price of a dead slave to Jesus' betrayer (Matt. 26:14–16). And later, after Jesus' death, the coins were brought back by a remorseful Judas and thrown into the temple. The chief priests picked up the coins and "decided to use the money to buy a potter's field as a burial place for foreigners" (Matt. 27:1–10). Thus the words of Zechariah found fulfillment in Jesus, as did the similar prophecy of Jeremiah (32:6–9).

With the Good Shepherd slain, the staffs of grace and unity are broken. He is replaced by worthless shepherds (14–17).

Thus the first section of apocalyptic oracles ends with the death of the Good Shepherd. But his death is not the end, for evil has not and will not overcome.

Chapters 12–14. The Final Intervention of the Lord
The Suffering

The second block of apocalyptic teaching continues from the first, and is linked with it (see "structure," p. 424). Now, however, the emphasis is on the suffering associated with the final intervention as the Lord acts to establish himself king of all.

Jubilation in Jerusalem; 12:1–9. God pictures a time when all the nations gather against Jerusalem and Judea. It is then that

God will act to shield those who live in Jerusalem. Her enemies will be consumed, but she will remain intact.

Mourning for the One Pierced; 12:10–13:1. Zechariah pictures a day of national conversion when the people of Jerusalem are "cleansed from sin and impurity" (13:1). This comes when "they look on me, the one they have pierced" (cf. John 19:34–37). Then the Good Shepherd is at last recognized, and all the people of Israel weep and mourn for the one they once rejected.

Rejection of Deceitful Leaders; 13:2–6. In that day all false prophets and deceitful leaders will be rejected. The false prophets who flee, when asked their occupation, will claim to be nothing but farmhands. When the self-inflicted scars associated with serving idols (cf. 1 Kings 18:28) are pointed out, these shamed prophets will lie and call them nothing but scars from wounds suffered in a brawl at the house of some friend!

The Shepherd Slaughtered; 13:7–9. Again the prophet returns to the death of the Shepherd. But this time the focus is on what happens to the sheep after his death. They are to be scattered, with two thirds struck down and only a third to live. This same language and proportion is mentioned by the pre-exilic prophets. It seems that the death of the Shepherd will initiate another scattering among the nations: a time of exile and suffering to last until the Shepherd returns.

Cataclysm in Jerusalem; 14:1–15. Again the prophet returns to the final battle. All nations are gathered against God's people. But God himself intervenes and fights for them, his "feet on the mount of Olives" (4). The picture of the split mountain and of the streams of living waters which flow from Jerusalem matches the picture of the new Jerusalem drawn in Ezekiel 40–48.

The destruction of the armies of the nations proves decisively that "the Lord will be king over the whole earth. On that day there will be one Lord, and his name the only name" (9).

The Lord King over All; 14:16–20. In the end all nations will go up to worship God in Jerusalem, and the city will be holy to the Lord.

MALACHI
The Faith That Waits

Malachi is the last of the OT prophets. He ministers to a people who have lost their sense of excitement and lost touch with God. The edge of eager expectation aroused by Haggai and Zechariah is dulled now, and the people have drifted from full commitment to God. For all of us who are caught in a waiting kind of life, Malachi has an important message.

Date and Author. Malachi is another of the unknown men of the OT. We have his words and through them can sense the character of his faith. But we know nothing more of his background and heritage.

We do know that Malachi is one of three prophets who ministered to the small community of Jews which returned from Babylonian captivity to live huddled around Jerusalem's ruins. His relationship with Ezra and Nehemiah has never been established, so the date of his book must be given in broad terms as originating some time between 465 B.C. and 430 B.C..

Background. The little company of some 50,000 Jews who returned from Babylon has been settled in Judah for over 70 years. These have been years of struggle and poverty, lightened only by the months of enthusiasm stirred by Haggai and Zechariah as they urged the completion of the temple of the Lord. The temple was finished, and the sacrifices and rituals of worship reestablished. But now the years slowly drift past. The Messiah Haggai and Zechariah spoke of has not come. The shaking of the nations those prophets promised has not arrived. Settled down over the years of waiting, all excitement about relationship with God has drained away. Even the worship of God now seems an empty chore.

This is the background against which Malachi speaks, and it is to a now lukewarm community of believers that he addresses his call to return to intimate relationship with God.

Structure. The whole book is an exploration of the relationship between a lukewarm people and their God. Through his hard-hitting blunt messages, the prophet weaves a series of unasked questions which nevertheless reveal the attitudes and actions of the Israelis.

Another feature is that 47 of the 55 verses involve God speaking with first person directness to his people. Thus Malachi is essentially

a reasoned call by God to his people to be faithful during a time
when heaven seems silent and still.

Outline

Value. Malachi contains a message to believers of all times. When
our relationship with God seems unreal, or unimportant, we can
turn to this prophet. In his teaching we can see the symptoms
that accompany drifting faith and also discover how to return to
a vital relationship with the Lord.

Chapter 1:1–5. The Chosen People

The book begins with an affirmation by God of love for his
people. This is particularly significant. It immediately establishes
the basis on which God seeks to relate to believers. It is love
that binds God to his own: it is love that God seeks from his
own.

But God's affirmation of love draws an incredulous response:
"How have you loved us?"

The next verses return to the covenant God gave to Abraham,
Isaac, Jacob, and their descendants (see *Covenant, OT,* p. 51). Looking back to the patriarchs God reminds his people, "Jacob have
I loved, and Esau have I hated" (2, 3). "Love" here is used in an
elective sense: God has chosen to transmit the covenant promises
through Jacob. The "love/hate" formula is reflected in wills of
OT times to communicate a parent's desire for distribution of property between family members. The claim of one is established;
claims of the other are decisively rejected.

Current history demonstrates the continuation of that elective
love. The descendants of Esau (Edom) were driven from their lands
by the Nabateans. Their ruins will never be rebuilt. But Jerusalem
has been rebuilt! The presence of this people in their land, with
the temple standing on its old site, is living proof of God's love.

II. The Chosen People . . . Neglect God

The love God has for his people is stable, but their love has cooled. How is this shown? First, by a pattern of neglect of God.

Neglect by the People; 1:6–14. Cooling love is clearly shown by priest and people who bring blind or crippled animals for sacrifice. They would never offer such an animal to their governor!

When people find it a burden to worship and offer God only what they do not want themselves, then clearly their love for him has drained away. God is a great king, and he deserves our very best!

Neglect by the Priests; 2:1–9. Cooling love by the priests is shown in their neglect of their ministry, and by drifting in their private lives. OT law charges the priests with responsibility to teach the law to the people, and to give guidance to individuals who seek to know God's will for their lives. But in Malachi's day these men not only fail to instruct others, they neglect to keep the law themselves! Commitment to living by God's Word is essential if anyone is to experience a personal, meaningful relationship with the Lord.

Chapter 2:10–16. The Chosen People . . . Break Commitments

God's faithfulness to his covenant promises is a clear indication of his love. But Judah has broken covenant, and this unfaithfulness indicates her loss of love. Intermarriage with pagans from the surrounding nations is an example of unfaithfulness to covenant relationship with God (10–12). But unfaithfulness also finds expression in the easy divorces some obtain as their wives grow older (14). God does "hate divorce," as unfaithfulness to life long commitment. When a people become unfaithful in their relationship to God, breakdown of relationships with one another will inevitably follow.

Chapter 2:17–3:5. The Chosen People . . . Doubt God's Involvement

Another indication of a drift from God is expressed in a cynical query the prophet picks up from the attitude of his countrymen. "Where is the God of justice?" Because God's hand is not seen in dramatic intervention in human affairs, the people begin to doubt his presence. But God reminds them that he *is* coming (3:2). When he does come it will be with judgment for those evil-doers who

now feel free to oppress others and have lost their fear of God
(3:2–5).

Chapter 3:6–4:3. The Chosen People . . . Doubt God's Significance

The drifting people of Malachi's day exhibit a hard-heartedness
all too familiar to God. He urges this generation to return to him,
but again they ask incredulously, "How are we to return?" They
are unable to see that they have turned away!

But the failure of the people to bring ordained tithes to the
temple for the support of the priests and temple sacrifices proves
that they doubt the significance of God in their lives. Their failure
to put God first is evidence of the low priority they give to relationship with the Lord.

But in Malachi's day, as in every other, there are individuals
who are spiritually sensitive. They respond to Malachi's message,
while the community as a whole remains dull to God's word. The
prophet's summary here is significant and epitomizes one of the
major messages of the OT about the personal nature of faith.

"Then those who feared the Lord talked with each other, and
the Lord listened and heard. A scroll of remembrance was written
in his presence concerning those who feared the Lord and honored
his name. 'They will be mine,' says the Lord Almighty, 'in the
day when I make up my treasured possession. I will spare them,
just as in compassion a man spares his son who serves him. And
you will again see the distinction between the righteous and the
wicked, between those who serve God and those who do not' "
(3:16–18).

When the day of the Lord comes, the reality of God's involvement in every life, and his significance to us all, will be fully known.

Chapter 4:4–6. Exhortation

The book closes with an exhortation to remember the law of
God while they wait for the promise of his coming.

There is also the promise of a prophet, an Elijah, who will
call God's people back to morality—or else God will come and
strike the earth with a curse.

Look at each of the questions Malachi puts in the mouth
of his people (1:6; 1:7; 2:14; 2:17; 3:6; 3:8; 3:13). How do
they reveal a drift from a love relationship? How does each suggest
we take corrective action to deepen our relationship with the Lord?

BETWEEN THE TESTAMENTS
Centuries of Preparation

Over 400 years passed between the writing of Malachi, the final book of our OT, and that bright winter night of 4 or 5 B.C. when the angels announced the birth of the Savior. These were silent centuries. No new prophet appeared to unveil more of God's plan. No more marvelous promises were given. But as the long years drifted by, God was at work. He was gradually shaping both world history and the Jewish homeland toward that time when a child born would also be the Son given (Isa. 9:6).

When we understand something of what was happening during those years, we gain fresh insights into the Gospels and the world which they describe.

World Powers in Palestine

Just as Daniel had revealed (see p. 364 f), empire followed empire as history marched toward God's appointed time. The Babylonian empire fell to the Persian. The Persian fell to the great Greek conqueror, Alexander. On Alexander's death in 323 B.C., his empire was divided between four of his generals. Although the world was no longer unified politically, Greek language and culture spread throughout. This was one of the most significant of God's preparatory steps. When the time came for the gospel to be preached throughout the world, there was a common tongue in which all men could hear and read the Word.

But in the meantime, Palestine lay squeezed between two of the empires carved out by Alexander's generals. To the south lay Egypt, under the rule of the Ptolemies. To the north and east lay Syria, dominated by the Seleucids. Nothing was more sure than the certainty that the Jewish homeland would once again be the focus of constant rivalry between two great powers.

For 122 years, from 320 B.C., to 198 B.C., the Ptolemies dominated Palestine. These were good years for the Jews. The faith of Israel was permitted and even encouraged, and the Jewish Scriptures were translated into Greek, in order that the many Jews in Egypt who understood only Greek could know the OT.

But finally, in 198 B.C., one of the many attempts by the Seleucids to win Palestine succeeded. Antiochus III defeated Egypt and replaced the pro-Egyptian high priest with a man named Jason. Jason was not only pro-Syrian but also was eager to make Jerusalem over on the pattern of a Greek city. Such Hellenization would involve acceptance of Greek dress, language, names, and morality. It was fiercely resisted by those Jews who rejected pagan ways and values.

Revolt against the politician-priest, Jason, led to a confrontation of the Jews with their Seleucid masters. A Syrian army was sent to take Jerusalem and the practice of Judaism was made a capital offense!

These brutal steps failed to stamp out the faith. Instead it stimulated a heroic resistance movement led by a man named Mattathias and his five sons. This family, the Hasmoneans, are best known by their nickname: the "Maccabees" (or "The Hammer!").

The Maccabean Revolt

The Maccabean revolt was not simply a war of liberation. It was also a civil war—a struggle between those committed to the ancient faith and the God of Israel, against the Hellenistic Jews who wanted to adopt the dominant world culture. Years of guerilla warfare preceded the decisive battle which defeated the Syrians. The Hasmonean family took back the high priesthood, purified the temple, which had been desecrated by the Syrians, and began to rebuild Jerusalem. But there was no peace for the family. The smaller nations that ringed Judea seemed always ready for war. Within the country opposition grew from the very Hassidim, or "pious," who had supported the revolt. Ambitious and hungry for political power, the Hasmonean family did maintain a kind of independent rule in Palestine for about a hundred years (143–37 B.C.). But the country was never truly free. By the time Jesus was born, power had passed out of Jewish hands entirely into the firm grip of the greatest empire the world has ever known: that of Rome.

In Jesus' day the old factions still exist. The men we know from the Gospels as Sadducees, associated with the priesthood and politically oriented, are the descendents of the Hasmoneans. Their zealous and religiously conservative opponents—the Pharisees of our Gospels—are in the tradition of the Hassidim (the Pious) who fought so strenuously against pagan culture.

But by the time of Jesus, neither Sadducees nor Pharisees held political power. That had passed into the firm hands of the conquerors who reached out from Italy to grasp the world.

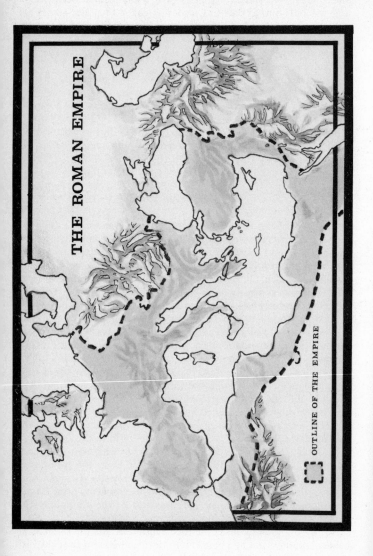

THE ROMAN EMPIRE

OUTLINE OF THE EMPIRE

Rome and the Herods

Palestine seethed with wars, rebellions, feuds, plots and counter-plots. But in the West an iron empire was hammered out—an empire which imposed its *pax* (peace) on Palestine as well as on the rest of the known world. That brutal peace entered Palestine with the invading army of Pompey in 63 B.C. At first vassal rulers were allowed to govern, and the fighting and rivalries continued. Then came one of the most astute plotters of history, Antipater. He was an Idumean, a descendant of the same Esau who once despised his birthright (Gen. 27). Antipater, by always taking the Roman side, managed to remain a dominant though hated figure in Judea. He also managed to have the Roman senate confirm his son, Herod, king of the Jews. Herod soon would earn his title, "The Great."

The twenty-six-year-old Herod took his kingdom by force. He held it by a mixture of brutality, scheming, and good administration. It is this Herod who ordered the butchery of the infants around Bethlehem in a futile effort to kill the Christ child (Matt. 2:7–23). His sons are the adult Herods mentioned in the Gospels as Jesus' contemporaries. And the Jerusalem temple which Herod beautified in an effort to silence Jewish grumbling is the temple in whose courts Jesus preached.

Herod's royal power was not absolute. There were Roman governors and Roman armies in this as in the other provinces. After A.D. 6 men like the man we read of in the Gospels, Pontius Pilate, would represent Rome's life-or-death authority in the land God had set aside for his chosen people.

The complex political history of Palestine and of the wider ancient world came into focus in Jesus' day. The world was uniquely prepared for the gospel. In the Holy Land, decades of struggle for the OT faith had fanned a deep desire for the promised Messiah. During the forty years that encompassed Jesus' life on earth, the iron fist of Rome maintained an uneasy peace in the violent Holy Land. At last there were quiet years during which Jesus could grow up and undertake his adult ministry.

But God's purposes in history are most clearly seen in his preparation of the wider world for the spread of the gospel. Greek culture and language linked the peoples of the world together, providing a common tongue in which the Word could be preached and written. Rome's armies maintained peace between peoples who had known nothing but war. There were no national borders to stop travelers: missionaries wandered freely over eastern and western

Roman Emperors	Roman Governors of Judea	
AUGUSTUS (27 B.C.–A.D. 14) who ordered the census related to Jesus' birth	Coponius	(A.D. 6–10)
	M. Ambivius	(A.D. 10–13)
	A. Rufus	(A.D. 13–15)
TIBERIUS (A.D. 14–A.D. 37) under whom Jesus ministered and was crucified	V. Gratus	(A.D. 15–26)
	PONTIUS PILATE	(A.D. 26–36)
	Marcellus	(A.D. 36–38)
CALIGULA (A.D. 37–A.D. 41) demanded that he be worshiped	Maryllus (Herod Agrippa I king between)	(A.D. 38–41)
CLAUDIUS (A.D. 41–A.D. 54) expelled Jews from Rome (Acts 18:2)	king between)	(A.D. 41–44)
	Cuspis Fadus	(A.D. 44–46)
	T. Alexander	(A.D. 46–48)
NERO (A.D. 54–A.D. 68) persecuted Christians, martyred Paul and Peter	V. Cumanus	(A.D. 48–52)
	M. Felix	(A.D. 52–59)
	P. Festus	(A.D. 59–61)
VESPASIAN (A.D. 69–A.D. 79) crushed Jewish revolt, city and Jerusalem Temple destroyed by his son Titus in 70 A.D.	Albinus	(A.D. 61–65)
	G. Florus	(A.D. 65–70)

Mediterranean lands (see map. p. 438). Good roads, protected sea routes, and a common coinage all made for speedy transmission of the NT's message across thousands of miles. At no time before or since have all these factors blended as they did in the first century. History had moved as God planned, and God was ready to step into a history prepared for the appearance of the Son.

First Century Judaism

The Jewish people remained fiercely nationalistic and passionately divided during the Roman years. The hatred of those without and the jealousies of those within the nation were as pronounced as during the years of struggle against the Seleucids. While there was a true zeal for the law, as it was understood, the Judaism of the first century was not molded on the classic pattern described by Moses. New groups and institutions had emerged; new beliefs and ideas formed the backdrop for the land described in the Gospels.

The Sects

All sects held continuing respect for the revealed law of the OT, but there were differing interpretations of that law.

The Sadducees. This was the priestly party: aristocratic, politi-

THE HERODIAN FAMILY

GENERATION I	GENERATION II	GENERATION III	GENERATION IV

HEROD THE GREAT
King of Judea
37–4 B.C.
Matthew 2:1-19
Luke 1:5

GENERATION II

Son of **Doris**
Antipater

Sons of **Mariamne**
Aristobulus
Alexander

Son of Mariamne of Simon
Herod Philip
4 B.C.–A.D. 34
(First husband of Herodias
—Matt. 14:3, Mark 6:17)

Sons of **Malthace**
*HEROD ANTIPAS
Tetrarch of Galilee
4 B.C.–A.D. 39
Luke 3:1, 19-20, Mark 6:14-29
Matt. 14:1-11
Luke 13:31-33, 23:7-12

*ARCHELAUS
Ethnarch of Judea
4 B.C.–A.D. 6
Matt. 2:22

Son of **Cleopatra**
*HEROD PHILIP
Tetrarch of Iturea
and Trachonitis
4 B.C.–A.D. 34
Luke 3:1

GENERATION III

Herod of Chalcis
A.D. 41-48

*HEROD AGRIPPA I
King of Judea
A.D. 37-44
Acts 12:1-24

Herodias
Consort of Herod Antipas
Mark 6:17
Matt. 14:3

GENERATION IV

Bernice
became consort of her
brother
Acts 25:13

*HEROD AGRIPPA II
Tetrarch of Chalcis and
of northern territory
A.D. 50-70
Acts 25:13—26:32

Drusilla
married *FELIX
procurator of Judea
A.D. 52(?)-59(?)
Acts 24:24

Salome
Matt. 14:1-11
Mark 6:14-29

Reigning rulers of New Testament note are in capitals, wives
and relatives by marriage are in bold face. Other members
of the house designated by *.

cally minded, rational, pragmatic. They doubted the supernatural and found it best to reject the idea of personal immortality as well as the notion of angels. They stressed the earliest books of the OT, but their cold and moralistic version of Hebrew faith left little room for a love relationship with God. They looked down on the passionate Pharisees and had contempt for the oral traditions which so delighted the other major sect. As pragmatic and political men, the Sadducees worked for an accommodation with Rome and the Herods which would preserve their own status and powers.

The Pharisees. This passionate and committed group of men were extremely influential with the general populace, who admired their zeal and looked to them as spiritually superior. It's likely that the beliefs of the Pharisees were in much greater harmony with those of the people as a whole than were the beliefs of the Sadducees.

The Pharisees were supernaturalists. They firmly believed in angels and demons, expected a bodily resurrection, and were convinced of personal immortality. In addition they valued the Scriptures highly. They believed that God wanted his people to carefully keep every small detail of the law. Their high level of commitment may have been admirable, but their focus on obedience to the law's details blinded them to the grace and mercy that shone through the OT. Salvation was not so much a matter of a relationship with a forgiving God as it was a climb toward perfection by constant efforts to obey. The stress on obedience was complicated by the fact that the Pharisees tried to keep not only the written law but an oral law, handed down by a tradition they believed went back to Moses himself.

In the NT the Pharisees who challenged Jesus so constantly and who tried to trap him are often called "hypocrites." Not all were hypocrites. First century documents report the nicknames given different types of Pharisees, which shows that the pretenders were recognized! Seven types noted include:

1. "Shoulder" Pharisees—who wear good deeds like a badge for others to notice.
2. "Wait-a-little" Pharisees—who ostentatiously ask others to pause while they do some good deed.
3. "Blind" Pharisees—who bruise themselves bumping into walls while their eyes are closed to avoid seeing a woman.
4. "Pestle" Pharisees—who hang their heads and fix their eyes on the ground to avoid temptations.

5. "Ever-reckoning" Pharisees—who keep count of good deeds to make sure they more than cover failures.
6. "God-fearing" Pharisees—who are truly righteous.
7. "God-loving" Pharisees—who have a personal relationship with God like that of Abraham.

In many ways the Pharisees were admirable men, but, as Paul points out, their zeal for God was not in accord with knowledge.

The Zealots. This terrorist group urged violence against Rome and a bloody war of revolution. One of the twelve Jesus chose as disciples is called "Simon the Zealot."

The Essenes. This group is not mentioned in the NT. They were an ascetic brotherhood which established communities where they could live quietly, by strict rules, while waiting the coming of Messiah.

The Common People. By far the greatest group, most people in Judea lived simply, worshiped God as best they could, took part in the temple sacrifices and synagogue. It is quite certain that they were closest to the Pharisees in the way they understood their religion.

Institutions

In the time of Jesus several institutions dominated the life of the people of Judea and are reflected in our Gospels.

The Sanhedrin. This group of 70 men was the highest court and Jewish governing authority. It was dominated by the aristocratic priesthood and thus packed with the Sadducee party. After Herod's death in 6 A.D., when Judea officially became a Roman province, this group controlled the internal affairs of the nation. Only when it came to the death penalty were Jewish leaders forced to appeal to the Roman governor, for him to pronounce sentence. After the rebellion of the Jews in A.D. 66–70 the Sanhedrin was dissolved and stripped of authority. But in the time of Christ the Sanhedrin was the officially sanctioned local governing body.

The Temple. The temple, which Herod expanded and beautified, dominated the Jerusalem of Jesus' day. The sacrifices commanded in the law were made there, and each year the people gathered at the temple for the festivals Israel was commanded to celebrate. Here Jesus came at age twelve, and here he later taught his disciples.

The Synagogue. During the decades that the temple lay destroyed and the Jewish people were captive in Babylon, a Bible study movement sprang up. People gathered weekly for study and teaching, and the synagogue became the social and religious focus of the community. Back in the land, the synagogue was retained as a neighborhood center. Here the children were trained, and here the men and women gathered for worship and for weekly readings of the Scriptures.

Jesus attended his local synagogue and gave a memorable sermon in his home town (Luke 4). As the missionaries later fanned out over the Greek world, they would go to a synagogue on entering any city, to share the good news of the Messiah's coming with the Jewish community first.

Rabbis. This term of respect means literally "my master." By Jesus' day it came to be a title accorded those who were recognized as gifted teachers of the law. Jesus is often called "Rabbi" by those who come to question or to test him. It was the dream of each rabbi to "fulfill"—that is, to explain accurately the meaning of God's Word. Not surprisingly, traditional interpretations were passed down across the generations, leading to the development of an extensive oral tradition.

Literature

The Jews were the people of the Book. It is not surprising that, as their lives were focused on the Scriptures, their thoughts and writings would be also.

Oral Traditions. The teachings of many rabbis during the silent centuries were remembered, memorized, and drawn together in a great body of oral teachings. The Pharisees revered this oral tradition as if it were itself Scripture and held that oral and written law had equal authority. After the time of Jesus, the oral traditions were written out and came to constitute the Talmud.

The Apocrypha. The Talmud was completed after the day of Jesus. But a number of religious writings did exist in the first century. These were read as religious treatises or moral instructions but were never considered to be "Scripture" by the Jewish community. None of them are quoted in the NT, as are the books of the OT.

Some of the apocryphal writings, whose name means "hidden" or "secret," were historical (I Esdras, I Maccabees, 2 Maccabees). Others were romantic novels whose theme was always the vindication by God of his persecuted people (Tobit, Judith, The Rest of Esther, History of Susanna, Bel and the Dragon). There were also philosophical books modeled after the Proverbs (Wisdom of Solomon, Ecclesiasticus), and devotional works (Song of the Three

Holy Children, Prayer of Manassas). These writings are included in some Catholic Bibles.

There are other Jewish writings as well, found by archaeologists or mentioned in first century documents, which reveal the development of Jewish faith, devotion, and imagination as the centuries of waiting slowly drifted past.

Summary. It would be a mistake to think of first century Judaism as a single, unified faith. There were common elements to Jewish theology. The law was revered by all. But within the broad framework provided by a common Scripture there were great differences in theology and many conflicts of values. Not everyone believed that a Messiah would appear to deliver Israel from Gentile domination. And not everyone hoped that it was true! For many who followed the legalism of the Sadducees or Pharisees, the Jewish faith was tragically drained of the dimension of a deeply personal faith. Reliance on human efforts and self-righteousness replaced reliance on the forgiveness God promised to those who would trust him. Few were spiritually sensitive enough to recognize the Savior when he did come. And many hated him as too great a challenge to their distorted beliefs to be allowed to live.

RELATIONSHIP BETWEEN THE
OLD AND NEW TESTAMENTS

The Old and New Testaments of our Bible form one organic whole. Together they tell the story of God's relationship with man and with the universe. Each testament looks back to the same Creator God. Each affirms that history is nothing less than the gradual unfolding of his good plan for mankind. Each looks forward to a time of endless blessing when God's rule is established and evil is eternally vanquished. The NT writers never doubted that they told one story with the OT. Over and over again they quote the writings of the older Scriptures, showing how first century events fulfill past prophecy and provide fresh insights into God's revealed purposes and plans. But the relationship between the two testaments is not a simple one. It is complex. And sometimes the basic harmony between the two can be missed as we focus on differences.

Differences between the Two Testaments. There are many obvious differences. The OT revelation came gradually, stretching out over at least a thousand years. Slow step by slow step, new truths were added to earlier revelations in a measured, progressive way. But the NT came with a sudden burst. In just fifty years the canon of the NT was complete!

Other differences are more obvious. The OT talks constantly about one people, Israel, and explores in depth God's relationship with the descendants of Abraham. The OT is land bound: its viewpoint is Palestine, and everything looks outward from that land which God promised to Abraham's seed. But the NT has a universal sweep. Its perspective is the whole world, and its urgent message, the gospel, is to be preached to every tongue and tribe and nation.

The OT looks ahead to a Savior who will rule over a redeemed Israel. The picture of a King from David's family dominates the expectations of the prophets as they describe the promised Messiah. The NT emphasizes a present relationship with God through one we look upon as crucified and risen Lord. We look ahead to Jesus' return, but focus on a gospel message which offers each individual a personal relationship with God through Jesus Christ, and urges each to accept blood-won forgiveness of sins.

The OT emphasis on righteousness and justice are strongly social. People and nations and communities are called on to do justice and correct oppression. The NT emphasis on righteousness is a strongly personal one. The believer is told that he has been made righteous by God, and is now expected to live a holy life, full of active compassion for others.

The OT knows a people whose community is a nation. The NT knows a new community, shaped from men and women who have different origins, nationalities, races, and social position. This community, both an extended family and a living body, exists as a colony in every nation, a living testimony to the living God.

These are just a few of the many contrasts which might be pointed out, and which so surprise the person who knows the OT well when he or she turns to the NT. The differences seem so great! Are these truly halves of one great, harmonious revelation?

The Complex Plan of God. In looking at the two testaments, it is important to keep in mind what the apostle Paul calls the "manifold wisdom of God" (Eph. 3:10). The word "manifold" means complex, or multi-faceted. It is as if we see a sparkling diamond and pick it up to examine it. The more closely we look, the more we realize that the brilliance of the gem is caused by the cutting of many complex facets, each catching and reflecting the light in a slightly different way. This is the nature of God's plan for mankind. He did not shape a single flat surface, like some mirror, but he designed history with great complexity, so that the full scope of his wisdom and his goodness could be brilliantly revealed.

It's important then that we look for complex relationships between the testaments, not simple ones. Although there is a basic shape to the reality revealed in God's Word, the plan and purpose of God is multifaceted rather than flat and plain.

The Basic Shape in Revelation. There are many dimensions of reality as revealed by Scripture that are completely consistent between the OT and the NT. These provide the basic shape, or the framework, of the one revelation given in the two.

In both testaments God is the underlying reality. It is he who has created the universe and shaped our planet to sustain life. This God created human beings to be the special object of his love. And he shaped us in his image so we would have a capacity for fellowship with him and with one another. In both testaments we learn that sin has shattered our fellowship with God and warped our relationships with one another. There is a principle of evil which warps and twists everything that men and societies do, confirmed in history and in each individual's life by the awful impact of separation from God.

Both testaments agree in their vision of God. As a moral being

God is committed to deal with evil. As a loving being, he is committed to care even for the twisted caricature of humanity that sin has made of man. Both testaments also agree that God has a plan. The universe not only sprang from his act of creation; it is also moving toward his intended culmination. He will deal with sin, the two agree. He will cleanse the universe of evil, and he will redeem man and society. The wounds of sin will be cured, the scars removed, and a transformed humanity will move at last into an eternity of joy-filled fellowship with God.

This common framework links our Old and New Testaments into one indissoluble whole. God's unshakable love and his commitment to redemption are the unchallenged foundation on which God's complex plan securely rests.

Harmony in the Differences between the Testaments. There are very apparent differences in significant details between the Old and New Testaments. There is also a common framework for both testaments; a single foundation of understanding about who God is and who mankind is, and where the world has come from and where history is going. But even more striking, the very differences between the testaments show an underlying harmony! The OT focus is on Israel, but God's plan always was that through Israel all mankind might be blessed (Gen. 12:3; Isa. 11:10). The NT focuses on a different kind of community, the church, but even in the NT God's ultimate plan for Israel is affirmed (Rom. 11). And in both testaments, the common principle is that God deals with believers not just individually but in community!

In the OT "salvation" is primarily deliverance from enemies in this world. In the NT "salvation" focuses primarily on forgiveness and personal redemption from sin. The OT knew and spoke of forgiveness, and the NT knows and speaks of a present deliverance to be worked out by God's people, in the assurance that it is God who is working his good purposes in each situation. In both Testaments the common principle is that God is the author of salvation: it is by his action in history that his people are rescued from dangers beyond their power to overcome.

The chart on the next page shows just a few of the "differences" between the testaments which are, in fact, simply different facets of a complex plan that express the same basic truths about God through both testaments. Understood as different ways of expressing common realities, we can see even in the "differences" testimony to the unity of these two great blocks of revelation, which show us one good and loving God.

History Is Not Over Yet. One last important consideration helps

Illustrative Differences between the Testaments and Unifying Principles Underlying Them

Unifying Principle	Old Testament Emphasis	New Testament Emphasis
Sin Warps Humanity	In Society	Individually
God Is Committed to Righteousness	Justice	Holiness, Compassion
God Commits Himself to His People	Abrahamic Covenant	New Covenant
God Is the Author of Salvation	Redemption from Egypt	Christ's Cross
God Deals with Man in Community	The Nation Israel	The Church as Family, as One Body
Relationship with God Is a Gift	Received through Faith	Received through Faith
Relationship with God Is Expressed in Daily Life	By Obedience	By Obedience
Believers Are Given God's Guidance for Daily Living	Mosaic Law	Holy Spirit
Jesus Is the Focal Point in God's Plan	As Coming Messiah	As Crucified Savior
	As Future King	As Lord
God Acts As Judge	Of Nations, Cultures	Of Individuals
History Is Moving toward a Culmination	After Messiah and World Judgments, Endless Blessing	When Jesus Returns to Judge the World, Endless Blessing

us see another vital fact about the two testaments. Each of them looks forward eagerly to history's end. Much of what each one speaks of so expectantly will not be fully understood until the end comes, and all the threads of God's great and complex tapestry have been woven into one whole.

For instance, the OT prophets spoke often about Jesus and revealed many details about his first coming. But what they said of him, and how it all fit together, could not be understood until Jesus was born, lived, died and rose again. Then history showed how the prophetic Word fit together, and how apparent differences were resolved.

It is the same for us today. Many of the apparent differences between the testaments seem contradictory because they deal with a future that we cannot yet see clearly. When history has run its course, and God's plan has been worked out in full, then the unity and majesty of the story told in Old and New Testaments will be known by man.

The ruins of the Roman Forum

Excavation and ruins at Corinth

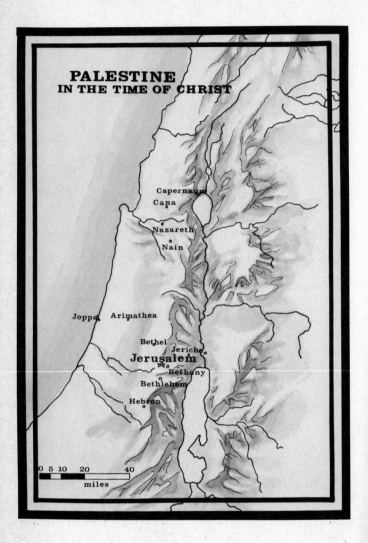

PALESTINE
IN THE TIME OF CHRIST

Capernaum
Cana

Nazareth
Nain

Joppa   Arimathea

Bethel
Jericho
Jerusalem
Bethany
Bethlehem

Hebron

0 5 10 20   40
miles

THE GOSPELS
Four Views of Jesus Christ

The long silence of God was shattered one winter night in 4/5 B.C. Angels announced to shepherds what Gabriel had whispered months before to Mary. The time had come. God was about to enter the world he had created, in the Person of his Son.

A little less than half our NT is made up of four Gospels: four tellings of the story of the birth, life, teachings, death and resurrection of Jesus.

Each Gospel deals with well-known facts, told and retold by the first century evangelists. Each was written by a person who was an eye-witness to most of the events described, or who had carefully questioned other eye witnesses. But the four Gospels, for all their common elements, are not the same. Each is shaped for a different audience in the ancient world; each gives a slightly different slant to the greatest story ever told. Matthew provides careful proofs to show Jewish readers that Jesus truly did fulfill the words of the OT prophets. Luke's equally careful presentation speaks to the hellenistic world, revealing Jesus as a historical rather than mythical figure, who is the ideal human being as well as the Son of God.

Three of the four Gospels are closely linked by content and manner of expression (Matthew, Mark, Luke). These three are called the synoptic Gospels, from a Greek term meaning "common view." Their many common elements have led some to believe that each writer drew from an earlier written source, or from Mark's "prototype" Gospel. But it is more likely the similarities rest on an established oral tradition. The early church concentrated on relating events and sayings of Jesus as they spread his story outward from Palestine. Many events would be told and retold word for word, typical for the poetry and traditions of the day. Also the authors of the Synoptics knew one another and surely shared their memories.

After all, the land in which Jesus lived and ministered was tiny. For over three years he traveled it, preaching and teaching the crowds as well as instructing his disciples. He would have preached the same sermons many times and repeated the same sayings. Even his healing ministry would have been repeated more than once. In tiny Judea and Galilee, so fervently focused on religion, the

Golgotha. Some scholars think Jesus was crucified here

A carpenter in his shop in Nazareth, where Jesus grew to manhood

reports of his sayings and doings would soon be known by all. (See map of Palestine in Jesus' day. p. 452).

A Harmony of the Events of Jesus' Life

It's difficult to agree on an exact chronology of Jesus' life and ministry. While the Gospels are generally organized in chronological sequence, each author selects and organizes his material for his own purposes and emphasis. In addition, the fact that Jesus must have preached his sermons and shared his illustrations many times during the years of ministry means that authors of the Gospels need not be reporting on exactly the same event even when their descriptions seem to overlap. Nevertheless the Gospels do tell a common story, and it is possible to outline the life of Christ through a harmony of the four Gospels. The harmony beginning on page 456, gives us an overview of the most significant life ever lived.

	Matthew	Mark	Luke	John
IV. GREAT GALILEAN MINISTRY				
Jesus Arrives	4:12–17	1:14	4:14	4:43–45
Heals Nobleman's Son				4:46–54
Calls First Disciples	4:18–22	1:16–20		
Jesus Heals the Sick	8:14–17	1:21–34	4:31–41	
Jesus Travels and Preaches		1:35–39	4:42–44	
Jesus Performs Many Miracles	8:1–4 9:1–17	1:30–3:12	5:1–6:19	
Jesus Confronts Pharisees	12:1–21			
The Twelve Appointed		3:13–19	6:12–16	
The Sermon on the Mount	5:1–7:29		6:20–49	
Jesus Heals a Soldier's Servant	8:5–13		7:1–10	
Jesus Raises a Widow's Son			7:11–17	
John the Baptist Doubts	11:2–30		7:18–35	
Jesus Anointed by a Prostitute			7:36–50	
Jesus Makes Another Tour			8:1–3	
Jesus' Family Protests	12:46–50	3:31–35	8:19–21	
Jesus Speaks in Parables	13:1–53	4:1–34	8:4–18	
Jesus Performs a Series of Miracles	8:23–24 9:18–26	4:35–5:43	8:22–56	
Jesus Rejected at Nazareth	13:54–58	6:1–6		
Disciples Sent Out to Preach	9:36–11:1	6:7–13	9:1–6	
John the Baptist Executed	14:1–12	6:14–29	9:7–9	
The Twelve Return	14:13		9:10	
Jesus Feeds 5,000	14:13–21	6:30–44	9:11–17	6:1–14
Jesus Walks on the Sea	14:22–33	6:45–52		6:15–21
Jesus Teaches on "Uncleanness"	15:1–20	7:1–23		

	Matthew	Mark	Luke	John
Jesus Warns against Pharisee Attitudes and Values			12:1–59	
Jesus at Feast of Dedication				10:22–39
Jesus Warns His Listeners			13:1–35	
Jesus Dines with a Pharisee			14:1–24	
Jesus Tells Cost of Discipleship			14:25–35	
Jesus Teaches on God's Compassion			15:1–32	
Jesus Teaches His Disciples			16:1–17:10	
Jesus Raises Lazarus				11:1–44
Enemies Plot to Kill Jesus				11:45–54
VI. JESUS TRAVELS TOWARD JERUSALEM				
Jesus Teaches About His Return			17:20–37	
Jesus Teaches About Prayer and Faith			18:1–17	
Jesus Teaches on Divorce	19:1–12	10:1–12		
The Rich Young Ruler	19:16–20:16	10:17–31	18:18–30	
Jesus Predicts His Death	20:17–19	10:32–34	18:31–34	
Jesus Teaches on Leadership	20:20–28	10:35–45		
Events Near Jerusalem	20:29–34	10:46–52	18:35–19:28	
Jesus Arrives at Bethany				11:55–12:11
VII. JESUS' LAST WEEK PASSOVER, A.D. 33				
Sunday				
The Triumphal Entry	21:1–9	11:1–10	19:29–40	12:12–19
Jesus Views the City	21:10,11	11:11	19:41–44	

	Matthew	Mark	Luke	John
Monday				
Jesus Curses a Fig Tree	21:18,19	11:12–14		
Jesus Cleanses the Temple	21:12,13	11:15–19	19:45–48	
Healings in the Temple	21:14–17			
Tuesday				
The Fig Tree Is Withered	21:19–22	11:20–25		
Jesus Challenged by the Elders	21:23–22:46	11:27–12:37	20:1–44	
Pharisees Condemned by Jesus	23:1–39	12:38–40	20:45–47	
The Widow Gives Her Mite		12:41–44	21:1–4	
Greeks Try to See Jesus				12:20–36
Jews Reject Jesus' Claims				12:37–50
Jesus Teaches on History's End	24,25	13:1–37	21:5–38	
Jesus Predicts Crucifixion	26:1–5	14:1,2	22:1,2	
Jesus Anointed by Mary	26:6–13	14:3–9		12:2–8
Judas Agrees to Betray Jesus	26:14–16	14:10,11	22:3–6	
Wednesday				
Thursday				
The Passover Meal Held	26:17–29	14:12–25	22:7–30	13:1–38
The Last Supper Teaching				14–16
Jesus' High Priestly Prayer				17
Prayer at Gethsemane	26:36–46	14:32–42	22:39–46	18:1
Jesus Arrested	26:47–56	14:43–52	22:47–53	18:2–12
On Trial before Annas				18:12–14 19–23
On Trial before Caiaphas	26:57–68	14:55–65	22:63–65	18:24
Peter Denies the Lord	26:69–75	14:66–72	22:54–62	18:15–18 25–27
On Trial before the Sanhedrin	27:1	15:1	22:66–71	
Suicide of Judas	27:3–10			

MATTHEW
Gospel of the Servant King

Matthew's Gospel has always been given priority by the church. Its richly textured portrait of Jesus, so clearly rooted in the OT, makes an ideal bridge between the two testaments. Matthew's Gospel is strongly theological. Directed to the Jewish people, it is designed to demonstrate that Jesus Christ truly is the Messiah promised in the OT. And it explains to a people who were awaiting a conquering king that royal glory is to be first revealed in a suffering servant, and then in disciples who follow the path of servanthood marked out so clearly by our Lord.

Author and Date. This is an early Gospel, written in the first century shortly after the death of Jesus in A.D. 33. The author does not identify himself in the body of the book. But the work has always been known as the Gospel "according to Matthew" and been recognized as Matthew's account of the gospel history.

Intended Audience. Matthew is the Gospel most frequently quoted by the Church Fathers of the first two centuries A.D. Origen sums up the view of the early church in his Ecclesiastical Histories (VI. 14.5): "The first gospel was written by Matthew, who was once a tax collector, but who was afterwards an apostle of Jesus Christ, and it was prepared for the converts from Judaism, and published in the Hebrew tongue." There is some doubt about Matthew's original appearance in Hebrew. But there is no doubt this book was directed to a Jewish audience. Compelling evidence is found in the 53 quotes from OT passages and 76 additional OT allusions. These quotes almost always are argumentative: that is, they are used to prove a point to Jewish readers. Many of the quotes are clearly messianic and are used to show that something in the ministry of Jesus, or some fact about his life and death, fulfill descriptions or predictions made by the prophets when they spoke of the Messiah. For instance:

Matt. 1:23	virgin birth	Isa. 7:14
Matt. 2:6	Bethlehem	Micah 5:2
Matt. 2:15	from Egypt	Jer. 31:15
Matt. 2:23	a Nazarene	Isa. 40:3
Matt. 8:17	bore infirmities	Isa. 53:4
Matt. 11:5	blind healed	Mal. 3:1

Matt. 12:18f	chosen servant	Isa. 42:1f
Matt. 26:64	2nd coming	Dan. 7:13
Matt. 27:34	cross	Ps. 69:21
Matt. 27:35	cross	Ps. 22:18
Matt. 27:39	cross	Ps. 22:7
Matt. 27:43	cross	Ps. 22:8
Matt. 27:46	cross	Ps. 22:1
Matt. 27:48	cross	Ps. 69:21

Matthew the Man. The author is Matthew, also called Levi. We meet him in his own Gospel, in Mark (2:14–17) and in Luke (5:27–32). He is identified as a tax collector, approached one day by Jesus with the commanding invitation, "Follow me!"

Tax collectors in the first century were in the same category as harlots and thieves, placed there by secular writers as well as the writers of the Gospels. These men bid for the right to collect Rome's taxes and then extorted personal fortunes for themselves from their oppressed peoples. In Palestine they were doubly hated: they were collaborators with the foreign enemy! Men such as Levi were scorned by all patriotic men. But Jesus went to Levi's home to share a meal with him and his outcast friends. As expected, the Pharisees eagerly condemned him, until silenced by this response: "It is not the healthy who need a doctor, but the sick. But go and learn what this means: 'I desire mercy, not sacrifice.' For I have not come to call the righteous, but sinners" (Matt. 9:12,13).

The power of mercy is dramatically demonstrated in materialistic Matthew. He left his wealth and his extortion to accept a totally new set of values as a follower of Jesus, and to be a chronicler of the life on earth of God's Servant King (Matt. 10:3).

Major Themes. The *theological* thrust of Matthew's Gospel is clear. The writer demonstrates the fact that Jesus fulfills the OT prophecies about the promised Messiah. A parallel concern is with the kingdom over which Jesus is to reign. Matthew shows that it is both present and future: that God's kingdom is now *and* coming.

There is also an *ethical* theme which runs strongly through this Gospel. Jesus said it to the Pharisees: God desires mercy. The ethical values which underlie the OT law are exposed in Jesus' teaching, as is the fraud of the pious of Jesus' day who exalted the letter of that law but denied its spirit. Matthew thus portrays an ethics of discipleship for those who are willing to become Jesus' followers. In this ethics, the humbleness of quiet compassion far outweighs the proud self-righteousness of those who were thought of as Israel's "holy" men.

A complementary theme is that of *servanthood.* Greatness is found in the ministry of a servant. Even the King of Glory stoops to serve. Thus for all time he makes glorious a simple life which finds it no shame to drop on one's knees to wash a weary traveler's feet.

A final theme is *eschatological.* The kingdom is now, found in a life of servanthood lived as a disciple of the King. But the kingdom is also coming. One day Jesus will return to rule, and then the One we know through Matthew's Gospel as a servant of men will be fully known as King in the glorious exercise of his divine power!

Thematic Outline of Matthew

Chapter	Theme	Contribution
1, 2	Birth of the King	Demonstrates that Jesus is the expected Messiah
3, 4	Baptism and temptation	Demonstrates Jesus' full identity with man—and victory over human weaknesses
5–7	Sermon on the Mount	Contains Jesus' exposition of Kingdom ethics
8–11	Jesus' authority demonstrated	Proves Jesus' authority over all that binds men (8, 9), and shows servant character of His authority (10, 11)
12–15	Growing opposition	Pinpoints opposition in Pharisaism (12, 15), and unexpected form of the Kingdom (13)
16–17	Kingdom's present focus	Develops contrast between expected and present form
18–20	Kingdom greatness	Examines Greatness to emphasize servanthood
21–23	Confrontation	Pronounces the King's judgment on His enemies
24–25	The future Kingdom	Gives Jesus' prophetic promise of the expected Kingdom's appearance
26–27	The King crucified	Records the execution of the King
28	Resurrection	Tells of the King raised to reign

Chapters 1–2. Birth of the King

Just a few short miles from Jerusalem, in a cave that served as stable for an inn, the long wait ends. God acts at last and a child is born, to be God's promised Servant King.

The Genealogy of Jesus; 1:1–17. The genealogy is important. The first thing Jewish believers would demand is proof that Jesus has a right to the messianic throne. Thus Matthew provides proof: Jesus is a descendant of Abraham (see *Covenant*, p. 51), and a descendant of David, with clear right to his throne (see *Davidic Covenant*, p. 177).

The names are organized in three groups of fourteen. It is common to Hebrew genealogy that some names be left out so that other more significant individuals might be emphasized. The first fourteen names culminate with David, the prototype King. The second fourteen end with Jehoiachin (Jeconiah), who forfeited his royal position and was dragged into captivity. The third fourteen ends with Jesus, who will regain the throne and fulfill the royal destiny.

The reference to Joseph deserves special mention. He only is not said to be the "father of" the next individual in line. Instead, Joseph is identified as "husband of Mary, of whom was born Jesus." Jesus inherits a legal right to Israel's throne through his foster father. But he is the Son of God, not Joseph (see *Virgin Birth*).

The Virgin Birth

Matthew and Luke each set down in clear, factual narrative the details of Jesus' birth. Both claim Jesus lacked a human father and was born of Mary, who was a virgin. The Greek term unquestionably means "virgin" and not simply "unmarried." The earliest Christian confessions are explicit: the Jesus the church knows and worships is virgin born. The same testimony is found in the earliest church fathers, who defended this basic doctrine against both Jewish and pagan objections.

But the most compelling evidence to Matthew and to us is biblical. Isaiah promised a virgin-born child who will be "Immanuel," a Hebrew word meaning "with us is God." Isaiah also foresees a promised deliverer who, though born a child, is a son when given (Isa. 9:6). Among the titles given the promised one are clear ascriptions of deity: he is "Mighty God," and "Everlasting Father," even though he is to "reign on David's throne and over his kingdom" as David's descendant (Isa. 9:7). This mystery was finally solved at Bethlehem. There the Son of God was born a child: God and man became one in the mystery of incarnation (See *Incarnation*, p. 542).

The Birth of Jesus; 1:18–24. Matthew emphasizes the unique aspect of Jesus' birth. He was born before Mary and Joseph "came together" (18) or "had union" (25). The Holy Spirit of God quickened Mary for the birth of the child, thus fulfilling the prediction of Isaiah some 700 years before that a virgin would have a child.

The Birth of Jesus

Joseph was told what had happened before the birth, so that he would go through with the marriage when Mary was discovered to be pregnant. Joseph was also told to name the child Jesus, "for he will save his people from their sins" (21). The name Jesus in Hebrew is Joshua and means "savior" or "deliverer." Israel looked for a political savior. But this child sent by God would deal first with mankind's greatest need: before he rules he will deal once for all with sin.

Visit of the Magi; 2:1–12. Some months after Jesus is born, travelers from the east come to Jerusalem asking about the new-born king of the Jews. The travelers are Magi, a class of wise men long associated with government in Persia. Over 500 years before Daniel had been one of this class of highly trained professionals. Now a group appear that has apparently studied Daniel's writings and quite possibly refers to Numbers 24:17 in speaking of the Messiah's "star."

This appearance terrifies Herod. The aged monarch has already killed several of his own sons to protect his throne from imagined threats. The mention of a "king of the Jews" seems to be a clear threat to this Idumean, who rules the Jews only at the pleasure of Rome.

Herod, fearing these Persian king-makers are plotting against him, reacts cleverly. He pretends to believe the story that they come only to worship this one who fulfills prophecy. Herod even aids them: scholars are called and asked where the Scriptures say the coming ruler will be born. The answer is found in Micah 5:2. It is Bethlehem out of which "will come a ruler who will be the shepherd of my people Israel" (6).

The crafty Herod sends the Magi on to Bethlehem to search for the child, first making them promise to report to Herod when they find him, "so I too may go and worship him."

The Magi are guided to the house where the family now lives (11). They find the young child with Mary and bow down to worship him. Herod has feared a political motivation. There is none. These are simply foreigners, men of faith, who believe the Word of God and have traveled for months to see and worship the Christ-child.

With their worship, they also give gifts that characteristically are presented to royalty. There is gold, incense, and an expensive cosmetic oil called myrrh.

The Magi were not shaken by the family's humble circumstances. Faith always looks beyond appearances.

The Magi do not return to Herod. Warned away in a dream, they return home by a different route.

The Escape to Egypt; 2:13–18. Joseph is warned in a dream to send the family to Egypt. Undoubtedly the gifts of the Magi will finance the trip! Joseph does not wait. That very night he rouses Mary and Jesus and leaves for Egypt (14).

The family remains in Egypt until the death of Herod the Great. Herod intended his death to be as bloody as his life. We learn this from other historic documents: angry that no one would mourn his passing, Herod ordered the chief men from every part of his kingdom brought to the palace. Then he commanded that they be slaughtered the moment he died! The Jews might not mourn Herod—but the whole land would weep when Herod died!

Herod's character, so clearly revealed in this last heartless plot, is expressed when the Magi do not return. Herod orders every male child two years old and younger in and around Bethlehem killed! Many die by Herod's cruel decree. But Jesus is safe.

Return to Nazareth; 2:19–23. Joseph is informed of Herod's death by another dream. He brings his family back but fears to settle in Judea, where one of Herod's sons rules. Again he is given divine direction and turns aside to settle in Nazareth of Galilee (see map p. 452). Matthew links each step of these travels to OT passages. He shows that, in detail after detail, the early life of Jesus fulfills prophetic visions of the Messiah and a future which now is being transformed into history.

The OT passages which Matthew quotes, or refers to, give us a fascinating portrait of the person about whom they speak. Look up these passages and from the context make a list of characteristics of the promised King. The list will help you understand the surprise of many when Jesus took the route of servanthood. The passages: Isaiah 7:14 (Matt. 1:23); Jeremiah 23:5; Zechariah 9:9 (Matt. 2:2); Micah 5:2 (Matt. 2:6); Hosea 11:1; Exodus 4:22 (Matt. 2:15); Jeremiah 31:15 (Matt. 2:18); and Isaiah 11:1 (Matt. 2:23).

Chapters 3, 4. Preparation of the King

Quiet years pass between chapters 3 and 4. Jesus grows up in Nazareth, works with Joseph as a carpenter, and lives quietly in the small Jewish community there. Then, at last, when Jesus is over thirty years old, more words of the prophets are fulfilled in the gaunt person of a fiery preacher called John the Baptizer.

The Baptist's Ministry; 3:2–12. John is nicknamed "the Baptist" because his practice is new. The people know of self-washings for purification and self-washing by converts to Judaism. But no one has baptized others or related that act to repentance.

Like the prophets of old, John boldly strikes out against the sins of God's people (cf. Luke 3:10–13). He calls on individuals and the nation to repent, warning them that the kingdom of heaven is almost upon them! There is little time: each person must make his choice—now!

John explains that he is the forerunner of another who will "baptize with the Holy Spirit and with fire." This is powerful imagry to listeners familiar with the OT. They know the promised kingdom of OT prediction is associated with dire judgments and with heart-purification, both accomplished by a pouring out of God's Spirit when Messiah arrives (Isa. 32:15; Ezek. 11:19; 36:26,27; Joel 2:28,29). The choice John demands is clear. They can repent and be purified by God's Spirit when Messiah comes. Or they can resist and be swept away in the roaring flames of the cleansing judgment.

Jesus Baptized. Jesus travels from Galilee to be baptized by John. John objects. Jesus, whom John knows intimately because the two are cousins, is a good man and needs no repentance! But Jesus is determined to take a stand with the messenger and his message. It is, he tells John, the right thing to do (15). As Jesus comes up out of the river waters, the Spirit of God (see *Holy Spirit,* NT. p. 516) visibly descends on Jesus, and God's voice of commendation is heard.

Repentance

Repentance is often misunderstood as "feeling sorry" about one's sins. The notion is that if a person feels sorry enough, God will forgive. While the NT does speak of a "godly sorrow" that leads a person *to* repentance, it also notes a "worldly sorrow" which is mere wallowing in grief and of no value (2 Cor. 7:10). The biblical doctrine of repentance does not focus on emotions, but on a person's decisions and choices.

Actually, repentance involves a complete change of moral and spiritual attitude toward God: one demonstrated by a change in a person's way of life. John the Baptist's preaching of repentance was a demand for an inner "about face" which would "produce fruit in keeping with repentance" (Matt. 3:18).

While the word "repentance" is not characteristic of the OT, there are many illustrations of the doctrine (cf. Ps. 51; Ps. 32; Amos 5:4,6,14). The clearest expression of repentance in the OT is found in Ezekiel 18. There individuals are promised "if a wicked man turns away from all the sins he has committed and keeps all my decrees and does what is just and right, he will surely live" (18:21). The repentance John and Jesus preached, and which the Scriptures know, is not an emotional state, but a complete turning from sin and to God, our forgiving Savior.

The Temptation of Jesus; 4:1–11. Soon Jesus will launch a preaching mission to tell others how to live in God's present kingdom (Matt. 5–7). But since man is his own worst enemy, Jesus proves his right to instruct others by demonstrating that he controls himself.

The Spirit leads Jesus into a desolate, empty desert lying between Jericho and Jerusalem. After a forty-day fast, when Jesus is physically weakened, Satan comes to tempt him (see *Satan,* p. 245). Jesus' response to the first temptation, a quote of Deuteronomy 8:3, shows us he will meet these tests in his human nature. We too, being "man," can overcome our temptations using the resources Jesus used.

Jesus' primary resource is Scripture. He does not quote it as some magical saying to ward off evil: he quotes a principle which then guides his decisions. When we permit God's Word to determine our choices, we too will experience victory.

Jesus' temptations focus on three areas in which human beings are especially vulnerable. The temptation to turn stones to bread (hunger, 2–4) focuses on man's physical needs and desires. Jesus' response shows that God's will, not the physical, will determine his choices. The second temptation, to leap from the temple (faith, 5–7), is answered by another quote (Deut. 6:16). This was spoken about a people who refused to take God's presence on faith but demanded that God prove himself. Jesus continues to trust God's love for him and refuses to doubt. The third temptation (abandon God's will) focuses on a shortcut to reach a good goal. One day Jesus will rule the kingdoms of the world which Satan offers him now. But God's plan calls for the cross before the crown. We too must take God's means to reach his ends.

Kingdom of Heaven

The Gospels speak often of a "Kingdom of Heaven" or "Kingdom of God." To the hearers of John and Jesus (cf. Matt. 4:17) the meaning seemed clear. That message, addressed to the Jewish people alone (Matt. 10:5–6), conjured up visions of Israel's earthly kingdom, to be ruled by Messiah (see *Old Testament Eschatology,* p. 372, 373. This impression, also held by Jesus' disciples (Matt. 20:20,21; Acts 1:6), was not corrected by the Lord. But though the notion was not wrong, this picture of the kingdom was incomplete.

The OT sees the entire universe as kingdom and God its sovereign Lord. But in speaking of kingdom, Scripture's emphasis is on the personal presence and righteous rule of God in the lives of his people. God seeks a relationship with human beings in which love motivates a willing response of obedience to him. In this sense—the sense of Jesus' personal presence with us, the sense of love relationship, and the sense of willing obedience to his rule—the kingdom is to be *now* for the church, and for you and me.

The disciples were not wrong to look for a coming earthly kingdom. But much of Matthew's Gospel goes on to show how you and I can live out our personal relationship with God as citizens of a hidden kingdom, ruled over by Christ our King (Eph. 1:22,23).

The temptations completed, and Satan defeated, angels come and attend Jesus (11).

To which avenue of temptation are you most vulnerable (through physical needs and desires, through doubt of God's presence, through desires for good things which tempt you to short-cuts that are out of God's will)? How does the verse Jesus quoted from the OT give you guidance? What must you do to overcome the temptation?

Jesus' Preaching Mission; 4:12–25. Jesus begins his preaching in the province of Galilee. His message is essentially the same as that of John: "repent, for the kingdom of heaven is near" (17). On this tour he calls four fishermen to be his disciples (18–22). His ministry also involves healing (23–25). As the news spreads, great crowds come from all over to see, and hear, and be healed.

Chapters 5–7. The Sermon on the Mount

Jesus' famous sermon has been interpreted in many different ways. It has been taken as (1) a statement of how to be saved, (2) a picture of how men will live when Jesus rules at last, and (3) as commandments for Christians. It is best understood in a fourth way: as a royal announcement by Jesus of the way men and women are freed to live when they commit themselves to Jesus as Lord. Because Jesus is the living King, and we live in relationship with him, we can abandon ourselves to the unique kind of life that Jesus describes in this sermon.

The Beatitudes; 5:1–12. Jesus introduces a new set of values by which his followers are to live. The values, implicit in such things as meekness and mercy, run counter to the values found in human societies and cultures. It only makes sense to try to live by these values if we truly believe that God does rule in our lives and that he does govern our circumstances.

Values Expressed in Action; 5:13–16. Any true value will find some expression in behavior. This is Jesus' point as he gives the illustration of the salt of the earth and of lights held high. The values which underly the Beatitudes must be acted on, so that men may "see your good deeds and praise your Father in heaven" (16). Jesus is not presenting a morality to which we can give lip service. He is teaching a morality which is to shape our lives!

"To Fulfill the Law"; 5:17–48. Many have misunderstood what Jesus says now: "I have not come to abolish the Law or the Prophets, but to fulfill them" (17). But his hearers understand! It is the ambition of every Rabbi (teacher) to give the true and full interpretation of God's word: something the first century rabbis call fulfilling it. Jesus promises this revelation! And he warns that his explanation involves a righteousness which "surpasses that of the Pharisees and the teachers of the law" (20). Jesus will not be satisfied to stop with the letter of the law, but will expound its deepest spirit and implications.

The Beatitudes. Matthew 5:3–10

Jesus' Values	Cultural Values
Blessed are those who . . .	Blessed are those who are . . .
(v. 3) are poor in spirit	self-confident
	competent
	self-reliant
(v. 4) mourn	Pleasure-seeking
	hedonistic
	"the beautiful people"
(v. 5) are meek	proud
	powerful
	important
(v. 6) hunger	satisfied
for righteousness	"well-adjusted"
	practical
(v. 7) are merciful	self-righteous
	"able to take care of themselves"
(v. 8) are pure in heart	"adult"
	sophisticated
	broad-minded
(v. 9) are peacemakers	competitive
	aggressive
(v. 10) are persecuted	adaptable
because of	popular
righteousness	"don't rock the boat"

Jesus now moves on to give illustrations. The law regulates, and thus focuses on, behavior. Thus law says, "Do not murder." Jesus explains that underlying this regulation is God's concern with human motives and intent. Anger, which leads to the harming of a brother, is also God's concern! A Pharisee might nurse anger against another person but not murder. By the letter of the law, he is guiltless. But by Jesus' "fulfilled" standards, he is in danger of judgment (21–22). Thus those who live as citizens of Jesus' kingdom must deal with interpersonal tensions even before they bring God gifts, such as those in which the Pharisees took such pride (cf. Isa. 1:12–17)!

Each case Jesus cites follows this pattern. Law regulates acts of adultery: God is concerned with lust (27–30). Law permits divorce: God is concerned with lifelong faithfulness (31–32). The Pharisees' traditions demanded binding oaths: God wants a people so honest that their word is their bond (33–37). The law permits revenge: God seeks a people who will act lovingly even to those who are enemies (38–48).

The kind of life style Jesus describes is impossible for mere men. But those who have a personal relationship with God as Father (48) will find his kingdom power at work within them.

The kingdom morality that Jesus teaches, then, requires exactly the inner transformation promised in the OT (Jer. 31:33–34). That transformation will issue in a godly behavior which flows from the heart and which far exceeds any righteousness found in keeping the letter of OT law.

The Kingdom Misplaced; 6:1–7:23. Jesus lives among a people who are hungry for God's kingdom—as they understand it. But now Jesus warns his listeners against pathways that appear to lead to God but which in fact lead a person further and further from personal experience of the kingdom's presence in our lives.

(1) *The Path of Visible Piety; (5:1–19).* Jesus warns against doing "acts of righteousness" in public. His three illustrations—almsgiving, prayer, and fasting—focus on what the Jews think of as important acts of devotion. He warns that such things are not to be done "to be seen by men." Outward religion is not the issue. It is an inner sensitivity to God, and a desire to please him, that is the secret to life in Jesus' present kingdom. The "Lord's Prayer" guides Jesus' disciples to that inner attitude (see p. 474).

Verse 19 has been sometimes misunderstood as teaching a conditional forgiveness. But when Jesus says, "If you do not forgive men their sins," your Father will not forgive your sins," he does not set a condition. He warns the religious, who measure themselves against the failings of others. They must become humble. A hard-hearted man, who judges rather than forgives, will never welcome the forgiving grace of God, or admit his own need for forgiveness. It is this reality of which Jesus speaks.

(2) *The Pathway of Material Success; 6:19–34.* In Jesus' day the people believe that wealth is a sign of God's blessing. The rich are near God; the poor are suffering his judgment. Jesus warns against focusing on wealth as an evidence of spiritual prosperity. God, a loving Father, meets the daily needs of his children (6:25–31). Freed from the need to constantly worry about the material, Jesus' followers can put God first and live each day for him (32–34). See also *The Christian and Money,* p. 527.

(3) *The Pathway of Authority over Others; 7:1–14.* This warning is for those who see the kingdom of God as an opportunity to exalt themselves over others. Jesus says, "Do not judge," and insists that his followers relate to each other as "brothers" (1,3). Rather than trying to climb to the heights by putting others down, Jesus calls on his hearers to realize the nature of their relationship with God. We are so close to God we only need "ask," knowing that "your father in heaven will give good gifts to those who ask him" (7–11). This intimate relationship with God frees us to serve others rather than judge them (12), for servanthood is the narrow way that leads to living in the kingdom of God's Son.

The Lord's Prayer
Matthew 6:9–13

THE PRAYER	THE KINGDOM ATTITUDE
* Our Father . . .	* Affirms personal relationship with God.
* in heaven . . .	* Recognizes him as Lord over all.
* Hallowed be your name . . .	* Honors God as living, powerful, real.
* Your kingdom come . . .	* Accepts God's right to rule in our lives.
* Your will be done on earth as it is in heaven . . .	Submits completely to God's will now as guide to life on earth.
* Give us this day our daily bread . . .	* Recognizes God's involvement in our daily experiences, supply of our needs.
* Forgive us our debts, as we also have forgiven . . .	* Expresses readiness to live as a forgiving and forgiven people.
* Lead us not into temptation, but deliver us from evil.	* Asks protection from the trials always associated with establishing God's kingdom on earth.

Understanding these pathways helps us recognize false leaders (7:17–23). They may speak in Jesus' name (21–23), but their character unmasks them. Their love of public piety, of money, and their pretension of authority to judge their brothers and sisters, are the bad fruit which identify them.

The Kingdom Discovered; 7:24–27. What then is the way to find God's Kingdom? We are to look to the King and follow his words. The wise man, whose life is built on solid rock, "hears these words of mine and puts them into practice."

Which of the popular but wrong approaches to spiritual achievement do you believe is most attractive to Christians today! How is it expressed in the contemporary church? How can you guard against it in your own life?

Chapters 8–11. The King's Authority

Jesus has claimed the knowledge needed to explain the inner meaning of God's law, and the wisdom to direct each individual's life by his words. Now, in a series of miracles, Jesus proves his right to royal command.

Willing and Able; 8:1–13. A leper asks Jesus to heal him, "if you are willing" (2). Christ touches the man and cures the disease. The King is willing to use his authority in our lives!

Then Jesus is approached by a Roman military officer. The man expresses belief in Jesus' ability to cure a sick servant who is miles away! Jesus speaks the word and the servant is healed. No distance can limit our Lord's power to act for those who have faith in him.

Power over All; 8:14–9:32. Matthew now crowds together reports of a number of events which demonstrate Jesus' authority over forces which hold man in bondage. You and I can live victoriously in Jesus' kingdom, for he has power to free us!

Jesus exercises authority over nature (he calms the storm, 8:23–27), over demons (who are cast into a herd of pigs, 8:28–34), over disease (he heals a paralytic, 9:1–8), over the grip of sin in a person's life (he calls Matthew the tax collector to a new life, 9:9–13), and even authority over death (a dead girl is raised, 9:18–26). A final incident emphasizes the basis on which Jesus' followers can experience Christ's freeing power in their lives. Two blind men beg for their sight. Jesus asks, "Do you believe I am able to do this?" They reply, "Yes, Lord." And so the principle of full experience of God's kingdom power is stated by our Lord: "according to your faith it will be done to you" (9:29).

Miracles, NT

The Bible affirms that God is, that God created, and that God can act in our world of space and time. He can affect the "normal course" of events. Jesus demonstrated this power when he commanded a storm to be stilled and restored sight, hearing, strength to paralyzed limbs, and even life itself. He may well have used natural means in these mighty acts. We only know that he exercised control over nature and control over men's bodies to cure their diseases.

These NT miracles of Jesus served two purposes. First and foremost, they served to authenticate Jesus as God's spokesman. Like Moses, Jesus brought new revelation from God. His words were authenticated by his miraculous acts. As a blind man, whose sight was restored, said to the Pharisees who called Jesus a sinner, "We know that God does not listen to sinners. He listens to the godly man who does his will. Nobody has ever heard of opening the eyes of a man born blind. If this man were not from God, he could do nothing" (John 9:30–33).

A second purpose of the miracles in the Gospels is didactic. God is teaching us how he desires to use his power. While some of the NT miracles of Jesus are nature miracles (John 2:1–11; Luke 5:1–11; Matt. 8:23–27; 15:15–44; 17:24–27), almost all deal directly with human needs. God demonstrates in Jesus his willingness to use his power for the healing of mankind!

The NT does not present miracles as normative for the church. There are a few miracles recorded in Acts, which also have an authenticating function (Acts 5:1–11; 6:8; 8:39; 9:3, 8, 18; 19:12). But, as the new revelation was gradually completed and recorded in our NT, such authenticating signs became less and less common. In fact, the NT even warns against looking again to miracles for authentication! Jesus says, "false Christs and false prophets will arise and show great signs and wonders, so as to lead astray, if possible, the very elect" (Matt. 24:24). Revelation gives the same warning (13:13; 16:14; 19:20).

What then can we conclude about miracles in the NT? First, the "authenticating miracle" is no longer a valid test of one who claims to be God's messenger. We have a completed revelation now and can test the message of every teacher against a trustworthy Word. Second, we recognize that God's power is no less now than in the second century. He can, and does, intervene on behalf of his people; he still has control over us and his universe. God is a God of miracles still, and each of us has access to him in prayer.

For study: See *Miracles, OT,* p. 79 and *Healing,* p. 499.

One additional insight in this passage is important. Jesus tells a paralyzed man, "your sins are forgiven" (9:2). Bystanders object to the "blasphemy," for only God can forgive sin. Jesus then asks which is easier: to say "your sins are forgiven," or "get up and walk" (9:5)? "Get up and walk" is much harder, for if the person does not walk, fraud is immediately exposed! When the lame man walks, Jesus' authority to also forgive sins is demonstrated.

But there is another demonstration! Matthew immediately moves on to his own case (9:9–13). There is another miracle that proves Christ's power over sin. He can take a sinner—even a materialistic tax collector like Matthew—and transform him into a godly man. Jesus still brings his transforming forgiveness to people like Matthew, and like you and me, today!

Read chapters 8 and 9 carefully. Which demonstration of Jesus' power seems most significant to you personally? What is God calling you to trust him for in your life?

A Shared Authority; 9:35–10:42. Jesus has used his royal authority to serve people trapped in bondage to sin, to demons, and to sickness. His motive is one of compassion (9:36). Now, to multiply his caring ministry, Jesus gives his twelve disciples authority to heal and free.

Matthew 10 defines the attitude of service that those given authority in God's kingdom are to adopt. There is no pomp or luxury for Jesus' followers. They are to go humbly among the common people as servants of those in need. Jesus' instructions to the disciples describe a life style appropriate for all his followers. Disciples depend on God, not on their own possessions or wealth (10:8–11). Disciples extend to others the freedom to accept or reject them and their Lord (10:12–15). Disciples can expect persecution from those who reject their Lord (10:6–25). Disciples can live without fear of men, for they are important to God (10:26–35). Disciples can expect conflict, but must put Jesus first (10:34–39). Disciples bring great gifts to mankind and will be rewarded by God (10:40–42).

When Jesus shares his authority with the twelve, he does not lift them above others. Instead, spiritual authority makes them the servants of others. Disciples are called to a humble life of service.

What in the instructions in Matthew 10 speaks most powerfully to you? What is Jesus calling you to do in your quest to grow as one of his modern disciples?

John the Baptist's Confusion: 11:1–30. Jesus has now proven his power. But he does not use it to set up the national kingdom promised by the prophets! Instead Jesus has used his power to heal the hurts of humanity. He does not claim royal glory but acts as a humble servant of all who seek his help. Even John the Baptist is confused. John sends messengers to ask Jesus if he really is the Messiah. Jesus points to his actions: "the blind receive sight, the lame walk, those who have leprosy are cured, the deaf hear, the dead are raised, and the good news is preached to the poor" (11:5). To John, the echoes of Isaiah's description of the Messiah will be clear (cf. Isa. 29:18; 33:24; 35:4–6; 61:1).

As John's disciples leave, Jesus identifies him as that "Elijah" who is to prepare Israel for the Messiah (7–10). He calls John the greatest of the prophets—but this generation does not respond to him (11–15). Israel is like changeable children, unable to decide what the Messiah should be like, and changing their expectations when each new candidate appears (16–19). Yet Jesus' miracles are conclusive demonstration of his messianic authority. Even Sodom would have repented if Christ's miracles had been performed there! But Israel remains unresponsive (20–24).

Jesus turns in praise to the Father. The nation will reject its king, but weary and burdened individuals will turn to the Lord. They will find rest in his gentle care (25–30).

Chapters 12–15. Opposition to the King

Israel has heard Jesus announce the ethical constitution of his kingdom. It has seen his authenticating miracles. But the common people have hesitated to acknowledge him—and now open opposition develops. This opposition comes from the Pharisees, who are respected by the crowds as religious men, but who are exposed in Jesus' teaching as men who have missed the point of the law they pride themselves in observing. For background, see p. 442.

Chapter 12. Attacked

Lawbreaker! 12:1–21. Jesus' disciples pluck some grain on the way to the synagogue and eat it as they walk. The Pharisees point this out to Jesus. By their interpretation, this is "harvesting" and against the Sabbath law! Jesus shows their interpretation is wrong and claims to be Lord over the Sabbath. The Pharisees are the true lawbreakers, for they condemn the innocent without mercy (1–8).

Then the Pharisees attack Jesus directly (9–14). In the synagogue is a man with a withered hand. They point him out to Jesus and ask if it is "lawful" to heal (e.g., work) on the Sabbath. Jesus' answer stuns them. Any one of them would lift one of his sheep out of danger on the Sabbath. A man is far more important than a sheep. Thus "it is lawful to do good on the Sabbath." Jesus heals the man and by his act exposes the Pharisees further. They are self-rightous men, without concern for the humanity God loves.

Inspired by Satan; 12:22–37. Jesus' miracles stimulate speculation that he might be the Messiah (22,23). To counter this, the angry Pharisees attack Jesus openly. They accuse him of being in league with the prince of demons (24). Jesus points out the foolishness of this charge. Could Satan maintain his power if he permitted his followers to publicly defeat one another? Oh, no. Jesus drives out demons by the power of God (25–28)!

Here Jesus introduces the much debated "unforgivable sin" (31). Many have wondered about this "blasphemy against the Spirit" that will not be forgiven. Can we commit this sin today? It is best to understand the unforgivable sin in the context of the unique blasphemy the Pharisees committed that day. Never before or since has God's Son stood among men and performed such clear authenticating signs in the power of the Holy Spirit! The Pharisees recognize the supernatural nature of Jesus' power. But they harden their hearts to Jesus' explanation and to all the evidence. Committing themselves to oppose God, they even label the Spirit's works the work of Satan! They have made an irrevocable choice, against compelling evidence. By their own decision they have passed beyond possibility of repentance (cf. Matt. 11:20–24).

No More Proofs; 12:38–50. Jesus now refuses to give more signs, "except the sign of the prophet Jonah." His resurrection, after a three-day burial, will be conclusive proof of his claims! Israel may have cleansed itself of idolatry, the evil that dominates the OT, but she has refused to welcome in God the Son to fill the cleansed dwelling. Now Israel will be filled with even worse wickedness than before (43–45). When Jesus' family arrives, he takes the opportunity to stress a basic truth. Relationship with the Lord is only for those who submit to the will of the Father.

Chapter 13. The Parables

The people will reject the King and his kingdom. Now Jesus uses a unique kind of parable, which both reveals and hides. The subject of these parables is truth not revealed in the OT (13:35). Before the time arrives for the earthly kingdom of the Messiah which the OT promises, the kingdom of heaven will take an unexpected form. Jesus speaks in parables so those who have rejected him will hear but will never understand what he is saying (13:13–15).

Jesus explains the meaning of two of the parables privately to the disciples. Those explanations, with the information that the subject matter is the "secrets of the kingdom of heaven" (13:11), gives us the principles and keys needed to understand the other parables as well (see chart, p. 481).

Demons

In classical Greek *daimon* was a general term for the hidden powers believed to control man's fate. The Mesopotamian culture personified demons: they were beings who lived in a dark world beyond ours and were responsible for all human misfortunes. In popular thought at the time of Jesus, demons were malignant beings infesting the air, seeking to do harm. In the Gospels, demons are portrayed as real: spiritual beings who are the enemy of God and man. These beings are called "demon," "evil spirit," or "unclean spirit."

Strikingly, the OT does not speak of demons. Nor did demons have a role in the thinking of God's OT people. But there are clear indications in the OT of spiritual personalities that are God's adversaries. Satan is the primary adversary. But he has followers, like the evil "prince of the Persian kingdom" who opposed an angel sent to Daniel (10:12–13). Fallen angels (see *Satan*, p. 245) are apparently the beings we know in the NT as demons.

Jesus' years of ministry are marked by a great outburst of demonic activity. The reason seems to be that Satan focused his forces to oppose the work of God in Christ. The charge that Jesus is in league with demonic powers (Matt. 12:22–37) may stem in part from the unusual concentration of demonic activity that surrounded him! Attacks of demons took the form of possession of persons, or oppression of them with various diseases and suffering. Prominent gospel examples are found in Matthew 8:28; 12:22; 15:22; and Luke 4:33; 11:14.

There are few references to demonic activity in Acts. And most uses of the word in the Epistles simply designate pagan deities (cf. Acts 17:18; 1 Cor. 10:20; Rev. 9:20). It seems clear that the "spirit of anti-Christ" mentioned in the Epistles takes a more deceptive form than immediate demonic confrontation.

One question which the gospel account often raises is of real concern to some Christians. Are we in danger today from these evil beings? Is modern demonic possession a reality? It would be wrong to suggest that possession or oppression cannot happen today. But it is important to remember that the Epistles do not portray demonic attack as a major problem for believers. What the Scriptures emphasize, and what the Gospels prove, is that Jesus is more than a match for the evil powers of our universe. We can be confident, with the apostle John, that through our relationship with Jesus Christ "you are from God, and have overcome them, because the one who is in you is greater than the one who is in the world" (1 John 4:4).

Parables of the Kingdom

The Parable	Expected Form	Unexpected Form
1. *sower* 13:3–9, 18–23	Messiah turns *Israel* and all *nations* to Himself.	*Individuals* respond differently to the Word's invitation.
2. *wheat/tares* 13:24–30, 37–43	The Kingdom's righteous citizens *rule over* the world with the King.	The Kingdom's citizens are *among* the men of the world, growing together till God's harvesttime.
3. *mustard seed* 13:31–32	Kingdom *begins* in *majestic glory*.	Kingdom *begins in insignificance;* its greatness comes as a surprise.
4. *leaven* 13:33	Only righteousness enters the Kingdom; other "raw material" is excluded.	The Kingdom is implanted in a different "raw material" and grows to fill the whole personality with righteousness.
5. *hidden treasure* 13:44	Kingdom is *public* and for all.	Kingdom is *hidden* and for individual "purchase."
6. *priceless pearl* 13:45, 46	Kingdom *brings all valued things* to men.	Kingdom demands *abandonment* of all other values (cf. Mt. 6:33).
7. *dragnet* 13:47–50	Kingdom begins with initial separation of righteous and unrighteous.	Kingdom ends with final separation of the unrighteous from the righteous.

Chapter 13:53–15. Resistance Continues

The next events recorded by Matthew show continuing resistance to Jesus and an increasing emphasis by the Lord on faith. Jesus' Nazareth neighbors are offended at the pretensions of this "carpenter's son" (13:53–58). John the Baptist is beheaded (14:1–12). Jesus continues to respond compassionately to the crowds, healing them and feeding them (14:13–21; 15:29–39), but the people still hesitate to commit themselves. A few recognize Jesus. Among them is a Canaanite woman whose faith wins her blessings intended first for Israel (15:21–28). But the disciples seem amazed when Jesus walks on the waters: even Peter pauses and doubts (14:22–34). When Jesus strikes out against the Pharisees, charging that their traditional interpretations actually distort God's law, the disciples fail to grasp his teaching (15:1–20). Jesus must rebuke them for being "still so dull."

Jesus' continuing miracles win praise for God (15:31). But the active opposition of the Pharisees and general spiritual dullness combine to withhold the commitment of the nation to the Servant King.

Read these chapters carefully. What role does faith seem to play? What does faith gain, and failure to have faith lose? How can you apply your discoveries to your own life?

Chapters 16–17. The Turning Point

Matthew now introduces the theological turning point in his Gospel. Before these chapters, Jesus' preaching has emphasized the kingdom and its ethics. After these chapters the emphasis shifts to discipleship and to the cross.

Pharisees and Sadducees; 16:1–12. These hostile sects have now joined to combat Jesus as a threat to both (see p. 440 f). They have rejected the evidence of Jesus' compassionate miracles. Now they demand a more "acceptable" sign. Jesus refuses to speak with these leaders who cannot read the signs of the times and warns his disciples against their approach to religion.

The Christ; 16:13–20. The disciples are asked who "people say" that Jesus is. The report is complimentary. All identify him with some great OT prophet. But they do not accept him for who he truly is—their King and Savior. Peter's confession of faith correctly identifies our Lord: "you are the Christ, the Son of the Living God" (16).

Simon is given the name "Peter," which means "stone." Jesus goes on to say, "upon this rock I will build my church." Even the Roman Catholic fathers disagree about the rock on which the church is to be built. "Stone" (petros) and "rock" (petra) are different words in Greek. In fact, the foundation is the reality which Peter affirms: Jesus truly is "the Christ, the Son of the Living God!"

The next verse speaks of "keys to the kingdom" (19), and the power of binding and loosing on earth and in heaven. Most Protestant scholars link the keys with Peter's privilege of opening the door of the gospel to both Jews (Acts 2) and Gentiles (Acts 10, 11). He is the first to preach the freeing message of Jesus to each group.

Crucifixion Ahead; 16:21–28. The theological turning point is found in verse 21: *"from that time on* Jesus began to explain to his disciples that . . . he must be killed and on the third day rise again." The nation has rejected its King: now the cross becomes the focus of Jesus' teaching.

The disciples too are taught (24–26). They must deny themselves, take up their cross, and follow Jesus. The cross speaks here of God's will. Just as Jesus turns toward the cross because it is God's will for him, so each disciple must daily commit himself to whatever God's will may be for him.

The normal translation of the next verses, making them seem to speak of the loss or saving of one's soul, is unnecessarily confusing. The Greek word means "life" as well as "soul." The use may also be Aramaic, where a parallel Hebrew term is used as a reflexive pronoun. Thus Jesus warns disciples not to be like the Pharisees, who hold tightly to their old selves, unwilling to lose the old in exchange for the new person that relationship with Jesus promises. What a loss it would be if you or I gained the whole world but lost the new person we might become through Jesus Christ!

Transfigured; 17:1–13. Jesus has promised that some of the disciples will catch a glimpse of the Son of Man in his kingdom glory (16:27–28). Six days later three accompany Jesus to a mountain top. There he is transformed: "His face shone like the sun, and his clothes became as white as the light." The promise has been kept. But then the brightness dims and Jesus returns to the crowds below.

Faith, Not Natural Relationships; 17:14–27. Back with the crowds, an epileptic boy is healed. Jesus explains that faith is the key to accomplishment in the hidden kingdom. God's people may not see their Lord revealed in shining splendor, but he will be with them, acting through their faith (14–23). A final incident reinforces this vital truth. The Jews have based their claim to relationship with God on physical descent from Abraham. But when Peter pays the annual temple tax, Jesus asks him from whom the kings of the earth collect taxes. Is it from their sons, or others? The fact that God requires a tax from his people shows that natural descent from Abraham makes no man a child of God! It has always been a faith like Abraham's which saves (cf. Rom. 4:13–17).

Chapters 18–20. Greatness in Jesus' Kingdom

These chapters are linked by a common theme, as Jesus explains how to recognize and achieve true greatness.

Chapter 18. Attitude toward Others

Greatness Introduced; 18:1–9. The disciples ask Jesus who is greatest in his kingdom. He does not answer but calls a small child over to him. To be great, the disciple must "become like little children" and "humble himself like this child" (3,4). Israel has heard the call of the King but refused to respond. Yet the humble child immediately obeyed when Jesus called him. Greatness for us is found in just such ready obedience to the voice of our Lord.

Jesus then warns against causing his "little ones" to sin (6) and underlines the seriousness of such an offense. In the rest of the chapter he shows how his followers can live together as "little ones" and help each other grow to greatness.

Three Illustrations; 18:10–35. The relational key to life together as God's little ones is found in the attitude believers take toward each other. We are to remember that, like sheep, we are likely to go astray. Then we are to be found and received back with joy (10–14).

Believers are also family. As in any family, hurts and sins will intrude. Every effort is to be made to reconcile those with disputes, and forgiveness is to be extended as often as necessary to heal the hurts (15–22).

A final illustration shows that believers, who have been forgiven so great a debt by God, are never to withhold forgiveness from others, who owe them for some comparatively insignificant hurt (23–55).

Thus we see that an attitude of acceptance and ready forgiveness is vital if God's people are to remain responsive to the word of the Lord. Those who persist in some Pharisee-like attitude will harm others and be disciplined by an angry Father.

Chapters 19:1–20:16. Three Detours

Matthew now reports events which explore three detours religious people sometimes take in search of greatness.

Careful Observance of Law; 19:1–15. The Pharisees took pride in observing the law more carefully than others. This is the ground of their claims to spiritual superiority. Now these men come to Jesus and ask a legal question: "Is it lawful for a man to divorce his wife for any and every reason?" Jesus goes back, before law to creation, and points out God's ideal of a permanent union. The Pharisees object. Why then does the law permit divorce? Jesus answers that God permits divorce "because your hearts were hard." The thought is that sin warps and twists the ideal, to the extent that divorce may become necessary. But this means that law is *not* God's highest standard at all! Law actually is a lower standard than the ideal, showing God's willingness to accommodate himself and meet man where he is (cf. Matt. 5).

Even the disciples misunderstand and think Jesus is laying down some more difficult, "no divorce" regulation (see *Divorce and Remarriage, NT,* p. 639). Jesus explains that "not every one can" accept the ideal. Underlining his point, Jesus directs attention to little children, to whom he says "the kingdom of heaven belongs." Even in the Mosaic law "little children" are not subject to regulation!

Thus the way of the Pharisees, which seeks greatness by strict legalism, is shown not to be God's way to greatness at all.

Doing Good; 19:16–30. The rich young ruler represents honest humanitarianism. But when he is challenged by Jesus to "go, sell your possessions, and follow me" (20) the young man turns away. His response shows that, for all his goodness, he puts his money before his God. Service to others will flow from relationship with God. But humanitarian effort apart from God is no pathway to kingdom greatness. Putting God first comes first!

Harder Work; 20:1–16. A parable illustrates the third detour. A landowner hires workers at different times during the day. But then each is given a day's pay, however long he has worked! When those who worked all day complain, the owner explains that he is generous. God does not evaluate by how long or hard we work, but is generous in rewarding whatever task (or time!) he calls us to. We cannot measure greatness by "full time" involvement in his service.

Chapter 20:17–34. Servanthood

The topic culminates in an exposition of servanthood. Jesus speaks again of his death (17–19). When James and John enlist their mother to beg for high place in his coming kingdom, Jesus asks first if they are able to share his cup. The anger of the ten when they hear leads to a clear statement of how to achieve greatness. Like Jesus, his disciples must give their lives for others! "Whoever wants to become great among you must be your servant, and whoever wants to be first must be your slave" (27).

A final incident illustrates. Jesus moves now toward Jerusalem, where he knows the cross awaits. In spite of this personal burden, Christ turns aside when blind men, ignored and hushed by the crowd, beg his help. Setting aside his own deep needs he quietly asks the blind men, "What do you want me to do for you?"

This is servanthood. This is the way to greatness.

Servanthood, NT

The OT builds its concept of servanthood on a conventional relationship of mutual responsibility between a lord and his servant. It also includes a large block of prophetic teaching on the Messiah as servant of the Lord (see *Servanthood, OT,* p. 306). The NT builds its teaching about servanthood on the example provided by Jesus Christ.

As a servant, Jesus came "not to be served but to serve, and to give his life as a ransom for many" (Matt. 20:28). His life on earth shows constant compassion and sympathy for those with every kind of need. In obedience to God, Jesus acts to meet the needs of the people who crowd around him. His gentleness, his humility, and his refusal to force others to accept him or his message, reveal the servant attitude which all believers are to adopt (cf. Matt. 10:13, 14; Phil. 2:1–8; 2 Tim. 2:24–26).

But Jesus also establishes a new model of authority, which is based on servanthood rather than on power. In doing so he insists that those who follow him reject the idea of "exercising authority over" one another. They are to build a life together in which leaders are recognized, and followed, for their servanthood.

Matthew 20:25–27 contains several striking contrasts between a servant and a ruler approach to authority:

Servant Leader	*Secular Ruler*
Is among others	Is over others
Serves others	Exercises authority
Leads by example	Leads by command
Gives to others	Receives from others
Never forces	Uses power
Achieves commitment	Achieves compliance

NT passages show the apostles leading as servants. Paul encourages the Corinthians to give, but refuses to command them (2 Cor. 8:8). What God desires is not forced actions, but spontaneous giving from a cheerful heart (2 Cor. 9:7). But how can leaders rely on servanthood to move others?

Paul shows us. He is confident, because he knows that "Christ is not weak in dealing with you, but is powerful among you" (2 Cor. 12:3). Spiritual leaders can lead as servants because they do not depend on fleshly means, but rely fully on the power of the living Christ at work among his people.

Chapters 21–23. Confrontation

Jesus entered Jerusalem on Passover Sunday, A.D. 33, to begin the last week of his life on earth. The next day saw a great confrontation with the religious leaders, who were about to set in motion the events that led to his crucifixion.

Triumphal Entry; 21:1–17. Jesus enters the city to the cheers of the crowd and fulfills Zechariah's prophecy (9:9). Going to the temple, Jesus drives out of the great temple court the businessmen who buy and sell sacrificial animals—and regularly cheat the worshipers who buy. Angrily he says the temple is to be a house of prayer, not a den for thieves!

Against the Pharisees; 21:18–22:14. The next day begins with Jesus' cursing of a fig tree. Like Israel, it appears green but has failed to produce fruit. Under Jesus' curse the fig tree withers (21:18–22). In the city the religious leaders challenge Jesus to cite his authority for the acts of yesterday (21:23–27). Jesus turns the question against them. "Was John's authority from God, or men?" Knowing the common people hold John a prophet, and aware that if they say "from God" Jesus will ask why they rejected his message, the frustrated "leaders" are still.

Jesus then tells a series of stories. He tells of a father with two disobedient sons, which makes a devastating point: even prostitutes and tax collectors have been more responsive to God than Israel's leaders (21:28–32)! Another story describes tenants who kill their landlord's messengers and finally murder his son. "I tell you," Jesus concludes, "the kingdom of God will be taken away from you and given to a people who will produce its fruit" (21:33–43). The furious chief priests and Pharisees realize Jesus is talking about them. But they are afraid to arrest him because of the people.

A final parable describes a banquet prepared by a king for his son. When the invited guests refuse to come, strangers come in to enjoy the feast instead of them (22:1–14).

Traps Set for Jesus; 22:15–46. Desperate now, the leaders try to trap Jesus into some admission which will turn the crowds against him. They ask about taxes. Should Caesar be paid? A "no" will let them accuse Jesus to the Romans. A "yes" will let them call him traitor and collaborator. Jesus simply asks for a coin, points to Caesar's picture, and tells them to give Caesar what belongs to him and God what is God's (22:15–22). Another faction, which denies resurrection, asks a riddle about a much-married woman. Whose wife will she be "in the resurrection"? Jesus quotes Scripture to show that the dead still live, and tells these Sadducees that their errors in doctrine come from failure to know either the Scriptures or God's power (22:23–33). Finally a Pharisee asks about the greatest commandment. Jesus turns and asks them about the Christ. If Messiah is David's descendant, how is it that in the inspired Scriptures David calls him "Lord"? The answer cannot be given, for it would involve admission that Messiah is both the son of David and of God. It would confirm Jesus' own claim to deity (see John 8:48–59). After this no one dares question Jesus.

Judgment Announced against Leaders; 23:1–37. The leaders have slunk away, and Jesus turns to his disciples. They are to permit no hierarchy to develop among them. "You have only one Master, and you are all brothers," Jesus explains. Titles such as "father" and "teacher" draw attention away from God the Father and Christ the Teacher. Human leaders are to find their greatness in servant-hood (23:1–12).

Seven woes are now pronounced against the Pharisees and teachers of the law. Here is the King's final judgment on the hypocritical leaders of his land.

What brings Jesus' condemnation on these men? Can you turn his words around, and from chapter 23 develop a list of ten positive commandments for Christian leaders today?

Chapters 24–25. The Future of the Kingdom

The disciples draw Jesus' attention to the temple buildings. Jesus dismisses the beauty: soon all will be torn down. The remark stimulates a series of questions about the future, and about the kingdom which all the OT prophets saw in the future.

Jesus is asked three questions. "When will the temple be thrown down? What will be the sign of your coming? And, what will be the sign of the end of the age" (24:3)? The questions are answered in reverse order.

The Sign of the End of the Age; 24:4–26. Jesus sketches a picture familiar to readers of the OT prophets. The years that stretch out toward the future will be marked by tension, disasters, wars, growing wickedness, and persecution for Jesus' followers. But these common disasters are only a foreshadowing of what is known in the OT as the "day of the Lord," which Jesus describes here as a time of "great distress, unequaled from the beginning of the world until now—never to be equaled again" (24:21). Jesus specifically links this period with a prophecy found in Daniel 9:25–27. That prophecy gives a time framework for the appearance of Messiah, speaks of his being "cut off," and then goes on to tell of a final seven-year period which begins sometime later. The sign in Daniel that the seven-year period has begun is the making, and breaking, of a treaty with the Jewish nation by a future ruler, who establishes an "abomination" (usually used in OT of an idol) in the temple itself. This, Jesus says, is the sign.

The Sign of Jesus' Coming; 24:27–35. Jesus identifies no special sign to mark his coming, except to note that it will be "after the distress of those days" (24:29). That return will be visible to the whole earth, for he will come "with power and great glory."

There are many interpretations of Jesus' promise that "this generation will not pass away" until the fulfillment comes (24:34). Some stress the fact that the Greek word for "generation" also means "race," or "lineage." To them the reference is a promise that the Jewish race will be preserved as a separate people until Christ returns. Another likely meaning is that the generation living at the beginning of the great tribulation period will survive, and a remnant will live to welcome the Lord.

The Unanswered Question. Jesus does not tell his disciples the answer to the first question they asked, about the destruction of the Jerusalem temple. But history answers that question for you and me. In A.D. 70 Roman armies under Titus crushed a Jewish revolt, destroyed the city, and tore down the temple, just as Jesus had foretold. Just before that seige, the large Christian community in Jerusalem, warned by its prophets, moved from the city to a place of safety.

New Testament Eschatology

The word "eschatology" refers to the distant future and history's end. Like the OT the New does speak of a culmination to life in this universe. As Jesus' teaching in Matthew 24 shows, the NT teaching about the future rests on the foundation laid in the Old.

But like OT prophecy, NT pictures of the future are incomplete. The writers describe different aspects of the time of the end, but they do not give a clear, simple, step-by-step statement of the sequence of the events described.

This has led to debate between Bible students. Will Jesus come for Christians before the tribulation described in Matthew 24? After it? How does Paul's picture in 1 Thessalonians 4, of Christ descending and believers caught up to meet him in the air, relate to Jesus' description of angels gathering God's elect in Matthew 24? Peter speaks of the universe itself flaming out of existence (2 Pet. 3:10). Revelation describes a new creation (Rev. 21), but also speaks of a thousand-year period during which Satan is bound, and Christ and his saints rule the earth (Rev. 20:1–6). How do these events all fit together?

Different schools of prophetic interpretation present charts and diagrams. But no one can speak with complete certainty about the sequence or the timing of these future events.

Exhortations to Watch; 24:36–25:46. Jesus does not dwell on the prophetic details. Instead, he turns the thoughts of his disciples to the life they are to live until he returns. "Watch," Jesus exhorts, "because you do not know on what day your Lord will come" (24:42).

In a series of illustrations, Jesus stresses the need to serve him faithfully, always expecting his coming. In one parable, wise virgins are prepared with plenty of oil, ready to serve however long they must wait till the bridegroom arrives (25:1–13). In another parable, commendation comes to servants who put their talents to use while their Lord is away on a journey. They use what he has given them, aware that they will have to account for their talents when he returns (25:14–30). In a final word Jesus speaks of judgment coming at his return. Then men's words will not be used to measure their faith. Instead faith will be measured by compassionate concern for those in need: for ministries of service performed as if for Jesus himself. This is what will show the reality of one's relationship with the Lord (25:31–46). Thus Jesus turns his disciples—and us— from curiosity to commitment. We are on a mission to mankind. The future is in God's hands. The present is committed to us!

The NT Picture of the Future

What then can we say about NT eschatology? Several things are important to keep in mind as we come to NT pictures of the future.

First, NT prophecy is clearly coordinated with that of the OT. The testaments do not contradict each other, although relationships are not always clear. Thus we must study the OT as well as the NT to understand the time of the end.

Second, the Bible does not give a systematic picture of the sequence of the events it predicts. Can we conclude that it is not necessary for us to have this information? Perhaps majoring on prophetic details is not one of God's priorities for us!

Third, when the Bible does speak of major prophetic events, the NT passage always applies the truth presented to present experience with God.

We will meet the Lord in the air, Paul says in Thessalonians, and "therefore comfort one another with these words" (1 Thess. 4:18). The universe will be destroyed, Peter teaches, and "therefore, what kind of people ought you to be" (2 Pet. 3:11). Our goal in studying NT prophecy should first of all be to apply truth to our life now.

Finally, both testaments assure us history moves toward God's intended end. We can trust as we live a life of faith and love.

Chapters 26, 27. Death of the King

Now events move swiftly. Unable to touch Jesus openly, the chief priests plot to arrest and kill him in "some sly way" (26:4). One of Jesus' own disciples, Judas, agrees to betray him for thirty pieces of silver—the price set in the law as the value of a dead slave (cf. Zech. 13:7)!

Jesus shares a final meal with his disciples and reveals that the promised new covenant (see *New Covenant,* p. 330, p. 653) is about to be written in his own blood (26:17–30). The burden is especially heavy as they travel to Gethsemane, a grove of trees on the slope of the Mount of Olives. Jesus predicts Peter's denial and desertion by the others, and then goes aside to pray. Here Jesus expresses his commitment to do the Father's will, however great the cost (26:31–45). And it is here that a crowd of armed rabble, led by Judas, comes to arrest the Lord (26:47–56).

The trial is swift and illegal. Jesus is taken at night before the Sanhedrin, Israel's court and governing body. There Jesus openly admits he is the Son of God, and the leaders of God's people shout, "Blasphemy!" (26:57–68). In the meantime Peter, who is outside in the courtyard, denies that he knows Jesus, terrified by the mere servants of the great men who persecute his Lord (26:69–75). Judas, remorseful now that Jesus has been doomed, flings his blood money on the temple floor and wanders away to commit suicide (27:1–10).

The Jewish court has no power to sentence a person to death. So Jesus is taken to Pilate, the Roman governor. He admits to being king of the Jews and refuses to defend himself. Pilate is convinced of Jesus' innocence, yet yields to pressure and pronounces the death sentence (27:11–26). Jesus is whipped and mocked (27:27–31), and led away to be crucified (27:32–44: see *Crucifixion,* p. 503).

The death of Jesus is one of the focal points of OT prophecy. Matthew is careful to show how the events that lead up to the cross, and what happens there, are predicted in the OT (see *Fulfilled*

Prophecy, p. 305). The dying is marked by a noontime darkness and earthquakes. As the earth shakes and the rocks split, the Son of God dies (27:45–55).

Jesus' body is taken down and laid in a nearby garden tomb. His apparently victorious enemies set a guard on the tomb. They want none of the disciples to slink about some night and steal the body of this pretender who prophesied his own resurrection (27:57–66)!

Matthew 28. Resurrection

Jesus' body lies in the garden tomb for three days. Then, on the first day of the week, the ground shakes again. An angel comes and rolls away the stone that blocks the door. The purpose is not to release the resurrected Lord, but to permit the disciples to see the place where the body lay!

The Resurrection of Jesus

The resurrection of Jesus is the central teaching of the NT. "If Christ has not been raised," Paul says, "your faith is futile; you are still in your sins" (1 Cor. 15:17). The literal resurrection of Jesus, to endless life in his own transformed flesh, is what Paul calls God's great declaration that Jesus truly is the Son of God (Rom. 1:4).

It is no wonder then that the earliest preaching of the gospel focused on the Resurrection in that proclamation's offer of forgiveness of sins (see Acts 2:24–32; 3:14–16, 26; 4:10; 5:30; 7:55; 10:39–43).

The Resurrection is well attested historically. All the apostles saw and talked with the resurrected Lord, as did many others listed in Scripture. In chronological order, these are: Mary (John 20:11f), several women (Matt. 28:9,10); Peter (Luke 24:34); two on the Emmaus road (Luke 24:13f), a group on resurrection day (Luke 24:33,34; John 20:19), Thomas (John 20:24–30), disciples on the seashore (John 21), over 500 gathered followers (Matt. 28:16; 1 Cor. 15:6), James (1 Cor. 15:7), and others at the Ascension (Acts 1:1–10). No fraud could have been perpetrated with so many eye witnesses alive all during the years the NT documents were being written and distributed.

But belief in the Resurrection has never rested on evidence alone. Faith that God exists, and that he acts in man's world, has always been necessary. Even incontrovertible miracles by Jesus could not convince the chief priests and Pharisees against their will. No evidence can force a person to believe.

What is the importance of Jesus' resurrection to us who do believe? First, Jesus' resurrection guarantees that he lives today, to accomplish all that God has promised in our lives. "Because Jesus lives forever," the writer of Hebrews explains, "he has permanent priesthood. Therefore he is able to save completely those who come to God through him, because he always lives to intercede for them" (Heb. 7:24,25).

Second, the return of Jesus to life, in a transformed body which can never die, is a preview of our own destiny in Christ! Jesus lives in a real body (cf. Matt. 28:9; Luke 24:30,31; John 20:16; 21:12,13). But it is also a glorified body, no longer limited as ours is now (cf. Luke 24:31, 36; John 20:19; 1 Cor. 14:42–50). We too can look forward to life in a body which Paul describes in 1 Corinthians 15 as imperishable, glorious, incorruptible, and immortal.

There are many mysteries associated with resurrection. But John, in his first epistle, puts the promise of Jesus' resurrection well. "What we will be has not yet been made known. But we know that when he appears, we shall be like him" (3:2)!

The Gospel of Matthew ends now, with Jesus' appearance to his eleven disciples, and with what has come to be called the "Great Commission" (Matt. 28:16–20). Raised, Jesus the Servant King rules over the hidden kingdom of God. While not visible to men of the world, "all authority in heaven and in earth" is his. Trusting in the power of the risen Lord, the eleven—and all other followers of Jesus—are commissioned to "go and make disciples of all nations. . . . teaching them to obey everything I have commanded you" (28:16–20).

His promise supports us to this very day. "Surely I will be with you always, to the very end of the age."

MARK
The Gospel of Christ in Action

Mark's picture of Jesus is shaped for the Roman mind. There is no time here to record the sermons that attract the attention of Matthew and Luke. Instead with vivid, headlong prose, Mark reveals Jesus to be a man of action. The vigorous Savior is conqueror of demons, disease, and death. This bold portrayal of Jesus' strenuous life, which so appealed to the practical Roman, draws us as well. It shows us a man whose commitment to servanthood can never mask his character as a person of strength and power.

Date and location. Most view Mark as the earliest of the four Gospels. It is typically dated in the A.D. 50s and tradition indicates it was written in Rome. This view is supported by the content. Mark carefully explains common Jewish practices as if for a foreign audience, and he translates Jewish terms into Roman equivalents (see Mark 2:18; 7:3,4; 12:18,42). The view of the early church is summed up by Papias, about A.D. 140. "Mark, being the interpreter of Peter, whatsoever he recorded he wrote with great accuracy, but not however in the order in which it was spoken or done by our Lord." Like the other gospel writers, Mark has a specific purpose in mind and organizes his material to achieve it.

Author. The earliest tradition assigns this Gospel to John Mark, but pictures him as a reporter of Peter's narrative preaching rather than as an eye-witness. We know something of John Mark from the Acts and various Epistles. Peter stayed in the home of Mark's mother in Jerusalem when he was released from prison (Acts 12:12). Later the young Mark traveled with Barnabas and Paul on their first missionary journey (Acts 12:25; 13:5). But Mark abandoned the party at Pamphylia (13:13). Later, when Barnabas wanted to bring Mark along on another mission, Paul absolutely refused. After a sharp argument the two old friends separated. Paul took a new partner and left without Barnabas (15:36–41). Barnabas, a man whose name "son of consolation" accurately reflected his character, took John Mark and set out on his own mission.

Barnabas' willingness to trust in the young man who failed Paul's sterner test was justified. John Mark became a valued missionary and a later companion of Paul (Col. 4:10; Philem. 24; 2 Tim. 4:11). Peter looked on him as a dearly loved son (1 Pet. 5:13).

And Mark was chosen by God to write the Gospel which carries his name.

Theme. Mark's clear, vivid narrative simply tells the story of Jesus Christ. Mark assumes no special knowledge by his readers of the OT, and he avoids theological speculation. Mark seems to speak as the simple evangelist or street preacher, telling the story of Jesus in plain terms. Mark relates the events of Jesus' life and leaves it up to his readers, knowing the facts, to make up their minds about this man and his claims. The Jesus Mark presents is a man of tremendous vigor and authority, yet one who "came not to be ministered to, but to minister, and to give his life a ransom for many" (Mark 10:45).

Structure and Outline. Mark writes a fast-moving narrative, over and over using the word "immediately" to move the reader ever on. He seems to want us to keep on reading—not to pause, but to see the story of Jesus as a whole. Thus Mark is best read at one sitting, as a single coherent whole. Those who do outline this brief Gospel, however, have marked out several special emphases in Mark's retelling of the gospel story.

Outline

I.	Introduction	1:2–13
II.	Jesus' Authority Demonstrated	1:14–5:43
III.	Jesus' Conflicts with Others	6:1–8:26
IV.	Jesus Instructs His Disciples	8:27–10:52
V.	Jesus' Journey to the Cross	11–13
VI.	Jesus' Death, and Resurrection	14–16

Chapter 1:2–13. Introduction

Only thirteen verses in Mark tell of preparation for Jesus' appearance. Matthew uses 76 verses, and Luke 183. Mark quickly passes over the ministry of John, to present Jesus, a man who came from Nazareth in Galilee, and is immediately introduced as the Son of God.

Chapters 1:14–5:43. Jesus' Authority Demonstrated

Mark plunges into description of a round of activities which show Jesus as a man of action, and a man with authority. This man Jesus is committed to his mission: he does not pause to rest, but gives himself totally to his work.

Chapter 1:14–2:17. Authoritative Acts

Mark describes a series of wide-ranging events in which Jesus acts decisively. Jesus speaks to several successful fisherman, and they leave their business to follow him (1:14–20). He not only "teaches as one who had authority," but also acts with authority. He speaks sternly to evil spirits, who are forced to obey his orders (1:21–28). He works late into the night healing those with various diseases (1:29–34). Before the next morning dawns, Jesus is up ahead of his disciples, praying in a solitary place (1:35–37). When the worried disciples find him, he urges them on and leads them throughout Galilee (1:38,39).

This Man, with his amazing stamina, is also sensitive. He feels a rush of compassion at the misery of a leper and reaches out to touch and cure (1:40–45). He announces forgiveness of a paralytic's sin, and to prove his right to do so commands him to "get up and walk" in "full view of them all" (2:1–12). Even hardened tax collectors and sinners yield to the dynamic personality of this Man who braves criticism to call them to repentance.

Chapters 2:18–3:30. Authoritative Teaching

Mark does not give extended accounts of what Jesus says as he travels. But he does focus on incidents which show Jesus speaking with compelling authority. On a fast day Jesus responds to criticism of his disciples by announcing that the new truth he teaches will not fit old molds (2:18–22). When the Pharisees (see p. 442) criticize Jesus' disciples for eating as they walk on a Sabbath day, he tells them that he is Lord of the Sabbath (2:23–27). When the Pharisees cruelly use a crippled man in an effort to trap Jesus into what they label "working" on the Sabbath, Jesus boldly calls the cripple to "stand up in front of everyone." Flushed with anger at the hardness of these "religious" men's hearts, Jesus heals the cripple, proclaiming that "to do good" is always lawful (3:1–6)!

The crowds respond to this man who cannot be cowed, and the press of those begging to be healed becomes so great that Jesus has to teach from a small boat, floating just off shore (3:7–12).

The work is now so great that the twelve he has called earlier are now appointed disciples and designated "apostles" (see *The Disciples,* p. 497). They are to remain with him and go out to preach where he sends them (3:13–19). But the press around Jesus continues. The pace is so frantic he has no time even to eat! Jesus has thrown himself so completely into his ministry that his family worries he has gone "out of his mind," and his enemies call him demon-possessed! They even suggest that his power over demons comes from the prince of demons himself (3:20–22)! Jesus shows up the foolishness of their argument and warns them. Calling the works which he performs in the power of God's Spirit the work of demons is a sin which will not be forgiven (3:23–30)!

Mark now concludes with a report of several of Jesus' parables. He explains that these sayings are designed to hide truth from those without spiritual perception, and that they are carefully explained to the disciples (4:1–33). (For a discussion of the parables, see pp. 479, 480). Mark reports only four of the parables, while Matthew gives fifteen and Luke nineteen. But in this Gospel of Christ in action, Mark finds room to report eighteen miracles!

The Disciples

The Gospels speak often of an intimate group of twelve men, chosen by Jesus, who accompany him everywhere (Mark 3:16–19). While the term "disciple" is often used in the Gospels to describe any of Jesus' followers, or those who associate themselves with the Lord, it is this small group of twelve who are *"the"* disciples.

Discipleship was a prominent element of Judaism in Jesus' day (cf. Matt. 9:14; 22:16; Acts 9:25). It involved a well-defined teaching process, marked by (1) a close teacher-learner relationship. The disciple was expected to live with his teacher and to share his experiences as well as to hear his teachings. (2) The disciple was also expected to "abide" in his teacher's words (John 8:31,32). This meant to take on the teacher's words as the pattern for his own way of life, putting all that he taught into daily practice. (3) The goal of discipleship was not simply knowledge. Instead, the disciple was expected to "be like his teacher" (Luke 6:40). Discipleship was designed to shape the character of the learner as well as his thinking.

All this is involved in the process by which Jesus trained the twelve. We can trace the process most easily in Mark's Gospel, as we see the twelve following the Lord, listening, asking questions, sent out on missions, encouraged and corrected. This teaching process, so different from the training we give those who prepare for ministry today, was successful. After some three years with Jesus these men became the spearhead of a missionary movement which carried the life-changing gospel of Jesus throughout Europe, Africa, Asia Minor, and deep into India as well.

Strikingly, the term "disciple" is not used outside the Gospels and Acts. But the term was revived immediately after the apostolic era as another name for Christians. Like the twelve, we today are called to live in close relationship with Jesus and one another, to live by Jesus' words, and to open our lives to God's Spirit for tranformation toward Christlikeness.

Read through Mark quickly, marking each time when the twelve seem to receive training. How can we train disciples today?

Chapters 4:35–5:43. Ultimate Authority

Mark brings his vivid pictures of Jesus' authority to a climax with three extended stories. A furious squall strikes as Jesus and his disciples cross the water. Jesus sleeps on, till roused by the frantic disciples. He calmly commands the wind and waves to "Be still!" The wind dies and the waters become completely calm (4:35–41). On the other side of the lake a demon-possessed man, whom no one is strong enough to subdue, falls on his knees before Jesus. The demons, tortured by the very presence of one they recognize as "the Son of the Most High God," are sent into a herd of pigs, which then hurtles off a cliff to destruction (5:1–20). Back on the Jewish side of the lake, Jesus heals an incurable illness while on his way to help a sick child. When he arrives at her house, the girl is already dead. Ignoring the wailing and words of ridicule, Jesus takes the girl by the hand. To the astonishment of his disciples and the parents, the girl responds and her life is restored (5:21–43). Jesus controls the awesome powers of nature, demons, and even death itself.

Chapters 6:1–8:26. Jesus in Conflict

It might appear that life would hold no challenges to a man with Jesus' powers. Mark goes on to show the many conflicts and tensions which placed great demands on the character of the Lord.

Jesus is rejected by his relatives and his old neighbors at Nazareth (6:1–6). When he sends out disciples two by two, some towns welcome them but others turn them away (6:7–13). John the Baptist, Jesus' cousin and also a prophet, is beheaded by Herod (6:14–29). When the crowds do come out, the press is so great that Jesus has no time even to eat. Jesus tries to lead the twelve to a quiet place where they can rest, but they are followed. Despite his own hunger and exhaustion, Jesus performs a miracle and feeds some 5,000 people (6:30–44). At night Jesus, in an attempt to be alone, sends the disciples across the lake in a small boat. When a storm comes up and the men strain at the oars because the wind is against them, Jesus comes to them, walking on the water. Again the sea calms. At the shore crowds of sick beg for healing (6:45–56).

The pressures on Jesus include open opposition. Pharisees and other religious leaders come to criticize and are boldly rebuked. Jesus corrects the distortions of God's Word that the traditions of these men have caused, but even his own disciples fail to grasp his point (7:1–23)! When Jesus does meet a person with outstanding faith, it is a foreigner and not one of his own people at all (7:24–36)! Later Jesus tests his disciples. He points to the great crowd that has been with them for three days, and is now hungry. The twelve never think of the earlier miracle of feeding five thousand, but object, "Where in this remote place can anyone get enough bread to feed them?" (8:1–10).

Again the Pharisees harry Jesus. When the Lord warns the twelve against their teachings, they misunderstand. Frustrated, Jesus twice cries out, "Do you still not understand" (8:11–21)? The series of frustrations culminates when, after another healing (8:22–26) Jesus asks who people say he is. The disciples report he is considered a great prophet! But he is not accepted as the Son of God (8:27,28).

Healing

Each of the Gospels describes many healings by Jesus. Acts also reports healings performed by the apostles, after Jesus' resurrection. And 1 Corinthians 12 mentions "gifts of healing" three times, although these gifts are not mentioned in other Epistles.

The most important question raised by the biblical account of healings is not "Can God heal?" Instead the question believers have asked is, "Is healing something I can expect for myself and my beloved ones?" God surely does desire the best for his dearly loved people. And God's work in our lives is designed to bring us to spiritual, emotional, and physical health. Thus Christians are encouraged in James' letter to pray when sickness comes (James 5:13–16).

But the Bible does not teach that miraculous healing is normative for the church. Or that Christians can expect to be healed of every and any illness. The healing miracles of the Gospels and Acts had specific purposes: they authenticated the person who performed them as a messenger from God, and they demonstrated that God's power would be used to meet the needs of the suffering and oppressed (see *Miracles, NT.*, p. 476). Such healings do not imply that every believer can expect healing miracles performed on his behalf.

Three NT passages illustrate this point. Paul urges Timothy to quiet an easily upset stomach by taking a little wine (1 Tim. 5:23). When Epaphroditus, a messenger from Philippi, is taken desperately ill the apostle Paul does not simply "heal" him. Instead he prays for recovery and is grateful to God when his friend gets well (Phil. 2:26–28). Most significantly, when Paul himself is stricken with a chronic illness, the healing he prays for is refused (2 Cor. 12:7–12). God has a purpose for that disease in the great apostle's life!

This perhaps is the most important perspective for us. God *can* heal us and often does. But God can also use our times of suffering to achieve some important purpose in our lives. When we or our loved ones become ill, we can and should turn to God in prayer. And we can pray confidently! Our loving God will either heal, or else he will use the illness as one of those "all things" which "work together for good to those who love the Lord" (Rom. 8:28).

Mark, in this series of sharp sketches, has shown us the pressures under which Jesus lived. There is exhaustion, there are pressing demands on his time and energy, there is the pain of rejection by the people nearest to him, there is frustration as his disciples fail to grasp the meaning of his words and actions, there are open attacks by religious leaders, and finally there is the failure of his nation to accept him for who he really is. Yet, in spite of these discouragements and the constant pressure, Jesus never falters. He continues to press on in his ministry of teaching and healing, demonstrating over and over again that he has come "not to be ministered to, but to minister, and to give his life a ransom for many" (Mark 10:45).

Chapters 8:27–10:52. Jesus Instructs His Disciples

The crowds do not recognize Jesus. But the disciples do. "You are the Christ," Peter affirms for them all (8:27–30). For Mark as well as Matthew, this is the turning point. Immediately Jesus "began to teach them that the Son of Man must suffer many things," be rejected, killed, and rise again the third day (8:31–33). Now the rapidly unfolding events are for the instruction of the twelve. Jesus tells them the cost of discipleship (8:34–38), and in his transfiguration shows them the glory disciples will one day share (9:1–13).

The healing of an epileptic boy in the grip of an evil spirit leads to private instruction on faith (9:14–32). When rivalry develops, Jesus teaches the twelve about servanthood (9:33–37). He also teaches the twelve not to reject others who believe, but who are "not one of us" (9:38–41). He warns of the seriousness of causing any who believe in him to sin (9:42–50).

When the Pharisees raise questions of law, Jesus shows that in some points even the law of Moses dips below God's ideal. Later, privately, Jesus shows his disciples they must go back to basic principles for guidance (10:1–12, see Matt. 19, p. 484). The next day the disciples are reproved for keeping young children away. "Of such is the kingdom of God," Jesus tells them (10:13–16). The rich youth who appears next illustrates Jesus' point. He asks what he can "do to inherit eternal life." The young man is moral and honest. But when Jesus tells him to give away his wealth and follow the Lord, he turns away. How unlike a trusting child (10:17–22)!

Later Jesus and the twelve discuss the incident, and Jesus points out the difficulty of the rich in abandoning trust in their wealth to trust in God. The disciples again misunderstand and Jesus reassures them. Salvation, impossible for man, is possible with God (10:23–31). As they move on together toward Jerusalem, Jesus speaks again of his coming death (10:32–34).

But the twelve still do not seem to understand. They maneuver to gain preferred places in Jesus' coming kingdom. Again Jesus stresses the importance of servanthood for his disciples. Jesus' followers will serve others, not rule them (10:35–45)!

As if to illustrate, Mark concludes this section with the report of one last incident. In Jericho, on the way to Jerusalem, a blind man cries out to Jesus. The crowd hushes him, but Jesus stops. "What do you want me to do for you?" The blind man begs for, and receives, his sight. And the disciples have a vivid demonstration of what it means to set aside one's own great burden, to give everything in service to others (10:46–52).

Chapters 11–13. Journey to the Cross

Mark has brought us to the last week of Jesus' life. He now relates the events which bring Jesus closer and closer to his death.

The week begins with a triumphal entry into Jerusalem, the air filled with the shouts of the crowd (11:1–11). When Jesus drives the sellers of animals and the money changers out of the temple, the enraged chief priests plot to kill him (11:12–19).

Jesus has cursed a figless tree, demonstrating the power of prayer (11:20–25) and the reality of an authority which the leaders of Israel challenge the next time he enters the city. As at other times, Jesus easily silences them (11:20–26). But a series of confrontations with the authorities follows. Jesus likens them to tenants whose landlord has sent his son to collect the fruit due at harvest. Wickedly they plot to kill the son (12:1–12). When the leaders try to "catch Jesus in words," he easily avoids their traps (12:13–34. See Matt. 22, p. 487 f). Then Jesus puts a question to them which they cannot answer except by admitting that Jesus must be God's Son as well as the descendant of King David (12:35–37).

Publicly Jesus warns against teachers of the law whose religion masks pride and greed. "Such will be punished most severely," he says, to the delight of the crowd (12:38–40). Privately Jesus points out a poor widow to his disciples. She slips in to put her last two coins in the temple treasury. Jesus tells the twelve that this gift from poverty means more than all the gold given by the rich (12:41–44).

Leaving the temple that day, Jesus describes the future that awaits the world. Wars and disasters will continue; Jesus' followers will suffer persecution (13:1–13). But finally the time of the end foretold by the prophets will arrive, marked by a desecration of a Jerusalem temple predicted by Daniel 9:25–27. After the dreadful sufferings of the end time Jesus will return, visible to all, "with great power and glory" (see *NT Eschatology*, pp. 489, 490). But when this will be is not known. Until the day comes, Jesus' followers are to watch and to be busy about the task assigned each by God (13:32–36).

Chapters 14–16. Jesus' Death and Resurrection

Each gospel writer deals at length with the final week of Jesus' life. Mark now gives graphic details about his last two days.

Chapter 14. Thursday

In Bethany an unidentified woman pours expensive perfume on Jesus' head. Some are indignant. Why wasn't the perfume sold and the money given to the poor? Jesus tells them to leave her alone. She has done a beautiful thing, preparing him beforehand for burial. As Jesus speaks Judas slips away to the chief priests and bargains to betray him (1–11).

In Jerusalem that evening, Jesus and the twelve share a Passover meal (12–26). There Christ identifies his betrayer and explains that his broken body and shed blood will institute the long promised new covenant (see *New Covenant*, pp. 330, 653). After the meal Jesus listens to Peter's declaration that, whatever others do, he will never desert his Lord. Jesus tells him Peter will disown him that very night (28–31).

The little company continues on in the darkness to an olive grove called Gethsemane. As the disciples doze, Jesus, "overwhelmed with sorrow to the point of death," prays (32–41). They are there together when Judas arrives with an armed mob. Jesus is taken and dragged to the home of the high priest, while his disciples all desert him and flee. Nighttime trials are illegal in Israel. But the whole Sanhedrin, the court of the Jewish people, is waiting.

When false testimony will not stand up, the high priest asks Jesus bluntly if he is the Son of God. Jesus answers clearly. "I am." To these men who reject and hate Jesus this is a clear case of blasphemy, and "all condemn him as worthy of death" (53–65).

Outside, Peter crouches in the courtyard and when questioned curses, swearing he doesn't even know that man, Jesus (14:66–72).

Thursday is over. The next dawn will bring the day of Jesus' execution.

Chapter 15. Friday

Very early in the morning Jesus is brought to the Roman governor, Pilate. The Sanhedrin cannot execute: only Rome has that authority.

Pilate questions Jesus, who admits being the King of the Jews but will not answer the other accusations of the chief priests. Pilate realizes that Jesus is innocent and recognizes the envy that has turned the leaders against him. But when the leaders and the crowd cry out, "Crucify him," Pilate turns Jesus over for execution (1–15).

The Roman soldiers in charge of the execution detail, as normal preparation for crucifixion, whip Jesus brutally and mock him. Then they lead him off to be crucified (16–20).

The Crucifixion

Crucifixion was practiced as a method of torture and execution by the Persians before it was adopted by the Romans. Roman law allowed only slaves and criminals to be crucified. Roman citizens were not crucified. The victim's arms are stretched out above him, fastened to a cross bar fixed near the top of a stake slightly taller than a man. Suspended this way, blood is forced to the lower body. The pulse rate increases, and after days of agony the victim dies from lack of blood circulating to the brain and heart. The Romans often placed a *titulus* above a sufferer, naming his crime. Scourging before crucifixion hastened death, as did breaking a victim's legs.

Thousands were crucified by the Romans. In 71 B.C. some 6,000 of the followers of Spartacus died at one time! But the death of Jesus was different. That death came about according to the "set purpose and foreknowledge of God" (Acts 2:23).

The Epistles concentrate our attention on God's purpose. "Christ died for sins," Peter explains, "to bring you to God" (1 Pet. 3:18). "We have forgiveness through his blood," Paul says (Col. 1:14; Eph. 1:7). The writer

The Crucifixion

to the Hebrews looks back on the OT sacrifices and realizes that all of them merely point us to the one final sacrifice by Jesus of himself on Calvary's cross. He says, "by one sacrifice he has made perfect forever those who are being made holy" (Heb. 10:14).

The message of the Gospel, then, is the offer to all of a salvation won for us by Jesus' death on the cross. Through simple faith in him, and confidence in the forgiveness earned by his blood, we are brought into personal relationship with God. We are forgiven and assured a future of eternal life, beyond every taint of evil, in the presence of God and the resurrected Jesus.

For study: Isaiah 52:14–53:12; Matthew 26:26–28; John 17:4; 19:30; Acts 2:22–39; 4:8–12; Romans 3:21–26; 1 Corinthians 1:18–25; Ephesians 2:14–18; Hebrews 9:11–10:18.

The execution ground is outside the city. Weakened by loss of blood from the beatings, Jesus is unable to carry the crossbeam of his cross. A watching visitor who has come to Jerusalem to keep Passover is pressed into service.

As Jesus' enemies mock him, and the disinterested soldiers gamble for the right to sell his clothing, Jesus hangs suspended between two robbers. Even one of these two joins the bystanders in heaping insults on the suffering Savior (21–32).

A sudden midday darkness shrouds the scene, hiding the figure on the cross. Those nearby hear a loud cry! Jesus has breathed his last (33–41).

At sunset one of Israel's holiest days will begin. Jesus' body is taken down from the cross in the late afternoon, carefully wrapped, and laid in a tomb carved into rock. A stone is rolled against the entrance (42–47). No matter how admirable this Man may have been, his story seems to be ended.

Chapter 16. Resurrection

But Jesus' story is not ended at all! The first verse in Mark's Gospel had announced "the *beginning* of the gospel about Jesus Christ, the Son of God." Now we realize that the gospel story will never end!

Mark simply tells the story. The women creep up to the tomb the first day of the new week, carrying spices to anoint the body that is no longer there. They find the stone rolled away, and angels point to the empty shelf carved in the rock where the body had been placed. "He is not here," they tell the women. "He is risen!"

Trembling and bewildered, and more than a little afraid, the women go away. They do not realize it yet, but they have entered a world made forever new by the resurrection of the Son of God.

Mark's Gospel is intended to be read as a whole. Read it through quickly several times. Then write down the impressions you receive of Jesus from this most evangelistic of the four Gospels.

Mark's Endings

Several different endings to Mark's Gospel have been found, added to chapter 16's eight brief verses. While the ending represented by verses 9–20 in our English versions is one of the oldest, the most reliable Greek manuscripts do not include it. Most NT scholars believe that these verses were not written by Mark.

LUKE
The Gospel of the Perfect Man

Luke is the longest book in the NT. In rich tones and with superb style, the author gives a careful historical account of Jesus' life, and continues in Acts with a history of the early church. Luke is not only concerned with historical accuracy, but also with an ideal: the ideal of excellence. Luke portrays the only perfect man who has ever lived for an idealistic people, who admired excellence above all. As Matthew wrote to the Jew, and Mark to the practical Roman, so Luke communicates a unique picture of Jesus to the Hellenistic Greek.

Author and Date. From earliest times the author of this Gospel and the Book of Acts has been identified as Luke, a Gentile convert to Christianity. Luke was a companion of Paul on various missionary journeys and is often mentioned in the Epistles (Col. 4:14; 2 Tim. 4:11; Philem. 24). The view of the early church is corroborated by the "we" sections of Acts. Elimination of other companions leaves only Luke as possible author of that book (Acts 16:10–17; 20:5–21:18: 27:1–28:16). In addition, Luke's use of medical language has been well documented, and this "beloved physician" makes frequent references in his Gospel and in Acts to illnesses, diagnosis, descriptions and details of sickness and cures, and even gives marks of recovery.

Luke wrote his Gospel before writing Acts (Acts 1:1), probably around A.D. 58 while Paul was in prison in Caesarea. There Luke would have had opportunity to consult his eye witnesses and talk with others in his careful investigation of the facts (Luke 1:2, 3).

Distinctives. Considering the Book of Luke along with Acts, this physician wrote more of our NT than any other person. Like the other Gospels, this one is an "orderly account" of Jesus' life (1:3). It follows the same chronological order as Matthew and Mark. But Luke contains much material which is not in the other Gospels. For instance, some six miracles and no less than nineteen parables are unique to Luke (see pp. 510, 511).

Luke places more stress than the other Gospel writers on Jesus' relationships with people. Christ is shown as a cosmopolitan, socializing comfortably with all sorts of people, and concerned about everyone. Luke is also filled with character sketches of the people Jesus meets, thus setting a much more "human" tone in his book.

But Luke is no humanist. A distinctive emphasis in Luke is his stress on the Holy Spirit. Jesus, as Son of God and perfect human being, lived his life on earth in dependence on the Spirit. The Spirit's work infuses events related to Jesus' birth, and it is a Jesus "full of the Holy Spirit" and "led by the Spirit" who later performs his miracles. Luke holds out hope to all of us for a life like Jesus' own, resting on Jesus' promise to clothe his followers with the Spirit. As Luke records, we will be given "power from on high" (24:49). This theme is picked up in Acts, which shows the role of the Holy Spirit in the continuing life of Jesus' followers.

A last distinction is the attention Luke pays to women. Mary, Elizabeth, and Anna are given priority in the birth story (1, 2). Women who support Jesus' mission financially (8:1–3), Mary and Martha (10:32–42), even an immoral woman (7:36–40), and the many present at the Crucifixion and Resurrection, are included by Luke in his account.

In what has been called the most beautiful Greek of the NT era, Luke gives us a warm and personal report, full of insight into the greatest life ever lived.

Structure and Outline. Luke, like the other Gospel writers, arranges events in a general chronological and geographical framework. Like the others he lists events within this framework to suit his focus and emphasis. The outline shows the geographical structure, which can be traced on the map on page 452.

Outline

Fishermen on the Sea of Galilee

The Damascus Gate in Jerusalem

Miracles of Jesus in the Gospels

Two blind men see	Matt. 9:27–31
Dumb spirit cast out	Matt. 9:32–33
Money in fish's mouth	Matt. 17:24–27
Deaf and dumb man cured	Mark 7:31–37
Blind man cured	Mark 8:22–26
Great netting of fish	Luke 5:1–11
Widow's son raised from the dead	Luke 7:11–17
Crippled woman healed	Luke 13:11–17
Dropsy cured	Luke 14:1–6
Ten lepers cleansed	Luke 17:11–19
Malchus' ear reattached	Luke 22:50–51
Water turned to wine	John 2:1–11
Nobleman's son cured of fever	John 4:46–54
Invalid cured	John 5:1–9
Man born blind cured	John 9:1–7
Lazarus raised from the dead	John 11:38–44
Great catch of 153 fish	John 21:1–14
Syro-phoenician's daughter cured	Matt. 15:28; Mark 7:24
Four thousand fed	Matt. 15:32; Mark 8:1
Fig tree cursed	Matt. 12:22; Mark 11:13,14
Centurion's servant healed	Matt. 8:5; Luke 7:1
Blind and dumb man healed	Matt. 12:22; Luke 11:14
Demoniac in synagogue healed	Mark 1:23; Luke 4:33
Leper cured	Matt. 8:2; Mark 1:40; Luke 5:12
Peter's mother-in-law cured	Matt. 8:14; Mark 1:30; Luke 4:38
Tempest stilled	Matt. 8:23: Mark 4:37; Luke 8:22
Demoniacs cured	Matt. 8:28; Mark 5:1; Luke 8:26
Paralytic cured	Matt. 9:2; Mark 2:3; Luke 5:18
Jairus' daughter raised	Matt. 9:23; Mark 5:23; Luke 8:41
Woman's issue of blood healed	Matt 9:20; Mark 5:25; Luke 8:43
Man's withered hand cured	Matt. 12:10; Mark 3:1; Luke 6:6
Devil cast out of boy	Matt. 17:14; Mark 9:17; Luke 9:37
Blind man cured	Matt. 20:30; Mark 10:46; Luke 18:35
Christ walks on the sea	Matt. 14:25; Mark 6:48; John 6:19
The five thousand fed	Matt. 14:15; Mark 6:34; Luke 9:10; John 6:1–14

Parables of Jesus

The tares .... Matt. 13:24–30
The hidden treasure .... Matt. 13:44
The pearl of great price .... Matt. 13:45,46
The fishing net .... Matt. 13:47,48
The unmerciful servant .... Matt. 18:23–34
Laborers in the vineyard .... Matt. 20:1–16
The man with two sons .... Matt. 21:28–32
The marriage feast (given by the king's son). .... Matt. 22:1–14
The ten virgins, the talents .... Matt. 25:1–30
The sheep and the goats .... Matt. 25:31–46

The blade, the ear, the full grain .... Mark 4:26–29
Watch for his coming! .... Mark 13:34–36

The two debtors .... Luke 7:36–50
The good Samaritan .... Luke 10:25–37
The friend at midnight .... Luke 11:5–8
The rich fool .... Luke 12:16–21
The watchful servants .... Luke 12:35–40
The wise steward .... Luke 12:42–48
The barren fig-tree .... Luke 13:6–9
The great banquet .... Luke 14:16–24
The tower and counting its cost .... Luke 14:28–33
The lost sheep .... Luke 15:3–7
The lost coin .... Luke 15:8–10
The prodigal son .... Luke 15:11–32
The unjust steward .... Luke 16:1–13
The rich man and Lazarus .... Luke 16:19–31
The master and servant .... Luke 17:7–10
The importunate widow .... Luke 18:1–8
The Pharisee and the publican .... Luke 18:9–14
The pounds.................................... Luke 19:12–27

House built on the rock .... Matt. 7:24–27; Luke 6:48,49
The leaven .... Matt. 13:33; Luke 13:20,21
The lost sheep .... Matt. 18:12–14; Luke 15:3–7

The candle under a
    bushel .... Matt. 5:14–16; Mark 4:21,22; Luke 8:16,17
The new cloth on
    old garment .... Matt. 9:16; Mark 2:21; Luke 5:36
New wine and old
    bottles .... Matt. 9:17; Mark 2:22; Luke 5:37,38
The sower........... Matt. 13:3–9, 18:23; Mark 4:3–20; Luke 8:4–15
The mustard seed .... Matt. 13:31,32; Mark 4:31,32; Luke 13:18,19
The vineyard and
    husbandmen .... Matt. 21:33–41; Mark 12:1–9; Luke 20:9–16
Young leaves of the
    fig tree .... Matt. 24:32–35; Mark 13:28–31; Luke 21:29

Chapter 1. Jesus' Birth Foretold

The Forerunner; 1:5–25. There is an air of expectancy in Judea.
Josephus and two other secular writers tell of the stirring. Many
realize that the 490-year-period predicted in Daniel 9:24–27 to
the coming of Messiah is drawing to an end. The angel Gabriel
appears to a priest named Zechariah, to announce that his wife
Elizabeth will bear a son who "will go on before the Lord, in
the spirit and power of Elijah" (1:17). This reference to a prediction
in Malachi 4:5 is clear evidence that the Messiah, focus of the
prophets' dreams, is about to appear. The child will be John the
Baptist and will be Jesus' cousin.

Jesus' Birth Foretold; 1:26–38. It was the "desire of women"
(cf. Dan. 11:37) in Israel to be the mother of the Messiah (see
Messiah, p. 255). Six months after John is conceived, the angel
Gabriel visits a young virgin named Mary, engaged to a man of
David's royal line named Joseph. The angel announces that Mary
is the chosen one. His message is clear. Conception will come by
the "power of the Most High" (35). The child, to be named Jesus,
will be both "the Son of God" and the one fulfilling the prophet's
promise of a king of David's family line—one who can as God
and man reign forever over a "kingdom" which "will never end"
(33). Like each teller of the Gospel story, Luke immediately establishes the fact that the person of whom he writes is God in the
flesh (cf. Matt. 1:23; Mark 1:1; John 1:14).

Mary's Reaction; 1:39–56. Mary hurries to visit an older relative,
Elizabeth, who is the wife of Zechariah. Elizabeth is moved by
the Holy Spirit to confirm Gabriel's message. Mary will be "the
mother of my Lord" (43). Mary's poetic song of praise lets us
see her inner reaction to this amazing privilege.

Mary's pregnancy was bound to be misunderstood by many.
Read her song of thanksgiving (46–55). What does it tell
you about Mary as a person and about her faith in God? What
concept of God is expressed here which helps explain how Mary
could accept such risks?

Birth of John the Baptist; 1:57–80. At John's birth Zechariah is also moved by the Holy Spirit to prophesy. This and other events surrounding John's birth fill the neighbors with awe; soon "throughout the hill country" of Judea people are gossiping about John's birth. These events undoubtedly help to intensify the sense of expectation that builds in Judea as the time for Messiah draws near.

This is one of the few sections of Luke in which he deals with OT prophetic background. To grasp the implications of Zechariah's prophecy see: with 68, 69, *Davidic Covenant,* p. 177; with 70–73, *Covenant,* p. 51; with 74–79, *Messiah,* 255, and OT *Eschatology,* 372, 373.

Chapter 2. Jesus' Birth and Childhood

NT Chronology. Luke is a careful researcher. He dates his events, following the practices of historians of his time. We know some pivotal dates precisely—others with less certainty. Herod's death can be confidently placed early in 4 B.C. Jesus' birth was in the winter of 5/4 B.C. (The B.C. date comes from the calculations by Dionysius Exiguus, who formulated the calendar we still use, but made errors in his calculations.) Other events are difficult to date, such as the census spoken of in Luke 2. Quirinius was in Syria twice, first as imperial legate around 7–5 B.C. Roman census figures were gathered every fourteen years, but often first censuses met with resistance. In Gaul (France) the first census took forty years! It is likely the Jews would also resist (cf. 2 Sam. 24). It's possible the "first enrollment" Luke speaks of began in 8 B.C. and was concluded in A.D. 6, the official date of a well-known Judean census. In spite of such difficulties with dating, we can give a probable NT chronology for the Gospels as follows:

6 B.C. (summer)	Angel appears to Zechariah	Luke 1:5–25
6 months later	Angel appears to Mary	Luke 1:26–38
	Mary visits Elizabeth	Luke 1:39–56
5 B.C.		
3 months later	Mary returns to Nazareth	Luke 1:56
	John the Baptist born	Luke 1:57–80
	Angel appears to Joseph	Matthew 1:18–24
5 B.C. (winter)	Birth of Jesus	Luke 2:1–7
	Angels tell shepherds	Luke 2:8–20
8 days later	Jesus circumcized	Luke 2:21

4 B.C.

32 days later	Jesus presented at temple	Luke 2:22–38
(spring)	Wise men visit	Matt. 2:1–12
	Flight to Egypt	Matt. 2:13–15
	Children slaughtered	Matt. 2:16–18
	Herod dies	
?	Return to Nazareth	Matt. 2:19–23
A.D. 29 (fall)	Baptism of Jesus	Luke 3:1–20
A.D. 33 (spring)	Crucifixion of Jesus	Luke 23

To Bethlehem; 2:1–7. Mary and Joseph travel to Bethlehem, for Joseph is from David's line and this is his home. The birth takes place in a warm cave, such as are commonly used for stables in that rocky land.

The Shepherds; 2:8–20. The miracle is not for the shepherds alone. Their report of the angels' visitation is something for Mary to "treasure up" and "ponder in her heart" as the long years roll by.

Presentation at the Temple; 2:21–40. Each first-born son of a Jewish family belongs to the Lord and must be redeemed (cf. Exod. 13–16). At the temple the family is approached by two devout persons, Simeon and the prophetess Anna. Each is moved by the Spirit to recognize Jesus as the promised Redeemer.

The fact that only two pigeons were offered in sacrifice (2:24) shows the family was poor. If able they would have offered a lamb (cf. Lev. 5:7).

Over and over Luke stresses the Holy Spirit's role in events surrounding Jesus' birth. Underline each place the Spirit's name appears in chapters 1 and 2. What are his different ministries?

Jesus at the Temple; 2:41–51. A final sketch shows Jesus at the temple on his first Passover trip to Jerusalem. He sits listening to the teachers of the law and asking questions, amazing all with his grasp of spiritual truth. Luke's last words about Jesus' childhood tell of his return to Nazareth with his parents, to live as an obedient son in the carpenter's family.

Luke has carefully blended two apparently contradictory themes. (1) Everything about Jesus' birth is unique, from his virgin birth to the confirming signs that cause such a stir of expectation in Judea. God is preparing not only his Son, but also his people. (2) Everything about Jesus' birth is also commonplace. He is born into a poor family, in a stable behind a Bethlehem inn. His parents, like thousands of others, do everything required by the law of the Lord and by custom. Jesus is just another Jewish child who is born, grows up, and lives quietly in a small town far from the

Nomads crossing the Sinai desert, reminiscent of the three wise men coming to worship the baby Jesus

An inside view of the Church of the Nativity built over the traditional sites of Jesus' birth

seat of power. For over thirty years Jesus lives this hidden and
normal life as a pious, hard-working Jew. His mother has only
memories of amazing events to ponder as she watches him grow
to manhood.

Chapter 3. John's Ministry

John the Baptist; 3:1–22. Jesus is in his early thirties when John
the Baptist begins his ministry. John preaches that the Messiah
will come soon. Like the OT prophets, he strikes out against the
sins of God's people, stressing an OT message of justice and compassion (3:11–14). John answers rumors that he may be Messiah
by promising "one more powerful than I" who will soon appear.
This person will also baptize, but with the Holy Spirit and fire
rather than water (see *John's Ministry,* p. 469). Then Jesus comes
to be baptized by his cousin and is identified by the Spirit as God's
Son.

Jesus' Genealogy; 3:23–37. This genealogy differs from the one
given by Matthew in two ways. (1) Luke traces Jesus' line back
to Adam, while Matthew focuses on Abraham and David. Luke's
purpose is to show the full humanity of Jesus, the perfect man.
Matthew's goal is to show the right of Jesus to rule, as inheritor
of the Abrahamic and Davidic covenants. (2) Several names differ,
for Luke traces the lineage through Mary, and Matthew through
Joseph. Thus Joseph who is Jesus' father ["so it was thought"]
is the son-in-law of Heli in Luke's genealogy rather than son. The
word "son" may indicate either.

The Holy Spirit, NT

The NT reveals the Spirit to be a Person, one with the Father and
Son in Trinity (cf. Matt. 28:19; John 15:26). He is also given a personal
name in the NT: Comforter. While the Spirit is mentioned in the OT
(see p. 356), the full revelation of his personality comes in the New.

Three NT lines of teaching about the Spirit are important to us. First,
the Spirit is seen in the Gospels as the one who superintends the birth of
Christ, and who is the source of Jesus' strength and power in ministry
(cf. Matt. 12:28; Luke 4:18; John 3:34). Jesus depended on the Spirit for,
while he is God, he is also truly man. Luke's emphasis on Jesus' humanity
explains why he places so much emphasis on the Spirit in his Gospel.

Second, the Spirit is promised to Jesus' followers and spoken of as the
source of our power (John 14:16,17; 16:5–15; Acts 1:8). In Acts we see
the impact of the Spirit who works through the men and women he baptizes
and fills with power. This theme of inner power is often repeated as the
history of the early church unfolds.

Third, the Epistles go into great detail about the role of the Spirit in the life of the individual believer and the Christian community. He is the one who leads us to understand and obey God's will, and he gives power for the control of our sinful nature (Rom. 8:5–11). The believer's new relationship with God is not through law but through the Spirit (Rom. 7:4–6). As we live, responsive to the Spirit's promptings, he works a transformation of our character (Gal. 6:22,23).

It is the Holy Spirit who empowers individuals for ministry today. He gives each believer a special capacity to contribute to the lives of others (1 Cor. 12:1–11). While Christians may debate how these spiritual gifts find expression today, the biblical emphasis is clear for us all: each of us is called and gifted by God to serve others for "the common good" (12:7). In the context of close and loving personal relationships, the Holy Spirit does his work building human lives (cf. Rom. 12; 1 Cor. 12–14; Eph. 4).

The vitality of our personal Christian life, and the vitality of our congregations, depends on the person and the work of the Spirit, whom God has given to be with us to fill our lives with his power.

Chapter 4. Jesus' Ministry Begins

Jesus' earliest ministry takes place in Galilee. It is preceded by a personal test, over which Jesus proves victorious. Luke moves on quickly to describe many pressures on this perfect man.

The Temptation of Jesus; 4:1–12. Luke gives a different sequence of the temptations than does Matthew (4:1–11). Matthew's theme is Jesus as the promised King. Thus to him the offer of all the world's kingdoms to Jesus by Satan is the culminating test. Luke emphasizes Jesus' humanity, and the culminating temptation is the suggestion to prove God's presence by leaping from the temple (9–12). All Gospel writers adjust the sequence of events to suit their theme and emphasis.

We can sense from Luke why the last temptation is so great. Jesus has been led by God into a desert. He has fasted forty days and been subject to Satan's pressures. How alone a person must feel in such a situation! How great the need to know that God is there. But Jesus returns to Deuteronomy and a rebuke given God's OT people for doubting the Lord's presence (Deut. 6:16; cf. Exod. 17:1–7). Jesus will obey the Word of God and trust in even this circumstance.

The two resources which you and I have in facing temptations are stressed here by Luke. The Holy Spirit who fills Jesus, and the Word which guides him, are both gifts God has given to you and me!

Jesus Rejected at Nazareth; 4:13–30. Luke immediately moves us to Galilee. Jesus returns there "in the power of the Spirit" (14). In his home synagogue at Nazareth Jesus reads an OT passage about the Messiah and applies it to himself! As the stunned congregation whispers, Jesus predicts that his own people will reject him and that he will turn to the Gentiles (24–27), who will receive many blessings associated with the messianic age. This stimulates a furious reaction, just as it does when Paul, speaking to another Jewish audience, tells them God sent him "far away to the Gentiles" (Acts 22:21).

Why were these people so angry they were ready to kill Jesus and the apostle? Israel suffered for centuries under the rule of Gentiles. Though the prophets speak of Messiah bringing blessings to all, these people have fastened on the predictions which speak of God's vengeance on Gentile persecutors! They want the Savior to appear, but not to save them from their own sins. They want him to come and punish the foreigners they have come to hate! The hearts of the Jewish people are not in tune with God: they will reject his Son and the message of forgiveness he brings.

Jesus' Ministries; 4:31–44. The OT prophets speak of Messiah's mission as one of saving and of judging. When Jesus reads from Isaiah 61 in the synagogue (4:17–20) he emphasizes release and stops just before reading these words: "and the day of vengeance of our God" (61:2). Now Luke demonstrates Jesus' mission to the oppressed. Christ frees a man gripped in the possession of a demon (see *Demons,* p. 480) and heals many of "various kinds of sicknesses." And he keeps on preaching the "good news" promises of the kingdom of God.

Chapter 5. Jesus and Sinful Men

The next series of incidents reported by Luke focuses on the ability of Jesus to deal with human sinfulness.

Disciples Called; 5:1–11. Jesus' command to the professional fishermen who became his first disciples leads to a great catch of fish, so astonishing that Peter falls down before Jesus and begs him to leave! Peter senses the hand of God in this man and becomes deeply aware of his own sin. None of us can see perfection in Jesus without awareness of how flawed we are. But Jesus does not leave, nor is he repelled by Peter the sinner. "Don't be afraid," Jesus says, and promises "from now on you will catch men" (10). Jesus not only will deal with sin but will introduce a dynamic new principle of life that enables the sinner to serve God.

Leper Healed; 5:12–16. Three Gospels tell this story. Each emphasizes Jesus' willingness to deal with this man, whose disease made him an outcast. Each one reports that Jesus *touches* the leper. In the OT this disease is symbolic of sin (cf. Isa. 1:5,6).

The Paralytic Forgiven and Healed; 5:17–28. Now Pharisees and other teachers of the Mosaic law come to observe this new preacher and healer. As they watch, a paralytic is brought to Jesus for healing. Seeing the faith of the man and those who carry him, Jesus announces, "Friend, your sins are forgiven" (20). Jesus has made it plain for all how he will deal with man's sin.

The teachers of the law see this as blasphemy. Only God can forgive sin, and they will not recognize Jesus as God's Son. So Christ shows his authority to forgive. He tells the paralyzed man to rise, pick up the mat on which he is lying, and go home. He is immediately healed and leaves praising God. Jesus' authority is demonstrated conclusively.

Levi (Matthew); 5:21–31. There is another demonstration of Jesus' authority to forgive. He calls a man we know better as Matthew, author of the first Gospel. Levi is a tax collector. This occupation is doubly condemned in Judea: tax collectors defrauded others and collaborated with the Roman conquerors. But Jesus calls Levi to follow him and even eats in his home. The repentance and changed lives of people who are known sinners is a powerful demonstration of Jesus' authority over sin—and of his power to cleanse and forgive (cf. Matt. 21:28–32; Luke 19:1–10).

Jesus and New Wineskins; 5:33–39. Jesus intends to initiate a new era. The new will not fit in the container for the old: new ways of life will come that fit the new revelation Jesus brings.

Chapter 6. The Value of Persons

Luke is especially sensitive to human beings. Here he groups several incidents and teachings which help us see the view of other persons which will underlie personal relationships of Jesus' followers.

Lord of the Sabbath; 6:1–11. The Sabbath is set apart in the OT as a day of rest, patterned on God's own rest after creation (Gen. 1). The Pharisees who now criticize Jesus and his disciples belong to a religious sect which places supreme value on keeping the details of Mosaic law, and on their traditional interpretations of the law (see p. 442). According to one Pharisaical interpretation, only a person at the point of death should be given medical treatment on the Sabbath! Now Jesus shows up the hard-heartedness of these men, whose religion fails to reflect God's values. Jesus claims the right, as Lord of the Sabbath, to establish its true meaning (5). Immediately he acts to heal a man with a shriveled hand, while the Pharisees and teachers of the law watch closely, hoping to accuse him. Boldly Jesus announces that it is "lawful to do good" on the Sabbath. Jesus' actions expose the uncaring attitude of the Pharisees and establish clearly the priority God places on meeting human need (cf. Matt. 23:23,24).

The Beatitudes; 6:12–26. In Luke the Beatitudes are directed specifically to the disciples. The culture in which they live values wealth and social acceptance. Yet Jesus, who has chosen common men as his followers (12–16), announces, "Blessed are you poor . . ." (20). Each Beatitude shows that Jesus values persons for themselves alone. Following Jesus means learning a new value system which puts disciples in conflict with society and often will lead to rejection. "Respectability" has never been a sign of spiritual achievement!

Love for Enemies; 6:27–36. What is a sign of spiritual achievement? Jesus now shows how great a priority Jesus places on human beings, in the dramatic command, "Love your enemies, do good to those who hate you" (27). Human interpersonal relationships are based on what is called the "norm of reciprocity": we treat others as they treat us (32–34). But Jesus says we are to model our relationships on God, who is merciful and "kind to the ungrateful and wicked."

Judging Others; 6:37–43. Relationships with others are to be free of judging (see *Judging*, p. 520), filled with forgiveness. The promise is that, as God's people set a new pattern of life, others will begin to respond in similar ways (38).

For this kind of life self-examination, not criticism of others, is important (39–42). Actually, it's never necessary for us to judge others. As time goes by, each life produces its own fruit: good fruit comes from those with good in their heart, bad from those who have evil stored within.

Foundation for Life with Others; 6:46–49. The foundation for life with others is not just knowing what Jesus says but practicing it. How clearly the words of Jesus in this chapter call us to live a life of constant love for one another.

Judging Others

Luke, James, and Paul all deal with "judging." Each says clearly that believers are not to take it on themselves to evaluate one another. "There is only one Lawgiver and Judge," James says, "the one who is able to save and destroy. But you—who are you to judge your neighbor" (James 4:12)? Paul develops this theme in Romans 14. He teaches that Jesus died and rose again "that he might be Lord of both the dead and the living. . . . why (then) do you judge your brother? Or why do you look down on your brother?" (14:9,10).

Paul carefully develops this teaching in Romans. We sin if we fail to help each other be responsible to God, our true Master, and snatch to ourselves his perogative of passing judgment (14:1–4). When believers do let a critical spirit and attitude intrude, the unity of the body of Christ is distorted, for we will look down on some and actively condemn others (14:3,10).

These sharp prohibitions of judging sometimes cause confusion when compared with two NT passages which speak on church discipline and the settlement of disputes (1 Cor. 5). In the case of discipline, the church is not called on to judge others but to take a stand with God against actions which he has clearly specified in his Word to be sin. In disputes between believers, the facts of the particular situation are to be evaluated. "Judging" involves a critical attitude toward the beliefs, motives, or convictions of another person. And judging is strictly prohibited by God.

We only owe others one debt, the Bible teaches: "the continuing debt to love one another" (Rom. 13:8). We do not owe it to others to stand in judgment over them—only to stand with them as members of a loving, supportive community in which each can grow to know God better. How wonderful it is to be able to look at a brother or sister uncritically, freed by God to love him or her unstintingly, and so to communicate the amazing grace of our Lord.

For study: Luke 6:36–45; Romans 14:1–15:8; 1 Corinthians 5.

Chapter 7. The Role of Faith

The next events in Luke's history illustrate something of the role of faith in our relationship with Jesus.

The Centurion; 7:1–10. The prime model of faith in Jesus is not a Jew but a Roman army officer. Though one of the conquering foreigners, he "loves our nation and has built our synagogue" (5). Messengers ask Jesus to heal a servant of this officer. As Jesus approaches, the man sends others to intercept the Lord. The Roman humbly states, "I do not deserve to have you come under my roof." He asks Jesus simply to say the word, and the servant will be healed. The officer explains that he is a man "under authority." That is, others obey him because ultimately all the power of Rome stands behind his orders. To see Jesus too as one "under authority" is to recognize that all of God's power stands behind what he says and does! Jesus does speak the word and heal the servant. And Jesus remarks, "I have not found such great faith even in Israel."

Jesus Raises the Widow's Son: 7:11–17. Now Jesus raises the dead son of a widow, and there is no mention of "faith." Why?

To make it clear that the power belongs wholly to Jesus. His works are not *dependent* on our faith. But faith will do for us what it did for the centurion: bring us to Jesus—and give us the confidence that he can act even when he is not physically present!

Jesus and John; 7:18–35. Faith is not easy, especially when God does not act as we expect! Even John the Baptist is shaken when Jesus does not set up the expected kingdom immediately (20). John's messengers are sent back with a report of miracles of healing. Messiah is to care for the oppressed as well as judge (cf. p. 520)!

It is difficult even for a great prophet like John (7:24–27) to have faith when God does not do what we expect or desire. But in Jesus' kingdom we find greatness by surrendering our expectations and trusting God to do what is best (7:28).

The religious people of Jesus' day show us what it means to be without faith (7:29–35). They accept neither John nor Jesus. Rather than submit their expectations to God, they pretend the right to set up criteria which God must meet before they respond.

Jesus Anointed by a Sinful Woman; 7:36–50. A final incident shows one more aspect of faith. Faith is always linked with forgiveness, and forgiveness with love. At a Pharisee's house, an immoral woman creeps in and, weeping, anoints Jesus' feet with tears and expensive ointments. The Pharisee hides a sneer, thinking that if Jesus were really a prophet he would know a sinner touches him— and pull away! Jesus answers the unspoken criticism. When a great debt is canceled, great love is generated. The faith of this woman, who knows herself to be a sinner, has brought forgiveness for sins— and awakened a great love for Jesus. We too must recognize our great need, find forgiveness through faith in Jesus, and know that love for him generated in our hearts.

Summary. Luke 4 through 7 deals with Jesus' earliest ministries and recurring biblical themes. Study each chapter carefully, and focus on these questions: Chapter 5: What is God's attitude toward you as a person who has personal sins and failures? Chapter 6: With what one particular person do you want to improve your personal relationships? What principle in this chapter can you put into practice to improve that relationship? Chapter 7: Faith is both simple and profound. From this chapter develop a one-sentence definition of faith.

Chapters 8, 9. Training the Disciples

The Parable of the Sower; 8:1–21. The crowds following Jesus are large. But this parable points out that only a few will respond to Jesus' words. Those who do will show the reality of response by their actions (16–18). Thus the "good ground," and family relationship with God, are related to a faith which, when it hears God's word, puts that word into practice (15, 19–21).

Four Miracles; 8:22–56. Jesus now performs four miracles, most witnessed primarily by the twelve. When Jesus calms the storm, his disciples' faith is shown to be weak (8:22–25). On the far side of the lake Jesus cleanses a man possessed by many demons (8:26–39). Returning to Jewish territory he heals a woman of a chronic illness while on the way to bring life to a twelve-year-old girl who has died (8:50–56).

This series of miracles shows the full scope of Jesus' power: over nature, over the demonic, over disease, and over death itself. The sequence is a special lesson for the twelve, whose weak faith needs to be shored up before they are sent out on their own mission.

The Twelve Sent Out; 9:1–9. Jesus now sends out the twelve with authority to heal and preach. His instructions to them are given in greater detail in Matthew 10. As they go the whole countryside is full of rumors, focusing on who Jesus might be.

Feeding the Five Thousand; 9:10–17. When Jesus feeds the crowds, it is the disciples who know the full scope of the miracle. They supply the five loaves and two fish, and they gather up the twelve baskets of food left after all have eaten. All these experiences strengthen the disciples' faith for the confession that now comes (cf. 8:25 with 9:20).

Peter's Confession of Faith; 9:18–27. The crowds identify Jesus with one of the great prophets of long ago. But the disciples are now ready to affirm him as "the Christ of God" (9:20). Immediately Jesus speaks of his death and resurrection—and the need for complete daily commitment by his disciples. But there is also a promise of glory at the end of the disciples' path.

The Transfiguration; 9:28–36. Jesus' transfiguration gives three of the twelve a glimpse of the glory about which Jesus has spoken. On a mountaintop Jesus' "face changed, and his clothes became as bright as a flash of lightning." Moses and Elijah appear with him "in glorious splendor." The message to the disciples is clear. Beyond the cross, glory awaits Jesus—and those who follow him.

A Healing; 9:37–45. Back in the valley, Jesus is met by a crowd and a man whose son is subject to convulsions. The disciples have been unable to heal the boy. Jesus does so now (9:37–43). But when Jesus speaks to the twelve about his coming death, while the crowd is still buzzing over the miracle, they do not understand him (9:42–45). All Jesus' power cannot release him from his coming suffering.

Following Jesus; 9:46–56. The disciples have realized who Jesus is but are still far from sharing his attitudes and values. They have not yet reached the goal Jesus states in Luke 6:40, to "be like their teacher." This is shown as the disciples fall to bickering over which of them will be greatest. They must be instructed in servanthood: that "the least among you—he is the greatest."

When some Samaritans, descendants of foreign peoples who live in territory that was once northern Israel, refuse to welcome Jesus and his followers into their village, James and John want to call down fire from heaven to destroy them. The disciples must still learn that Jesus' way is to give one's life for others, not snatch life from them (9:51–55). Belief in Jesus is simply a beginning for a disciple. Progress along the way requires a transformation of attitudes and values, until the follower reflects his Lord.

The Necessity of Choice; 9:57–62. This chapter concludes with three brief sketches. One man wants to follow Jesus but turns away when told that discipleship can involve privation (9:57,58). Another is commanded to follow but asks Jesus to wait until his father dies (9:59). Yet another offers to follow—conditionally. To each there is a single message. Unconditional commitment to Jesus is a requirement of discipleship.

Put yourself in the place of the disciples as you read through these chapters. How does each event affect you? What part does each play in helping you become a better disciple of Jesus? What section of these chapters do you believe is most important for modern, present-day disciples? Why?

Chapter 10. Priorities for Disciples

Seventy-two Missionaries Sent Out; 10:1–23. Earlier Jesus sent out the twelve. Now seventy-two are sent out in pairs to preach and heal. The teams return, excited about the powers they have exercised. But Jesus tells them to rejoice in their relationship with God (20). He himself, full of joy, praises God for the individuals who have responded to his gospel (21,22).

The Good Samaritan; 10:24–37. OT law places love for God in the place of highest priority. But a corollary of love for God is love for one's fellow men (27). Jesus' familiar story of the good Samaritan points up the fact that any human being in need is our neighbor and is to be loved.

Mary and Martha; 10:38–42. One last incident helps to establish priorities. In the home of some of his followers, two sisters respond differently to Jesus. One is distracted by all the work that must be done to prepare for Jesus' visit: the other sits at Jesus' feet and listens to what he says. Mary, the listener, has "chosen what is better."

How beautiful. Jesus affirms Mary in a disciple's role—a role reserved by the Rabbis for men alone. And with equality, he affirms an important priority. Any work we do "for" God must flow from a significant personal relationship with the Lord.

Chapter 11:1-13. Jesus on Prayer

Jesus' own life of prayer leads his disciples to ask for instruction. His teaching comes in a series of brief but vital sayings, which put this vital aspect of Christian experience in clear perspective.

The "disciples' prayer" (2) begins with confidence in the unique relationship we have with God in Christ. He is "Father" as well as Sovereign Lord! The rest of the prayer stresses dependence on the Lord (3) and a life lived humbly with others (4).

Jesus' illustration of the man who knocks at a friend's door to ask for bread involves teaching by contrast. One who needs to borrow from a neighbor may get what he wants simply by making so much noise the bread is given to be rid of him! But, Jesus goes on, God is our *Father*. What father would refuse a son, or give what is bad for him? No, all who come to God as Father in prayer will receive (see *Prayer, NT*, p. 526).

Chapter 11:14-53. Opposition Develops

Jesus' growing popularity alarms the religious leaders, who feel their place and authority threatened. Rumors are started: Jesus has power over demons only because he is in league with their prince (14-28). Also these leaders demand additional miraculous signs (29-32). Jesus answers the foolish charge and refuses more signs. There will be only the "sign of Jonah": as Jonah was in the whale, so Jesus will lie for three days in the grave. But Jesus also speaks in sharp condemnation. He is greater than Jonah. Yet Nineveh, the capital of a pagan nation, repented when Jonah preached. Now God's own people will not respond to this one who is "greater than Jonah." Great condemnation for this generation must follow.

The Light Is Darkness; 11:35-53. The teachers of the law claim to have insight into truth through God's law. But the Pharisees and leaders are blind to the true meaning of that law. Their blindness darkens their whole life (33–36).

It is while dining at a Pharisee's house, not before the crowds, that Jesus scathingly exposes the spiritual darkness he has just spoken of symbolically. But the listeners do not respond with repentance when Jesus catalogs their sins. Instead these Pharisees and teachers of the law "oppose him fiercely."

Chapter 12. Jesus on Materialism

One characteristic of the Pharisees who oppose Jesus is their grasping love of status and wealth. Jesus now speaks openly against them, warning his listeners to guard against their attitudes.

Prayer, NT

The NT speaks often about prayer and includes many prayers which can serve as models for us to study. But the emphasis in the NT, established in Luke 11 and often reflected in other passages, rests on the fact that prayer is an expression of personal relationship. In Jesus we are children of God, and God to us is always "Father."

Thus the pagan approach, which emphasizes empty repetitions in the vain hope of attracting attention (Luke 11:7,8; Matt. 6:7,8), is not for us. Instead we are free to come to God in the confidence that we are welcomed and heard (Heb. 4:14–16). We *know* that God will give us his good gifts and meet our needs.

This is the basic perspective on prayer maintained throughout the NT. God does not run us through some obstacle course of "conditions" before he will hear us! Instead God invites us to come as a child to a Father, knowing that he loves us, will hear us, and that God the good Father will give us what is best.

For study: Model NT Prayers. Matt. 6:9–14; John 17; Acts 4:23–31; Ephesians 1:15–22; 3:14–21; Colossians 1:3–14. See also *Prayer, OT,* p. 216.

On Guard; 12:1–12. The disciples of Jesus are to be on guard against the ways of the Pharisees. Only confidence in our value to God can free us from fear of other human beings (4–7) and help us to take a bold stand that openly affirms our trust in Jesus.

The Rich Fool; 12:13–21. Two things link the story of a rich man who plans to build larger barns to hold his possessions, but dies suddenly that night. His greedy materialism reflects an attitude common to the Pharisees. And freedom from materialistic concerns come from that same thing which frees us from fear of others— the confidence that God values us highly.

Do Not Worry; 12:22–32. Jesus develops this second link. God cares for the flowers and the birds. We, "much more valuable" to God than these, need not worry or set our hearts on "what you will eat or drink." Without the pressure of worry about future needs, we are able to give freely to others. By giving we put our treasures where our hearts are: with God himself, and the glorious future to which he leads us.

Watchfulness; 12:33–48. As Jesus' servants, disciples are entrusted with material possessions which are, ultimately, God's own. We are not to use them to harm others, or to indulge ourselves (45). Instead we are to use possessions as God's stewards.

What are your own feelings and attitudes about material possessions? Is there something in this chapter especially for you?

The Christian and Money

Jesus' basic teaching on material possessions is put simply in Luke 12:15: "a man's life does not consist in the abundance of his possessions." Jesus' followers are freed, by relationship with God, to concentrate on that of which life *does* consist.

Freedom comes when we grasp how greatly God loves and values us. Thus he will meet our needs (12:30,31). Freedom is expressed by use of our possessions to meet the needs of others (12:32; 2 Cor. 8:13–15).

The Bible says that love of money is a "root of all kinds of evil" (1 Tim. 6:10). But riches are not evil in themselves. The danger is always in our attitude. Those who "want to be rich fall into temptations and a trap and into many foolish and harmful desires" (1 Tim. 6:9). If the rich resist the temptation to arrogance, and resist resting their hope in their riches, wealth can be used. Those who are "generous and willing to share" (1 Tim. 6:18) have a valid ministry to others. What is really important then? To not let money distract from what Scripture shows us is the true center of life for Jesus' followers. We are called to love and to trust God—and to value persons above our possessions.

Dangers to Be Faced; 12:49–59. Jesus does not promise an easy life, for his own life is filled with stress and tension. Turning to the crowds, Jesus speaks of the storm about to break over them (54–56) and the necessity for each person to make his own decision about what is right. No one will suffer punishment *for* another individual: each one must act now to step beyond the danger of that judgment which looms for those who do not recognize the Lord.

Chapter 13. Call for Repentance

Repentance; 13:1–9. A short time before, the Roman governor had sent disguised soldiers into an unruly crowd of Galileans. On a signal his men threw off their cloaks and beat the Galileans with clubs. The point Jesus makes is that the Galileans, who were not better or worse than his listeners, met a sudden, unexpected fate. His hearers must repent or they too will perish (1–5). God has given Israel her last opportunity to produce fruit (6–9).

Healing on the Sabbath; 13:10–17. The need for repentance is graphically demonstrated in an incident Luke now relates. A woman, crippled for eighteen years, comes to a synagogue while Jesus is teaching. He heals her—and is criticized by the indignant synagogue ruler. Jesus has again "worked" on the Sabbath! Jesus lashes out against this heartlessness and hypocrisy, humiliating his opponents.

Two Parables; 13:18–21. Each suggests that God's kingdom begins with the small, and grows only gradually.

The Narrow Door; 13:22–35. The narrow door Jesus refers to is repentance, and willingness to associate oneself with the small and apparently insignificant. Few will be able to enter (22–30). Jesus will take no pleasure, however, in the judgment that falls on those who drive him away (31–33). Instead Luke shows us Jesus weeping over Jerusalem and the people he longs to gather to himself, "but you were not willing."

Chapter 14. Disciples in Contrast

At a Pharisee's House; 14:1–14. The same old conflicts between Jesus and the religious people of his time again emerge. Jesus challenges them concerning Sabbath healings, but these teachers of the law remain silent (1–6). The way the guests seek out places of honor at the table shouts in silent language of the pride of these people. Jesus corrects them and appeals for the poor and the outcasts.

The Parable of the Banquet; 14:15–24. The sullen unresponsiveness of the religious leaders causes Jesus to tell a story about a great banquet and the guests who are invited to come. One after the other they hang back until, angry at all the excuses, the homeowner sends his servants out to fill the hall with the outcasts of society.

Jesus' disciples may not be "socially acceptable." But they are those who respond to God's invitation to come!

The Cost of Discipleship; 14:25–35. Discipleship is demanding. While Jesus invites followers, there should be no doubt that allegiance to Jesus will represent the disciple's first commitment. The use of "hate" in the passage is simply a graphic and colloquial way of stating complete commitment (cf. Rom. 9:10–13). Each listener is invited to consider the cost before making his or her commitment.

Chapter 15. Parables of God's Love

Luke includes many parables. Most of them are not found in other Gospels. These parables, unlike the parables of the kingdom in Matthew 13, are designed to unveil rather than obscure truth. Speaking of commonplace experiences, Jesus expresses many truths which have infused his whole ministry.

The Lost Sheep; 15:1–7. The parable of the lost sheep shows that God does welcome sinners—and rejoices when even one turns to him.

The Lost Coin; 15:8–10. Like a woman who recovers a lost coin, God rejoices over a single sinner who repents.

The Lost Son; 5:11–31. The two earlier stories have prepared the way for what we know as the story of the "prodigal son." The young son is given the freedom he demands by his father, even at the risk that the freedom might be misused. But the choices he makes lead to personal disaster. Finally the son comes to his senses. He returns to his father, ready to confess his sin, and hoping to be accepted as a hired man. But he is not a hired man; he is a son. And the father welcomes him back with joy and orders a feast prepared for him.

But there is also an older son, who is angry that the father is so forgiving. Like the Pharisees, the older son will neither see his own attitude as sin, nor will he take any joy in the rescue of his brother from sin's bondage.

What does the picture of the father in this story teach you about God? What warnings do you see here about attitudes toward others?

Chapter 16. Use of Possessions

The parable of the prodigal son raises a question which Jesus now explores. The father seemed unconcerned about what most irritated the older brother: "this son of yours has squandered your property with prostitutes." Not only is the property wasted but wasted immorally! Yet God in the guise of the father welcomes back the son! What then is Jesus' view of the man's possessions?

The Shrewd Manager; 16:1–18. A business manager about to be fired goes to his employer's creditors and has them falsify their debts. The employer later commends the manager, not for his dishonesty, but because he looked ahead and tried to use possessions in his care to prepare for his future! Jesus remarks that the people of the world are more shrewd in this than the "people of light."

The money-loving Pharisees who hear the story sneer (14–15). But Jesus is speaking of them. Love of money means devotion to one of this world's idols (13) and conflicts with love of God. Like the dishonest manager, his hearers should at least have sense enough to look ahead, beyond the present, and use possessions to prepare for the eternity that awaits them.

Jesus emphasizes this in verses 16–17. All that the OT prophets have foretold will surely happen: all that has happened since John testifies to the kingdom's rapid approach.

Thus what Jesus teaches here is that possessions should be used but with eternity's values in view.

The Rich Man and Lazarus; 16:19–31. The story Jesus now tells underlines the importance of eternity. When death comes to a rich man and a beggar, the two find themselves still "alive"! But they are separated. The rich man is in torment (see *Hell, NT,* p. 531), while the beggar is with Abraham in a place reserved for the blessed.

The story does more than stress the importance of preparing for a future every person must one day face. The rich man asks to be allowed to return and warn his brothers. He is rejected. They already have the Scriptures. Those who reject the clear testimony of the Word of God will not believe even if (and when!) one returns from the dead.

Chapter 17. The Coming Kingdom

Forgiveness No Option; 17:1–10. Jesus tells his disciples that they are to extend unlimited forgiveness to each other (1–4). They are shaken by what they view as a difficult command and beg for more faith (5). Jesus corrects them. Faith is for moving mountains (6). Those who are servants, and hear their master's command, have only duty (7–10). This matter of forgiving is not a matter for faith but for obedience. Forgiveness has been commanded by our Lord.

Ten Healed; 17:11–19. When ten lepers are healed, only one turns back to thank Jesus. And he is a foreigner. How typical!

The Coming Kingdom; 17:20–37. The Pharisees ask Jesus when the kingdom of God will come, and Jesus warns them not to look for a visible coming. He tells them that the kingdom is "among you," and in this he means the kingdom is now present in the person of the King. Later Jesus talks with his disciples. The time will come when Jesus is no longer with them. Then his return will be visible—as obvious as a flash of lightning which brightens the night sky (24). But his return will be sudden—and unexpected by the people who live on the earth (28–37).

Hell, NT

The word translated "hell" in the Gospels refers to a place of punishment for the ungodly. The Bible clearly teaches that life, as the conscious continuation of the individual personality, does not end with physical death. Jesus mentions this a number of times and speaks of a place where the ungodly will suffer.

In the teaching of Jesus both fire and darkness are recurring figures used to picture hell's terrible reality. References to hell by Jesus in the synoptic Gospels can be found in the following passages: Matthew 5:22, 29,30; 7:19,23; 8:12; 10:28; 22:13; 23:15; 25:30,41; Mark 9:42,43; 12:40; Luke 12:47,48; 16:19–31. Surely these many references demonstrate that this grim teaching is confirmed from the mouth of Jesus, who we know to be the supreme expression of God's deep love for humankind.

The Epistles add to Jesus' teaching. They tell of a judgment that comes to men when this life is ended. There is no attempt to obscure the fact that "wrath and fury" await evildoers when they face God the Judge (Rom. 2:3–9). Other NT passages that speak of this judgment are: 1 Thessalonians 5:3; 2 Thessalonians 1:6–9; 2 Peter 2:4–9; Jude 6–7; Revelation 14 and 21.

How do we reconcile the doctrine of hell with Scripture's clear affirmation of God's love? On the one hand we need to realize that we do not sit in judgment over God's moral sensibilities. He is just and loving. If we find it difficult to accept the fairness of hell, we must simply face the fact that we do not understand all that is involved in either God's love or his justice. We must trust him and his decision concerning eternal punishment.

There are things that we can understand. We can understand that God does not speak of hell to frighten us but to help us face one of the most basic issues of life. We can also bow before the Lord in wonder. It is only because God's love for us is so great that he stepped into our world to take on himself the punishment due us. In Jesus' suffering on Calvary, he rescued from deserved punishment all who will come to God through Jesus. As a free gift, God offers not only forgiveness of sins but also the transformation of our character to reflect his own holiness, goodness, mercy, and love.

The doctrine of hell is one of the great mysteries of our faith. It is an awesome reminder of the fact that each individual does have an eternal destiny, which stretches far beyond our brief days on earth. And it is a reminder of the love of Jesus Christ, who suffered and died that you and I might be released from the threat of punishment.

Chapter 18:1–19:15. Various Incidents

It is nearly time for Jesus to enter Jerusalem for his last week. Luke groups several incidents that are not closely related.

The Persistent Widow; 18:1–8. Here, as in Luke 11:5–9, Jesus teaches by contrast. God, so unlike the unjust judge who dispenses justice only to be rid of a persistent widow, will act for his people.

The Pharisee and Tax Collector; 18:9–14. It is not the individual self-righteously proud of his own goodness whom God accepts, but the person who acknowledges his sins and seeks mercy.

The Rich Young Ruler; 18:15–30. Little children who come to Jesus provide an example of simple trust and faith. In contrast a wealthy ruler asks Jesus what he can "do to inherit eternal life"? The ruler misunderstands the nature of goodness; true goodness is an attribute of God alone. To reveal to this "good" man his own need, Jesus tells him to sell his possessions and give all to the poor. This is not a general command for all believers. It is a specific command to a specific individual, designed to show him that, for all his "goodness," he values his money more than his God (22,23).

Riches can be a hindrance in building relationship with God. No one who abandons the pursuit of possessions to follow Jesus will suffer loss; each will gain more than is surrendered (24–30).

Jesus' Death and a Healing; 19:31–42. Jesus again tells his disciples of his rapidly approaching death (31–34). But his own personal burden does not keep Jesus from responding to the needs of others (35–43).

Zacchaeus Is Converted; 19:1–10. Zacchaeus is an outcast because, as a tax collector, he is considered a collaborator with Rome. His conversion and response to Jesus is witnessed by a change in his values. He gives half his possessions to the poor and repays those he has cheated the four times over commanded in the law.

Parable of Service; 19:11–27. Several servants of a nobleman who is absent in a distant country will be given sums of money to put to work for their master. Those who use the money wisely are given more responsibility when the master returns. But the servant who does not put his resources to work loses what he has.

In Jesus' story those who do serve are each given the same praise and proportionate rewards.

It is not how much you and I have to work with but what we do with the gifts God has given us that earns praise from the Lord.

Chapter 19:29–21:4. The Last Week: Final Conflict

Jesus' last week on earth begins with sharp conflict between the Lord and the religious leaders in Jerusalem.

The Triumphal Entry; 19:29–48. Jesus enters Jerusalem early Sunday morning. The crowds shout praises, calling Jesus "the king who comes in the name of the Lord" (19:38). Onlooking Pharisees insist Jesus rebuke his followers! Instead, Jesus warns the Pharisees! Because they refuse to recognize him the city of Jerusalem will be crushed and they will die. The prediction will be fulfilled in less than forty years. In A.D. 70 a Roman army besieges a rebellious Jerusalem and destroys it.

Jesus enters the temple and drives out the merchants. This further arouses the chief priests, who take a percentage of the income. The leaders are eager to kill Jesus but hold back because the people "hung on his words."

Jesus' Authority Questioned; 20:1–19. Jesus refuses to respond when the chief priests and elders demand to know the source of his authority. Instead he tells a story. Some tenants, living on another man's land, refuse to surrender some of the fruit as rent. They beat his servants and finally kill his son. Jesus' authority is that of the Son of the Owner of all: the leaders are usurpers, who will be punished severely when the Lord returns.

Traps Avoided; 20:20–39. Judea has a history of rebelliousness. And Rome is always quick to put down threats to its power. One group tries to trick Jesus into open conflict with Rome by asking questions about taxes. Jesus easily avoids the trap. Coins bear Caesar's image. Let Caesar have what is his. But be sure to give God what is his!

The second trap involves an old religious argument between the Sadducees—who deny a resurrection—and more conservative Jews. This first group comes to Jesus and asks about a much-married woman: whose wife will she be "at the resurrection"? Jesus explains that, like angels, the resurrected do not marry. This verse has been taken by some to suggest that the saved *become* angels. It only suggests one point of resemblance. As for resurrection, Jesus shows from the Scripture that to God, "all are alive."

Hypocrisy and Faith; 20:21–21:4. Jesus now turns on his questioners. He demands these religious leaders, who claim the right to interpret Moses, explain how the Christ can be both David's descendant and David's Lord. The only possible answer is that the Christ is both God and man. But the "leaders" remain silent.

In the hearing of everyone, Jesus warns against the "teachers

of the law." They make a great show of their religion, but all
the while foreclose on the homes of poor widows (20:41–44). The
difference between the leaders and true religion is revealed when
Jesus points out a poor widow, placing two tiny copper coins among
the golden gifts of the rich in the temple treasury. The others
give what they can afford; she gives her all.

Chapter 21. Predictions of the Future

Each of the synoptic Gospels contains Jesus' teachings to his
disciples about what will take place after his death and resurrection.
The most complete teaching is found in Matthew 24, 25 (p. 488–
491.

Chapter 22. The Last Supper

Jesus' final night begins with supper with his friends. John chapters 13 through 16 tell us what was said there.

Betrayal! 22:1–6. Judas, one of the twelve, has gone to the chief
priests and arranged to betray Jesus for money. Against the dark
background of betrayal the intimate final gathering takes place.

The Meal; 22:7–38. Luke emphasizes three things which happen
at this meal. Jesus announces that his body and blood will institute
the long promised new covenant (17–23; see pp. 330, 653). Jesus
again must emphasize servanthood as his disciples argue over who
of them is greatest (24–30). And Peter must be told of his weakness—and his denial by Jesus be predicted (31–38).

This report emphasizes the insensitivity of the disciples of Jesus,
and their continuing misunderstanding. It is only the work of the
Holy Spirit, which Luke will trace in his companion history, Acts,
which transforms these men into the courageous and wiser men
who spearhead the growth of the early church.

The Long Night; 22:39–71. The supper ends and Jesus is launched
on a final night on earth. He is arrested while praying, "exhausted
from sorrow" (39–53). Peter alone follows the mob that takes Jesus
away. But in a courtyard outside the building where Jesus is being
tried, Peter denies Jesus three times (54–62). Mocked and beaten
by the temple guard, Jesus admits openly what he has often
taught—he is the Son of God (63–71).

Chapter 23. The End

Before Pilate; 23:1–25. The leaders of the council bring Jesus
to Pilate and charge him with "subverting the nation" by his claim

to be king. This is a politically sensitive charge. Though Jesus admits being king of the Jews, Pilate refuses to condemn him. During that morning Jesus is moved from one jurisdiction to another (see chart on p. 441). Neither Pilate nor Herod, who might have jurisdiction because he rules in Galilee, will condemn Jesus. Pilate announces that he will punish (beat) Christ but then release him.

But the leaders loudly shout their demand: "Crucify him!" Pilate finally bows to the pressure and turns Jesus over to be executed (for background see John 19:12, pp. 560–561).

The Crucifixion; 23:26–43. Crucifixion is an especially painful form of death (see p. 503). But Jesus is hung on a cross between two criminals and sneered at by those who stand and watch. This man who has shown such compassion for others is mercilessly ridiculed and jeered at. "He saved others," some wags joke, "let him save himself if he is the Christ of God, the Chosen One" (35). What these observers do not understand is that only by refusing to save himself can Jesus truly save others!

Luke alone reports that one of the crucified thieves, after joining in the insults, falls silent. Then, with awakened faith, he rebukes his companion. "We are getting what our deeds deserve. But this man has done nothing wrong." Turning to Jesus he asks to be remembered when the Lord comes into his kingdom. Jesus' response to his confession of faith is an encouragement to us all: "I tell you the truth, today you will be with me in paradise" (43).

It is never too late to turn to Jesus in faith. For those who do, death no longer need be feared. For believers, death is an entrance into paradise.

Jesus' Death and Burial; 23:44–56. Jesus' life was not torn from him. He did not die under protest, struggling against the inevitable. After several hours on the cross, as a curtain of darkness is drawn over the scene, Jesus commits himself to his Father and dies.

There is a sense of hushed awe that silences the mockers as darkness shrouds the cross, and Jesus' voice is heard calling out to God. Even the Roman officer in charge of the execution detail "praised God" and said, "this was a righteous man." The others are gripped by a strange sense of anguish and loss. They "beat their breasts" (in mourning) as they go away.

Jesus' death came long before the normal two to three days expected for crucifixion. One of the council of elders, who did not agree with the verdict against Jesus, boldly goes to Pilate and asks permission to bury the body. Because the next day is the first day of the religious festival of Passover, the body must be buried without preparation, which would involve winding the body in linens packed with various spices. Jesus' body is laid in a tomb cut into the rock near Calvary, and his sorrowing followers leave to observe the days of rest.

Chapter 24. Resurrection: The New Beginning

The Discovery; 24:1–12. The Sunday following the crucifixion several women go out to the tomb. They find the stone rolled away and are told by angels not to "look for the living among the dead"! Just as Jesus promised, he has been raised.

It is only then they remember what Jesus has told them. How empty the past three days must have seemed, with Jesus' promises forgotten. But even when the women report to the disciples, the eleven do not believe. The report "seemed to them like nonsense."

The Emmaus Road; 24:13–35. The blindness of the disciples is linked to a common blindness to one OT truth: that the promised king would also be a suffering Savior (Isa. 52:14–53:12). When two of Jesus' followers walk home that afternoon to a village called Emmaus, the Lord joins them, unrecognized. The two share their dashed hopes—that "he was the one who was going to redeem Israel." And they tell of resurrection rumors which they do not believe (cf. 24:17). Jesus then traces through the OT those passages which tell of Messiah's suffering. Finally, together in the Emmaus home, the disciples' eyes are opened and they recognize Jesus! He disappears but they do not hesitate. They rush back to Jerusalem to join the eleven, who have also at last realized, "It's true!"

Jesus on Trial

Religious Trials
Before Annas .... John 18:12–14
Before Caiaphas .... Matt. 26:57–68
Before the Sanhedrin .... Matt. 27:1–2
Civil Trials
Before Pilate .... John 18:28–38
Before Herod .... Luke 23:6–12
Before Pilate .... John 18:39–19:6

Crucifixion Events at Calvary

Jesus offered drugged drink to lessen
   suffering .... Matt. 27:34
Jesus crucified .... Matt. 27:35
Jesus cries, "Father, forgive them" .... Luke 23:34
Soldiers gamble for Jesus' clothing .... Matt. 27:35
Jesus mocked by observers .... Matt. 27:39–44; Mark 15:29

Other Appearances; 24:36–53. Luke carefully reports other post-resurrection appearances of Jesus. He tells how the disciples touch him; how they see him in a body of flesh and bones; how he even eats with them. But the body is different, for this resurrected Jesus can appear and disappear among them at will.

But most important to Luke, Jesus now "opens their minds so they could understand the Scriptures." Before, Jesus had spoken to men who had no grasp of what he was saying. But the resurrection puts the whole OT in a new perspective. Realities hidden there suddenly appear in fresh and startling relief (see *Fulfilled Prophecy,* p. 305).

Resurrection Events

Additional Appearances of Jesus

Jesus is with them only for a short time. When the appointed days pass, Jesus returns to the Father. But he leaves his followers with a great promise. He will send them the Spirit and soon each one will be "clothed with power from on high."

How that promise is fulfilled, and the impact of it on our lives, is shown in Luke's companion history, the Acts of the Apostles (p. 564 f).

JOHN
The Gospel of the Son of God

John's portrait of Jesus is richly theological, focusing on the deity of our Lord and the meaning of faith in him. John's purpose is clearly stated: "these are written that you may believe that Jesus is the Christ, the Son of God, and that by believing you may have life through his name" (20:31).

Date and Author. John's Gospel is the latest of the four, written in the last twenty-five years of the first century. The book was highly valued by the early church and the source of much of its theology. All early traditions assign the book to the disciple John. Irenaeus tells of a personal acquaintance with Polycarp and others who had known John, and says, "John, the disciple of the Lord who also leaned upon his breast, did himself write a gospel during his residence at Ephesus in Asia."

John the Man. John was the son of a man who operated a successful fishing business in Galilee. He employed others beside his sons. John's sentence structure, and many expressions, show that he was familiar with the way the rabbis approached biblical interpretation. It would be wrong to think of him as an "ignorant fisherman."

All the Gospels portray John as one of the inner circle of the disciples, with Peter and James. They also portray him as ambitious and volatile! It is John who whispers with his brother James about ways to gain the chief places in Jesus' coming kingdom (Matt. 20:20–28). And it is these same two who earn the nickname "Sons of Thunder" by their eagerness to "call down fire from heaven" on a Samaritan village to avenge an insult (Luke 9:51–55). Like many successful individuals, John seems highly competitive and achievement-oriented.

But this same John is also "the disciple Jesus loved," and who becomes known through his writings as the Apostle of Love! John's Gospel and his three Epistles uniquely lift up love, not only revealing the love of God for us, but also that love for others which is to infuse the life of every believer. How beautifully John's own personal transformation testifies to the truth of his teaching. Jesus *is* the Son of God. One of his most notable miracles was to take the volatile, self-centered John and transform him into the tender and sensitive person we know through his writings.

John's teaching is true. Belief in Jesus is the doorway to a new life of love for you and me.

Comparison with the Synoptics. John's Gospel differs in several ways from the other three. John ignores the time Jesus spent in Galilee, to focus on his ministry in Judea and Jerusalem. The others report only one Passover visit to the temple; John tells of three times that Jesus comes up for this annual festival. The others give brief sketches of many of Jesus' sayings and doings. John focuses on a few events and goes into detail on longer teachings. Only John gives a detailed report of what Jesus says at the Last Supper (13–16). And only John takes care to interpret what he reports, using key theological terms over and over in his books. These differences in emphasis and approach make the Gospel of John particularly important, for it gives a unique perspective on the life and ministry of Jesus.

Theology of John. John has been called the "theological Gospel." He builds this book and his letters around key theological concepts, expressed in terms he uses over and over again. John's approach is to teach by contrast—to set one concept against its opposite and thus to reveal the meaning of Christ's coming. Some of the key terms in John, paired as he uses them, are: Life/Death; Light/Darkness; Belief/Unbelief; Truth/Falsehood; Love/Hate. Other key theological terms are Know, World, Word, and Glory. Perhaps *the* key word in John is Belief, or Faith. This word occurs ninety-eight times in the Greek text of John's twenty-one-chapter Gospel!

A careful study of these theological terms in John's writings will give clear understanding of basic NT revelation.

The Deity of Jesus. It has sometimes been claimed that "Jesus never said that he was God." This statement is incomprehensible in view of the clear testimony of all the Gospels. While each teaches the deity of Christ, John gives this doctrine greatest stress.

Each Gospel affirms many times that Jesus is the Son of God. John makes it clear that this means "making himself equal with God" (John 5:18). More than once Jesus states his deity in an absolute way (Mark 14:61,62; John 9:35–37; 10:36). Jesus also claims to be the preexistent "I AM" (*Jahweh,* see p. 75) of the OT (John 8:58). He claims that he existed with God "before the world was," (John 17:5). He claims a oneness with the Father so complete that "he that has seen me has seen the Father" (14:9). Nor does Jesus hesitate to claim God's prerogative to forgive sins (Mark 2:10). The people of Jesus' day clearly understood his claim to be God, and that claim was one of the charges against him at his trial (cf. Matt. 14:33; 26:63–65). Even demons trembled before him and acknowledged him as the Most High God (Matt. 8:29; Mark 3:11; 5:7; Luke 4:41). There is no doubt that Jesus claimed to be—and is shown to be—God himself. It is as God he promises us, "I am with you always, even to the end of the age" (Matt. 28:20).

Structure and Outline. There is no agreement on how to outline John's Gospel, largely because it lacks the chronological organization of the others. Some have suggested a structure based on the theme of belief; others suggest structures around Jesus' discourses, or the seven miracles that John reports. The very lack of agreement suggests that there is an essential unity to the book which resists any attempt to impose external organizing principles. Our best approach is simply to list the book's contents and the theological concepts John develops, without any attempt to produce a normal outline.

CONTENTS OF JOHN'S GOSPEL

The Word Becomes Flesh (Light)	1:1–18
Testimony about Jesus	1:19–2:25
Jesus and Nicodemus (New Birth)	3:1–36
Jesus and the Samitarian Woman (Belief)	4:1–54
Jesus' Discourse on Life	5:1–47
Jesus' Discourse on the Bread of Life	6:1–70
Jesus Faces Opposition (Unbelief)	7:1–52
Jesus Claims Deity (Truth)	8:1–59
Jesus Heals the Man Born Blind (Darkness)	9:1–41
Jesus as the Good Shepherd	10:1–42
Jesus Raises Lazarus (Life)	11:1–57
Jesus Predicts His Death (Unbelief)	12:1–50
Jesus Washes the Disciples' Feet (Love)	13:1–38
Jesus' Last Discourse (all themes)	14:1–16:33
Jesus' Final Prayer (Glory)	17:1–26
Jesus' Crucifixion	18:1–19:42
Jesus' Resurrection	20:1–21:25

One other feature of the structure of John's Gospel is worthy of note. John's dialogues follow a pattern. Someone asks Jesus a question. He answers briefly and obscurely. The puzzled listeners misunderstand, and Jesus then goes on to explain the issue at length. It will help to understand the discourses of Jesus if we keep this pattern in mind.

Value of John's Gospel. John focuses our attention on the need for a personal response to Jesus. The other Gospels invite us to watch as observers while Jesus performs his miracles or teaches the crowds and his disciples. We are moved to awe, to wonder, and then to worship at their portrayal of the Son of God. But in John each of us is directly confronted with the claims of Jesus: claims which demand a personal decision on our part. The issue of personal response is clearly drawn, and each one of us is invited to Believe!

Chapter 1:1–18. The Word Becomes Flesh

John launches us back before Creation to introduce Jesus. Jesus is "the Word": God himself, who existed before the beginning (1:1). The title focuses our attention on Jesus as the One through whom God has always expressed himself (cf. Luke 10:22; John 14:19). In the past Jesus revealed God in the Creation itself (1:3; cf. Ps. 19:2–4), in the unique gift of life (1:4) which transformed the barren universe, and in "light" (1:5). In John, "light" and "darkness" are moral terms. The very fact that human beings have moral awareness is a powerful testimony to the existence of God (cf. Rom. 2:15).

This person, God himself, ventured unrecognized into the world he formed: Jesus "became flesh and lived for a while among us" (1:4).

John leaves us with no doubts. The one who lived as Jesus of Nazareth is the eternal Son of God. Through incarnation he communicates God's glory in an entirely new way. The God who spoke in creation, in life itself, in moral awareness, and through human intermediaries in the written Word (1:17) has now come in Person, communicating a glorious message of grace and truth (1:17).

Incarnation/Is Jesus God?

Although this term is not found in the Bible, the doctrine it expresses is clearly taught. In Jesus, God became a human being. He continues forever God and man in the person of our resurrected Lord.

John says clearly that he who "was God" became flesh. Matthew and Luke each tell the story of Jesus' birth and explain how Jesus came to bear both the human nature of Mary and the divine nature of God the Father. Paul describes this event in his famous *kenosis* (self-emptying) passage: Jesus, "in very nature God," took on "the very nature of a servant, being made in human likeness" (Phil. 2:6–11).

This truth must remain an object of awe-filled wonder for believers. As Paul says to Timothy, "beyond all question, the mystery of godliness is great: He appeared in a body . . ." (1 Tim. 3:16). Others too are filled with wonder. "Since the children have flesh and blood, he too shared in their humanity so that by his death he might destroy him who holds the power of death . . . and free all those who were held in slavery by their fear of death" (Heb. 2:14,15). Jesus came for a purpose, and he continues as God/Man to free us for all time.

There can be no doubt. The full deity and full humanity of Jesus is taught clearly and unequivocally by the Word of God.

For study: Virgin Birth, p. 465; *Messiah,* p. 255; John 1:1–18; Philippians 2:6–11; Hebrews 1:1–2:18.

Chapter 1:19–2:25. Testimony about Jesus

John has boldly presented Jesus as God incarnate. Now he reports several testimonies to that identity.

The Testimony of John the Baptist; 1:19–34. John the Baptist appeared in wilderness areas to preach repentance and to warn of the coming of God's kingdom (Luke 3:1–18). John is recognized as a prophet, and many come to hear him. Those who do repent are baptized by John as a visible confession. When John is questioned about his identity, he tells his listeners he is neither Christ nor one of the old prophets returned to life. He is, however, one foretold in Isaiah who prepares the way for the coming of the Lord (1:23; Isa. 40:3). As a prophet, John's testimony can be trusted.

The testimony is given the day after Jesus comes for baptism. God has told John that one who is the Son of God will be revealed to him when the Holy Spirit, in the form of a dove, comes from heaven and rests on him. When Jesus is baptized, John sees the Spirit come. "I have seen," John says, "and I testify that this is the Son of God" (1:29–34). So fully was the Son of God a man that John had never dreamed his cousin, while truly good (Matt. 3:13–15), was the Messiah (1:31).

The Testimony of Personal Experience; 1:35–51. John tells of five disciples who spent time with Jesus. Invited by the Lord to "come and see," Andrew rushes to share his discovery with his brother, Peter. "We have found the Messiah!" When Philip brings Nathaniel to Jesus, and Jesus knows this stranger, Nathaniel confesses, "Rabbi, you are the Son of God; you are the king of Israel" (1:49). The men who knew Jesus personally add their testimony to the Baptist's.

The Testimony of Miracles; 2:1–11. Jesus' first miracle, turning water to wine, is one of many which "revealed his glory." John looks on their testimony as decisive. As Jesus says, "The miracles I do in my Father's name speak for me" (John 10:25).

The Testimony of Scripture; 2:12–25. In Jerusalem a furious Jesus drives those who conduct business out of the temple court at Passover. His zeal for God's house reflects a prophetic statement in Psalm 9:9. But the ultimate testimony of Scripture will come with Jesus' death and resurrection. Then the full meaning of the OT (see *Fulfilled Prophecy,* p. 305) and of Jesus' words are understood, and the disciples will "believe the Scriptures" (2:22).

This early testimony to Jesus was accepted, but superficially (2:23–25). Belief had not become commitment, and Jesus would not entrust himself to the crowds who had not trusted themselves to him.

What is the most convincing testimony that you have ever received to the truth that Jesus *is* the Son of God?

Chapter 3. Jesus and Nicodemus

You Must Be Born Again; 3:1–8. When Nicodemus comes at night to Jesus, he makes a startling revelation. He admits that the ruling council and the Pharisees "know you are a teacher who has come from God" (2). Nicodemus, then, represents all religious men who rely on their own efforts for salvation (see *Pharisees,* p. 442). The fact Nicodemus comes by night suggests that opposition is already strong and he does not want to be seen. Jesus goes immediately to the heart of the issue and proclaims the need for a new birth. Startled, Nicodemus asks, "How can this be?"

Jesus explains two births: flesh can only give birth to flesh. The Spirit must give birth to spirit. "Water" in verse 5 speaks of the bag of water that breaks to mark the entry of an infant into the world. The presence of the Holy Spirit marks birth into God's kingdom.

How Can This Be? 3:9–14. Nicodemus, as one of Israel's teachers (10), should have understood, for the OT prophets foretell a new inner life for mankind (cf. Jer. 31:33). Jesus, coming from heaven, speaks with authority about this reality: God will give new and eternal life to "everyone who believes" in Jesus his Son.

Reference to an OT incident illustrates the role of belief in new birth. When thousands of poisonous snakes infested Israel's wilderness campground (Num. 21:4–9), Moses was told to make a bronze serpent. This was placed on a pole in the center of the camp. God promised that all who would come to look would be healed and protected against future bites. There was no therapeutic value in the bronze image. But those who trusted God's word responded and were released from the danger of that death. Soon Jesus will also be lifted up on Calvary's cross. He will become the object of faith for those today who believe God's promises.

God So Loved the World; 3:16–21. This is Jesus' great Gospel promise. "Whosoever" simply trusts himself to the Son of God will be given eternal life. Condemnation's grip on mankind is broken by the Son of God. Now only one issue remains: "whoever believes in him is not condemned, but whoever does not believe stands condemned already" (18). There are only two destinies: the destiny of death and the destiny of life. Faith in Jesus Christ releases us from death and brings us life.

John's Further Testimony; 3:22–36. John the Baptist is full of joy as the crowds that followed him turn away to gather around Jesus. He too affirms, "whoever believes in the Son has eternal life."

📖 Now is a good time to praise God for your new birth. Or if you are not yet born again, to simply tell God you do trust his Son.

Born Again

Jesus introduces this striking phrase in John 3. Theologians have a more obscure term: regeneration. Each affirms the same vital truth. Human beings must experience a radical inner transformation.

The Bible describes humanity as stiffened in a spiritual state that is like death (Eph. 2:1–4, see *Death, NT* p. 612). Nothing we can do, no good deeds we perform, can change this reality. What each of us needs is an infusion of spiritual life. Only a new life within can counter the grip of death on our personalities.

The OT introduces the theme of renewal and hints at the great revelation Jesus unveils in John 3. More than one prophet communicated a promise that God would one day transform hearts, taking away the stony and unresponsive, and giving human beings a new heart which will be alive and responsive to God (cf. Deut. 30:6; Ezek. 11:19; 36:26; 37:1–14; Jer. 31:11).

The NT likens this inner renewal to a new birth. Our spiritually dead nature was derived from our parents who also lived in the grip of sin (cf. Rom 5:1–11). Our new nature comes from God himself. Inherited from him, that new life will be transforming and eternal! "You have been born again," Peter teaches, "not of perishable seed, but of imperishable, through the living and enduring word of God" (1 Pet. 1:23).

The beautiful picture of a new birth is an apt illustration of what God does in our lives, and is full of hope and excitement. First, birth speaks of an intimate relationship. "How great is the love the Father has lavished on us," John exults, "that we should be called the children of God. And that is what we are!" (1 John 3:1). John goes on: "*everyone* who believes that Jesus is the Christ is born of God" (1 John 5:1). In Christ we are now members of a great family, blessed with brothers and sisters to love and to love us.

Second, new birth makes us "new creations" (2 Cor. 5:17). Transformation to newness is not instant: all who are born into any life must grow (1 Pet. 2:2). But the implanting of new life from God within is a promise that life will change—that we will grow toward Jesus' likeness. Again John says it: "We know that we have passed from death to life . . ." and "no one who is born of God will continue to sin, because God's seed remains in him: he cannot go on sinning, because he has been born of God" (1 John 3:9,14).

All this is portrayed in the simple phrase, "born again." And this new birth is available to whoever will trust himself to Jesus, the Son of God (John 3:16; see *Belief/Faith,* p. 562).

Chapter 4. Jesus and the Samaritan Woman

Background. Samaria lay between Jerusalem and Galilee, on the west side of the Jordan. The district was populated by a mixed people, brought into the land by the Assyrians when the old northern kingdom of Israel fell in 722 B.C. These peoples retained elements of their pagan religions but adopted the worship of the God of the new land as well. Their claim to be worshipers of Jahweh was sharply rejected by the Jews when they returned to Jerusalem after the Babylonian captivity, and a deep hostility between the two peoples existed up to Jesus' day. Jews often crossed the Jordan river and traveled many extra miles on a trip to Galilee to avoid "contamination" in this land of a people whom they felt mongrelized their faith.

Now Jesus not only leads his disciples into Samaria, but he even stops near the town of Sychar! Jesus rests beside a well dug nearly two millennia before by the patriarch Jacob, and there he speaks with a woman.

The Conversation: 4:1–26. Jesus speaks of a water that will forever satisfy the woman's thirst. He lets her know that he is aware of her sins but is not repelled by her (15–18). When she introduces one of the theological differences between the Jews and Samaritans, he affirms the accuracy of the OT revelation but quickly moves on. God is not concerned with the externals of religion. Even now God is seeking "true worshippers, who will worship the Father in spirit and truth" (21–24). Then Jesus identifies himself as the promised Messiah, expected by the Samaritans as well as the Jews.

The Birth of Faith; 4:27–42. Jesus is so moved by the incident that he is no longer hungry when the disciples return. He has been satisfied in doing the Father's will, gathering another person ripe for harvest into God's great crop stored up for eternal life (34–37). The Samaritan woman hurries to her village and tells of her encounter with the Lord. Some believe her: all hurry out to see Jesus. Jesus stays with them for two days. A new community of faith is born as many affirm, "we know that this man really is the Savior of the world."

This passage has been called the model "personal evangelism" story in the Bible. What do you learn from it about sharing faith in Jesus with another person? Particularly, what is Jesus' constant attitude toward the woman?

Jesus and the Official's Son; 5:43–54. Some who saw Jesus' Jerusalem miracles want him to perform in Galilee (43–45). But one official begs Jesus to act, not out of curiosity but out of fear for his dangerously ill child (46–49). Jesus promises the boy will recover, and the man "took Jesus at his word and departed" (50). Jesus would not act for show. But he did act to meet a human need.

Chapter 5. Jesus' Discourse on Life

A Paralytic Healed; 5:1–15. Jesus finds a man who has been paralyzed for thirty-eight years. He lives, but his life is a frozen one, his personality trapped in dead flesh. Jesus heals the man, releasing him from the grip of his disease. How appropriate an incident with which to introduce Jesus' discourse on eternal life. For mankind lies trapped in the grip of sin. Men live, yet are dead to God.

Life through the Son; 5:16–30. Jesus makes a series of claims.

* Jesus and the Father are one in Jesus' miracles. The Jews may criticize his Sabbath healings, but when they do they criticize God! This is correctly understood as a claim by Jesus of deity (16–18). As God, Jesus will do greater works than this healing. He will give life to those who are dead (19–21).

* Jesus and the Father give one judgment. The critics implicitly claim the right to judge Jesus. But God has given Jesus the right to judge them! Only those who "hear my words and believe him who sent me" can cross over from death to life, and so escape condemnation (22–24).

* Jesus and the Father are one source of life. By the Father's choice, Jesus is the source of all life. The life Jesus gives others will be fully expressed at the resurrection. The reality of the distinction between eternal life and eternal death will be fully demonstrated then (25–31, see *Life,* p. 548).

Testimony to Jesus; 5:31–46. The truth of what Jesus says is witnessed by John and by Jesus' own miracles (36). But God himself is the strongest witness. Those who are responsive to God will recognize Jesus as the one spoken of in the OT. Those who refuse to believe show that they "do not have the love of God" in their hearts.

Chapter 6. Jesus' Discourse on the Bread of Life

Jesus Feeds Five Thousand; 6:1–24. When Jesus feeds five thousand persons on the shore of the Sea of Galilee with just a few loaves of bread and two small fish, the excited crowds intend to "come and make him king by force" (15). To escape them the disciples cross the sea by boat: Jesus joins them walking on the water (16–21). The next day the crowds follow around the lake.

The Bread of Life; 6:25–59. Jesus openly tells the crowds they have followed because he fed them—not because they believe in him. They suggest Jesus should provide a sign, specifying "bread from heaven" as appropriate, because Moses provided manna during Israel's wilderness years (25–31). This breadlike substance, which God himself miraculously provided each day during the forty years Israel wandered in the wilderness, provided the background for Jesus' discourse on himself as the bread of eternal life (cf. Exod. 16). Jesus himself is God's supernatural provision both of eternal life and of all that is needed to sustain that life up to the very time of our resurrection (40, 53)

Life

This word is difficult, because it is so rich and full of meanings. But let's begin with a common meaning and think of "life" as the self-consciousness of a person who realizes, "I am." In this sense, every human being has received his gift of life from God, and so each human being is to be cherished and valued. This human identity is the only lasting thing in our universe: long beyond the end of time, each individual will continue to exist.

But in the Bible "life" speaks of far more than existence. Life speaks of relationship with God. Here images like life and death, health and paralysis, light and dark, affirm something essential about the quality of each human being's existence. Because of God's love for us, he invites each human being into a personal relationship with him through which "existence" is transformed into "eternal life."

Outside of personal relationship with God lies a dark realm of death, where sin maintains a cold grip on human beings and holds them under condemnation. Death, like life, can be eternal. Endless separation from God is man's tragic destiny unless faith in Christ breaks the bondage and we "cross over from death to life" through trust in God's Son (John 5:24; see *Hell, OT* 375, *NT,* 531).

"Eternal life" is God's promise of freedom from endless bondage. It is a vivid word picture which means far more than forgiveness of past sins. When God gives us eternal life, the life he gives us is Jesus' own (Gal. 2:20). A human personality enriched with the gift of Jesus' life begins a beautiful transformation. In place of fear and alienation, there is now rich fellowship with God as our Father. In place of the dark and grim scars caused by sin, there is the flow of a warmth which heals. From God we receive love, joy, peace, goodness, and gentleness. These take root in our lives and gradually transform our experience on earth (Gal. 6:22,23). Yes, eternal life is a promise of an eternity in heaven. But eternal life is something we receive now. It holds out the promise of a rich new experience for you and me here on earth as well.

To understand the real meaning of eternal life, the Bible invites us to look at Jesus. In his personality, his love, and his compassion, we see the kind of person God will enable you and me to become. In Jesus' resurrection we see power for our new life—power to break through whatever holds us back, and lead us triumphantly toward an eternity we will spend in the presence and in the image of our God (cf. Rom. 8:29; *Born Again,* p. 545).

For study: see *Death, NT,* p. 612; Rom. 5:12f; 1 Cor. 15:20f; Col. 3:3,4,

---

Many Desert Jesus; 6:60–71. Many grumble about the difficulty of this teaching. Jesus explains that he does not expect a literal eating of his flesh and drinking of his blood but a spiritual appropriation of the life he offers (61–65). The God who nurtured physical life in the wilderness can and will sustain the eternal life offered through Jesus.

Several times in this passage Jesus speaks of God as enabling, or drawing, those who come to Christ through faith (43,65). God the Holy Spirit plays a vital role in every conversion, opening the understanding of sin-darkened human beings to life in Jesus. But the response of faith in Jesus is never made by a person against his will.

Compare this passage with Exodus 16. In what ways is Jesus, "the bread of life," comparable to the manna provided by God?

This passage contains a number of promises related to relationship with Jesus. See how many benefits of relationship you can see in John 6.

Chapter 7. Jesus Faces Opposition

Jesus is now the focus of speculation. He has been endorsed by John the Baptist and has performed many miracles. Jesus has also boldly pressed his claims in Galilee to be the giver and sustainer of life—the one sent by God to become the object of faith for his people. But many will not believe. Their reaction is a hostility so great that the leaders are already determined to see Jesus killed (7:1,20,25). The different reactions of the unbelieving show the nature of the death which Jesus has taught grips all those who will not believe: such persons are unresponsive and antagonistic.

Ridicule and Fear; 7:1–13. Unbelief by Jesus' own brothers produces accusations and ridicule. They urge him to hurry to Jerusalem, since he "wants to become a public figure." When Jesus does slip quietly into the holy city, everyone is whispering about him, divided over whether he is a good man or a deceiver. But the antagonism of the leaders (whom John usually calls "the Jews" in his Gospel) is so well known that everyone is afraid to talk openly.

God's Authority Rejected; 7:14–24. Jesus begins to teach openly, claiming that his message is from God who gave the law through Moses. The crowds accuse Jesus of being demon-possessed! Yet none of them have kept the law, and even now they plot to kill Jesus in violation of the law. Their objection to healing on the Sabbath shows how the people of Israel have twisted the intention of God's OT revelation.

Moral Cowardice; 7:25–52. Many are moved to believe as Jesus teaches. Hearing the whispers that identify Jesus as the Christ, the chief priests and Pharisees are furious but fear to confront him openly. Instead they send temple guards to arrest him. But the guards are so awed they will not carry out their orders. When Nicodemus objects to condemning Jesus before he is given a full hearing, the other leaders strike out at him.

Unbelief produces nothing admirable. There is no love or compassion here. There is only hardness toward God, a climate of fear, and moral cowardice. There is only hostility as men strike out at Jesus and one another. How much these people need the gift of eternal life that Jesus offers them!

 Review chapter 7 carefully. What are the marks in character and interpersonal relationships where unbelief reigns?

Chapter 8. Jesus Claims Deity

John continues his report of events at the Feast of Tabernacles (7:2) and shares what is called Jesus' "Temple Discourses"! Now John focuses on a sharp conflict in which Jesus makes a clear claim to deity and explains the nature of truth.

The Adulterous Woman; 8:1–11. The best Greek manuscripts do not include this incident, but it is in fullest harmony with the character of Jesus and his opponents. They know where to catch a woman "in the act" of adultery. They bring only the woman and release the man. They care only about using her against Jesus. Jesus' character is also revealed. When the accusers slink away, Jesus refuses to condemn. He releases the woman to live a new life, freed from her past sins.

Testimony to Jesus; 8:12–30. As Jesus speaks he is challenged by the Pharisees. They refer to a dictum of OT law: any fact must be established by at least two witnesses. Jesus' claims are unsupported and must thus be rejected (23). But Jesus *is* supported by the active testimony of God the Father! One day that testimony will be open and visible to all (27,28). Now the testimony is within the hearts of those who hear Jesus' words and believe (30).

Knowing Truth; 8:31–47. Biblically, "truth" involves knowing and experiencing reality (cf. *Truth,* p. 552). Jesus promises his disciples that they will come to know the truth by personal experience when they keep his words and thus will find freedom (31,32). This is bitterly opposed by other hearers. They claim they are already free (33), for they are related to Abraham (33) and to God (41). But these claims do not meet the test of truth! In reality they are enslaved by sin (34–38). They show their lack of relationship with Abraham by failure to respond as Abraham did (39–41). And they show their lack of relationship with God by hating Jesus instead of loving him as one coming from the Father (42–47). In reality they are related to the devil, for they love lies just as he does!

Jesus the I AM; 8:48–59. When Jesus claims to be the I AM known by Abraham millennia ago, the crowds grasps for stones to kill him for blasphemy. "I AM" is the revelation name of God in the OT (see *Jehovah/Jahweh,* p. 75), and Jesus' statement is a bold and unequivocable claim to deity. John presents Jesus as the "I AM" in several passages, in each case linking Christ with one of the new revelations he brings (such as "I am the resurrection and the life"). "I AM" revelations are found in John 6:35; 8:12; 9:5; 10:7,11,14; 11:25; 14:6 and 15:1. Each is another affirmation by Jesus that he is God.

Truth

The Hebrew and Greek words for "truth" share a common meaning: each suggests that a thing is "true" when it corresponds to reality. In the Bible "truth" is no abstract ideal or philosophical concept. Thus when in each Testament God's word is called "truth" (cf. Ps. 119:142; John 17:17), a striking claim is being made. The claim is that all the Scriptures teach is in fullest harmony with reality. God has unveiled in his Word the way things really are and how life is meant to be lived. All that Scripture shows us about ourselves, about relationship with God, and about relationships with others, is a revelation of reality as God knows it.

This kind of truth is a dynamic and freeing thing. Men wander about in a world of illusions, guessing at the nature of the universe and struggling with moral judgments, without knowing which of the many competing philosophies of life is best. But when we come to the Word of God we are freed from uncertainty. Scripture directs us to reality, pointing us toward what is good and away from all that is wrong and harmful.

In its biblical sense as reality, truth is something which is to be experienced by Jesus' followers. We are to let his words define the issues of life and to act on his words obediently. As we practice God's words we come to know truth in a personal way—and to gain all its benefits. When Jesus speaks of revealing God's truth, he never speaks of simple possession of information. He speaks of an unveiling of reality, to which we are to commit ourselves by faith.

For study: John 8:31–59; Psalm 119; 1 Corinthians 2; Romans 1:24–32.

Chapter 9. Jesus Heals A Man Born Blind

The Healing; 9:1–12. The Jewish people view God as a moral judge and illness as a punishment (see *Job,* p. 244). But who has sinned when a man is born blind? Jesus says that neither the blind man nor his parents are being punished. Instead the blindness, like much of our suffering, is an opportunity for God to bless. So saying, Jesus gives the man sight.

The Pharisee's Reaction; 9:13–25. The frustrated Pharisees cannot deny the miracle. At last they give up interrogating the blind man and simply insist, "we know this man (Jesus) is a sinner."

Hypocrisy Revealed; 9:26–34. Others fear to contradict them (22). But the now-sighted man openly confronts the Pharisees' hypocrisy. "If this man were not from God, he could do nothing." Earlier Nicodemus had told Jesus these same leaders "know you are a teacher who has come from God. For no one could perform the miraculous signs you are doing if God were not with him" (3:2).

The leaders are so furious at this new evidence that they willfully shut their eyes to the truth.

Spiritual Blindness; 9:35–41. Later, as the blind man kneels in worship before Jesus, the Lord observes that the nearby Pharisees— who claim that they are able to see—are blind to the only release . . . man will ever have from the guilt of sin.

 Meditate on 9:41. What do you think Jesus is saying here to us today? To whom do you think this statement applies?

Chapter 10. Jesus, The Good Shepherd

The OT uses the image of a shepherd to represent both political and religious leaders of God's people (Isa. 56:11; Jer. 25; Ezek. 34). One of the great messianic promises in the OT is that the Lord, whom David knew as "my shepherd" (Ps. 23), will come to personally care for his people (Isa. 40:11; Ezek. 34:23; 37:24). Now Jesus announces that he is the promised Good Shepherd— a claim which was understood by these people who knew the OT so well.

Shepherd Recognized; 10:1–6. As a Palestinian shepherd knows each of his sheep by name, and as they recognize his voice, so those who belong to God will recognize and follow Jesus.

Thieves and Robbers; 10:7–10. The leaders of the Jews are like thieves and robbers because they harm and use the sheep. Jesus has "come that they may have life, and have it to the full."

Good Shepherd Gives Life; 10:11–13. The true shepherd is recognized by his willingness to give his life to preserve the sheep from danger. Soon Jesus will lay down his life on Calvary for you and me.

Jesus Willingly Gives His Life; 10:12–21. Life will not be torn from Jesus as an unwilling victim. Jesus' life will be *given,* that people from every nation may become God's "one flock."

Jesus' teachings are heard but rejected. "He's raving mad."

Unbelief; 10:22–42. Jesus again plainly tells the Jews (e.g., the leaders) that he is the Christ. When he claims oneness with the Father the Jews attempt to stone him, "because you, a mere man, claim to be God" (33). The OT in Psalm 82:6 refers to God's people as "elohim" (gods) because of their relationship with God the Father. Jesus asks how then the leaders can call him a "mere" man, when his own relationship with God is that of eternal Son?

 Study this passage and OT "shepherd" references. What do you learn about your relationship with Jesus as one of his sheep?

Chapter 11. Jesus Raises Lazarus

Jesus has claimed authority over death as giver of eternal life. Now the claim of authority is authenticated in Bethany.

Return to Judea; 11:1–16. Jesus is in Galilee when he receives word that a beloved follower named Lazarus is desperately ill. He waits two days and then heads for Bethany, in Judea. The disciples view returning to Judea as so dangerous to Jesus they will "die with" him. But Jesus goes to raise the dead, "so that God's Son may be glorified" and "so that you may believe" (4,16).

I Am the Resurrection and the Life; 11:17–37. Jesus arrives and comforts the two sisters. Each affirms faith in Jesus as the Son of God. Each is sure if Jesus "had been here, my brother would not have died" (21,32). But they have not yet grasped what it means for Jesus to be "the resurrection and the life" (24). Jesus' resurrection power is not limited to the last day! God can act in human lives now and even break the grip of death and advanced decay.

Lazarus Raised; 11:38–44. When Jesus orders the stone blocking the tomb of Lazarus moved, Martha objects. After four days "there (will be) a bad odor." But they obey. Jesus calls, and the dead man comes out, alive again.

Jesus' Death Plotted; 11:45–57. The raising of Lazarus stimulates faith in some. But the chief priests and Pharisees, who admit he is "performing many miraculous signs," still will not believe (47,48). The high priest announces that Jesus must die (49–53). Hatred has hardened into a determined plot to destroy Jesus.

What do you see as the main teaching of this passage? What did it mean to the people of Jesus' own day? What does it mean to us now? Is it valid to apply Jesus' resurrection power to spiritual death?

Chapter 12. Jesus Predicts His Death

Jesus Anointed; 12:1–10. At a dinner in Lazarus' home, Mary anoints Jesus with expensive perfumes. Jesus says this speaks of "the day of my burial." The last Passover is near, and the hatred of the leaders is so great they even plan to murder Lazarus!

The Triumphal Entry; 12:11–19. With the recent raising of Lazarus, Jesus' popularity is at its peak. When he enters Jerusalem, Jesus is lauded as the promised Messiah and King of the Jews.

Jesus' Death Approaches; 12:20–36. Jesus again predicts his coming death, but promises it will produce a harvest of life for all who trust and follow him (20–26). Many ask how, if he is the Christ, he can die? Doesn't the Scripture teach "the Christ will remain forever"? The answer is resurrection. Even though they have just seen Jesus raise Lazarus, no one sees the implication of this event. They are determined not to believe.

Continued Unbelief; 12:37–50. Again and again Jesus presents himself as the object of faith, and warns that God, who has sent Jesus, will judge those who reject him. But even those who do believe are now afraid to confess their faith openly. How vital that you and I care more for God's good opinion than for the approval of men!

Chapter 13. Jesus Washes His Disciples' Feet

John now moves to the last night of Jesus' life on earth and tells of an intimate supper Jesus shares with his disciples. Chapter 13 tells of several events as that evening begins: chapters 14–16 are a record of what Jesus taught his followers that evening.

An Example of Servanthood; 13:1–17. The relationship between a disciple and his teacher was well established in Judaism. The disciple actively served his master. Now, at the beginning of the evening meal, Jesus puts aside his outer clothing and stoops to wash his disciples' feet! This is a shocking reversal of roles—doubly shocking when the Master is the very God at whose feet the disciples worship! The emotional impact of the act is so great that Peter at first refuses (8). But Jesus insists. Only by this dramatic act is Christ at last able to convey to his disciples that he really intends his followers to *serve* one another (13–17).

Betrayal Predicted; 13:18–30. Now, before the teaching, Jesus identifies Judas as the betrayer (22–26). Realizing he is known, Judas surrenders fully to Satan and slips away to make final arrangements for Jesus' arrest (27–29). John reports that it is now night (30). Only when the Resurrection is an accomplished fact will John report that a new day dawns (20:1).

The New Commandment; 13:31–39. Warning his disciples that he will soon leave them, Jesus introduces what he calls his "new commandment." When he is gone, the new community which will be established is to be marked by love for one another: a love modeled on Jesus' love for his own (see *Love*).

This instruction is followed immediately with Peter's honest affirmation that he will "lay down his life" for Jesus. But Jesus knows human weaknesses and predicts Peter will disown him that very night. Self-sacrifice, whether giving up our life or living out a selfless love like that of Jesus (13:33,34), is beyond us. Only the coming of the Holy Spirit will lift Peter beyond himself, or give you and me the ability to love others as Jesus has loved us. It is to the work of the Spirit that Jesus now turns in his extended teaching. Look in a concordance for "one another." Then look in each passage that uses the word, to see how love is to be lived by Christians.

Love

John, the Apostle of Love, most fully develops this theme, which is also expressed by most OT and NT writers. In speaking of love the NT does an unusual thing. It takes a mild Greek word for love, *agape*, and fills it with dynamic new meaning.

The biblical meaning of "love" is defined for all time by Jesus' self-sacrifice on Calvary. "This is how we know what love is:" John puts it, "Jesus Christ laid down his life for us" (1 John 3:16). OT and NT writers both speak of God's love for mankind. The nature and extent of that love is made unmistakably clear in Jesus.

Being loved by God is just a beginning. When we accept the love of God in Jesus and are given eternal life, God plants love within our personality. John puts it this way: "Dear friends, let us love one another, for love comes from God. . . . Dear friends, since God so loved us, we also ought to love one another . . . if we love each other, God lives in us and his love is made complete in us" (1 John 4:7-12).

God's love then is intended to find living expression in the community of those who know Jesus. In fact, the NT emphasis is placed on the love we are to express to one another. The Epistles speak even more of that love, intended to infuse relationships between believers, than it does of God's love, although it is clear that love for one another is only possible because of Jesus.

What a privilege to share with others the love that God has lavished on us! And what a model of selfless love we have in our Lord.

Chapters 14–16. The Last Supper Discourse

Many topics are covered by Jesus in this significant passage, which touches on vital aspects of the new relationship of believers with Jesus.

Jesus the Way; 14:1-6. Jesus is the only way by which men can approach the Father, or through whom men can come to know God.

Jesus Will Continue to Work; 14:7-14. Jesus emphasizes his unity with the Father and promises that Jesus will continue to work in answer to his disciples' prayers. The work God accomplishes through us will be "greater than what I have been doing." How? God will perform his new works on earth through weak and fallible human beings, rather than the sinless Son of God!

Love Motivates Obedience; 14:15–24. Love for Jesus will move his followers to obey the Lord, and this will deepen the experience of our personal relationship with God (see also *Obedience*).

Obedience

OT law portrays obedience as the pathway which God's people take to find his blessing (Deut. 28:1–14). Those who knew God best also found it a pathway full of delight (Ps. 119:41–48). The NT emphasis includes this and stresses another dimension. Now we see that obedience can only flow from a personal relationship with God. As Jesus says at the Last Supper, "If you love me, you will obey my commandments" (John 14:15). "If anyone loves me," Jesus goes on, "he will obey my teaching" (15:23). Thus obedience is not a test of love: it is an outgrowth of a deepening love relationship with the Lord.

God's insistence that we learn to obey him also is motivated by love. He knows what is best for us. He knows what will harm us and what will help. It is love that impels him to share his commands and guidelines in the Word of God.

This love of God is shown in discipline when we fail to obey. "The Lord disciplines those he loves," the OT and NT agree (cf. Prov. 3:11,12; Heb. 12:1–11). Loving discipline from God is intended to lead us back into his paths and "produce a harvest of righteousness and peace for us" (Heb. 12:11).

When we discern the tones of love in all of Jesus' commandments, our love for God is awakened and we want to obey him. How freeing it is to realize that God is no tyrant, and that obedience is not a burden, to be grudgingly offered God out of fear. Knowing God's love, and returning it, we can joyfully trust ourselves into his hand, and trust our lives to the guidance given in his Word.

For study: Deuteronomy 4:1–14; 28:1–14; Psalm 119:41–48; John 14:15–24.

Not Left Alone; 14:25–31. Jesus will leave, but he will not desert his followers. He will send the Holy Spirit to be with them, and he himself will come again.

Jesus the Vine; 15:1–17. The picture of a vine shows the nature of our relationship with Jesus. As the vine, Jesus supplies each branch with the nourishment needed to bear fruit. Apart from an intimate and close relationship, expressed in the word "abiding" ("keeping close"), we can do nothing (1–5).

Jesus' reference to branches that wither and are burned is not a reference to hell. Jesus is speaking about fruitfulness, not salvation. God's desire is that we do not live a worthless, barren life, but "bear much fruit, showing yourselves to be my disciples" (6–8).

How do we abide in Jesus? We obey his commands. And the command Jesus emphasizes here is "love each other as I have loved you." We have been chosen by God to bear the fruit that comes from a life of love.

The Holy Spirit Promised

One theme that runs through the Gospels is Jesus' promise to give his followers power from on high, in the person of the Holy Spirit (cf. Luke 24:49; John 7:37–39). After the Ascension the disciples are told to wait in Jerusalem for the gift of that power (Acts 1:5).

The Holy Spirit has been active through the OT and especially in Jesus' ministry on earth. But the relationship of the Spirit with God's OT people, and with the disciples through the days of Jesus on earth, is a relationship Jesus calls "with you" (John 14:17). Jesus calls the new relationship with the Spirit one in which "he will be in you" (John 14:17). What that relationship will mean is explored in five blocks of teaching in the Last Supper discourse.

John 14:15–17. The new relationship is promised and the Spirit is given a personal name: Comforter. The Greek word, *Paraklete,* means one who comes alongside to support.

John 14:25,26. The coming Spirit will be the teacher of Jesus' followers, who will remind of and help to understand Jesus' words.

John 15:26,27. The Comforter will give inner testimony to Jesus as his disciples proclaim their Lord to others.

John 16:5–11. The coming Spirit will work in the world of men, convicting of guilt and authenticating the messages of sin and judgment.

John 16:12–15. The Holy Spirit will be the guide which Jesus' followers need to lead them into the experience of truth (see *Truth,* p. 552).

The promised Spirit has now been sent by Jesus to those of us who are his followers. God's Spirit is in us, to support, teach, empower, and lead us into the full experience of God's Truth.

Persecution Ahead for Disciples; 15:18–16:4. The hatred men have felt for Jesus will also be directed against Jesus' disciples. But his followers are to testify to their Lord, knowing that the Spirit will add his inner testimony within the hearts of those who hear.

The Work of the Holy Spirit; 16:5–16. Jesus is the one in whom the Bible's teachings about sin, righteousness, and judgment all come together. It is the Spirit who deals with these issues, presenting Christ to the world and convicting those who will not believe.

The Spirit also is at work for believers. He is the living Voice of Jesus to us, who guides us into an experience of God's truth.

Joy Ahead for the Disciples; 16:17–24. The first reaction of the disciples when Jesus is gone will be heartbreak. But after mourning, grief will be transformed to joy. Then the implications of relationship with the resurrected Jesus and the power of prayer will be known. Then "the Father will give you whatever you ask in my name."

This does not mean simply tacking "in Jesus' name" on after every prayer. In Bible times, the "name" summed up the identity and the character of a person or thing. To ask in Jesus' name means to pray in full harmony with all that Jesus is, and in harmony with his character and purposes.

Jesus Returns to the Father; 16:25–33. Whatever happens in the next hours, Jesus will not be alone. "My Father is with me," he tells the eleven. This Jesus, who will soon go back to the Father, will return the victor: "I have overcome the world."

Chapter 17. Jesus' Final Prayer

This is often called Jesus' "high priestly" prayer, because it is primarily a prayer of intercession for his followers.

Coming Return to Glory; 16:1–5. The time has come for Jesus to be glorified. This word when applied to God usually speaks of the splendor of deity's disclosure. Jesus had glory with the Father when he existed before the world's creation (see *Incarnation,* p. 542). At his second coming he will also be seen in "power and great glory" (Mark 13:26). On earth Jesus' glory was both hidden and revealed in the Incarnation. The great splendor of God's overwhelming presence was masked by Jesus' human flesh. But Jesus has shown a new aspect of God's glory: a glory known only through servanthood and by "completing the work" God the Father gave him to do.

Jesus Prays for His Disciples; 17:6–19. Jesus asks that his followers might be kept safe and receive "the full measure of my joy within them" (13). Because of relationship with Jesus his followers are no longer part of the world (see *World System,* p. 797). Jesus' desire is that we might be sanctified ("made holy") through experience of the Word of God as truth (see *Truth,* p. 552).

Jesus Prays for All Believers; 17:20–26. Jesus makes it clear that he includes all who will ever "believe in me through their message" in this great prayer for his disciples (20). Looking into the future the focus of Jesus' prayer is "that they may be brought to complete unity."

Many debate the nature of this Christian unity. Jesus, however, says that it is to be modeled on his own relationship with the Father: "that they may be one as we are one" (22). It is clear that organizational unity is not in view, for members of the God-head are distinct in their identity as persons. So differences may exist which give identity to different Christian groups. The essential identity is that, as God has a common life shared by the Three in One, so believers through Jesus also share in a common life (see *Born Again,* p. 545). This life, the very life of God, will always find expression in a love for one another which is like the Father's love for Jesus (23). Our differences must never be allowed to create barriers which might prevent us from acknowledging other Christians as our brothers and sisters, and from loving them as family.

Chapters 18, 19. Jesus Is Crucified

John now reports the all-too-familiar story told in each Gospel. The sequence of events is the same, but John adds special insights.

Jesus Arrested; 18:1–11. A mob led by Judas arrests Jesus. Jesus allows himself to be taken, first negotiating the release of his disciples (8,9). John tells us that Peter boldly struck out to protect his master but succeeded only in cutting off the right ear of a servant of the high priest. Jesus rebukes Peter. What happens now is the will of the Father.

Jesus on Trial; 18:12–27. Jesus is taken at night to the residence of various Jewish leaders. Peter trails behind and in a courtyard fulfills Jesus' prediction: he denies any relationship with Jesus. For a sequence of events and trials see page 536.

Jesus before Pilate; 18:28–40. Jesus has several confrontations with Pilate, the Roman governor of Judea. Only he has the authority to pass the death sentence. The Jews thus must bring Jesus before him.

On careful examination he determines that Jesus' kingdom is "not of this world" (36). Pilate refuses to make any judgment on the truth of such a claim (37,38). He announces to the Jews that there is no basis for their charges against Jesus!

The Sentence of Crucifixion Is Passed; 19:1–16. The angry Jews shout their demands for crucifixion, finally revealing that the real reason they want Jesus killed is that he claims to be the Son of God. This revelation frightens Pilate, who questions Jesus again and then tries to set him free. But the Jews threaten Pilate and he gives in.

John portrays Pilate as a weak man, terrorized by the people he is supposed to rule. This is strikingly out of character with the Pilate we know from secular sources as a ruthless man, quick to crush any who affronted him. What is the explanation for the weak behavior we observe in the Gospels?

Pilate was a protege of a man named Sejanus, who rose to near supreme power as commander of the Praetorian guard under the Roman emperior Tiberius. But shortly before Jesus' trial in A.D. 33 the anti-Jewish Sejanus fell. All those associated with him were under suspicion. Already Tiberius had angrily ordered Pilate to remove shields bearing the image of the emperor (which he had brought to Jerusalem over the objection of the Jews, who saw this as idolatry). Pilate's position was now delicate. If the Jews should gain the emperor's ear again, and accuse him of being "no friend of Caesar" (12) for releasing a man who claimed to be a king, Pilate's position and possibly his life would be in danger.

Under this threat, Pilate surrendered to the Jews and turned Jesus over to them for crucifixion.

The Crucifixion; 19:16–27. Pilate orders a notice identifying Jesus as king of the Jews attached to the cross. As Jesus hangs in anguish from the torment of this cruel method of execution (see *The Crucifixion*, p. 503), he commits his mother to the care of the John who writes this Gospel.

The Death of Jesus; 20:28–42. Jesus' death corresponds to OT prophecies found in Exodus 12:46, Numbers 9:12, Psalm 34:20, and Zechariah 12:10. The flow of blood and water is characteristic of one who dies in this way (34). Jesus is laid in a new tomb in a garden near the public execution grounds.

Chapters 20, 21. The Resurrection of Jesus

The Empty Tomb; 20:1–9. John is with Peter when the two run to the garden tomb after Mary of Magdala reports the stone has been rolled away. John tells how Peter goes into the tomb and sees the empty linens in which Jesus was wrapped lying there. The disciples still do not understand, but they know that Jesus is risen.

Jesus' Post-Resurrection Appearances; 20:10–31. Christ has now performed the ultimate miracle. To prove it he appears to Mary of Magdala (10–18), to the disciples with Thomas absent (19–23), and to the disciples with Thomas present (24–31). Thomas has sworn not to believe unless he touches Jesus' nail-pierced hands and puts his hand in the gash torn in Jesus' side by the Roman soldier's spear (19:34). But when Jesus appears, Thomas drops to his knees in worship, acknowledging Jesus as "my Lord and my God" (20:28). Many millions who have not seen what Thomas saw that evening have believed on Jesus since. And the report penned by John has accomplished its purpose (20:31) and led many to saving faith (see *Belief/Faith*).

Jesus and the Great Catch of Fish; 21:1–14. After these events Jesus meets seven disciples who have gone fishing. On his directions they throw their net on the other side of the boat, and the nets are filled. On shore Jesus shares a meal with his followers.

Belief/Faith

In his Gospel John speaks some 98 times of belief or faith. But he is not alone in emphasizing faith: it is stressed by other writers of both Old and New Testaments.

We see faith most sharply in the OT in a report of Abraham's response to God's covenant promises. "Abraham believed the Lord, and it was credited to him as righteousness" (Gen. 15:6). Here faith is seen to be personal response to God. And here faith is seen to be something which God can accept in place of a righteousness no human being possesses.

Each of these emphases is developed in the NT, and is expressed in the use NT writers make of the "belief/faith" word group. In normal Greek usage one would speak of believing "that." James uses the word in the normal way when he says, "you believe that God is one? Good!" But James goes on, "Even the demons believe that—and shudder" (2:19). Faith as intellectual assent or mere agreement with facts is not the kind of faith the Scriptures invite us to have.

To express their meaning the NT writers coined a new phrase: to "believe *in*." It is not enough to agree. There must be response to the object of faith—a believing *in*. This faith response is not made to information, even to true information. This faith response is made to God himself, just as Abraham's faith was not just a response to information but to God personally. It is this personal response of trust in God which the Bible knows as saving faith. We have no righteousness to offer God that he might accept us. And he does not demand good works from us. Instead the Bible says, "It is by grace you have been saved, through faith—and this is not from yourselves, it is the gift of God—not by works, so that no one can boast" (Eph. 2:8).

The promise of salvation by faith was not just for Abraham, "but for us also, to whom God will credit righteousness—for us who believe in him who raised Jesus our Lord from the dead" (Rom. 4:24). Today you and I have that same wonderful privilege given Abraham: to hear the message of promise from God, and to put our trust in him.

For study: Romans 4; Hebrews 11.

Peter Reassured; 21:15–25. Peter had denied Jesus three times. Now Jesus asks Peter three times if he loves him. Three times Peter affirms his love for the Lord. And three times Peter is reassured. His denial of Jesus in a moment of weakness has not disqualified him from service. Peter will shepherd and care for many of Jesus' lambs.

Jesus then speaks of Peter's death (18,19). Tradition tells us that Peter was later crucified in Rome, upside down, after a long life of loving service to Jesus' flock.

John also reports that Peter asked Jesus about the future of another disciple. Jesus rebukes him: "What is that to you? You must follow me" (22). What a truth for each of us to remember! The resurrected Jesus is Lord. Each disciple is committed to follow Jesus and to give others the freedom to be personally responsible to our risen Lord (cf. Rom. 14:1–4).

ACTS
The History of the Early Church

Acts vividly portrays the emergence of the new Christian community. Here the author of Luke's gospel continues his careful report of first century events, documenting for us the swift expansion of the new faith as it reaches out beyond the tiny district of Judea to penetrate to the heart, and to the borders, of the great Roman Empire. Acts gives us insight into the growing awareness that Christianity is a universal faith and shows us the dynamic power of the Word of God and the Holy Spirit in the lives of all peoples, everywhere.

Date and Author. A clear tradition and solid internal evidence make it clear that the author of Acts is Luke the physician, the careful historian who gave us the third gospel (see p. 507). Most agree that the book was completed during, or shortly after, Paul's last imprisonment, A.D. 66–67. It is likely that Luke met his own death shortly after the execution of his friend, the great apostle.

Historical Background. The events of the Book of Acts can only be understood against the background of the great Roman Empire. During this period Rome embraced the Mediterranean world and reached into Britain in the west. Because of Rome, the Western world was at peace. Population centers were linked together by a network of land and sea trade routes. The resultant freedom to travel safely from place to place was vital to the missionaries who carried the gospel message throughout the empire.

Just as important was a common language, Greek, which all civilized peoples spoke, beside their national language. The gospel could thus be preached to all and, in our NT letters, the teachings of the apostles of Jesus could be recorded for all to read or to hear it read when believers gathered in their house-churches.

There was also considerable religious freedom within the empire. For most of the three decades covered by Acts, Christianity was viewed as a sect of Judaism, known as "the way." This was important, for Judaism was an officially recognized, or licit, religion. Thus there was no early governmental opposition to the spread of Christianity, and in fact there was protection from religious persecution.

Several different emperors ruled during the years between A.D. 33 and A.D. 68, the maximum years with which Acts can be concerned. Tiberius ruled from A.D. 14 to A.D. 37. His main contribution to the gospel story is seen in the impact of the fall of Sejanus, the guard commander who plotted against him, in A.D. 31. That fall and the relationship of Pontius Pilate to Sejanus is important to help us understand the motivation of the man who ordered Jesus' execution (see *Sentence of Crucifixion* pp. 560–561).

Caligula followed Tiberius briefly, ruling from A.D. 37–41. While his mad and violent rule terrorized the Roman nobility, it had little impact on the story told in Acts.

Claudius ruled Rome from A.D. 41 to A.D. 54. He reorganized the administration of the empire and began the conquest of Britain. Claudius was hostile to all foreign cults and attempted to reestablish the old Roman religion. The historian Seutonius states that he expelled the Jewish population of Rome when some riots were stimulated "at the instigation of one Chrestus." This may indicate a reaction in Rome's Jewish colony to the early preaching of Christ in the capital. It is this expulsion order which probably led Aquila and Priscilla to move from Rome (cf. Acts 18:2).

Nero ruled wisely for the first five of his fourteen years (A.D. 54 to A.D. 68). To divert a suspicion that Nero himself caused the great fire which destroyed much of the city of Rome in A.D. 64, the Christian community was accused. An intense but local persecution followed at the center of the empire. Tradition says that both Peter and Paul were executed during this first official reign of terror.

Chronology. Luke is a careful historian and uses the methods of his time to date many of the events he describes. But Luke wrote a contemporary history. His dating references would be understood by the people of his own day but are more difficult for us, nearly two millennia distant, to reconstruct. Nevertheless, much work has been done by scholars working with secular documents and records to give us a realistic framework of chronology for the events described in Acts. The following chart shows probable dates.

The Crucifixion	A.D. 33
Paul's Conversion	A.D. 36
Famine Visit to Jerusalem	A.D. 45
First Missionary Journey	A.D. 46–48
Jerusalem Council	A.D. 49
Second Missionary Journey	A.D. 49–52
Third Missionary Journey	A.D. 53–57
Paul's Arrest at Jerusalem	A.D. 57

THE ROMAN EMPIRE

OUTLINE OF THE EMPIRE

Imprisonment at Caesarea	A.D. 57–60
First Imprisonment in Rome	A.D. 61–63
Second Imprisonment in Rome	A.D. 66–67
Death of Paul/Peter	A.D. 68

Distinctive Contributions. Acts is an exciting book to read. We thrill as we see the story of the early church unfold, and many have been aroused from a superficial faith to seek the power and vitality that Acts reveals as our Christian heritage.

Luke develops two themes with special care in his selective story-telling. One theme is the transformation of biblical faith. Up to the resurrection of Jesus, biblical faith was narrow, held in tight custody by the Jewish people. In a few short decades, a transformation of that faith to a universal religion was accomplished. A dynamic new community was formed—a community of believers which cut across the cultural, social, racial, and economic barriers which divide humankind. Luke gives us an intimate picture of this transformation. He tells of the first preaching of the gospel message to the Jews and the growing fellowship that formed within Judaism (ch. 2–7). He tells of the unexpected conversion of many in Samaria (ch. 8), and the absolutely stunning conversion of Cornelius, the first Gentile to come to Christ (ch. 10,11). Luke reports on the establishment of a Gentile church at Antioch, and the vision of the gospel which led Paul and Silas to set out on their first missionary journey (ch. 13–14). And Luke tells of the council that struggled with the question of how the Jewish majority, and the OT law, should relate to the churches being formed by Gentile converts (ch. 15). Luke goes on then to describe the great outreach in the West that transformed Christianity, as the Gentiles became the vast majority.

Another theme in Acts is the work of the Holy Spirit in the men and women of the new Christian community. The new movement was infused with a dynamic and a power that touched its members. The great expansion was not due to a more compelling philosophy, but to a great work of God, which was dramatically visible in the lives of the men and women who responded to the gospel message. In Acts we learn much of the "normal Christian life" and realize that through the working of this same Spirit within us, we too have power from on high that enables us to triumph.

For all its exciting contribution to our understanding of the early Christian movement and the potential for spiritual power in our own lives, we must remember that Acts is a book of history.

Luke is not teaching doctrine: he is telling a story. We do not build doctrine on our interpretation of the events Luke reports. Instead we study the Epistles, which do teach doctrine, and let their teachings help us interpret the meaning of the historical events.

When we read Acts for what it is, and are sensitive to the themes which Luke himself stresses, we gain a clearer vision of our great missionary faith—a faith which offers hope to all mankind.

Structure and Outline. There are two common approaches to analysis of the structure of Acts. One is to build an outline around the individuals who are Luke's central characters. The other is to build an outline around the ever expanding borders of Christian outreach.

It's clear that Acts is the story of the early church told through the ministry of two men: Peter and Paul. Peter dominates chapters 1–11 of Acts. The impetuous disciple of the Gospels has matured, and he is the dominant figure as the gospel invitation is extended first to the Jews and then to Gentiles in Palestine. The second part of the book, chapters 12–28, is dominated by Paul. This persecutor of early Christians experiences a conversion which transforms him into the new faith's greatest missionary and theologian.

But Luke's organization of his book also reflects a careful attention to surges of expansion in the church. Each surge is examined, and following each a summary statement is given. The summary statements, found in Acts 6:3; 9:31; 12:24; 16:3, and 19:20, provide the framework for the outline below.

Outline of Acts

I.	The Jerusalem Church	1:6–6:7
II.	Expansion in Judea, Galilee and Samaria	6:8–9:31
III.	Inclusion of First Gentiles	9:32–12:24
IV.	Period of Gentile Evangelism	12:25–16:5
V.	Establishment of the Gentile Church	16:6–19:20
VI.	Paul's Imprisonment	19:21–28:31

Chapter 1:1–5. Introduction

Luke addresses Acts to the recipient of his gospel, Theophilus. This is a common Greek name. The title "most excellent" (Luke 1:3) suggests he was a high government official, or perhaps the patron who supported the writing and copying of Luke's histories.

Acts takes up the gospel story, moving from what "Jesus began to do and teach," to report on Jesus' post-resurrection ministry through his disciples. Christ has been "taken up into heaven." But he continues to minister through his followers on earth.

Luke immediately picks up one of his major themes: the Holy Spirit. The disciples are to wait in Jerusalem for his "baptism." This is defined in 1 Corinthians 12:13 as the Spirit's ministry of uniting all who believe in Jesus in an organic relationship with God and one another (see *Body of Christ*, p. 646). Thus the Spirit's coming at Pentecost is the beginning of the NT church.

I. The Jerusalem Church (Acts 1:6–6:7)

At first the church contained only Jewish believers, who continued to worship at the Jerusalem temple and to live according to OT law. They were distinct only because they worshiped Jesus as God and recognized him as the one who fulfilled the OT messianic promises (see *Messiah*, p. 255). These believers formed a unique community within Judaism, marked by a great love for one another and by a sharing of their lives. This supportive community, with evangelistic preaching and miraculous healings performed by the disciples, stimulated a great turning to Jesus in the holy city.

Chapter 1:6–26. Preparation

Power for Ministry; 1:6–11. Just before Jesus returns to heaven, the disciples ask if he is about to establish the promised earthly kingdom (6). Jesus tells them they are not to know the date or time (7). They are to concentrate on their mission: "you will receive power when the Holy Spirit comes upon you, and you will be my witnesses in Jerusalem, and in all Judea and Samaria, and to the ends of the earth" (8). God's plan for this age of ours is one of aggressive witness to our Lord, empowered by the Spirit of God (see *Holy Spirit, NT*, p. 516).

A Twelfth Apostle Chosen; 1:12–26. A man named Mattathias is chosen to take the place of Judas. The term "apostle" now replaces the familiar "disciple" of the Gospels to identify the small group of men who followed Jesus "the whole time the Lord Jesus went in and out among us" (21,22). "Disciple" means "learner." "Apostle" means "one sent on a mission." Two candidates for the apostleship are put forward, and Mattathias is chosen by drawing lots (cf. Prov. 16:33). This is the last time such a method of decision-making is mentioned in the NT. When the Spirit comes,

he guides the choices of God's people in a direct, personal way
(cf. Acts 13:1–3).

☐☐ Read ahead through Acts 1–5. What evidences do you find
🙰 that the Holy Spirit's coming did bring power for witness
to Jesus?

Chapter 2. The Holy Spirit Comes

Pentecost; 2:1. This is the OT harvest festival known as the "feast
of weeks" (Exod. 34:22; Deut. 16:9–12). It is one of three religious
festivals all Jews are to attend in Jerusalem, during which an offering is to be returned to God, according to his blessing of his people.
In Jesus' surrender of his life on Calvary the ultimate blessing
has been given. Now it is time for God to receive the first of a
great harvest of believers, to be his own special people.

The Coming of the Spirit; 2:1–4. The promised coming of the
Spirit (cf. 1:5) is marked by three unmistakable signs. There is a
sudden roaring sound (2:2), visible tongues of fire rest on each
of the 120 gathered for prayer (2:3, cf. 1:15), and all begin to
speak in foreign languages (2:4). Jesus' followers will often be filled
by the Spirit (cf. Acts 4:8,31; 9:17; 13:9). But these three distinctive
signs mark only the Spirit's initial coming to be "in" rather than
"with" Jesus' followers (John 14:17).

Tongues; 2:5–13. In the first century some 150 Jewish colonies
were established in major population centers throughout the Roman Empire. Many Jews came from them to Jerusalem for the
feast of Pentecost, popular because the date was well into the Mediterranean sailing season. Crowds of these visitors now stand stunned
as "each one" hears Jesus' Galilean followers "speaking in his
own native language" (2:8,11). Only to those who did not understand the foreign tongues did the speaking seem like drunken bab-
bling.

Peter's Explanation; 2:14–21. Peter quotes a long passage from
Joel to explain the phenomenon. Before the Day of the Lord comes
(see *OT Eschatology,* pp. 372, 373) God promised that the Spirit
would be poured out on all peoples (2:14–18), and that in those
days "everyone who calls on the name of the Lord will be saved"
(2:21). What all see is evidence that the Spirit has at last come!
Peter moves on immediately to tell his hearers that they can be
saved by calling on the name of Jesus as Lord.

Peter's Sermon; 2:22–39. Acts records two early gospel sermons
preached by Peter (2:22–39; 3:12–26). These reveal the basic elements of early apostolic preaching.

(1) Jesus, the historic person all the hearers know.   2:22

(2) Was crucified and raised from the dead.   2:23,24   3:13–15

(3) In accordance with prophecy.   2:25–35   3:18

(4) He is God's Messiah.   2:36   3:20

(5) All who turn and believe on him will receive remission of sins and be given the Holy Spirit.   2:37,38   3:19,21–26

Response to the Gospel; 2:40–47. Peter's preaching leads to the conversion of some 3,000 people! These form a devoted company, so committed to loving one another (cf. John 13:33,34) that they are willing to sell their possessions to meet one another's needs. How does this picture of the fellowship of the early church (2:42–47) reflect a pattern for Christian life together today?

The Healing at the Temple

Chapter 3. A Healing Miracle

A Crippled Beggar Healed; 3:1–10. One "miraculous sign" performed by the apostles (cf. 3:43) is the healing of a cripple who begged at one of the temple gates. The spectacular Jerusalem temple, completed now after a forty-year expansion and beautification project, is the focus of Israel's religious life. Now, at the time of afternoon prayers, there are a host of witnesses to the healing performed in Jesus' name (see *Healing,* p. 499).

Peter's Sermon; 3:11–26. Peter's message after this healing is the same as his Pentecost sermon (2:22–41). Israel has turned the Messiah (Christ) over to execution. But God has raised him from the dead (14,15). It is Jesus' power that has been exercised to make "this man whom you see and know" whole. Each listener has the opportunity through Jesus to "turn to God, so that your sins may be wiped out" (19). Peter seems to suggest (20,21) that if the nation will turn to God now, Jesus' return may be hastened.

Chapter 4. The First Persecution

Before the Sanhedrin; 4:1–22. The Sanhedrin is the governing body of Judea, with limited civil as well as religious powers. This group of leaders was responsible for forcing the cruicfixion of Jesus. Understandably, they are "greatly disturbed" at the miracles and the announcement of Jesus' resurrection. There are now some 5,000

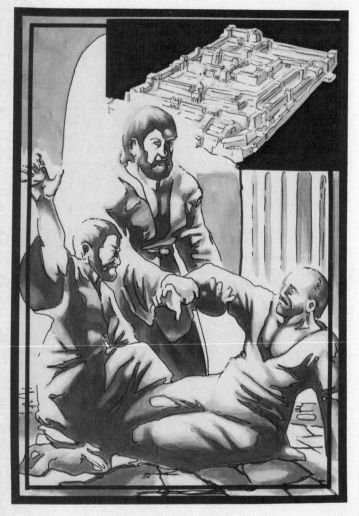

The Healing at the Temple

believers and the leaders are determined to stop the movement from spreading beyond Jerusalem (16).

Peter and John boldly confront the leaders of their people, proclaiming Jesus "whom you crucified but whom God raised from the dead" (10). Fearlessly they announce that "salvation is found in no one else, for there is no other name under heaven given to men by which we must be saved" (see *Salvation,* p. 574). Although the leaders threaten Peter and John, the two openly announce that they will do what is right in God's sight.

The Believers' Prayer; 4:23–31. Peter and John report these threats to the believing community and all turn together to God in prayer. God is addressed as "Sovereign Lord." The rulers of Israel may claim authority but are powerless against the maker of heaven and earth (24)! All the rage of the leaders and their plot against Jesus has been in vain. God's will has been accomplished, through their hatred! Now the believers ask God as Sovereign Lord not for protection, but for boldness and power to speak out in the name of Jesus.

Prayer, and confidence in the sovereign power of our God, is still a source of great strength for the people of the Lord.

The Close Knit Community; 4:32–37. This first threat of persecution caused the early church to draw even closer together. It stimulated not only prayer but also the willingness of each to help meet the needs of others (34). The description here and in 2:42–47 is not of some "Christian communism." It is instead a demonstration of Jesus' kind of selfless love for others (cf. John 13:33,34) and of a trust in God which frees us to put persons before our material possessions (see *The Christian and Money,* p. 527, and *Giving,* p. 656).

Second Corinthians 8:1–9 tells of another Christian community that responded to needs in a similar way. Compare the two churches.

Chapter 5:1–6:7. Early Church Problems

The first days of the church were not a time of unmixed blessing. Now Luke shares some of the inner and external tensions that arose as the Jerusalem church grew.

Hypocrisy; 5:1–11. Internal tensions held the greatest danger for the young church. Seeing the honor in which those who gave all for their brothers and sisters were held, one couple sells land and agree together to lie about the amount when they present part to the apostles for the church. This hypocrisy and dishonesty is a serious threat to the unity of prayer and love that exists (4:23–37). God acts and judges Ananias and Sapphira immediately. The awe inspired by the sudden deaths (5:11) deepens the awareness of the church and the community that God is among this people.

The Apostles Persecuted; 5:12–41. The crowds continue to gather to hear the apostles and be healed. This rouses the jealousy of the high priest and his associates. The apostles are arrested and brought before the Sanhedrin. Peter and the others boldly present Christ and his offer of forgiveness of sins (5:31,32). But there is no repentance from the leaders who murdered the Lord. Gamaliel persuades the Sanhedrin not to press for execution. This most influential rabbi, the teacher of the apostle Paul before his conversion (Acts 22:3), argues that if the movement is not of God, it will fail. If the Christian movement is from God, the leaders will not be able to stop it. Temporarily persuaded, the court settles for beating the apostles.

This persecution does not harm the church. The believers draw even closer together and "never stop teaching and proclaiming the news that Jesus is the Christ."

Disputes; 6:1–7. Another serious internal problem develops when some Greek-speaking Jewish Christians complain that their widows are not given a fair share in the daily food distribution. The apostles ask the whole community to choose seven "known to be full of the Spirit and wisdom" to oversee this ministry. The twelve will be free to devote themselves to prayer and teaching. The community chooses seven, each of whom has a Greek name! No factionalism can take root when the very group that complains is entrusted with distribution to all.

Salvation

Most OT references to salvation speak of deliverance from man's enemies. Escape from death (Psa. 6:4,5; 107:13), from troubles (Jer. 30:7), and from sickness (Isa. 38:21) are typical examples of the way the OT saint thought of "salvation." There is a deep OT awareness of need for protection from national and personal enemies. And there is the sure confidence that one can rely on God alone to provide salvation (cf. Exod. 14:30; Isa. 43:11).

The NT continues the theme that salvation is a work of God. But in the NT we find a distinctive emphasis. Now salvation is primarily viewed as God's action to deliver us from sin (cf. Luke 1:77; Acts 2:38; 3:19). In Christ God has at last taken steps to deal with mankind's greatest enemy: his sinful self.

Salvation as revealed in the NT has past, present, and future aspects. We have been saved, are being saved, and will be saved. Salvation in each of these senses rests on the death and resurrection of Jesus and is ours through trust in him.

We have been saved. Christians can look back and affirm that they "have been" saved. There may be no particular point of time at which an individual consciously trusted Christ as Savior. But those who have been saved did experience what Jesus calls being "born again" (see *Born Again,* p. 545). Life from God was received as a free gift and the individual has passed from death to life (John 5:24), released forever from sin's guilt and punishment. I can't remember my physical birth, and it is often the same with those who are born again. We may not remember the event, but our relationship with Jesus tells us that we have life.

We are being saved. God is presently at work in our lives, delivering us from the power of sin that we might live a new holy life. This is what is meant as "being" saved. The NT gives us many pictures of the life from which, and to which, we are being saved (see Rom. 8:1–5; Col. 3). The transformation is gradual, involving growth (2 Pet. 3:18). But as we grow in Christ toward that person the Lord is helping us become, we know the meaning of present-tense salvation.

We will be saved. One day the very presence of sin in our lives, and every reminder of its pull, will be gone. The universe will be cleansed from every taint of evil (cf. Rom. 8:18–25), and we ourselves will be like Jesus (Rom. 8:28–30). Then we will know the fullness of the salvation that God has won for us in his Son. Then we will know completely the meaning of this most significant Bible word.

The writer now summarizes the first Jerusalem phase of the early church: "So the Word of God spread. The number of disciples in Jerusalem increased rapidly, and a large number of priests became obedient to the faith" (6:7).

What guidelines for dealing with internal or external pressures on churches today do you find in this chapter? What are the dangers today to which the guidelines you find should be applied?

II. Expansion in Judea, Galilee, and Samaria. (Acts 6:8–9:31)

After a period of consolidation, the new faith burst out of Judea, spilling over into the surrounding regions. The expansion was stimulated by sharp persecution which followed the stoning of Stephen, one of the seven "full of the Spirit and wisdom" (6:3) who were chosen to care for the food distribution.

Chapter 6:8–7:60. The Stoning of Stephen

Stephen Seized; 6:8–15. Stephen's witness to Jesus is so powerful that his frustrated opponents seize him and bring him before the

Jewish court, the Sanhedrin. They have arranged for perjured testimony to be given against him.

Stephen's Defense; 7:1–53. Stephen recites the history of Israel's relationship with God. He demonstrates from the OT that the Hebrew people have always resisted the Lord. And he applies this truth pointedly. The present generation is just like the fathers They killed the prophets who foretold the coming of the Holy One. Now this generation has betrayed and murdered their Messiah.

Stephen Stoned; 7:54–60. When Stephen announces that he sees Jesus now, standing at God's right hand in heaven, the yelling crowd drags him out of the city. They stone Stephen to death. There has been no trial, no verdict, and the Sanhedrin lacks authority to condemn anyone to death. Stephen has been murdered by a mob.

The NT here introduces the word "sleep" for death (7:60, cf. John 11:23–26; 1 Cor. 15; 1 Thess. 4:13–18). This becomes the way Christians think of death; the term affirms the conviction that Jesus has provided his followers with immortality.

> Stephen emphasizes how Israel's response to God revealed the people's character. What do God's actions reveal to you of his character?

Chapter 8. Evangelism Explosion

Persecution; 8:1–3. The persecution of believers which follows the murder of Stephen scatters Christians across Judea and Samaria. One of the chief persecutors is a man we will come to know well: Saul, who became the apostle Paul.

Philip in Samaria; 8:4–25. Luke traces the ministry of Philip, one of the seven of Acts 6:5, to illustrate the witness of the scattered believers. Philip proclaims Christ in a Samaritan city and there is a great response (8:7,12).

Report of the revival brings Peter and John from Jerusalem. The Samaritans are descendants of pagan peoples imported by Assyria after their conquest of the old kingdom of Israel in 722 B.C. The newcomers adopted a form of Jahweh worship, since he was viewed as the God of their new land. But they and their mongrelized faith were deeply resented by the Jews. The response of the Samaritans to the message of Jesus must have been disquieting to the all-Jewish Jerusalem church!

In this instance the Holy Spirit is given by the laying on of the apostles' hands (8:15–17). This is not a normal thing in the early church, but here serves two important purposes. (1) It establishes the authority of the apostles, and (2) it demonstrates to the Jewish believers that God has welcomed the Samaritans into the Christian community as full members. The unity of the new Christian movement is thus protected.

This chapter also tells of a sorcerer, Simon, who had convinced the Samaritans he has some great power (a deity: 8:10). Stunned by the real miracles of Peter and Philip, he professes faith and follows them, to learn the secret of their power (8:13,18–23). But his old motivations are strong and he tries to buy power from Peter. Simon may have been a believer. But he was not able to share in the ministry, for his motives and character were still in the grip of sin (20–23). Salvation is for all who believe. Ministry is for those whose faith brings them significant inner transformation.

Philip and the Ethiopian; 8:26–40. Philip is led away from the revival in Samaria by God to witness to an individual. The man is an official in the court of the Ethiopian queen—a Jew or Jewish convert who had come to Jerusalem to worship. Philip interprets the passage he is reading in Isaiah 53 and leads him to faith in Jesus. The conversion is sincere, and at the Ethiopian's urging, Philip baptizes him along the roadside.

Twice in this chapter Acts speaks of converts undergoing water baptism. See *Baptism,* p. 580. Why do you feel this practice was important in the early church? Why might it be important to us today?

Chapter 9:1–31. The Conversion of Paul

Paul's Background. He was born as Saul, in Tarsus, of well-to-do Jewish parents who had won Roman citizenship (Acts 16:37, 38; 22:25–29). As every Jewish boy, he began his study of the Scriptures at five. Around thirteen he went to Jerusalem and there studied under Gamaliel (22:3), "thoroughly trained in the law of the fathers" and "zealous for God." His later writing and preaching show that young Saul also received a classical Greek education. But it was to Judaism that Saul was committed, heart and soul. He watched with full approval as Stephen was stoned (8:1). As the young church grew, Saul became one of its chief persecutors.

Saul's Conversion: 9:1–19. The high priest has legal authority from Rome to arrest those Jews who break the Jewish religious law. Saul obtains letters of authority from him and heads toward Damascus where there is a colony of some 16,000 Jews. He intends to arrest "any there who belonged to the Way" (9:2). Six times

Acts uses the phrase "the Way" to identify early Christians (9:2; 19:9,23; 22:4; 24:14,22) as those who followed Jesus.

On the road to Damascus, Christ appears to Saul in blazing light. Blinded, Saul must be led to Damascus. There the Lord sends a believer to restore his sight. Three great convictions which will rule Saul's life are born in this experience. Saul now knows for certain that Jesus is Lord. Jesus must be preached. And Saul is God's chosen instrument to carry the name of Jesus to the Gentiles.

Saul's Early Preaching; 9:20–31. At once Saul begins to preach in the synagogues of Damascus, boldly showing that Jesus is the Son of God. As Saul learns, his preaching becomes more powerful and compelling. Soon the life of the zealous convert is threatened and he barely escapes the city.

He returns to Jerusalem, but the Christians there fear a trick and will have nothing to do with him. Finally Barnabas, who later will be his first missionary companion, accepts the risk and brings him to the apostles. Within weeks Paul's bold and fearless preaching seems about to arouse a fresh wave of persecution! The brothers "take him down to Caesarea and send him off to Tarsus."

Now there is another time of consolidation, and Luke summarizes this stage of his history. "Then the church throughout Judea, Galilee and Samaria enjoyed a time of peace. It was strengthened; and encouraged by the Holy Spirit, it grew in numbers, living in fear of the Lord."

How does Saul seem different after his conversion? How does he seem the same? What kind of person do you think this man is?

III. Inclusion of the First Gentiles (Acts 9:32–12:24)

The church has spread to Jewish communities beyond Jerusalem. Even the Samaritans have been accepted in the new community. But no one who is a Gentile—a pure pagan, and thus one of the Jews' hated enemies—has responded to the gospel. But the church is to be a universal fellowship. The old barriers that divide peoples must be broken down (cf. Eph. 2:14–22). Luke now continues his history to tell of the first Gentile convert, the consternation his salvation caused, and the first Gentile congregation.

Chapter 9:32–10:48. Cornelius' Conversion

Peter's Ministry; 9:32–43. Peter travels about the country, teaching and healing as he visits the saints. His ministry brings him to Joppa, where he stays with a tanner named Simon. Because tanning involves the handling of dead bodies, it is considered an unclean occupation by the Jews. The fact that Peter would stay with Simon shows clearly that some old social attitudes are breaking down, as the dynamics of the new relationship between Christians call each believer to view others as beloved brothers and sisters.

Cornelius' Vision; 10:1–8. Cornelius is a Roman army officer. The term "God-fearing" is a technical term for a person who believes in God and worships him, but who has not been circumcised or converted to Judaism. This man now has a vision in which he is told to send to Joppa and summon Peter.

Peter's Vision; 10:9–23. "Uncleanness" is a religious concept from the OT. One who is ritually unclean is unable to participate in worship or other religious practices until he or she has been cleansed. The Jews avoided anything which could cause them to become unclean, and especially avoided unclean foods. Gentiles were considered to be unclean by the Jews of the first century, and a pious Jew would not enter a Gentile home or eat with him.

As the messengers of Cornelius travel to Joppa, Peter falls into a trance on the roof of Simon's home. He sees a great canvas sheet let down from heaven, filled with unclean animals. A voice from heaven commands Peter to kill and eat. Shocked, Peter refuses, objecting, "I have never eaten anything impure or unclean!" (14). Three times this experience is repeated, with the voice telling Peter, "Do not call anything impure that God has made clean" (15). As Peter ponders the meaning of the vision, the Holy Spirit tells him of Cornelius' messengers and says specifically, "do not hesitate to go with them, for I have sent them." God is about to announce that he has made clean a people the Jews have considered impure!

At Cornelius' House; 10:23–48. Peter tells Cornelius how God has "shown me that I should not call any man impure or unclean" and asks why he has been sent for. Cornelius tells of his vision and, for the first time, Peter preaches Jesus to a Gentile audience (34–43).

As Peter is speaking the Holy Spirit comes on these new believers, making his presence known with one of the three signs present at Pentecost: they speak in other languages in praise of God (44–46; cf. Acts 2:1–4). Peter recognizes the meaning of this event. It is a sign given to the Jews—compelling evidence that these Gentiles are to be accepted as full participants with them in the new community of faith! Peter accepts this evidence and baptizes the new believers in the name of Jesus Christ.

[📖] Compare the presentation of the gospel to Cornelius with the early preaching of Acts 2 and 3 (see p. 571). Has the message changed?

Baptism

The OT knew a washing with water to cleanse from ritual uncleanness (see p. 97). In later Judaism, self-baptism was part of the service of conversion. But when John the Baptist appeared preaching his message of repentance he introduced something totally new: water baptism became a profession of commitment to change.

The gospel preaching of early Acts also stresses repentance. Repentance does not mean mere sorrow for sin, but a change of heart and mind. Those who heard of the resurrected Jesus in Jerusalem were to reverse their opinion of him—and to acknowledge him now as the Son of God. It was appropriate, in view of the meaning of this symbol introduced by John the Baptist, to continue the practice as an open confession of faith: a public testimony to the fact that the individual has changed his or her mind about Jesus and now acknowledges him as the Christ, God's Savior from sin.

But when John introduced baptism, he also announced that when Jesus came he would "baptize with the Holy Spirit" (Matt. 3:11; Acts 1:5). This promise was kept at Pentecost. From that time on believers have been united to Jesus and one another by the baptizing ministry of the Holy Spirit (1 Cor. 12:13). Thus for the Christian, baptism implies more than repentance. It is a picture of a work which God performs deep within the human personality.

Paul explains the inner reality which water baptism mirrors in Romans 6:1–7. Speaking of the work of the Holy Spirit, Paul teaches that Christians are united with Jesus in his death, so that Jesus' death is considered ours. Likewise, we are united with Jesus in his resurrection, so that his new life is also ours! The baptism practiced by the early church, which was most likely baptism by immersion (cf. Mark 1:10), pictured graphically the burial of one's old life with Christ and the raising of the believer to a new life, to be lived in Jesus' power.

There is no NT passage that instructs us on the mode of baptism which the church is to practice. Church history shows us that at different times baptism has involved sprinkling, pouring, and immersion. What is important is to realize that, beyond the symbolism of the rite, there lies a great spiritual truth which water baptism is intended to picture. We *have* died to sin in Christ. We *have* been raised in him to a new life.

When we accept water baptism we make a public commitment. We will turn our back on all that is evil, to live a holy life that reflects the goodness and the love of our Lord.

Chapter 11. Peter's Defense

The Reaction; 11:1–3. Even though Peter is an apostle, his visit to Cornelius stimulates strong criticism. The basis is legalistic: "you went into the house of uncircumcised men, and ate with them." The believers in the early Jewish church still see the basis for fellowship in the church the same as the basis for relationship which existed before Christ came: strict observance of Mosaic law.

Peter's defense lays a new basis for acceptance of other believers and leads toward the realization that relationship with Jesus and not the Mosaic law provides the foundation for fellowship in the universal church.

Peter's Defense; 11:4–18. Peter simply reports what has happened. He emphasizes five historic facts. (1) Through a vision God taught him not to think of other men as "unclean." (2) The Holy Spirit directed him to go to Cornelius' house. (3) An angel was sent by God to Cornelius. (4) The angel promised that Peter would share the message of salvation. And (5), there was outward evidence that the Holy Spirit baptized these Gentiles "as he had come on us at the beginning."

This evidence is compelling. The stunned Jewish believers can only praise God, saying "So then God has even granted the Gentiles repentance unto life!"

The relationship between Jewish and Gentile believers will cause tensions in the future, tension which will need to be resolved. But the reality of Gentile salvation is accepted.

The Antioch Church; 11:19–26. When Gentiles in the Greek city of Antioch turn to Christ in great numbers, the Jerusalem believers accept the movement as a work of God. Barnabas is sent to Antioch. He recognizes God's hand, brings Saul from Tarsus to help, and the two stay to teach and minister in this first Gentile congregation. It is here the name "Christian," which means "little Christs," is coined for the followers of Jesus.

Famine Relief; 11:27–30. The Gentile church demonstrates its sense of oneness with the Jewish church of the holy land when prophets foretell a famine. All "decide to provide help for the brothers living in Judea" (29). The years of famine fall between A.D. 43 and 47. It is only a little over a decade since the crucifixion of Jesus, and already the first colony of God's people has been established in the Gentile world.

Lifetime attitudes are always hard to break. Yet God carefully and graciously acted to show Jewish believers that he intends them to accept others, who are different, as brothers. What differences tend to divide Christians today? What are we to learn from the lesson God taught the early church?

John 17 records Jesus' prayer for unity among his disciples. What evidence is there here that his prayer "that they may be one, as we are one" is answered? What do we learn about the nature of Christian unity from these Acts passages?

Chapter 12. Peter's Escape from Prison

The focus of history is about to shift to Paul and to his mission to the whole world. But first Luke gives one final report on the life of Jewish believers in Jerusalem.

Peter Imprisoned; 12:1–4. The Herod who initiates the third persecution of the believers (cf. 4:1; 5:17 and 9:1,2,29) is the grandson of Herod the Great, and nephew of that Herod who beheaded John the Baptist. His harassment, begun to please the Jewish leaders, led to the death of John's brother, James. Now Herod seizes Peter as well.

Peter Is Released; 12:5–19. An angel frees Peter from his prison the night before his trial is scheduled. Peter joins a group gathered at the home of John Mark's brother to pray for him.

Herod's Death; 12:20–25. Shortly after Peter's release, Herod dies suddenly. The date, fixed from secular sources, is A.D. 44. This ends the third wave of persecution in Jerusalem, which probably began about A.D. 41 when Herod began his rule. Luke now adds one of his typical summary statements: "the Word of God continued to increase and spread" (24).

Little is known of Peter's ministry after this date. The NT indicates that it focused on ministry to Jews, in Palestine and scattered across the empire (Gal. 2:7). Peter died some twenty years later, in Rome.

IV. The Period of Gentile Evangelism (Acts 12:25–16:5)

A vision of the universal church has now gripped Paul. Soon he and Barnabas are launched by the Holy Spirit on a missionary journey to spread Christian faith throughout the Roman Empire. The success of Gentile evangelism raises a question which was sure to emerge following the conversion of Cornelius: What is the relationship of the new faith to its OT roots?

Acts 13. Missionary Methods

Set Aside by God; 13:1–3. Barnabas and Saul return from Jerusalem, to which they have delivered relief funds (12:25). Now they are called by God to a special work. Their commission from the Holy Spirit is affirmed by the church (13:3), and they set off together on their first missionary journey (see map, p. 585).

Cyprus; 13:4–12. Cyprus has been an important trading center from the nineteenth century B.C. It has had a large Jewish population for at least 200 years. Paul proclaims the Word in the Jewish synagogues and travels the whole island preaching the gospel. On these travels he meets the Roman governor of the province, a proconsul named Sergius Paulus. At Paul's word, the Lord strikes a false prophet who advises Paulus, with blindness (see *False Prophets,* p. 326). The governor, amazed at the message of Jesus, becomes a believer.

Preaching in Pisidian Antioch; 13:13–41. This inland city was included in the Roman province of Galatia. It had a large Jewish population and also a large group of Romans, for it was a colony city to which Roman army veterans were retired after their twenty years of military service.

On the Sabbath the missionaries attend the synagogue and, as is the custom, are invited to share a "message of encouragement for the people" (15). The message which Paul preaches clearly parallels the early preaching of Peter and Stephen (see p. 571). God's OT promises are reviewed (17–22), Jesus is shown to be an historical person and descendant of David (23–25), and the death and resurrection of Jesus are announced (26–31). These events are shown to be in harmony with the teaching of the OT (32–37), and "forgiveness of sins through Jesus" is proclaimed (38–40).

The response of the hearers will be duplicated over and over again across the years of missionary endeavor. The Jews debate the message among themselves; the Gentiles respond enthusiastically. When "almost the whole city" gathers to hear the Word of the Lord the next Sabbath, the Jews grow jealous and angry. Jealousy shuts their hearts to the gospel, and they stir up persecution against the missionaries.

Missionary Strategy. The patterns which mark the efforts of NT missionaries can already be seen in this chapter.

* A missionary team visits an area where the Word has not yet been heard.

* They choose population, political, and trade centers.
* They begin by sharing the gospel with the Jewish community and with those Gentile "God-fearers" who attend synagogue services.
* They spend a few weeks or months teaching the new believers—and then trust their growth to the Holy Spirit.
* Typically, persecution develops in the community, often at the instigation of unbelieving Jews, and the missionary team moves.
* Later the team or their representatives will revisit the new church to confirm the leaders who have emerged and to teach.
* Still later letters of instruction will be written to the young churches, and these epistles will be gathered together and circulated to make up most of our NT.

The rest of the Book of Acts tells the story of one group of missionaries as it carries out this strategy, which enabled the early church to reach their world for Christ.

How are modern missions similar to or different from first century missions? What are the implications of the missionaries moving on, rather than remaining to "pastor" the new churches they establish?

Chapter 14. The First Missionary Journey

Barnabas and Paul continue on to several key cities in Asia, preaching the gospel and establishing new churches.

Iconium; 14:1–7. This ancient settlement is the principal city of Lycaonia, a district containing a distinct national group in the process of being absorbed into the wider Hellenic civilization. The missionaries stay in the city for some time, until its population is deeply divided and their enemies plot to kill them.

Lystra and Derbe; 14:8–20. Lystra is a small rural mountain town, well off the major trade routes. There is a tradition that it was once visited by the gods in human form. When Paul and Barnabas heal a cripple there, the two are believed to be gods themselves. Sculptures from the area suggest something about the looks of the two missionaries. They show Zeus (with whom the people identify Barnabas) as a tall, bearded man. Hermes (with whom they identify Paul) is slight and agile.

The apostles stop the crowd from sacrificing to them, and preach the gospel. Soon some Jews from Antioch and Iconium turn the

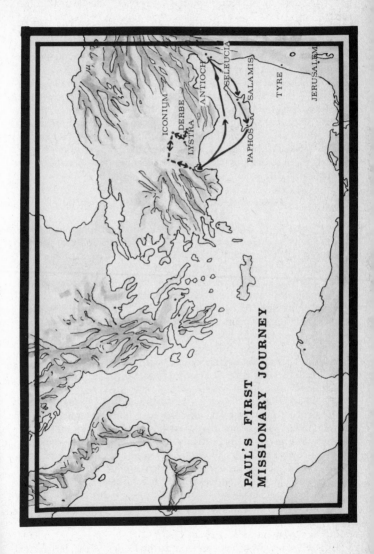

PAUL'S FIRST
MISSIONARY JOURNEY

people against them. Paul is stoned and left for dead outside the town.

Return to the Antioch Church; 14:21–28. After some two years on mission, the team returns to the Antioch church which sent them out. They report "all that God had done through them" and how the door to faith is wide open to the Gentiles.

Leaders Appointed. Verse 23 speaks of Paul and Barnabas "appointing" elders when they revisit the newly established churches. The word in Greek does not require hierarchical interpretation. Instead it probably suggests official recognition or ordination of those whom God has put forward and the people have recognized as their leaders. It is likely the process used in Acts 6:3–6 was used in NT times for the selection of local leaders (see *Local Church Leaders,* p. 720).

Chapter 15:1–16:5. The Jerusalem Council

The Council; 15:1–21. Now at last the issue of relationship between Jewish and Gentile believers becomes clear. Some converted Pharisees (cf. 15:1 with 15:5) come to the Gentile churches and teach that to be saved believers "must be circumcised according to the custom taught by Moses." Their ultimate goal is to impose the Mosaic law, and thus Judaism, on the whole church (15:5). This teaching stimulates a serious debate. Does a believer have to surrender his own culture and become a Jew to be a Christian? Must Gentile believers adopt the life style laid out in the Mosaic law?

Paul and Barnabas are appointed, with others, as a delegation to go to Jerusalem and discuss the issue with the apostles and elders.

The Pharisee party insists on law-keeping. But, as many share in the process of prayer and discussion, a different conclusion is reached. Peter points out that God has accepted the Gentiles as they are and given them the Holy Spirit just as he has given the Spirit to Jewish believers. Both are saved not by law but by faith. What right then has the Hebrew Christian church to impose the Mosaic law, "a yoke neither we nor our fathers have been able to bear" on the Gentiles (6–11)?

Then Barnabas and Paul add their testimony of God's work among the Gentiles, reporting the miraculous signs that authenticate the movement as a work of God (12).

Finally James, who has emerged as the leader of the Jerusalem church, speaks up. This James is the brother of Jesus and the writer of the Book of James. He quotes God's words from Amos 9:11,12 showing that God predicted the salvation of Gentiles *as Gentiles*. The Jewish church then should also accept their Gentile brothers as they are (13–18), without insisting they adopt Judaism.

James sums up the sense of the council. They should not "make it difficult" for the Gentiles who are turning to God. He suggests only that four guidelines be passed on to the Gentile churches. They should abstain from all association with idol worship, reject sexual immorality, give up unbutchered meat (a prohibition which may be related to Lev. 17:10–12), and abstain "from blood." Some in the post-apostolic church took this last to refer to military service and suffered execution rather than serve in the Roman army.

The Official Letter; 15:22–35. The letter sent out by the apostles and elders is no authoritative command. Instead it simply tells the Gentile churches that any who came from Jerusalem "and disturbed you" did so without authorization of the leaders. Led by the Spirit, the Jerusalem congregation has been led not "to burden" the Gentiles with "anything" other than the four issues James suggested.

Messengers are sent with copies of this letter, encouraging and strengthening the Gentile believers who are recognized as "brothers."

The Jerusalem council has dealt wisely with a basic issue: an issue Paul recognized and writes of in Galatians. Not only is the unity of the church on the sole basis of faith in Christ reaffirmed, but the Mosaic law is beginning to be seen by believers in a new perspective. The decision not to "burden" the Gentiles with the law did not imply they were free to live unrighteously. Instead, as Paul will show in his writings, freedom from the law will lead to a new and dynamic righteousness for all (see *Law, NT,* p. 617, and *Righteousness, NT,* p. 611).

Paul and Barnabas Separate; 15:36–41. A sharp disagreement breaks up the missionary team of Paul and Barnabas. The tragic dispute (described on p. 711, see "author") shows that even the great apostle is fallible.

Timothy Joins Paul and Silas; 16:1–5. Paul forms a new team and sets out on another journey. He first visits Gentile churches, sharing the conclusion of the Jerusalem council. Again now there is a pause—a time of consolidation. Luke makes his familiar summary statement: "So the churches were strengthened in the faith and grew daily in numbers" (16:5).

Do Christians today ever seek to impose their own standards on other believers as the price of acceptance? What are some

"tests of fellowship" modern Christians may insist on? What principles do you see in the decision of the Jerusalem council that we
can apply today?

V. Establishment of the Gentile Church (Acts 16:6–19:21)

At this point Luke joins the missionary team. From Acts 16:10
on he reports the journeys in Acts as something which "we" under-
took. Perhaps as many as eight years of ministry are summarized
in these few chapters, which tell of Paul's work in many of the
major European cities of the empire.

Chapter 16. Imprisoned in Philippi

The Macedonian Call; 16:6–12. Paul and his team are led by
God into Europe. They cross the waters and travel the main highway that cuts across Macedonia, coming first to the commercial
center of Philippi. The population is largely retired or active-duty
military personnel.

Lydia's Conversion; 16:13–15. There are too few Jews in this
city to establish a synagogue. But Paul finds a few worshipers of
the Lord gathered by a river on the Sabbath. The first European
convert is a woman named Lydia.

Imprisonment; 16:16–40. When Paul casts a demon out of a
slave girl used as a fortune teller, her furious owners accuse the
missionaries of "throwing our city in an uproar." A crowd joins
in the attack, and the city magistrates have Paul and Silas beaten
and thrown into prison. When an earthquake opens the prison
doors, the jailer intends suicide. This is something Stoic philosophers of the day recommend to escape execution.

But no prisoners are gone, and the jailer, who has apparently
heard the missionaries' preaching, asks Paul how to be saved. The
answer is as simple as ever: "Believe on the Lord Jesus Christ,
and you will be saved—you and your household" (16:31, see *Belief/
Faith,* p. 562). The "household" reference is best taken to relate
to the role of the father in the strict Roman family: as *pater familias*
his own decision would release his family to believe also. Verse
34 makes it clear that each family member did make a personal
decision to trust the Lord. In many cultures missionaries have
found conversion comes by family or tribal groups, as decisions
by the leaders open the door to faith for all.

The next day the missionaries are discovered to be Roman citizens! Their beating without trial was illegal. Humbly the city magistrates come and apologetically request that Paul and Silas leave.

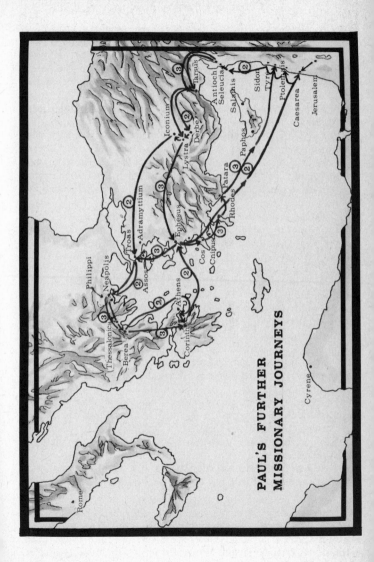

PAUL'S FURTHER MISSIONARY JOURNEYS

Chapter 17. On to Athens

In Thessalonica; 17:1–19. The pattern seen earlier is now repeated in this, the largest and most important city in Macedonia. The team of missionaries goes first to the synagogue. Gentiles respond enthusiastically. The jealous Jews stir up trouble. Two NT letters are later written by Paul to the church established during this short visit to Thessalonica (1 and 2 Thessalonians).

In Berea; 17:10–15. Berea is a small city some sixty miles from Thessalonica. The Jews there listen for three Sabbaths to Paul teach from the OT. Many of these Jews are convinced and, with prominent Greek men and women, become Christians. All goes well until the Jews of Thessalonica send agitators to stir up trouble.

In Athens; 17:16–34. Paul's stay in Athens is brief—but important to our understanding of missions. Here his preaching is appropriate to an audience which is very different from the Jews and God-fearing Gentiles whom Paul usually approaches first.

Athens is the ancient home of Plato and Aristotle and still the center of philosophical speculation in the ancient world. So Paul begins his talk with reference to an altar to an "unknown God" which he has observed among their many objects of worship (22,23). Paul presents this God as the Creator and source of all life (24,25). The direct Creator of humanity, he desires that mankind should seek him (26,27). Quoting some of their own Greek poets Paul argues that since man has been created in God's image, it is wrong to think of God as being gold or silver or stone fashioned by men (28,29). This is ignorance and has been overlooked in the past. But now God has set a day of judgment and calls for repentance. To prove this, God has raised Jesus from the dead (30,31).

Paul has done what many missionaries today argue should be done in our outreach efforts. He has contextualized the gospel. He has not changed the message of Jesus and resurrection. But he has put the message in a form suited to the thought patterns of his listeners.

Most who hear Paul ridicule the idea of resurrection, so foreign to Greek thought. But a few believe in the Lord (32–34).

Chapter 18. In Corinth

Corinth. Corinth is a bustling port city, the capital of Achaia. It is very prosperous and is a center for worship of the love goddess, Aphrodite. Corinth is well known for its easy immorality and extravagances. Paul comes to this city shortly after the emperor Claudius has expelled the Jews from Rome (18:2, A.D. 49) and while Gallio, who is the brother of the philosopher Seneca, is proconsul (18:12, c. A.D. 51). Paul is to stay in Corinth for at least eighteen months and later will write letters of instruction to the church here.

Missions Principles. A study of Acts 16–19, and of Paul's letters to the Thessalonians and the Corinthians, helps us see the principles practiced by the early missionaries in establishing new churches. The chart below summarizes the NT principles revealed in these documents. These same principles are vital to the life and mission of Christ's church in our own day.

	Establishing a Healthy New Church	
Acts 16–19	Gospel Communication	Contextualize core truth
1 Thessalonians 1–2	Love	Loving interpersonal relationships provide a climate for hearing God's Word.
1, 2 Thessalonians	Transformation	The new community of faith promises its members personal transformation.
1 Corinthians 1–4	Maintaining Unity	Approach differences with God's point of view, recognizing Jesus as central, and human leaders as merely God's servants.
1 Corinthians 5–6	Discipline	Deal firmly with sin in the family and resolve disputes fairly.
1 Corinthians 8–10	Doctrinal Disputes	Love and truth are both required for a resolution. Being "right" does not remove the obligation to love others and build them up.
1 Corinthians 12–14	True Spirituality	Possession of certain spiritual gifts should not be mistaken as indication of spiritual maturity. Love is the true evidence of growth in Christ. Believers, as members of one body, are interdependent. Each spiritual gift is important, and each individual's ministry to others is needed.
1 Corinthians 7, 11	Women's Identity	Women are to be affirmed as persons and valued in the body. Equality does not mean "sameness" but does imply importance.
1 Corinthians 15	Resurrection Coming	Ultimate transformation is sure!

Ministry in Corinth; 18:1–17. Paul is protected from the Jews by God and by the disinterest of the proconsul Gallio in "questions about words and names and your own law." Paul teaches in Corinth for some eighteen months before moving on.

Apollos; 18:18–28. Apollos is a learned Jew who has heard only the message of John the Baptist. He vigorously preaches that the Messiah is coming. When Apollos comes to Ephesus and gives his message in a local synagogue, Priscilla and Aquila from Corinth hear him and invite him to their home. There in private they "explain the way of God more adequately." Many believe that this powerful new convert and later leader of the NT church (cf. 1 Cor. 1:12) is the unknown author of the Epistle to the Hebrews.

When the Bible refers to the couple who shared Christ with Apollos it is the wife, Priscilla, who is listed first. She is evidently recognized as one of the leaders of the early church (cf. Rom. 16:3; 1 Cor. 16:19; 2 Tim. 4:19; Role of *Women in the Church*, p. 625).

Acts 19. In Ephesus

Ephesus. Ephesus is known as the gateway to Asia. It is situated on a geat harbor, which has in Paul's day begun to fill with silt. And it is the terminus of a major highway between the coast and central Asia Minor. The city also contains one of the seven wonders of the ancient world: the great temple of Artemis, whose image is reputedly formed from a meteorite. This is the religious center of all Asia, and metal workers make a rich living from the sale of shrines and miniature silver images of the goddess.

John's Followers; 19:1–7. Entering Ephesus, Paul finds others who know of John the Baptist's ministry but have not yet heard of Jesus (cf. 18:24–26). They believe, and the tongues speaking, which signifies the coming of the Spirit on them, is evidence that Jesus truly is the one whom John foretold.

A Great Response; 19:8–22. Many respond to the missionary team. This passage shows the dramatic impact of the gospel on the life of a typical pagan city (13–20), and also reveals more of Paul's missionary strategy. By choosing capital cities and trade centers for their preaching, the missionary team makes it sure that converts will carry the word through their own provinces. Within two years of the concentrated effort in Ephesus, the gospel has been spread throughout the province of Asia (cf. 19:10).

Here Luke inserts another of those summary phrases, which tell us he is finished with this phase of his history and is about to launch on another. "In this way the word of the Lord spread widely and grew in power" (19:20).

Paul's Imprisonment (Acts 19:21–28:31)

Luke now focuses his history even more sharply on the apostle Paul, relating the sequence of events which brings him to Rome as a prisoner. Many churches have been established in Asia and Europe through Paul. Now the apostle will fulfill the other part of the mission to which God originally called him: "this man is my chosen instrument to carry my name before the Gentiles and their kings and before the people of Israel" (Acts 9:15).

Chapter 19:21–20:38. Paul's Farewells

Riot in Ephesus; 19:21–41. Paul has decided to travel to Jerusalem and then on to Rome. Before he leaves Ephesus there is a riot, led by a silversmith whose idol-making business is being ruined by the mass conversion of the population (23–28)! The magistrates finally quiet the crowds, insisting that if anyone has a grievance it should be handled through the courts or in a legal assembly (35–41). The response of the city officials shows the great value of Roman authority to the early church. Rome controls the western world and Rome insists on legal due process (cf. 19:40).

Through Macedonia; 20:1–12. Paul revisits the churches he has established in Macedonia and Greece. His sense of urgency to impart all he can to these young believers is illustrated by an incident at Troas. A young man who sits up with others till midnight to listen to Paul's teaching falls asleep. He tumbles from a third story window. Paul restores him to life and then goes on with his teaching until daylight. Others might sleep. Paul is driven to accomplish all he possibly can.

Farewell to the Ephesian Elders; 20:13–38. Luke shows us more clearly the sense of urgency that now drives Paul. He is unwilling to take time to revisit Ephesus and sends messengers to have the elders of that city meet him as he passes by. Paul reviews his ministry with them (17–21) and shares that he is "compelled by the Spirit" to go to Jerusalem, aware that danger, imprisonment, and hardships await (22–31). Paul commits these dear brothers to the Lord, sure that they will never see one another again (32–38).

Earlier Luke has shown us the scope of the work Paul has accomplished. Now Luke begins to unveil the heart and soul of the great apostle, inviting us to come to know him as a person.

What impression have you had of the apostle Paul as a person? Read Acts 20 carefully. How does this strengthen or change your view of Paul the man? For further insights into Paul as a person read 1 Thessalonians 2, Philippians 3, and Galatians 2.

Chapters 21–23. Witness to the Jews

In Jerusalem; 21:1–26. The trip to Jerusalem is marked by other warnings of the dangers facing Paul (1–11). But Paul is firm. Though the tears of his brothers and sisters break his heart, Paul will die for Jesus' name if this is God's will (12–15).

In the holy city Paul is welcomed and told of thousands of Jews who now believe in Jesus. These Christian Jews also are zealous adherents of the law of Moses. Because Paul is a Jew, the leaders suggest Paul show his piety by joining several brothers who have made a vow in the old way. He will thus show "that you yourself are living in obedience to the law" (24). Paul does as they advise.

Paul Arrested; 21:27–36. Paul is recognized in the temple and his companions are taken to be Gentile converts! For Gentiles to enter the temple area where only Jews are permitted was a great desecration. Paul is dragged out of the courtyard and barely rescued by Roman troops that rush down from the nearby fortress Antonia to break up the riot.

Paul's Speech to the Crowd; 21:37–22:22. Paul receives permission from the Roman officer to speak to the crowd. He identifies himself and tells of his background (22:3–5). He reveals his conversion to Jesus (6–13). But when Paul reports a vision in which God commands him to go with the gospel to the hated Gentiles, the riot explodes again (14–22, cf. Luke 4:27–30).

Paul, the Roman Citizen; 22:23–29. The military commander orders Paul beaten with the *flagellum,* a weighted whip used for torture, to discover what he has done to set off the riot. Paul appeals to his Roman citizenship. The commander immediately sends away the examiners. Under the empire, no Roman citizen could be so examined until legally convicted in a court of law.

Before the Sanhedrin; 22:30–23:11. The Roman military commander of Jerusalem orders the Sanhedrin to gather and brings Paul to the assembly. He is determined to find out the cause of the rioting.

There Paul identifies himself as a Pharisee, inducing a dispute between members of this sect and the Sadducees (see pp. 440, 442). The two groups fall to arguing and the dispute becomes so violent that the commander is "afraid Paul would be torn to pieces by them." He again rescues Paul and returns him to the military barracks.

That night an angel announces that Paul has fulfilled his mission to the Jews (9:15). Now he must testify in Rome itself.

The Plot to Kill Paul; 22:12–35. Paul's nephew, hearing of a conspiracy by over forty men to murder Paul, warns the apostle. When the plot is reported to the military governor, he acts immediately and sends Paul with a guard of several hundred troops to the Roman governor in the port city of Caesarea. The commander also orders Paul's accusers to go there, if they have a case to present against the apostle.

Chapters 24–26. Witness before Kings

The Trial before Felix; 24:1–27. Secular sources tell us much about Felix, who was procurator of Judea from A.D. 52 to 59. This childhood friend of the Emperor Claudius apparently felt safe because of that relationship and was extremely corrupt. Tacitus says that he "had the power of a tyrant and the temper of a slave," and that he was known for his lust and cruelty.

In five days Paul is arraigned for trial before this man, charged by the high priest and some of the Sadducee party who have come down from Jerusalem (1–4). Several charges are brought against Paul. He is called a political agitator, the leader of a subversive movement masquerading as a sect of Judaism, and a person who has desecrated the temple (5–9). As Roman governors carefully consider the customs of subject peoples as a matter of imperial policy, these are serious charges and must be examined.

Paul defends himself skillfully. He caused no uprising. He has only been in Jerusalem for about two weeks, for the purpose of worship. Paul did not enter into a single argument until he was mobbed (10–13). The Christian movement is not subversive but rests on and is an outgrowth of OT faith, whose Scriptures are believed by all (14–16). As for desecration of the temple, Paul was undertaking a vow and was ceremonially clean when he was attacked by accusers who are not even in court (17–21)!

As governor of this religion-mad province, Felix is "well acquainted with the Way," as Christianity is known locally. Felix refuses to make an immediate decision. Later he confers with his Jewish wife, Drusilla, and listens with some terror as Paul talks with him about faith in Jesus and coming judgment.

Felix keeps Paul confined in Caesarea for some two years, hoping to be offered a bribe by the apostle. In the meantime, keeping the apostle locked up is a favor to the Jewish leaders.

On Trial before Festus; 24:1–12. In A.D. 59 Felix was replaced in Judea by Porcius Festus. His honorable rule lasted only two

Paul before Festus

years, as he died in office. Josephus speaks of his effort to put down crime and the robber bands which had run wild under Felix.

Festus no sooner arrives in Judea than the chief priests bring up the case of Paul and demand it be settled. In Caesarea the Jews bring a number of false, but serious, charges against Paul. When Festus asks Paul if he is willing to go to Jerusalem for trial, Paul recognizes the danger of another conspiracy (see Acts 23:20,21), and officially appeals to Caesar. The right of legal appeal to Caesar is an important perquisite of Roman citizenship, resting on some five centuries of legal precedent. By the act of appeal, Paul takes himself out of the jurisdiction both of the Jewish court (the Sanhedrin) and the jurisdiction of Festus as well.

Festus Consults King Agrippa; 25:13–22. A few days later Herod Agrippa II, son of the Herod mentioned in Acts 12:23 and a high Roman administrator in Judea, visits the new procurator. (Apparently at this time the title *king* is a courtesy title only.) When Agrippa and his sister Bernice arrive, the frustrated Festus asks for advice about the unfamiliar Jewish customs and beliefs which complicate the case of this Roman citizen, Paul. Festus is also confused about Paul's strange statements concerning "a dead man named Jesus who Paul claims is alive" (19). Agrippa is eager to hear Paul speak, and Festus promises to arrange a meeting for the next day.

Paul Before Agrippa; 25:23–26:32. The next day all the important people in Caesarea assemble with the Roman administrators to witness the interrogation. Agrippa and Bernice enter with great pomp. Festus introduces Paul's case and the apostle is then invited to speak out for himself.

Paul acknowledges Agrippa's intimate knowledge of Jewish affairs (26:2, 3), and tells of his own early life as a member of Judaism's strictest sect, the Pharisees. This group has believed in resurrection and thus should not have been shocked when God raised Jesus (26:4–8). But, like others, Paul at first reacted by persecuting the church (26:9–11). He tells of Jesus' appearance to him on the road to Damascus (26:12–16), and of his commission to witness to the Gentiles "so that they may receive forgiveness of sins and a place among those who are sanctified by faith in me" (18). Then Paul makes a direct appeal to Agrippa. All Paul has said is just what Moses and the Prophets foretold would happen (26:19–23).

All this seems like utter madness to the Roman Festus (26:24). But Paul insists that "what I am saying is true and reasonable." Again he challenges Agrippa to make a personal commitment (26:25–27).

Agrippa puts Paul off. "Do you think that in such a short time you can persuade me to be a Christian?" Boldly Paul replies that he prays each listener will be converted (26:29). At this the king and Festus leave. Whatever Paul's beliefs, there is nothing in them that deserves death or imprisonment under Roman law. If Paul had not appealed to Caesar he could have been set free.

How does Paul's preaching match other Acts sermons? Compare this with Acts 2, 3, 17 and 26 for common elements.

Chapters 27, 28. Paul in Rome

Shipwreck; 27:1-44. Luke's graphic description of travel on the Mediterranean in the time of Christ has been studied carefully. Every detail matches—and adds to—the understanding of ancient sea trade and travel gained from other sources.

Most important to us is the picture Luke gives of Paul. He is being taken under guard to Rome, yet clearly this prisoner is the dominant personality, to whom all look for support and encouragement. His unshakable faith in God gives him a confidence which causes the others to trust him even in the most dangerous situations.

On Malta; 28:1-10. The survivors winter on Malta, a small island some seventeen miles long, about sixty miles south of Sicily. When Paul survives the bite of a poisonous snake and cures many who are ill, the whole company is made welcome.

Paul in Rome; 28:11-16. When the company arrives in Rome, the missionaries are met by Christians living there. Paul is allowed to rent his own quarters and to live there with a military guard.

Paul's Prison Ministry; 28:17-31. For two years Paul waits for his case to be heard. He welcomes visitors to his home and shares the gospel with both Jews and Gentiles, "boldly and without hindrance" preaching the kingdom of God and teaching about the Lord Jesus Christ.

After Acts

Luke's history of the early church ends here. What happened to Paul afterward? While in prison Paul wrote our NT books of Colossians, Ephesians, and Philemon. Apparently the Jews in Jerusalem did not forward any charges against him. After the statutory wait established by Roman law, Paul was simply released in A.D. 63.

For the next few years Paul continued to evangelize, perhaps going to Spain as he had wanted (cf. Rom. 15). Paul wrote letters to Timothy and Titus during this period.

Paul was later rearrested. He writes his second letter to Timothy during this imprisonment, and it is clear he expects death. Tradition tells us that Paul was executed in Rome, probably around A.D. 68.

But when Paul went to meet his Lord, he left a church which had spread throughout the Roman empire, with hundreds and hundreds of thousands who had come to know Christ through the missionary effort begun by this small but great man.

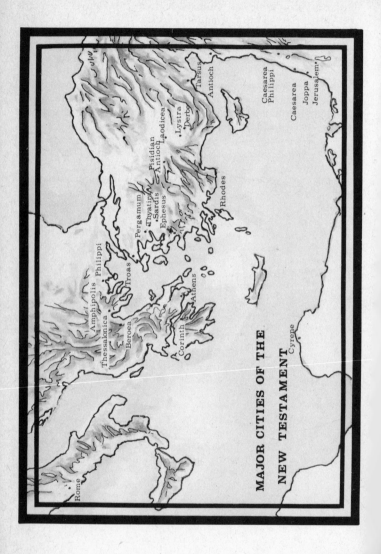

MAJOR CITIES OF THE
NEW TESTAMENT

THE NEW TESTAMENT EPISTLES

The bulk of the New Testament is made up of epistles: letters written by leaders of the early church to various Christian communities throughout the whole Roman world. These letters have different purposes, but each comes out of specific needs that emerge as the expanding Christian movement struggles to resolve a variety of problems. Some of the letters are written to individuals, some to congregations divided by strife, some to believers facing persecution. But all were quickly copied and circulated among all the churches. All were recognized as Scripture: as an authoritative Word not just from a man but, through a man, from the Holy Spirit of God.

Each of these Epistles is a *teaching* letter. In each the Holy Spirit is speaking to communicate, to the believers of the first century and to us today, basic principles on which our lives together as God's people are to be based.

We study the Epistles differently than we study the OT and NT books of history. In narrative portions of our Bible, the authors have carefully arranged the sequence of incidents they report to illustrate their themes. We study that history by watching unfolding events and listening for statements of truth which help us interpret their meaning. In the Epistles a more direct approach is taken. The authors explain, argue, illustrate, exhort, and instruct. To study the NT epistles we carefully trace the "argument"—the flow of thought—of each writer.

We are not to take isolated verses of the Epistles out of their context and try to understand them as if they stand alone. The individual verses do *not* stand alone. Each verse is intimately related to the sentences around it, to the paragraph in which it rests, and to the purpose of the whole letter in which it is found. To understand the NT epistles we must study them in this way—in the flow of the argument as the author deals with real historical problems or situations in first century church life.

Handbook notes on the NT Epistles are designed to help you trace this argument and to explain the flow of thought of the writer so that each verse can be better understood.

There are two groups of NT Epistles: the Pauline (letters of Paul) and the General (the letters of others). An overview of the epistles is given in the chart on page 602.

Overview of the NT Epistles

Title	Author	Probable Date	Source	Destination
James	James, brother of Jesus	44–49	Jerusalem	Jewish Christians
Galatians	Paul	48–49	Antioch	Central Asia Minor
1 Thessalonians	Paul	51	Corinth	Thessalonica
2 Thessalonians	Paul	52	Corinth	Thessalonica
Romans	Paul	57	Corinth	Rome
1 Corinthians	Paul	57	Ephesus	Corinth
2 Corinthians	Paul	58	Macedonia	Corinth
Ephesians	Paul	62–63	Rome	Ephesus
Colossians	Paul	62–63	Rome	Colossae
Philemon	Paul	62–63	Rome	Philemon
Philippians	Paul	63	Rome	Philippi
1 Peter	Peter	64–65	?	Jewish Christians
1 Timothy	Paul	65–66	?	Timothy
Titus	Paul	65–66	?	Titus
2 Peter	Peter	66	?	Jewish Christians
2 Timothy	Paul	67	Rome	Timothy
Jude	Jude, brother of Jesus	80–90	?	Jewish Christians
Hebrews	unknown	?	?	Jewish Christians
1, 2, 3 John	John	90–95	Ephesus	Believers

ROMANS
The Explanation of God's Righteousness

Romans is a theological treatise, which carefully explains for the many Jewish and Gentile Christians living in Rome the dynamic nature of God's righteousness. Israel has futilely sought righteousness through a Mosaic law, whose purpose is misunderstood. But now the longed-for righteousness has been made available to all through faith in Jesus Christ. This foundational epistle is perhaps the most basic exposition of Christianity in the NT.

Date and Author. The letter was written by the apostle Paul, from Corinth, probably about A.D. 57. This places its writing toward the end of Paul's missionary work in Asia Minor and Greece. It came nearly a decade after the Jerusalem council (Acts 15) affirmed the principle that the law of Moses was not binding on Gentile believers. During this period Paul had come to understand clearly the answer to the great question raised by that decision: How can a Christian be free from the law, and not released from the righteousness the law expresses? Paul's careful explanation is contained in the Book of Romans.

The Church at Rome. From the second century B.C., Rome had a Jewish colony. After Judea was incorporated into the Roman Empire in 63 B.C., the Jewish population expanded. Cicero, writing in 59 B.C., speaks of the Jews of Rome as a large, powerful, and influential group.

Acts tells us that Jews from Rome were in Jerusalem in A.D. 33, at the birth of the church (Acts 2:10). They surely carried back a report of the events and of Peter's preaching. It is possible a small nucleus of Christians was formed in Rome even at this early date. Apparently Aquila and Priscilla were already believers when driven from Rome by Claudius' edict in A.D. 49 (Acts 18:2).

The Jewish community was expelled from Rome several times. Each time the edict lapsed and the Jews returned. This was the case with the edict of Claudius as well. In A.D. 57, when Paul wrote, there was a large Christian community, and the report of their faith was "proclaimed in all the world." It also seems likely that when Paul wrote, the faith had begun to penetrate the elite of Roman society. In A.D. 57 the wife of Aulus Plautius, conqueror of Britain, was charged with a "foreign superstition." From the specifications associated with the charge, she appears to have become a Christian. This is made more likely by archaeological evidence which shows the family members in the next century were believers.

In A.D. 64 the first great persecution, under Nero, struck the church at Rome. It was only seven years after this letter had been sent to them by Paul. Pagan historians of the period tell of the torture and execution of "a huge multitude" of Christian martyrs. The gospel of God had been heard and believed in the very center of the empire. No persecution would ever stamp out the new community of faith which the gospel brought into being. No threat of death would ever overcome the dynamic power of the righteousness of God.

Theme. The theme of Romans is clearly stated in Paul's introduction to his letter. "In the Gospel a righteousness from God is revealed, a righteousness that is by faith from first to last, just as it is written: 'The righteous will live by faith' " (1:17). Reading this great NT book, we gain a vivid impression of the vital new life which God gives us in Christ: a life infused by the gift of a righteousness which is from God (see *Righteousness,* p. 611).

Structure and Outline. The Book of Romans is a theological treatise as well as a letter. Thus it is a very carefully developed, logically organized document. The outline on page 605 traces the flow of the argument which Paul develops in this book.

Value. Romans has been one of the most highly valued of the books in our Bible. It was through Romans that the monk, Martin Luther, rediscovered the great truth of justification by faith, and began the Reformation which reshaped much of the Western World. It was while listening in Aldersgate Chapel to the reading of Luther's commentary on Romans that John Wesley, who had struggled with his own deep sense of alienation from God, felt his heart "strangely warmed." Thrilled, and filled with the gift of righteousness which he then received by faith, Wesley began a fifty-year ministry in England. The great revival that swept the British Isles is believed by historians to have prevented the kind of bloody revolution that swept France.

The Word of God communicated to us in Romans still has power to warm our hearts. Power to launch us on a life, as new and significant as the lives of Luther and Wesley have been to the world, is explained in this great NT book.

Before Reading. Here are several questions answered in Romans. Which of these questions is important to you? Read Romans for the answers. *How can I receive God's righteousness? *Are non-Christians really lost? *What is the real nature of sin, and what does it do to me? *Why do I have so much trouble doing what is right—even when I want to do it? *Do the OT and NT disagree about how to be saved? *What does a "righteous life" for me really involve? *What is my attitude to be toward others with different convictions than mine? *How do I have close relationships with other Christians?

Outline

I. Introduction (Romans 1:1–17)

Greeting; 1:1–7. Paul, as always, immediately directs our attention to Jesus. He is the one promised beforehand in the Holy Scriptures. He is the one "declared with power to be the Son of

God by his resurrection from the dead." Jesus is Lord. All of life must now be understood and experienced in relationship to Jesus Christ, for as believers we are "called to belong to Jesus Christ."

Personal Items; 1:8–15. Paul expresses his longing to visit the believers at Rome for whom he prays (8–10). Such a visit would be an opportunity for mutual ministry: each will strengthen the other's faith. Paul does recognize his own unique gifts for upbuilding others (11) and feels a deep obligation to share the gospel with all human beings (14).

Theme Stated; 1:16–17. Paul has experienced the power of the gospel at work in himself and in others. He shares it then with full confidence, sure he will never be embarrassed (16). The phrase "first for the Jew, then for the Gentile" is historical; Paul's missionary strategy (see p. 591) followed this pattern.

In this gospel about Jesus a unique righteousness is revealed: a righteousness that "is by faith from first to last." Righteousness that comes to us through Jesus, and is appropriated by faith, is the theme of Paul's letter to the Romans.

What is Paul's attitude toward the Christians at Rome? How does he seem to view them and his relationship with them?

II. Universal Need of Righteousness (Romans 1:18–3:20)

The Jewish people assumed that righteousness was theirs, for they possessed the law of God and thus knew God through revelation. The pagan peoples around them simply stumbled after God in darkness. First, then, Paul must show that no one lives without some knowledge of God. In point of fact it is the way that Jew and Gentile both have responded to God, when they knew him through revelation, that demonstrates so clearly the need of all mankind for a righteousness which can only come through faith.

Chapter 1:18–32. Need of the Gentiles

Knowledge Possessed; 1:18–20. Paul makes a bold statement. God's righteousness is revealed in his deep-seated anger against mankind, for men wickedly suppress the truth about him. God can be known, for he communicates himself in the Creation (cf. Ps. 19:1–4). Paul's thought here goes beyond external evidence. The apostle indicates that God presents himself directly to the human conscience. Thus there is no excuse. All have at least some knowledge of the Lord.

Man's Response; 1:21,22. It is the response of men to God which

demonstrates so clearly humanity's need for righteousness. Rather
than turn toward God, or thank him, men turn away. With their
ability to reason darkened, they even stoop to the worship of idols
shaped like mortal man or animals.

Moral Results; 1:23–32. Society demonstrates the impact of this
rejection of God. Sexual perversion (23–27) and every kind of
wickedness is expressed in interpersonal relationships (28–31). Each
individual and culture adds tragic testimony to sin's demonstration
of our need for a righteousness which the human race does not
possess.

   Glance through any newspaper. How do current items demonstrate Paul's point and show man's need of righteousness?

Chapter 2. Need of the Jews

Paul has just shown that the Gentiles *do* have truth about God
but have turned away from him. He will now show that, while
the Jews have more extensive knowledge about God, they have
responded no better than the pagans they scorn!

Judgmentalism; 2:1–13. Paul immediately exposes an attitude
which is prevalent in first-century Judaism. It is an attitude of
brittle pride; a judgmentalism which looks down on and condemns
all non-Jews (1–13). Great knowledge of God should have produced
humility and repentance (4). It is not immorality but "your stubbornness and unrepentant heart" which shows the Jewish people
have responded no differently to God than have the Gentiles! God
will judge all men, not by what they know, but by what they do
(6–13)!

Man's Moral Nature; 2:14–16. These often misunderstood verses
teach that God made human beings moral "by nature" (14). This
does not mean all know the specific moral standards revealed in
Scripture. But it does mean that every society recognizes the same
general "moral issues" and sets moral standards. Paul's point is
that no human being lives up even to his own standards, much
less God's. God is even willing to judge a man by his own standard
and not the Lord's. Even with lowered standards, every individual's
conscience testifies that he has fallen short, for his thoughts make
excuses for his behavior or try to avoid responsibility by blaming
others (15).

The Jews and the Law; 2:17–29. To have the law of God does
mean having a superior standard of morality. But moral superiority
cannot come "because you are instructed by the law," or even
because you approve of it (17–20). In fact Israel violates the very

law she teaches, and "God's name is blasphemed among the Gentiles because of you." The Jews have the law but have not kept it (21–24).

Paul then mentions circumcision (25–29). This important OT rite was given by God as the symbol of descent from Abraham and thus of membership in God's Covenant people (see *Covenant*, p. 51). Many Jews counted on this physical relationship as a basis for relationship with God (cf. John 8:33–47). Paul argues that circumcision guarantees nothing. Those who are circumcised and fail to keep the law stand condemned by the law. It is not a physical and outward sign of relationship God seeks, but a heart that is responsive to his Spirit.

Chapter 3. The Testimony of Scripture

Advantages of the Jews; 3:1–8. The fact that both Gentile and Jew need righteousness does not imply the Jews have no advantages. They do—in their possession of God's very words in Scripture. The failure of some to respond to those words of revelation does not alter the truth of the words (1–3). Nor will Israel's failure dishonor God, for the Jews will be judged by the law in which they trust, and thus God's faithfulness to his Word will be established.

Proof of Need for Righteousness; 3:9–18. What then does the OT say about righteousness? Paul has earlier pointed to empirical evidence of mankind's need. Now he proves his thesis by quotes from the very OT law in which the Jews mistakenly hoped: "There is no one righteous, not even one."

Purpose of the Law; 3:19, 20. This teaching is stunning to the Jew of NT times, who thinks of law as God's way of salvation. If the law is not God's way to make men holy, what then is its purpose? To Paul the answer is clear. Law reveals God's standards of right and wrong behavior in order to make men *conscious of sin!* When we honestly measure ourselves against the holiness revealed in the law, we are all silenced, for we all fail to keep that law and thus stand guilty before God.

III. The Gift of Righteousness (Romans 3:21–5:21)

Paul now makes a clear and powerful statement about God's way of salvation and the role of faith. The righteousness which humanity desperately needs and cannot find through the law is available to Jew and Gentile alike through faith in Jesus Christ.

Chapter 3:21–31. Righteousness Provided

The notion that righteousness comes through faith is not new. It is an open secret, unveiled in the OT but ignored by the Jews (cf. Gen. 15:6). Christ, however, brings this righteousness into sharp focus, for his death reveals how God can be "just" in his offer of a salvation by faith to those who have sinned (21–24). God has not permitted sin to go unpunished! Instead God chose, in Jesus' sacrifice of atonement, to himself bear the punishment which justice decrees (25,26).

Righteousness is now available to Jew and Gentile alike through faith. Thus it is clear that justification is a matter for faith and something totally apart from "observing the law."

Paul adds one more thought for the stunned Jew who might read his argument. Faith does not make law irrelevant. Instead it "upholds the law," by giving it the role God always intended for it, as a revelation to humanity of each person's need for a righteousness which can only be found through faith (cf. 3:19,20).

Chapter 4. Justification by Faith Illustrated

Paul goes back now to the OT to show that the faith principle has always operated in the same way. Abraham's faith was credited to him for righteousness, according to Genesis 15:7 (4:1–5). And in Psalm 32:1, 2 David speaks of the same truth (4:6–8). As for circumcision, Abraham was justified by faith before the rite was given (Gen. 17:3–14). Thus Abraham's justification by faith sets the pattern for both Jews and Gentiles (4:9–12). Paul goes on to show that God's covenant promise (see *Covenant*, p. 51) was received by faith and thus is not related to law either (4:13–17).

Justification

"Justification" is courtroom language. To understand this great theological term we must imagine an individual standing before God the judge, his life and character and every activity under examination. Paul tells us in Romans that, if a human being were to "do good" and keep either the law of conscience or Moses, God would declare him righteous (2:12–16). But Paul shows us that all have sinned and fallen short. How then can God the judge declare a verdict of "not guilty" over any man?

Paul goes on to explain that God has already announced a stunning verdict! We "are justified freely by his grace, through the redemption that came by Christ Jesus" (Rom. 3:24). God has accepted the blood of Christ as an atoning sacrifice for our sins and because of Jesus has declared man justified (3:25, 26).

In an objective sense Christ died for all, and the verdict of "not guilty" has been pronounced over all humanity. In a personal sense, each individual must accept the announced pardon. This pardon, the Bible says, is accepted by faith—simply by trusting in the God who has extended forgiveness to us in Jesus.

What then is "justification"? It is a judicial act of God by which he declares us righteous. It is intimately linked with forgiveness of sins. And it is the beginning of a new life of faith in which we desire to please God.

For study: Romans 3:21–31; 4:13–15; 10:14–17; 2 Corinthians 5:18–21.

It is clear then from this analysis that justification by faith is boldly affirmed in the OT! So Paul goes on to analyze the nature of faith. When God's promise of an offspring was made to Abraham he was nearly a hundred years old, and his wife Sarah ninety. Abraham faced these facts. But he also took into account the fact of God! He was "fully persuaded that God had power to do what he had promised." For you and for me, too, faith—the conviction that the God who raised Jesus from the dead will credit us with righteousness through him—is also the way to forgiveness and a new life (4:18–25).

Look at the brief explanation of *Faith/Belief* on p. 562. Some say it is the "sincerity" of a person's faith which is important. How do you think Paul would respond to that idea? What is the relationship of "faith" to what one has faith in?

Righteousness

To "justify" is to declare righteous as a judicial act. But God does more than this for us. He acts in our lives to actually *make* us righteous.

Three strong emphases on righteousness are found in the NT, and each is linked to Jesus: *Jesus' death has demonstrated God's righteousness, revealing him to be a gracious and holy person (Rom. 3:24–26). *Jesus himself is the object of faith, through whom individuals are declared righteous by God. And *Jesus is the source of a dynamic new life for those who exercise a believing trust in him. In our relationship with Jesus a "righteousness that is by faith from first to last" (Rom. 1:17) begins to possess us, bringing us new thoughts, new motives, and a new way of life.

In Romans 6 Paul outlines an option facing believers. We can choose continued bondage to sin, or by faith commit ourselves to God and be servants of righteousness. By offering ourselves totally to God, to respond to his Spirit, we are released to experience a truly righteous life which reflects the very character of our Lord (6:1–14).

James goes even further. The dynamic of righteousness which faith introduces into our lives *will* find expression in our lives. God's righteousness is a dynamic, vital force, and thus true faith will lead always to the kind of good works that bring honor and definition to the goodness of God.

For study: Romans 3:21–31; 6:1–14; James 2:14–16.

Chapter 5. Justification for all

The Joyful Certainty of Justification; 5:1–11. Faith awakens a sense of rejoicing confidence in our acceptance by God. There is peace where fear ruled; there is hope even in difficult circumstances; there is a growing awareness of God's love, communicated by the Holy Spirit (5:1–5). Our inner experience is confirmed by objective evidence. God has "demonstrated his love for us, for while we were still in our sins, Christ died for us" (5:6–9). Now that we have been brought into harmonious relationship with God (reconciled), we are sure that God will complete the saving work he has begun and preserve us from all that is destructive.

Read this passage to discover the benefits of justification. Which are you experiencing now? For which do you want to thank God?

Death

The Scriptures consistently view death as an enemy which men fear and seek to avoid (cf. Ps. 6:1–5; Isa. 38). But to the writers of the NT "death" means more than dying. In the Epistles, "death" is often used to describe the spiritual condition of mankind. The appropriateness of the analogy is clear. A body without physical life is cold and unresponsive to the natural universe. Just so a human being without spiritual life is cold and unresponsive to God and to those realities the Scriptures unveil (cf. *Truth,* p. 552).

The Bible traces both forms of death back to sin, and to Adam and Eve. The spiritual death which struck the first pair has been communicated to all their offspring. Man's inner bent toward sin demonstrates the fact of death, for acts of sin are an expression of the deadness—to God—which holds humanity in a merciless grip. Only the gift of spiritual life from God can shatter the grip of death (see *Born Again,* p. 545). Apart from new life through Christ, death is the dark and endless destiny of every person.

But Jesus Christ has become a man, experienced death for us, and has been raised to life again! In his resurrection Jesus broke the grip of death on us. Through faith you and I can participate in a resurrected life which will free us from our own personal spiritual death even as we live now in our mortal bodies.

The image of death is a powerful one. But a powerful image is needed to help us grasp what it means to be alienated from God—unresponsive to him and to all that is truly good. Understanding death, we turn eagerly to Christ to receive his gift of life.

For study: Romans 5:12–21; Ephesians 2:1–3; 4:17–19; Hebrews 2:14–18.

Availability of Justification; 5:12–21. This NT passage is one that theologians puzzle over in an attempt to understand the origin of sin and spiritual death. The basic point of Paul's analogy is clear. All human beings have been affected by Adam's first act of sin, which brought spiritual death to all. Now all humanity is affected by Christ's act of obedience, which makes it possible for God to justify sinful man (see *Justification,* p. 610). Adam is the first member of a lost race, bringing mankind under condemnation. Jesus is the first member of a saved race, bringing forgiveness and release from the judgment merited by each man's sins.

Paul is saying that the sins which every individual commits document the reign of death and the grip of death on mankind. Now, as individuals respond in faith and accept the gift of life offered by Christ, the quality of righteousness will be expressed in their actions and will document the transforming grace of God.

Paul again brings up the issue of the law in these verses. This is necessary, for it is his view of law which so troubles Jewish readers. The apostle argues that death was the condition of humanity from Adam to Moses, before the law was given. And death continued to be the condition of humanity from Moses to Christ! Law was introduced alongside to magnify (increase) the trespass (sin) and so to vividly demonstrate the reality of death. Only when men realize that they are truly dead will they be likely to turn to God in search of life!

IV. Righteous Living Now Is Possible (Romans 6:1–8:39)

It is only natural that Paul's reinterpretation of law would frighten many of his readers. Law is an expression of the holiness of God. In setting aside the law is the apostle also setting aside the need for holy living? Paul answers these objections by teaching that only a "righteousness which is by faith from first to last" (1:17) can make holy living a possibility for God's people. God has not abandoned his ideals. In fact, it is through Christ that we are now at last able to achieve the ideal of righteousness in daily life.

Chapter 6. Union with Christ

Our Real Union with Jesus; 6:1–4. Freedom from law does not mean freedom to sin. Paul points to the baptizing work of the Spirit of God (see *Baptism,* p. 580) and teaches that he unites us with Jesus in a real though mystical way. An illustration may be found in marriage. A woman who marries a millionaire becomes legally one with him, so that his wealth becomes hers just as if she had participated in earning it. A believer who is united by faith with Jesus becomes one with him, so that he is considered to have participated in Christ's death and in his resurrection. "We were therefore buried with him," Paul affirms, and "just as Christ was raised from the dead through the glory of the Father, we too may live a new life."

Sin Rendered Powerless; 6:5–10. The old pull of sin will still make itself felt within us. There will be temptations to sin. But our mystical union with Jesus in his death and resurrection has a freeing impact in our daily life. The "old self," with its package of warped and sinful responses, is "rendered powerless." Passions may swirl within us, but the spiritual death which once held us in an unbreakable grip is no longer master! We are free now to respond to God and to choose righteousness.

New Life Lived by Faith; 6:11–14. Paul carefully shows us how to experience the freedom he promises. We are to *know* the meaning of Christ's death in relationship to our sin nature (5–7). We are to *count ourselves dead* to the pull of sin when we sense it within (11). And we are to *not let* sin rule but rather *offer yourselves to God* to do his will (12–13). The way to freedom is thus clear. We are to hear God's promise of freedom, believe it, and act on it.

Old Man/New Man

Several terms in the Epistles introduce the concept that each Christian is fighting an inner war. We live, the Bible suggests, a life of constant tension between an inner pull toward sin and an inner desire for righteousness. Bible words like "flesh" and "old man" and "old nature" speak of that whole bundle of desires and responses which are sinful. Words like "spirit" and "new man" and "new nature" speak of new desires and responses which reflect the righteous character of God himself.

Paul lays the basis for understanding this inner war between the old and the new in Romans 5:12–21, where he teaches that sin is a "nature" as well as actions. We inherited from Adam that core of unresponsiveness to God which the Bible calls death. Acts of sin are expressions of humanity's deadened condition. But in Christ God has offered us the gift of life! The new birth introduces to each believer's personality a new nature, a core of responsiveness to God. There is growth for the new life and a gradual replacement of the old pattern of passions and responses. But there is always struggle.

How can we have victory over all within us that is from the old and is so attracted by sin? Paul answers this question in Romans 6–8. The basis of victory is our union with Christ. The old in us was crucified with Christ and its authority over our will forever ended. Freed now from the power of the old, we can resist its passions and choose to obey God. We are freed from the power of sin which once mastered us—freed to choose to respond to God and to grow toward everything our best selves have always yearned to become.

For study: Romans 6–8; Colossians 3:1–11; Galatians 5:13–26.

Slaves to Righteousness; 6:15–23. But someone is sure to object. Who would want to choose righteousness if law did not force him or her to do so? Paul answers this question that he expects to be in the minds of his readers. Man, Paul says, has only two choices he can make. He can lend his heart and mind and body to serve sin—or he can surrender all these capacities to serve righteousness. Sin may seem attractive, but to choose it means to go on living in the empty realm where death reigns. It is freedom, and promise of experiencing now that eternal life which Christ has won for us, which will attract the believer and motivate holiness.

Is there some temptation or sin which seems to have a grip on your own life? What will you do to put the teaching of this passage into practice?

Chapter 7. Released from Law

In Romans 6, Paul made a shocking statement. "Sin shall not be your master, because you are not under law, but under grace" (6:14). Clearly Paul sees a link between release from law and freedom from the control of sin! This concept plunges us into a section of the NT which is contrary to the common notions about the law held by Israel—and held by many Christians today.

How Can We Be Released from Law? 7:1–3. Paul uses marriage as an illustration. Under law a married couple become one, bound together till one of them dies. But the death of one partner frees *both* from the law of marriage—and the survivor can remarry! We who are in union with Christ (Rom. 6:1–4) died with him and Law has no authority over a dead man. Thus Christ's death legally releases us from the authority of God's law.

Why Must We Be Released from Law? 7:4–6. Paul now returns to what he has said earlier about the purpose of law (3:19,20; 5:20). Law not only reveals sin, it also "arouses the sinful passions" (7:5). We see this energizing principle everywhere. Even a child, told not to touch some cookies, will be hungrier for them than before! The do's and don'ts of law simply charge the old nature with energy and lead to acts of sin.

What Is Wrong With the Law? 7:7–13. There is nothing wrong with law. As an expression of God's character law is "holy, and the commandment is holy, righteous and good." What is wrong is man's nature (see *Old Man,* p. 614). Law acts on the old nature to "produce in me every kind of covetous desire," so that sin "springs to life" and shouts for domination.

Does the Believer Experience This Reaction too? 7:14–25. To answer, Paul shares his own experience as a believer trying to keep the law. A paraphrase points up the key elements of his argument.

"I don't understand my own actions. I don't do what I want— I do the very thing I hate. Because I don't want to do the things I do, it's clear that I agree that what the law says is good and right. I'm that much in harmony with God. But somehow I'm not in control of my own actions! Some sinful force within takes over and acts through my body. I know that nothing good exists in the old me (see *Old Man,* p. 614). The sin nature is so warped that even when I desire good I somehow can't do it. Sin, dwelling in me, is to blame for this situation. It all seems so hopeless! The fact is that when I want to do right, evil lies close at hand. In my inmost self I delight in God's law. But another principle wars with the desire to obey and brings me to my knees, a captive to the principle of indwelling sin."

Paul's struggles as a Christian to keep the law did not lead him to a life of righteousness.

📖 Think of several times when you experienced the kind of struggle Paul describes in 7:14–25. How did you try to resolve your problems? Do you have a sense of victory yet, or is your life still being lived in Romans 7? The way out is found in Romans 8!

Chapter 8. The Spirit's Power

New Life Through the Spirit; 8:1–17. Romans 8 affirms our release from condemnation. Our new life, energized by the Spirit (the "law of the Spirit") overcomes the principles of sin and death (1,2). Romans 7, in explaining attempts to relate to God through an impersonal code, mentions "law" 20 times, "I" 22 times, and "I do" 14 times! Its conclusion is, "I try, but I cannot!" In Romans 8 a dramatically new perspective is introduced. "Law" is mentioned only 4 times and "Holy Spirit" 20 times! Its conclusion is "I cannot, but the Holy Spirit within me will!"

Paul describes the difference in relational terms. Through Christ's death sin has been condemned and the Holy Spirit given. He is now within to guide us (3, 4). When we live in harmony with his promptings (5) we find that he controls the sin nature within (6,7).

It is the Spirit of God within us, who raised Jesus from the dead, who is able to lift us up too, to a new and righteous kind of living (9–11). Our obligation is not to "try," but to trust the Spirit of God within us and let him lead us (12–14). After all, we are God's children now, and heirs to a righteousness which is his.

Law, New Testament

In the NT "law" is sometimes used to mean customs, sometimes natural principles, sometimes the whole of God's revelation, and sometimes it means the Mosaic code which regulated the life style of Israel. In Paul's letters to the Romans and the Galatians he examines the Mosaic law and makes many startling statements. According to the NT, the law of Moses was temporary, limited in its purpose, and actually stimulated human beings to sin. The law of Moses condemns rather than helps mankind to find righteousness!

Theologians distinguish three functions of the Mosaic law. (1) Law reveals God. Seeing the "holy, righteous, and good" standards which God has communicated, we understand more of the moral character of the God who gave it. And we receive a partial explanation of righteousness. (2) Law convicts of sin. When man hears God's law, the old nature is even stimulated to acts of sin! The great contrast between what law says is good and what human beings do is underlined, and thus mankind stands silent in the dock, condemned before God. (3) Law is a guide for the believer. It is this "third function of law" which theologians debate. Are we to be guided by law today? Do we seek to please God by acting on his commandments—or is there some other way?

Paul in Romans and Galatians rejects this "third function" concept. He teaches that law always relates to the old nature. In fact law energizes or stirs up that nature. No wonder 1 Corinthians 15:56 says that "the power of sin is the law!"

What does the Bible put in place of law as the Christian's guide to holy living? Jesus said it when he promised his disciples the Spirit: "he will guide you into all truth" (John 16:13, see *Truth,* p. 552). This is the reality Paul turns to in Romans and Galatians. It is the Holy Spirit who energizes the life of God within: it is those who live "in accordance with the Spirit" in whose lives the righteous requirements of the law are fully met (Rom. 8:5).

The saints of both testaments trusted God and relied on him rather than on their own efforts. But all too many have misunderstood the dynamics of personal relationship with God. Man does not need to *behave* righteously: man needs to *be righteous* (see *Righteousness*, p. 611). It is not the law written in stone but the law he is writing on our hearts with which God is concerned (2 Cor. 3). Laws may tell us how to behave. But only God's Spirit can make the loving kind of life law describes a spontaneous expression of a personality which God is reshaping from within.

For study: Romans 6–8; Galatians 5; Hebrews 8; 2 Corinthians 3.

Final Glorification; 8:18–39. The promise of righteousness is for now—and for forever. What now seems a struggle will become full liberation when Jesus returns, when the fact of our sonship is made plain to all. Then even the Creation will share in a great purification, as every trace of sin is removed (18–25). In the meantime we have the assurance that the Spirit "helps us in our weakness." We have the confidence that whatever enters our life is designed for good, that we might grow toward likeness to Jesus and our destiny (26–30).

Now, also, a great promise is ours. We are beyond condemnation. Christ has died for us and is risen for us, and nothing will ever be able to separate us from the love of God in Christ Jesus our Lord.

V. Righteousness in History (Romans 9–11)

Paul has referred to sacred history to demonstrate that righteousness comes by faith (Rom. 4). He has looked back and put the law of Moses in fresh perspective (Rom, 3, 7). But those familiar with the OT will have other questions. What about Israel? How does all Paul's talk of righteousness square with what appears to be spurning of the people to whom God gave solemn covenant promises? What has happened, and what will happen, to Israel?

Chapter 9. Israel's Present Rejection Is Just

A Proud Heritage; 9:1–6. Paul is a Jew, proud of his race and heritage. He is deeply aware of the gifts God has given Israel: relationship with him, the covenants, the law, temple worship, the patriarchs, and so many other blessings. The present rejection of his people is a great sorrow to Paul. But it does not cast any doubt on the faithfulness of God or suggest his Word has failed.

Not All Israelites Are Included in the Promise; 9:7–13. To show the righteousness of God's actions, Paul points out that mere physical descent has never been involved in possession of God's promises. Not everyone born an Israelite is really an "Israelite." To prove this point Paul notes that offspring of both Abraham and Isaac are specifically *not* included in the line of those who inherit the promises. This was done purposely by God to show that his grace always rests on promise and not on works—that the active agent is God and not man. God's sovereign freedom to choose some and not others has always operated in Israel's history. Clearly then God is not inconsistent in his present rejection of Israel. And, as Israel has been the beneficiary of his past choices, she can hardly object now or cry out "unfair!"

Predestination/Election, N.T.

In Romans 9 the apostle Paul strongly defends the right of God to choose and says, "God has mercy on whom he wants to have mercy." In saying this he raises an issue that theologians call "predestination": the idea that God has looked ahead and destined some individuals to become believers and thus to be saved. "Election" is a parallel term: it is the act of choice by which God predestines.

There are few doctrinal concepts which have caused more dispute in church history. The whole idea has been condemned as unfair. In fact, it has at times been misunderstood as "double predestination" (e.g., choosing some to go to hell as well as choosing others for heaven). Teaching about predestination has led some to agonize over their relationship with God and to wonder if they are among the chosen. Missionary work has been abandoned in more than one period of church history because of the stern conviction that "if God wants to save people, he will do it himself."

But does this idea rob us of freedom to choose Christ, or of the privilege of communicating the gospel to all?

Two NT passages, Romans 9 and Ephesians 1, do unquestionably speak of God's active choice of those who come to know him. Several verses in John's Gospel add to the impression (6:35–43; 17:1–6). But, to be understood, this truth must be kept in balance with other truths revealed in Scripture:

* God loves all, and does not want "anyone to perish, but everyone to come to repentance" (2 Pet. 3:9). Yet not all will be saved.

* We receive Christ by faith, and even faith is the gift of God (Eph. 2:8,9). Yet no one believes against his will.

* God is seen throughout Scripture as sovereign. Yet man is viewed as responsible, with a truly free will (see p. 350).

When we deal with truths which seem to be mutually exclusive (sovereignty and free will/predestination and "whosoever will may come") we have entered the realm of paradox. There are issues here which we simply cannot understand. We are finite and limited. Some things can only be understood and reconciled by God.

What then do we do with paradox? We remain confident that the God we know through Jesus is both fair and loving. We commit ourselves to an active life of faith, living in a responsive relationship with the Spirit who speaks to us through the Word.

And we accept the fact that there are some things about which we must say, "I do not understand. But I do trust God to know best."

For study: Romans 9; Ephesians 1; Isaiah 48; Job 38–41.

The troubling mention in 9:13 of "hate" reflects an ancient legal formula, by which a person making his will affirmed one person as heir and decisively rejected the claims of others.

God Is Free to Act; 9:14–22. In the most stark way Paul insists that God be recognized as God. He is free to use his power as he chooses. However the exercise of that power might appear to those who cry "unfair," God's choices flow from his purposes and from his merciful love.

God Has Chosen to Have Mercy on the Gentiles; 9:23–33. The OT taught that God would one day have mercy on Gentiles (23–26). As far as Israel is concerned, the OT makes it clear that not all but only a remnant (a few "survivors") of that nation will be saved (27–29). The nation as a whole has rushed after righteousness "as if it were by works," and missed the principle of faith (30–33).

Paul's argument from history can be summed up in brief statements. *Physical descent from Abraham never guaranteed an individual a right to God's grace. *God retains the right to choose and the freedom to be merciful to whomever he chooses. *Scripture reveals that God chose long ago to bring salvation to Gentiles. *The Jewish nation has lost its place because of its failure to seek righteousness through faith. On no count, then, can God be charged with unfairness in the way he has dealt with Israel. Every principle of action that he has taken in Christ is clearly laid down in the OT. The sacred history vindicates God.

Chapter 10. Israel's Present Rejection Explained

Paul again expresses his deep desire for the salvation of his own people and restates the reason for Israel's rejection: "they did not submit to God's righteousness" (10:3). It is because Israel is unwilling to approach God on the basis of faith, and insists on misusing the law, that rejection has come—and is deserved (10:1–4)! Paul again states the gospel. Christ has come down from heaven, has died, and is risen again. All that is left for any person to do is to believe. Jew and Gentile must relate to God through faith, knowing he will bless all who call on him (10:5–11).

This universal gospel is now being proclaimed throughout the whole world. Israel too will hear, but most will not believe (10:14–18). For Paul the proclamation of the gospel to the Gentiles is not evidence of God's rejection of the Jews but evidence of the Jews' rejection of God! Paul hopes that some of his nation will be moved to jealousy and so awakened from their obstinate disobedience (10:19–21).

Chapter 11. Israel's Present Rejection Incomplete

A Remnant Remains; 11:1–10. This is an important statement by the apostle. Israel has *not* been completely rejected. Paul himself is a Jew and yet he is a believer. For its first decade the early church was a Hebrew church. There are thousands upon thousands of Jewish Christians when Paul writes his letter to the Romans. As always in history, there is a remnant that has been chosen by grace.

A Restoration Is Coming; 11:11–24. Paul reveals in this passage that Israel's rejection is also temporary. God has opened the door of faith to the whole world, but he has not rejected the people who were the original branches, growing from that tree of faith which has its historic roots in God's first great acts of self-revelation. The day is coming when Israel will be grafted back into that original vine.

A Redeemer Will Return; 11:25–32. Paul promises that "all Israel will be saved" when "the full number of Gentiles has come in." His quote from Isaiah 59 and 27 makes it clear that Paul believes the promises of the OT prophets to Israel will be literally fulfilled. For a picture of those promises, see *OT Eschatology,* p. 372, 373.

A Doxology of Praise; 11:33–36. Paul concludes this section with a doxology that links the words of Isaiah 40:13 and Job 41:11. God's plan is great and complex. Its very complexity shows us the depth of the riches of his wisdom and knowledge.

VI. God's Righteousness Expressed in the New Community (Romans 12–16)

Romans 1–3 demonstrates mankind's need for righteousness. Romans 4–5 examines the faith through which a person is declared

righteous by God. Romans 6–8 shows how faith releases the power
of the Spirit of God to do what law could not do—to transform
from within so that believers actually become righteous. Chapters
9–11 is a digression, demonstrating from history that God has
been fair to the Jewish people and really has not "changed the
rules in the middle of the game." Now, in Romans 12–16, Paul
returns to his major theme and shows how God's righteousness
is to find expression in his new community, the church. The life
of faith is not something any of us is called on to live alone. We
are intimately linked to one another in a single body, the body
of Christ. It is just as vital to understand how to live our new
life together as to understand personal victory over sin.

Chapter 12. Relationships in Christ's Church

An Appeal for Commitment; 12:1, 2. When we offer ourselves
to live for the Lord (cf. 6:15–23), we begin a process of inner
transformation which will lead to an entirely new outlook on life.
Only by refusing to be squeezed into the ways in which people
of this world relate to others will we be able, together, to experience
the good and pleasing will of God for us.

True Interdependence; 12:3–8. The world's way is competitive,
with each individual seeking to be superior to others. In Christ's
body a new way is made possible: a way of cooperation and true
interdependence. In Christ each person is valued, for each has a
spiritual gift which enables him to contribute to others. There is
no room to "think of yourself more highly than you ought," for
we are all needed and all important.

Sincere Love; 12:9–21. The climate of the new community is
to be marked by a sincere love for one another. It is this climate
which makes possible maximum growth in righteousness. Such a
love is so dynamic a power that it enables us to "overcome evil
with good."

Which of the indicators of sincere love (12:9–21) are you
presently experiencing from other Christians? Which are you
practicing with others? Do these verses suggest any person or persons
who may need to be shown this kind of love by you?

Chapter 13. Relationships with Society

Submission to Secular Authorities; 13:1–7. God has introduced
the institution of human government as a restraining influence
on sin and has permitted it the use of force (cf. Gen. 9:6). But

the function of government is clearly limited: it is commissioned to restrain wrongdoing. Christians are to subject themselves to secular authorities "for conscience sake," and not just for fear of possible punishment. The Christian is to live as a good citizen of his country and society.

God's Colony; 13:8–14. At the same time, God is concerned with far more than good citizenship! God is building a new community: a colony of righteousness, settled in the dark and twisted world of lost men. This community is not marked off by its ideals or even by its rules and high standards: it is marked off by a deep love for one another which makes rules irrelevant, for "love does no harm to the neighbor. Therefore, love is the fulfillment of the law" (10).

Paul closes with an urgent call to his readers to awake to the importance of the present time. God calls us, now, to clothe ourselves with Christ, and to build his new community of love.

How would you characterize your local church: God's colony, or a mirror of society? How can you make it more of God's colony?

Spiritual Gifts

The words immediately communicate their meaning. Spiritual gifts are *spiritual,* because they refer to the operation of the Holy Spirit through the believer's life. They are *gifts,* because God himself chooses how he will equip each of us to serve others. The exciting reality they communicate is that each Christian is divinely enabled to serve God and others!

Two lists in the NT give illustrations of spiritual gifts (Rom. 12; 1 Cor. 12). In Ephesians a slightly different list focuses on persons and calls individuals with distinctive enablements, gifts to the whole body. What you and I can do to build others up is a gift, and we ourselves are God's gift to others.

It is tempting to examine the gift lists, to define each, and to try to find our role in the body by attraction to one or another. It is more important to approach spiritual gifts with a perspective provided by the context of the passages in which gifts are discussed. When we approach gifts this way, we make striking discoveries.

First, each context stresses personal relationships and highlights the importance of love. It is in the climate of close, loving personal relationships that God's Spirit works to build up members of the new community. Gifts are *not* primarily designed for institutional roles or settings. "Teaching" in the NT does not speak of Sunday schools (which did not exist in NT times or for the first 1800 years of the Christian era). "Teaching" speaks of helping another believer put God's truth into practice, and this ministry can take place in the home, at lunch, over the phone, in a home Bible study—or the Sunday school.

Second, each context focuses on the church as a body and growth as building up one another. In these contexts each person is a minister. There is no division between "clergy" and "laity," but growth and health come "through that which every part supplies" (Eph. 4:16). True interdependence is possible only because each individual has an important role to play in the life of others. Like cells in a living body, each of us makes a contribution to health of those around us.

How can you discover your spiritual gift? Take time to know and to love your Christian brothers and sisters. As you love them, you will reach out to support, encourage, rebuke, pray, share, instruct, and care. It is as you care and seek to help that God the Holy Spirit will work through you. Then others will be able to affirm the gift you have, for they will experience the Holy Spirit working in their life through your ministry.

For study: Romans 12; Ephesians 4; 1 Corinthians 12–14.

Chapter 14:1–15:13. Principles of Life Together

What are the basic attitudes toward other members of the body of Christ that will help us build a unified, loving community? Paul spells them out in this passage, aware that he is picturing a radical transformation of the way the world approaches relationships (12:1,2).

Nonjudgmental Attitude; 14:1–13. Human associations are based on conformity: we "belong" because we conform to the interests, or the rules, or the way of thinking of our group. The church is radically different—so different that conformity is not to be required or expected. Thus Paul insists we abandon judgmental attitudes and neither condemn or look down on brothers or sisters whose convictions or practices differ from our own. Paul is terribly blunt here. Christ died and rose again so that *he* might be Lord (14:9). No one proclaimed you or me God. How then dare we to judge others (14:10–12)? Christ, the master of each of us, is able to bring each of us to obedience and to maturity: "he will stand, for the Lord is able to make him stand" (14:4).

Self-sacrificial Attitude; 14:14–15:4. In any community there will be carnal believers who have not yet come to realize that things are not "unclean" in themselves (cf. Matt. 15:16–29). The freedom of others to engage in "eating and drinking" practices with a clear conscience may lead such people either to judgmentalism or to follow practices that are against their own conscience. While Paul firmly upholds the principle of freedom and teaches that we have no right to judge one another, he balances this truth with another: "we who are strong ought to bear with the failings of the weak and not to please ourselves" (15:1). Our goal is to build up the brother whom we love, not to flaunt our freedom or our superior knowledge.

Accepting Attitude; 15:5–13. Underlying the teaching of this section is the fact that Jesus has accepted us, imperfect as we are. "Accept one another, then, just as Christ accepted you" (15:7). If this is our attitude toward one another, unity will be achieved, and we will become a community which loves and praises God together, filled with joy and peace and hope.

What are some of the things about which Christians tend to criticize each other, or which they make criteria for acceptance? How can you respond to Scripture's invitation to work toward unity by building a nonjudgmental, self-sacrificing, and accepting attitude?

Chapter 15:14–16:31. Personal Notes

Paul's Motivations; 15:14–33. Paul closes by sharing several revealing personal matters. He expresses his confidence in the believers of Rome. They have the Spirit: they are "complete in knowledge and competent to instruct one another" (15:14). Paul's letter is an expression of his own giftedness (15:15,16), not a suggestion that he has no confidence in the giftedness of the body in Rome.

Paul also shares his desire to travel to Spain, to pioneer there as a missionary. Paul asks the prayers of these believers about dangers he may soon face in Judea (cf. Acts 19:21–28:31), and tells his plans to visit them in Rome on his way to Spain.

Personal Greetings; 16:1–27. Paul's personal greetings help us catch a glimpse of his view of the role of women in the church, for clearly he values women as well as men as fellow workers (see *Role of Women in the Church,* below).

Role of Women in the Church

What was the place of women in the first century church? Were they viewed as inferior to men and ruled out of significant ministry? This is what some believe today. But while it is obvious that the apostles and other visible leaders, such as Timothy and Titus and Luke and James, were men, a little exploration shows us that there were women leaders as well—and that the NT writers, like Luke and Paul, affirm their importance.

There are several indications in Romans 16 of this reality. The most striking is found in 16:1, which says literally, "I commend to you Phoebe our sister, being deacon of the church, the one in Cenchrea." This is the same Greek word, deacon, used to identify Paul, Timothy, Tychicus, Epaphras, and the church leaders spoken of in 1 Timothy 3:8,12! Most translations tend to blur this fact, reflecting quite possibly a male chauvinistic orientation indicated also in slanted translations of such verses as 1 Corinthians 11:3,10, and 14:34.

In Romans 16 Paul lists people who are significant to him and to the body of Christ. With his eighteen men are six women, of whom he says of several, they "work hard in the Lord."

Other NT passages strengthen the impression that women are full partners in the life of the church. Paul is specific in ruling out the old social distinctions which evaluate others by race, or wealth, or social status—or sex (Gal. 6:26–28). Like every male believer, every woman has a spiritual gift and is to exercise it (cf. 1 Cor. 12:7). According to Peter's Pentecost sermon, in this day of the Spirit the gifts given to women include those that Christians have always viewed as the most significant: "your sons and your daughters will prophesy," Peter says in Acts 2:17. On close examination even those passages most often quoted to suggest a restricted role for women (1 Cor. 11:1–16; 1 Cor. 14:33–36 and 1 Tim. 2:1–13) have been misinterpreted. Today as in NT times, each believer has a vital role in the life of the church, and women are as important as men.

For study: Male and Female, p. 32; Woman's Role, OT p. 267.

Paul includes a word of warning against those who would cause divisions or would contradict the principles of Christian experience which the Romans have been taught (16:17, 18; cf. 2 Peter and Jude).

Paul's last words commit the dear brothers and sisters at Rome to the care of God, who alone "is able to establish you by my gospel and the proclamation of Jesus Christ." In this gospel the impact of Jesus on the past, the present, and the future of every believer has been made known! The good news is that righteousness is now ours, through faith.

1 CORINTHIANS
Solving Problems in the Church

Some idealize the church of the first century. But, as today, there were many problems the NT church had to solve. Paul's first letter to Corinth is a problem-solving letter. It gives the brothers and sisters at Corinth guidance on how to deal with a variety of conflicts which have emerged there. It is a letter which might have been written yesterday, for it deals with issues that trouble many churches today.

Corinth. In Paul's time, Corinth was the finest city in Greece. It had existed for centuries before it was destroyed by Rome in 146 B.C. Refounded by Caesar in 46 B.C., it quickly regained its ancient place as a center of industry and trade, and as capital city of Achaia. The population of this seaport city was some 250,000, composed of native Greeks, a large number of Jews and other orientals, with Roman settlers, government officials, and businessmen. Corinth was a notorious city. It was so known for wantonness that "to live as a Corinthian" was used throughout the empire to denote a sexually immoral life style. This was reflected in worship at Corinth. Over a thousand priestesses served in the temple of Aphrodite as sacred prostitutes! Some of the problems experienced by Christians reflect the moral climate of the society in which they lived.

Paul spent some eighteen months in Corinth, in A.D. 50–52. In this time he founded a large congregation of believers (Acts 18:1–8). Some five years later, Paul had heard by letter and from messengers of problems which were tearing at the unity of this large body of believers. Quickly he sat down to write words of guidance, which we have preserved for us today in this fascinating NT book.

Date and Author. The author of this letter was Paul the apostle who founded the church at Corinth on his first missionary journey (Acts 18). Paul wrote the letter from Ephesus, probably in A.D. 57.

Theme and Structure. The church at Corinth is a fascinating body. Its members had a full range of spiritual gifts (1:7) and had a long period of instruction by the apostle himself. But it was a church whose members Paul calls "carnal," for they lived just like the people of the pagan world, without discerning the spiritual realities by which God's people are to guide their actions. The bickering, open sin, and pride of these people reveal them to be unspiritual.

The disturbing things which happened at Corinth still happen in modern congregations. There are still divisions, as believers exalt this or that human leader. There is still open immorality, for our society, too, is lax and wanton. Disputes between believers still lead to bitterness and law suits. Families break up. Doctrinal disputes divide. And debate over speaking in tongues still shakes our fellowship. Misunderstanding of basic truths still raises doubts and uncertainties. These facts make this letter of Paul to Corinth one of the most relevant of the NT epistles for us today.

Paul's logical approach in dealing with these problems helps us to outline this lengthy NT letter. In the Greek text, each new problem is introduced with the phrase *peri de,* "now concerning." While the phrase is not always marked out clearly in the English text, its presence in the original lets us outline 1 Corinthians with great confidence. And it helps us to study the argument (the flow of thought) of each section. The problem structure is reflected in the outline on pages 629–631 and throughout this discussion.

Values. First Corinthians is of great value to the church today, for it deals with many of the same problems that plague our congregations. In 1 Corinthians we have specific guidance for dealing with seven common congregational problems.

But there is another great contribution that 1 Corinthians can make to your life and mine. It reveals for us a Christian approach to problem-solving! This is illustrated in the way Paul approaches each problem area. In each case he analyzed the issue carefully, to uncover the underlying issue. Then he searched out the basic revealed truth which is to be applied to guide our actions.

But can you and I use the method applied by the great apostle? The answer of 1 Corinthians is, "Yes!" In the Holy spirit who is present within us to interpret God's Word, we have the very mind of Christ (1 Cor. 2:10–16)!

Before Reading. Here are several questions answered in 1 Corinthians. Which of them is important to you? Read 1 Corinthians for the answers. *Should I pick a particular denomination or Bible teacher, and be loyal to it or to him? *How should I react to fellow Christians who are openly living an immoral life? How should our churches react? *What happens if a person's spouse refuses to live with him or her? Can he or she remarry? *What should I do if I think another person is wrong doctrinally? Is it important to insist he be correct? *What about my own personal rights? Should I insist on them? How hard should I fight for my rights? *What is the place of women in the church? Are they really somehow inferior? *Is "tongues" a spiritual gift for today? Should everyone speak in tongues? What does tongues really say about a person? *What is the sign of spiritual maturity? *What spiritual gifts are more important? *Do I have a spiritual gift, and what is it?

Outline

Salutation: 1:1–9

The tone is set immediately. These believers have been set aside ("sanctified") in Christ Jesus for a holy life (2). Although they have been enriched by God and "do not lack any spiritual gift" (7), Paul must call the congregation "mere infants in Christ" (3:1). Yet the apostle is sure that God is at work in Corinth and will strengthen his people, for God is faithful (9).

As Paul begins this problem-focused letter he is not discouraged. Whatever our problems, we too can remain confident in the Lord.

I. The Problem of Divisions in the Church (1 Corinthians 1–4)

Paul first deals with the nagging problem of cliques and party factions that exist in Corinth. Like some today who identify themselves first by denomination or a favorite preacher, persons in Corinth began to see themselves as "followers of" Paul, or Peter, or another, rather than as Christians. To resolve the problem Paul goes back to basics. He examines the difference between natural and divine wisdom, urging the believers to look at all things from Christ's point of view. If God's wisdom is applied to the problem of divisions, it is clear that human leaders are simply servants of Jesus. Jesus, not a man, is to have our full allegiance.

Chapter 1. Foolish Wisdom

Divisions in the Church; 1:10–17. Factions and party divisions harm the unity of the church, so believers are no longer "perfectly united in mind and thought" (10). The error is revealed when one simply asks, "Is Christ divided? Was Paul crucified for you" (13)?

Foolish Wisdom; 1:18–25. The cross of Christ has shown God's approach to solving spiritual problems to be at odds with mankind's "wise" ways. Neither the Jew's "do a miracle" approach, or the Gentile's rational philosophical approach, can grasp the power and wisdom God expressed in the cross. Thus it is clear that God's wisdom and man's wisdom are completely different—and contradictory.

Superior Wisdom; 1:26–31. The superiority of God's wisdom is shown in its success: in Christ we have "righteousness, holiness, and redemption" (30). Clearly then we should seek God's wisdom in approaching any problem and not rely on the foolish "wisdom" of man.

Chapter 2. Wisdom from God

Paul's Preaching; 2:1–5. Paul simply presented Jesus, without using oratorical skills. In Paul's day many were highly trained in the art of persuasion; some of the books on swaying an audience from the time exist today. But Paul relied only on the simple truth, to show that God's wisdom and power can be trusted.

Access to Divine Wisdom; 2:6–10. Human beings have no way to deduce or discover God's thinking. But his very thoughts have been communicated to us in the words of Scripture by the Spirit (see *Inspiration,* p. 729).

Application of Divine Wisdom; 2:11–16. The Holy Spirit, living in the believer, serves as interpreter of the written Word. This enables us to make judgments about all things on the basis of God's wisdom. Both the written Word and the Spirit are needed to operate by God's wisdom. But through these two gifts from God, we have access to the very mind of Christ (15,16)!

Wisdom, New Testament

In the language of the NT as well as our own tongue, "wisdom" does not speak of knowledge, but of interpretation and application. Knowing "what the Bible says" is not as important as putting our knowledge into practice in daily life!

First Corinthians 1 identifies and illustrates two kinds of wisdom. "Foolish" wisdom looks at the facts and reaches the wrong conclusions. By this foolish wisdom, Jesus' death was a tragedy, or an injustice, or a politically expedient act—and nothing more. But God looks at the cross in a very different way. He sees it as a sacrificial offering by which we who believe are given "righteousness, holiness, and redemption" (1:30). For you and me, wisdom involves accepting God's interpretation of things and acting on that interpretation.

But how do we know God's interpretation? This is what Paul explains in 1 Corinthians 2 in his talk of "God's secret wisdom." God has given us in the words of Scripture not only historic facts but also God's own thoughts and interpretation of the facts. The Bible is not just a book about "what" Christians are to believe. It is a book that helps us see the way God looks at and interprets all the issues of our lives.

God has given us more than the Word. He has also given us the Holy Spirit, who will help us understand and apply the written Word. Because the Spirit is in us and the Word with us, we can know God's viewpoint on any situation in which we find ourselves. In the Bible and the Spirit we have access to the very mind of Christ, to give us guidance for daily living (2:15,16).

What a privilege when we face a difficult situation, to know that we can look into the Bible, and ask God's Spirit to give us the wisdom we need to find God's way.

Chapter 3. The Place of Human Leaders

Evidence of Unspirituality; 3:1–4. The quarrels and bickering over leaders show the Corinthians are not "spiritual" but "worldly." That is, they are not acting on God's wisdom but like "mere men."

The Divine Perspective; 3:5–9. God is the source of spiritual birth and growth. Human leaders are "only servants," each performing the task God has assigned. It is God, not the men, who are important.

The Divine Foundation; 3:10–15. Jesus is the foundation on which every life and ministry must be built. Certainly each person's service is important: it should be performed carefully and will be judged. But the foundation for all is Jesus.

The judgment mentioned here has nothing to do with salvation. It is to determine rewards which God will graciously provide for those believers who serve him (cf. 2 Cor. 5:10).

The Divine Priority; 3:16, 17. It is not the builders (the leaders) who are important, but the building! God places great value on each individual, for each of us is a living temple—a residence for the Spirit. How foolish to exalt some believers over others when each of us is privileged to be a living temple and dwelling place for God!

Focus on Jesus; 3:18–23. It is futile and foolish to make distinctions between human leaders and boast about one or another. In Christ all has been given to us—life, death, the present and future, and many different leaders to serve us. All this is ours because of Jesus. He should be the focus of our lives, and be the One of whom we boast.

Chapter 4. Privileges of Leaders

The Privilege of Faithfulness; 4:1–7. Believers should view leaders simply as "servants of Christ" (1). As such, Jesus will evaluate their work when the time comes, and the criteria he will use is simply that of faithfulness (2–5). God does not evaluate us on the basis of the different gifts or tasks he has given us. We should not boast about these differences either, as if our assignments reflected some personal superiority rather than simply a gift or calling given us by God.

This is encouraging for each of us. You or I may not have a gift the worldly person views as important. But what counts with God is our faithfulness in using the gifts and abilities we do have to serve others.

The Privilege of Suffering; 4:8–13. Rather than build little empires, spiritual leaders abandon all and willingly accept suffering to better serve God and other believers.

The Privilege of Modeling; 4:14–17. Leaders model the life they teach. The Corinthians are to adopt the attitude Paul has taken and follow his example in thinking of leaders.

The Privilege of Authority; 4:18–21. Paul concludes with a warning. Spiritual leaders do have authority, and this matter of unity is so vital that any who remain arrogant or divisive will be disciplined when Paul next visits (see *Spiritual Authority,* p. 658).

Make a summary list of the "thoughts of God" in these four chapters relating to (a) divisions and factions which destroy unity, (b) attitudes toward human leaders, and (c) ministry priorities.

Ask God's Spirit to show you how each of these principles of wisdom which you have listed can be applied in your own relationships with others.

II. The Problem of Church Discipline (1 Corinthians 5, 6)

The second problem area dealt with by Paul involves discipline. How are Christians to react when a fellow believer persists in sinning? What happens when disputes between Christians can't be resolved? The pattern Paul sets out is clear, simple, and powerful!

Chapter 5. Immorality

Open Immorality; 5:1–8. Corinth is known throughout the Roman Empire for its loose sexual standards (see *Corinth,* p. 627). But one of the Christians is now involved in a sexual relationship even the pagans abhor! Paul has "already passed judgment" on this individual and demands that he be "put out of your fellowship" (2, 3).

In such a case, passing judgment simply involves agreeing with God that a practice, identified in Scripture as sin, is sin (see *Judging Others,* p. 520). Discipline relates specifically and only to such sin.

When Paul speaks of handing the man over to Satan, he expresses the conviction that persistent sin will lead to physical death. Satan can have his handful of dust in the dead body. If the individual is a believer, God will take his spirit (5)!

Paul is greatly concerned because of the indifference of the Corinthians to sin in their fellowship (6–8). The whole community is called to be holy. Undisciplined, sin will spread, as yeast does in dough, to corrupt the whole congregation.

Immoral Nonbelievers; 5:9–13. Christians are not to withdraw from immoral non-Christians. That would mean isolation in our society. We are not called to judge nonbelievers, but to share Jesus. We *are* called to judge those who call themselves "brother" and yet practice sin. Purity and holiness are to mark each community of God's people.

> What would be the impact if all local churches were committed to the practice of church discipline? What if none practiced it?

Chapter 6. Lawsuits

Civil Disputes; 6:1–8. Believers embroiled in lawsuits against each other are told to let committees of believers settle the disputes, rather than pagan courts. "Even men of little account" who are in the church could settle such "trivial cases" fairly (1–5).

What disturbs Paul is the fact of the suits in the first place. They show that believers are actually trying to cheat and wrong each other! It would be better to be cheated than to be a cheater (6–8)!

God's Kingdom; 6:9–11. God's kingdom is more than a place or time. It is a relationship with God, in which he is free to act in and through us (see *Kingdom of Heaven,* p. 470). Paul says flatly that no one who habitually practices sin can enter into this experience. But Christ has cleansed us from what we were, to live new lives as citizens of his kingdom.

Immorality; 6:12–20. Paul now restates a principle developed in Romans 6:15–27. A believer *can* do anything. But our body is designed to serve and glorify God. Thus we choose to serve righteousness, not sin.

Sexual immorality is particularly abhorrent to Paul. Jesus lives within each believer. Our body is a temple of God, won at the price of Christ's own blood, and must be committed to uses which honor God. No wonder Paul is so troubled when sexual sins are simply ignored by the members of the Corinthian fellowship!

III. Problems Relating to Marriage (1 Corinthians 7)

Background. In the immoral society of Corinth, warped attitudes toward sex were reflected in the church. One extreme is seen in chapter 5, in the open immorality practiced by a believer. Another extreme provides the background for this chapter.

Some in Corinth felt that Paul's condemnation of immorality was a condemnation of sex. They either sought divorces or insisted on celibate marriage. Some there felt that when Paul's Christian teaching lifted women to the place of personhood (rather than simply being sex objects), that the physical side of man/woman relationships was ruled out.

Divorce also caused problems. The believers remembered that Jesus had called for a permanent marriage relationship. But often conversion meant that a person's non-Christian spouse deserted or divorced him or her. What about divorce? And what about remarriage for those who had been deserted?

All of these issues provide the background against which Paul gives his brief but pointed instruction concerning marital relationships.

Church Discipline

You and I are each charged by God to help others grow in godliness. But how can we help a person who has chosen to practice sin? This is the question addressed in church discipline. The purpose of discipline is to help a brother or sister to turn back to God's ways. What then is involved in church discipline?

* Discipline is administered *only* in cases where persons are habitually practicing sins, and will not acknowledge the actions as sin or try to reform.

Discipline is not administered to force others to do things the way a leader or the majority wants, or for doctrinal differences. Only when a person's practices are clearly and unmistakably identified as sin by the Scriptures is discipline to be evoked.

Infrequent failures, or even a series of failures where there is an honest effort at change, is no cause for discipline. When sin is acknowledged it can be forgiven (see *Confession of Sins*, p. 794). Then forgiveness, warmth and support are to flow from the Christian community to the person trying to break away from his old life.

* Discipline is intended to communicate reality to the person under it. Scripture teaches that sin interrupts fellowship with God. In discipline, fellow believers refuse to have fellowship with (eat with, talk with) the person disciplined. Thus we communicate on earth the reality of that person's interrupted fellowship with God in heaven.

* Discipline is designed to encourage repentance and restoration, not to punish. When the individual is willing to acknowledge his acts as sin and to turn from them, the Christian community is to gather around him or her again with warmth, forgiveness, and loving support.

* Scripture outlines a process to be followed when discipline is required. One person, who knows the situation, goes to the individual to share his or her concern. If the individual refuses to listen, that person returns with another brother or sister. Next the leaders of the church are called in. Finally, if the individual still refuses to respond, the whole congregation is told of the problem and instructed by the leaders not to fellowship with the one under discipline.

As this outline of the process shows, discipline is the responsibility of all Christians and not just local church leaders. At every step the administration of discipline is to be loving. It is because of love we go to an individual (rather than gossip about him!). It is because of love that the congregation turns away from the person under discipline. And it is because of love that he or she is welcomed back with joy and without recriminations when repentance comes.

For study: 1 Corinthians 5; 2 Corinthians 2:1–11; 1 John 1; Matthew 18.

Sexuality; 7:1–7. Paul begins by quoting a position taken by one group at Corinth. Yes, he says, it is "good for a man not to marry." But he immediately corrects the impression that marriage and sex are wrong (see *Sex*, p. 100). Both men and women have sexual needs: spouses belong to each other physically as well as in other ways. To those who have taught that Christian marriage should be sexless, Paul says that sexual relations can be abstained from only when three conditions are met: it is by mutual consent, for a short time only, and for the purpose of devoting oneself to prayer (1–5).

It is important here to note that Paul speaks of the wife possessing the husband as well as the husband possessing the wife (4). Christian women are persons, not playthings, and their needs are to be given as much consideration as the needs of men!

Paul himself prefers the unmarried state and knows that not everyone is called to be married. Each person must seek his own calling, to marriage or singleness, and view it as a gift from God.

Marriage Not Wrong; 7:8, 9. Those presently unmarried are free to marry and should do so if their sexual drive is strong.

Divorce Problems; 7:8–16. Some believers have left non-Christian spouses, misapplying Paul's teaching that one should marry only those belonging to the Lord (cf. 7:39). Other Corinthians have been deserted by their spouses and now torment themselves with guilt because Christ taught marriage should be permanent. How can these problems be resolved? Paul lays down principles to cover several of the situations common in Corinth.

* Christians who divorce in spite of Paul's instructions to the contrary should remain unmarried and seek a reconciliation (10–11).

* The Christian is not to initiate a divorce, even if the spouse is an unbeliever (12–13). The presence of the believer is an important factor is setting aside any children for faith in the Lord (14).

* A believer abandoned by an unbelieving spouse who refuses to live with him or her is to consider himself unbound. The implication is the person is free to remarry; the reason given is that "God has called us to live in peace." There is no need to wait forever, just in case the spouse should return (15–16).

The passage is not intended to cover every possible marital situation. But there is a strong stress on faithfulness, and on grace. When one person's faithfulness is rejected and a spouse abandoned, release is given for remarriage.

Opportunity to Serve; 7:17–24. Both married and unmarried states are equally "spiritual," for God calls individuals to each. Each gives us opportunities to serve. Neither state is superior to the other.

Advice for the Unmarried; 7:25–35. Paul is careful to note that he is not passing on a divine command when he observes that there are advantages to being unmarried. The married must, rightly, think of how to please his or her spouse. The single person can concentrate on pleasing the Lord. To Paul the single state seems better. But again he makes it clear that God will guide each individual into his or her own calling.

Divorce and Remarriage

The Bible makes it clear that God's ideal for marriage is a lifetime union of one man and one woman. In this intimate relationship God has provided for mutal support and love, for growth, and for satisfaction of human sexual needs. But at times the ideal is not realized and a divorce comes. What then?

In OT times the law of Moses provided for a "bill of divorce." And it was expected that a divorced person would remarry. In the NT Jesus reaffirms the original ideal. He points out that divorce was permitted "because of the hardness of your hearts" (Matt. 19:8). That is, God understood the grip of sin on humanity and knew that marriage has great potential for harm as well as for healing. Some marriages become so distorted that divorce is the best option. Then, even though remarriage, as falling short of the divine ideal, may involve adultery, it is God himself who provides for it as a gracious gift to his OT people.

The same theme of graciousness pervades Paul's discussion of marriage in 1 Corinthians 7. The ideal has never been changed. Christians should seek to deal with problems within the marriage and not initiate divorce. But some in Corinth found themselves in agonizing situations. Some struggled to hold the marriage together—and were deserted by spouses who simply refused to live with them! At times even Christians took this course of abandoning the marriage, despite Paul's exhortation to work out the problems. To these people God shows an extremely gracious face. He encourages them to do everything they can. But he announces release for those victims of divorce whose spouses simply will not continue with them: "a believing man or woman is not bound in such circumstances" (1 Cor. 7:15). This surely is a word of grace; a healing word of peace to those torn apart by feelings of guilt and failure concerning something over which they have had no control.

It is normal today to take Jesus' expression of the marriage ideal as an announcement of a higher law, which absolutely prohibits divorce or remarriage for any reason. We may forget the fact that it is God who permits both under Moses' law, and who speaks so graciously in the Epistles. Certainly no Christian should rush into divorce, or choose it as an easy way out of difficulty. We should seek to love our spouse fully and be careful not to hurt. But when a divorce does shatter the life of a Christian brother or sister, we need to be supportive rather than judgmental. It is not at all sure that God is as absolute in his prohibition of divorce and remarriage as some of his people seem to be, or so forgetful of forgiving grace.

For study: Divorce, OT, p. 131, Matthew 19:1–14; 1 Corinthians 7.

Free to Remarry; 7:36–40. Paul says those who are widowed and unmarried are free to marry another believer. Couples should marry if not doing so would harm or hurt one of them (36). But Paul cannot resist expressing again his feelings that there are great advantages in not being married.

One of the key questions raised in this chapter is, Does "unmarried" here include those who have been divorced? (see *Divorce and Remarriage,* OT, p. 131, NT, p. 639).

IV. Conflicts over Doctrine (1 Corinthians 8–10)

In first century cities animals were offered as sacrifices at pagan temples. Part of the meat was burned; much of it was sold in the temple meat market, like the market shown on page 641. Some Christians in Corinth regularly bought this meat, convinced that the idols had no real existence except as lumps of rock or metal. Other Corinthians associated idol worship with demonic powers and were convinced that to eat meat sacrificed to idols was to associate with demons. Each side rested its case on doctrine. Idols are not real, said one. Evil spiritual powers *are* real, answered the other. Each side argued strongly that its doctrine, and thus practices, were correct.

In dealing with this doctrinal dispute Paul goes back again to basic principles. He shows first how doctrinal disputes are to be dealt with by Christians. Then he shows which doctrinal position in the dispute is right.

Chapter 8. Food Sacrificed to Idols

Knowledge, or Love? Paul argues first that we must approach such disputes from the perspective of love, rather than asking "Who is right?" The attitude that we *know* tends to puff up and create pride. This is foolish, for while we all have some knowledge, no one has complete or perfect knowledge. We must then hold our doctrines humbly, confessing imperfect knowledge. On the other hand, the attitude that we will *love* builds others up—and opens everyone up to the Lord.

Paul's point is important. Whenever there are doctrinal disputes each party must give love for the other high priority.

The Problem; According to Knowledge; 8:4–8. Paul agrees that "we know an idol is nothing at all in the world, and that there is no God but one." Strictly speaking this position is doctrinally correct.

The Problem According to Love; 8:9–13. But being "right" is not the only issue. Some who do not see this truth are being harmed by those buying from the temple market! When the practice of a correct doctrine seems to justify wounding a brother, it is sin!

Buying Meat at the Temple Meat Market

One can be wrong even when his doctrine is correct. Look at chapter 8 carefully. Have you ever experienced anything similar?

Doctrine

The word means simply, "the teaching." In its NT usages, "doctrine" is closely related to ethical practices (cf. Titus 2). But theologians and most Christians think of doctrine as the content of faith: what we believe. Thus the virgin birth, the deity of Christ, the resurrection of the body, and many other things taught in the Bible are thought of as doctrines.

Church history shows that Christians have often had different ideas about various Bible teachings. This has led to doctrinal disputes. Too often believers have separated from others with whom they could not agree. Often local churches split over doctrinal differences.

It is obvious that doctrine is important. Some doctrinal errors are extremely serious. But how do we deal with doctrinal disputes? How do we relate to someone with whom we disagree doctrinally?

In 1 Corinthians 8 Paul says we must begin by affirming our love for those with whom we differ. Christians are Christians because faith in Jesus has brought them his new life. It is faith and not doctrinal agreement which makes us brothers. But Paul's goal is not compromise. He wants believers to begin a process through which they will move to a more accurate understanding of truth!

If we confront one another over doctrine, each claiming to know the truth better than the other, pride and closed minds results. If we affirm our love and acceptance for each other, and approach the issue humbly, each admitting his knowledge is limited and concentrating on helping the other love God better, then both are open to the Lord and the teaching ministry of the Spirit. It may take time. But when we give each other time and love, better understanding will come.

Truth is important. But doctrine is never to be exalted at the expense of love. Thus Paul tells Timothy, "The Lord's servant must not quarrel: instead he must be kind to everyone, able to teach, not resentful. Those who oppose him he must gently instruct" (2 Tim 2:24,25). Love and humility open the door for the discovery of truth.

Chapter 9. Love vs. "Rights" Illustrated in Paul

Paul admitted that the doctrinal foundation on which the meat eating party based its practice is correct. This implies that these people have a right to purchase from the temple market (8:4–8). But then Paul shows that love should lead these Corinthians to surrender their "right" for the sake of their weaker brothers (8:9–13).

Paul also shows that he himself has chosen to surrender many of his own "rights"—which he might have demanded on biblical grounds!—for the sake of others. He has given up the right to marriage (9:3–5). He has given up the right to be financially supported by those he ministers to (9:6–14). He has even given up his right to freedom from the Mosaic law when he is with Jews, so as not to offend them (9:20–23). He has done this, to "make myself a slave to everyone, to win as many as possible" (15–19).

Paul concludes by pointing out that only by setting a goal and working toward it can an athlete win the prize. As a Christian, Paul has the goal of ministry; he will sacrifice everything to achieve it.

Paul was not just preaching self-sacrifice to the Corinthians. He lived a self-sacrificial life for their sake!

Chapter 10. Idolatry Reexamined

Earlier Paul admitted that "an idol is nothing at all in the world" (8:4). But he also said that our knowledge is incomplete (8:2). Now he raises issues that those who frequented temple markets, and some who even went to feasts dedicated to idols, had not considered.

Israel's Errors Repeated? 10:1–22. Israel too enjoyed many spiritual privileges, but most did not please God. They turned to idolatry and the immorality associated with it (1–8). In Corinth, too, idolatry is associated with immorality. Israel's experience provides a warning for Christians. It is unwise to test God by associating with that which stands for evil, and which is likely to stimulate and to tempt us as well (9–13).

As sensible people the Corinthians should flee idolatry. The idol may be nothing. But there are demonic powers behind paganism. The Lord's Supper and feasts for idols simply do not mix (14–22).

Freedom to be Used Constructively; 10:23–11:1. Paul now returns to his basic theme. Freedom is to be used for the benefit of others (24). Meat is irrelevant and can be eaten with a clear conscience. But if for instance an unbeliever announces the meat was offered to an idol, it should not be eaten for that person's sake (28,29).

In his summary, Paul suggests that "rights" are really irrelevant. God has called each of us to live for his glory. God gains no glory by our being right. He *is* glorified when we do not seek our own good but the good of others (31–33). In choosing the way of love we will be following the path in which Paul walked—and he tried only to follow close behind Jesus our Lord (11:1).

Summarize the key teachings of chapters 8–10. Can you express in your own words how to relate to a person with whom you differ doctrinally? Can you explain why a person who is "right" may be far from following Jesus?

Which of the truths you discover has the greatest impact on your life right now? How will you apply it this week?

V. Problems over Worship Customs (1 Corinthians 11)

Two issues related to worship practices caused divisions in Corinth. One involves the Lord's supper, and the other gives us insight into what was perhaps the first "women's lib" movement stimulated by Christian teaching!

Chapter 11:2–16. Women at Worship

Background. In the first century culture a veil covering was a symbol of respectable womanhood: something a wife might wear to affirm herself as a woman of dignity. The Corinthian women, thrilled at Paul's teaching that in Christ they were equal to men in worth and value (cf. Gal. 4:26–28), wanted to symbolize this status by removing their veils in church meetings. Paul does not put down their aspirations: he praises them for affirming their value (2). But he does want to show them why removal of the veil is an inappropriate symbol of equality and shows a misunderstanding of the meaning of equality.

Denial of Identity: 11:3–10. Paul returns to creation to point out that God has made men and women different. The order of creation shows the difference. The charge to men to function as "head" shows the difference. Note that "head" here does not connote superiority or suppression (see *Headship,* p. 685). In the context, Christ's headship implies the exaltation of mankind as the "image and glory" of God. Thus to say man is head implies the exaltation of women as the glory of man (7). Women then can take pride in their identity as women!

In fact, what wearing a veil as a "sign of authority" really symbolizes, to men and to angels, is that in Christ it is no shame to be a woman. Each time these Corinthians participate *as women* in the life and ministry of the church, they affirm their own worth and value as women. No woman has to be "like a man" to be equal!

True Interdependence; 11:11,12. Paul does not want anyone to think his argument from creation implies that men are "better" than women. "Woman came from man," he says, but "so also man is born of woman." Neither sex is adequate or whole without the other, and so neither can be more important than the other.

A Cultural Illustration; 11:13–16. In the first century, long hair was regarded as feminine. No Corinthian woman would think of cutting off her hair and appearing in public. She would be ashamed and in some significant way would deny her identity as a woman. Paul wants the Corinthian women to think of taking off their veil in church not as a symbol of equality, but as a denial of their worth and value as women. How unnecessary to be ashamed of being a woman! In Christ women have been lifted up, to once again be the glory of humankind.

What are some ways that women today struggle to symbolize their equality with men? Which ways involve a denial of their identity and value as women?

Do you think that Christians and our churches give true recognition to the worth and value of women? How do men sometimes try to make women ashamed of their identity as women? How can we affirm women, as Paul does here in 1 Corinthians?

Chapter 11:17–34. The Lord's Supper

The Corinthians have turned the Lord's Supper into a feast at which the rich eat like gluttons and the poor go without. Paul restates his simple instructions for this great sacrament of remembrance and warns those who engage in it casually that because they have failed to take communion as an opportunity for self-examination and turning from sin, many experience God's judgments and some have died.

VI. The Problem of Misuse of Spiritual Gifts (1 Corinthians 12–14)

In the first century it was universally accepted that trances, ecstatic speech, and bizzare behavior indicated a special closeness to the gods. It's easy to understand why epilepsy was named the "divine disease"! In view of this cultural notion, it is not surprising to find many Christians at Corinth viewed those who spoke in tongues as especially spiritual. This assumption led to problems, and it led Paul to include a long section in this letter instructing the church about true spirituality. In the process Paul puts all spiritual gifts in perspective, helping us all to understand the nature of true spirituality and how to recognize spiritual maturity.

Chapter 12. Spiritual Gifts

Spirituality; 12:1–3. The word "gifts" is not in the Greek text of verse 1. Paul is writing of spirituality and countering the pagan notion (2) that anyone making an ecstatic utterance is "speaking by the Spirit of God" (3). Apparently some Corinthians even viewed such utterances as having more authority than Scripture! In chapters 12–14 Paul will thoroughly discuss all aspects of spiritual giftedness, of spiritual maturity, and of ministry.

Spiritual Gifts; 12:4–11. Paul teaches that each believer has a gift which involves the Spirit working through him to serve and build up others (see *Spiritual Gifts,* p. 623). Since the same Spirit is at work through every gift, no gift should be singled out as "special."

One Body and Its Members; 12:12–31. God the Spirit unites every believer with Jesus and one another to form a single, living body (12, 13). The members of the body are interdependent, and the whole needs what each part contributes (14–19). The teaching has two applications: in the body every member and his gift is indispensable. Thus all should be honored "so that there should be no division in the body" (21–26). And, since gifts are distributed, everyone should not expect to have the same gift (27–30). Against the background of the Corinthian preoccupation with tongues, and the desire of many for this more spectacular gift, this last reminder was important.

The Body of Christ

This is one of the dominant NT images used to convey truths about our relationship with other Christians and with Jesus Christ. Several important truths are emphasized in the image and in passages where it is used in the NT.

* *Christ Is Head.* As Christians, we are to recognize and submit to the guidance of Jesus in our lives. We are to be aware that decision-making is done by the Head of the Church—and to seek his will. To let Jesus be Lord means searching out his will by prayer and exploration of the Scriptures, ever sensitive to the leading of the Holy Spirit. We are not to rely on human approaches to planning and goal-setting.

* *We Are Christ's Living Body.* Today Christians actually are the living incarnation of Jesus on earth. We represent Jesus to others, and we have his life within us. The work of Jesus is continued on earth through the members of his living Body.

* *Health Is Vital to the Body.* The NT speaks often of how the body grows and remains healthy. As any living organism, the body of Christ must be healthy to carry out the will of its Head. Two things are vital

to health of the body of Christ. There are to be close and loving relationships between its members. Each member is to use his gifts to serve and minister to each other. How important it is that each of us learn to see ourselves as God sees us: as persons enabled by the presence of Jesus to serve and to build others up.

For study: 1 Corinthians 12; Ephesians 4; Romans 12; *Spiritual Gifts,* p. 623.

Paul's final statement is to the Corinthian church as a whole and not to individuals, and is an exhortation to them to give their attention to the "greater gifts" (see chapter 14).

Chapter 13. Love

This brief chapter presents the priority of love in understanding spirituality. No gifts benefit the users if they are not motivated by love (1–3). Love is not shown in the use of a gift, but in the patience, kindness, selflessness, and forgiveness which infuse a person's character (4–7). Spiritual maturity is revealed by love, and maturity comes through loving. This, rather than the childish approach of the Corinthians and their focus on gifts, is the "more excellent way" (12:31) to gauge and to grow in true spirituality.

Chapter 14. The Place of Tongues

More Important Gifts; 14:1–5. Paul compares the gift of tongues with the gift of prophecy (teaching God's Word authoritatively). As the purpose of gifts is to build up the body (1 Cor. 12), Paul would "rather that you prophesy," for this edifies the church. The Corinthians have been majoring on a minor gift!

Limitations on Tongues; 14:6–19. Paul does not forbid the expression of tongues. It is a valid spiritual gift. But he does insist that unintelligible speech in church must be interpreted for the edification of the congregation (cf. 14–27).

Purpose of Tongues; 14:20–25. This debated passage is best understood in the context of the Greek culture where ecstatic utterances were taken as signs of divine presence. Unbelievers may take tongues as such signs, even though believers are not to (22). So an outsider might come to a Christian meeting through hearing of such a miraculous event. But if everyone at the meeting is shouting out in tongues, the impression given is likely to be, "What a madhouse!" (23). If an unbeliever comes to a meeting and hears the Word in plain speech, he will be convinced by the Spirit and converted (24,25).

Conclusions about Tongues; 14:26–33a. Paul concludes by describing what happens at a typical gathering of the NT congregation. Many participate, and one or two—at most three—may contribute in a tongue, if an interpreter is present. No one should excuse bursting out in a tongue by saying he "couldn't help it," for this is just not true (32,33). In general, Paul affirms the validity of tongues as a spiritual gift, restricts their use in public meetings, and helps the Corinthians see that this is not a particularly significant gift.

Compare 1 Corinthians 14 with Acts 2. Do you notice anything different about the "tongues" the two seem to be describing?

What feelings and ideas have you had about "tongues" and about believers who speak in them? How have these chapters corrected or strengthened your views? Your attitudes?

Women Remain Silent? 14:33b–35. This comment is hard to understand, particularly as Paul in 11:5 instructs women how to pray and prophesy in the church. As no OT law suggests women should not speak in religious meetings, the word here may refer to some civil law or to a custom of the Greeks or Romans about women and public speaking. It is also possible that the early women's liberation movement, noted in chapter 11, was particularly vocal, and these instructions, in the context of Paul's stress on orderly worship (32), were to correct abuse. Surely our interpretation must be in harmony with the voice of the NT as a whole on this question (see *Role of Women in the Church,* p. 625).

VII. Uncertainties Relating to Resurrection (1 Corinthians 15)

Some at Corinth continued in the typical Greek attitude toward the idea of resurrection: disbelief. Paul firmly presents resurrection as a doctrinal keystone of Christian faith (cf. chart on p. 537).

Resurrection Basic to the Gospel; 15:1–11. Jesus' resurrection is critical to the gospel message and well attested by witnesses (see chart on p. 537).

Our Resurrection Attested by His; 15:12–19. Jesus' resurrection was literal, and ours will be also. Otherwise Christian faith is an empty shell.

God's Plan Hinges on Resurrection; 15:20–28. It is in the resurrection that God's plan to defeat the powers of death and sin will be carried out. In God's time the end will come, and with it victory.

Impact on Daily Life; 15:29–34. Paul's willingness to endanger his own life for the gospel makes sense only in view of resurrection. Even those who practice baptism on behalf of the dead (something that Paul does not endorse, and speaks of as "their" practice) shows that belief in resurrection influences present behavior.

Nature of Resurrected Bodies? 15:35–49. While few analogies exist, Paul points for illustration to a dry, dead looking seed which, planted in the ground, reappears vital and green. There will be relationship or similarity between our mortal and resurrection bodies, but there will also be transformation. Then we will not be like Adam, but "we shall bear the likeness of the man from heaven" (49).

Transformation Ahead; 15:50–58. Paul is caught up in a vision of the glory coming, and the great moment when all that is mortal in us is transmuted to immortality. Then we will fully experience the victory won for us through Jesus. Until then, we are to commit ourselves to the work of the Lord, knowing that our labor is not in vain in him.

Chapter 16. Parting Instructions

Paul closes this letter with a reminder to continue collecting funds for the relief of other believers (1–4; cf. 2 Cor. 8, 9). He mentions his plans and the friends he hopes to send to the Corinthians soon (5–18). And he conveys the greeting of the churches of Asia.

2 CORINTHIANS
New Covenant Ministry

This is the most personal and revealing of Paul's NT letters. In it he opens his heart to the believers of Corinth, many of whom are still critical of him. But he must share openly to communicate the attitudes and principles which are at the heart of Christian ministry. This is a vital letter for all who seek to serve and build others.

Date and Author. The letter was written by Paul to the believers at Corinth. They have his first letter. A report of the church's reaction to that letter of A.D. 57 has stimulated this follow-up letter, written from Macedonia in A.D. 58.

Background. Paul's first letter dealt graciously but bluntly with issues tearing at the unity of the Christian community in Corinth. (For background on the church there, see *Corinth* p. 627). In general the response to his letter was heartening. But there were still pockets of hardness and antagonism. In this warm letter, Paul wants to communicate his love to those who were hurt by what seemed to them the harsh tone of the earlier letter, and also to warn those who still rebel against his authority. In the process, Paul gives us all a clear picture of the principles on which his, and all spiritually effective ministry under Christ's new covenant, is based.

Structure and Outline. Paul's thoughts are organized around the principles of ministry on which he has operated for so many years.

Outline

Values. This NT book is exceptionally important. It opens our eyes to the nature of Christian ministry and shows us how to minister. It also teaches us vital truths about the transformation we experience under the new covenant, and about the way that spiritual authority is to be exercised in the church of Jesus Christ.

Chapter 1. Comforting Others

Communicating God's Comfort; 1:3–11. The person who has known trials and suffering, and has experienced God's comfort, is in a unique position to comfort others when they suffer. Paul is willing to share openly his own times of "great pressure, far beyond our ability to endure," so that others can sense the overflowing comfort of God which sustained him when he felt despair.

Sharing human weaknesses, so that others sense we can identify with them in their need, is a vital aspect of communicating the reality of Christ's comfort.

Paul's Change of Plans; 1:12–23. When Paul sent his first letter rather than visiting Corinth personally, as he had told the church he intended, some accused him of being afraid to face them, or at best of being untrustworthy. Paul explains that his change of plans was motivated "in order to spare you" (23). Paul wanted to give these people time to respond freely to his instructions, and wanted to avoid appearing to "lord it over your faith." When they do respond freely, they will "stand firm" in their own faith, and know joy.

Chapter 2. Deep Love

No Painful Visit; 2:1–4. Paul's deep love for the believers at Corinth moved him to delay his visit. He did this with full confidence that the church would respond to his letter, and thus when he did come all might rejoice together (2,3). Paul also shares the feelings of anguish and pain that gripped him as he wrote about their problems.

Forgiveness Encouraged; 2:5–11. The first letter to Corinth called for discipline of a brother living in an immoral relationship (1 Cor. 5). The church did discipline him—so effectively that he repented. Now Paul urges them to forgive the brother and "reaffirm your love to him." Paul assures the Corinthians that he trusts their judgment, so completely that he will forgive whomever they do.

Triumphant Ministry; 2:12–17. God is leading his ministers in a triumphal procession, for they bear a gospel message which always produces response. There is the fragrance of life where it is received,

and the fragrance of death where it is rejected. Clearly, Paul feels
the responsiveness of the Corinthians is a sweet fragrance.

📖 Review chapters 1 and 2, looking for words and thoughts
which reveal Paul's feelings and his character. What kind
of a man was the apostle? What were his relationships with others?

📖 Two principles of ministry that will be explained later are
revealed here: transparency (1:3–11) and a delicate sensitivity
to freedom (2:1–4). What do you learn of each from Paul's actions?

Chapter 3. Transparency

Ministers of the New Covenant; 3:1–6. Paul views himself as a
minister of the long promised new covenant. Evidence of his ministry is found in the lives of those he has touched with the gospel,
for transformed Christians are letters from God, written by the
Spirit not on stone tablets but on the human heart.

The Glory of the New Covenant; 3:7–18. Paul contrasts the glory
of the old and the new covenant. When Moses returned from Mount
Sinai with the tablets of stone, his face shown with a brilliant
radiance. But the glory faded. Moses hid his face with a veil to
mask that deterioration from his people. Paul says that Christians,
"not like Moses," can remove the veils that hide us from others.
We do so because we know that God's Spirit is at work within
us, and "we are being transformed into his likeness with ever increasing splendor, which comes from the Lord, who is the Spirit"
(18).

The point is that transparency, an honest sharing of our lives
with others, is the best way to "reflect the Lord's glory" (18).
Others will not see Jesus in our facades of perfection. It is the
process of transformation that witnesses to the Lord. How comforting this must have been to the blemished believers in Corinth.
And how comforting to us to know that, with all our faults, we
can glorify our Lord.

📖 Do you know another Christian whose growth in Christ is
a witness to Jesus' presence? How important is it to live
transparently and share our true selves if we want to reflect Christ?

Chapter 4. Confidence

Clay Jars; 4:1–12. Paul is completely aware of the human weaknesses which mar him as well as his readers. But still he renounces
"secret and shameful ways." He will be honest and never use deception (1,2). An honest awareness of our humanity, and even honest

communication of pressures, perplexities, and the struggles that mark our lives, shows to all that our enablement "is from God, and not from us." The Christian, of all persons, should be most willing to admit his weaknesses and thus reveal that his strength comes from God.

Never Lose Heart; 4:13–18. Whatever troubles may come, Paul never loses heart. He knows that within, where none can see, God the Spirit is at work. Thus "we fix our eyes not on what is seen, but on what is unseen. For what is seen is temporary and what is unseen is eternal" (18). We too need to realize the promise of the new covenant, and to hope.

Often Christians are discouraged by their weaknesses, or by the failures of others. Paul is fully aware of human weakness, but is not discouraged. What reasons can you find here that encourage you?

New Covenant

The people of Israel were in the final months of that siege of Jerusalem which led to its destruction when Jeremiah uttered his prophecy of the new covenant (Jer. 30–33). The disasters threatened in the Mosaic law (cf. Deut. 28) were falling on God's disobedient people with crushing weight. They were about to be carried into Babylonian captivity when the prophet promised, "I will make a new covenant with the house of Israel and with the house of Judah. It will not be like the covenant I made . . . when I took them by the hand to lead them out of Egypt" (Jer. 31:31,32).

That new covenant was made with Israel, and with all mankind, at Calvary in the death of Jesus Christ (cf. Luke 22:20). Since Christ's resurrection, all believers have been called to a life governed by the new covenant, and not by the old Mosaic code.

What are the provisions of the new covenant? How do we live a new covenant life? This is the theme of the whole NT. But three NT books are especially revealing. Romans explains how a person becomes righteous and lives a righteous life under the new covenant. Second Corinthians explains how believers live with one another in a ministering relationship under the new covenant. Hebrews explains how we relate to God, as his new covenant priesthood.

But we must begin our understanding of new covenant living by noting that both testaments state decisively that it is "not like" the old law covenant of Moses. How is the new "not like" the old?

*The old covenant carved God's Law in stone, as a standard of living no man could achieve. The new covenant promises inner transformation, as God the Spirit writes righteousness on the responsive hearts of his trusting people.

*The old covenant of law provided penalties for those who did not keep it. The new covenant provides immediate forgiveness as a vital part of the process through which God commits himself to work in our lives and makes us righteous.

*The old covenant provided limited access to God, through a priesthood and a sacrificial system served by one small family of Israel. The new covenant provides immediate access to God for all believers and calls every believer to a priestly ministry.

There is no more basic area of study for those who wish to grasp the wonders of the new life God has provided for us in Christ. The new covenant is the key to understanding the NT.

For study: Covenant, p. 51; *Law, OT,* p. 87; *Priesthood, OT,* p. 103; *New Covenant,* OT, p. 330; *Law, NT,* p. 617; *Priesthood,* NT, p. 749.

Chapter 5. Motivation

The confident expectation of success is a vital thing for all in new covenant ministry. Paul now unveils the basis on which he is so sure that the Corinthians, and all believers, *will* experience that transformation toward Christlikeness the new covenant promises.

Ultimate Transformation Assured; 5:1–10. Paul is sure that all believers will know full transformation under the new covenant. He sees death as dismantling of a temporary tent, to be exchanged for a building constructed by God (1). The Spirit's presence is a guarantee of the splendor to be ours in the hereafter (2–5). The future state is to be preferred, for then we will be with the Lord (6–8). Being confident of our destiny, we can give full attention to living now to please God (9), sure that all our actions will be evaluated and rewards given "for things done while in the body" (10). In this context the "judgment seat" or tribunal of Christ is not related to salvation, but to rewards (cf. 1 Cor. 3:10–15).

Present Transformation Also Assured; 5:11–21. Paul is deeply aware of his responsibility to encourage commitment by others to obedient new covenant life (11–13). But he understands the principles on which his ministry must be based. First, he must count on the fact that the Holy Spirit is truly present in the heart of the believer (12). Second, he must realize that only love for Christ will stimulate a believer to the inner responsiveness so central to new covenant living (14a). Third, he knows that the purpose of Jesus' death was to work the inner transformation, moving believers to "live no longer for themselves but for him who died for them and was raised again" (14,15).

The practical implications are exciting. Paul no longer looks at behavior or evidence of carnality in evaluating those he serves. Instead he knows that "if anyone be in Christ, he is a new creation"

(16,17). Paul also realizes that his ministry is a ministry of reconciliation: a ministry to bring the life of the believers he serves into harmony with the inner reality of Jesus in the heart.

How is the ministry of reconciliation accomplished? The model is provided by Christ and involves "not counting men's sins against them" (19). Thus Paul will never use guilt or shame, or reminders of failure, in an attempt to motivate change. Instead Paul will constantly assure those he serves of his and God's unconditional love, and of forgiveness. Paul will appeal and implore. And Paul will communicate his own confidence, knowing that Jesus died that "we might become the righteousness of God" (21). Christ has not died in vain!

Why is the teaching of this passage important for ministers? How might it be applied by parents? How is it relevant to you?

Chapter 6, 7. New Covenant Ministry Exemplified

Servanthood; 6:1–13. Paul, as a minister of the new covenant, has relied on new covenant principles to motivate the Corinthians to follow Jesus. One such principle is implicit in servanthood: the willingness to provide an example rather than to command others to act (see *Servanthood, OT,* p. 306, *NT,* p. 486). Paul's sufferings and hardships on behalf of those he serves both show the Corinthians how to follow Jesus (3–10) and demonstrate his affection for them (11,12).

Commitment to Righteousness; 6:14–7:1. On the basis of his own commitment to righteousness and from the Scripture, Paul exhorts the Corinthians to seek holiness.

Transparency and Trust; 7:2–16. Paul shares the joy that the response of the Corinthians to his letter has caused. That response (8–13) was made freely and justifies the trust the apostle has shown in the Spirit's working within the Corinthian believers.

How many of the principles of ministry which Paul has discussed in chapters 1–5 can you see exemplified in these two chapters? Do you see other guidelines for ministering with others that you might apply in your interpersonal relationships?

Chapter 8, 9. Giving under the New Covenant

Giving Encouraged; 8:1–7. The churches of Macedonia were in the grip of poverty. But they actually pleaded for the privilege of contributing to the needs of other brothers. Paul encourages the Corinthians to also excel in "this grace of giving."

Giving Explained; 8:8–9:5. Paul sees giving as following the example of Jesus, who was willing to become poor to enrich us (8:8,9). Such sharing is never to be measured by "how much" but rather by "how able." We share in proportion to what we have (9:10–12). Finally, the goal of giving is to distribute within the body of Christ so that the needs of all will be met (9:13–15, see *Giving,* below). Paul then shares the fact that a delegation is coming soon to accept their contributions. Earlier the Corinthians made a commitment to set money aside. Now Paul expressed confidence in them. But he wants to be sure they avoid embarrassment by being ready, for Paul has already told others of their eagerness to contribute (9:1–5).

Benefits of Giving; 9:6–15. God wants no one to give because he feels he has to, or to give grudgingly. To help motivate joy-filled and willing sharing, Paul reminds the Corinthians of the many benefits of generosity. One basic principle is revealed throughout nature: one reaps only what he sows (9:6). God is totally able to meet the needs of every believer, freeing Christians to "abound in every good work." Believers do not need to grasp tightly every loose coin, for no one can outgive the Lord (9:9–11)!

In addition to supplying the needs of God's people, generosity will move others to praise God. And it will move those who receive to pray for their benefactors (9:12–14). Thus Paul looks on the privilege of giving as God's indescribable gift—a gift he offers to the giver (9:15)!

What motivates your giving? How do you determine what you give, and where you direct your contributions? What do you see in these chapters that might guide you?

V. Authority under the New Covenant (2 Corinthians 10–13)

The final chapters of 2 Corinthians are especially revealing. They explain Paul's understanding of his authority as a minister of Christ's new covenant. And they help us understand the great care he has taken to communicate respect for the freedom and responsibility of individuals and the local Christian community (cf. 1:24; 2:8; 6:4; 7:1; 8:8; and 11:7). The principles revealed as Paul shares so openly and personally in these chapters are vital for all who have been called to leadership in Christ's church.

Giving

OT law prescribed a tithe, to be paid by every Israeli for the support of the temple and the priesthood. The NT mentions no similar requirement. Instead, entirely new new covenant principles are introduced.

First, there is no "ten percent for God, ninety percent for me" notion in the NT. We are God's servants, and all we have belongs to the Lord. We merely hold it in trust for him.

Second, "giving" is intimately related to the concept of the body of Christ. The basic word used in the NT is not "give" but "share." The image is one of distributing resources through the whole body so every member can function effectively. Paul states the ideal this way: "not that others might be relieved while you are hard pressed, but that there might be an equality" (2 Cor. 8:13).

Third, NT sharing has a strongly personal focus. There is nothing in the NT about (or against) the support of institutions or facilities. But there is a strong emphasis on meeting human need. Funds shared within the body to meet needs will help every believer function effectively.

Finally, there is to be no pressure exerted to force or shame others to share. "Each man should give as he has decided in his heart to give, not reluctantly or under compulsion, for God loves a cheerful giver" (2 Cor. 9:7). One who sees all he has as the Lord's, and who loves others, will be moved by the Spirit to share and so meet their needs.

For study: The Christian and Money, p. 527; 2 Corinthians 8, 9.

Chapter 10. Appeal, Not Command

Meekness and Gentleness; 10:1–6. Paul has been accused by some in Corinth of being a "weak" leader. Even now he appeals rather than commands (1). It seems they expect leaders to be more forceful and demanding. Paul notes that Christ himself was meek and gentle—but never weak! Paul is engaged in a spiritual warfare, so he can never rely on worldly methods. It requires divine power to demolish the inner strongholds and bring hearts and minds into an obedient relationship with the Lord.

True Authority; 10:7–11. The Corinthians "look only on surface things." Paul's authority is real, for it has been given him by God. The Corinthians should be respectful, though not frightened (cf. 13:1–4). It is significant that Paul identifies his authority as "authority the Lord gave us for building you up rather than pulling you down" (8). No spiritual leader is called to lord it over others and thus keep them in spiritual childhood. Authority is for building others toward spiritual maturity.

Divine Commendation; 10:12–18. Apparently some in Corinth are comparing themselves with others and boasting of their leadership ability. Paul seeks no commendation, except from the Lord. The salvation and the growth of the believers in Corinth, and Paul's years of ministry, speak for him.

Spiritual Authority

God's goal under the new covenant is to accomplish inner transformation. He does not require conformity. He seeks to produce commitment. Thus human authority structures, such as the "chain of command," which are designed to control others' behavior, simply have no place in the life of God's people. Those with spiritual authority claim no right to control others. Instead they exalt Christ as Lord and seek to build allegiance to him (cf. Rom. 14:9–13).

How is spiritual authority, given by God to leaders to build up the body of Christ, exercised? The two primary sources of influence are teaching and example, each communicated in a context of love.

Thus Paul's instructions on recognizing spiritual leaders in the local church focus on evidence of an individual's personal growth as a follower of Jesus (1 Tim. 3; Titus 1). Even in teaching, the leader is to be gentle and to rely on God to convince others (2 Tim. 2:24–26). In every aspect of the leader's ministry he must trust God to move within others and to produce response. Never are leaders to "lord it over" the faith of their brothers and sisters in Christ (cf. 1 Pet. 5:1–4; Matt. 23:8–12).

Believers are told to be responsive to their leaders (1 Pet. 5:5; Heb. 13:17). This is wise, for their authority is authenticated by Jesus himself, and he is "not weak in dealing with you, but is powerful among you." Because Christ *is* real, spiritual leaders can abandon worldly approaches to leadership, and trust him (see *Servanthood*, p. 486).

Chapter 11. Serve, Not Exploit

Allegiance Is to Christ; 11:1–6. Paul seeks to win no one to allegiance to himself. He has "promised you to one husband, to Christ." The "super apostles" in Corinth, who want allegiance to themselves, lead believers away "from your sincere and pure devotion to Christ."

Leadership Is Serving; 11:7–33. Paul has chosen to "lower myself in order to elevate you" (7), even to the extent of taking no support from the Corinthians when he was with them. There are too many counterfeit leaders, masquerading as "angels of light," but actually eager to exploit their fellow believers (19).

Willingness to suffer for Christ in the service of others (21–29) and willingness to reveal weaknesses (30–33) are both indicators of spiritual leaders who practice new covenant leadership.

What practices of modern leaders might indicate seeking to build allegiance to Christ and not themselves? Commitment to serve others rather than to exploit them? What practices might indicate those whom Paul calls "deceitful workmen, masquerading as apostles"?

Chapter 12. Weakness, Not Strength

Weakness Is Strength; 12:1–10. Despite the many revelations Paul has received, God has taught Paul to reject conceit and to appreciate weakness. Many believe the vision he refers to in verses 1–4 was given to Paul himself when he was stoned and left for dead in Lystra on his first missionary journey (Acts 14:8–20). To help Paul learn the value of weakness, Paul was given a "thorn in the flesh." Many believe this was an eye disease which made it hard for Paul to see and was most unattractive. Whatever the problem, it helped Paul realize that God's "power is made perfect in weakness." It is when Paul is weak that he is strong.

The natural talents so many rely on may only be hindrances to new covenant ministry, in which all success must come from Christ and from him alone.

Persons Have Ultimate Value; 12:11–21. Paul resorts to gentle irony when he points out the foolishness of those who try to undermine his ministry. The Corinthians have seen the miracles that mark an apostle (11,12). Yet they have half believed the claim that Paul only wants to use the church or exploit it—and this despite the fact that neither Paul nor his associates have accepted any money (26–28).

In fact, only the Corinthians themselves have any value in Paul's eyes: "What I want is not your possessions but you" (14). Paul has actually spent himself and his resources to serve them, because he loves them (14,15). Indeed, Paul can say with complete candor that "everything we do is for your strengthening" (19).

Paul's only worry is that those in Corinth who have sinned might not have repented from their impurity by the time he comes, and that anger, factions, and disorder may still mar the fellowship. How much better to praise than to discipline those we dearly love.

Does Paul's sharing of his motives and values in this chapter bring to mind anyone in your church? Is this person recognized as a leader? What suggests that he or she might be God's kind of leader? What criteria are used in your church to distinguish leaders?

Chapter 13. Warning!

This exposition of new covenant ministry closes with a warning. Paul has appealed and not ordered. But he does speak with authority! The Corinthians have demanded "proof that Christ is speaking" through Paul. If the members of this church refuse to respond and continue sinning, they will not be spared when Paul returns.

But what can Paul do? What he has always done. In this as in other aspects of his ministry, Paul will not rely on the sanctions or the manipulations used by worldly leaders to force conformity. No, Paul explains that Christ "is not weak in dealing with you, but is powerful among you" (3). Paul possesses true spiritual authority. He is a leader called by God. Christ does speak through him. Therefore the Lord himself, "powerful among you," will vindicate Paul's spiritual authority and act to discipline those who refuse to respond! Just as Paul relies on Christ in the heart to motivate obedience (ch. 5), so also Paul relies on Christ in the heart to discipline his own people.

Paul's farewells are brief. "Aim at perfection," he urges. "Listen to my appeal, be of one mind, live in peace. And the God of love and peace will be with you" (11).

Review 2 Corinthians. What do you learn about how to live your own life under the new covenant? What do you learn about how to motivate others to follow Jesus?

GALATIANS
In Defense of Christian Freedom

Few documents have had the impact of this short letter, a tract on Christian freedom. It stunned those in the early church who insisted that for salvation believers must add keeping of the law to faith. It stunned the medieval Catholic Church, as the teaching of justification by faith alone was articulated by Martin Luther. And it continues to pulse with life-changing vitality, communicating its message of freedom. In the freedom from law that Galatians proclaims, you and I find the key to a life of true goodness and holiness.

Date and Author. Paul wrote this short letter. It is best dated just prior to the Jerusalem council of A.D. 49 which dealt with this same issue of the relationship between the believer and the law.

Background. Paul and Barnabas have finished their successful first missionary journey, which established many new churches in Asia and the Phrygian (southern) region of the Roman province of Galatia (see map, p. 585; cf. Acts 16:6). When the missionaries returned to Antioch they found that some "men came down from Judea to Antioch, and were teaching the brothers, 'Unless you are circumcised according to the custom taught by Moses, you cannot be saved' " (Acts 15:1). These men were converted Pharisees from Judea and wanted to impose more than circumcision: they actually insisted that Gentile Christians must be "required to obey the law of Moses" (Acts 15:5). In essence these Judaizers, or legalists, insisted that the gospel was a message of grace *and* law; of salvation by faith *and* works.

Paul and Barnabas realized this was a critical distortion of the gospel, which "brought Paul and Barnabas into sharp dispute and debate with them" (15:2). Soon after a delegation went to Jerusalem to confer with the apostles and elders there. This led to the council reported in Acts 15 (see p. 586). And to the discovery that the Judaizers had not been sent by the apostles or the Jerusalem church! The conclusion of the matter was agreement that Mosaic law and Jewish life style should not be imposed on Gentile Christians (15:19).

Galatians 2 does not mention this council, so it seems the letter was written before it. Paul had to move quickly to counter the influence of the Judaizers who had already infiltrated the newly planted churches in southern Galatia. This brief letter, confirmed by the council decision, underlines justification by faith alone and a freedom to live for the Lord which is found with release from law.

Theme. Like the Book of Romans, Galatians explores righteousness and the problem of how a people not under law can experience personal holiness. To the Jews, who relied on the law as both the way to salvation and the way to holiness, the announcement of freedom from law was frightening. Liberty was viewed as a license, and Paul's call to freedom seemed to them an invitation to abandon morality. But the law of Moses had never produced righteousness in any human being. And no one had ever been justified by keeping that law. The NT insists that what law cannot do God is able to accomplish through personal relationship with Jesus Christ and through faith in him.

In Romans Paul explains how God has provided righteousness in Christ. In Galatians Paul exhorts believers to hold firmly to the principles through which we find salvation and holiness. We have exchanged law for a personal relationship with God, and it is that relationship which provides freedom and true goodness. "It is for freedom that Christ has set us free," Paul announces. "Stand firm, then, and do not let yourselves be burdened again by a yoke of slavery" (Gal. 5:1).

Structure and Outline. The Judaizers who demanded Christians live under law attacked Paul's gospel of freedom on three grounds. *They attacked Paul personally. "This man is not really an Apostle," was their argument. *They pointed out that God authored the law. How then could Paul say it should be set aside? *They accused Paul of licensing sin. How could an "outlaw" people have morality? Each attack is answered in Galatians, as reflected in the outline below.

Outline

Before Reading. For background to this book study the following Theology in Brief articles: *Law, OT,* p. 87; *Law, NT,* p. 617; *Righteousness,* p. 611. Here are several questions answered in the Book of Galatians. Which of them seems most important to you? Read Galatians for the answers. Is the Christian life summed up in moral do's and don'ts? Should I feel boxed in as a Christian or free? How do I learn to feel free? Since the Mosaic law is in the Bible, how can it be wrong to try to keep it? What does it mean to "fall away from grace"? How can I tell if God is really working in my life? How do I tell if I am doing something morally wrong? What does it mean to "do good"?

Introduction. 1:1–5

Paul immediately affirms his position as an apostle, authenticated and sent by Jesus himself. He also refutes the moral accusations made against his gospel. There is no immorality associated with grace. In fact, Jesus died for our sins to rescue us from the power of that evil which infects human society.

Chapter 1. Paul and His Gospel

No Other Gospel; 1:6–10. Paul uses the word "gospel" some sixty times in his letters. Six of them are found in this brief paragraph!

The Greek word means "good news." The earliest presentation of the gospel, found in Acts 2 and 3, emphasizes the historic life, death, and resurrection of Jesus. It shows that all this happened in accordance with OT prophecy and proclaims forgiveness of sin for all who believe in Jesus. This is the unmixed "gospel of grace" which Paul preached in Galatia and which these new believers "are so quickly deserting" (Gal. 1:6) for a different and perverted gospel.

The "other gospel" is a mixture of faith and works, of grace and law, taught by Judaizers (see *Background,* p. 661) who insisted that faith in Christ is not sufficient for salvation. They also taught that faith does not provide sufficient guidance for holy living, and that OT law must be added to Paul's teaching to complete it. This issue is not a minor one. It is so vital to true Christianity that Paul pronounces anathema on those who teach it: "let anybody preaching a gospel other than what you accepted, let him be eternally condemned" (1:8,9).

Paul's Commission; 1:11–24. One objection to Paul, raised by the Judaizers, was that he had no real authority to present his "incomplete" gospel. He had never been authenticated by the leadership in Judea.

Paul responds to this argument here, and in chapter 2. He begins by reviewing his calling. Paul did not receive the gospel he preached from any man (so obviously no human "authentication" of his authority was possible). Instead he "received it by revelation from Jesus Christ" (11,12). Both his message and his call come direct from God, the highest of all authorities!

After Paul's conversion he spent time alone, studying out the meaning of Christ's first coming. The "revelation" Paul speaks of here may have been Spirit-guided understanding of the OT prophets.

After this his early contact with the apostles in Judea was a brief visit with James and Peter. Then Paul returned to Syria, and there boldly preached the gospel of Jesus, whose followers he had once persecuted. This witness caused only praise in Judea.

Chapter 2. Standing for the Gospel

Apostolic Acceptance; 2:1–10. Paul reports a brief visit to Jerusalem some fourteen years after his conversion. He was directed by God to make the trip (1) and "set before them the gospel that I preach among the Gentiles" (2). Even then the law issue was raised by some "false brothers" who "infiltrated our ranks to spy on the freedom we have in Christ Jesus." But there was no retreat from grace (3–5).

In fact, the Jewish apostles and elders added nothing to Paul's gospel. Instead they affirmed Paul as apostle to the Gentiles (6–8). Thus "James, Peter and John, those reputed to be pillars" recognized the grace given Paul and "gave me and Barnabas the right hand of fellowship" (9). They only asked that the Gentile churches remember to make contributions for the poor (10).

Thus the charge laid by the Judaizers that Paul was out preaching "on his own" was doubly deceptive. Paul did have the recognition of the leaders in Jerusalem as an apostle. And by their charge, the Judaizers implied that *they* represented the Jerusalem church, when actually they were acting without any such authorization (cf. Acts 15:24)!

Paul Confronts Peter; 2:11–21. Paul shares another instance when the issue of mixing law and grace emerged. Peter was visiting Antioch, the first Gentile church (cf. Acts 11:10–30). There Peter at first mingled with the Gentile brothers, which was in harmony with what God had taught him earlier (cf. Acts 10, 11). However, when some of those Christian Jews appeared, who insisted that believers must observe the Mosaic law, Peter began to "draw back and separate himself from the Gentiles." The other Jewish Christians in Antioch "joined him in this hypocrisy" (11–13).

To Paul these believers were clearly "not acting in line with the truth of the gospel." Immediately Paul confronted Peter. He argued that "we who are Jews by birth" know "a man is not justified by observing the law, but by faith in Jesus Christ" (15, 16: note that "justified" means to be declared righteous by God, cf. p. 610).

The fact that Christians do fail and are sinners does not mean that law ought to be reestablished (17,18). Paul's comment that "through law I died to the law" (19) is explained in Romans 7:1–4. But Paul's basic argument is that through the gospel God has provided a new dynamic which infuses the life of the Christian and has nothing at all to do with law. "Christ lives in me," Paul says. And "the life I live in the body, I live by faith in the Son of God" (20). To return to law would mean setting aside the grace of God, the only hope mankind has to achieve righteousness (see p. 611). Paul now moves on to develop this point in the next chapters of Galatians.

Chapter 3. Law, or Faith?

Paul has answered the first charge. He is an apostle, sent by Jesus himself. Now he turns to the second charge leveled by the Judaizers. How dare he set aside the law, which was given by God? The summary of Paul's argument is seen in the chart on pages 666 and 667.

Testimony Concerning Law; 3:1–15. Paul begins by pointing out that even though law was given by God, it has nothing to do with the new life which comes from Christ. He reminds these "dear fools of Galatia" of their own experience. Did the Spirit come to touch their lives through law, or faith? Wouldn't it be strange, since the Spirit was received through faith, if Christians could "attain your goal by human effort"? No, law has nothing to do with life (1–5).

Paul points to Abraham. He too was saved by faith (cf. Gen. 15:6; Rom. 4). The principle of faith that brought Abraham salvation is the faith principle that operates in Paul's gospel now preached to the Gentiles (6–9).

Paul quotes the testimony of the Scripture. The law brings a curse, not life. The very OT the Judaizers accuse Paul of abandoning testifies that "the righteous will live by faith" (cf. Hab. 2:4). In the death of Christ he experienced the curse of the law—for us. His death was a redemption—a purchase which takes the thing bought off the market! The death of Christ was for the purpose of making the blessing that came to Abraham available to all, so that we might receive the promised Spirit through faith (10–15).

Paul adds one devastating observation. Abraham's faith came in response to an unconditional promise made to him by God (15, 16; cf. *Covenant*, p. 51). The law, introduced some 430 years after the promise was made, could not replace or set the promise aside (15)! The promise speaks of what God will do and implies inheritance through his action. Law speaks of what man must do and implies inheritance through human performance (17,18). We must make a choice between law and promise, for they rest on mutually exclusive principles!

Since in fact God "gave it to Abraham through a promise" it is clear that law is totally irrelevant to our new life in Christ.

The Function of Law; 3:19–25. Paul now underlines the fact that law is unrelated to life. Law was "added because of transgressions" to reveal the sinfulness of sin (cf. Rom. 3:19,20; 5:20,21). Thus law has always related to sin, not righteousness (Gal. 3:19). This same verse points out that law was always intended to be temporary. It was introduced long after Abraham and passed away when Jesus, the object of the Abrahamic promise, appeared.

The next verses show that while the promise imparts both life and righteousness, law can impart neither (3:21). All law accomplished was to make the world aware that man is a prisoner of sin and turn his eyes toward Christ. Aware through law of our desperate condition some at least might seek justification by faith (3:22–24). Now that faith has come with Jesus, law is no longer in charge of us (3:25).

Law at a Glance
Galatians 3–5

I. Law is unrelated to life (3:1–18). This is proved
   A. by how we receive spiritual life (3:1–5)
   B. by how OT saints were made righteous (3:6–9)
   C. by Scripture's testimony of contrast between promise and works (3:10–14)
   D. by Scripture's testimony that law does not void the earlier promise (3:15–18)

II. Law has always had a severely limited role (3:19–4:8). This is proved
   A. by the fact law is temporary (3:19,20)
   B. by the fact law cannot make alive (3:21,22)
   C. by the fact law pointed toward faith and now believers are released from it (3:23,24)
   D. by the fact believers now have the full rights of sonship (3:25–4:7)

III. Law is an inferior way (3:8–5:12) that will lead believers to
    A. loss of joy (4:8–19)
    B. loss of freedom (4:20–5:1)
    C. loss of power (5:2–12)

The last few verses of this chapter (3:26–28) belong with the argument developed in chapter 4.

Chapter 4. The New Relationship

Sonship; 3:26–4:7. Paul's announcement that "you are all sons of God through faith in Christ Jesus" (3:26) had special meaning for those who lived in the world of the NT. "Sonship" was a socially significant term. The young child of a well-to-do family was placed in the care of a pedagogue (the "guardian" of 4:2). This family slave accompanied the child everywhere and was responsible for his actions. The pedagogue both controlled and punished the child. In essence such a child lived as the slave of a slave!

Then came the great day when the child was legally recognized as "son." At that moment the individual was freed from the authority of the slave. He became directly responsible to his father and was expected to live responsibly as an adult. It is against this cultural background that Paul now presents his image of the law. Law once kept us enslaved, but now has no power over us. In Christ we have received "the full rights of sons" (4:1–5).

With full rights we have received the Spirit as a direct link to God, so we can speak with him and hear his voice directly rather than through law (4:6). As an heir, we also have the full resources of God himself, available to enable us to live the new life to which we have been called in Christ (4:7).

Enslaved Again? 4:8–20. In view of the glorious freedom and joy the Galatians have experienced through their intimate relationship with God, Paul cannot understand why they are now turning to law to pattern their lives (8–11). How different is Paul's goal: that "Christ (be) formed in you." The inner transformation that this phrase portrays is vastly different from a return to childhood and to control of behavior by external rules and regulations (17–20).

An Analogy; 4:21–31. Abraham had been promised by God that his son would inherit the covenant promises made to him (cf. Gal. 3:15–18). When the years passed, and Sarah's body was no longer able to conceive, she insisted that Abraham follow a common custom then and father a child by her slave, Hagar. The birth of Ishmael to Hagar brought much conflict and unhappiness (Gen. 16:5–14; 21:8–14). Thirteen years later, when—humanly speaking—it was impossible, Sarah had a child. God had kept his promise to Abraham.

These well known OT events are now applied by Paul. Ishmael represents human effort: Isaac represents the working of God. The intense rivalry between the two boys reflects the antagonism between human effort and promise. God directed a reluctant Abraham to do as Sarah urged and send Hagar and Ishmael away, "for the son of the slave shall not inherit with the son of the free woman" (Gal. 4:3). The principle of human self-effort, and that of by-faith appropriation of God's promise, can never operate together. A person must either relate to God through the law, or reject law and the self-effort it requires, to rely on the supernatural power of God operating through our relationship with God as his sons.

Freedom

It's not surprising that most people think of freedom as *from* some kind of restriction. "If I could only do what *I* want to do" may sum up the common impression. For anyone aware of the desires and impulses that surge in human beings, the notion of freedom may be frightening. What would people do if limits were removed? It's easy to understand why, for Christians, the idea of law is rather comforting. The "thou shalt not's" are like the bars of a cage that keep us safe from the tiger in us and in others. No wonder the Bible's statement that we are "no longer under the supervision of law" (Gal. 3:25) seems to some to imply an irresponsible or immoral life.

But fear of freedom is based on a radical misunderstanding. Yes, the Bible does teach we are "not under law but under grace" (Rom. 6:14). But this is not license to sin. Instead, it is our title deed to experience true morality and righteousness. You see, God has taken the bars away and left us uncaged, because in Christ he has released us from the power of that tiger that rages in every man! In Christ we are free to be truly good—in motives and desires as well as actions! What then is freedom?

Freedom is release from the dominance of sin over our reactions and our responses. This is explained in Romans 8 and Galatians 5.

Freedom is release from the need for external regulations found through our new, inner relationship with God. This is explained in Romans 7 and Galatians 4.

Freedom is a union with Christ by which the tiger in us is bound and the best in us unchained. This is explained in Romans 6.

There is no need through legalism to build again a dismantled cage. We are freed to concentrate on loving Jesus and so experience the changes God is working within.

Chapter 5. Freedom in Christ

Necessity of Freedom; 5:1–2. Paul urges the Galatians to "stand firm" and not permit themselves to be led by Judaizers back into a slavery to law. "It is for freedom that Christ has set us free" (1,2).

At this point Paul has begun to respond to the third charge of the Judaizers. Paul has demonstrated his apostolic authority (Gal. 1,2). He has shown that his "lawless" gospel is in full harmony with the OT (3,4). Now he will show how that freedom from law which so repels the Judaizers is actually the key to becoming righteous. First, however, Paul again declares that law and grace are opposing principles. When he says that if they turn to law "Christ will be of no value to you at all" (5:2), he is not threatening the Galatians with the loss of their salvation. All his phrases— "alienated from Christ" (4) and "fallen from grace" (4)—relate to the problem of becoming truly good persons. The new relationship believers have with Christ will not benefit them at all if they insist on seeing Christian living as a law-keeping, self-effort kind of thing. "In Christ" such externals have no value. "The only thing that counts is faith expressing itself through love" (6).

These words reaffirm Paul's theme. The issue lies within the human heart, not with standards or behavior. True goodness is the spontaneous expression in action of holy motives and desires. It is this and this alone that has value in God's eyes.

As for those troublemakers who are running around with knives, eager to circumcise the bodies rather than the hearts of the Galatians, Paul wishes they would "go the whole way and emasculate themselves" (7–12)!

Freedom to Live Love; 5:13–26. Paul's explanation is based on a truth introduced in 2:20. "Christ lives in me." The new relationship of the Christian with God as son means that we share his heredity. The life of God within responds to the Spirit and must be lived by faith. The old, identified here as the "sinful nature," responds to law. For background, see *Born Again,* p. 545 and *Old Man/New Man,* p. 614. The conflicting characteristics of these two inner realities is summed up in the chart on page 670.

Paul's teaching can be understood when we realize that his call for freedom is an invitation to live by faith and thus to become the new person we are in Jesus Christ. In summary:

* The new person is never found by indulging the impulses of the old nature, but by loving. Law shows how love would act. But law has never produced love within our hearts (5:13–15).

* The Holy Spirit is unmoved by sinful cravings. Thus if we follow the Spirit's lead and live in the strength he provides, we will not "gratify the desires of (our) sinful nature" (5:16–18).

* The acts and attitudes which the law takes a stand against all flow from the old, sinful nature. It follows then that if the Spirit within us controls the desires of our sinful nature, law has no function in our lives (5:19–21).

* Actually, the Spirit will produce fruit within us which stand in stark contrast to the dark products of the sinful nature. God the Spirit produces love, joy, peace, patience—all those things that men long for and dream about, but have not achieved. If we live in a responsive relationship with the Spirit, he will produce just these things in us (5:22,23).

GALATIANS 5
Our New Life in Christ

"sinful nature" (old life)	"Spirit" (new life)
Characteristics	
* not responsive to God	* responsive to God
* in conflict with the Spirit	* in conflict with sin
* ruled by cravings	* ruled by God
Products	
immorality	love
impurity	joy
debauchery	peace
idolatry and witchcraft	patience
hatred	kindness
discord	goodness
jealousy	faithfulness
fits of rage	gentleness
selfish ambition	self-control
factions	
envy	
drunkenness	
orgies	
Relationship to the Law	
Law is "against such things" (5:23) and was added "because of the transgressions" (3:19)	NONE! "Against such there is no law" (5:22)

---

* How does law relate to a person living in the Spirit? It doesn't! No law has ever been passed to regulate kindness, goodness, and gentleness. Law only stands against sin, and the Spirit produces goodness.

The Christian life, then, does not focus on rules but on relationship. Our goal is not to practice do's and don'ts, but to love God, and to please the Holy Spirit who guides us and enables us from within.

Chapter 6. Living the New Life

Life by the Spirit does not provide guaranteed success. Freedom, to be real, must give individuals a real choice. Paul knows that believers are given the freedom by God to respond to the Spirit or to the sinful nature. How do we deal with this reality in our own lives and in the lives of our brothers and sisters?

Dealing with Failures; 6:1-6. Under law a person "caught in a sin" was to be punished. Under grace "you who are spiritual should restore him gently" (1). The picture given is one of a supportive concern that accepts and loves while encouraging a commitment to righteousness. It is a burden to have immature Christians in a local fellowship. But when we "carry each other's burdens" by unconditional love we "fulfill the law of Christ" (cf. John 13:33,34).

It is important, however, to avoid excusing sin. It is this sense of personal responsibility for one's choices Paul stresses when he says each should "test his own actions" and "carry his own load" (5).

Dealing with Discipline; 6:7,8. The legalistic person is eager to punish the failures of others and does not understand how God is at work within to preserve the integrity of the gospel. A person who sins is not "getting away with" something, and thus mocking God. The believer who misuses his or her freedom, and lives by the impulses of the sinful nature, will experience alienation and the emptiness always associated with death. The person who seeks to please the Spirit will know the enriching gifts which are the mark of eternal life (see *Death,* p. 612 and *Life,* p. 548). The passage is not speaking of salvation but of the quality of the believer's experience now.

Dealing with Growth; 6:9-10. Man's inner transformation is never accomplished suddenly. It involves growth. Thus the encouragement to not become "weary in well doing" is important. A full experience of the blessings of life in Christ will come "at the proper time." Our task is to "do good to all people, especially those who belong to the family of believers," and realize that growth will come.

Concluding Remarks; 6:11–18. Paul's final remarks are brief. He warns again against those who want to bring believers under the bondage of law (12,13). In the cross Christ dealt decisively with such issues so all that now counts "is a new creation" (14,15).

God has planted his new life within. As we live out our relationship with the Spirit of God, that new life will become full and strong. The whole process rests on relationship and has nothing at all to do with keeping the law.

Galatians is a book which must be grasped as a whole before its parts can be understood. To test your understanding of the message of this key NT book, try to answer the questions raised under "before reading" on page 663.

EPHESIANS
The Living Church

The theme of Ephesians is something which Paul calls a great mystery (3:3,6)—a thing unrevealed in the OT but unveiled now after the resurrection of Christ. That mystery is the church, not as an institution, but a living organism of which all believers are members, and Christ is the Head. Because the church is more than an association or an institution, believers must learn to think of themselves and of each other in new and different ways. The exciting difference in being members of Christ's living body is shared in this great NT letter.

Date and Author. The letter was written by Paul to believers of the congregation established in Ephesus on one of Paul's later missionary ventures (Acts 19). It was written from Rome, in A.D. 62 or 63.

Ephesus. The city was known in ancient times as "the Landing Place," and its people were proud of its role as a port city and gateway to Asia. But by the first century, the harbor of Ephesus was nearly filled with silt. The proud city was anxious, experiencing economic decline.

One source of both pride and income to Ephesus was religion. Ephesus was the site of the great Temple of Artemis. That temple was four times the size of the magnificent Parthenon of Athens: it was a great shrine, reverenced throughout the province of "Asia and the world" (Acts 19:27). Multitudes of tourists and worshipers visited Ephesus to see the temple, and the city's commercial life and prosperity depended on these visitors. Tradesmen and souvenir makers, as well as those providing food and lodging, all depended on the temple trade. In addition the temple served as a treasury— a bank in which cities and kings as well as individuals made deposits and from which they drew loans. Pagan religion was a great success in Ephesus. Religious institutionalism was the heart and center of Ephesian social and economic life.

It is against this background that Paul writes about an entirely new thing. He tells of a faith which cannot be expressed through its buildings and institutions, or the kind of success which glorified Asia's gateway city. It is people who are God's treasure. The relationship of these people with God, and with each other, expresses a glory that can never be reflected in structures of stone, no matter

Temple of Artemis at Ephesus

how magnificent. How appropriate that the Ephesians who knew successful worldly religion so well, received this explanation of the church of Christ, which can only be seen through the lives of a people who live in intimate relationship with God.

Theme. The theme of Ephesians is the living church. Paul examines in detail the implications of viewing the church as a living organism, not as an institution. Many times in the Christian era the truths taught here have been mislaid. Christians have thought of the church in institutional terms—as a hierarchy, as buildings and property, as programs and activities. Today too many Christians have no grasp of the truths taught in this great book. How exciting to look into it now, to understand who we are as Christ's people, and to learn how we can draw together as his living church.

The vision of the living church often moved Paul to worship. He includes a number of paragraphs apparently used in the liturgy of the early church as hymns or as confessions of faith (cf. 1:3–12, 20–23; 2:4–10, 14–18).

Outline. The following outline builds on the theme of the living church and captures the major truths taught in this beautiful epistle.

Outline

Before Reading. Here are several questions answered in Ephesians. Which of them is important to you? Read Ephesians for the answers. Why should I be part of a local congregation? How can being a member of a church be significant? What should I look for as signs of a healthy local church? What is necessary if Christians are to help each other grow? How is the church as a body important to me? As family? How does Jesus express himself in and through my life?

Chapter 1. A Chosen People

Saints; 1:1–2. Paul gives the believers in Ephesus a common NT title: saints. This word has come to suggest some moral or spiritual superiority. In the NT, however, it means someone "set aside for the exclusive possession and use of God." The temple of Artemis at Ephesus contained many objects set aside in this same way. Many were made of gold studded with jewels. But human beings are the peculiar treasure of our wise and loving God.

The Importance of Persons; 1:3–4. We can never understand the church until we sense the great value of persons and have some concept of what God has done for us and our fellow believers. In this great NT passage, Paul shows how each person of the Trinity was deeply involved in winning us for God's treasury. Through God's action we have been lifted up and blessed "with every spiritual blessing" in Christ (3).

To accomplish this, the Father: chose us (4) and predestined us to be adopted as sons (5). In context the subject is the whole company of saints, not individuals. Paul's point is that God carefully planned before creation to transform human beings through relationship with his Son. God knew who and what we are. But still he determined to win us to become his most treasured possessions!

To accomplish this, the Son died, that through his blood we might have redemption and forgiveness (7). The price was freely paid—a necessary part of God's plan to draw everything together in and under Christ as sole head (8–11). Our selection in Christ was to make it possible that we, who have been so marred by sin, might actually be "for the praise of his glory."

To accomplish this, the Spirit came: "when you heard the word of truth, the gospel of your salvation." The word "heard" here implies hear and receive. Thus "having believed," the presence of the Spirit is the stamp of God's ownership, guaranteeing our ultimate redemption (1–13).

How important are you and I and other Christians to God? We are so greatly valued that God has shaped the plan of the ages to win us to himself. Nothing that man can construct of brick or stone or glass can compare with the value that God places on those human beings who become his saints.

Thanksgiving and Prayer; 1:15–23. Paul's vision of the people of God as the Lord's treasure stimulates prayer for the saints at Ephesus (15,16). Paul asks the Lord to help them know Him better (17) and to realize the "riches of his glorious inheritance in the saints" (18). When you and I grasp how important we are to God, our attitude about ourselves and others changes dramatically!

Paul also wants the believers at Ephesus to know God's "incomparably great power for us who believe." It may be difficult for those familiar with the successful, wealthy, and powerful cult of

Artemis, to realize that true power is that resurrection life of Jesus which works changes within humanity (19,20). But true power is the Lord's—and is ours in him. Jesus is exalted in heaven, above "all rule and authority, power and dominion, and every title that can be given." There he lives as "head over everything" to the living church—human beings who are his treasure, and his body (21–23).

What concepts today distort the vision of Christ's church as people? What are five ways that viewing other Christians as God's great treasures might affect life in our local congregations? What problems might be caused by Christians perceiving "the church" as a building or as a hierarchy?

Chapter 2. A Transformed People

Life from Death; 2:1–10. God has no illusions about the human beings he has chosen as his treasured possession. He knows that his saints "were dead in your transgressions and sins." He knows that our life style was one of disobedience, acting as we were moved by the cravings and thoughts of our sinful nature (1–3). But God loved us in spite of ourselves (4). He chose to make us "alive with Christ even when we were dead in transgressions" (5; see *Death,* p. 612). God has done even more than give us life: he has lifted us up in Christ, working such a transformation that throughout the coming ages we will display the "incomparable riches of his grace" (6,7). All this has been done on God's initiative—a gracious act that does not rest on any merit of our own, since even faith must be viewed as a gift from God (8,9).

But God's transformation is not simply something future. God *has* transformed us. As his new creations we are actually fitted to "do good works." As those set aside for God's use, we are assigned to good works that he has planned in advance for us to do.

Our value then is not just related to the fact that God has chosen us. It is related also to God's working in us, transforming us now so that we can do good works. This gives a striking new focus to our lives. We are no longer in our old, powerless state! We can begin to glorify God now by a commitment to those good deeds for which we've been remade in Jesus (see *Good Works,* p. 677).

Harmony from Hostility; 2:11–22. The Gentiles to whom Paul writes had no historic claim to relationship with God, for the covenants that promised relationships were made with Israel (cf.

Covenant, p. 51). But now "you who were once far away have been brought near through the blood of Christ" (11–13).

This has won an "at peace" relationship for all believers, with God and with each other. The hostility that existed between Jews and Greeks was abolished when the law which stimulated that hostility was superseded by the new covenant (15, cf. *Law,* p. 617). Members of different and even hostile cultures now have been united in "one body." Our common access to the Father by one Spirit shows that we are now in fact a unified community (14–18).

Paul adds two more quick images which impress upon us the unity of the church. Believers are members of a single household (family) headed by the Father (21). And believers are building blocks, fitted together as in a living temple "being built together to become a dwelling place in which God lives by his Spirit" (21,22). Each of these images stresses the unity of the church, found in a common experience of salvation and a common relationship with God. All the differences which cause hostility between persons— race, culture, social status, education, sex—are no longer relevant. In the living church all believers can know a unity and harmony that is impossible for natural man, for it is based on a shared relationship with God.

This chapter suggests two ways in which the church can be "for the praise of his glory" (1:12). Chapter 2:1–11 suggests we demonstrate God's grace by good works; 2:12–23 suggests we demonstrate God's grace by unity. From these passages discover: What makes good works a demonstration of grace? What makes unity such a demonstration?

If good works and unity were given priority in your own life, what might you do differently? If good works and unity were given priority in local churches, how might church activities differ?

From Ephesians 1 and 2 develop two lists. On one show what God has done for believers. On the other show what we possess in him.

The Church

Originally the Greek word we translate "church" meant an assembly of citizens, called out to conduct public affairs. In the NT the word identifies all believers everywhere, as well as local groups of believers who come together as God's people. This sense of a "people called together" is important in the NT.

"Church" is never used in the Bible of a place or building. For the first 120 years of the Christian era there were in fact no "churches." Believers gathered in homes or out of doors or, in times of persecution, in caves. They did not construct buildings.

What is unique about the NT concept of "church" is that the word always focuses our attention on people: on believers who are called together to experience a unique relationship with God and each other.

Ephesians gives us three images to help us understand the church. The church as a body emphasizes our calling to be ministering to people, who continue Christ's ministry to others inside and outside the fellowship of believers. The church as a family emphasizes our calling to be a loving community, rich with supportive relationships in which individuals can grow to maturity. The church as temple emphasizes our calling to be a holy community, a beacon of light shining in a sin-darkened world.

How important that we view the church and our churches as God does, placing his priority on ministering to and loving our brothers and sisters. When we understand that the church is people, our commitment to Christ is given a very different focus from that of those who mistakenly see the church as buildings or programs or other constructions of mere men.

For study: see *The Body of Christ,* p. 646, *The Family of God,* p. 680.

Chapter 3. A Loving People

The Church As Mystery; 3:1–13. Four times in these verses Paul speaks of the church as a "mystery." In the NT this word does not refer to the unknowable or to the kind of secret knowledge claimed by religious cults. Instead "mystery" in Scripture designates information communicated by revelation from God. Paul's emphasis in this passage is on the fact that the church, as the living body of Christ in which all believers are united, is a completely new revelation "which for ages past was kept hidden in God, who created all things" (9). Thus we cannot learn about the church by looking into the OT. We must understand the church from the NT alone.

This new revelation is a stunning expression of the "manifold wisdom of God." The idea behind "manifold" is "complex, many-faceted." God's plan was more complex than was revealed in OT times, although the church was always a part of his eternal purpose (10,11). For all angelic beings the church is an amazing surprise (10): for us the new relationship with God experienced by members of the church is direct access to the Lord "with freedom and confidence" (12). The intimacy of our shared relationship with God is his jolting surprise!

The Church As Family; 3:14–19. It is our intimate relationship with God which gives us our identity (from which we "derive our name"). He is Father, so we who are in relationship with him must be family (14,15). Paul prays that we will experience all this relationship offers. He prays that we may be strengthened within by the Spirit as a dwelling place for Christ (17). He is convinced that as we are rooted and grounded in love for each other we will, "together with all the saints," grasp the extent of Jesus' love. Experiencing that love, we are "filled to the measure of all the fullness of God" (17–19). As we live together as family, loving one another as Christ loved us, we will grow together toward all that it means to be a Christian.

God's Work Within; 3:20,21. Living and loving each other as family is our heritage in Christ. But it is only possible because God is able to do immeasurably more than we can imagine, "according to his power that is at work within us."

Have you experienced this "family" identity with other Christians? How can you be "family" to others who may need to be grounded in a growing relationship of love?

The Family of God

One of the most beautiful images of the church seen in Ephesians and other NT epistles is that of a loving family, over which God is Father. Whenever this particular image is used, the emphasis of the passage is on the quality of relationships which are to exist within the Christian community.

The family into which a child is born is intended by God to provide a context in which he or she can mature. Thus the family has always been recognized as critical in the growth and development of persons. In the same way, a person who is born again is intended by God to have a place in God's extended family, the church. Loved and supported by others who really care, the individual matures in Christian faith.

When we see the church as people rather than an institution, we can begin to sense the importance of belonging. And we can grasp the vital necessity of building close and warm relationships with other believers. For healthy spiritual growth requires a rooting and establishment in love, spoken in Ephesians 3, which enables us to experience "together with all the saints" Christ's incomprehensible love. Christ's love, the greatest of all stimulants to growth, is communicated as Jesus loves us through one another.

For study: Ephesians 3:14–18; Colossians 3:12–17; 1 Thessalonians 2:7–12.

Chapter 4:1–17. A Ministering People

Live in Unity; 4:1–6. Ephesians has stressed the fact of Christian unity. Now Paul urges the believers who read his letter to live together in a way that is worthy of their calling. It is humility, patience, and a love that is willing to put up with others that make the experience of unity possible. The body *is* one. We are to "make every effort to keep the unity" by our relationships with others.

Serve in Unity; 4:7–16. Unity is vital as the context of ministry. In Jesus' resurrection he distributed gifts to all believers (see *Spiritual Gifts,* p. 623). Leaders were placed in the body to "prepare God's people for works of service" (12). Like every cell in a living organism, every believer in the body of Christ has a contribution to make. It is by the contribution of each that we "all reach unity in the faith . . . and become mature, attaining the whole measure of the fullness of God" (13). The relational climate of loving honesty (15) is vital for our shared ministry to each other, for the body will "grow and build itself up in love, as each part does its work" (16).

This is one of the most significant passages in the NT. It helps us understand what it means for you and me to be one of God's people. We have been chosen by God, given his life, and equipped for good works. We have been united with others in a church that is body and family—a context for intimate and loving relationships. And each one of us is called and gifted to build up our brothers and sisters in Christ. There is no laity/clergy division in the Bible's vision of the church of Jesus Christ. Each one of us is important. Each of us gifted. Each of us can serve.

How is the importance of each individual as a ministering person expressed in your local congregation? How is the unity of the Spirit expressed through your interpersonal relationships?

Chapter 4:17–5:20. A Christlike People

This section contains an exposition of one of the most amazing of the NT's teaching. As members of the body of Christ, the living church of which he is the head, believers are the present incarnation of Jesus in our world. It is in and through us that Jesus continues to love, heal, and communicate the good news to others. This has been called the "practical" section of Ephesians. Actually it is one of the most significant theologically. Here God shows us that we are called to be, individually and collectively, the living expression of Jesus himself.

The New Self; 4:17–25. Ephesians 2 portrays believers as those once dead who have been raised to life in Christ. Now Paul calls on the Ephesians to abandon the sensuality and impurity that marked their lives ("put off the old self") and to take an entirely new approach to living. Taking their lead from Christ, these believers are to "put on the new self, created to be like God in true righteousness and holiness" (24, cf. *Old Man/New Man,* p. 614). To represent Jesus we must be like him in our commitment to righteousness.

The New Relationships; 4:25–5:2. We are to be "imitators of God . . . as dearly loved children, and live a life of love." Thus we will live a life like that of Jesus (5:1,2). Paul describes the relationships that Christians have with others in the church. He places great stress on "speaking truthfully" to our neighbors (4:25). This is not truth in contrast to lies, but truth as living honestly with others, not trying to deceive them about ourselves. Even anger is to be dealt with honestly, by going to a brother and working out the conflict before it leads to sin—and that before the sun goes down! (4:26, see Matt. 5:21–24). In our fellowship, bitterness and malice are to be replaced with kindness, compassion and forgiveness "just as in Christ God forgave you" (4:32). If we are like Christ in our relationships with others, the church will truly become a community of love!

The New Life Style; 5:3–20. Like Christ, we are to be filled with the Spirit and live as "children of the light" (18,8). Paul's emphasis here is on holiness, which is vital—for we represent Jesus. Those things which are unlike him are "improper for God's holy people" (3–5). In fact, our lives, marked by goodness, righteousness, and truth, will expose the "fruitless deeds of darkness." Paul's point is that as we live a Christlike life, the great contrast between good and evil, light and darkness, will clearly reveal sin for what it is (11–14).

How can we help each other grow toward this incarnational life style to which we are called? Paul concludes with a call for believers to help each other focus their lives on Jesus and as a worshiping community deepen our shared relationship with him (19,20).

List each way suggested in these chapters that Christians can be like Christ, and so communicate him to others. What would be the most convincing quality of a community of Christlike people that might communicate Jesus to the world around us?

Maturity

The word translated "mature" or "adult" in our NT is a Greek word associated with reaching a goal. In the context of human development the image is of a person living as God intended: one who is mature for his age in Christ. Maturity should not be confused with perfection. The ultimate goal toward which we are moving, full likeness to Jesus, will be reached only when Christ returns (cf. 1 John 3:2).

Several exciting concepts are linked with maturity. Our life really does have a goal! We are to move toward likeness to Jesus, experiencing more and more of what it means to share our Lord's thoughts, values, and emotions, (cf. 2 Cor. 3:18; Gal. 4:19; Eph. 4:22–24; Col. 3:10).

Our life can be one of constant growth. Maturity is something that comes gradually and is gained through experience (cf. Heb. 5:14). We may know enough so that just hearing Christian truths is no longer exciting. But because we can grow more and more toward Christ's likeness, there is always a fresh newness to the life that lies ahead.

And, since our faith is about Jesus, and about growing more like him, there is real purpose to coming together with others. Ephesians makes it clear that growing toward maturity is something Christians do *together*. When we build warm and loving familylike relationships with other believers, and when we actively serve or minister to each other, we are helping each other grow toward that maturity promised to each of us in Christ.

Chapter 5:21–6:9. A Submissive People

On earth Jesus lived humbly, submitting to the will of God and the restraints of his society. Paul now explores a variety of relationships within which Christians live, within which we are to "submit to one another out of reverence to Christ" (5:21). Whether slave or free, each relationship gives us an opportunity to serve. As we serve others we incarnate the servant attitude of Christ (cf. Phil. 2:5–8).

Husbands and Wives; 5:21–33. This passage suggests that husbands serve their wives by taking the lead in loving, and wives serve their husbands by taking the lead in submission. Each concept is important for us to understand.

The husband's ministry to the wife is modeled by Christ, who as head of the church "gave himself up for her, to make her holy." The image is one of selfless giving and seeking what promotes the growth of the body in holiness. Applied to marriage, the husband exercises his headship when he acts toward his wife as Christ acts toward the church. To be head, he is to give himself up for her, put her needs first, and seek always to help her mature as a Christian person. There is no hint here of the distorted "chain of command" concept which views headship as power, and insists man is master.

The wife's ministry to the husband is modeled by the church, which is submissive to Christ. The word "submission" is a beautiful one in the NT. When applied to Christian interpersonal relationship it speaks of "voluntary yielding in love." We are responsive to Jesus because we know how greatly he loves us. In the marriage relationship, the wife is called on to take the lead in submissiveness, not by mindless or grudging obedience, but as a special ministry to her husband.

What does "the husband is head of the home" mean to most people? What in this passage helps give "head" a distinctly Christian meaning? What can be done in your relationship with your spouse to serve him or her as this passage suggests?

Parents and Children; 6:1–4. Children model Christlikeness by honoring and obeying parents (cf. Luke 2:51,52). Parents model Christlikeness by using Christian discipline (cf. Heb. 12:5–12). There is no thought here of "make your children obey." Instead the emphasis is to use Christian principles of relationship so parents do not overcontrol ("exasperate") their children.

Slaves and Masters; 6:5–9. Slavery was a fact of life in the first century world. The NT does not call for a social revolution, nor does it justify slavery. Instead each believer is called to see his state in life as an opportunity to serve. Christian masters can serve and treat their slaves with respect. Christian slaves can view their bondage as an opportunity to do good (6:8). Whether one is "superior" or "subordinate," every relationship provides opportunities to serve.

Parallel passages which develop this concept are shown on the chart.

Submission As Serving in the NT

Relationship	Ephesians	Colossians	1 Peter
Husband/Wife	*5:22–33*	*3:18–19*	*3:1–7*
Parent/Child	*6:1–4*	*3:20–21*	
Master/Slave	*6:5–9*	*3:22–4:1*	*2:18–21*

Think about relationships in which you are subordinate. What opportunities does each give you to do good, and thus serve others? Think about relationships in which you are superior. How do these give you opportunities to serve?

Headship

The NT uses the word "head" some 75 times. In most cases it refers to the literal head of a person or animal. At times "head" is used to show the mystical or hierarchical relationship between Christ and the church which is his body. At times the term describes human relationships (Eph. 5:21–33; 1 Cor. 11:2–15).

Like many other Bible terms, the concept of headship has been warped by importing secular notions. To call someone head of a corporation or project identifies him as a person with control over others. But the NT term is not used in this sense. Instead the biblical emphasis is on the head as "source" or "origin." Thus Jesus, as "head over everything for the church" (Eph. 1:22) is seen as source and sustainer of the life of his body. As "the Head . . . from him the whole body, joined and held together by every supporting ligament, grows and builds itself up in love" (Eph. 4:15,16), Jesus is the harmonizer of the body, who blends each member into relationships with others in which he or she can best love and serve. Headship does not speak of power but of serving!

This is particularly important for an understanding of what the Bible teaches about husband/wife relationships (see Eph. 5:25–33). Men are not given control over the lives of their wives. Rather they are given the privilege of taking the lead in serving and giving themselves for the benefit of the wife, just as Christ as Head loved and gave himself for the church.

To know that Christ is our living Head is to receive his promise of constant support and sustenance. To speak of headship in the family is intended to communicate that same promise of selfless love, offered by the husband to his wife.

Chapter 6:10–20. A Strong People

Ephesians closes with an exhortation to "be strong in the Lord and in his mighty power" (10). We are a people called to spiritual warfare, and like Paul we are to fearlessly declare God's gospel (19,20). God has equipped us with every resource needed (12). Each item of armor that Paul lists is best understood in the context of his teaching in Ephesians, about our life together as the living Church.

The belt of truth is that openness and honesty which enable us to experience our unity as members of one body (4:25).

The breastplate of righteousness is the holy life style to which we are to be committed (5:3).

Feet fitted with the gospel of peace speaks of that harmony which maintains the unity which has been created by the Spirit (4:3).

The shield of faith is our confidence in our God who "is able to do immeasurably more than all we ask or imagine, according to his power that is at work in us" (3:20).

The helmet of salvation is an understanding of the new identity that salvation has brought us, as family and as body of the living Christ.

The Spirit's sword is identified for us as "the Word of God" (6:17). Why is this piece of equipment alone identified in the passage? Because it alone has not been discussed in Ephesians, as have each of the others.

Fully equipped, believers who make up the church can glorify the God who has chosen us to find new life in him.

PHILIPPIANS
The Sharing of Christian Joy

This brief NT epistle is a warm personal letter to believers in the church at Philippi. In it Paul explains no great doctrine but rather shares the sources of joy that sustain him. He is writing from prison to close friends who are deeply concerned about him.

Date and Author. The writer is the apostle Paul. He writes from Rome in early A.D. 63.

Background. Philippi is identified by Luke as "a Roman colony and the leading city of Macedonia" (Acts 16:12). The city had a famous medical school which Luke probably attended. The first convert in Europe, Lydia, was won to Christ in Philippi, and a small Christian community was established there.

Paul maintained a deep affection for the believers at Philippi. They kept in contact through messengers from Philippi, like Epaphroditus, and Timothy was sent there at times to minister and report to the apostle. This letter was stimulated by simple friendship, not a need to communicate some corrective or instructive truth.

Structure. As a personal letter, Philippians shows no tight or logical structure. Thus it is less important to outline than other letters which contain a definite logical argument (flow of thought).

Values. Two themes found in Philippians are particularly helpful. Paul speaks constantly of joy and rejoicing, even though he is in prison and in danger of execution. What is the source of joy for Paul, and for us, when we have none of those things the world believes necessary for happiness? Paul also includes in 2:5–11 a great hymn or confession of the early church affirming the deity and exaltation of Jesus.

Chapter 1. Joy in the Gospel

Thanksgiving and Prayer; 1:2–11. Paul's first words quickly set the tone of warmth. "I have you in my heart," he tells these believers who have been his partners "in the gospel from the first day until now" (4–7). He prays that they may abound in love, and have the insight to know "what is best" that they may "be pure and blameless until the day of Christ" (10).

Paul's Imprisonment; 1:12–30. Paul wants his friends to see his imprisonment as a good thing, for it has advanced the gospel.

His witness has been heard through the "whole palace guard" (the Praetorian guard, which were the Emperor's personal troops). According to 4:22, even members of Caesar's household had become believers! In addition, others have been stimulated to greater zeal in evangelism through Paul's imprisonment. Some are apparently motivated by personal ambition or rivalry, but the important thing is the gospel being preached, and this leads the apostle to rejoice.

What do you learn about joy from Philippians 1? How is joy different from happiness? What would you say Paul's motives and his values have to do with the experience of joy?

Chapter 2. Joy in Following Jesus

Christlike Attitudes; 2:1–11. Paul exhorts his friends to increase his joy by "being like-minded, having the same love, being one in spirit and purpose" (2). This is possible only by adopting the attitude Jesus displayed in "making himself nothing" to take on human nature and then humbling himself further to die on the cross (3–8). The humility was the doorway to exaltation for Jesus (9–11) and the way to fulfillment for believers.

This early church hymn or confession of faith (6–11) is called the *kenosis* (self-emptying) passage by theologians and is one of the clearest biblical statements of the full deity of Jesus (see *Incarnation/Is Jesus God?* p. 542).

God at Work; 2:12–18. Paul's encouragement to "work out your salvation with fear and trembling" is a reference to present tense salvation: that is, to meet each situation in a way that expresses the new life God has given us (see *Salvation,* p. 574). This is possible only because "it is God who works in you to will and to act according to his good purpose" (11–13). As believers remain committed to a Christlike life style, Paul has evidence that his life has not been lived in vain (14–18).

Epaphroditus; 2:19–30. This is a personal note about a messenger from the Philippians who has become ill and almost died. Paul commends him: "Welcome him in the Lord with great joy, and honor men like him."

In what relationships do you find it difficult to maintain the attitudes described in chapter 2? How is 2:12,13 significant to you in these relationships?

Chapter 3. Joy through Commitment

To a Resurrection Life Style; 3:1–11. Paul warns against Judaizers who want to introduce Jewish Law and life style as a basis for

Christian living (see *Galatians*, esp. p. 661, 665). Paul considers the things in which legalists take pride to be rubbish (8), for he has found a dynamic power for righteous living which comes through faith in Christ (9–11). Paul's reference to "attain(ing) to the resurrection from the dead" expresses his desire to experience the resurrection power of Jesus in his present life, not doubt about his eventual salvation (cf. Rom. 8:11).

To a Meaningful Goal; 3:12–4:1. Paul focuses his efforts, to "take hold of that for which Christ Jesus took hold of me." His goal is to be obedient to God's will and accomplish it daily (12–14). Each of us has a similar calling, and maturity involves commitment to doing God's will, thus finding meaning and purpose in our life (15,16). This goal-oriented living is contrasted with that of those whose mind is "on earthly things" (19). All who look eagerly and expectantly for Jesus to return will never be deceived by empty earthly values.

What goals are you committed to in your life? What, using Paul's criteria in this chapter, would characterize "mature" goals?

Chapter 4. Joy in the Lord

A Plea for Perspective; 4:2–9. Paul speaks of joys that are found through relationship with the Lord (4). In Christ we have release from anxiety, for we can express every need to God and experience peace (5–7). In Christ we can concentrate our attention on the true, noble, right, pure, lovely, admirable, and praiseworthy (8). In Christ we can put godly living into practice, and have the assurance that the God whose presence means inner peace will be with us (9).

What a wonderful perspective to maintain on life, and what a source of constant joy!

An Expression of Thanks; 4:10–23. Paul concludes by thanking the Philippians for a contribution they had made for his support. What he most appreciates is the love and willingness to share that the gift expresses. Paul has learned that, whatever his finances or situation, "I can do everything through him who gives me strength."

This short chapter is filled with rich promises which are ours through our relationship with the Lord. Which have become reality in our own life? Which do you want most to experience now?

COLOSSIANS
Fulfillment in Christ

Colossians is a brief but significant letter. It was written to combat false teachings which were beginning to corrupt the churches of Asia. Many concepts that marked that false system are no longer a threat to Christianity. But the basic issue raised in Colossae is still vitally important to believers. That issue is, How can we experience a truly fulfilling Christian life? The answer is given to us by Paul in this great exposition of the life that is ours, to be lived in Christ.

Date and Author. Paul the apostle is the author of this letter. Like Ephesians, it was written while he was in prison in Rome, and sent in A.D. 62 or 63.

Colossae. The city lay inland from Ephesus, on the main road east at the junction of highways to Sardis and Pergamum. The city had a large and cosmopolitan population, which included many Jewish settlers. The threat to the church lay in a syncretistic approach to faith, which intruded ideas drawn from Judaism, from pagan philosophy, and from the mystery religions. These were used to interpret and distort foundational Christian doctrines.

Background. Most believe that this letter was written to combat concepts that later grew into a heretical movement known as Gnosticism. That name comes from the Greek word for knowledge, *gnosis,* for the cult claimed to possess a special, secret knowledge not available to simple Christians. Only through their secret knowledge could a person enter into the full experience of spiritual reality.

We know of this developed Gnosticism from the writings of two second century church fathers, Irenaeus and Tertullian, who argued against it. We clearly see its echo in many key Gnostic words and phrases used by Paul in Colossians (such as "fullness"). Thus an understanding of what the Gnostics believed helps us grasp the full impact of the powerful truths about Jesus, and about life in Christ, which fill this great, Christ-centered epistle.

We can summarize Gnostic beliefs by noting their answers to three questions: What is God like? How do we gain access to him? And, How can we experience the fullness of life which relationship with God must promise?

What is God like? The Gnostics saw everything categorized under two opposing principles. There was good, which they associated with the spiritual, or immaterial. There was evil, which they associated with the material universe. In this system God, to be good, must be "spiritual" and have no contact with the material. To God the pure spirit, this world would be alien and contaminating. No wonder the Gnostics rejected incarnation: God would never become man, or step into man's world. Thus Christ must either be a lower being, or perhaps a shadow image cast on some screen.

This perspective also determined the Gnostic's view of mankind. Human beings contain some spark of the divine, but this is trapped in our bodily form. Salvation involves release of the inner person from the material prison, and thus bodily resurrection was repelling.

How does a person gain access to God? Because of God's great distance from the universe, the Gnostics believed that God must be approached through a series of angelic intermediaries, each more distant and more spiritual than the other. If Christ were supernatural, he must have been of a lower order because he had contact with the world.

Most Gnostics believed that these powerful intermediary spirits held the destiny of individuals in their hands. Thus worship of angels, or rituals designed to placate them, had an important place.

How does a human being have a fulfilling life? The answer again was found in the Gnostic's basic dualism. Since the inner man is good, and the physical is evil, spirituality must be a matter of knowledge alone. Life in the body could be ignored, or else perhaps the evil physical shell could be controlled by ritual, asceticism, abstinence, and rigid regulation of life.

These ideas, summarized on the chart below, are all challenged in Colossians. There we read of an entirely different view of true spirituality and the fulfilling life.

The Gnostic Way	God's Way in Christ
Christ: low intermediary	Colossians 1:15–23; 2:9–12
Man: divine spark in evil body	Colossians 1:21–22
Salvation: release from body	
Way of Salvation: through special knowledge, asceticism	Colossians 1:9–13
Morality: ascetic self-denial of needs and desires	Colossians 3:1–14,18–25
True religion: subjective, speculative, intellectual	Colossians 1:9–13
Angels: powers bridging gap between man and God	Colossians 1:19–20

Value Today. Today, too, many Christians are eager for a fulfilling Christian experience. Some seek fulfillment through an ecstatic experience, some through knowledge of the Bible or a system of interpretation, some through discipline or ritual observance or ascetic self-denial. But the unmasked secret of spirituality is shared in Colossians. Here we see that Jesus is the center of the believer's spiritual life. True spirituality means simply to meet the common events of our life with that servant attitude lived out by Jesus before us.

Structure and Outline. The questions supposedly answered by gnostic teaching give us the framework for outlining Colossians. Here Paul explains clearly what God is like and explains his relationship with the material world. Paul shows how believers approach God and enter his presence. And Paul explains the life that believers are to live to find fulfillment as Christians. The following outline of Colossians traces this structure.

Outline

Before Reading. Here are several questions answered in Colossians. Which of them is important to you? Read Colossians for the answers. How can I find spiritual fulfillment? Why won't asceticism or legalism help me grow spiritually? What is the process by which we grow to spiritual maturity? How can I experience Christ's fullness in my life?

Chapter 1. Christ, the Full Expression of God

The Fruitful Gospel; 1:3–7. Paul begins with an expression of thankfulness for the faith and love of the Colossians (4). Paul notes that these "spring from" two sources: the "hope stored up for you in heaven" and the gospel message (5). In the NT "hope" speaks of confident expectation and of a patient, disciplined waiting for fulfillment which spurs believers on to holy living (1 John 3:3; Heb. 12:14). It is disciplined and expectant waiting for fulfillment that has produced fruit among them, and "all over the world this gospel is producing fruit and growing" (6). There is no reason for these believers to abandon the simple gospel and dabble in Gnosticism, hoping for immediate fulfillment. The simple gospel is already producing results in their life.

The Growth Process; 1:9–14. Paul's prayer for these believers who are so eager for spiritual fulfillment unveils the process of Christian growth. Christians have been rescued from the "dominion of darkness and brought into the kingdom of the Son" (13). Jesus has redeemed and forgiven sins (14), thus qualifying believers "to share in the inheritance of the saints in the kingdom of life" (12). This is just the inheritance the Colossians so eagerly sought! Paul's prayer shows how to enter our inheritance, and how to know God in a deeply personal way.

The Growth Process

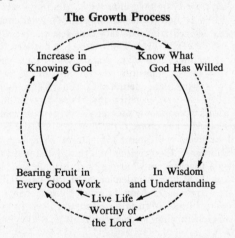

The growth process begins with a knowledge of what God has willed (9): that is, the content of revelation. Unlike the speculative, abstract theories that so fascinated the Gnostics, such knowledge is to be held in "all wisdom and understanding" (9). These terms focus attention on application of knowledge: God's revelation is to be used to guide daily life in the present, material world (see *Wisdom,* p. 632)! By acting on truth we "live a life worthy of the Lord and please him in every way" (10). So too we "bear fruit in every good work." This kind of life has a vital, experiential impact on our relationship with God. As we do God's will, we come to know him better in a personal way.

This approach to spirituality is diametrically opposed to the things taught by the false teachers in Colossae. Paul says that spirituality is necessarily linked with life in the world, thus fusing the material and the divine. What's more, this kind of life requires "great endurance and patience." But God has promised us the power, "according to his glorious might" (11), to live a truly spiritual daily life.

God in the Flesh; 1:15–23. Paul has shown that spirituality links the divine and the material, as God's Word is practiced in daily life (1:9–11). Now he affirms that Jesus is God come in the flesh, destroying forever the structure of dualism erected by the Gnostics.

Paul calls Jesus the "image of the invisible God" (15). In Greek thought "image" shares in the reality of what it portrays. The Colossians understood Paul to mean that Jesus perfectly represents God, for he is God. In the same way, "firstborn" (15) does not imply a created being. It affirms superiority over creation. That superiority is derived from the fact that Jesus created "all things in heaven and on earth" (16). There is no gap between the spiritual and material realms. Jesus takes responsibility for creation of the material world and is supreme over the immaterial as well. With stroke after stroke, Paul demolishes the philosophic structure erected by the Gnostics, crushing their false concept of the nature of God. Jesus is preeminent, not some lower-order being (17). He is head of his body, the church: the first to know the bodily resurrection all believers will share (18). Jesus is in fact the one in whom the fullness of God resides. All things material and immaterial are drawn together and harmonized through the blood which God the Son shed on a wooden cross in this material world the Gnostics so despise (20). Man is not a "good" being, locked in an evil prison of flesh. Man is a sinner, alienated from God, and an enemy of God through wicked thoughts as well as evil behavior (21).

The capstone of Paul's presentation is in verse 22. God has acted to bring sinful man into harmony with himself, not through some secret knowledge that frees the inner, intellectual man, but "by Christ's physical body through death."

This then is the God who promises salvation in the gospel. This is the God to whom the Colossians must hold fast. And it is this God, who was unashamed to suffer in the material universe, who calls us to live a blameless life in that same world.

Paul's Ministry; 1:24–29. In his body, the church, Jesus is still active in this world. As servant of the church, Paul is commissioned to "present to you the word of God in its fullness." There is nothing hidden within the gospel. Instead the gospel is God's disclosure "to the saints" of what was once unknown, but is now openly revealed. Paul shares the heart of the gospel: it is "Christ in you." It is Christ within the life of the believer who brings "hope for all the glorious things to come" (27, Phillips *Letters to Young Churches*). By focusing on Jesus, and by teaching the meaning of life in him, Paul is committed to help these Colossians, so eager for the fullness of life, to become "perfect" (mature: see *Maturity*, p. 682).

What is the most important thing you learn about Jesus in this passage? What does it mean to you?

Chapter 2. Christ, The Way to God

Fullness; 2:1–7. Paul again affirms that the "full riches of complete understanding" are contained in the simple gospel, all ours now in Christ (2). All the "treasures of wisdom and knowledge" (3) are found in Jesus. Paul here uses the language of the Gnostics, challenging their empty promises of "complete understanding" of "mystery" and of "hidden treasures of knowledge." Every fine-sounding argument of these false teachers is empty and deceitful (4,5). The reality is Christ, and Christ has come to dwell within us.

Paul expresses confidence in the firm faith of the Colossians (5). He urges them to continue to live in Christ, "strengthened in the faith as you were taught" (6,7). In the next chapter Paul will review his teaching on how to live in Christ. But now he evaluates the principles that underlie the two contrasting ways offered by Christianity and by Gnosticism.

"In Christ"; 2:8–15. The gnostic concepts are an amalgam of "hollow and deceptive philosophy" which rests on "human tradition and the basic principles of this world" (8). In fact, every element of the gnostic system can be traced to pagan philosophers and religions.

In contrast, Christ himself, "the fullness of the deity in bodily form" (9) is the one on whom all experience of Christian faith rests. The phrase "in Christ" has been called the "mystical dative." This grammatical construction was never used by the Greeks prior to the NT. It indicates a unique personal relationship, so close that it involves full union with Jesus. Jesus is the fullness of God: through our new relationship "in Christ," we now possess all that God is! How tragic that some in Colossae turned away from the source of spiritual fulfillment, to seek God in the empty speculations of mere man.

What does union with Christ mean for us? Union offers no ritual relationship, symbolized by circumcising the flesh. Instead we are offered inner transformation: a putting off (literally, "put off and lay aside") of the sinful nature, and lifting up to a new life won for us by Jesus' resurrection (11–12: see *Old Man/New Man,* p. 614).

The new life given us in Christ is the key to our experience of God, not the "written code, with its regulations" on which some rely (13). All such things have been set aside by Jesus, for it was opposed to our search for God, not an aid (see *Law, NT.* p. 617). Now everything and everyone that claimed authority over humanity has been "disarmed." Christ's cross has shown all such things to be empty and powerless. It has thus made a "public spectacle" of them (14,15).

Emptiness; 2:16–23. Paul insists that life's fullness is found through relationship with Jesus. Christians must permit no one to impose empty religious practices or restrictions, which will only distract them from the Lord. Some of the practices of early and later Gnosticism are listed here. They include special diets and days of religious observance (16,17) and the worship of angels, who were supposed to serve as intermediaries between man and God (18). Such things may seem to express humility by suggesting one is not worthy of approaching God directly. But in fact this denies our connection with Christ. We are already linked to him as members of his body, and he is the one who supports and guides our growth (19,20).

Paul looks over the regulations suggested by the early Gnostics for spiritual discipline. Most demand asceticism, or self-denial (21). But those are totally worthless. God never asked for ascetic restrictions. They are based on human commands and teachings (22). Despite any appearance of wisdom such things may convey, "they lack any value in restraining sensual indulgence" (23). This is surprising only if "sensual indulgence" is taken to be gross acts of sin. As soon as a biblical perspective is adopted, and "lust, evil desires, and greed" along with "rage and malice" are understood to belong to the earthly nature (3:5–8), we can see how a person who is rigidly ascetic may still rage with uncontrolled desires. It is not the appearance of holiness that God promises us in Christ. It is holiness itself, as our personalities are transformed by his presence.

How have you been seeking to grow as a Christian? What clues do you find in Colossians 1:19–11 to help you better understand the process God has called you to follow?

📖 Paul calls the religious practices of the early Gnostics useless,
based on "principles of this world." What notions held today
would you put in the same category? Why?

Chapter 3. Christ, The Pattern for a Fulfilling Life

One Focus Only; 3:1–4. Paul speaks of our lives as hidden with
God in Christ. The source of fulfilling Christian experience is in
heaven, not in "earthly things" (2). That which seemed to offer
so much to the Gnostics is worthless to Christians. In contrast
we are to fix our attention on "the things above" where Christ
sits at the right hand of God, his very position showing his authority
(1).

There is another sense in which our lives are hidden with God.
The full glory of relationship with Jesus will only be understood
when Christ appears. Then we will appear with him in glory (4).
Until then the glory of the Christian life may continue to be misunderstood by those who, puzzled, look on and insist there must
be "something more."

The Glory of Love; 3:5–14. The glorious promise of Christian
life is expressed in the fact that we can now "put to death" what
belongs to our earthly nature (5). This is explained in Romans
6:1–14 and involves counting our death with Christ as a reality.
This frees us to conduct our lives without the old sinful responses
of immorality, greed, anger, slander, and other evils (5–8). Now
a whole new way of life is possible. We have actually been given
a new self, and our new personality is in the process of a renewal
which will express "the image of its Creator" (10). The picture
is striking. In us Christ still lives in man's dark world! It is Christ
in us, not the religious notions drawn from Jewish and pagan cultures (11), that is the key to a fulfilling life.

What is a truly spiritual life like? It is simply a daily walk in
which we forgive others as the Lord forgave us; in which we are
compassionate, kind, humble, gentle, and patient (12–14). It is
simply living with others the kind of life that Jesus lived when
he walked on earth, and thus to reveal the loving and holy character
of our God. Fulfillment and spiritual reality are not found in the
exciting and the spectacular. What counts with God is a life of
love lived in the real world. This is the life that Jesus yearns to
live within us.

The Glory of Shared Worship; 3:15–17. Because so much of our
life in Christ and its glory is hidden, we need to come together
as God's people. Together we reaffirm the great truths of our faith,

encourage each other in holy living, and praise God in prayer and song. The uneasy sense of need for something more fades as we worship and together focus our lives on the Lord. Here we experience Jesus, wrapping our hearts in peace.

The Glory of Servanthood; 3:18–4:1. As in Ephesians, Paul now looks at the most significant of human interpersonal relationships. These are significant because they are both basic and common. In each relationship we are to concentrate on serving others as a context in which we can live out Christ's love (cf. p. 679).

From chapter 3, how might you define "true spirituality"? In what ways is the pathway which Paul here describes to a fulfilling Christian life superior to the pathways suggested by the early Gnostic?

Chapter 4. Personal Notes

Paul concludes with encouragement and personal notes. He wants the believers in Colossae to pray for him as he shares the message of Christ (2–6). He introduces Tychicus, who is to carry the letter and bring along Onesimus (7–9, cf. also p. 738). Paul sends greetings from others with him who are also deeply concerned for the welfare of the believers in Colossae (10–15). Finally Paul instructs the church to share his letter with others in the area. The whole church in NT times, like the church today, needs to be constantly reminded of the simplicity, the beauty, and the life-changing power that is ours in the gospel of Jesus Christ, our Lord.

1 THESSALONIANS
The Hope of His Coming

This brief letter is one of Paul's earliest epistles and the only NT book to speak of Jesus' return in each chapter (1:10; 2:19; 3:13; 4:13–18; 5:1–11,23). The letter, however, is not tightly reasoned teaching. It is a warm reminder of truths already known and an exhortation to live blameless lives while looking expectantly for the Lord to come again.

Date and Author. Paul wrote this letter to the Thessalonians in the early 50s, probably in A.D. 51 or 52.

Thessalonica. This city was capital of the Roman province of Macedonia and site of a great Mediterranean naval base. Its location made it a prosperous commercial center. These characteristics made it an important focus for missionary activity, and it was reached early on Paul's second missionary journey. Paul and his team spent only a short time there (estimates vary from three weeks to three months, cf. Acts 17:2). They were driven out by opposition organized by a hostile Jewish population. Still, the small Gentile congregation established in Thessalonica grew rapidly and spearheaded the sharing of the gospel throughout the whole province (1:8).

Occasion. Paul kept in close touch with all the churches he helped to establish. Members of his missionary team, such as Timothy (3:2,6), were sent to visit and encourage the new churches. This letter is written after a report brought by Timothy of one such visit. In the letter Paul touches on a number of matters. He particularly encourages the believers to a commitment to holy living and adds insights into the meaning of Christ's return for those who wait eagerly for him.

Outline

Before Reading. Here are several questions answered in 1 Thessalonians. Which of them is important to you? Read 1 Thessalonians for the answers. What indicates that the Word of God has been heard and received by a group of people? What kind of relationships

will help me communicate God's Word effectively? What difference
does the Second Coming make to me now? What are some specific
things God wants me to do?

Chapter 1. The Word Heard

Cause for Thanksgiving; 1:1–3. After a brief salutation (1), Paul
mentions three reasons why he thanks God whenever he thinks
of the Thessalonians (3): your "work produced by faith, your labor
prompted by love, and your endurance inspired by hope in our
Lord Jesus Christ." These three are often linked in Paul's writing
(cf. 1 Cor. 13:13; Col. 1:5). Each has a special function in Christian
experience. Faith, as daily trust in God, enables us as we do good
works. Only love can motivate us to serve. And hope, as confident
expectation of a glorious future, strengthens us to endure and keep
on serving despite discouragement and persecution.

Evidence of Response; 1:4–10. Paul points to more evidence for
his confidence that the Lord loves and has chosen these brothers.
The evidence is linked to their response to the Word. Paul traces
the progression: they heard the word (5), welcomed the message
with joy (6), and then the "message rang out from you" (8). A
similar progression is seen in the same verses. Paul brought the
message and lived a life in "imitation" of the Lord. The word
"imitate" means an example or a pattern to be followed. Paul
patterned his conduct on Christ (6); the Thessalonians learned
from Paul how to follow Jesus (6); then their own lives set an
example for the many in Macedonia and Achaia they won with
the gospel message (7).

Living a life patterned on Jesus meant a great change in the
lives of these believers. They turned to God from their idols. They
now lived to serve "the living and true God" while they waited
for his Son to come back from heaven (9,10). All this was in
spite of the persecution and suffering which their new faith brought
them! How clearly the lives of Jesus' followers reveal the power
of the Word of God and the message of the gospel.

What indications might show today that the Word of God
has been heard by an individual or congregation? What is
there in your own life that shows the gospel "came to you not
simply with words, but also with power, with the Holy Spirit and
with deep conviction" (1:5)?

Chapter 2, 3. The Word Shared

Paul has reviewed the impact of the word which reached the
Thessalonians. Now, in a significant passage, Paul reviews the rela-

tionship that grew up between him and these believers. This passage is important for us today. It helps us understand the climate of warm and loving interpersonal relationships in which the Word of God is best shared. To share the gospel effectively, and to build others up in the faith, we need to develop the kind of relationships described by Paul.

Transparency; 2:1–6. Paul writes about this theme in 2 Corinthians 3 (p. 652). He reminds the Thessalonians that they knew him well (5). There were no impure motives, no trickery (3), no flattery or hiding behind a mask to cover greed (5). There was not even a desire for praise from men (6). Instead Paul's motive, as one "entrusted with the gospel," was simply to please God. God does not focus on what men do for him, but on what is in their hearts (4).

Love; 2:7–12. Paul's life was transparent, so that God might approve all that was in his heart. What was there was clear: love. Paul selects the family as an illustration of the relationship which he had with the believers of Thessalonica. He was gentle, as a nursing mother caring for a tiny infant (7). That gentleness was an expression of love, as was the fact that Paul shared not only the gospel but himself, "because you had become so dear to us" (8). He keeps up the family image and reminds the believers that "we dealt with each of you as a father deals with his own (nearly grown) children." This means more than giving time to individuals ("each of you"). It means coming to know each individual so well that each can be given just the guidance, or encouragement, or urging needed to stimulate growth (12).

In all this ministry, Paul's goal was to see these children in Christ grow to maturity, enabling them to "live worthy of God, who calls you to his kingdom and glory."

Sharing the gospel with others is no impersonal, "say the words" kind of thing. Sharing the gospel effectively calls for bonds of love and open communication with those we serve, not because we seek praise from men, but because "we loved you so much!"

Thanksgiving; 2:13–20. Paul again speaks of the joy he has because of the Thessalonians' response to the gospel. They have recognized Paul's message as the Word of God (13) and patterned their life on Christ. Even the reaction of the unbelievers around them shows the pattern which emerged in Judea, as their own people persecuted them just as believing Jews were persecuted in Palestine. Even this suffering and opposition is something Paul takes as evidence of God's grace—and as proof that judgment will soon fall on those who "heap up their sins to the limit" (16).

Paul has longed intensely to see his dear brothers and sisters again. But he has been prevented (17–19). Still, nothing can keep them out of his thoughts and prayers, for a great surge of glory and joy will be his when he sees them, standing in Jesus' presence when He comes.

Search chapter 2 and carefully describe the relationship that existed between Paul and the Thessalonians. Include clues to how it was built. Compare and contrast the relational climate you see here with that between you and any persons to whom you witness.

Timothy's Visit; 3:1–12. Paul knows that these young believers are suffering persecution and strong opposition (2:14; 3:3–4,7). Paul's love for them is further demonstrated by his concern. Twice he shares that it was "when I could stand it no longer" (1,5) that he sent Timothy, a member of his missionary team, to encourage and strengthen the young Thessalonian church. Now Paul is filled with joy, for "Timothy has just now come to us from you" (6). Timothy told of their steadfastness and their affection for Paul. Paul loves these believers deeply. But he does not pray that their persecution might end. Instead he asks God that their intimate relationship of love, so vital to growth in holiness, might "increase and overflow" (12,13).

What is most important to you? Avoiding difficulties? Or having those who love you there to support and care? Why?

Chapter 4. Live to Please God

Holy Living; 4:1–12. Each of Paul's letters to a young congregation includes instructions on holy living. It's clear that teaching "how to live in order to please God" was a basic part of the early church's mission. Thus Paul reminds the Thessalonians, "you know what instructions we gave you by the authority of the Lord Jesus" (1,2).

Three areas are reviewed in this passage. The Thessalonians are to abstain from sexual immorality. The heathen may be driven by lust, but believers are to control their passions and are never to wrong or take advantage of another person. God's will is that we be holy, and it is not holy to surrender to sensuality (3–8).

They are also to continue to practice love for each other. Paul realizes they have already learned this lesson from God. Still "we urge you, brothers, to do so more and more" (9,10).

The third reminder comes when Paul urges these believers to a "quiet life" in which each person tends to his own business and does his own work. He wants them to fit unobtrusively into their society and culture. Holiness is expressed in the normal activities of daily life and in honest work. Paul's call is for believers to live as responsible and mature adults, fitting into their society. This kind of life will "win the respect" of non-Christians as well as develop personal responsibility (11–12).

The Lord's Return; 4:13–18. Paul uses the term "asleep" to describe death (13,14,15). He knows the bodies of believers will awaken when Jesus returns. This is something misunderstood by the Thessalonians. When friends and loved ones died, they grieved for them. Paul explains that the "dead in Christ" will be raised to join living believers and be caught up to greet Jesus. What a message of comfort for us today.

The Rapture

The event described in 1 Thessalonians 4:3–17 is called the "Rapture of the Church." It tells of the day when Jesus returns to earth. He comes down from heaven, the trumpet of God sounds its call, and the dead in Christ are raised. Then, along with living believers, the whole congregation is caught up in the clouds to meet the Lord in the air. The picture is clear, but it has stimulated much debate.

Just the Dead "in Christ"? The phrase "in Christ" is only found in the NT. It speaks of the special relationship believers now have as members of Jesus' body, united with him. Many believe that the saved of OT times have a different (not "better" or "worse," but "different") role in God's plan for the future than those believers who make up his body. So the first debate is over whether this is a special resurrection, just for those who have become believers since Jesus' incarnation, with resurrection for OT saints coming at a different time.

Pre, Mid, or Post? Closely related to the first debate is the question of whether the Rapture will come before, in the middle of, or after the "great tribulation." The Tribulation is a period of time spoken of in both testaments, believed from Daniel 9:24 to be seven years in length. Predictions in both testaments concerning the end of time, when God's plan comes to its fulfillment, focus on this Tribulation period. And so the question is raised. When will those in Christ be caught up to be with the Lord? Before this time of intense sufferings? In the middle of it? Or after the great Tribulation has passed?

Which position should we accept as correct? Before we join the prophetic debating society, it's helpful to note that the Bible itself does not fit future events into clearly defined sequences. Instead, wherever major future events are described there is a clear focus on the meaning of that teaching for the present life of the reader! The picture of the Rapture was drawn by Paul to console those whose loved ones have died, and who are grieving because they believe the dead have missed the blessing of meeting Jesus. But we will all welcome Jesus back! The believing dead will be caught up with us to meet Jesus and be with him forever. "Therefore," Paul says, "encourage each other with these words."

No doubt one school of prophetic interpretation is more correct. But

there is even less doubt that God shared this vision of the Rapture with
us to comfort us as we too mourn loved ones who have died. That comfort
is more important than which prophetic system is right.

For study: see *OT and NT Eschatology,* pp. 372, 489; and *Prophetic
Systems,* p. 812.

Chapter 5. Be Alert

A Sudden Coming; 5:1–3. Paul continues with the theme of Jesus'
return. Paul pictures the return as sudden and unexpected, and
thus imminent. No one knows when Jesus will return, but it might
be at any moment. That coming, which brings joy to believers,
will bring destruction to others.

Be Alert; 5:4–11. Jesus' coming means destruction of the dark
world system in which we now live. This fact provides believers
with a completely new perspective on life and motivates self-controlled commitment to a faithful and loving life style (4–8). When
our perspective ("mind") is shaped by the hope of salvation, we
understand that nothing in this world will survive the coming destruction, but we will "live together with him." Living now in
light rather than darkness, we recognize what is truly important
and can "encourage one another and build each other up" (9–
11).

Views of the prophetic future are to have an impact on present experience. Paul describes two events in 4:13–5:11: Jesus
will come to meet his saints, and Jesus will come to destroy the
wicked world in which we live. Check in this passage for ways
that Paul expects knowledge of these future events to affect Christians. How does conviction that these events are part of God's
plan for the future affect you?

Additional Instructions; 5:12–28. Paul urges love and respect
for leaders. The original word translated by the phrase "who are
over you" is better taken as "those who protect and care for"
rather than as those who preside over or lead (12,13). Paul is
concerned about the idle: they are to be warned and sent back
to work (see 2 Thess. 3:6–13). Paul again commends the Christian
life style he teaches in all the churches: helping the weak, patience,
thanksgiving in all circumstances, and responsiveness to the Spirit.

Paul closes with a typical expression of confidence. "May your
whole spirit, soul and body be kept blameless at the coming of
our Lord Jesus Christ. The one who calls you is faithful, and he
will do it" (23,24).

A view of modern Thessalonica

A close-up of a city gate in downtown Thessalonica

2 THESSALONIANS
The Day of the Lord

This short epistle is closely linked to Paul's first letter to the Thessalonians. It clarifies further the picture of the future Paul had taught them but about which they were still confused. The letter is meant to be strong encouragement to those who are now experiencing persecution for their faith in Christ. It is especially meaningful to all who undergo such sufferings.

Date and Author. Most believe this letter was written within three or four months of the first, giving us a date of A.D. 51 or 52.

Occasion. The growing persecution of the believers in Thessalonica led some to believe they were living in the troubled "day of the Lord" about which Paul and the OT taught. Paul writes to correct this misunderstanding and to instruct them in living under persecution.

Outline

Greetings		1:1,2
I.	Persecution and Judgment	1:3–12
II.	The Day of the Lord	2:1–17
III.	A Request and a Warning	3:1–15
	Final words	3:16–18

Before Reading. The question to ask before reading this book is, How do I respond to pressures or persecution? There is information here about the future that God has in store for us. But the emphasis of the book is on living for Jesus in troubled times.

Chapter 1. Persecution and Judgment

A Word of Praise; 1:3–4. Paul praises the Thessalonians for their perseverance in spite of "all the persecutions and trials you are enduring." In spite of everything, their faith and their love for each other are growing. The persecution Paul speaks of is local. It was initially stirred up by the Jewish population (Acts 17:5) but is continued by their own Gentile countrymen (I Thess. 2:14).

Judgment Sure; 1:5–10. Paul shares an important perspective on persecution. He notes first that faithfulness under persecution vindicates God's calling of these believers and thus "is evidence that God's judgment is right." Also faithfulness through suffering shows that these believers are worthy of their call into God's kingdom.

But Paul also wants the Thessalonians to know that God has not deserted them and is not ignoring them in their trials. "God is just," Paul says, and will "pay back trouble to those who trouble you and give relief to you who are troubled." What is important here is God's timing. "This will happen when the Lord Jesus is revealed from heaven in blazing fire with his powerful angels" (7). God does not promise to remove the pressures, or to punish evil-doers now!

This does not mean that God never acts as judge as history moves toward the end of time. He does (see *Judgment of the Wicked,* p. 322). But we have no basis to demand that God act now, when we suffer. Instead, we are to hold fast to the vision of a just and holy God. All human experience will be put in sure perspective when Jesus returns. Then there will be punishment for the wicked (7–9) and great blessing for God's people (10).

Paul's Prayer; 1:11,12. The long-range perspective Paul holds now shapes his prayers for the Thessalonians. The apostle does not ask God to relax the pressures. Instead he asks that the believers might be found worthy of their calling. He asks God to empower them, enabling them to fulfill the good purposes he has in mind for them in their tribulations. It is by living for the Lord *in* tribulations that "the name of our Lord Jesus" will be glorified. Through suffering we will find glory waiting for us when Jesus comes.

How have you looked at your own times of trouble or persecution? From this chapter list five things that suggest how Paul might evaluate your situation. How does this chapter help you face the prospect of future suffering?

Chapter 2. The Day of the Lord

This chapter builds on an OT prophetic framework and features an OT phrase ("the day of the Lord"), which tells readers of the older testament that the prophets are speaking of the end times, when all God's purposes are summed up in great acts of judgment. For orientation before reading this chapter, see *Old Testament Eschatology,* pp. 372, 373 and *New Testament Eschatology,* pp. 489, 490.

Has the Day of the Lord Come? 2:1–4. The Day of the Lord is

marked by great tribulation (cf. Matt. 24:9). The trials the Thessalonians now experience have been taken by some as evidence that
"the day" has already begun (2). Paul urges these believers not
to be unsettled by such rumors, or even reports that this is his
teaching. Paul reminds them that the Day of the Lord, according
to Jesus' teaching in Matthew 24:15–24, begins with the appearance
of a long predicted apostate leader, the "man of lawlessness." The
name identifies this mocking counterpart of Jesus, often called the
antichrist, as a person who acts contrary to all expressed in the
OT. The Thessalonians should have remembered from Paul's teaching that this individual's appearance begins the Day of the Lord.
And that antichrist is unveiled when he enters God's temple and
proclaims himself to be God (4).

The Secret Power of Lawlessness; 2:5–12. There is, however, a
relationship between present trials and the great Tribulation of
the end time. The "secret power of (behind) lawlessness" is already
at work in man's world (7). The full expression of evil is now
"held back" by God's Spirit (7). But a time will come when the
Spirit's restraining influence is removed. It is then that the antichrist, who is destined for destruction by Jesus at his coming (8),
will be unveiled. Paul wants these believers to know that God
continues to be in control of his universe and is sovereign even
over the secret powers that energize the tormenters of the Thessalonians.

Paul identifies the hidden source which empowers lawlessness
now and whose released energy will be fully displayed when the
lawless one appears. This source is Satan, who will authenticate
the antichrist by "all kinds of counterfeit miracles, signs and wonders, and in every sort of evil that deceives those who are perishing"
(9,10). Then Satan's vast energies will be focused on rallying humanity to follow his substitute Jesus (see *Satan,* p. 245).

Paul knows that there is no hope for those who fail to respond
now to the gospel and so be saved (10). They have no defense
against Satan when God withdraws the influence of his Spirit.
Indeed this release of mankind to follow its own tendencies is
like sending a great delusion, "so that they will believe the lie,
and so all will be condemned who have not believed the truth
but have delighted in wickedness" (11,12).

Stand Firm; 2:13–15. Against the background of the terrible
destiny awaiting the darkened unsaved world, Paul is moved "always to thank God for you." These men and women in the Christian
community were snatched from destruction by God, who "chose
you to be saved through the sanctifying work of the Spirit and

through belief in the truth" (see *Election/Presdestination, NT.* p. 619).

This is an important reminder for any who are presently suffering trials or persecution. God has called us in the gospel to "share in the glory of our Lord Jesus Christ." This hope, and an understanding of the destiny toward which the world is hurtling, encourages all believers to "stand firm and hold to the teachings" communicated to us by the prophets and apostles (15).

Benediction; 2:16,17. The benediction is in keeping with Paul's teaching. May God who "loved us and by his grace gave us eternal encouragement and good hope, encourage your hearts and strengthen you in every good deed and word."

Chapter 3. A Request and Warning

Please Pray; 3:1–5. Paul asks the Thessalonians to pray for his missionary team. He does not seek relief from troubles, any more than he would seek release for them from theirs. Instead he asks prayers that the gospel may spread (1), and that the team might be delivered from the hands of wicked and evil men (2). Paul shares what he prays for the Thessalonians and expresses confidence. God will keep on working in them so they can live as he commands. And God will protect them from the evil one (3–5).

Satan's secret power may be at work in the world now. It will be unleashed in the coming Day of the Lord. But Satan has no power over those who are God's own.

Review 2:1–3:5 and identify how you can apply to your life the perspective shared by Paul on the future. Note what values and attitudes are appropriate. And how you need to live in view of the future the NT describes.

Warning against Idleness; 3:6–15. Some in Thessalonica took Paul's teaching of Jesus' imminent return as an excuse for idleness. They stopped working, sponged off fellow Christians who did work, and spent their days as busybodies, meddling in other's affairs. This is not what Paul had taught by either word or example (6–9). In fact he laid down a rule to cover such situations: "If a man will not work, he shall not eat" (10).

This does not mean that the truly needy should be turned away. But it does mean that work is a moral issue and thus subject to church discipline (see *Church Discipline,* p. 636). Godliness requires honest labor and toil as well as prayer and praising!

Final Greetings; 3:16–18. Paul concludes as he begins, affirming the gift of peace that comes "at all times and in every way." This is not a peace that depends on external circumstances. It is a peace that is ours even in tribulation, because the Lord himself is "with all of you."

1 TIMOTHY
Shaping the Local Church

Timothy was a close companion of the apostle Paul, a member of his missionary team. He was often sent to revisit and to teach churches planted by the great apostle. In this letter to Timothy, Paul shares principles of order for the churches which are emerging throughout the first century world.

The Pastorals. Together, 1 and 2 Timothy and Titus are called the Pastoral Epistles. The name is deceptive. Neither Timothy nor Titus had what we would today call a pastoral ministry. Instead, each served as an itinerant troubleshooter sent by Paul to believers in various cities or larger areas when guidance was needed. As the Christian movement and its opposition took sharper form, this ministry was required often.

It is clear from these three letters that various false teachings and false teachers troubled the congregation. Problem areas are noted in the letters and correctives outlined. But most emphasis is placed on how the younger Timothy and Titus can help the churches establish order and a solidly Christian life style. Thus there are instructions on the selection of local leaders, stress on the importance of good works and godliness, and guidelines for the conduct of various groups within the fellowship of God's people.

The Pastorals are highly valued today. They are encouraging letters of guidance for our own younger leaders. And they are a source of principles to be applied in shaping modern life together in our own local congregations.

Date and Author. The earliest traditions all agree with the content of this letter that its author is the apostle Paul. It was written to Timothy, probably near the end of Paul's life. Although the chronology is uncertain, most date the letter after A.D. 64.

Timothy. Timothy shared an intimate relationship with Paul, who looked on him as a dear son (1 Tim. 1:2,18; 2 Tim. 1:2). Timothy was a companion of Paul's second and third missionary journeys.

Timothy was born in Lystra, of mixed parentage. His mother Eunice was a Christian Jewess and his father a Greek (Acts 16:11). He had been carefully instructed in the OT by Eunice and by his grandmother, Lois (2 Tim. 3:15). His call to a special ministry with Paul was apparently confirmed by some prophetic utterances (1 Tim. 1:8, 4:14).

Timothy was sent on a number of missions by Paul (1 Cor. 4:17; 16:10; Acts 19:22; 2 Cor. 1:1,19). He was not always successful.

While Paul trusts Timothy and sees him as the one who will take up the mantle of leadership on his own death, Paul also is aware of Timothy's weaknesses. Timothy is young and apparently somewhat shy and hesitant. Paul warns him in his letters against being overawed by his opponents and their teachings. Paul carefully instructs him on how to relate to believers in the churches to carry out an effective corrective ministry.

For all who are young, and yet feel called to serve God among his people, this letter and the other pastorals are rich with guidance and encouragement.

Theme. The first letter to Timothy speaks warmly and with encouragement to the young leader, instructing him and advising him as he seeks to help local congregations set their lives together in godly order.

Structure and Outline. Paul's letter, while filled with personal references and notes, does deal with specific aspects of church life.

Outline

I. The Goal of Sound Teaching	1:1–20
II. Instructions for Worship	2:1–15
III. Instructions Concerning Leadership	3:1–16
IV. Importance of Godliness	4:1–16
V. Instructions for Personal Ministries	5:1–6:2
VI. Concluding Exhortations	6:3–21

Common Elements in the Pastorals. The outline of 1 Timothy shows the general areas with which Paul is concerned in each of the pastoral letters. In Titus particularly there is mention of many NT doctrines. But Paul lays his emphasis in these letters on the life style which is to mark out the church and its leaders as they live the truths all believers are taught. The common emphases of the pastoral Epistles are shown on the chart on pages 714 and 715. It is adapted from the book, *Pass It On* (published by David C. Cook) written by the author of this handbook. Examine the chart before studying the pastoral epistles for an overview of Paul's concerns as he nears the end of his life and his ministry. Note particularly the relationship between local church leadership and godly living.

Before Reading. Here are several questions answered in 1 Timothy. Which of them is important to you? Read 1 Timothy for the answers. Why is it important to be doctrinally sound? What should I do to become a leader in the church? What does it mean to live a "godly" life? How should I view wealth—my own, or that of others?

Chapter 1. The Goal of Sound Teaching

Greeting; 1:1–2. Paul's identification of Timothy as his "true son in the faith" is significant. Timothy's father is a Gentile and his mother Jewish. According to contemporary Jewish teaching he would be considered illegitimate. His mission in Ephesus (1:3,4) demands he stand against those very legalists in the church who would be most likely to reject him on genealogical grounds! So Paul reassures Timothy. His new birth, and thus his relationship with God in Christ, is "true": literally—legitimate or genuine. Timothy can minister confidently, secure in the knowledge of his relationship with Jesus.

The Goal of Sound Doctrine; 1:3–7. Timothy has been posted to Ephesus to combat false teaching. Legalists, basing their false doctrine on misinterpretations of the OT, are corrupting the church. They concentrate on irrelevancies, insisting that believers abstain from marriage and restrict their diets (4:1–5). In majoring on minors, they have distracted believers from the true issue of Christian faith. This Paul identifies as "love which comes from a pure heart and a good conscience and a sincere faith" (5). Paul's point is that love overflows when our personal relationship with God, as defined in the doctrines of Scripture, is maintained. Then our purified heart (cleansed by God's forgiveness), our good conscience (maintained by personal commitment to live righteously), and our unhypocritical daily trust in God will issue in that love which marks the Christian community as Christ's dwelling place (see *Conscience,* p. 759; *Love,* p. 556).

Function of Law; 1:8–11. The law teachers in Ephesus "do not know what they are talking about" (1:6). This is shown by the fact that law is always "against" sinners and was never intended for the good. To make law-keeping out to be a way for spiritual achievement is to use law improperly (see *Law, NT,* p. 617). It is not law but the "glorious gospel of the blessed God" which transforms.

Common Content in the Pastoral Epistles

THE LIFE OF THE CHURCH 1 Timothy		THE WORK OF LEADERS 2 Timothy		THE WAY OF THE BODY Titus	
1:3-7	Goal of ministry: love from pure heart	1:3-12	Called to holy life, fervent love	1:1-4	Concern for "knowledge of the truth that leads to godliness"
1:8-11	Life-style *contrary to sound doctrine* described	1:13-14	Must guard *sound doctrine*		
1:12-17	Paul an example of a saved sinner; "eternal" life	1:15-18	Onesiphorus an example		
1:18-20	Timothy's goal to be a minister of the faith	2:1-7	Timothy to entrust truth to faithful men who will minister		
2:1-7	Pray and live to bring salvation to others	2:8-13	Paul's endurance for the salvation of elect		
2:8-9	Examples of godly life	2:14-19	Leaders must live godly lives		
2:11-15	Special limits placed on women's role	2:20-21	Limits placed by individual's response		
3:1-15	Leaders' qualifications	2:22-26	How a leader lives, teaches, and corrects	1:5-9 1:10-16	Leader's example Leader's duties

4:1-5 False life-style	3:1-9 False leaders	
4:6-10 Danger of distraction from godliness		
4:11-16 Need to set example in faith, speech, life, etc.	3:10-17 Need to continue in godly life and teaching	
5:1-8 Respect toward others in the family: "put religion into practice"	4:1-5 Need to preach and live true doctrine	2:1-15 Godly life and doctrine applied
5:9-16 Widows' role		
5:17-20 Elders' responsibility		
5:21-25 Various injunctions		
6:1-2 Slaves' attitude		
6:3-10 False doctrine; wrong motives		
6:11-21 Charge to pursue godliness, truth, love, etc., keep faith in Christ central	4:6-18 Paul an example of persevering workman, athlete	3:1f Practical results of our common salvation

God's Grace Demonstrated; 1:12–20. Paul himself is a living testimony to grace. Though once "a blasphemer and a persecutor and a violent man" (12–14), Paul has become a display of God's goodness and patience (15–16). As always, experience of grace evokes thankfulness (17).

But to experience transformation one must hold both to the faith and a good conscience. Paul names two who have deliberately and violently pushed both of these away from them. Paul portrays the results as shipwreck. Their lives are ruined and the slander of God which the abandonment involves has placed them in the hands of Satan, to experience the strong punishment that comes from following his ways.

What tests can you see here which might help you recognize sound doctrinal teaching in a local congregation?

Grace

The concept has its roots in Greek culture, long before the NT age. There *charis* were associated with things which produce a sense of well being. It characterized a relationship between persons marked by acts of generosity, which in turn stimulated gratitude and thanks. Aristotle defined the word as "helpfulness towards someone in need, not in return for anything, nor that the helper may get anything, but for the sake of the person helped." But the Greeks saw this relationship as something possible only between human beings. It was not seen as something that might exist between men and the gods.

Even in the OT the term most frequently translated "grace," *hen,* fails to reflect the depth of NT meaning. The Hebrew term is closer to "mercy" and pictures a strong person, moved by the needs of a weaker, coming to his or their aid. The OT seldom uses the Hebrew word *hen* of God.

So it is the NT which takes the idea of *charis* and adds exciting new meaning. The word appears 155 times in the NT, with 100 of these occurrences in the Pauline letters. It is here, in Paul, that the theological meaning of "grace" finds fullest expression and definition. Certainly the OT and cultural shades of meaning still exist. But now "grace" describes decisive action taken by God on behalf of a mankind which is not merely weak but powerless without him.

In the NT, God's grace is often set in contrast to law. While law demands that a human being perform perfectly to win God's approval, grace makes great promises of pardon and love. "That is why it depends on faith," Paul explains in Romans 4. Salvation must be a matter of faith "in order that the promises may rest on grace and be guaranteed to all his [Abraham's] descendants" (4:2,25). Only by making salvation a free gift could the saving promise be extended to all mankind.

The Christian life is also a matter of grace. Because we live under grace rather than law (Rom. 6:14) we can experience righteousness. The power of sin has been drained and Christ, living in us, can act through us to make us truly good (cf. Gal. 2:20; Eph. 2:8–10).

It is appropriate then that what we call spiritual gifts are, literally, *charismoi*, or "grace gifts." The emphasis is on the fact that it is God who is working in and through believers. Our ministry to others as Christians does not depend on ourselves or our talents, but on the powerful working of God who acts through us as we trust him.

Grace *is*, as it is often defined, the "unmerited favor of God." But most importantly, it is God acting powerfully to do for you and for me all those things which we could never do for ourselves.

Chapter 2. Instructions for Worship

Prayer and Peace; 2:1–7. Paul urges prayer for all men when believers gather. One focus for prayer is prominent officials, and one request is that believers might be left alone to live tranquil lives, marked by devotion to holiness (2). Believers are also to pray for leaders' salvation. This is appropriate because God "wants all men to be saved and come to a knowledge of the truth" (4). The verb stresses God's wish or desire but does not suggest that he has determined to save all. What Paul provides as a basis for confidence in our prayers for the salvation of others is this: the door to God is open! The Mediator exists in the person of "the man Christ Jesus, who gave himself as a ransom for all men" (6). Thus while we cannot know if a given individual will respond to the gospel, we can pray freely for any person, knowing that in Christ the ransom has been provided. The Savior stands ready to bring any who will believe to God.

Paul quickly adds one more thought. He sees himself as a herald, announcing the true faith to the Gentiles (7). The first century herald was commissioned to bring important news to others. His task was to proclaim his message accurately, in a strong and clear voice, without lingering, for all must hear. It is important that, as well as pray, we communicate clearly the message that the ransom has been paid. God is now ready to welcome all who will respond to the gospel message with faith.

Men and Women; 2:8–15. Paul now speaks of behavior at worship gatherings. It is likely this passage is corrective, stressing proper behavior for men and women who are violating it. Male members of the congregation are to avoid disputes and quarrelsomeness. The hands they raise to God in prayer are to have been engaged only in clean and holy actions which fit the gospel (cf. 1:10). Women are urged to dress modestly and to show self-controlled and quiet

behavior. They are to be ready to respond (submissive), in contrast
to holding unbending or domineering attitudes (9–11).

Paul makes a point of not permitting a woman "to teach or to
have authority over a man" (12). "Authority" here means to "have
mastery, to be dominating or an autocrat." Paul goes back to Adam
and Eve in explaining this limitation. The interpretation and application of this passage is much debated. Some take it to restrict
women from any participation; others as an affirmation that only
men are to fill the position of an elder (one who teaches with
authority). Those who hold this last view note that Jesus chose
only men to serve as apostles and that the human authors of the
Scriptures were men.

It is clear from the rest of the NT and from Paul's own writings
that women are fully gifted and significant members of the body
of Christ (see *Role of Women in the Church,* p. 625). However
the passage is understood, it must not be applied in such a way
that it denies other clear teachings of the NT about the value
and worth of women and the importance of their ministries in
the church.

The obscure reference in verse 15 is perhaps best explained by
noting that the Greek text states "the" childbearing. It may thus
be a reference to the birth of Jesus and parallel to the promise
of present tense salvation given to Timothy himself in 1:18, 19.

The Early Church at Worship

What happened when believers of the first century came together on
the Lord's day? Several NT passages give us intimate insights into these
meetings which, for the first 120 years of the Christian era, took place
primarily in homes (cf. Rom. 16:5).

We know that there was prayer, with believers standing together, arms
upraised and hands outstretched to God (1 Tim. 2).

We know too that mutual exhortation and encouragement played a part,
for believers are urged to "consider how we can spur one another on toward
love and good deeds." Meetings are important, for mutual support is vital
(Heb. 10:24–25).

Paul gives us another fascinating picture in Corinthians. There he describes a gathering marked by both order and spontaneity, as a number
of the believers speak out, sharing a "hymn, or a word of instruction" or
even, if there is an interpreter present, speaking in a tongue. It is clear
that there is an emphasis on teaching, for Paul says that "two or three
prophets should speak, and the others should weigh carefully what is said"
(1 Cor. 14:26–32).

A similar picture, of a closely knit and ministering group, is found in
Colossians. Here Paul exhorts, "let the word of Christ dwell in you richly

as you teach and admonish one another with all wisdom, and as you sing psalms, hymns and spiritual songs with gratitude in your hearts to God" (Col. 3:12–17).

The dominant impression communicated in the NT pictures of the gathered church is one of intimacy and active participation. Spiritual gifts are in full operation, and the dynamic growth of the Christian movement may be traced in part to the fact that the whole body "grows and builds itself up in love, as each part does its work" (Eph. 4:16). We need not reproduce the forms of the first century church today. But we do need to recover the intimacy and the vitality which comes as each of us takes an active ministering part.

For study: see *Spiritual Gifts*, p. 623, *Priesthood, NT*, p. 749.

Chapter 3. Church Leadership

The Character of Overseers. Leaders in the early church were normally recognized within local fellowships and then confirmed as leaders (see Acts 15:23). Qualifications for leadership were not educational, or the possession of particular spirit gifts, but instead were character traits. The reason for the stress on character is that leaders are to provide an example of Christian life style as well as to teach sound doctrine (cf. 1 Tim. 4:11–16). A comparison between the Christian life which Paul describes in the pastorals, and qualities of Christian leaders, makes the reason for this stress clear. It takes an individual marked by the traits on the left to effectively teach the way of life described on the right!

Christian Leaders Are. . .	*Christian Life Style Involves. . .*
* above reproach	* godliness
* temperate	* faith
* self-controlled	* temperance
* respectable and upright	* love
* hospitable	* self-control
* not alcoholics	* endurance
* not competitive but gentle	* dedication to good
* not quarrelsome and not quick tempered	* integrity
	* seriousness
* not materialistic	* response to authority
* well respected by nonbelievers	* trustworthiness
	* humility
* lovers of good	* consideration
	* peaceableness

The terms in this passage which describe an individual suited for leadership show he must be calm and collected, fair in his treatment of others, and not insistent on his own way or personal rights. The "husband of one wife" (2) does not mean the leader must be married, but that he must be either monogamous or celibate. Leaders are not to be materialistic or motivated by money, but are to be generous and hospitable. Quarrelsome and competitive persons are ruled out, as are those whose lives do not represent Christ well to outsiders. New Christians are not to be considered for leadership, in part because it takes time for these qualities to mature, and also because early recognition as a leader may cause a recent convert to become conceited.

Leaders in the Church

The spiritual leaders of the NT Church are identified by three terms: *elder, bishop* (or "overseer") and *pastor* (or "shepherd"). Each describes a person, not an office or managerial role. Each stresses a distinctive relationship with members of the local body. Each pictures a mature Christian character—and a person-oriented individual who cares about the growth and well-being of others.

The NT carefully guards against exalting spiritual leaders to some position of authority "above" others. "You are not to be called 'Rabbi,'" Jesus warned his followers. "You have only one Master, and you are all brothers. Do not call anyone on earth 'father,' for you have one Father and he is in heaven. Nor are you to be called 'teacher,' for you have one Teacher, the Christ." In contrast to this hierarchical order, Jesus says "the greatest among you will be your servant" (Matt. 23:8–11). This stress is constant throughout the NT. For instance, Peter writes to elders, "Be shepherds of God's flock that is under your care, serving as overseers—not because you must, but because you are willing, as God wants you to be; not greedy for money, but eager to serve; not lording it over those entrusted to you, but being examples to the flock" (1 Pet. 5:2–4).

Leadership is provided in part by example (which explains the great emphasis in 1 Timothy 3 and Titus 1 on character as a qualification for leadership). The other tool of leaders is the sound doctrine of the Word of God. But even their teaching is to be done gently (2 Tim. 2:24–26), though with conviction and authority (1 Tim. 4:11–16).

The overseeing role expressed in the terms *elder, overseer,* and *pastor,* seems to be applied only to men in the NT. However, a leadership role is expressed in the term *deacon,* and both men and women undertake this service (cf. 1 Tim. 3:8–10; Rom. 16:1). The word deacon literally means servant, and a number of tasks related to the function of a local church are entrusted to these deacon leaders. The best example of their ministry is found in Acts 6:1–14.

Today these NT terms are applied to offices in a number of church organizational systems, but the NT does not support any particular form of church government. Instead the NT stresses the way that leaders minister to others in the church, and the commitment of leaders not to lord it over their brothers, but to serve them and build them up. When our leaders show a NT character and a concern for others, God's work will prosper, whatever their office may be called.

For study: see *Servanthood, NT* p. 486, and *Spiritual Authority,* p. 658.

The Character of Deacons; 3:8–13. Character is the living evidence of the work of the Spirit in a believer's life. Thus character is also the first consideration in selecting those who will "serve as deacons" (10). The distinction between the ministry of deacons and overseers, or elders, is illustrated in Acts 6:1–4. There, responsibility for an important temporal matter, the distribution of food to those dependent on the church, is seen as a task for deacons. The deacons thus released the apostles (note that Peter identifies himself as an elder in 1 Peter 5:1) "to give our attention to prayer and the ministry of the Word" (Acts 6:4). This and "directing the affairs of the church" (1 Tim. 5:17) seems to be the distinctive ministry of elders.

God's Household; 3:14–16. It is because the church is God's household (family) that it's so important we conduct ourselves well. The great mystery of the Incarnation (16) is, in one sense, continued in the people who together compose "the church of the living God."

Compare qualifications listed here with Galatians 5:22, 23. What is the relationship between the two lists? Why do you think Paul does not simply list the "fruit of the Spirit" here?

Who in your local church embodies the qualities spelled out here? Is he or she recognized as a spiritual leader? If not, why not? If so, what leadership ministries does this person have?

Chapter 4. Importance of Godliness

Abandoning the Faith, 4:1–5. Now, in the mid-sixties A.D., there is a clearly defined Christianity. "The faith" is understood to include both doctrinal content and a distinctive code of Christian conduct, marking out how a believer is to live to please God (cf. Titus 2). The attack of the false teachers, against which Paul warns Timothy here, is focused on Christian conduct. The source of false teachings is demonic (1), and they are communicated by "hypocriti-

cal liars, whose consciences have been seared as with a hot iron"
(3). The particular content is a legalism which demands that the
believer abstain from marriage and follow other ascetic practices.
This actually involves rejecting gifts which God intends to stimulate
us to thanksgiving (4,5) and ought to be accepted.

Train Yourself in Godliness. 4:6–10. Timothy is to point out
their error and to affirm "the truth of the faith" and its "good
(useful) teaching." The empty myths followed by the credulous
are in fact ungodly, in conflict with true godliness. "Godly" is
seldom found in the NT, except in the Pastoral Epistles. Here it
denotes a moral attitude: a reverent responsiveness to God which
expresses itself in a life filled with Christian virtue and good works
(cf. 1 Tim. 2:10; 5:4). The "physical training" mentioned here is
the rigorous discipline of the body encouraged by the ascetic false
teachers, not exercise. This, Paul says, has only small and brief
value. But discipline in godly living promises great achievements
now and for eternity (8). Unlike these others, Paul and Timothy
have fixed their hope not on self-effort but "in the living God,"
who is able to deliver now and hereafter (9,10).

The Mission of Leaders; 4:11–16. Timothy, despite his youth,
is not to hesitate to transmit truth as a command (11). In NT
culture a leader would be considered "young" if between 30 and
40 years old. Timothy's resources as a leader are the Scriptures,
which he is to preach and teach, and the example he sets by his
own godly life style. Thus his behavior is to be godly "in speech,
in life, in love, in faith and in purity" (12). Total commitment to
his ministry, with careful attention to "your life and doctrine"
(16), is important. This approach to life and ministry will rescue
both Timothy and his hearers from the empty and ungodly life
recommended by the false teachers (see *Salvation, NT,* p. 574).

> Read through the Pastoral Epistles and jot down a descrip-
> tion of a godly life. In what areas do you most need to
> grow?

Chapter 5. Instructions for Personal Ministries

Paul now gives instructions related to the ministries of several
groups in the local congregations.

Respect for All; 5:1,2. Leaders must remain sensitive to others.
Spiritual authority never implies superiority or disregard for the
dignity of brothers and sisters (see *Servanthood, NT,* p. 486).

Widows; 5:3–16. In the first century world there were no opportunities for women to be employed. It was normal then for widows to become a part of their children's family (3,8,16). Younger widows were expected to remarry, and Paul advises this course, both because of normal sexual needs and desires and to provide women with meaningful work of their own to accomplish (11–14). The widows who lacked family to care for them were supported by the church. Even here there was an opportunity for a fulfilling personal contribution. Older widows who had been faithful to their husbands and well-known for good deeds, who wished to dedicate themselves to Christ's service, were given special recognition. They served by training the younger women "to love their husbands and children, to be self-controlled, and pure, to be busy at home, to be kind, and to be submissive to their husbands" (Titus 2:3–5).

The pattern then preserves the dignity of every individual. The younger widows remarry and build a new life. Those with relatives become members of an extended family. Those supported by the church do not receive "charity" but are freed for a significant ministry to the younger women of the Christian community.

Elders; 5:17–22a. Paul encourages respect for elders, especially those whose work is preaching and teaching (18). It is appropriate to support an elder so he can concentrate fully on ministry (19). Rumors about elders are to be disregarded, but if an elder does sin he is to be rebuked publicly, and without partiality (20,21). It is especially important not to "be hasty" in ordaining a person to leadership in the church (cf. 5:24,25 below).

Wine; 5:23. Timothy is encouraged to add wine to his drinking water for medical reasons. In NT times, wine was usually diluted with between three and six times as much water.

Trailing Sins; 5:24,25. This warning may be related to the verse 22 warning against hasty ordination. Paul notes that while the sins of some are obvious, those of others only show up later. In time a man's sins and his good works both become evident.

Slaves and Masters; 6:1,2. In a culture where people can be property, Paul urges Christians to take another perspective. Slaves whose masters are now brothers can be ministered to and offered "even better" service. Masters can minister to slaves by showing them respect as persons and caring for them.

How might Paul's instructions about widows differ in today's culture? What might be the same? How can we today protect the dignity of individuals who receive their support from others and help them to contribute?

Chapter 6. Concluding Exhortation

Love for Money Discouraged; 6:3–10. It is not money itself but love for money that "is a root of all kinds of evil." Paul encourages believers to concentrate on godliness and be content with that, for godliness brings with it true contentment (see *The Christian and Money,* p. 527).

Paul's Charge to Timothy; 6:11–16. As a man of God, Timothy is to bend every effort to pursue "righteousness, godliness, faith, love, endurance and gentleness." In keeping this commandment, Timothy, and you and I, will win all that is truly important in life.

Commands to the Rich; 6:17–21. The use of money for good is approved by God, and thus is one distinct opportunity for the rich to serve God and others, by being "generous and willing to share."

2 TIMOTHY
The Call to Commitment

Paul's final letter, written just before his execution in Rome, is an exhortation to his younger friend and follower, Timothy. Paul calls on Timothy to live as a good soldier of Jesus Christ in the face of growing opposition. Paul can look back over his own life with satisfaction, knowing that he has "kept the faith." The crowning righteousness is soon to be his. And so this letter marks the passage of leadership from one generation to the next.

Date and Author; Paul writes this letter to Timothy during his last imprisonment in Rome, probably about A.D. 67. For background see pages 711–712.

Theme. Last words of famous people are often revealing. Here Paul unveils, not only his parting advice, but also the values and the commitments that have shaped his own life—and can shape ours!

Outline

Before Reading. Here are several questions answered in 2 Timothy. Which of them is important to you? Read 2 Timothy for the answers. What are the chief duties of Christian leaders? What might a life of full commitment cost me? What are reasons why full commitment is the wisest choice an individual can make? How shall I respond to the evils around me and to people who oppose what I believe in?

Chapter 1. The Call of Commitment

Initial Encouragement; 1:3–7. Paul expresses deep love for Timothy and confidence in him. Like Paul, whose life has been distinguished by unbroken service (3), Timothy has a heritage of sincere

faith, transmitted from grandmother to mother and now to Timothy
(5). Paul's reminder to "fan into flame the gift of God, which is
in you" is not a rebuke. In the first century fires were kept alive
as glowing coals, which could be fanned into flame by bellows
whenever needed. With Paul's death approaching, the situation
now places new demands on Timothy. But Paul is confident. God's
gifting brings with it power, love, and self-discipline (7). No one
called to leadership need hold back timidly or fearfully.

A Herald and Apostle; 1:8–12. Paul sees his calling as testifying
about the Lord (8,11). This is glorious, not something of which
to be ashamed. But commitment does involve suffering, which in
the culture is viewed as shaming. Paul's perspective is completely
different. It is the living of a holy life rather than a "successful"
one that is in harmony with God's purpose and his grace (9).
The true glory of Christian life and commitment is unveiled in
Jesus, who has "destroyed death and brought immortality to light
through the gospel" (10). It is because Paul knows Jesus that he
is never ashamed. Using a legal term for something which a person
places on trust in another's keeping, Paul expresses his conviction
that Jesus will faithfully guard him against "that day" of Jesus'
return.

Guard the Deposit; 1:13,14. But faith not only means entrusting
ourselves to God. It means that God entrusts "the pattern of sound
teaching" to us! "Pattern" indicates a ground plan used by an
architect, or a rough draft in literature. In Scripture we have a
clear outline of God's truth: now we are to build on it and fill
out its details by our lives and by exposition. With the help of
the Holy Spirit, Timothy will guard this trustworthy foundation
and later pass it on to other faithful men (2:2).

Faithful Friends; 1:15–18. Some have deserted Paul and the gospel (13). But others have shown a love and concern which risked
danger by identifying themselves with him.

What does calling to leadership seem to involve? How much
of what Paul writes here applies to every Christian and not
just leaders? What specifically do you see applying to you?

Chapter 2. The Life of Commitment

Commitment Described; 2:1–7. Paul calls on Timothy to be empowered by the grace which flows from Christ (1). He will need
strength, for the mission of teaching and training (2) involves both
hardship and self-discipline. Paul uses three figures to explain. Like
a soldier, Timothy must be willing to take his share of rough treat-

ment, concentrating on pleasing his commander. In the Roman world, the general was responsible to provide equipment, food and shelter for his soldiers. Timothy, under Christ's command, need not become entangled in "civilian affairs." He, and we, can give wholehearted devotion to the mission set by the Lord (3,4). Like an athlete, who must compete under strict rules, the Christian is unable to bypass God's principles to "lighten" his struggle (5). Like the farmer, who must often work until exhausted, the committed Christian will receive his share of the crops. But the harvest may not be immediate (6). Each of these analogies is commended by Paul for reflection, so that Timothy might gain insight into the commitment called for by ministry.

Jesus Lives, 2:8–13. Timothy is challenged to remember Jesus as risen, living Lord (8). In view of Christ's Lordship and his concern for the people of God, Paul even accepts chains, knowing that although he may be bound, the Word of God is free (9,10). The next verses are a confession of faith, part of the liturgy of the early church. That confession stresses the fact of our resurrection with Jesus (11), the glory to be won in his service (12), and the faithfulness of Jesus despite our failures (13).

The Word of Truth; 2:14–19. Paul tells Timothy to take a stand against those who are waging a war of words against the gospel, subverting the faith of those who listen (15). God's servant plows a straight furrow, guided by the Word, and avoids the "godless chatter" which leads further and further from a life filled with Christian virtues and good works (*Godliness,* cf. p. 722). Those who war against the truth plant heresies which spread like a cancer and corrupt the health of the whole body (17–19). But despite inroads such false teachers may seem to make, God's work rests on a firm foundation. From God's perspective, he knows those who are his own. From man's perspective, God's people will validate their confession of faith by turning away from all wickedness (19).

Faith at Work; 2:20–26. Paul encourages all believers to commit themselves to becoming instruments fit for God's use. Paul then describes both the cleansing process and the good works (22). Especially significant is the attitude with which the believer ministers to others (23,24), and the confidence that only by the supernatural working of God can spiritual results be achieved (25,26).

What about the commitment described here seems attractive to you?

What about it seems difficult or distasteful? What reasons can you find in this chapter why full commitment is the wisest choice?

Chapters 3, 4. Difficulties to Face

Terrible Times; 3:1–9. Paul does not picture a gradual victory of Christianity, transforming the world toward some just moral society. Instead he pictures increasing moral deterioration among those who are "lovers of pleasure rather than lovers of God" (4). Men may adapt a form of religion, but their values and lives will deny the power of godliness (6). The general culture decline is reflected in the popularity of false leaders whose character shows them to be "men of depraved mind" (see *Recognizing False Prophets,* p. 326).

The Godly Life; 3:10–17. The "way of life, purpose, faith, patience, love, endurance, persecutions, and sufferings" of the believer stand in sharp contrast to human society. Because of this, "everyone who wants to live a godly life in Christ Jesus will be persecuted" (12). But the Christian's values and guidance for living are not taken from society. They are found in the "holy Scriptures," which give us wisdom needed to experience God's present-tense salvation (15). As our lives are corrected and disciplined by the inspired Word, we are completely outfitted for "every good work."

TITUS
The Call to Good Works

Titus, a young member of Paul's missionary team, is ministering to unruly believers on the isle of Crete. Paul's brief letter of instruction, the third of the "pastoral epistles," outlines the mission of Titus and gives us insights into the importance of good works as an expression of living faith.

Date and Author. The letter was written by Paul to Titus and is usually dated A.D. 65 or 66. See page 711 for background on the Pastoral Epistles.

Titus. Titus was a member of Paul's missionary team and is mentioned twelve times in the NT. A fascinating picture of him and his ministry can be constructed from these references. We know that Titus was a Gentile, an uncircumcised Greek. He joined the missionary team sometime before Paul's second missionary journey. Like Timothy, he was often sent on special missions to deal with difficulties in various churches. He was apparently quite successful in helping to resolve tensions between Paul and the Corinthians—a mission at which Timothy had earlier failed. Among his ministries was the collection at Corinth of gifts for the poorer churches of Palestine.

When Paul writes this letter, Titus is working in Crete. There he deals with a particularly difficult group of believers. Paul expresses no concern for Titus, whom he praises highly in 2 Corinthians. Instead he gives advice which has been highly valued by Christian leaders through the centuries.

Inspiration of Scripture

First Timothy 3:16 describes the Scriptures as "God-breathed" or inspired. From OT times, it was understood that the Spirit of God spoke through the prophets so that their words originated not with them but with God. This same conviction was shared by the early church and by Christians across the ages. Because of their inspiration by God, the Scriptures are trusted as both reliable and relevant.

Theologians have used several words to describe Scripture and God's relationship to it.

Revelation affirms that the Bible contains an unveiling of the thoughts and the person of God, permitting us to know that which would otherwise remain hidden (cf. 1 Cor. 2:6–13; Col. 1:24–2:5).

Illumination affirms that the Holy Spirit who superintended the writing of the Scriptures also works in the lives of believers to enable us to apply the truths God has unveiled. Illumination does not mean mastery of Scripture as a system of belief and doctrine. Instead illumination focuses on application of the Word, as the Holy Spirit works in us to show us which principles and truths apply in specific life situations (cf. 1 Cor. 2:14–16; see *Wisdom, NT,* p. 632).

Inspiration makes a statement about the Scriptures themselves, not about the prophets or apostles who penned them. It is not the men who are inspired: it is the writings. Thus the doctrine of inspiration guarantees that the words, as written, accurately communicate the thoughts of God as he intended. Certainly the personalities and the background of various writers are reflected in the books of our Old and New Testaments. Inspiration does not suggest dictation. But inspiration does teach that the men God used to record our OT and NT were so guided by the Spirit that the product, our Scriptures, are completely trustworthy. They are his word and thus "useful for teaching, rebuking, correcting and training in righteousness," able to prepare us fully for "every good work" (2 Tim. 3:16,17).

For study: see *Understanding Your Bible,* pp. 13–21.

Crete. This island, 160 miles long and 35 wide, lies in the Mediterranean southeast of Greece. It was populated from prehistoric times, and was the center of the great Minoan culture that developed during the Middle and Late Bronze Ages. There was a large population of Jews there by the second century B.C., and Jews from Crete were present in Jerusalem on the Day of Pentecost described in Acts 2. It is not known who planted the Christian faith on Crete, but it seems likely that it was Paul or members of his missionary team.

The Cretans were viewed in the ancient world as a rather depraved and an unruly people. This view is summed up in the quote from the poet Epimenides (c. 600 B.C.) which Paul includes in Titus 1:12: "Cretans are always liars, evil beasts, lazy gluttons." It is these people whom the gospel will transform by grace into men and women who "devote themselves to doing what is good" (Titus 3:8).

Theme. The theme of Titus is the transformation which the gospel effects in human lives, and instruction to a young leader on how to call an unruly people to disciplined commitment to good works.

Distinctives. Titus contains a striking blend of doctrinal and life style emphasis. No less than fifteen basic doctrines are referred to, including: the personality of God (2:11; 3:6); God's love and grace (2:11; 3:4); Christ's Saviorhood (2:10, 13; 3:4); the Holy Spirit (3:5); the Trinity (3:5,6); the deity of Christ (2:13); the vicarious atonement (2:14); salvation offered to all (2:11) by grace, not works (3:5); justification by faith (3:7); sanctification (2:14); the inheritance of eternal life (3:7) and Jesus' return (2:13). In addition, there is a summary of Christian life style, described in terms of godliness (1:1), faith (1:2; 2:2), temperance (2:2); love (2:2,4); self-control (2:2, 5,6,12); endurance (2:2); dedication to good (2:7; 3:1, 8, 14); personal integrity (2:7, 10); seriousness (2:7); submissiveness to authority (2:9; 3:1); trustworthiness (2:10); humility (3:2); consideration (3:2), peaceableness (3:2) and unity (3:10). Both doctrine and life style are included as the content of Christian teaching.

Outline

Before Reading. Here are several questions answered in Titus. Which of them is important to you? Read Titus for the answers. What is "teaching"? Can I have a teaching ministry? How do "good works" fit into the Christian life? What are the "good works" that I am called by God to perform?

Chapter 1:1–4. Greeting

Paul sees himself as a bondslave of Jesus, set to a specific task by his Master. This task is to further the faith of God's people and to further that "knowledge of the truth" which leads to godliness (1). This is an important note, for it reflects the thrust of the book. Titus is charged with teaching a body of truth that is to radically affect the lives of those who embrace it (1). This transforming faith rests on the confident expectation ("hope") of God's promised eternal life, so that confidence in God's promises becomes the foundation on which the Christian life can be constructed.

Chapter 1:5–16. Mission to Crete

The Ordination of Elders; 1:5–9. As new churches were established in the first century, it was the practice of the missionaries to move on to new fields. Later team members would return to give added help. Particularly, they would oversee the selection and ordination of elders (see *Leaders in the Church,* p. 720). These leaders were chosen on the basis of their growth in Christ, as demonstrated in godly character. Paul carefully defines, here and in 1 Timothy, traits which indicate spiritual maturity.

Here Paul says one place to look is the family (6). The one-woman kind of man who is suitable will have believing children, who themselves are believers and do not extravagantly squander their means on luxury ("being wild") and who are not independent to the point of insubordination ("disobedient"). Paul suggests this is a logical necessity, as are other personal traits (cf. 1 Tim. 3:1,2). His reason is that an elder is "entrusted with God's word." The word here is "manager," but manager in a distinctive NT sense and not in the modern corporate sense. The "manager" then was a household servant, responsible for care of his owner's estate. To manage well, the Christian leader must operate in harmony with principles of leadership laid down by God in Scripture. Such management requires a man of special character. He cannot be an obstinate man, who asserts his rights over the feelings and interests of others ("overbearing"). Nor can he be quick-tempered, a heavy drinker, or the kind of person who makes money discreditably (7). In contrast, the person who can manage by God's principles must be hospitable, devoted to all that is best, have complete self-mastery so that his will is in submission to God's will ("self-controlled"), and in short be an upright, holy, and disciplined person (8). As always, life and teaching must correspond. Thus the spiritual leader must steadfastly apply Christian truth as it has been taught, using the biblical message to encourage, and to refute whoever objects to it (9).

The Opposition; 1:10–16. The urgency of recognizing a core of elders is underlined by Paul's description of the situation in Crete. Many who are "rebellious" are "ruining whole households" by their false teaching (10,11). "Households" is probably a reference to the house churches in which the early church invariably met. Paul's next words are striking. Not only is the content of the teaching false, but the character and motivation of the false teachers is depraved, the opposite of the character of the Christian elder (11).

Apparently the false teachings were quickly responded to, in part because of Cretan national character. Paul makes no charge but instead quotes Epimenides, a Cretan religious teacher of the seventh century B.C., who was considered on that island to be a prophet. Paul can only agree with his assessment of the depraved character of the Cretans (12,13). This means a need for strong leadership, which will take a stand against sins so common in their society, including "lazy gluttony" (uncontrolled greed). Paul looks at the culture and sees "both their minds and consciences" as corrupt (15). "Mind" here speaks of their whole outlook on life, while "conscience" refers to the capacity for moral discrimination (cf. *Conscience,* p. 759). Even those things which are intrinsically pure are corrupted and distorted in the polluted thoughts of these people, whose lives deny relationship with God, and who disgust Paul by their hypocrisy (16).

How striking that the gospel of Christ can and will take such a people and motivate them to live holy and godly lives!

How do you see the situation in your own community in relation to Paul's description of Crete? Like, or unlike?

In view of the situation in Crete, what do you think the elders there could or should do to build that "knowledge of the truth which leads to godliness" (1:1)?

Chapter 2. The Teaching Ministry

To correct the situation in Crete, Titus must "teach what is in accord with sound doctrine" (1). The following verses show that what is being "taught" is not doctrine itself, but a life style marked with virtues which, in Paul's words, make the "teaching about God our Savior attractive" (10).

Teaching. Words for teaching in this passage help us understand what this ministry meant in NT times. This is important, for the NT ministry of "teaching" is often clouded for us by the different meanings given to it in our society. The different Greek words behind terms used in the RSV translation of this chapter are: "teach" (1,7), meaning simply to speak, or communicate. "Bid" (2,3,9) does not appear in Greek, but reflects a common construction which means to communicate an urgent need. "Teach what is good" (3) is no classroom exercise but advice and encouragement given privately, by word and by example. "Train" (4) is a word commonly used for the teaching of morality, and it means to encourage, urge, and advise. "Urge" (6) is to exhort or encourage, and it implies an "alongside" relationship between the teacher and learner. To "set them an example" (7) is to make oneself visible as a pattern or an example to be followed. "Training" in verse 12 is different from the word translated "train" in verse 4. Here it implies daily guidance and the correction of behavior designed to lead another to maturity. "Declare" (15) is simply "to speak." "Reprove" there means to put out or bring to light, thus convincing and, if needed, to reprove. Clearly, Paul here does not see teaching as drilling believers until they master information. His focus is on the application of truth to reshape the life style of believers, until lives are in fullest harmony with the doctrines that Christians believe.

An Attractive Gospel; 2:1–10. Paul's stress on behavior is in part to "make the teaching about God our Savior attractive" (10). In a society marked by depraved self-centeredness, Christian character and interpersonal relationships will stand out in bright contrast. Thus older men are to be "temperate, worthy of respect, sound in faith and self-control" (2). Older women, instead of being addicted to slanderous gossip and alcohol, will be reverent; literally, "like those engaged in sacred service" (3). Integrity and healthy talk will mark the lives of young and old, and Christian slaves will be responsive to their masters, never talking back or stealing, but showing they can be fully trusted (9,10). What will make the gospel attractive is the beauty of the lives of those who are transformed by it!

The Gospel's Impact; 2:11–14. The Gospel of grace makes salvation available to all men (11). But it also brings with it the power and the obligation to say "No" to ungodliness. God's people, their hope fixed on Jesus' appearing, are called to live upright and godly lives (11,12). This moral imperative flows from theology. Christ gave himself for the express purpose of ransoming us from our life of wickedness. As his possessions now, we are to be "eager to do good" (14). Thus "good works," and the beauty of a life committed to goodness, is basic to the gospel itself! One cannot be "doctrinally orthodox" without a full commitment to a loving life style.

Education, NT

Among the Jewish people the center of education was the home, and the goal of education was holiness (cf. *Education,* OT, p. 124). In contrast, Greek education stressed development of a cultured person and was entrusted to a number of community institutions. The Greek concept of a cultured person was, however, flawed, for it despised work and built society on slaves, whose labors freed the cultured class for idleness. Among the Romans, primary education was carried out in schools, where repetition and corporal punishment dominated. Higher education was training for public speaking, since the power to sway others was viewed as its highest goal. Christianity, established in this pagan world, found the roots of both educational method and goal in the OT. There is no NT repetition of OT passages dealing with nurture, for the church accepted the OT as authoritative. Likewise no contrast is drawn between knowing the content of faith and living a holy life. The early church linked these two, knowing with Paul that "knowledge of the truth . . . leads to godliness" (Titus 1:1).

Children in the first centuries were trained in the educational system of the Roman empire, with full responsibility for Christian nurture resting on the home. As Jerome writes to a parent in one of his letters (107.9), "never let Paula see either in you or in her father that which she cannot imitate without sin." The character of the parents, like the character of elders, was to lead toward good.

Both the location and the goal of NT education helps us to realize that "teaching" in the NT is a unique ministry, quite different from assembling individuals in a classroom to be given information they are expected to learn and repeat. Titus 2 gives us a good insight into the NT meaning of "teaching." Here Titus is told to "teach what is in accord with sound doctrine" (2:1). He is to communicate, with content, the implications for daily life as truth is applied. A number of words are used in this brief, fifteen-verse chapter, which give us insight into "teaching" as it is understood in the Christian community. Believers "teach," "bid," "teach what is good," "train," "urge," "show yourselves in all respects a model," "declare," "exhort," and "reprove" (RSV).

Thus in a NT sense, "apt to teach" does not speak of an ability to lecture, nor does education indicate school. Teaching is guiding others into godly living by an application of the Word of God to the practical issues of life. This exciting kind of ministry is open to each of us—in our homes, in our relationships with friends, and in our sharing with others in our local congregations.

For Study: see *Education, OT,* p. 124; *Truth,* p. 552.

In view of the concept of "teaching" seen in this chapter, what opportunities do you have for a teaching ministry? What do you see in this chapter that defines the qualifications necessary for a teacher of that which "is in accord with sound doctrine?"

Chapter 3:1–11. Good Works

Paul stresses the practice of good works, to reflect the work of grace God has performed within the believer. These involve good citizenship (1) and living with others as good neighbors (2). The phrase "true humility" means a patient, trusting attitude. Whatever we once were, trapped in our passions and deceived and enslaved, our relationships infected by malice and hatred (3), we are now made new. God's salvation is said to be an expression of his kindness. Literally this is generosity, which inscriptions from that age show to be the virtue most praised in rulers. God acted out of his own goodness and love to save us. He did not act because of anything we have done (5), for salvation is a gracious, generous gift.

In fact, salvation demanded that God's Spirit wash us so thoroughly that his work constitutes a rebirth, making us new persons (6). The result of this work is that now we are God's heirs, confident possessors of an eternal life which floods us now, as well as guarantees eternity (cf. *Life,* p. 548).

Paul now wants Titus to stress "these things" as a spur to the good works to which believers are to be devoted (8). A life in which a person is constantly busy with good works will be both praiseworthy and meaningful (8).

But Titus is warned to avoid those who see faith as a matter of works, and argue and quarrel about the OT Law. If they will not abandon such a useless and futile approach to Christianity, such persons are to be avoided; for their own actions show they are still in the grip of sin (9–11).

Why does a life of good works seem so important to Paul? What underlies his conviction that good works must be a vital concern of Christians? What emphasis on good works have you experienced in your own Christian life and training?

Chapter 3:12–15. Final Greetings

Paul closes with a few personal notes about friends. But he can't help repeating again the burning passion that moves him with concern for all the churches. "Our people must learn to devote themselves to doing what is good, in order that they may provide for daily necessities, and not live unproductive lives" (14).

Good Works

The word Paul uses in the pastorals when he writes of good works is *kalos.* Its root meaning is "beautiful, noble." In Greek thought it implies that which is aesthetically pleasing as well as morally good. It ultimately came to mean "the total state of soundness, health, wholeness and order" that were to rule within and without a person.

In Titus, Paul argues strongly that God's people are to eagerly pursue acts and deeds which are in every sense, "good." The basis for a believer's good works is deeply rooted in theology. Jesus died to rescue us from wickedness, to purify us, and to make us zealous for good works (2:14). This he accomplished by saving us, not on the basis of our works, but by the supernatural intervention of the Holy Spirit. The Spirit worked an inner transformation, through rebirth and renewal (3:4,5). Good works, then, are the natural overflow of Christ's work for us and the Holy Spirit's work within us. Because good works are integral to salvation itself, all who have "trusted in God" are to "be careful to devote themselves to doing what is good" (3:8).

What are actions which reveal the beauty as well as the moral purity of God, and makes teachings about him so attractive (2:10)? Titus is filled with illustrations. Paul speaks of hospitality (1:8), self-control (1:8), encouraging others (1:9), temperance (2:1), love (1:9), love for husbands and children (2:4), kindness (2:5), trustworthy service (2:10), upright and godly lives (2:11), peaceableness and true humility (3:2), and many other graces which enrich the lives of others as well as our own.

"Good works" then is no suspicious phrase, nor a denial of grace. Instead, good works and beautiful lives are seen as the necessary expression of the work of God in a human life. We need to recover the totally biblical emphasis seen so clearly in Titus on "good works."

For Study: Born Again, p. 545; *Faith and Works,* p. 736.

PHILEMON
A Personal Appeal

This brief letter from prison is a personal appeal from Paul to Philemon on behalf of a runaway slave, Onesimus. Paul has met this young man in Rome in prison and led him to Christ. Now he sends him back to his old master, a beloved brother.

Date and Author. Paul is the author of this brief letter. It was written while Paul was in prison in Rome, probably about A.D. 62 or 63.

Occasion. Onesimus is a runaway slave, who apparently stole from his Christian master, Philemon. He then fled Colossae where Philemon lived (Col. 4:9,17) and found his way to Rome. There he met Paul and became a Christian.

Paul's brief letter, just 335 words in Greek, is an appeal to Philemon to forgive Onesimus and to welcome him back as more than a slave, as a brother.

Values. This letter shows the gentle persuasion Paul used with a brother whom he had once won to Christ. As always the apostle is eager that the response of believers be free and wholehearted, and that no action flow from a sense of compulsion (cf. 2 Cor. 9:7).

The letter also gives us insights into the way Christianity deals with the social issue of slavery. In the first-century world, slavery was an entrenched institution, with the economy resting on slave labor. Historically slave rebellions had been fearsome bloodlettings. Practically, wholesale freedom of slaves would have meant abandoning great segments of the population to starvation, for there were no social mechanisms which could have provided them with employment and a place to live.

Christianity's response was not to mount a crusade against this admittedly evil institution. Instead Christianity introduced a new dynamic: a relationship in which love and respect for others as brothers in Christ eroded antagonism and showed the impossibility of treating human beings as mere property. It is this dynamic that we see revealed so clearly in Paul's short but striking letter to Philemon.

Greetings; 1–3. Paul writes out of an intimate relationship that is both personal and based on shared ministry (1). There is no indication in the rest of the NT of where they may have worked together, unless it was Philemon's home city of Colossae.

Thanksgiving and Prayer; 4–7. This is a common greeting used by letter writers in Hellenistic culture. A number of secular letters show similar thanks to the gods for the health of the addressees and assurance of prayers. Paul fills this typical greeting with distinctive Christian content and adds a special note of appreciation for Philemon as a person (7).

Paul's Plea; 8–22. Paul refuses to make a command of what he is about to request (8). Instead he bases his appeal on love (9). The apostle's concern is for Onesimus who "became my son" while Paul was in prison (10). Although Onesimus has been worthless to Philemon, Paul now assures him that he will prove profitable to both of them (11).

Even though Paul would have liked to keep Onesimus with him (12,13) he returned him so there might be no pressure involved in whatever Philemon chooses to do now (14). In coming back, Onesimus will be a slave but, more than that, a brother (15). Gently Paul encourages Philemon to accept him "both as a man and as a brother in the Lord" (16). It is this dynamic of Christianity, which has power to transform the most warped of relationships, which has throughout history motivated emancipation.

Paul's appeal continues in a deeply personal vein (17–22). He concludes with the hope that he will soon be able to visit Philemon if released from his imprisonment (22).

Final Greetings; 23–25. As is typical, Paul concludes by sharing greetings from their common friends.

Background. One tradition reports that Onesimus later became the bishop of Ephesus in the second century. While the tradition is uncertain, the possibility is intriguing and suggests, in a beautiful way, the transforming power of the gospel, which touched not only individual lives but the very fabric of society.

HEBREWS
Present Ministry of Jesus Christ

This letter was written to Jewish believers who were certain
that God had spoken through the OT, but were shaken as the
radical nature of Christianity became apparent. Legalistic Jews
infiltrated all the churches, and Christian leaders, like the writer
of this letter, ministered to the Jewish Christians whose faith was
wavering. Christian teaching showed the superiority of Jesus, and
how relationship with him promises a full experience of realities
OT institutions could only foreshadow. A study of this fascinating
book helps us to understand the OT. But more important, it helps
us to realize how completely Jesus meets our every need.

Author and Date. In many ways this book remains a mystery.
No author is mentioned in it, and while the early church fathers
speculated about its writer, by the later half of the second century
they were forced to conclude, "God knows the truth of the matter."
So while Barnabas, Apollos, and even Priscilla have been suggested,
we simply do not know who wrote Hebrews. We do know he
was solidly grounded in the OT and in traditional Hebrew exegesis.
From the masculine participle in 11:32 we believe the author was
a man. But that is all.

The date too is uncertain. Hebrews is referred to by Clement
of Rome about A.D. 96, so it was surely written earlier than this.
Many believe the references to temple worship indicate it was written prior to the destruction of Jerusalem in A.D. 70.

Background. While there is no particular location to which this
letter is addressed, it is clear the author speaks to Jewish believers
who had a firm trust in the OT, and a deep affection for the faith
and worship of Judaism. The writer constantly compares the old
covenant and new covenant, carefully pointing out the superiority
of the New. The writer's arguments help us sense the deep yearning
to return to the familiar which troubled Christian Jews who felt
cut off from their roots as the church became more and more
Gentile.

This yearning is understandable. The first excitement associated
with recognizing Jesus as the Messiah had passed. The early return
of Jesus, which all expected (Acts 3:19–21), had not yet taken
place. There was no mass conversion of the Jewish people; many
friends and relatives continued in the old ways, enjoying the pattern

of worship and the fellowship of the synagogue from which Christians were now cut off. In many cities, the flood of Gentile believers imposed a great strain on Jewish believers who, even though they were spread across the Roman world, had always lived in pious separation from Hellenistic culture. Perhaps more serious, the authorities were beginning to view Christianity as something other than a sect of Judaism. The Jews practiced a licit (legally recognized and protected) religion, but antagonism to Christians and persecution of believers was increasingly common. All these pressures caused some Jewish Christians to waver, pondering whether they should turn again to their roots.

It is against this background that the Book of Hebrews was written, with the intent of making clear what abandonment of Jesus for Judaism would involve. For Jesus is the fulfillment of all the OT promises. Only relationship with a living Jesus, who ministers today to his people, promises us an experience of God, and of all the benefits to be found in knowing him.

Values. The Book of Hebrews is especially helpful for Christians today. It helps us to understand the OT. But more important, Hebrews helps us realize what it means for us to be linked with a living Savior! When we understand the full promise of relationship with him, we, like these wavering first century saints, find a great and wonderful release. Hebrews' major themes are outlined in the chart on pages 744 and 745.

Outline

Before Reading. Here are several questions answered in Hebrews.
Which of them are important to you? Read Hebrews for the answers. Does the OT teach that Jesus is God? What is my personal
destiny as a Christian? What does the present and future hold
for me? Can I hear God speaking to me today? What is God's
attitude toward me when I fail him? Is there any way I can be
free from a sense of guilt over past sins? How is faith supposed
to function in my daily life? What does it mean for God to "discipline" me? What resources has God provided to help me grow
as a Christian?

I. Jesus, the Living Word. Chapters 1–4

The Jewish Christians to whom this book is written knew that
God had spoken to their fathers through Moses and the prophets.
The OT was unquestionably the Word of God. Thus, the writer
begins his closely reasoned appeal for full commitment to Christian-
ity by pointing out that Jesus is the ultimate expression of God's
Word, for he is himself God. These chapters contain an appeal
to these Hebrew believers to listen to Jesus as the living Voice of
God, who guides each of us into God's rest in our own "today."

Chapter 1. Superior to Angels

The Revealer of the New; 1:1–4. The OT revelation came in a
progressive and fragmentary way (1). But now a final, authoritative
message has been given, which draws the whole of God's purposes
together, and has in fact been spoken to us by the Son of God.
The phrase, "in these last days," is a rabbinic expression meaning
the age of the Messiah, who is now revealed to be Jesus, the Son
of God (2). There is a strong affirmation here of the full deity of
Jesus. He is the radiant source of that Glory which, in the OT,
marks the very presence of God (see *Glory of God,* p. 345). He
is the exact reproduction of God's essence (3). It is he who is
carrying the ages along toward God's intended end, and who has
provided purification for us from sins (3). He is vastly superior

to even the angels, whom the Jews revered as the messengers who mediated the gift of God's Word to men (4, cf. Heb. 2:2). The word translated "much superior" occurs thirteen times in this letter as a comparison of Christ and the new covenant to the old covenant (for background, see *New Covenant, OT,* p. 330 and *New Covenant, NT,* p. 653).

Testimony of the OT; 1:5–14. A series of quotes from the OT now demonstrate that it too recognizes the superiority of the Son to the supernatural messengers the Jews so deeply respected (see *Angels,* p. 370). How eager then we should be to hear this person who is the Son, and how quick to heed his final, authoritative word.

Chapter 2. Man's Destiny

The First Warning; 2:1–4. There are four warning sections in the Book of Hebrews (see chart, p. 753). This first warning focuses on the importance of heeding the salvation message brought by Jesus. The first verse contains two nautical terms, and means, "We must eagerly anchor ourselves to the truths we've been taught, or we are likely to drift away from our moorings" (1). The reference to punishments is historical: the Mosiac law, conveyed by angels, carried penalties for those who violated it (2: cf. Deut. 28). To what then can these Hebrew believers flee ("how shall we escape") if they turn away from the "great salvation" which has been announced by God himself (3)? And then was confirmed by miracles and by the distribution of spiritual gifts (see *Miracles,* p. 476 and *Spiritual Gifts,* p. 623)! Turning back to Judaism holds out no hope at all!

The Promise of Great Salvation; 2:5–18. Turning back to Judaism also means abandoning a great salvation which promises much to every believer. This salvation can be found only in Jesus.

The "world to come" (5) in rabbinic thought is the age when Messiah will rule from David's throne. The writer points out that God intends to subject that world to men, not angels. He quotes Psalm 8:4–6 to demonstrate God's determination to lift mankind up and give us dominion. Jesus' resurrection, and his exaltation after suffering death for us, is conclusive proof that Jesus is the key to humanity's destiny (5–9).

The suffering of Jesus was always hard for the Jews to accept. Now the writer argues that his suffering was appropriate. God intends, through Jesus, to bring humanity to its intended destiny. Thus Jesus chose to share fully in our human condition. He ac-

Hebrews' Message to Me

HEBREWS	THEME	CONCEPT	KEY VS.	KEY WORDS	MEANING
CH. 1	Jesus' identity	Jesus is God	Heb. 1:1-2	whole, complete	Jesus is enough . . . there is nothing more I need.
2	Our identity	We are Jesus' brothers	Heb. 2:11	mastery, dominion	I need to see myself raised to mastery of life in Jesus.
3 & 4	Life-principle	Experience our position	Heb. 4:10	rest, faith, response	When I trust and obey God I enter His rest.
5	High Priest	Jesus links us with God	Heb. 4:16	weakness, link	When weak, I can come confidently to Jesus for forgiveness and aid.
6	Maturity	Security stimulates growth	Heb. 6:18	insecure, foundation	I can forget myself and launch out in reckless trust that the atonement is complete.

7	Priesthood	Relationship is assured	Heb. 7:25	guaranteed relationship	I can have assurance of salvation: Jesus is my guarantee!
8 & 9	Law	Righteousness is necessary	Heb. 8:10	commandment law, inner law	I can trust Jesus to make me progressively more righteous as I trust and obey Him.
9 & 10	Sacrifice	Holiness is ours	Heb. 10:14	guilt, cleansed	I can see myself in Jesus as a holy, not a guilty person.
10	Warning	Maturing takes time	Heb. 10:35-36	process, persevere	I can know that daily commitment to God's will will produce maturity.
11	Faith	Faith enables	Heb. 11:6	enablement, obedience	I can meet any challenge enabled by faith in God.
12	Discipline	Faith becomes commitment	Heb. 12:10	patience, holiness	I can discipline myself to full commitment to faith's life.
13	Love	Faith produces love	Heb. 13:20-21	externals, grace	I can find life's real meaning in others and in Christ.

cepted the sufferings to which all of us are subject as part of what it means to be of the "same family" (10–13). The implications here are stunning. Jesus stooped to share all that we are, identifying himself fully with us, so that he might then lift us up to share all that he is! We are of one family now, inheriting through our relationship with Jesus—our elder brother—the very life of God (see *Born Again*, p. 545).

The thought expressed in making Jesus "perfect through suffering" (10) does not imply adding to his nature. It means qualifying him for his mission. To serve as the pioneer of our salvation, Jesus had to be a true human being and to suffer (cf. Heb. 4:14–5:10).

Finally, the writer points out that, through sharing in our humanity and dying as a human being, Jesus destroyed the hold of Satan over mankind. The fear of death and the one who wielded it no longer holds us enslaved, for Jesus has nullified Satan's power (14–16). The word "destroy" in verse 14 means to make impotent, as though no longer existing. Thus a relationship with Jesus frees us from our bondage, and Jesus becomes the dominant person in our life. Because Jesus has suffered as a man, he is deeply sensitive to our needs. He is willing to help us in the hour of our temptation (17,18).

This then is the destiny of redeemed humanity: to be lifted up to dominion and, until then, to live each day linked to a compassionate Jesus, who stoops to help us in our hour of need. This truly is a great salvation, for never did the old covenant promise such a destiny, or offer a stricken mankind such aid.

How has Jesus won this "great salvation" for you? What can you experience now of the exaltation that is promised in Christ?

Chapter 3:1–4:13. Hearing God's Voice

The writer has presented Jesus as one who brought word of the great salvation he himself won for us (ch. 1). That salvation not only promises the ultimate fulfillment of humanity's destiny (2:1–13), but also contains the promise of present aid (2:14–18). The writer now explores the promise of present aid, one benefit of living daily in relationship with a living Jesus.

Greater Than Moses; 3:1–6. Moses was honored above all men by the Jews. He was viewed by the rabbis as even greater than the angels, because of his role as giver of God's law. Jesus is superior to Moses, just as the person who plans, designs, builds and pays for a house is greater than a butler who serves in it (4,5).

There is another reason for the comparison with Moses. The law code that bears Moses' name patterned all of life for the Jewish people. It should follow then, since Jesus has come with his superior message, that he will also introduce a superior way of life! This thought is now developed as the writer urges believers to listen for Jesus' living voice which speaks "today."

The Danger of Unbelief; 3:7–19. The writer returns to an incident from Moses' time to demonstrate the urgency of responding to each fresh word from God. The children of Israel had been poised on the borders of the Promised Land when God called on them to enter. But they refused to listen. Rebelliously, they hardened their hearts. As a result they were unable to enter the land of rest but were turned away to wander and die in the wilderness (7–11). Today a fresh word from God has come through Jesus. Today, too, it is vital to guard against an unbelieving heart, which expresses itself by turning away from God (12). Christians need constant mutual encouragement to keep each other tender toward God (13). The next phrase makes it clear that the writer views his readers as true believers. "Share in Christ" in the original indicates those who have become and are now partakers in a real relationship with Christ (14). It is failure to hold firmly to this relationship that is the danger, for a return to the life style of Judaism would be a rebellion against God's contemporary voice. Such a return would place these Jewish Christians in the same condition as the ancient Jews who sinned, and whose bodies were buried in the desert. Like them, the present generation would forfeit God's promised rest (15–19).

It is important in interpreting this passage to remember that the generation to which the writer refers was redeemed, and its sins were covered by the atoning sacrifices God provided for them (see *Atonement, OT,* p. 99). What ancient Israel forfeited was not salvation but an experience of the blessing which would have been theirs in Canaan. So too with the believers to whom Hebrews is written. Turning back is rejecting God's present voice, intended to guide them today to God's place of blessing and rest.

Rest Today; 4:1–12. This complicated passage is based on the repeated affirmation that God always speaks in the "today" of his people (1,7,8). Always God speaks to his people, eager to guide them into his rest.

"Rest" is used in three senses in Hebrews 3 and 4. First, it is used to describe life in the Promised Land: a life in total contrast to the bondage the old generation had known as slaves. In the Promised Land were vineyards Israel had not planted and homes they had not built, all waiting for them to take possession. Second, the word is used in relation to God's rest, which he entered on completing Creation. Jewish teachers noted that the seventh day was not marked by an "evening" (Gen. 2:1,2). The rabbis took this to mean that God's work was completed. He is not inactive but every contingency is planned for so that he is at rest. The third use of "rest" is an application of these first two to Christian experience. The promise of a "Sabbath-rest for the people of God" (9) indicates that we can cease from our struggles and enter into God's own rest (10). That is, we can let him guide us into these places of blessing which he has already prepared for us. Our "effort to enter that rest" (11) does not mean struggle against circumstances but instead constant attention to our hearts, lest we become like unresponsive Israel and refuse to listen to God's voice. We must obey when he speaks to us.

To the writer of Hebrews, this is the essential nature of faith: faith is a responsiveness to God which expresses itself as obedience to his voice in each of our "todays."

There is both an objective and a subjective aspect to this message. Objectively, the "today" message of God is the gospel of Jesus which these Jewish Christians had begun to doubt. Subjectively, because Jesus lives and serves as our high priest (see *Priesthood, NT,* p. 749), Jesus does give personal guidance to each believer. If we are to experience the blessings of the Christian life, we need to be obedient to God's promptings whenever we recognize his voice, believing that there is no problem we face which he cannot solve—and no uncertainty for which he does not have the answer.

The Living Word; 4:12,13. The writer now describes God's Word as alive and active today. God's voice moves deep within us, penetrating to the level of our inmost thoughts and attitudes. The word "judge" (12) means "capable of making a decision, discerning" and, in this sense, able to judge. All is open and known to God, and it is his word "which applies to us" (not "to whom we must give an account"). God, who knows all, is present within to guide us daily by his living and active contemporary voice.

What problems are you struggling with now? Have you asked God to guide you? You can commit yourself to obey and know that through the written Word, a Christian friend, or inner certainty, God the Holy Spirit will speak to you and show you God's solution.

In what ways is "rest" an appropriate term to describe what would happen within a person if he or she approached difficult decisions with the confidence that God knows the situation and has a solution which he will reveal by a living Word when it is time?

Have you found it an effort to keep a believing attitude (4:11)? What is the difference between this struggle and other struggles you have known as a Christian?

II. Jesus, Our High Priest (Chapter 4:14–8:13)

The writer has shown one superiority of Christianity. OT and NT messages are both the Word of God. But the NT message has been delivered by the Son of God himself! Also, the NT word is a living and active word, capable of penetrating our deepest thoughts and motives—and guiding us daily into God's rest. How important that we maintain our trust in Jesus, sensitive and obedient to his voice as he speaks to us in our today.

Earlier the writer called Jesus our "merciful and faithful high priest" (2:17). He now picks up this theme. The priesthood, and the comfort found in always having a Mediator to stand before God in the temple, was vital to Jewish believers: something Jewish Christians felt had been lost. Now, to all those yearning for the old order, the writer of Hebrews unveils the wonderful meaning of having Jesus as our ever-living high priest.

Chapter 4:12–5:10. Jesus' Priesthood

A Sympathetic High Priest; 4:14–16. Even though our high priest is "Jesus the Son of God" (14), he is able to "sympathize with our weaknesses." The meaning is "share in the experience": to be present with us in our weakness. This is because Jesus has been put to the same tests we are, yet never sinned. This point is important. We never know the full power of the temptation unless we resist it. Jesus experienced the full impact of every temptation that can be known by humanity, but he never surrendered to them (15). It is because he knows our weaknesses so thoroughly that we never need draw back from him in shame. He knows what it means to be human, so we can come with bold confidence to the throne of grace. We can be sure that he will extend us mercy when we fail and will provide help to meet our need when we require strength to overcome as he did.

Priesthood, New Testament

The OT priests represented God to man, and represented man to God. The priests were entrusted on God's behalf with teaching his word and

with judging the actions of his people. On humanity's behalf the priests
were entrusted with the offerings and the sacrifices by which a sinner might
approach God to find forgiveness or to offer praise. The priests were media-
tors: they linked an estranged humanity with a loving, yet holy God.

In the NT we see all these functions carried out by Jesus. In his own
person as true God and fully man, Jesus links God and man in indissoluble
union. Thus Jesus is able to perfectly represent God to man, communicating
to us by his living Word in a voice we can recognize in our every "today"
(Heb. 3, 4). At the same time he stands in God's presence to guarantee
us access, forgiveness, and aid.

Jesus supersedes, in his own person, all the functions that in OT times
were carried on by the priesthood. With Jesus as living high priest, the
OT priesthood becomes completely unnecessary!

But there is more to the priesthood as taught in the NT than the priesthood of Jesus. There is also a "priesthood of believers." This reality is
best understood when we realize that Jesus continues his mission to mankind
through Christians. So our priestly ministry may involve sharing a word
of correction or of encouragement which is recognized by a brother or
sister as a living word from Christ. Or our priestly ministry may be exercised
in prayer, representing others before the throne of grace. Priesthood is
no longer for a few (the family of Aaron). It is for all believers.

When we understand the priesthood of Jesus, explained so beautifully
in Hebrews 4 through 8, we better understand our own personal ministry
to others as underpriests, serving both our Lord and one another. But
best of all, we realize how free we are to come confidently to God.

For study: Hebrews chapters 4–8; 1 Peter 2:4–10; *OT Priesthood,* p. 103.

The Priestly Ministry; 5:1–9. The writer now builds on what
these Jewish Christians already know about a high priest. He is
chosen from the human family, to represent mankind to God (1).
He is to have a controlled sympathy for sinners, but to deal with
sins by sacrifice rather than overlook them (2,3). The honor of
the high priesthood goes only to one selected by God, as was
Aaron (4). Just so God, in the OT, appoints the Son a "priest
forever, after the order of Melchizedek" (5,6; cf. Heb. 7:1–21).
Now the writer explains that Jesus has already functioned as a
high priest. He offered up what was, to the rabbis, the most significant kind of prayers ("with tears"). And his resurrection proves
that God heard him (7)! The note that he "learned obedience"
and was "made perfect" (8,9) speaks of Jesus' full personal experience of the cost of obedience when his suffering was involved.
He was "made perfect" in the sense that he retained his integrity
under every assault and thus fully established his qualifications
for sympathetic priesthood. Then, as the culminating ministry of
a high priest, he offered a sacrifice which made him the "source

of eternal salvation for all who obey him" (9,10). "Obey" in this context and in others where "obedience to the truth" is spoken of, indicates a response to God that is rooted in faith (cf. Heb. 4:1–3).

Chapter 5:11–6:20. Falling Away?

This is the second of the four warning sections in Hebrews. It has been the focus of much theological debate as well as personal concern. We need to carefully trace the writer's thinking.

Immaturity; 5:11–14. The writer first expresses frustration. These people, so knowledgeable about the OT priesthood, seem unable to grasp the meaning of Christ's priesthood (11). They are like unskilled infants, blindly sucking at milk when they should be mature and spiritually sensitive, having grown by constantly distinguishing between what is good (beneficial) and evil (dangerous or injurious). The warning, then, is against continuing in immaturity.

On to Maturity; 6:1–3. The writer urges these believers to move on to maturity. "Leaving" the elementary teachings does not mean to abandon them, but to view them as a beginning. Christians are to build on elementary truths as a foundation, taking them as givens rather than constantly and doubtfully returning to them.

No Option; 6:4–6. There have been four interpretations of this difficult passage. One: the writer speaks of Jews who have stopped just short of faith in Christ. Two: he speaks of believers who have fallen into sin and will lose their reward. Three: he refers to believers whose unbelief means loss of salvation. Four: he gives a hypothetical illustration, to show how foolish it is to think of a return to Judaism. The following paraphrase highlights the fourth interpretation, which picks up the image of immature believers, struggling to "lay again the foundation" (6:1) of faith.

"Think how impossible! Imagine a believer—one who has been enlightened, tasted heaven's gift, shared in the Holy Spirit, experienced the goodness of God's Word and the spiritual resources still to be revealed—imagine him to fall away and be lost again. What will he do to get back to God? Crucify Jesus all over again? Shame!" There is no going back: the only way a believer can go is on to maturity, building on the firm foundation God has laid for us in Christ.

Encouragement; 6:7–9. The writer turns again to maturity and to the products of maturity. God is concerned that a useful crop grow from the land he waters (cf. Isa. 5:1–7). Thorns and thistles on cropland are worthless and must be burned off so the land can be productive. This image may speak of discipline, or of the final evaluation of the Christian's life (1 Cor. 3:10–15; 2 Cor. 5:10). These Jewish Christians must go on to maturity (6:1) and fruitfulness (6:7,8).

As though he senses this warning might shake his readers, the writer expresses confidence in them. He is persuaded that the better things which are always associated with salvation (9) do and will mark their lives as well (10). But, he explains, "we do not want you to become lazy." It will take earnest endeavor and patient endurance for these Hebrew Christians to "inherit what has been promised" (that is, the maturity and fruitfulness response to God will produce).

God's Sure Promise; 6:13–20. The writer concludes by affirming the security of the Christian's foundational truths. God has spoken and given his oath (13–18; cf. *Covenant, OT,* p. 51). Thus he has made the "unchanging nature of his purpose" very clear. God's promise is "an anchor for the soul, firm and secure" (19). The anchor chain which links us to the promise stretches beyond the sanctuary curtain (20).

This last image is of vast significance for Jewish Christians. Once a year, on the Day of Atonement, the high priest entered the inner sanctuary of the temple which was blocked off by a thick curtain. There, in the very presence of God, he offered a blood sacrifice for the sins of the people. The writer is saying clearly that Jesus' priestly ministry, fulfilled when he went before God with the offering of his own blood, has forged an unbreakable chain, linking the believer with Jesus who stands today in the very presence of God.

Chapter 7. A Priest Forever

In Hebrews 5:6 the writer noted that Christ's priesthood is "after the order of Melchizedek." Now he explains two vital implications.

Melchizedek; 7:1–10. The argument of this passage has deep roots in rabbinic interpretation of the OT. The person named appears only briefly, in Genesis 22:7. He is identified as both a king and priest. No genealogy is given; no birth or death are recorded. He simply stands there for a timeless instant, his greatness demonstrated by the fact that Abraham paid him a tithe and that Melchizedek blessed Abraham. In a sense, the writer says, even Levi, from whose family OT priests came, recognized Melchizedek's superiority too.

The Warnings of Hebrews

Keys	Hebrews 2:1-4	Hebrews 5:11-6:8	Hebrews 10:19-39	Hebrews 12:14-20
Section Theme	JESUS the Living Word	JESUS our High Priest	JESUS the Perfect Sacrifice	JESUS, the Object of Faith
Who is warned?	those who have heard the gospel	immature believers	those turning back to a Jewish life style	those weakening under difficulties
What are they to do?	hold to what was heard	go on to maturity (6:1)	persevere in living by faith (10:32-37)	respond to God and not refuse his calling (12:25)
Consequences of not heeding?	drift from life's moorings	fruitless and unproductive lives (6:7,8)	ruin of their hopes (10:39)	build life on that which will be destroyed (10:27)
Benefits of heeding?	experience God's great salvation	experience what God has promised (6:12)	experience of rich reward (10:35)	receive the unshakable kingdom (12:28)
How do they heed?	respond obediently (3:7-4:13)	trust God's oath as a firm foundation (6:13-20)	make commitment to love and good works as Christians	live by faith

Jesus Like Melchizedek; 7:11–28. The writer now points out to these Hebrew Christians so eager to return to the Aaronic priesthood of Judaism, that if that priesthood could have brought perfection, then there would have been no OT promise of a priesthood "in the order of Melchizedek" (11–17). But there is! Jesus has come and now has been raised to "an indestructible life." Thus Jesus is qualified for the long-promised new priesthood!

The writer also argues that this change in the priesthood means the entire OT law covenant is set aside, for its commandments, priesthood, sacrifices and life style are a single fabric. Jesus' superior and endless priesthood means the coming of a superior covenant (18–24: see *New Covenant, OT* p. 330 and *New Covenant, NT* p. 653). Under the new covenant, the superior priest, Jesus, is "able to save completely (both "for all time" and "to completeness") all who come to God through him" (25). At last we have a high priest who meets our every need! Jesus, so powerful and perfect in his own right, has been brought, through his experience of suffering and death, to the place where he can function as the ultimate high priest (26–28).

In four ways then Jesus' priesthood is superior to the OT priesthood which so attracts these converted Jews. One: Jesus is qualified by his resurrection to endless life for an eternal priesthood. OT priests were only qualified by physical descent (15,16). Two: Jesus' priesthood is guaranteed by God's oath. No oath guaranteed permanence to the OT priesthood (17–22). Three: OT priests lived and died. Jesus is a permanent priest who "always lives to make intercession for us" (23–25). Four, the priests of the OT were themselves weak and sinful men, for whom sacrifices must be made. But Jesus' perfection stands as a visible guarantee that he is able to save us "completely" (26–28).

How foolish the Jewish Christians would be to abandon reliance on Jesus as their high priest, to return to an ineffective institution.

Chapter 8. The New Covenant

The priesthood of Aaron's family is an integral part of Mosaic law. Law, the "old covenant," encompassed the whole of the commands given by God: the worship, sacrifices, temple, priesthood, and every other OT institution. Because every element was linked, a change in priesthood implies a corresponding change in the whole and in every other element (cf. 7:12). The writer now goes on to argue that, since Jesus' priesthood is superior, it follows that his whole new covenant will be superior!

The Reality, not the Shadow; 8:1–6. The OT sanctuary in which the priests ministered was constructed on a pattern delivered by God. That pattern symbolically represented ("is a copy and shadow of") heavenly realities (3–5). Because the covenant which Jesus administers is founded on reality and not shadow, it is vastly superior and promises much more to mankind (6).

The Obsolete Replaced; 8:7–13. The OT is itself the source of the term "new covenant" (Jer. 31:31–34). The very name "new" marks the old Mosaic code as something which was temporary, due to become obsolete and to be replaced. The author's quote shows two vital areas in which the new replaces and is superior to the old. Under the new God "will put my laws in their minds and write them on their hearts" (10). OT Law was written on parchments and stone tablets. It stood outside man, pointing out what men must do and condemning when men failed. But the living Word of the new covenant is written within the believer's very personality, freeing us to spontaneously do the good and the moral (for background see *Law, OT,* p. 87; *New Covenant, OT,* p. 330; *Law, NT,* p. 617; and *New Covenant, NT,* p. 653). This is one stunning superiority of the covenant that Jesus administers. The second great difference, which the writer goes on to develop in chapters 9 and 10, is that under the new covenant there is complete forgiveness for sinning humanity. Because the old has passed, and the new has come, there is at last assured transformation for humankind.

Chapters 5–8 must have been as thrilling for the Jewish believers to whom it was penned as it is difficult for us today. We know little of the meaning priesthood had for OT worshipers. Here, however, are key verses which sum up the meaning to us of Jesus' present ministry as high priest: 4:15,16; 5:8,9; 6:18; 7:24,25; 8:10,12. Read each. At what times in your life would each ministry have special meaning?

Return to the warning section (5:11–6:8). Why do you suppose it is inserted in this section dealing with Jesus' ministry as high priest? How might confidence in Jesus as high priest free these hesitant believers to move on to maturity?

III. Jesus, the Perfect Sacrifice (Chapters 9, 10)

The writer has now demonstrated that Christianity has a word from God which is superior to the OT word (Ch. 1–4). He has shown that Jesus is a vastly superior high priest, compared with the OT priesthood (Ch. 5–8). Now the writer will show that the sacrifice on which forgiveness rests is also superior to the sacrifices of the old covenant.

The OT speaks of blood sacrifice in these words: "the life of a creature is in the blood, and I have given it to you to make atonement for yourselves on the altar: it is the blood that makes atonement for one's life" (Lev. 17:11; see *Atonement,* p. 99). Throughout the OT, the blood of sacrifical animals taught that giving a life is a necessary, God-given avenue to forgiveness. Now the full promise of the old system has been realized in the One of whom all the sacrifices spoke.

Those familiar with the OT should have been prepared for the writer's explanations. From the moment God slew an animal to cover the guilty Adam and Eve (Gen 3:21), sacrifice had been taught.

Chapter 9. The Blood of Christ

Old Covenant Sacrifices; 9:1–10. The OT tabernacle, and the temple which followed, were designed for sacrifice. They were the setting for an annual drama, which took place each Day of Atonement (cf. p. 99). On that day the high priest entered the curtained inner chamber to present a blood offering to God, first for his own sins and then for the sins of the people (1–7). Earlier the writer showed the sanctuary was a symbolic representation of heavenly realities (8:3–6). Now he says this atonement drama was also symbolic—an "illustration for the present time" (9). OT sacrifices covered over sins ("cover over" is the literal meaning of "atone") but were not able to clear the consciences of the worshipers (see *Conscience,* p. 759). The fact that a thick curtain continually blocked off the inner sanctuary showed that "the way into the Most Holy had not yet been disclosed" (8).

The writer does not mention it here, but the Gospel of Luke reports that at the moment of Jesus' death "the curtain of the temple was torn in two" (Luke 23:45). With the sacrifice of Jesus on Calvary, the "time of the new order" (Heb. 9:10) had finally come!

The Blood of Christ; 9:11–28. The next verses develop striking contrasts. Jesus entered the true holy place, not the copy on earth (11). Jesus entered with his own blood, not the blood of animals (12). Jesus' blood provided no temporary covering, but won eternal redemption for us, cleansing not the outer, material man but the innermost personality of those he sets apart to God (13,14). With our consciences thus cleansed, we are freed at last to serve the living God (14).

Forgiveness

There are few more awe-inspiring teachings in Scripture. This is particularly so when we grasp the full impact of what God has done for us and what he teaches us in this distinctive Bible term, which carries the same meaning in Hebrew and in Greek.

The root meaning in both languages is to "cancel," "release," or to "send away." There is no hint of leniency here, as though God were ready to overlook evil. Instead the word "forgive" speaks of firm, direct action taken by God to "send off" not the feelings of guilt associated with sin, but the sin itself!

When God forgives sin, he cancels it completely. So completely that even he "will remember their sins no more" (Heb. 8:12). A sin which God has forgiven no longer has existence. It no longer blocks intimate relationship with God, because it has been removed. It no longer locks us in the paralyzing hold of remembered guilt, because it has been removed. It no longer blocks growth and change. When we understand and accept by faith the truth of the way that God has dealt with sin through Jesus, we experience a flooding sense of joy and know release from bondage to our past.

One of the great contributions of the Book of Hebrews is to help us understand more fully the meaning of Jesus' sacrifice of himself for us, and the meaning of the forgiveness that sacrifice has won. The chart below sums up the emphasis of Hebrews:

An Act of Sin . . .	Generates	Jesus Deals With Sin As . . .	Providing
	Shame	Compassionate High Priest	Ready Access To God (Heb. 5–8)
	Guilt	Perfect Blood Sacrifice	Forgiveness (Heb. 9–10)
	Guilt Feelings	Perfect Blood Sacrifice	Cleansing of Conscience (Heb. 9–10)

If our conscience troubles us, or we feel a sense of guilt and shame, we need only come to Jesus. He has won us forgiveness. We are free, for God's promise is "their sins and lawless acts I will remember no more" (Heb. 9:17; cf also *Guilt,* p. 95).

The writer turns to analogy. We "inherit" after a person dies. The blood sacrifices demanded under the old covenant to cleanse objects associated with it served as a continual object lesson that "without the shedding of blood there is no forgiveness." The old always looked ahead to, and spoke of, someone's coming death (16–22).

This is just what happened! Jesus died and entered heaven itself bearing his own blood, being both priest and sacrifice. The sacrifice was so excellent that he suffered only once. His one sacrifice was sufficient to take away the sins of the many. When Jesus comes again it will not be to make another sacrifice but to complete the salvation that is in store for all who await him (23–28).

Chapter 10:1–18. One Sacrifice Sufficient

The writer continues his explanation of the superiority of Christ's sacrifice of his own life for our sins.

Annual Reminder of Sins; 10:1–4. The very fact that the OT sacrifices had to be endlessly repeated proves they did not cleanse from sin. The sacrifices were in fact constant reminders of Israel's guilt. But Jesus' one sacrifice cleanses his worshipers "once for all." Our sins truly are gone, and we are freed from guilt! We can forget our past.

Full Satisfaction; 10:5–10. The writer quotes an OT passage which shows God could never be satisfied with the sacrifices the law required. Christ's coming revealed what God had determined from the first to be necessary to deal with sin. By Jesus' one sacrifice, he has set apart and made holy all who believe in him.

Forgiveness in Full; 10:11–18. The effectiveness of Jesus' sacrifice is demonstrated in three ways. First, Jesus "sat down" at God's right hand. OT priests never sat in God's presence and always returned to make another sacrifice (11,12). Second, Jesus "made us perfect." This phrase means that he completed what God intended for us; that his act has a present and continuing impact on us. He is even now writing his law within our hearts and minds, demonstrating that we are "being made holy" (13–15). Third, the effectiveness of Jesus' sacrifice is shown in the fact that God has forgiven, and thus forgotten, our "sins and iniquities." We stand before him in Christ and are pronounced holy (14,17–18)! No more sacrifices are required.

All of us are bothered at times by conscience and nagged by the memory of past sins or failures. What in Hebrews 9–10 proves that you can forget your past? What gives assurance that there is hope for your future? What helps you realize that God himself does not condemn you, or feel disappointed in you?

Conscience

Today we use "conscience" in two primary ways; one to indicate moral awareness, and the other to suggest a sense of guilt. Conscience is used in both ways in the NT. Some NT passages warn of evils which "sear" the conscience. Others warn that an inadequate understanding of biblical principles makes for a "weak" conscience (cf. 1 Tim. 4:2; Titus 1:15; 1 Cor. 8:7, 10). Thus conscience is not regarded as an adequate guide even though it is a moral sense.

The Bible also uses conscience in the sense of guilty remembrance of past sins. It is important to the apostles that believers refuse to sin knowingly. There is a confidence and freedom which come from having a clear conscience (Acts 23:1; Rom. 13:5; 1 Tim. 1:5,19; 3:9; 2 Tim. 1:3; 1 Pet. 2:19; 3:16).

The most significant use of conscience as guilty remembrance is found in Hebrews. There it carries the meaning most uniformly given to it in the common speech of the first century. In common speech "conscience" spoke of a deep pain felt when a human being does wrong. For the Greek-speaking world the "bad conscience," marked by relentless inner anguish and the nagging awareness that moral wholeness had been lost, was of deep concern.

While there is no OT word for "conscience," the term "heart" often functions there as a "bad conscience," reminding of guilt (1 Sam. 24:6) and causing both sorrow and regret (Ps. 51:3–10). This is also the way the term is used in Hebrews 9 and 10. Because of sin man is locked in the grip of his past, paralyzed from doing good by the realization that he is evil at heart. Nothing the ritual of the OT could do could free an individual from the awareness of his guilt and from a bad conscience.

Yet Jesus in his sacrifice of himself at Calvary dealt with just this bondage. His blood paid for the past sins that trouble our conscience. Cleansed from such sins, our consciences now are purged of our past acts. We can now act as holy people, for we have actually been made holy by Jesus' sacrifice (Heb. 10:10).

If we are to experience the joy and freedom that are our heritage in Christ, it's vital to realize that our past sins *are* gone. We no longer need to look back with regret and anguish; we are no longer the person we were then. Instead of looking back and feeling helpless, we can look forward with perfect confidence and hope. Because of Jesus our conscience has been cleansed, and we realize that we truly have been made new.

For study: Forgiveness, p. 757; Hebrews 9–10.

Chapter 10:19–39. A Call to Persevere

Faith's Life Style; 10:19–25. The writer calls on his Hebrew Christian readers to live together in light of all Jesus has done as high priest and as a sacrifice. Now a believer can enter God's very presence and need not look to an earthly priest to represent him (19–21). Because we are truly forgiven, we can put our guilty consciences behind us (22,23). It is important for believers to gather, to help each build a godly life marked by love and good works on this foundation which Jesus has laid (24,25; 6:1–13).

Where to Turn? 10:26–31. The writer now strongly warns Hebrew believers who have given up "meeting together" (10:24) and who are even now turning back to Judaism. His argument takes a common rabbinic form, reasoning from the lesser to the greater. Those who rejected Moses' law "died without mercy" when convicted (28). How much more deserving of judgment are those who despise God's own Son and treat his self-sacrifice as empty and useless? Those who turn back to Judaism deliberately reject the living word, the high priesthood, and the sacrifice of God's Son (29–31).

In OT times the sins of all God's people were covered by a sacrifice offered on the Day of Atonement. But the sins individuals committed between such sacrifices interrupted fellowship with God and called for the individual to offer his or her own sacrifices. But OT law made no provision for cleansing from individual acts of deliberate sin. Verse 26 ("there is no more sacrifice for sins") builds on this OT concept. It argues by analogy that there is no way for a person to deliberately abandon Jesus—and then find fellowship with God and growth toward holiness (cf. Gal. 3:1–14; 5:2–6).

Persevere! 10:32–39. The writer looks back at the evidence. These very people did boldly follow Jesus in "those earlier days" (32–34). He now begs them not to "throw away" their confidence. Only after a person has done the will of God can he expect to receive the promise (25,26). Jesus will come, and then all that God has promised will be received. Until then we must live by faith (37).

The writer concludes his warning with an expression of confidence in his readers. "We are not those who shrink back and are destroyed (ruined). We are those who believe and experience salvation!"

IV. Jesus, the Way to Sanctification (Chapters 11–13)

The writer of Hebrews has demonstrated the superiority of Jesus as the living Word (Ch. 1–4), as high priest (Ch. 5–8), and as the perfect sacrifice for sin (Ch. 9–10). Again and again he has urged these Jewish believers to live by the great truths he has explained. He has just concluded his last warning with an exhortation to live by faith. Now this great NT book concludes with an extended discussion of faith's life style.

Chapter 11. By Faith

The Nature of Faith; 11:1–2,6. The validity of "faith" does not rest on the sincerity of the believer, but on the reliability of what is believed. Truths revealed by God's Word cannot be seen, but we can still be confident about them (1). It is in the nature of our faith to take God's Word for what we can't see, just as we believe that he shaped the visible universe from nothing, although there can be no witnesses (2). Without the confidence that God exists and wants a relationship with man (6), no one can be pleasing to him.

The Evidence of Faith; 11:3–40. We may not see the object of our faith. But we do have evidence. Faith has a visible impact on human experience. Over and over again, those who have trusted God have demonstrated by their lives the validity of their faith. Here then is a great hall of fame. It is peopled with OT heroes and heroines whose significance in salvation history shows the Jewish Christians to whom this book is written, that those who follow Jesus by faith (10:35–39) place their feet on a path well-marked by the men and women they revere.

Look at each individual in this hall of fame. How did faith function in each person's life? What did faith enable him or her to accomplish? What does God want you to accomplish this week "by faith"?

Chapter 12:1–13. Discipline

Run Your Marathon; 12:1–3. The saints who across the ages have lived by faith are a great crowd of witnesses who give a common testimony. In view of their evidence (Ch. 11), we are to "run with perseverance the race marked out for us" (1). Jesus' own example of committed obedience serves to encourage us and to strengthen us. We continue to live by faith, despite opposition (2,3).

Opposition As Discipline; 12:4–11. The Jewish Christians to whom this is written had become discouraged and had lost heart, even though their struggle had not even bloodied them (4) as it did Jesus and many OT saints. Rather than be discouraged by such events, Christians need to understand opposition and difficulties as training provided by God. The writer points out several things concerning God's discipline, which these Christians—and we!—need to keep in mind.

God's discipline is always loving (6). Difficulty is not an indication that God is displeased with us. It is evidence of his love!

God's discipline is a family matter (7,8). A father only accepts responsibility for the training of legitimate children! The fact that God disciplines shows that we are really his own.

God's discipline is purposive (10). God never acts on impulse. He always looks ahead and has our benefit in view. His purpose is that we might grow to "share his holiness."

God's discipline is effective (11). God's training may bring a temporary pain, but it will produce righteousness and peace.

God's discipline calls for response. Rather than becoming listless or falling into paralyzed inactivity, we are to continue vigorously on, sure that the discipline will not disable us but bring healing.

What difficulties do we face now? How have you responded to them (10,12)? Which of the truths taught in 11:5–14 is most helpful to you?

Chapter 12:14–29. Do Not Refuse God

Will these Jewish Christians respond to the writer's call and turn again to a life of faith? One last warning is now included (cf. 753). The writer begins by pointing out three dangers. The interpersonal danger (14) is that we will fail to live in peace with our brothers and sisters and so turn aside from holiness. The inner danger (15) is that we will not see God's grace in what happens to us and become bitter. The outward danger (16,17) is that we will choose immorality and other sensual pleasures instead of our spiritual birthright.

The contrast is further developed. The OT shows God breaking through into the physical universe at Sinai. Fire, darkness, gloom and storm warned of his holy presence (18–21). But in Jesus we are lifted into a heavenly realm, marked as a truly "better world" by joy and righteousness (22–24). The Jewish believers have a choice. Will they refuse God, who is calling them to a heavenly life style (25), and try to build their lives in the material world? That world is only a copy of reality (cf. 8:1–6) and soon will be shaken out of existence (26: cf. 2 Pet. 3:3–12). Or will they heed God's voice and live "by faith," thus "receiving a kingdom that cannot be shaken" (28)? The appropriate response to God is not to turn back to Judaism, but to be thankful and reverently worship the Lord.

What are some "shakable" things that Christians sometimes rely on for security? What from Hebrews 11 and 12 do you believe God really wants us to rely on? In what ways are these things "unshakable?"

Chapter 13. Love and Good Deeds

Earlier in this section, the writer urged his readers to build a life together which focuses on "love and good deeds" (Heb. 10:24). Now he closes with a brief series of exhortations. Each helps us picture the life of faith which God has in mind for citizens of his unshakable kingdom.

Keep on Loving; 13:1–3. Hospitality and visiting those who are in prison or suffering are examples of "loving each other as brothers."

Be Holy; 13:4–6. Personal holiness involves forsaking sexual immorality and love of money. Victory is won through the confidence that God is with us and that he will never forsake us.

Be Responsive to Leaders; 13:7–10,17. The lives and the faith of leaders are to be observed and imitated. "Strange teachings" are to be rejected. Verse 17 should be understood: "Be responsive to those whom God has given to guide you and remain open to their persuasion" (see *Spiritual Authority,* p. 658). Leaders do not command. The respect they earn should make commands unnecessary.

Bear the Disgrace; 13:11–14. Jesus suffered a death which was considered shameful by Israelites. He was even taken outside Jerusalem so his execution would not contaminate that holy place. Now these Jewish Christians want to return to Judaism!? The writer urges them instead to bear the disgrace of exclusion from the OT community. In doing so, they will be going out to join Jesus.

Offer Praise; 13:15,16. The rabbis taught that in the messianic age the only required sacrifices would be thank offerings. The writer mentions this belief when he points out that all believers can now offer God is praise and the sacrifice of their own dedication to "doing good" (see *Good Works,* p. 736).

Prayer, and Benediction; 13:18–25. The writer, as the apostle Paul often does, closes with a request that the recipients of the letter pray for him. And he commends them to God (20,21).

The reference to brother Timothy suggests that Timothy was imprisoned some time after Paul's execution in A.D. 67 or 68, but won his release.

Look over the benediction (20–21). How is each phrase related to the subjects covered in this great epistle?

How does the life style described in this final chapter compare to and differ from the life style of those who still followed Judaism? What seems most important in each system? Why is this life style outlined here so far superior?

JAMES
Faith at Work

This is probably the earliest of the NT letters. It is written to a young church, composed only of Jewish believers. The author is James, the brother of Jesus. James is not an evangelistic book or a doctrinal book. It is simply a letter of exhortation, written to the family of God, urging the believers to live out their faith in ways that honor God. It is a helpful book for all of us who want to make Jesus the center of our lives and honor him in all we do.

Author. There are several different men named James in the NT. One is the brother of John, martyred by Herod Agrippa I about A.D. 44 (Acts 12:1–3). Another is James the son of Alphaeus, also one of the disciples. Many believe this person is also called James the Less (Younger). The most prominent James is identified as "the Lord's brother." Paul mentions him as a leader of the Jerusalem church (Gal. 1:19). In most NT references he is simply called James (Acts 12:17; 15:13; 21:18; 1 Cor. 15:17; Gal. 2:9).

James, like the other children of Mary and Joseph, did not respond to the early claims of Jesus (John 7:2–5). But James was later converted and achieved great influence in the Jerusalem church. His influence extended to Christian Jews throughout the empire. Tradition nicknames James "the Just." It describes him as a man of great piety and constant prayer. This James, who played such a significant role in the Jerusalem council (Acts 15), wrote this letter that provides such insight into the earliest days of the church, when believers "devoted themselves to the apostle's teaching and the fellowship, to the breaking of bread and prayers" (Acts 2:42).

Date. The book itself is undated. It was certainly written prior to James' death in A.D. 62, but nothing else is certain. It seems best to view it as written before the Jerusalem council, probably between A.D. 45 and 48.

History and Background. James was very lightly regarded by Luther and the other reformers. They were drawn to NT books which provide clear expositions of salvation by faith. The reformers were suspicious of James, because his book speaks so much of works and is practical rather than theological. Some even argued

that James contradicts Paul's teaching of justification by faith alone
and thus should be removed from the canon of Scripture.

But James was written in the earliest days of the church. Then
the believing community was Jewish. They were distinguished primarily because they believed in Jesus as Messiah and Lord, and
by the intense love that marked their community. In those days
the issues with which Paul deals in Romans and Galatians simply
had not been raised. As Calvin pointed out, "It is not required
that all handle the same arguments."

What then is James' concern? Like Paul, he is concerned with
faith. In fact, James uses the word "faith" more often than Paul
did in Galatians! But what James explores is the impact of faith
in the life of a believer. A comparison between the thrust of James
and the thrust in Paul's theological letters is helpful.

James writes . . .	Paul writes . . .
to explore how faith finds expression in the life of a believer.	to explain saving faith in relation to the work of Christ on Calvary.
out of a concern that faith produce fruit (2:10), so that no one confuse mere creeds with vital Christianity.	out of a concern that faith be placed in Jesus alone, unmixed with any reliance on law or an individual's supposed "works of righteousness."
shortly after Jesus' resurrection, when the church is still Jewish and OT truths known by all.	when the conversion of Gentiles has raised many theological questions never before explored.

When we take the Book of James in the context of its own
time and understand the concerns of the writer, the supposed "contradictions" between James and Paul are quickly resolved.

Structure and Outline. James is often classified as "wisdom literature." This short, pithy exhortation on a variety of subjects more
resembles pearls strung on a common thread than closely reasoned
argument. But there is a logic to James. The book builds on the
conviction that there is a distinctive life style appropriate to faith
in Jesus. This logic is reflected in the outline on page 766.

Distinctive Contributions. Aside from the practical advice which
is of great value to every Christian, James also serves as a corrective
to an intellectualized view of "faith." Those who see Christianity
as simply a matter of "believing the right things" are jolted when

they read James' blunt assertion that "that kind of faith" is worthless! It is only a faith demonstrated to be real by growing transformation of the individual which is true Christian faith. It is not that works save. Instead the truth is that saving faith will work!

Faith's Life Style

Before Reading. Here are several questions answered in James. Which of them are important to you? Read James for the answers. What really is "temptation," and how do I overcome it? What is "true religion"? How do works relate to salvation? Why is gossip such a serious matter? How do I show God's wisdom in my life? What is Satan's impact on a believer's life?

Chapter 1:1–18. Trials and Temptations

Greeting; 1:1. James writes to Jewish Christians who live outside Palestine. He will give them the same instructions he has given the believing community in Jerusalem, where he serves as a leader.

His first exhortations (1:2–18) focus on how the individual believer should respond to trials and to temptations. James then moves on (1:19–2:13) to the relationships which mark the Christian community as a household of faith.

Response to Trials; 1:2–8. Christians everywhere face many kinds of external trials and internal temptations (2). These should not cause panic. Instead we can view them with joy, for we know God's intention is to develop a mature capacity to live a life of undivided obedience (3,4). When the pressures are great, and we do not know how to cope, James says simply, "Ask God." He assures us that God is not upset by our weaknesses or uncertainty. Instead of rebuke, God unconditionally offers us guidance (5). But James adds a warning. We cannot hesitate, turning from the world to God and back again in our search for a solution. A vacillating individual will not "receive anything from the Lord"—not because God is unwilling to give, but because failure to commit ourselves to God's way makes us unable to receive (6–8).

A New Identity; 1:9–11. Relationship with God actually frees believers from one source of temptation. The poor man throws off his old attitude of anger at his poverty when he realizes with joy that God has made him rich. And the rich throws off his attitude of pride, to realize that God loved him despite his spiritual destitution. For each, the material is no longer relevant.

Understanding Temptation; 1:12–18. The blessing available in temptation is found only by enduring it (12). It helps us to endure when we realize that our surging inner passions are not from God. They are rooted in our sin nature. Since God is never attracted by evil, any attraction we feel to wrong cannot be from him. There is a temptation process. We feel an inclination to evil; we submit and engage in an act of sin; then a pattern of sin takes root in our life. James wants us to recognize that first inclination for what it is—and resist acting on our passions (13–15). Luther said: "I can't stop the birds from flying around my head, but I can keep them from building nests in my hair."

But through every temptation God gives his good gifts and he remains "unshadowed." Nothing can cut off or interrupt the light he gives (16,17). He has given us his life: he intends to see us ripen and mature to fruitfulness. Just as "firstfruits" were early ripening grains and fruits brought to God's temple as a special thank offering, so our good works in spite of temptation honor him.

Temptation

Several Hebrew and Greek words express the idea of trial, test, or enticement, and thus of temptation. Temptation is not always viewed as bad in the Bible. Temptation may lead to acts of sin. But temptation is also an opportunity for obedience and thus a chance to affirm our personal commitment to God.

There are two aspects of testing and temptation. One aspect is external, involving pressure situations in which we find ourselves. James and Peter both view suffering and persecution in this light. A difficult decision to make may fit in this category. Even desire for a good goal which can only be achieved by questionable ends sets up tensions and can be described as a temptation. We are never deserted even in the most difficult of circumstances. James writes that whatever the temptation, we can ask God for wisdom and be sure that he will give us guidance.

There is also an internal aspect of temptation. James describes what happens within us: "each one is tempted when, by his own evil desire, he is dragged away and enticed. Then after desire has conceived, it gives birth to sin" (1:14,15). That inner pull toward sin is an expression of man's sin nature and is always with us (see *Old Man/New Man*, p. 614). No attraction we feel to evil comes from God, but from within us. God may place us in a situation where great pressure is felt. But God is never responsible when our impulse is to respond wrongly!

It is at this point that temptation provides us with opportunity. We can follow the sinful tendencies pressure situations bring out, or we can choose to be responsive to God. The Bible says that "No temptation has seized you except what is common to man. And God is faithful; he will not let you be tempted beyond what you can bear. But when you are tempted, he will also provide a way out so that you can stand up under it" (1 Cor. 10:13). By drawing on God's wisdom and making godly choices, in spite of external circumstances or internal pressures, we grow to maturity (James 1:4). It is by godly choices that we demonstrate the genuineness of our faith, and so bring "praise, honor and glory" to God and to ourselves (1 Peter 1:3–9).

It's helpful for us to remember that Jesus too suffered temptations. His testings came directly from Satan and yet were permitted by God so Jesus might be seen to be a perfect man. When our testings come, they too are permitted. For God wants you and me to know the joy of victory, and the satisfaction that comes from remaining true to him.

For study: James 1:2–8, 13–18; 1 Peter 1:3–9; 1 Cor. 10:13; Matt. 4:1–11.

How have you felt about yourself when undergoing some test or under temptation? How have you felt about God? What in this passage helps you understand yourself and him better? How will you respond in the future when you experience temptation?

Chapter 1:19–2:13. Life Together

Faith calls us to a special life, to be lived in community. Most NT epistles have a "practical" section dealing with interpersonal relationships. James is no exception.

Quick-tempered; 1:19–21. Competitive attitudes that express themselves in anger, or quickness to take offense, are ruled out in God's new community. Anger is always contrary to God's righteousness, in individual and community. These reflect a morally filthy attitude. God's implanted Word expresses itself as patient submission. God's work in human lives shapes a people who live without malice and are free from any drive toward revenge.

Living the Word; 1:22–25. God's Word has brought us life. But for the Word "planted in you" to grow, and so reshape us, we must "do what it says," not simply bend over and peer into it. Only by "doing" will God's promised blessings come.

True Piety; 1:26,27. Doing the Word should never be understood as "being religious" or performing rituals. Instead true religion means caring for others, looking after widows and orphans, and rejecting the values of the world around us (see *The World,* p. 797). James develops his comment on the tongue in chapter 3:1–12.

No Favoritism; 2:1–7. In the Christian community the very rich and the poverty stricken are both significant as persons. Neither is to be given preferential treatment (1–4). In the world, the poor are generally exploited by the rich. Can believers ever be found favoring the exploited over the oppressed (5–7)? Not without becoming "judges with evil thoughts."

Just Love; 2:8–13. The Christian community is to be distinguished by love. James calls love the "royal law," for Jesus himself commanded it (John 13:33,34). Thus each person must be loved, without favoritism, for favoritism violates this law and is sin (8,9). When James warns that "whoever keeps the whole law and yet stumbles at just one point is guilty of breaking it all" (10), he confirms an important insight of the rabbis. Sin is by nature offense against God, and God gave every point of the law. Law is thus like a balloon, in that a prick at any point bursts the whole (11).

But James has, as a believer, deliberately chosen a "law of liberty." That law relies on God's mercy and not the ruthless demands of the old code. It follows that if we are to enjoy mercy, we must apply mercy to others. To judge others is to deny them the liberty and the mercy on which we rely (12,13).

No, love makes a simple demand. We are to value each person for himself or herself. Since favoritism involves judging some as less worthy of our love and concern, it is totally ruled out in the believing community.

In what ways besides judging others by wealth or poverty does favoritism find expression today? Who do you know that God wants you to stop judging, and simply to love?

Chapter 2:14–26. Faith and Life

In this significant paragraph, James argues that a "faith" which fails to produce good works is empty. Scornfully James asks, "Can *that kind* of faith save him?" (14). Any faith unaccompanied by actions is dead (17), for true faith will always be revealed in what one does (18: cf. *Good Works,* p. 736).

James makes a clear distinction here between "belief about" and "trust in." Demons are convinced that God exists. But the thought of him causes them to shake in terror (18,19). What a contrast this is with Abraham, who not only believed that God exists, but who trusted himself to God to the extent that he "offered his son Isaac on the altar" (20–21, cf. Gen. 22; Heb. 11:17–19). This response of Abraham to God showed the nature of faith: "his faith was made complete by what he did" (22). James' thought is that faith is like the roots and trunk of a tree, which is "perfected" or made complete when it produces fruit. The fruit of good works, produced by the dynamic power of faith, justified ("vindicated") Abraham as a righteous person (23,24). God had pronounced Abraham righteous (Gen. 15:6), but it was only the works he did which enabled others to see the reality of the change within him.

In just this way, James says, Rahab was justified in the days when Israel invaded Palestine (Josh. 2). The reality of the inner work of God was demonstrated by her actions in hiding the spies and helping them to escape (25,26).

James then is not contrasting faith with works, or teaching a salvation by works. He is simply pointing out that biblical faith involves a dynamic inner transformation, which by its nature *must* be evidenced by a change in one's life. In this sense faith and works are always complementary.

How would you justify your own faith by pointing out the changes trusting God has made in your behavior?

Chapters 3, 4. Evidence of Faith

Faith is to find expression as good works. Now James looks at specific problem areas in developing a faith life style.

Taming the Tongue; 3:1–12. James views control of the tongue as an individual's most difficult challenge (3:2). Like many small things (a bit in the mouth of a horse, or a rudder of a ship), the tongue sets the direction of life and thus has great potential for evil (3:3–7). Since the tongue cannot be tamed, it must be guarded (7,8). Particularly we must guard against the habit of speaking ill of other human beings, while praising God. James sees this as contradictory, for man is made in the image of God (Gen. 1:26,27).

Subduing the Self; 3:13–4:10. James contrasts two kinds of "wisdom." The word speaks here of practical, moral wisdom, not theoretical knowledge. The one "wisdom" is rooted in man's natural instincts and expresses itself in envy, selfish ambition, and all evil practices that grow up when members of a group demand personal rights and operate as partisans (3:13–16). The other wisdom comes from above and expresses itself in a moral purity which is demonstrated by eagerness for peace, by gentleness, and by a humble patience ("submissive") which submits without hatred or malice (3:17,18).

James traces chronic interpersonal warfare to its source in earthly wisdom. The source is hot selfish desire: a passion to possess something an individual does not or cannot have (4:1,2). The implication is that the desire is wrong. This is not something one asks God for. Even if one does, God will not give it because "you ask with wrong motives, that you may spend it on your pleasures" (4:2,3). In a context where "selfish ambition" is condemned, it seems likely that status or recognition as a leader, rather than something material, is the consuming passion of those who sow disorder in the Christian community (cf. 3:16).

James uses an OT symbol for idolatry in calling such persons "adulterous." They are unfaithful to God, deserting him for the values of the world (4:4). But God is jealous over his people and eager to give grace to the humble who align themselves with his authority ("submit," v. 7).

When believers are responsive to God, they will take a stand against the devil, who will then flee (7). They will draw near to God. Coming to God will mean facing themselves, and the pain of repentance (8,9). But those who do humble themselves before God will be lifted up by him (10).

How striking! The recognition ambitious people so yearn for can only be achieved by self-humbling. The "wisdom from heaven" that seems to demand setting aside our own concerns for others is the way to exaltation by God (compare Phil. 2:1–11).

📖 Compare the marks of the two "wisdoms" described by James in 3:13–18. How do these wisdoms show up in your life?

📖 What are some things that you desire? How do you react when you do not receive them? What would the results be if you followed the course of action outlined in 4:1–5? What would they be if you took the course of action outlined in 4:6–10?

Judging; 4:11, 12. James returns again to slander and speaking evil of others (cf. 1:26; 3:9–12). To judge another person means taking to oneself the privilege of God! God gave the law: he alone is to judge. No human being has the right to judge another (cf. Rom. 14:1–18; *Judging Others,* p. 520).

False Pride; 4:13–17. Now James speaks briskly to merchants, who boast arrogantly of their plans and profits. This is wrong, for it fails to recognize the fleeting nature of life. It fails to acknowledge God as sovereign in men's affairs.

Chapter 5. Faith's Prospects

James concludes his letter by speaking of hardships ahead for the believing community. There will be suffering, but God will one day intervene. Until then, believers are to be patient and to wait.

Future Redress; 5:1–6. James describes the profiteering rich who withhold the wages of their workers. This is one of four sins the OT says continually cry out to God for redress (Lev. 19:13; Deut. 24:14). James warns such rich. They will cry out violently in grief and misery, and the wealth they hoard will testify against them. Their greed has condemned innocent persons to death, while they lived in luxury and self-indulgence.

Patience; 5:7–11. Now James turns to the oppressed. He counsels an attitude of quiet but firm endurance. As a farmer waits for a valuable crop to ripen, so believers are to wait for Jesus' return (7,8). The command "don't grumble" indicates an inner and unexpressed attitude toward others. Even this is inappropriate, for the judge stands just outside the door.

The patient endurance of current sufferings which James calls for is nothing new. Modern believers have an example in Job, and the end of his story illustrates the compassionate nature of God. The implication is that God will also bless us, for "the Lord made him prosperous again, and gave him twice as much as he had before" (Job 42:10). But our blessings cannot be expected until Jesus comes (8).

Do Not Swear; 5:12. The prohibition is not against cursing. It is against swearing an oath as security for one's word. The simple "yes" or "no" of a believer should be his bond.

The Prayer of Faith; 5:13–18. This often debated passage links sickness with prayer and anointing with oil. What does it really teach?

In NT and OT times, olive oil was commonly used as a medicine.

"Anoint and pray" (14) may simply mean: use both spiritual and medical resources when sickness comes. It is clear that in any case the healing will come from the Lord (15).

The elders have a special role in the ministry of prayer for the sick. The confession of sin spoken of here (15,16) is "to each other." This suggests perhaps that the illness is related to bitterness against someone wronged, and cleansing that relationship is vital for healing. Health is an inner and spiritual state as well as a physical one.

Prayer is also vital. God wants us to see prayer as a "powerful and effective" resource. The point of the Elijah illustration is that Elijah too was "just a man like us." Yet Elijah's prayer brought a three-and-a-half-year drought, and another prayer released the rains. How then can we doubt the efficacy of prayer for the sick?

Restore the Sinner; 5:19,20. James concludes on a common note. A brother who sins is not condemned. Instead he is sought out, so we can "bring him back." God loves all, and wants only to save.

1 PETER
Steadfast in Suffering

The church was entering an era of persecution when Peter wrote this letter for circulation. No less than seven different Greek words for suffering indicate the growing pressures under which Christians lived. Peter's letter offers words of hope, a call to holiness, and an explanation of the role of suffering in Christian experience. These themes help to make this brief letter a vital one for every believer, for each of us lives, in some way, under pressure.

Destination. The letter is to the "scattered." This is a term long associated with Jews who lived in foreign cities. This, plus the fact that Peter is the "apostle to the Jews" (cf. Gal. 2:7), leads many to believe the letter was written to Jewish Christians. But Peter speaks of "futile ways inherited from your fathers," and records a list of typically Gentile vices (1:18; 4:3–6). It seems best to view 1 Peter as a letter for all believers, everywhere.

Date and Author. The letter is from the apostle Peter, written near the end of his life. The commonly accepted date is A.D. 64 or 65. The letter is believed to have been written from Rome where, according to a strong tradition, Peter was executed.

Peter the Man. Peter is well known from the Gospels as the leading figure among the twelve disciples. He is pictured there as impetuous and often foolish, but quick to affirm Jesus as the promised Savior and Son of God (Matt. 16:15,16). Yet Peter was erratic, as shown in a number of incidents (Matt. 16:23; 14:28–31). While Peter is easy to admire, he does not seem to be the kind of person others would trust to lead.

The Peter we meet in Acts is a man transformed by the coming of the promised Holy Spirit. He is not perfect (cf. Gal. 2:11–14). But he quickly emerges as the dominant apostle, taking the lead in preaching and healing, and dealing maturely with a number of difficult situations (cf. Acts 10, 11).

Little is known of Peter's life after the early chapters of Acts. We do know that he was married (Mark 1:29–31) and that his wife traveled with him in his ministries (1 Cor. 9:5). We also know that, while his ministry focused on Jewish Christians, as Paul's focused on outreach to Gentiles, Peter and Paul traveled to the same cities (cf. 1 Cor. 1:12). A clear and early tradition establishes the fact that Peter, like Paul, died in Rome during Nero's persecution of the church.

Background. The early surge of Christianity into the pagan world had carried the faith throughout the Roman Empire. In the decades after the first missionary efforts in the late 40s, the impact of Christianity on society became more clear. No longer was Christianity viewed as a sect of Judaism and thus a legal (licit) religion. Now Christianity was viewed as a foreign faith, threatening the established religions, and even bringing the city of Ephesus near economic ruin (cf. p. 673)! Official hostility began to develop. The Emperor Claudius had struggled to restore the old, austere Roman faith, and was antagonistic to all foreign religions. The half-mad Nero was soon to torture and kill thousands of believers in the city of Rome. It was clear when Peter wrote that the decades ahead would hold great suffering for anyone who was willing to identify himself with Jesus and his people.

It is against the background of troubled times, with persecution ahead, that Peter penned this call for a commitment to holiness. In it he shared his understanding of the purpose of suffering in the believer's life.

Values and Emphases. Across the ages there has always been a suffering church. Today as well, in many parts of the world, allegiance to Jesus means suffering, discrimination, and ridicule. The letter of Peter is especially helpful for all who know such sufferings, or for those whose personal experience of suffering has caused doubts. The first letter from Peter helps us see God's prescription for those who suffer. It calls for holiness, for submission, and for acceptance of the amazing truth that suffering can be a gift from God.

Outline

Before Reading. Here are several questions answered in 1 Peter. Which of them is important to you? Read 1 Peter for the answers. What is the "goal of my faith"? What does holiness really mean, and how can I be holy? When is "submission" compromise? When should I stand up for my rights? What happens when I do what

I think is the right thing, and something terrible happens? Was I wrong?

Chapter 1:1, 2. Greeting

Peter writes to the Christian communities now scattered throughout the Roman Empire. The phrase, "God's elect" (1), means his "choice possessions." At the same time, Peter does view believers as specially selected by God (see *Predestination/Election*, p. 619). As in similar passages, Peter's concept of election emphasizes the purpose for which believers have been selected. God's Spirit is at work, producing in us a holiness expressed as obedience to God. (2).

These first verses capture the thrust of Peter's message. God is committed to demonstrate our holiness. Through it all, believers will discover abundant grace and peace.

Chapter 1:3–12. Our Living Hope

The Foundation of Christian Hope; 1:3–6. Peter writes of a "living hope." No circumstances can extinguish it, for it is based on great spiritual realities. These are: First, we have experienced a new birth and been given God's own life (3, 1:23–25, cf. *Born Again*, p. 545). Second, the resurrection of Jesus guarantees an inheritance that is reserved for us in heaven (4). Third, God's own power is continually exercised to guard us till Jesus comes (5). While these are not realities which can be touched or handled, there is evidence: the unexplained joy believers know despite mental anguish ("grief") from "all kinds of trials" (6) is testimony to what cannot be seen.

The Purpose of Trials; 1:7–9. Peter pictures trials that believers endure as intense heat, used to refine gold. Fiery trials demonstrate the genuineness of Christian faith (7). On the one hand, the truth will be known when Jesus comes, and faith will "result in praise, glory and honor." On the other hand, the value of faith is demonstrated now within each believer. Under trial, Christians experience deepening love for Jesus, and "are filled with an inexpressible and glorious joy" (8). Only a genuine faith—genuine because its object is real—could produce such results. What happens within us is proof that we are "receiving the goal of" our faith: salvation (9).

The phrase "salvation of your souls" does not refer to some immaterial and separate part of man, or to the future. "Soul," in Hebrew and in NT usage, normally either means "self" or speaks of the whole person in reference to his present life. Peter's point is that what happens within the Christian is positive evidence that God is at work, and salvation is an experienced reality.

Salvation, Now; 1:10–12. The OT spoke of a coming salvation (see *New Covenant, OT,* p. 330). Peter reports that the prophets struggled to understand that time and circumstances (11). How humbling to know that *now* we experience something promised for ages, desired by the prophets, and the object of the angel's amazed wonder.

List the key truths presented in this chapter. Which seem most important to you as a help to meet suffering?

Chapter 1:14–2:12. Our Holy Calling

The inner reality of salvation calls us to live holy and obedient lives. Peter, in a section filled with exhortations, lays out the nature of a life which is in harmony with holiness.

Obedient Children; 1:13–16. We have been born again and are God's children now (1:3,14,23). As such, it is appropriate for us to bear a family resemblance to God, and so to "be holy in all you do." This is no threat, nor warning. It is a wonderful promise. Because God's life is in us, we *can* be holy. Why? "Because I am holy" (6).

Reverent Awe; 1:17–21. The call to holiness should not occasion terror. It should lead to a deep awareness of all that is involved in our relationship with God. We are redeemed from our old way of life by Christ's own blood (18,19). God shaped the ages from eternity past for our benefit (20). Our relationship with God is certified by Jesus' resurrection and glorification (21). All this has been done that our faith and hope might be in God (21). In view of these realities we can never dismiss God's call to holy living as something insignificant or unimportant.

Imperishable Seed; 1:22–2:3. We are not to settle down as though this world were our home (1:17). This is only reasonable. We have been born again "through the living and enduring word of God" (23). The thought here is that we have a new identity. We share God's heredity. While human life withers, that which is born of God's Word is, like the Word itself, imperishable. We then are linked with eternity, not with time. Certainly our lives should give evidence of the living presence of the divine.

What marks God's presence? Deep love for other believers (1:22). A craving for God's Word, to nourish our new life (2:2). And a complete rejection of wickedness ("malice"), deceit, pretense ("hypocrisy"), of grudging others what we do not possess ("envy"), and of any talk which disparages or runs another person down ("slander").

Our New Identity; 2:4–10. Peter relates our new identity to Jesus. He is the cornerstone; we are living stones being built into a house for the Spirit (5). As a "people belonging to God" we are intended to be "a royal priesthood" (2:9). The priestly ministry Peter has in mind is a ministry to God, "offering spiritual sacrifices acceptable to God" (5). These sacrifices include praise and thanksgiving (9) and also the love and goodness which Peter associates with holiness (1:22; 2:12).

Live Good Lives; 2:11,12. This is the second time in this passage Peter calls believers "strangers." The word means "temporary visitors," in contrast to residents (cf. 1:17). But we are not isolated from society. This world is an arena, in which we fight a continual warfare against strong desires that surge within us. The Christian solution is to live good lives among pagans. We will never be free of accusations. But our good deeds will be observed. When Jesus returns, our good deeds will be acknowledged, to his glory.

What have you thought "holiness" to be? What is the most important thing you learn about holiness from this passage? What would you say if you were asked to describe a truly holy way of life?

Holiness, NT

The Greek word group associated with "holy" speaks of consecration—of being set apart. God is himself the Holy One. He is completely separated from any association with sin and actively committed to good. To "be holy, because I am holy" (1 Pet. 1:16) calls on us to reflect the character and the commitment of God in all that we do.

In the OT "holy" described objects, places and persons set apart for God's service. In the NT "holiness" is a relational concept. What is understood to be sacred are neither places nor things. What is sacred are the persons whose lives are infused by the Holy Spirit and who are thus set apart by his presence.

There's no doubt that it is the blood of Christ which makes us holy. In his death, Jesus dealt finally and fully with sin. The forgiveness he won for us, and the righteousness he gives us, are what makes us holy in God's sight (Heb. 10:1–14).

The key to experiential holiness is the Holy Spirit whom God has sent into believers. It is the Spirit's presence that makes us "saints" (literally, "holy ones"). It is his guidance that leads us into righteousness. It is his power that enables us to live a holy life. It is the manifestation of the Spirit's gifts that enables us to have an enriching, sanctifying impact on others.

Holiness is not in itself an ethical term. It is relational: an affirmation that we are cleansed by Christ and linked with the Holy Spirit. But God's dynamic power does free us to live an ethical and godly life. Because we are God's people, and because God's Spirit does live in us, our actions and choices will increasingly express the true goodness that is so perfectly and fully experienced in God.

For study: Holiness, OT, p. 101; *Holy Spirit, NT,* p. 516; Hebrews 10:1–14; Romans 6:19–22; 8:1–11; 1 Peter 2:13–2:12.

Chapter 2:13–3:7. Call to Submission

To Human Authorities; 2:13–17. We believers are aliens, visitors in a world where we do not belong. But courtesy demands that the laws and customs of the foreign land we are visiting be honored. Thus Christians are to submit themselves to human institutions and rulers (13,14). Peter points out that only by constantly doing good can we silence the accusations of those who in vicious ignorance slander Christian faith (15). God only is our master. But freedom is not to be a pretext for doing evil. Thus we owe human authorities proper respect and obedience, and we owe the household of God brotherly love.

Slaves to Masters; 2:18–25. Peter calls on slaves to submit voluntarily to their masters. He states a principle. Submission does not depend on the character of the master. The harsh master as well as the considerate is to be served (18,19). Peter is aware that a harsh master will beat a slave unjustly. He points out that while there is nothing admirable in enduring when we are punished for doing wrong, bearing up under unjust treatment is commendable (lit. "wins reputation, credit").

Peter's argument must be traced carefully. He says that Christians are called to follow Jesus (21). And Jesus suffered unjustly. "He committed no sin, and no deceit was found in his mouth" (22). Jesus even accepted injustice without retaliating, sure that God would vindicate him (23). And God did vindicate. God used Jesus' death "so that we might die to sins and live for righteousness" (24).

Peter's argument is clear. Christians are to do nothing that would merit punishment. If suffering comes, Christians are to bear it in a godly way, without retaliating. We are to remain confident that God is a person who "judges justly" (23). When we respond to suffering in these ways, we fulfill our calling to walk in Jesus' footsteps.

Husbands and Wives; 3:1–8. These remarks to wives are directed to those with non-Christian husbands. We know this, for the "if" in Greek assumes that "do not believe the word" is the actual case. Such wives are to seek to win their husbands "without talk," by the beauty of their lives (2–4) and by responsiveness to their husbands (5). It is never easy for Christian wives in this situation. But they are to keep on doing right. "Give way to fear" means to become perturbed, to be flustered and/or frightened (6). What is called for is a patient, steadfast doing of good.

Believing husbands are to be consciously sensitive to their wives' needs and show them honor ("treat them with respect") as joint heirs.

What are the most important reasons given here why we need to be submissive to those who have authority in society?

Suffering

To the Greek philosophers, suffering seemed the inevitable consequence of being trapped in a world over which mankind has no control. Suffering was the essence of tragedy; often the fates blindly decreed that unintentional acts would bring inevitable doom. In the OT a very different outlook is found. Suffering is no trick of fate. Suffering is evidence of the moral nature of the universe, and the consequence of evil deeds. Suffering is no accident, but comes as the verdict of God the moral judge.

The OT does add to the concept of suffering as punishment. Job suffered at God's hands, and Job was not guilty. Instead God used suffering to teach Job about the Lord. Clearly, then, suffering can have a positive purpose. The OT also introduces the idea of vicarious suffering: the suffering of punishment for the sins of others. This is seen most clearly in Isaiah's portrait of the suffering Savior, in Isaiah 53:4–6. The great contribution of the OT, and its sharpest contrast with pagan thought, is that suffering is supervised by the living God. The OT knows nothing of accidental suffering, or "fate."

In the NT the primary focus is on the suffering of Christ. This too is no accident: it comes "by God's set purpose and foreknowledge" (Acts 2:23). All of Jesus' sufferings had purpose, from the sufferings that prepared him for his high priestly ministry (Heb. 5:8–10) to the suffering at Calvary which won our salvation. In Jesus' case there could be no question of punishment, for he was sinless. Instead, his suffering was used to accomplish a great good.

The NT also speaks of the suffering of Christians. We're warned to do good, for there is no value in suffering that comes as a deserved consequence of our actions. But we're told that suffering *will* come. The world that hated Jesus will be antagonistic to his followers (John 17:14). Yet suffering as a Christian *does* have value. Our suffering always has some purpose, and God will use it in our lives. God uses suffering to purify our faith and help us experience his own presence in our lives. God uses suffering as a witness to the world that will bring God and us glory when Jesus comes again. Each of these truths, and others, are taught in 1 Peter, which contains the NT's clearest exposition of Christian suffering. In this same NT book, in chapter 3:8–4:19, God guides us to understand suffering and how to respond to it.

Suffering is never easy for us. But as Christians we can be sure that God is in control when suffering comes. God loves us and he permits our suffering, for our good.

Chapter 3:8–4:19. Call to Suffering

Peter suggested in 2:20,21 that suffering for doing good has value. He now goes on to develop this thought.

Doing Good; 3:8–12. The Greek phrase translated "finally" (8) actually introduces new material, not summarizes old. Now Peter describes the good life, listing virtues stressed in most NT letters: unity, brotherly love, compassion, and humility. The OT quote (10–12) is from Psalm 34:12–16. It explains Peter's comment that we are called to "inherit a blessing" (9). Because God's "eyes are on the righteous" (that is, he is actively supervising our lives), doing good can be expected to lead to blessing.

What a contrast with situation eithics, which says Christians should look ahead, calculate the probable outcome of decisions, and do what will result in good. Peter says concentrate on doing good, and God will take care of the results!

Suffering for Doing Good; 3:13–18. Normally no one will "harm you" for enthusiastically doing good (13)! In the unlikely event ("even if") suffering follows doing good, "you are blessed" (14).

How should we react if we do good and suffering follows? One, don't be frightened (shaken, or disturbed: 14). Two, remember that Christ is Lord. Our sovereign God is still in charge (15). Three, be ready to explain to all who "ask you to give the reason for your hope." The "ask" here indicates an inquisition or perhaps abusive questions from hostile neighbors. Under questioning we are to simply share our faith, with gentleness and respect (15,16). Four, keep a clear conscience, making sure there is no basis for anyone's slander (16). It's better, if suffering comes, that it not be caused by doing evil!

Christ, an Example of the Innocent Suffering; 3:19–22. Peter points to Jesus as one who did only good. His suffering was not a result of his sins but of the sins of others. Yet look at the result. God used his suffering "to bring you to God." Jesus then is the perfect example of doing good, of suffering according to God's will, and of subsequent blessing (18).

The reference to Noah is understood when the points of analogy are matched (see chart, page 782). Peter insists that in Christ we

have been delivered from our old civilization and lifted to live a
resurrected life, marked by submission to God's will.

Christ, an Example of Choosing God's Will; 4:1–6. Peter now
examines Jesus' suffering as a moral choice. Christ voluntarily accepted his suffering (1). We are to reject human passions, desires,
and motivations, and voluntarily submit to the will of God (2).
The old sinful things which once characterized our lives (3,4) are
to be rejected, and we are to live godly ("according to God")
lives led by the Spirit (6).

Peter, then, examines Jesus' death from two perspectives, each
of which is vital if we are to understand and to respond appropri-
ately to suffering. In Chapter 3 he looks at Jesus' death as an
occurrence. From a human point of view, it involved a terrible
injustice. But from God's perspective, it was in accord with God's
plan. It also had a wonderful outcome for us (he "brought us to
God," 18) and for Jesus ("who has gone into heaven," 22). Peter
applies this to us. When we suffer for doing good, we too can
know it is by God's plan, and that there will ultimately be good
results.

In Chapter 4, Jesus' death is examined as a moral choice. From
a human point of view, it involved a foolish decision. Jesus could
have escaped the cross. But from God's perspective, it was an
act of submission to God's will, and the outcome of Jesus' obedience
shows that doing God's will brings blessing. Peter applies this to
us as well. When we make moral choices, we are to be guided
only by God's will, confident that his will is the pathway to blessing.

---

1 Peter 3:18–22. Does Baptism Save?

Passage	Identification	Parallel
"spirits in prison, who formerly did not obey" (19,20)	Men of Noah's day who rejected the message God announced through Noah (cf. 1 Pet. 1:11)	The "unjust" (3:18) who rejected Jesus' message and crucified him
"eight souls saved" (20)	Noah's family, who did believe and enter ark	"you" (21) who believe in Christ
"water" (20)	The Genesis Flood, the means of judgment	God's coming judgment on sin

Passage	Identification	Parallel
"baptism" (21)	Union with Christ (1 Cor. 12:13). ("Water" speaks of judgment, not salvation.)	In Christ we are carried through judgment to resurrection
"which corresponds" (21)	The two pictures of deliverance correspond, not "water" and "baptism"	As Noah was given a new world, in Christ we are too

The Truly Moral Life; 4:7–11. Peter has argued that morality is choosing to do the will of God. What kind of life is God's will for us? With our minds cleared of confusion and armed with self-control, we are to choose to love each other deeply (8) and serve each other faithfully with our spiritual gifts (9). We are to do this "with the strength God provides" so that the praise and the glory may be his (10,11).

Summary of Suffering; 4:12–19. Peter now draws together the lessons he hopes his readers have learned from his teaching. The lessons are seen best when listed separately, as below:

* Don't look at suffering as something foreign to Christian experience. It isn't (12).
* Realize that it is a great privilege to share Christ's sufferings, and rejoice (13).
* Remember that the outcome of suffering is blessing, although this may not be apparent until Jesus comes (13).
* Accept persecution and insults for your faith as a blessing, and respond by praising God for the privilege (14,16).
* Do nothing criminal or petty, so you will never deserve suffering as a punishment (15).
* Know that God's judgments are purifying for us, but mean destruction for those who do not obey the gospel (17,18).
* Commit the situation to God when you experience suffering, and continue to do good (19).

How dramatically different the Christian's understanding of and response to suffering is from those who do not know God, and who cannot see his hand in every experience.

Think back over experiences of undeserved suffering you have known. Can you see blessing in them now? Which truth in this important passage seems most significant to you personally? How will you apply it to your own life?

Chapter 5. Exhortations

The exposition of Christian suffering (Ch. 2–4) is the major theme of this letter. But now Peter closes with brief bits of advice to different groups and individuals.

To Elders; 5:1–4. Elders are appealed to. They are to willingly guard God's flock, motivated by eagerness to serve (1,2). They are particularly warned against authoritarianism, as though Christian leadership involved some right to lord it over others and control their behavior (3). Instead, spiritual leaders operate by example (3), always mindful that Jesus himself is the Chief Shepherd (4). See *Servanthood,* p. 486 and *Leaders in the Church,* p. 720.

Humility; 5:5–7. A submissive attitude is appropriate for younger persons (5). It is in fact appropriate in all Christian interpersonal relationships, as an expression of trusting oneself to God (6). How good to know the release from anxiety which comes from the conviction that God cares for us (7).

Be Alert; 5:8,9. Believers are to remain alert, for Satan is always eager to make us his prey. We resist by taking a firm stand on "the faith"; in this context, the truth is that we can trust God despite the sufferings which Christians throughout the world undergo.

Benediction; 5:10,11. Peter commends his readers to God, sure that God has called us to eternal glory, and sure too that God will heal any damage which suffering causes. He will make us strong and provide a firm foundation for our lives ("steadfast").

Final Greetings; 5:12,13. Brief personal words conclude this letter of encouragement, which has meant so much to all who have shared in the sufferings of Christ.

2 PETER
Warning against Heresy

Peter's last, brief letter speaks in blunt warning. His first letter spoke of persecution from outsiders, and of suffering. Now he speaks of dangers within: of false teachers, and of relaxing our moral commitment to holiness. This short word from Peter is very meaningful to us as well as to Peter's first century readers, for we need to grasp the truths he shares.

Date and Author. There are many uncertainties about this letter, which is addressed to no particular group. Most assume from 1:13,14 it was written by Peter just before his death in A.D. 67 or 68. There was some uncertainty in the early church as to whether Peter wrote this letter, and some modern scholars have rejected it outright. However, 2 Peter is quoted by very early church fathers, and had won full acceptance by the fourth century. There is no compelling reason to doubt Petrine authorship.

Background. Second Peter is a book of warning and encouragement. Like Paul's last letter (2 Timothy) and like the Book of Jude, 2 Peter looks at emerging dangers from within the church and tells how to meet them. Second Peter is closely related to Jude: some 19 of Jude's 25 verses parallel Peter's teachings here.

Peter is concerned with two primary dangers. The first comes from false teachers. The danger of the second is failure to live those holy lives which accord with belief in Christ. This book is very helpful for understanding heresy and knowing how to deal with false teaching.

Structure and Outline. This brief letter is organized logically around Peter's twin concerns.

Outline

Before Reading. Here are several questions answered in 2 Peter. Which of them are important to you? Read 2 Peter for the answer.

Why don't Christians just attack false teachers and drive them
out? What does the end of the world mean to me today?

Chapter 1:1–11. Productive Lives

After a brief greeting (1,2), Peter launches a description of godly
living, which is an appropriate expression of reverence to the "divine power" (a title of God) who gives us such enabling gifts (3).
The "promises we have been given" (4) is a reference to salvation.
It was long promised in the OT and has now been given to us
(cf. 1 Pet. 1:10–12). In this age of fulfilled promise, the new birth
has become a reality. We have "been born again . . . through
the living and enduring word of God" (1 Pet. 1:23). Peter's thought
is that we are no longer mere mortals. Through new birth, God
has planted his own life in us, and thus we share his nature. Christ
in us is the power through whom we "escape the corruption in
the world caused by evil desires" (4). This is how we are enabled
to live godly lives.

But we are to "make every effort" to bring the life we live into
harmony with inner reality (5). The qualities Peter exhorts are:

* faith	loyal commitment to Christian teaching
* goodness (virtue)	moral energy or excellence
* knowledge	understanding gained from revelation
* self-control	the ability to "hold yourself in"
* perseverance	continuing on in spite of opposition
* godliness	reverent conduct in view of God's presence
* brotherly kindness	affection for fellow believers
* love	commitment to act for the other's good

When these qualities are growing and expanding in our lives, they
keep us from being "ineffective and unproductive" Christians (8).
Lack of them, however, indicates shutting our eyes to the meaning
of redemption (9).

Peter urges, "make your calling and election sure." His point
is that a holy life is a guarantee; it demonstrates to us and to
others that God has called us to himself (10). How great an encouragement it is to know that a "rich welcome" awaits us when we
enter Jesus' coming kingdom (11)!

Chapter 1:12–21. God's Sure Word

Transformation of our lives by Christ is one confirmation of
God's calling. A second secure basis for confidence is the Word
itself. About to die (12–15), Peter is confident that his generation

of leaders, who were eyewitnesses to Jesus' majesty and actually heard God's voice (16–18), can trust the Scriptures to confirm that witness. The Word will guide future generations of believers. Peter views the Scriptures as "more certain" than experience (19). The phrase "prophetic word" ("word of the prophets") is an expression used to indicate the Scriptures as a whole. Paying attention to that Word will provide light and guidance in the present dark world (19). In Greek and Roman times the phrase "morning star" was used of royal and divine persons. Here it refers to Jesus at his return.

Peter stresses the importance of continuing to trust the Scriptures. God's Word is not of human origin. It is from God, and its writers were "carried along" by the Holy Spirit (21). The phrase is used of ships, carried along before the winds on the Mediterranean sea. The prophets opened their lives to God, and he metaphorically filled their sails, carrying them in their efforts. The result is that the Scriptures can rightly be said to be God's Word (see *Inspiration of Scripture*, p. 729).

The testimony of transformed lives and the testimony of the Scriptures are both available to confirm our calling to Christ. How is each testimony related to your own Christian experience? How would you respond if asked to "make your calling and election sure"?

Chapter 2. False Teachers

Deep emotion is revealed in the bold, graphic phrases with which Peter warns of danger to Christian faith and characterizes the false teachers.

Danger Ahead; 2:1–3. Peter warns that false teachers will come from among professing Christians (1). They will introduce heresies (1) and will set an example of immorality that will discredit the faith (2). Tragically, many will follow them, even though their stories are "made up." This term was used in the first century of forged documents (3). Still, Peter wants us to know that the process of judgment has already been set in motion by God (3).

Historical Perspective; 2:4–10. The principle of divine judgment on the immoral is well established in sacred history. In each case referred to here, judgment came by direct action of God. Believers are *not* invited to judge others for God.

The cases Peter refers to as illustration are: First, judgment of fallen angels (4). Peter confirms a rabbinic belief that fallen angels are restrained, awaiting judgment. The word translated "hell" is Tartarus, taken over from Greek mythology by the rabbis because of its association with the punishment of supernatural beings. Second, judgment by the Genesis Flood (5). The ancient world was not spared. Third, judgment on Sodom and Gomorrah (7,8). Each destruction shows what will happen to the ungodly. It is important that in two cases the righteous were delivered as the ungodly were destroyed. Peter's point is that God distinguishes between beneficial suffering, which comes to Christians, and the punishment due the ungodly (9). In this context Peter notes two marks of false teachers. They "follow the corrupt desire of the sinful nature" and they "despise authority." What a contrast with believers whose "election is sure" and is so demonstrated by their godly lives and obedience to Scripture—the thrust of 2 Peter!

Character of False Teachers; 2:11-16. Peter speaks of these men as shameless and daring in their arrogance, ready to defy what even angels speak of with respect (10,11). The exact reference is obscure, but the basic charge is not. These false teachers have no more understanding of the spiritual than brute beasts, whom they resemble in that they, too, are controlled by their animal instincts. Like animals, they are "born only to be caught and destroyed" (11,12).

Bluntly Peter describes the dissipation that characterizes their lives. They are sinful and greedy, like the OT seer Baalam (Num. 22-24), who chose what he knew was wrong because he thought he could profit from it (13-16).

Heresy

The word appears several times in the NT, often in a nontheological sense as "sect" or "party" (such as the "party of the Pharisees," cf. Acts 15:5,7). The word can also mean a party or faction within the church which separates itself from others (cf. 1 Cor. 11:19). Galatians 5:20 identifies such "party spirit" as an expression of man's fleshly, or sinful, nature.

In 2 Peter the word is used in its developed theological sense. Here the aged apostle warns against the introduction of "destructive heresies" (2:1). These are introduced by false teachers, who deny basic doctrines and who encourage sinful behavior.

The early church fathers used the term in its theological sense. They always used it to denote groups within Christianity which taught errors hostile to the true faith. The existence of heresy in the church was a distinct stimulus to efforts, early in church history, to attempt to define truths or at least to distinguish areas in which differences of opinion are relatively unimportant.

How are Christians to deal with heresy? The basic approach in the NT is to keep on teaching sound doctrine. Thus false teaching will be shown to be out of harmony with truth. There are no instructions to undertake a crusade to purify the church by excluding heretics. Instead there is the confidence that, when the truth is presented clearly and firmly and with gentleness, God the Holy Spirit will make the contrast between the false and the true clear. Those who follow false teaching will separate themselves from God's people.

For study: 1 Peter 2; Jude; *Recognizing False Prophets,* p. 326.

Course of False Teachers; 2:17–22. Even though the false teachers have nothing with which to nourish growth (17), they snare young believers with empty talk and by appealing to "the lustful desires of sinful human nature" (18). They promise a "freedom" to do whatever natural passions decree. But they themselves have been defeated by their own passions and so are enslaved to depravity (19, cf. Rom. 6:15–23). Peter's summary reflects his earlier teaching: We have been delivered from the sinful world to live holy lives (cf. 1 Pet. 2:11,12; 4:1–11; 2 Pet. 1:3–11, esp. v. 4). To return to the world's corruption means turning one's back on "the sacred commandment that was passed on" (20,21). Two common proverbs capture the disgust Peter feels: such a thing is like a dog eating its vomit, or a sow wallowing in filth and slime (22).

What can you learn from this chapter that will help you recognize false teaching? For instance, it promises a certain "freedom" (19). List other characteristics. What do you learn about false teachers? How might you recognize them?

Chapter 3. The End of the World

Peter has spoken strongly on twin themes: the Scripture can be trusted, and God has called us to live holy lives. False teachers not only reject the authority of Scripture, they also encourage loose or undisciplined lives. They actually find satisfaction in the sinful pleasures the world offers.

Peter now raises an issue the false teachers ignore. What is in store for this world? What does the future hold for those who find this world so attractive?

Unbelief in the Last Days; 3:1–6. Peter's letter is written to stimulate believers to wholesome ethical thinking (1) and to full commitment to God's word (2). This will be increasingly difficult in view of growing skepticism and moral abandon (3). The skeptics will attack God's prophetic picture as unreliable. They will view the physical universe as a natural phenomenon. Everything in it will be explained as the product of continuing natural processes. Thus God is not required to explain origins or to undergird morality. Nor is talk of Jesus' "coming" meaningful. In essence, "God" will be taken as an empty word, as far as impact on life in this

world is concerned (4,5), and replaced by naturalistic and evolutionary concepts.

Peter predicts that such people will deliberately shut their eyes
to the fact that God has intervened in history. They will forget
that there was a Genesis Flood, whose waters "surged over completely" the old world as an act of divine judgment (6). God does
have his impact on the physical universe, for the flood came "by
God's word" (5)! God's historic act of judgment stands as proof,
consciously ignored, of God's real involvement in the physical universe.

The End of the World; 3:7–10. The present world will not perish
by water. But God will judge. When the day of judgment comes,
the world will be destroyed by fire (7). Our human notions of
"soon" or "slow" do not apply when evaluating God's timing.
We must interpret what seems to us to be delay as patience, motivated by God's desire to see that all have an opportunity for repentance (9, cf. Rom. 2:4). Peter describes the day of unexpected
judgment with graphic words. He speaks of a roaring, crackling
sound as the physical elements that compose the universe melt
in volcanic heat, disintegrating as they are exposed to the divine
judgment (10).

God acted once in judgment. God will act again. No matter
what the scoffers say, our universe did burst into being at God's
word, and it will end when he chooses to speak again.

"What Kind of People;" 3:11–18. Peter applies his teaching force-
fully. In view of the coming destruction of this world, "what kind
of people ought you to be?" To Peter it is clearly appropriate
that we commit ourselves to live godly and holy lives (11). Nothing
of this universe will remain when God judges: righteousness alone
will carry over into the new heavens and earth he will create (13).
If we see the future clearly how empty the words of the false
teachers seem, as they entice us to join in the corruption of this
world. Looking toward the new and lasting world, we will be motivated to godliness (14).

Peter's reference to Paul in verse 15 is significant. He identifies
Paul's letters with "the other Scriptures" the false teachers twist.
This shows clearly that apostolic teaching was viewed as authorita-
tive in the first century church and on a par with the OT.

  Can you identify the attitude and beliefs of the skeptics described in 3:1–6 with any current beliefs or attitudes?

  What motivates you for godly living? How does Peter's talk
of the future of the world relate to your own personal values?

1 JOHN
Fellowship with God

The word "fellowship" means literally, "sharing." That is what this warm NT letter is about: a life of intimate sharing of ourselves with God and with each other. For all who want to know and experience God in a deeply personal way, John's first letter is full of promise. In it the aging apostle of love invites us to come and journey into joy.

Date and Author. Early traditions assign this book and the two brief letters that follow it to the disciple John, and suggest that he wrote them from Ephesus near the end of the first century. John himself lived out that century, spending his last 25 or 35 years in Ephesus, except for a time of exile to the isle of Patmos (see *Revelation,* p. 818). For background on John, see the introduction to his Gospel, p. 539.

Background. The latter part of the first century saw serious persecutions of the church. From the crowning of Domitian in A.D. 81, persecution became state policy. Although harassment was less intense in Domitian's last years, it flared again under Trajan, who ruled from A.D. 98 to 117.

Despite the suffering of the church, John's warmly pastoral letters do not deal with external dangers. John seems confident that if God's people hold fast to Christ, and live a life of love, their Christian experience will be vital and healthy. It is the inner life of the people of God which is most significant. "He that is in us," John says, "is greater than he that is in the world" (1 John 4:4). If we live in intimate relationship with the Lord, we too will overcome the world (5:1–5).

Structure and Outline. John's epistles are distinctively different from those of Peter and Paul. Other NT books typically use closely reasoned, step-by-step argument. But John does not set his themes out in order and apply each in turn. Instead John introduces concepts, like light and love, and then keeps returning to them. This makes the book difficult to outline but adds to the impact of its exploration of fellowship with God.

John's brief statements, made in simple words, feature contrast. He speaks of light against darkness, truth against error, God against Satan, life against death, love against hate. These few images, introduced and then returned to, blend in a powerful rhythm to impress

on us the wonderful message of this short letter. We are invited
by God to a unique experience of shared life with him. God calls
us to fellowship, and we are eager to respond.

Outline

Values. This first letter of John is of special value to all who
have doubts or who yearn for a deeper personal experience of
God. John's Gospel reports that Jesus promised "the world will
not see me anymore, but you will see me." When a disciple asked
how Jesus intends to show himself to us and not to the world,
Jesus replied that the person who "loves me, he will obey my
teaching . . . and we (Jesus and the Father) will come to him
and make our home with him" (John 14:19–24). John's first epistle
can be understood as an explanation of Jesus' answer: as an outline
of the life style which enables a believer to experience living fellowship with the Father and with his Son, Jesus Christ (cf. 1 John
1:1–4). Thus this warm pastoral letter continues to speak to our
uncertainties, to provide both comfort and guidance for our lives.

Before Reading. Here are several questions answered in 1 John.
Which of them are important to you? Read 1 John for the answers.
What can I do if I sin as a Christian? What does it mean to
"walk in the light"? What does it mean to be "worldly"? When
am I acting in a worldly way? How can I know that I am a
child of God right now? What happens when I pray: does God

really hear? What should I do if a friend of mine falls into sin? Does it mean he's not a Christian? How can I help him?

Chapter 1:1–4. Invitation to Joy

This letter, like John's Gospel, goes back beyond creation to affirm a pre-existing Jesus (cf. John 1:1–13). John's message is always Jesus: Jesus as God's life-giving word (1). John also proclaims the Incarnation: life was unveiled in Jesus, and the aging apostle looks back on the days when he himself saw and touched and heard this divine expression (2: cf. John 1:14–18).

John stresses the fact that his experience with Jesus has had a continuing impact in his life. He is over 80 as he writes, yet even now John continues to have fellowship with God the Father and his Son Jesus. It is this continuing fellowship John wants other Christians to share (3). John writes warmly and urgently. He knows that fellowship with God is our only hope to know real joy.

These opening verses set the tone of the letter and define its direction. John writes about fellowship with God. His words are designed to guide us into that fellowship and thus into joy.

I. Walk in the Light. Chapter 1:5–2:29

"Light" is a key term in John's Gospel and in his epistles. It always appears in contrast with darkness. In one sense "light" is a moral term. But there is a more basic and ascendant meaning. Light, like Truth, speaks of reality. To walk in darkness is to be lost in a world of illusion, never able to penetrate to the true meaning of things, and never able to honestly face ourselves. On the other hand, to walk in the light is to face reality and to live in accordance with it.

The first section of 1 John explores a number of realities which believers must face and learn to live with if they are to experience fellowship with God. Since God is light, to walk with him we must walk in his light and evaluate all of life by his truth.

Chapter 1:5–2:2. Being Honest with Ourselves

Revelation is the source of all John knows about God and the basis of his teaching. The foundation John lays is the fact that God is unclouded light, in whom there is no darkness (5). John quickly moves on to make five statements about a believer's life in relationship to light. Each situation described is considered to be an option for us.

* A believer may claim to have fellowship with God, but walk in darkness. In such a case, when a person lives by his own moral insights rather than by truths revealed in Scripture, the claim to be in fellowship with God is a lie. To have fellowship with him we must "live by the truth" (6; see *Truth*, p. 552).

* A believer may be walking in the light. In this case we "have fellowship with one another" and the blood of Christ "purifies us from every sin" (7). Walking in the light does not mean to be sinless. Even when walking in the light we need the application of Christ's blood to "keep on cleansing us" from sin.

* A believer may claim to be sinless. But this is self-deceit, for God's truth reveals men to be sinful (8). We cannot be in fellowship with God if we reject his truth and the light it sheds on human experience.

* A believer may confess his acts of sin. In this case God faithfully and justly forgives the sin and continues the purifying process that has begun in the believer's life.

* A believer may insist "I haven't sinned" (when an act of sin has been committed). This actually makes God out to be a liar! Such a person has refused to give God's Word a place in his life.

These five statements give us a clear picture of how to evaluate our own Christian lives. We need to recognize our sinful nature and hear God's Word as it defines acts of sin. When we do sin, we must not hide that fact from ourselves or from God. Instead we are to come to God in confession. When we acknowledge our sins, fellowship is uninterrupted. God not only forgives the sins, but he continues his purifying and cleansing work in our lives.

John explains that he does not write this way to encourage believers to sin (2:1,2)! In fact, a realization of God's grace and love will motivate Christians to holiness. Most importantly, the promise of forgiveness is the truth! Jesus *is* the atoning sacrifice for our sins. We and the whole world are invited to come to him and to know the transforming power of forgiveness.

Which of the five conditions described above is most characteristic of you? How does *knowing* that you will be forgiven and cleansed when you acknowledge sin to God affect your motivation and attitude?

Confession of Sins

Confession is often misunderstood, being confused with "being sorry" and even with "promising never to do it again." But the biblical meaning of the word is clear: it means to acknowledge or to admit. In essence, confession means to take a stand with God and evaluate a particular action of ours as a sin.

The opposite of "confession" is denial and thus rejecting responsibility for our actions. Strikingly, denial is completely unnecessary. God has given a wonderful promise to Christians, and it is only our failure to admit our sins that keeps us from enjoying that promise.

The promise is linked to Scripture's basic teaching about sin and forgiveness. Scripture teaches that we are sinners and that there is nothing we human beings can do about our guilt. But God has acted in Christ to win us release. Jesus paid the penalty for sin. His blood not only wins us forgiveness, but also releases God's own dynamic, transforming power within us. Because God has already dealt with sin in Jesus we do not need to cloak our failures or to deny responsibility for our wrong actions.

God's call to confess sins is issued especially to Christians, who already *are* forgiven through faith in Jesus Christ. Confession relates to specific acts of sin we may commit as we follow Jesus, and is made available to us so we might enjoy fellowship with God. Salvation is by faith: fellowship follows confession.

How wonderful it is to know that we need not pretend with God. He is not shocked by our failures. He knows all too well what we sometimes hesitate to face: that we are sinners, and still need his forgiveness and his cleansing touch. When we come to God, honestly admitting our faults, he is always ready to touch us with forgiveness and to cleanse us within. *For study:* 1 John 1:8,9; Hebrews 9:10

Chapter 2:3–11. Being Loving

The second area in which John urges us to walk in the light speaks of relationships between Christians.

Obeying His Commands; 2:3–6. John begins with a general statement. The Greek tenses help us understand exactly what the apostle is saying. Growing obedience to God's commands provides increasingly clear evidence that we do know Jesus (3). Love for God is not something abstract or mystical. Love is practical and finds expression in a responsive obedience to God (5). Thus a person who claims to know (in the sense of experience fellowship with) God, but is not obedient, simply is not telling the truth. Obedience actually helps us in two ways: it provides objective evidence that we know God and, as we obey, we grow in our experience of him (cf. John 14:15–24). It's really simple. Anyone who lives in (close relationship with) Jesus will live as Jesus lived.

The Command to Love; 3:7,8. There is one particular command that John stresses as vitally important. This is Jesus' own command that his followers love one another (cf. John 13:33,34).

In the Light; 3:9–11. Just as admission of sin is a "walking in light" issue, so is love. One who hates his brother is stumbling, lost in darkness, and blind to the true light.

What do you think "loving your brother" means? Feeling something about him? Being committed to him? Caring about his needs?

Chapter 2:12–17. Being Separate from the World

John's Confidence: 2:12–14. John expresses confidence in his readers. Their sins have been forgiven, they know God and have overcome the evil one (Satan) by the power of the indwelling Word.

Love Not the World; 2:15–17. But there is a danger that can turn believer's hearts away from the Lord. This danger is the "world"—not as a place, but as human society with all its godless values. John focuses on three things which characterize the world system (16). These are: One, the "cravings of sinful man." The phrase means instincts and desires that spring from the sinful nature. Two, the "lust of his eyes." The phrase suggests desires for things that lie in the world of experience, which can be touched and seen. Three, the "boasting of what he has and does." The phrase speaks of arrogance caused by possessions and of a boasting designed to impress others. This is "worldliness."

None of this comes from God. It is, in fact, contrary to godliness. Significantly, this world and its passions are already in the process of passing out of existence. What is in the world is not reality! Only by looking to God and living by the pattern his will provides, can our lives stand the test of eternity.

Chapter 2:18–29. Being Alert for Antichrists

The last of the four issues explored in this first section of John's letter warns against those who would turn a believer's confidence away from Jesus.

Antichrist and Antichrists: 2:18,19. The Bible speaks of an individual, empowered by Satan, who will counterfeit Jesus as object of faith at the time of the end (cf. 2 Thess. 2:8–12). John's point is that even now others who oppose Christ are arising (18). An important point is made in verse 19. These opponents of Jesus do not stay in the fellowship of Christians. In fact, it is by separating themselves from the community of believers that their hostility to Jesus is unmasked. When members of the Christian community love one another and walk in the light of Jesus' commandments, those who do not belong will choose to depart.

Jesus Is the Christ: 2:20–25. John is not afraid for believers, for they have a living link with Christ ("have an anointing"). To deny that Jesus is the Christ (Savior) marks a person as a liar who does not accept truth (21). "Such a man is the antichrist" (22). We are to acknowledge the Son, holding fast to the truth we have heard about him. It is only through linkage with the Son and the Father that we have eternal life (23–25).

Jesus Is Coming; 2:26–29. The intimate relationship of the believer with Jesus is our protection. We "do not need anyone to teach you." This does not mean Christians cannot learn from each other, or from those with the gift of teaching. It means that God himself is present within us, to confirm and authenticate truth (26,27). Thus John exhorts his "dear children" to continue in fellowship with Christ. When Jesus comes again, he wants there to be that perfect openness to him which comes from a clear conscience (28). John returns to the theme of obedience. God is righteous. All who have received the new birth will reflect God's presence by doing right.

What bases for confidence in Christians, that they will not be led astray, can you find in these verses? How are you protected from dangerous false teachings?

The World

The Greek word "world" is used in our NT with several meanings. It refers at times to the whole universe. At others it means all beings above the animals and at still others the planet on which we live. "World" may also simply mean all human society, and in some contexts it means the scene of our earthly life, with all the sorrows and joys that human beings know.

There is also a moral sense in which "world" is used by the apostles Paul and John. In this moral sense, "world" means everything depraved and corrupted: the sum total of the values, the attitudes, the passions, and the desires which move sinful man and energize sinful society. In this moral sense, Satan is seen as "the prince of this world" (John 12:31), and John insists that the "whole world is under the control of the evil one" (1 John 5:19).

To "love the world," then, means to be drawn to and to actually choose the values, the ways, and the passions that move men and women who do not yet know God.

For study: 1 Peter 3:2–6; 1 John 2:15–18.

II. Walk in Love (Chapter 3:1–4:19)

John returns again to a theme he has already presented as vital if we are to walk in the light: love. In this extended section John relates love to obedience, to caring, and to allegiance to God. He shows us that God's love is the source as well as the example for our own.

Chapter 3:1–10. Children of God

Children of God; 3:1–3. There is a firm foundation for the life of love to which believers are called. This is found in the fact that we actually are the children of God. The full meaning of this relationship has not yet been made known, although we know that when we see Jesus we will bear his likeness (cf. Rom. 8:28,29; 2 Cor. 3:18, also *Born Again,* p. 545). This great expectation launches us into a process of purification in which we gradually grow to become what we are.

Righteousness Now: 3:4–6. We will not be perfected now, but there will be a change in our life style. We will not "habitually practice" sin, which John calls lawlessness—living in total disregard of God's standards. Jesus came to take away our sins (5). No person living in Jesus can keep on sinning as a way of life (6).

God's Children Recognized; 3:7–10. To John, the implications are clear. The life of God's child is marked by increasing righteousness. Continual practice of sin marks a person as a member of Satan's family. The new life God gives believers is vital and dynamic: it *will* lead to a righteous life style.

The Greek verb tenses in this passage make John's meaning perfectly clear. He is speaking of the tendency or direction of a man's life, not of isolated failures. Because we *are* God's children, the direction of our lives will be toward righteousness and away from lawlessness.

Have you seen the lives of others change direction as a result of becoming a Christian? What is the direction of your life now?

Chapter 3:11–20. Caring for Others

Hostility; 3:11–15. John often teaches by contrast. Here he says that love will characterize the believer's life. He explains by citing Cain, who hated his brother and murdered him. This was because Cain's acts were evil and his brother was righteous (cf. Gen. 4; Heb. 11:4). John's point is that those who are evil and belong to Satan will hate the righteous (11,12). It follows that lives which are marked by a growing love for God's children show we have "passed from death to life." Here, too, John uses verbs that make it clear he is not speaking of isolated incidents, but of the direction of our lives. We are becoming lovers of God's children.

Active Loving; 3:16–18. But what is "love"? It is not just a feeling. It is commitment expressed in action. Jesus sets the standard for love, for he "laid down his life for us." When John goes on to say that we "ought to lay down our lives for our brothers," he speaks of moral necessity. No other course is thinkable but to follow Jesus' example and to give ourselves for others (cf. 1 John 2:6). To give ourselves does not mean martyrdom. It does mean willingness to surrender those things which make up our life in the world. We will willingly surrender our possessions, moved deeply by the sight of a brother in need (17). "Love" is never a "words or tongue" kind of thing. Love calls for "actions and truth" (18).

Impact of Love; 3:19,20. John teaches that a life characterized by active love for others will help to "set our hearts (used in the sense of conscience) at rest" before God, whenever our "hearts condemn us." His thought is that conscience is an untrustworthy guide. It may accuse us unjustly. When it does, we can appeal to God, whose Word reassures those who are practicing a life of love.

How does the reaction to believers identify an individual? What in your own life helps you "set your heart at rest" before God?

Chapter 3:21–24. Confidence

John pauses briefly to apply what he has been saying. A life style marked by righteousness (3:1–10) and by love for fellow believers (3:11–20) gives us great freedom in approaching God (21). Because our lives are in tune with God, we "receive anything we ask" in prayer (22). John is not making a condition we have to meet to receive answers to our prayers. He is simply stating a fact. When our lives are in harmony with God, our prayers will be too, for what we desire will be in harmony with God's will (cf. James 4:1–3).

Again John repeats themes he has spoken over and over. Put your trust in Jesus; love one another; obey his commands (23). This is how we live in him and this is how we will know he lives in us. God's Spirit will be a living witness within us, and we will experience our fellowship with God.

Chapter 4:1–6. Allegiance to God

John returns to the theme of false teachers (cf. 1:18–27). They are animated by a "spirit" (supernatural power), but not by God's

Spirit (1). John gives two tests by which the spirits can be tested. The first is, do they acknowledge that Jesus is God come in the flesh (2,3)? Failure to acknowledge Jesus as God is sure proof of the satanic origin of any religious teaching.

While John recognizes the seriousness of satanic treat, he also reassures. "The one who is in you is greater than he who is in the world" (see *The World,* p. 797). The Holy Spirit is greater than Satan, so Christians meet satanic attacks from a position of strength and not weakness (see *Satan and the Believer*). The second test relates to the Word. Those who recognize its authority are from God (6).

Chapter 4:7–21. God's Love: Source and Example

Love Defined; 4:7–12. John turns again to love. Love can only be understood by God's great act in sending his "one and only Son" to be the atoning sacrifice for our sins (9,10). Love in human experience originates in God: it is his self-sacrificial gift that establishes the meaning of love.

Through Christ, love burst into the world of men. Those who are born of God, and know him (7), find his love reproduced in their love for one another (11). This is in fact the goal to which God's love was directed: to see us transformed, and loving one another (12).

Love Essential; 4:13–16. The central reality of revelation is God's love for us, made plain in Christ. It is so central that acknowledging Jesus as the Son of God marks the dividing line between life and death. A person who relies on God's love in Jesus has established a relationship with the Lord, through which "God lives in him and he in God" (15).

God Is Love; 4:16–18. John builds on the fact that God is love. It follows that loving is key to intimate relationship with the Lord! A person whose life style is loving "lives in God, and God in him." The word "punishment" (18) refers to disciplinary chastising. John says that as we grow in love, fears that God will punish us for wrongdoing diminish (cf. Rom. 13:8–10).

God Loved First; 4:19–21. Love does not arise from man's nature. Love is created in us by God's work. God's love *does* awaken love. Thus anyone who claims to love God, but fails to love other believers, simply is not telling the truth. The love of Christians for God is expressed as love for one another!

List seven things you learn about love from this passage. Which of them are true in your own experience?

Satan and the Believer

Satan is a powerful fallen angel, intensely hostile to God and antagonistic to God's people (cf. *Satan*, p. 245). The Bible warns us against Satan and his "devices." These are his ways of turning us away from God. They range from marshalling the enmity of non-Christians, who are instinctively antagonistic to godliness, to tempting believers to sin by the attractiveness of the world's possessions or values (see *The World*, p. 797); to sending false teachers whose doctrines distract us from the love and righteousness which enable us to live in close fellowship with God.

Satan's approach in temptation is best seen in the temptation of Adam and Eve (Gen. 3) and in the temptation of Jesus (Matt. 4:1–11). In each case he tried to raise doubts about the trustworthiness of God's Word. He held out the promise of something which seemed to be good but could only be achieved by adopting a wrong means. This kind of temptation, to take the shortcut of questionable means to achieve a supposed good, is still one of Satan's most effective strategies.

While Satan is a powerful person, Christians are taught not to be terrified of him. God is greater than Satan. Because Christ comes into the life of the individual who trusts him, security and victory over Satan can be found in our relationship with Jesus. James tells us to "resist the devil" and promises "he will flee from you" (4:7). This theme of alert watchfulness, with firm resistance, is also found in Ephesians 4:25–27; 6:10–17, and 1 Peter 5:8,9.

An important NT teaching tells us that Satan is now a defeated enemy (Col. 2:13–15; Heb. 2:14,15). By faith in Jesus, we can claim his victory over Satan (1 John 4:4; Rev. 12:11). Our new birth means that the whole direction of our lives is changed by the indwelling Christ, so that we need no longer make a practice of sin. That same presence means that "God keeps him safe, and the evil one does not touch him" (1 John 5:18,19).

Our relationship with God does mean that we are safe from Satan and possess all the resources needed to defeat him. But it does not mean that we are immune to Satanic attacks. Job was a believer whom God permitted Satan to assault (Job 1,2). God even permitted the loss of Job's wealth, family, and health. But Job continued to hold fast to his integrity and to God. In the end God used the attack of Satan to build Job's faith. We too may experience attacks from Satan and the world system he controls. But when we do, we can rest in the assurance that God is still in control. He will never permit us to be tested beyond our ability to stand (1 Cor. 10:13).

III. Walk by Faith (Chapter 5)

John continues to explore the kind of life that enables us to experience fellowship with God. He touches again on the themes so often repeated in this letter: love for one another and obedience to God's commands. But the focus of John's teaching now becomes faith. To John here, as in his Gospel, faith is more than mental assent. It is an active trusting of oneself to God, sure that God does love us and has provided salvation in Jesus (see *Belief/Faith*, p. 562). Trust in God's testimony about his Son not only brings us salvation; it brings us the assurance that we belong to the Lord.

Love and Obedience; 5:1–5. John states that "everyone who believes that Jesus is the Christ is born of God" (1). This is a statement about the present, not the future. Salvation is something we have *now* (cf. *Salvation*, p. 574). Evidence that we possess salvation is found in our experience: we find we love the children of God and that we obey his commands (2,3). This happens in us despite all the pressures of the world around us (see *The World*, p. 797). It is our belief in Jesus that is key to the victory we win over the world through love and obedience.

Who Jesus Is; 5:6–12. John has earlier pointed out the crucial test of religious teaching: does it "acknowledge that Jesus Christ has come in the flesh" (4:2)? Many interpret the phrase affirming that Jesus has come "through the water and the blood" as a reference to Jesus' nature as God in the flesh. "Water" refers to his birth from above (cf. John 6:37–39) and "blood" to his human nature. Another interpretation suggests that "water" speaks of the human nature taken on in incarnation (cf. John 3:5–8), while "blood" speaks of his bloody death for man's sins. Whichever is correct, it is clear that all the evidence—his incarnation, his humanity, his deity, his death and his resurrection—points to Jesus as God's Son. And God the Holy Spirit continually adds his own confirming testimony.

The Spirit's inner witness is in every believer (10). Any who reject Jesus as God's Son make God "out to be a liar" (11). Thus belief in Jesus' deity becomes the guarantee (the way in which "testimony" is used here) that we have been given eternal life as a present and continuing possession.

To John the issue is clearly drawn and the outcome sure. Life is in the Son. We who have the Son through faith in him have life. Whoever does not have the Son does not have life (12).

We Know God Hears Us; 5:13–15. John wants Christians to have no doubt about their relationship with God or their acceptance by him. John writes to us "that you may know you have eternal life" (13). Belief in Christ establishes a family relationship: we are God's children now (3:1), so we can approach God with confidence (14). John wants us to be able to pray confidently, secure in the knowledge of our relationship, knowing that God hears us.

The prayer "according to his will" speaks of harmony with God's purposes. Prayer is not so much telling God what we want as it is sharing, through relationship with him, in his own purposes and desires. The closer we are to God, the more clearly we will sense his will, and the more confidence we will have that our prayers are answered. How good when we know that what we ask is what God wants (15)!

We Are Freed from Sin's Control; 5:16–21. John has spoken emphatically about believers, insisting that our lives will tend away from sin toward righteousness. How then should we react if we see a Christian brother or sister commit a sin (16)? John says we should pray for such a person and that life will be granted to him. John has already shown that acts of sin are to be acknowledged to God and will be cleansed and forgiven (1 John 1:8,9).

The "sin that leads to death" in this passage speaks of physical death as a possible outcome of sinning (cf. 1 Cor. 5:4,5). While all wrongdoing is sin, John wants us to realize that not all acts of sin set us on the path that leads to death (17).

The reality which John wants us to focus on is, we who have been born of God are freed from sin's controlling power. We do "not continue to sin" (18). God's power is at work in the believer's life, and even Satan cannot touch God's children, for all that Satan controls the world around us (19). Freedom from sin's power comes to us through Jesus, who has come into the world that we might know him, the true God and the source of eternal life (20).

What in this section is the central content of our faith? What are the benefits that we experience through faith?

This brief letter from John is notable for the repetition of several basic themes: among them love, obedience, faith, and life. Read through this letter several times and jot down everything said on each theme. Summarize your findings and note which of them are particularly important for your own walk with God.

2 JOHN
Encouragement and Advice

Author and Background. The unnamed author of this brief letter is John the apostle. This is established by early tradition and by the repetition of the themes which appear over and over again in his first letter. Each of John's letters shows that the aging apostle's later ministry focused on encouragement of love and obedience among believers. Linking these two qualities together, John sees them as summing up the Christian's "walk." "Walk" in NT usage is a word for the believer's whole life style.

Like the first letter, this letter was probably written in the 90s A.D., when the apostle was well over 80 years old.

Salutation; 1:1–3. John identifies himself simply as "the elder." The word probably refers to his position in the church rather than his now advanced age (see *Leaders in the Church,* p. 720).

The term "elect" (2) when used as an adjective seems to have come to simply mean "Christian" (for background, see *Predestination/Election,* p. 619, and 1 Peter 1:1). This is an intimate letter, written to a friend whose family John has come to love. She is linked to the apostle "because of the truth, which lives in us and will be with us forever." Christian friendships are lasting, spanning time and eternity.

The initial blessing (3) is common to correspondence of this time, but here has specific Christian content.

Walking in the Truth; 1:4–6. John expresses joy at finding the elect lady's children "walking in the truth" (4). The phrase indicates a consistency in Christian living.

In reviewing Christian living, John focuses on two basics: loving one another (cf. 1 John 2:3–11; 3:11–20; 4:7–21), and being obedient to God's commands (cf. 1 John 2:3–8; 3:1–10). Love and obedience are intimately linked, for God has commanded his children to love one another.

Beware of Deceivers; 7–11. John's first letter also spoke about antichrists—individuals energized by spiritual powers antagonistic to Christ, who engage in false teaching and seek to deceive God's people (cf. 1 John 2:20–23; 4:1–6). John repeats the central truth which such false teachers deny: they "do not acknowledge Jesus Christ as coming in the flesh" (cf. 1 John 2:22, 4:2). John writes that such persons, who are not faithful to the apostolic teaching about Christ (9) do "not have God" and are not to be taken "into your house" or to be welcomed (10).

John is speaking of the common practice in the first century for traveling teachers to circulate from group to group and city to city, sharing their ministries. As the church in the first 120 years of the Christian era met in homes, it is likely that John's reference to "home" is to a house church. His instruction is that no false teacher is to be permitted to bring any teaching.

Desire to Visit; 12,13. John himself circulated among the churches of Asia from his headquarters in Ephesus. He excuses the shortness of this letter by expressing his hope to visit and "talk with you face to face." He desires the opportunity "that our joy may be complete" (12). This is a characteristic expression of the apostle's (cf. 1 John 1:4). It suggests that there is a fulfillment to be found in Christian experience, as love grows between believers (cf. 1 John 4:7–12).

3 JOHN
Letter to Gaius

Author and Background. The author is the apostle John, identified here, as in 2 John, simply as "the elder." The conclusion of this letter (v. 13) is so similar to that of 2 John that many commentators believe it was written about the same time, just before a planned trip by the apostle. The actual date, and the location to which the letter was sent, is unknown. But the common themes emphasized by John in his later years, and his emphasis on truth (see *Truth,* p. 552), mark this brief epistle as the work of the great apostle of love.

Greeting; 1. The name Gaius was a common one in the first century. There are three persons by this name mentioned in the NT (Rom. 16:23; Acts 19:29; 20:4). There is no reason to suppose that this Gaius should be identified with any of the others.

Best Wishes; 2–4. The wish that "all may go well with you" is a reference to prosperity. It may well mean prosper financially, "even as your soul is prospering." This would be appropriate in Gaius' case, because his acts of hospitality and support of Christian workers (6) demonstrate that he is generous in sharing his material possessions (cf. 1 Tim. 6:18,19).

John uses the same words that he uses in 2 John 4 to express his joy that this brother is "walking in the truth" (living by God's Word).

Commendation; 5–8. Gaius is commended for helping "the brothers, even though they are strangers to you" (5). In the early church those with missionary or special teaching gifts traveled, to share their ministries with many churches. The phrase "send them on their way" here, as in Acts 14:3; 1 Cor. 16:5,11; 2 Cor. 1:16 and Titus 3:13, speaks of supplying these itinerant ministers with food and money, and helping them in other ways. This is appropriate, as such persons have abandoned their secular occupations "for the sake of the name." Thus they merit hospitality. Helping to support them is one way that Christians as a body can "work together for the truth" (8).

Diotrephes: 9–11. The early church was no more ideal than are Christian churches today. In Gaius' town or city, a man named Diotrephes, "who loves to be first," has misused leadership. To hold his place and influence, he tried to insulate the group he led from other Christians, even bringing unjustified charges against John himself. He also refused to welcome the traveling brothers, whose itinerant ministries were so significant in the early church. Diotrephes took it on himself to control other believers and put them "out of the church" if they would not do what he said. This was a terrible misuse of spiritual leadership (see *Spiritual Authority*, p. 658). When John comes to the area, he will confront Diotrephes.

Demetrius; 11,12. For every Diotrephes who selfishly warps Christianity, there is a Demetrius who is "well spoken of by everyone," because he "does what is good." How clearly relationship with God is seen in the lives of those who live—or who fail to live—by God's truth.

Conclusion; 13,14. John hopes to visit Gaius soon and to talk with him face to face (cf. 2 John 12). In the meantime John passes on greetings to friends they have in common and blesses Gaius with peace.

JUDE
Contending for the Faith

The Book of Jude contains only 25 verses. It is a dark letter—a warning written by a man who wanted to encourage but who felt compelled instead to urge his readers to contend for the faith. His warnings, and his descriptions of false teachers, are as appropriate for us today as for the first century church.

Date and Author. It is difficult to establish the time this brief letter was written. However, its subject matter parallels that of 2 Timothy and 2 Peter, which suggests a late date of writing. Many believe it was written in the decade of the 80s A.D.

The author is known. He was accepted in the early church to be the person indicated in the first line of his writing: Jude, the brother of James. This is the James who was leader in the church of Jerusalem; thus Jude is also the half-brother of Jesus. This identification was firmly believed in the early church and is authenticated by mention of Jude by name as one of Jesus' brothers in Matthew 13:55 and Mark 6:3.

Background. With the early period of missionary expansion past, Christianity had become established throughout the Roman world. There were waves of persecution, some past and many still to come (cf. 1 Peter). But already a much more serious threat was developing. Jewish and pagan false teachers were creeping in among the brethren, corrupting the faith through reinterpretation and by introduction of pagan views of reality. There was a real danger that Jesus might be robbed of his deity, and that Christians might be turned away from the life of love and godliness which linked them in intimate fellowship to the Lord.

Jude's letter of warning seems addressed primarily to Jewish Christians. It notes that in the OT, too, the enemies of God tried to subvert the faith of Israel. Jude challenges the believers of this new age to contend against subversion and to reject the false teachers who twist the truth.

Apocryphal Quotes. There were a number of religious writings from pre-Christian Jewish sources circulating in the first century. These writings, called apocryphal or pseudepigraphal, were never accepted as Scripture. But they did affect the beliefs of the Jewish people and color their impression of OT events. A unique feature of Jude is that it contains quotes from these sources (vv. 6,9,14,15). Some have argued that Jude should not be accepted in the canon of Scripture because of these quotes.

But Jude is not quoting his sources as authorities. He quotes to demonstrate that the false teachers misinterpret even these stories. When rightly understood, even the apocryphal and pseudepigraphical writings support a traditional understanding of the OT.

Greeting; 1,2. Jude identifies himself (1) and identifies his readers. They are believers, the object of God's continuing love and watchful care (2). Both these assurances of God's protection will be important as Jude goes on to describe the dangers faced by the young church.

Secretly Slipped In; 3,4. The danger does not come from official governmental hostility. Instead, Jude has been forced to write this letter urging his readers to contend for the faith because individuals seeking to pervert Christianity have infiltrated the church. Jude's language is strong. The word "urge" was used to exhort hesitant armies to do battle—and "contend" indicates a struggle demanding intense effort.

It is important to contend, because the faith has been "entrusted" to the new generation. This same word is used of passing on the faith in OT times. It affirms the NT message of the apostles as the "once for all" standard of Christian belief (3). But this deposit of truth is threatened, by men who are already doomed to punishment (4a). Their own godlessness is demonstrated by a denial of Jesus' deity and by warping grace into license for immorality.

Judgment on Immorality; 5–7. Jude reminds his readers of familiar judgments God brought on the disobedient and immoral in the past. Peter also pointed back to sacred history, to warn the present generation in a similar exhortation to godliness (cf. 2 Pet. 2:4–10).

Rejection of Authority; 8–10. Jude links moral pollution with refusal to recognize valid authority. Those who behave this way are "dreamers": they are deluded and completely out of touch with reality. To "despise the glorious ones" is a reference to the characteristic teaching of first century heretics that the world was made by angels. But these beings are actually the servants of God and are defamed by this false doctrine (8). Jude points out that even in the apocryphal "Assumption of Moses," the archangel Michael is not pictured as rebuking Satan, who was created in a higher order (see *Satan,* p. 245, and *Angels,* p. 370). To speak abusively of authorities, with no more perspective than is provided by animal instincts, reveals the very quality that brings these men to destruction.

Jude's point is that the talk of the false teachers, their rejection of the reality of the spiritual world unveiled in Scripture, and their lack of respect for supernatural authority is a mark of their character and a basis of their coming judgment.

Their Character; 11. Three OT personalities illustrate the character of the false teachers. "Traveling along Cain's path" speaks of hatred for a brother. "Balaam's error" was to surrender any integrity he might have had as a spiritual leader in a greedy passion for money. "Korah's rebellion" was a demand to be recognized as a spiritual leader when not called to leadership by God. In each of these sketches we see a reflection of false teachers: loveless, greedy, and insubordinate. And in each illustration, we see that destruction is sure to come to such persons.

Judgment Coming; 12,13. In another series of word pictures, Jude describes the worthlessness of these men and their teachings. They are empty of value, contributing nothing of benefit to any man. Using a figure from the book of Enoch, Jude pictures them as shooting stars whose momentary appearance is simply a dying flash as they tumble from the sky to be engulfed in the darkness.

Enoch's Prophecy 14–16. Even the pseudepigraphical book of Enoch describes a judgment to take place when the Lord comes with his "holy ones" (angels). He will judge the ungodly (14,15). The false teachers who grumble and complain and follow their own sinful passions while spewing out boasts and flattery (16) fit the category of "ungodly" and will surely be judged.

Call to Persevere; 17–23. Jude concludes his warning with an exhortation. Believers are to remember that the divisive attacks of false teachers were predicted by the apostles, who gave warning (cf. 2 Tim. 3:1–8; 2 Peter 2:1–22; 1 John 4:1–6). Christians need to know the characteristics of false teachers and recognize them (18,19).

How then do believers "contend" for the faith? Jude is very clear. Build yourselves up in your most holy faith. Pray in the Holy Spirit. Keep yourselves in God's love (defined in 1 John as loving one another and obeying, cf. 1 John 5:1–4). Wait expectantly for Jesus to come. Be tender with those who waver. Snatch others from the judgment (by evangelism). Maintain an attitude of pity and concern—but keep clear of corruption.

Doxology; 24,25. Jude's last words are of praise, focusing on God as able to keep us from falling into the traps set by false teachers. God is also able to bring us through danger into his very presence without fault. All this is due to Jesus Christ, who sums up in himself the majesty, the power, and the authority of God.

From this book, 2 Peter 2, and 2 Timothy 2, build a complete description of false teachers, their character, and methods. How can following the advice given in 17–23 defeat them?

PROPHETIC SYSTEMS

The NT, like the OT, contains glimpses of the future. These range from general warnings ("there will be terrible times in the last days," 2 Tim. 3:1) to portraits of specific events ("the heavens will disappear with a roar," 2 Pet. 3:10). The glimpses of the future given in the Gospels and the NT epistles are invariably applied to Christian living. Knowing God is in control, we are to trust him. Knowing the end God has planned, we are to be holy. Or reevaluate our attachment to the world. Or comfort one another. Or accept present sufferings without doubting God's justice. Or commit ourselves to active service. Words of prophecy are thus woven into the fabric of NT teaching. Our curiosity about the timing and sequence of events is seldom satisfied. But God does want us to have information about the future and to apply that information to our lives now.

However, when we come to the last book of the NT, Revelation, many different questions are raised. Is this a book of prophecy? If so, does it describe a series of events in a chronological framework? If so, how long a period of time? It thus becomes important if we are to interpret the book correctly to know when the events it describes take place. Are they in the far future? Do they describe the time the book was written? Or is this a preview of world history from the first century to Jesus' return?

The question is made more significant when we look back into the OT. That Testament too contains prophecy. In fact, the future dominates the visions of the prophets. While some of the events the OT predicts (especially those related to Jesus' first coming) have already happened, many clearly have not been fulfilled. This is particularly true of prophetic visions of the end time, a period still future in our own day.

A significant question, then, is whether these OT prophecies should simply be dismissed, or taken as allegory, or whether they should be included when we study Revelation and other NT prophecy. Should they be integrated with NT prophecy? If so, will OT and NT together give a comprehensive picture of the return of Christ and of the end of the world?

To explore these questions, and before reading Revelation, it is helpful to review the history of prophetic interpretation and to describe systems of interpretation.

The History of Prophetic Interpretation

The Early Church. The *Didache* was probably written about A.D. 100. It gives this picture of the future as understood in the postapostolic church: "Watch for your life's sake. Let not your lamps be quenched, nor your loins unloosed; but be ye ready, for ye know not the hour in which our Lord cometh. When lawlessness increaseth, they shall hate and betray and persecute one another, and then shall appear the 'world-deceiver' as Son of God, and shall do signs and wonders, and the earth will be delivered into his hands, and he shall do iniquitous things which have never yet come to pass since the beginning. Then shall the creation of men come into the fire of trial, and many shall be made to stumble and shall perish, but they that endure in their faith shall be saved from under the curse itself. And then shall appear the sign of the truth, (a) first, the sign of an opening in heaven, the outspreading of the heaven; (b) then the sign of the sound of the trumpet; and the (c) third, and resurrection of the dead, yet not of all, but as it is said: The Lord shall come and all His saints with Him. Then shall the world see the Lord coming upon the clouds of heaven" (Ante-Nicene Fathers, Vol. VII, 382).

In A.D. 140–160 Justin Martyr write, "I, and as many as are orthodox Christians, do acknowledge that there shall be a resurrection of the body, and a residence of a thousand years in Jerusalem, adorned and enlarged, as the prophets Ezekiel, Isaiah, and others do unanimously attest" (Fathers, Vol. 1, 239).

Irenaeus, a great missionary and church father, who died in A.D. 202, summed up the picture of the future taught in his day. "When the Antichrist shall have devastated all things in this world, he will reign for three years and six months, and sit in the temple at Jerusalem; and then shall the Lord come from heaven in clouds, in the glory of the Father, sending this man, and those who follow him, into the lake of fire; but bringing for the righteous the times of the kingdom, that is, the rest, the hallowed seventh day; and restoring to Abraham the promised inheritance, in which the kingdom of the Lord declared that 'many coming from the east and from the west should sit down with Abraham, and Isaac, and Jacob' " (Fathers, Vol. 1, 560).

It is clear from these early fathers, as well as from the writings of Tertullian, Cyprian, Lactantius and others, that for some 300 years the church did integrate OT and NT prophetic pictures and took them in their literal sense. They expected Christ's return to precede a time of blessing, promised in the OT, before the world would end. For background see *Eschatology, OT,* 372, 373, *NT,* 489, 490.

To the Reformation. A review of commentaries on the Book of Revelation shows a shift in understanding prophecy occurred after the early centuries. A leader of the African church, Tyconius, wrote a commentary around A.D. 390 in which the events Revelation describes were spiritualized. His allegorical approach was adopted, and later used to justify the development of the papacy as a political power. The allegorical method of interpreting Revelation was followed by Pirimasius (c. A.D. 550), Alcuin (A.D. 735–804), Maurus (A.D. 775–836), and Strabo (A.D. 807–859).

Joachim of Fiore (c. A.D. 1130–1202) challenged the dominant allegorical interpretation by introducing a chronological division. He divided all of history into three ages: the age of the Father (Creation to Christ), the age of the Son (Christ to his own day), and the age of the Spirit (his time until final judgment). When the Reformation came, this chronological approach was fastened on by Luther, Calvin, and others. The antichrist-beast (Rev. 13) and the harlot (Rev. 17,18) were interpreted as the papacy, and as Rome. Events in the history of western Europe were linked to the various seals and trumpets of the book.

The Catholics responded with a commentary on Revelation in which Francisco Ribera (A.D. 1537–1591) argued that the antichrist was an individual who would come in some future time, not the pope. Other Catholic writers argued that Revelation applied only to events before the fall of Rome in A.D. 476.

Neither the medieval scholars, the Reformers, or the later Catholic theologians attempted to relate Revelation to the prophetic picture found in the OT and so to build a unified picture of the future.

Prophetic Systems Today

There are three dominant prophetic systems today, two of which are reflected in current interpretations of the Book of Revelation. Each has developed in Protestantism out of conflicts that took place during the Reformation.

Premillenial. This view, renewed in the nineteenth century by the Plymouth Brethren, is represented in most of the books on prophecy to be found in bookstores today. It integrates OT and NT prophecy, which it accepts and understands in a literal way.

The premillenialist sees a future appearance of the antichrist, a time of great tribulation, the return of Jesus to earth, a thousand-year rule of peace, a final rebellion, and then an eternity spent in a freshly created and sinless universe. The premillenialist camp is divided as to the rapture of Christians described in 1 Thessalonians 4:13–18 (see *The Rapture*, p. 703). Some believe Christians will be removed from the world before the great tribulation period, which begins at the appearance of the antichrist (pre-tribulationists). Others believe the Rapture takes place only at the end of that period, when Jesus is ready to stand on this earth again (posttribulationists). There are others who argue that the Rapture will take place in the middle of this seven-year time, foretold in both testaments (mid-tribulationists). Each group sees a period of blessing following Jesus' return (see chart, p. 816).

Postmillenial. Those who hold this system foresee a gradual growth in godliness as the Christian gospel is heard throughout the world. They view Jesus' first coming as the central fact of history and see him establishing then a new and powerful expression of God's eternal kingdom. The gospel, in this view, is more than the power of God for the salvation of individuals: it is the power of God for the salvation of society. Despite the record of history, the post-millenialist remains confident that God's purposes for the redemption of this world will be achieved through the preaching of the gospel. He expects a time when most persons will be Christians, and society purified. Most, but not all postmillenialists, foresee a sudden outburst of evil just before Jesus returns to judge (see chart, p. 816).

Amillenial. The final prophetic school rejects the idea of a long period of blessing on earth (a millenium). Like the postmillenialist, the follower of this school spiritualizes the prophecies of the OT. He sees them as representations of present blessings, not to be understood in any literal or national sense. Christ is now working out his salvation purpose, and when he comes again it will be to judge the world and welcome his saints into glory.

Amillenialism sees NT prophecy as symbolic also. In particular, Revelation is treated under this system as a completely symbolic book, whose seven sections each cover the same period of time, from Jesus to judgment, from differing points of view.

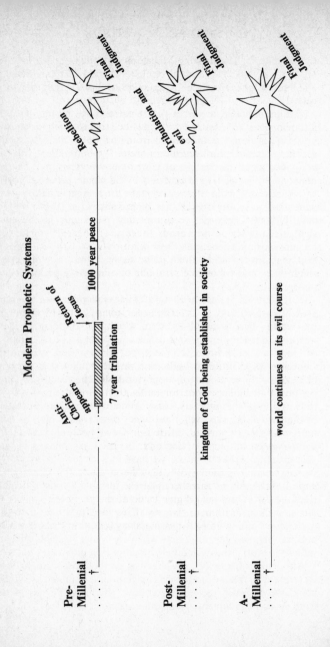

Modern Prophetic Systems

Pre-Millenial

Anti-Christ appears

7 year tribulation

Return of Jesus

1000 year peace

Rebellion

Final Judgment

Post-Millenial

kingdom of God being established in society

Tribulation and evil

Final Judgment

A-Millenial

world continues on its evil course

Final Judgment

Evaluating Prophetic Systems

The dividing line between prophetic systems is found in a single issue. How are prophetic passages to be interpreted? If they are to be taken literally, all agree that a premillenial picture emerges. But many contend, with St. Augustine, that prophetic passages should be interpreted differently from the rest of Scripture. The fact that so much prophecy incorporates symbolism seems, to this group, to suggest that prophecy is by nature intended to communicate something other than is found by taking the literal meaning.

On the other hand, those who do take prophetic passages literally argue that prophecy which has been fulfilled has been fulfilled literally. Simply because we cannot understand every aspect of a prophetic utterance, they argue, does not mean we must reject the part we do understand! They point out that if we do not take prophetic utterances in their plain sense, how can we ever tell which of the many possible symbolic or allegorical interpretations is correct?

Which prophetic system is right? That is a matter for each individual to study, and to determine for himself or herself. This is not one of those areas of teaching which is critical to Christian faith and doctrine. It is an area in which sincere and godly believers will continue to disagree. The fact that there are many prophecy books in every Christian bookstore makes it clear that disagreements exist. And they give us opportunity to explore each position.

What is more important for us to grasp is that the Bible does make one truth completely clear. Whether or not we agree on the details of the future which prophecy portrays, Scripture teaches that God *is* in control. The future is in God's hands, and all history is moving toward his intended end.

Every glimpse of the future we have in Scripture communicates this wonderful assurance. We may never agree on the details of how future events fit together. But the insights we can gain from what the Bible does tell us give us comfort, encouragement, hope, and a fresh dedication to live our lives in this world in the full awareness that the world is passing away, and that there is a world to come.

REVELATION
Jesus Unveiled

The final book of the Bible takes its name from the first word in the Greek text, which means "an unveiling, or disclosure." For most who read the book, the name seems inappropriate. The vivid scenes of cataclysm, and of disasters which strike planet earth, are powerful beyond imagination. Also the author steps beyond the physical universe. He shows us events taking place on another plane: one which touches our world, but which cannot be known today through our senses. It is this look beyond space and time rather than our understanding of it all which makes "Revelation" an appropriate title. Interpreters will differ on the meaning of the images seen here. But each reader is suddenly confronted with a vision of Jesus in unveiled majesty. His glory and the judgment of evil by his own action are clearly seen. However we may interpret the Book of Revelation, there can be no doubt that Jesus himself *is* unveiled.

Date and Author. The writer identifies himself simply as John. He tells of receiving his vision while "on the island of Patmos because of the word of God and the testimony of Jesus" (1:9). The earliest traditions identify this John with the writer of the Gospel and Epistles that bear his name. The weight of early testimony favors this view.

The most likely and the traditional date of writing is just before John's release from exile on Patmos. This took place on the death of the emperor Domitian, in A.D. 96. Thus Revelation is the last written as well as the final book in our NT.

Interpretations. Interpreters continue to differ when explaining the Book of Revelation. Some 278 of Revelation's 404 verses refer to or make allusion to the OT, and many of these allusions are obscure. When we add the use of symbolic language, we can see why it is impossible to be dogmatic about details. There have been, however, four general schools of interpretation into which interpreters can be divided.

(1) PRETERIST. This approach views Revelation as a description of conditions existing when the book was written. Those who hold this view argue that symbolism was used by the writer to avoid stirring up more persecution than had already been generated by

the demand of the emperor Domitian (A.D. 81–96) to be worshiped as God. In this view, the Roman state is the enemy represented by Babylon and by the beasts mentioned in Revelation. This view discounts any predictive element in the book.

(2) HISTORICIST. This approach sees Revelation as depicting the course of Christian history. The trumpets, seals, and bowls of judgment represent stages of the history through which the church has passed or is passing.

There are two branches of historicists. The older branch, represented in the Reformation, attempted to identify historic events in European and church history with the events described in Revelation 4 through 16. Revelation was thought to march chronologically from the first through the eighteenth centuries.

The younger branch is common today among Christians of Reformed background (Presbyterian, Reformed, and Christian Reformed), among Mennonites, Southern Baptists, and others. This branch sees Revelation as a nonchronological panorama of history. Revelation is divided into seven separate visions, each parallel to the others in that it spans the time between first and second comings. The perspective in each vision differs, but each reinforces and restates the primary message of the others.

(3) FUTURIST. This approach sees material in Revelation 4 through 16 as a picture of future events, which relate specifically to the end of the age. None of the material in these chapters is linked with the past or the present. Instead, Revelation is understood to portray the Great Tribulation period spoken of by the OT prophets and by Jesus (Matt. 24–26).

(4) IDEALIST. This approach takes Revelation as symbolic, with no relationship to events or persons in history or at the end of time. Instead the book is taken to use figures familiar to first century readers to represent the general conflict between good and evil.

Two of these schools have a number of adherents today. These are the futurist view, argued by the premillenialist and the parallel historicist view, typically held by amillenialists (see the discussion of *Prophetic Systems,* p. 812). Adequate presentations of these positions are found in two books: *The Revelation of Jesus Christ,* by John Walvoord (premillenialist) and *The Consummation of History,* by George G. Weeber (parallel historicist).

Structure and Outline. It is clear that the approach to the interpretation of Revelation taken by an interpreter will determine any outline of the book. The futurist will see chapters 4 through 16 as sequential, and his outline will express that interpretation. The parallel historicist will see the entire book as a series of seven parallel visions, and his outline must express that conviction. Thus outlining the book is only possible if one wishes to make a commitment to one school of interpretation. For this reason, rather than an outline, a list of the major subjects taken up in each chapter is provided below:

Contents of Revelation

Symbolism. Everyone who even glances at Revelation is quickly aware that it is filled with symbolism. Some of the symbols are explained in context. Many more are drawn from the OT and can be understood by examining the OT context. Interpreters of both modern schools agree on the meaning of a number of these symbols. A list of symbols concerning which there is agreement is helpful to anyone studying this book and is included here.

Symbols Explained in Revelation

Chapter	Symbol	Represents
1:20	seven candlesticks	seven churches in Asia Minor
1:20	seven stars	seven angels (messengers) of these churches
4:5	seven lamps of fire	the Spirit of God
5:8	bowls of incense	the prayers of the saints
7:13,14	great multitude	those who came out of the great Tribulation
12:9	great dragon	Satan
17:9	seven heads of the beast	seven mountains on which the woman sits
17:12	ten horns of the beast	ten kings
17:15	the waters	peoples, nations
17:18	woman dressed in purple	a great city that reigns over the kings of the earth

Symbols Drawn from the Old Testament

Chapter	Symbol	Represents
2:7; 22:2	tree of life	symbol of eternal life, from Genesis 2:9
2:17	hidden manna	from Hebrews 9:4
2:27	rod of iron	rule of Christ in judgment, from Psalm 2:9
2:28	morning star	reign with Christ, from Daniel 12:3 (?)
3:7	key of David	authority of Messiah, from Isaiah 22:22
4:6	the living creatures	represent highest of God's creations, from Ezekiel 10:14
6:1	the four horsemen	execution of God's purposes, from Zechariah 1:8; Ezekiel 5:17; 14:21
10:1	the mighty's angel's cloud rainbow	God's judgment, Psalm 97:2 God's mercy and faithfulness Genesis 9:8–17

Not every symbol is interpreted the same way by each school. Here are two examples of differences between them, though they draw from the same OT passages for their interpretations.

Chapter	Symbol	Represents
13:1–10	the first beast	the antichrist (futurist) anti-Christian world governments (historicists) both from Daniel 7
13:11–18	the second beast	the false prophet (futurist) anti-Christian religions (historicists)

Most of the symbols, even those explained, are unfamiliar to modern readers, and so add to the mystery associated with Revelation.

Values. In spite of differences between interpreters, and despite the unfamiliarity of many of the symbols used in Revelation, this last book of the Bible does have great value to modern believers. As the prologue to Revelation states, "blessed is the one who reads the words of this prophecy, and blessed are those who hear it and take to heart what is written in it" (1:3). The cataclysmic judgments Revelation portrays, and the overwhelming impression of the power of this God who merits our worship, create an unforgettable impression. One who reads and takes this book to heart, even if there are parts that he or she does not understand, will increasingly appreciate the majesty of God. One day soon his sovereign power will forever put away sin, and he will call us into eternity.

Methodology of Our Study. Because the Book of Revelation is understood differently by Bible students, the commentary on Revelation in this handbook will take the following form. Events in each chapter will be described, with insights to be gained from the original language shared, as in discussion of the other books of the Bible. But following the commentary on each chapter a brief summary will show how each of the two major interpretive systems understands the teaching of that chapter.

Whichever interpretive system you may prefer, there is value in understanding the perspective of the other. If a person has no preference, and wants to study Revelation in depth, books like the two suggested in the next to last paragraph on page 819 can be consulted.

Chapter 1. Jesus Glorified

Prologue; 1:1–3. This book is a revelation by and of Jesus (1). The phrase "must soon take place" uses a word indicating rapid execution (2, but see 2 Pet. 3:8,9). The phrase in verse 3 tells us that Revelation was intended for public reading in congregations, a practice the early church adopted from the synagogue. God has a special blessing to be given to his people through this book and its apocalyptic visions (3).

Greetings and Praise; 1:4–8. John intends this letter for the seven major centers of Christianity in Asia Minor (see chart p. 825). His greeting is a typical one, including a blessing and also a clue to the thrust of his letter. In this greeting John pictures God as summing up past, present, and future (4), and presents Jesus as "ruler of the kings of the earth" (5). To many interpreters this seems to provide the key for understanding Revelation. It separates Revelation's contents into past, present, and future concerns, and suggests the book describes the process by which Jesus establishes his sovereignty over all.

John breaks into praise at this announcement, blessing Jesus for his work on our behalf. Again past, present, and future provide the framework (5–7). This division is repeated four times in chapter 1.

Verse	Past	Present	Future
4	God was	God is	God is to come
5–7	Jesus freed us from our sins	Has made us priests to serve God	Jesus is coming and all will see him
9	The Lord was	and is	and is to come
19	John to write what he has seen	what is now	what will take place hereafter

John's Vision of Jesus; 1:9–20. John's vision came on the island of Patmos, a rocky and desolate speck in the Aegean Sea, used by the Roman government as a penal colony. John had been sentenced there "because of the word of God and the testimony of Jesus" (9).

He speaks of his vision taking place on the Lord's Day. This phrase may mean Sunday, or it may mean that John is transported in his vision to the eschatological "day of the Lord" to come at history's end (10: cf. p. 287). John is told to write what he sees in his vision to seven churches in Asia Minor (11).

John turns to see from where the voice instructing him comes, and sees a scene full of reminders of the OT worship center. As in the tabernacle and temple, there are lampstands (cf. Zech. 6:2) and among them a person in priestly clothing (cf. Exod. 28:4; Ezra 9:2). The person himself is described in terms that reflect OT visions of God (cf. Dan. 7:9), and John falls at his feet, stunned by his splendor. The figure identifies himself as the glorified Jesus (17–20). John is told to write what he has seen, what is now, and what will take place later (19). With this sudden vision the Book of Revelation begins.

The Sevens. There is a constant repetition of "seven" in this chapter and throughout the book. It is generally agreed that seven indicates completeness or perfection. Thus the "sevenfold spirit" of verse 4 is taken to represent the Holy Spirit, and the "seven lampstands" to indicate heaven, the true worship center of which the OT tabernacle was merely a copy (cf. Heb. 8:1–6). The selection of seven churches is taken to indicate that in some way they, or the messages to them, sum up what God has to say to all his people.

Futurist Interpretation of Revelation 1. The futurist sees chapter 1 as the "what you have seen" aspect of John's vision. He takes the letters to the seven churches (cf. 2,3) as the "what is now" part of Revelation, and thus chapters 4 through 22 become "what will take place later." Chapter 1 then is understood to provide the key to interpreting the rest of the book.

Historicist Interpretation of Revelation 1. The historicist stresses the repetition of the number seven. He says this number is not used chronologically, but stands for completeness or perfection. He sees this number as the key to outlining the book, and as evidence that Revelation is *not* to be studied as though it were organized chronologically. To the historicist Revelation 1 is also understood to provide the key for interpreting the entire book.

Chapters 2,3. Letters to Seven Churches

The content of these letters is summarized on the chart on page 825. There is no doubt these churches did exist in John's day, in what is now Turkey. There were, however, many other churches in Asia Minor. Apparently these seven were selected because of conditions which existed in each congregation and because of the need created by those conditions for a special word from God.

Futurist Interpretation. The futurist tends to view these letters as having multiple meaning. There is clearly a historical application to churches which existed in the days of John. There is also an application which can be made by believers of every age. The warnings and exhortations given to each church apply wherever we find similar conditions today. The futurist also is likely to suggest a third interpretation—a prophetic one. Many futurists take these churches to provide a panoramic view of church history, from the first century to the second coming. In this view, each church represents a time period. The churches and the periods they represent are usually identified as follows. Ephesus: the apostolic church of Acts. Smyrna: the church in the age of early persecutions. Pergamos: the development of the priestly hierarchy and Catholicism. Thyatira: the church of the dark ages. Sardis: the church of the Reformation. Philadelphia: the "true church" of every age. Laodicea: the lukewarm church of the twentieth century.

Historicist Interpretation. The historicist agrees that there were historical churches to which John wrote. The historicist also believes that the message of the churches is applicable today. To the historicist these churches are representative of the prevailing problems which are to exist throughout church history and until Jesus returns. Thus to the historicist it is important to study the characteristics of the churches and to relate that study to our own day and congregations, so that we can "hear what the Spirit says to the churches" (2:7).

Church	Characteristic	Description of Jesus	Desired Response
Ephesus, the Steadfast Church (2:1–7)	works hard, perseveres, rejects wicked, endures, left first love	walks among the seven lamps (is in heaven)	return to first love
Smyrna, the Persecuted Church (2:8–11)	undergoing suffering, poverty, persecution	the one who died but is alive again	remain faithful
Pergamum, the Morally Compromising Church (2:12–17)	remains true, faithful to death, tolerates immorality	holds sharp, double-edged sword (Word of God)	repent of evil ways

Church	Characteristic	Description of Jesus	Desired Response
Thyatira, the Doctrinally Compromising Church (2:18–25)	doing more than at first, tolerates immorality, false teaching	eyes of fire, feet of bronze (is Judge)	hold to the truth
Sardis, the Counterfeit Church (3:1–6)	has reputation as live, but is dead; deeds incomplete	holds the Spirit, angels in his hand	wake up, obey what has been heard
Philadelphia, the Obedient Church (3:7–13)	has little strength, yet kept the word; patiently endures	holds key of David (royal authority)	hold on to what you have
Laodicea, the Materialistic Church (3:14–22)	neither cold nor hot, wealthy but spiritually poor	ruler of creation	be earnest, repent under discipline

Chapter 4. God in Heaven

Now John is brought up into heaven itself, to be shown "what must take place after this" (1). The sight that draws his eyes is a great throne (2), such as kings and judges use when making official pronouncements. A transparent crystal rainbow circles the throne, reflecting prismatic colors. Twenty-four smaller thrones circle the central one, each occupied by a crowned "elder" dressed in white. Thunder rumbles and lightning flashes from the central throne, while blazing lamps identified as the sevenfold Spirit of God obscure the dazzling person seated there (5,6).

Standing close to the throne, surrounding it, are four "living creatures." They have the same aspect as creatures described in Ezekiel 1:10–28. They are usually taken to represent the highest expressions of animate creation (6,7). Each constantly worships the Lord, praising him with: "Holy, holy, holy, the Lord God Almighty, who was, and is, and is to come" (8). The 24 elders join in the praise, prostrating themselves before the one on the throne, praising him as worthy to receive worship "for you created all things."

Futurist Interpretation of Revelation 4. John's call to "come up" is suggestive of the rapture of the Church (see *The Rapture,* p. 703), and the chapter itself introduces the "things that shall be hereafter." The elders with crowns are taken by the futurist to represent the redeemed (cf. 2 Cor. 5:10; Rom. 14:10).

Historicist Interpretation of Revelation 4. The vision suggests awe-filled worship of God. The 24 elders are a panoramic representation of the church of all the ages, combining the 12 patriarchs of the OT and the 12 apostles of the NT. They join with all creation, represented by the living creatures, to offer worship and praise to God.

Chapter 5. Presentation of the Lamb

John sees that the still indistinct figure on the throne holds a document in his right hand. It is covered with writing and sealed with seven seals (1). The seals are stamped wax impressions, which authenticate a first century document. Roman law directed that a will should be sealed by seven seals of seven witnesses.

No one is found who is worthy of opening this document (2–4) until a voice announces the triumphant Lion of Judah, the Root of David. Each is an OT designation of the Messiah, who is from the tribe of Judah and David's royal line (cf. Isa. 11:1).

Now the Lamb appears. This particular word for lamb is used exclusively in the NT of the resurrected Jesus (6). Now too a new theme is introduced in the praise of the living creatures and elders. They earlier praised God as Creator (4:11). Now the Lamb is praised "because you were slain, and with your blood you purchased men for God . . . to be a kingdom of priests to serve our God, and they will reign on the earth" (vv. 9,10).

The hymn of praise is joined by myriads of angels, proclaiming the worthiness of the Lamb (11,12), and they in turn are joined by "every creature in heaven and on earth and under the earth and on the sea" offering God and the Lamb "praise and honor and glory and power, for ever and ever" (13,14).

Futurist Interpretation of Revelation 5. The futurist sees the scroll as the key to interpretation. He relates this scene to Daniel 7:13,14 and sees the scroll as the title deed to the kingdom Jesus will institute on earth after the seals, unleashing preliminary judgments, are opened.

Historicist Interpretation of Revelation 5. The historicist also sees the scroll as the key. But he sees it as symbolic of redemption. Thus the time of the vision is understood as just after the crucifixion, when Jesus returned to heaven to unlock redemption for all mankind. The victory song is sung because even now, in Christ, every believer *does* rule on earth (cf. Eph. 1:20–23). Thus there is no need to postulate some distant millennium.

Chapter 6. The Seals and Horsemen

As the Lamb breaks the seals, great disasters strike the earth. Horsemen are released who mount warfare (1–4), famine (5,6), and all sorts of devastating plagues that destroy a quarter of the earth (7,8). As the fifth seal is broken, John sees thousands "slain because of the word of the Lord" who calls out to God to avenge them (9,10). They are "under the altar," the place where the blood of OT sacrifices was poured out. John sees them clothed in white robes and is told to wait "until the number of their fellow servants who were to be killed was complete" (11).

With the breaking of the sixth seal, nature itself is jolted, and the fabric of the universe begins to tear (12–14). Then earth's inhabitants realize that the day of God's wrath is coming at last (15–17). The seven groups listed in verse 15 represent the seven classes which made up first century society, and thus show that all mankind is stricken by the judgments.

Futurist Interpretation of Revelation 6. To the futurist, this passage seems to initiate the events described in Matthew 24:5–8, which precede the appearance of the antichrist. The futurist sees these preliminary judgments as the subject of Revelation 6–12. The martyrs described in verses 9–11 are usually taken to be believers killed for their faith during the Tribulation period.

Historicist Interpretation of Revelation 6. The historicist believes this passage describes the impact of the gospel on earth. The first rider is taken to be Jesus, come to conquer through the gospel message, but followed by struggle with the world, culminating in God's judgment on his enemies and final victory. The historicist sees the martyred believers as the saints of all the ages.

Chapter 7. The Redeemed in Heaven

The chapter describes two scenes, one on earth and one in heaven. On earth the winds of judgment are held back until an angel can "put a seal" on the foreheads of the servants of God (1–3). The "seal" in the first century would speak of the tattoo worn by a slave or soldier or member of a guild. It was a mark of ownership, which here identifies the bearers as God's servants. There are 144,000 who are sealed. Their Jewish origin, with 12,000 from each of 12 Jewish tribes, is emphasized in the text (4–8).

Back in heaven, John sees an uncountable multitude "from every nation, tribe, people and language" gathered before the throne to praise the Lamb (9,10). Their worship is joined by the angels, the elders, and the living creatures (11,12). One of the elders tells John they are those "who have come out of the great tribulation and washed their robes and made them white in the blood of the Lamb" (13–15) and now possess great blessings (15–17).

Futurist Interpretation of Revelation 7. Futurists take the Jewish identity of the 144,000 literally and understand them to be Jewish converts, who serve as missionaries during the tribulation period (cf. Dan. 12:3). The great multitude of those saved are taken to be those who are saved during the Tribulation, through faith in Christ (Rev. 7:14).

Historicist Interpretation of Revelation 7. Historicists see the 144,000 as a perfect number (12 × 12 × 1000) representing the church of all the ages. The tribal identity is dismissed with the observation that in Christ there "is neither Jew, nor Greek" (Gal. 3:28). The redeemed multitude are the saved, who are in God's presence in heaven.

Chapter 8. The First Trumpets

The breaking of the seventh seal brings a hushed silence: an ominous pause that lasts for half an hour (1). Then seven angels standing before the throne are given trumpets (2).

Before the trumpets sound, however, another angel beside the altar offers incense and the prayers of the saints up to God. The prayers are best taken as prayers for vengeance (cf. 6:12). The prayers ascend and immediately the angel takes coals of fire from the altar and hurls it on the earth, accompanied by thunder, lightning and earthquakes (3–5).

Now the angels begin to sound their trumpets in sequence. As each sounds, a fresh judgment strikes the reeling earth. A third of the land area is devastated by fire (7); a burning mountain pollutes a third of the seas (8,9); a flaming star turns a third of the fresh waters bitter, taking many lives (10,11); the sun and moon and even the stars darken (12). As John watches, a great vulture (not "eagle") drifts through the gloom-shrouded skies, crying out in a loud voice, "Woe! Woe! Woe to the inhabitants of the earth" (13).

Futurist Interpretation of Revelation 8. The futurist sees further descriptions of the initial judgments of the tribulation period.

Historicist Interpretation of Revelation 8. The historicist believes that this chapter introduces the third of seven parallel segments in Revelation. The trumpets thus do not continue the judgments of the seals but are parallel to them. The thrust is to point out that God uses natural phenomenon to warn the ungodly of final judgment.

Chapter 9. The Fifth and Sixth Trumpets

The judgment of the two trumpets described in this chapter are called woes. The first woe comes as the Abyss is opened (1,2). This "bottomless deep" was considered to be a prison for demons and disobedient spirits. The creatures released are described as locusts, which sting like scorpions, and are given power to torment men (3–6). The description seems to indicate they are more than insects (7–11). The figure of locusts is appropriate. In his *Natural History,* Pliny wrote "this plague is interpreted as a sign of the wrath of the gods; for they are seen of exceptional size, and also fly with such a noise of wings that they are believed to be birds, and they obscure the sun, making the nations gaze upward in anxiety lest they should settle over all their lands."

The second woe pictures a mounted cavalry released to kill a third of mankind (13–16). The mounts are no natural animals, for they have lionine heads and breathe out sulfurous flames (17–19).

Despite these two awesome woes, the survivors of mankind refuse to turn to God, or to repent of their idolatry and immorality (20,21).

Futurist Interpretation of Revelation 9. The enemies described in the chapter are viewed as demonic. They bring a supernatural but literal judgment on those living at this time. The refusal of the remnants of mankind to repent even under obviously supernatural judgment is taken as a revelation of man's unbelieving nature.

Historicist Interpretation of Revelation 9. The historicist sees this vision as a representation of the present time. The locusts are demons from the pit; the dark clouds—a satanic smokescreen for the "invasion of demonic, anti-Christian forces." The second woe is also thought to represent demonic forces operating in the spiritual world today, the reason why the believer must put on the whole armor of God (Eph. 6:11,12).

Chapter 10. Angel and Scroll

John sees a mighty angel coming down from heaven. He holds a small scroll which has been opened (1,2). Part of the angel's message is not to be shared (3,4). But John reports that the angel announces that now, at last, history is about to close "just as he

(God) announced to his servants the prophets" (5–8). John eats
the little scroll and stands ready to "prophesy again about many
peoples, nations, languages, and kings" (9–11).

The Futurist Interpretation of Revelation 10. The futurist sees
this as an interlude, preparing John for the final, bitter revelations
to come.

The Historicist Interpretation of Revelation 10. The historicist
also sees this as an interlude. However, the message is for the
church. It is a promise that God has not abandoned believers
as they wait for the final judgment, which will come at time's
end.

Chapter 11. The Two Witnesses

Now John is given a task and very specific time periods are
specified. These correspond with time periods in Daniel 9 and
12.

He sees Jerusalem trampled for 42 months (1,2) and two unnamed witnesses who prophesy for 1,260 days (3). They are divinely
protected from their enemies and given power to bring drought
and plagues (5,6).

When they have finished the work God set for them, "the beast
that comes up from the Abyss" attacks and kills them (7). The
world rejoices as the witnesses lie dead in the streets of Jerusalem
where the Lord was crucified (8–10). Then after three-and-a-half
days, they are resurrected and called up to heaven in a cloud as
their enemies look on (11,12). Their departure is marked by earthquake and destruction, which so terrify the survivors that they
acknowledge God's hand (13). This marks the passing of the second
woe (14). God is about to take his kingdom (15–19).

Futurist Interpretation of Revelation 11. The two witnesses are
unidentified, though sometimes thought to be Moses and Elijah
(cf. Matt. 17:1–13). They are real persons, who testify in Jerusalem
for an actual three-and-a-half-year period before being killed by
the antichrist at the end of the first half of the tribulation period
foretold in the OT.

Historicist Interpretation of Revelation 11. The three-and-one-
half-year period is symbolic. It is taken from Elijah's life and represents periods of affliction. The trampled-down Jerusalem symbolizes
false Christianity. The two witnesses are not individuals but represent the whole church collectively as filled by the Spirit. The death
of the witnesses symbolizes the church silenced by persecution.
The resurrection represents its ultimate vindication by God.

Chapter 12. The Woman and the Dragon

Now John reports a vision that appears in the heavens and is clearly identified as a "sign" (1). The vision is of a pregnant woman, about to give birth. A dragon (Satan) seeks to devour the child who "will rule the nations with an iron scepter" (2–4). The child is snatched up to heaven and the woman hides in the desert. Again a 1,260-day period is specified (5,6).

John then observes a war in heaven, in which Satan and his angels are hurled down to earth (7–9). Then a voice announces from heaven that "the salvation and the power and the kingdom of our God have come" (10). Satan is overcome but furiously strikes out "because he knows his time is short" (11,12).

The dragon seeks to destroy the woman who gave birth to the child, but she is safely hidden by God (13–16). The raging dragon turns to make open war on those who "hold to the testimony of Jesus" (12:17–13:1).

Futurist Interpretation of Revelation 12. In the drama acted out here Satan and Christ are clearly identified. The woman who gave the child birth represents the Jewish people, who will be preserved during the last half of the tribulation (1,260 days) foretold by Daniel. The hostility of Satan, shown throughout history in anti-Semitism, is directed against all believers in fiercest persecution during this final period of world history.

Historicist Interpretation of Revelation 12. The historicist also sees the woman as Israel, the idealized church of the OT. The war in heaven is a picture of Jesus' victory on Calvary. Thus this chapter begins yet another recapitulation of the repeated message of this book, using different symbols. The chapter teaches that in spite of the hatred of Satan, the church will be preserved.

Chapter 13. The Beast from the Sea

Now John watches as a horned beast emerges from the sea (1). His shape reflects the form given Gentile world powers in Daniel 7. This beast is energized by Satan and followed by a worshiping world (2–4).

Again the 42-month period is specified. During it the beast holds power and makes war on the saints (5–10).

John then sees another beast, emerging this time from the earth. He resembles a lamb but speaks like the dragon (11). He performs miracles to authenticate the claims of the first beast (12–14) and forces the people of the beast to worship his image (15–17). The "number" of this beast is given as 666.

Futurist Interpretation of Revelation 13. The chapter introduces two more individuals. These are known from the OT prophets to play key roles in the great tribulation at the end of time. The first beast is believed by futurists to be the antichrist (cf. 2 Thess. 2). He will link the Common Market countries (the ten horns, or governments) to form a unity of those territories held by the old Roman Empire. The second beast is the false prophet. Together with Satan they form a mocking trinity that counterfeit Father, Son, and Holy Spirit.

Historicist Interpretation of Revelation 13. The historicist sees the chapter as a symbolic exposition of Satan's attack on the church. The first beast is thought to represent anti-Christian governments which emerge from the surging human sea. The second beast represents false religion and false teachers, whose heresies fall far short of the divine revelation (the significance of 666). The 42 months represents the entire gospel age.

Chapter 14. The Hour of Judgment

John's next impression is of the Lamb, returned to earth and standing on Mount Zion (1). The 144,000 are with him and are honored for their total commitment in following him (2–5).

At this point three angels are seen. The first announces to all humanity the good news (gospel) that the hour of judgment has come (6,7). The second announces the fall of Babylon the Great (8). The third announces the endless doom and torment of all who worship the beast and exhorts patient endurance on the part of the saints (9–13). Here a voice from heaven is heard, pronouncing a blessing on the dead "who die in the Lord from now on" (13).

When John looks up, he sees a figure, crowned and seated on a cloud (14). Angels, equipped for harvest, cry out to him. The gathering and the trampling out begin, and blood gushes from the city for a distance of some 180 miles!

The Futurist Interpretation of Revelation 14. The futurist sees this vision as an overview, or preview, of the final day of wrath. The details are developed in subsequent chapters. "Babylon the Great" speaks of consolidated political or religious power under the antichrist in the last days, with the name chosen because throughout Scripture Babel (Gen. 11:1–9) and Babylon represent unification and world empire.

The Historicist Interpretation of Revelation 14. The historicist sees Revelation 14 as another parallel image of final judgment. The elements in this chapter are taken to represent the purity of the church throughout history in the midst of a pagan world, and the destruction of God's enemies. Babylon is all the ungodly and unholy powers of the world.

Chapters 15, 16. God's Wrath

Again John peers into heaven and sees seven angels who will bear the "seven last plagues" that complete God's wrath (15:1). God is praised for his holiness and the vindication of his name that will come when at last all nations must prostrate themselves before him (15:2–4). The seven angels now come to receive seven golden bowls filled with God's wrath (15:5–8).

On command the angels pour out the bowls of wrath on the earth (16:1). Sores break out on the followers of the beast (16:2); all living things in the sea die (16:3); all the fresh waters turn to blood (16:4–7); the sun flares and sears the earth (16:8,9); darkness and anguish follow (16:10,11); finally demons are loosed to move the leaders of all the nations to gather for battle against God (16:14). The armies gather and assemble at a place called in Scripture Armageddon (16:15,16).

Futurist Interpretation of Revelation 15, 16. These are graphic but literal descriptions of what will happen on earth at the end of the coming tribulation period.

Historicist Interpretation of Revelation 15, 16. These are symbolic and not literal descriptions of final judgment.

Chapter 17. The Woman on the Beast

John is now shown the punishment of someone identified as the "great prostitute" who commits adulteries with the kings of the earth (1,2). John sees a woman seated on the scarlet beast. She is dressed in purple, laden with jewels, and drunk with "the blood of the saints, the blood of those who bore testimony to Jesus" (3–6). The angel explains the mystery, again identifying the beast as the antichrist (6–8). Aspects of the beast with symbolic meaning are explained. The seven heads are hills "on which the woman sits" (9–11). The ten horns are nations that will give their sovereignty to antichrist and make war on the Lamb (12–15). The woman, identified as "the great city that rules over the kings of the earth," will in time be destroyed by the beast, who wants sole possession of all power.

Futurist Interpretation of Revelation 17. The futurist identifies "mystery Babylon" as the religious aspect of mankind's final consolidation. Futurists see a close relationship between a coming western